P9-CAL-182

Instructor's Solutions Manual

to accompany

College Algebra with Trigonometry

Seventh Edition

Raymond A. Barnett
Merritt College

Michael R. Ziegler
Marquette University

Karl E. Byleen
Marquette University

Norma James
New Mexico State University

Special thanks to Jeanne Wallace for the preparation of this manuscript.

Boston   Burr Ridge, IL   Dubuque, IA   Madison, WI   New York   San Francisco   St. Louis
Bangkok   Bogotá   Caracas   Lisbon   London   Madrid
Mexico City   Milan   New Delhi   Seoul   Singapore   Sydney   Taipei   Toronto

McGraw-Hill Higher Education

A Division of The McGraw-Hill Companies

Instructor's Solutions Manual to accompany
COLLEGE ALGEBRA WITH TRIGONOMETRY, SEVENTH EDITION
RAYMOND A. BARNETT/MICHAEL R. ZIEGLER/KARL E. BYLEEN

Published by McGraw-Hill Higher Education, an imprint of The McGraw-Hill Companies, Inc.,
1221 Avenue of the Americas, New York, NY 10020. Copyright © The McGraw-Hill Companies,
Inc., 2001, 1999, 1993, 1989, 1984, 1979, 1974. All rights reserved.

The contents, or parts thereof, may be reproduced in print form solely for classroom use with
COLLEGE ALGEBRA WITH TRIGONOMETRY, SEVENTH EDITION, by Raymond A. Barnett,
Michael R. Ziegler, and Karl E. Byleen, provided such reproductions bear copyright notice, but
may not be reproduced in any other form or for any other purpose without the prior written consent
of The McGraw-Hill Companies, Inc., including, but not limited to, network or other electronic
storage or transmission, or broadcast for distance learning.

This book is printed on acid-free paper.

6 7 8 9 10 QPD QPD 0 9 8 7 6 5

ISBN 0-07-240606-2

www.mhhe.com

PREFACE

Part I of this manual contains solutions to the even-numbered problems in the exercise sets at the end of each section in the textbook. The solutions to the odd-numbered problems in these exercise sets and to all problems in the chapter review and cumulative review exercise sets can be found in the Student Solutions Manual that accompanies this textbook. Thus, taken together, this manual and the Student Solutions Manual provide solutions to all problems in the textbook.

Part II of this manual contains the answers to all the problems in the textbook in one convenient location.

TABLE OF CONTENTS

PART I—SOLUTIONS

CHAPTER 1: BASIC ALGEBRAIC OPERATIONS 1

CHAPTER 2: EQUATIONS AND INEQUALITIES 19

CHAPTER 3: GRAPHS AND FUNCTIONS 58

CHAPTER 4: POLYNOMIAL AND RATIONAL FUNCTIONS 101

CHAPTER 5: EXPONENTIAL AND LOGARITHMIC FUNCTIONS 132

CHAPTER 6: TRIGONOMETRIC FUNCTIONS 150

CHAPTER 7: TRIGONOMETRIC IDENTITIES AND CONDITIONAL EQUATIONS 178

CHAPTER 8: ADDITIONAL TOPICS IN TRIGONOMETRY 214

CHAPTER 9: SYSTEMS OF EQUATIONS AND INEQUALITIES 240

CHAPTER 10: MATRICES AND DETERMINANTS 267

CHAPTER 11: SEQUENCES AND SERIES 286

CHAPTER 12: ADDITIONAL TOPICS IN ANALYTIC GEOMETRY 308

PART II—ANSWERS

CHAPTER 1: BASIC ALGEBRAIC OPERATIONS 329

CHAPTER 2: EQUATIONS AND INEQUALITIES 337

CHAPTERS 1 & 2   CUMULATIVE REVIEW EXERCISES 351

CHAPTER 3: GRAPHS AND FUNCTIONS 353

CHAPTER 4: POLYNOMIAL AND RATIONAL FUNCTIONS 391

CHAPTER 5: EXPONENTIAL AND LOGARITHMIC FUNCTIONS 405

CHAPTERS 3—5   CUMULATIVE REVIEW EXERCISES 419

CHAPTER 6: TRIGONOMETRIC FUNCTIONS 425

CHAPTER 7: TRIGONOMETRIC IDENTITIES AND CONDITIONAL EQUATIONS 455

CHAPTER 8: ADDITIONAL TOPICS IN TRIGONOMETRY 467

CHAPTERS 6—8   CUMULATIVE REVIEW EXERCISES 485

CHAPTER 9: SYSTEMS OF EQUATIONS AND INEQUALITIES 493

CHAPTER 10: MATRICES AND DETERMINANTS 509

CHAPTERS 9 & 10   CUMULATIVE REVIEW EXERCISES 519

CHAPTER 11: SEQUENCES AND SERIES 523

CHAPTER 12: ADDITIONAL TOPICS IN ANALYTIC GEOMETRY 531

CHAPTERS 11 & 12   CUMULATIVE REVIEW EXERCISES 549

PART I
SOLUTIONS

CHAPTER 1

Exercise 1-1

2. Since 6 is an element of $\{2, 4, 6\}$ the statement $6 \in \{2, 4, 6\}$ is true.

4. Since 7 is not an element of $\{2, 4, 6\}$ the statement $7 \notin \{2, 4, 6\}$ is true.

6. Since 2 and 6 are both elements of $\{2, 4, 6\}$ the statement $\{2, 6\} \subset \{2, 4, 6\}$ is true.

8. Since $\{7, 3, 5\}$ and $\{3, 5, 7\}$ contain exactly the same elements the statement $\{7, 3, 5\} = \{3, 5, 7\}$ is true.

10. The commutative property $(\cdot)$ states that in general $uv = vu$. Comparing this with $uv = ?$ it follows that $?$ may be replaced with vu.

12. The associative property $(+)$ states that in general $a + (b + c) = (a + b) + c$ from which $3 + (7 + y) = (3 + 7) + y$ and comparison to $3 + (7 + y) = ?$ gives $? = (3 + 7) + y$.

14. The identity property $(\cdot)$ states that in general $1 \cdot a = a$ from which $1(u + v) = u + v$ and comparison to $1(u + v) = ?$ gives $? = u + v$.

16. Associative $(\cdot)$. $7(3m) = (7 \cdot 3) \cdot m$ is a special case of $a(bc) = (ab)c$.

18. $-\dfrac{u}{-v} = \dfrac{u}{v}$ is a special case of Theorem 1 (#6) on the properties of negatives $\dfrac{-a}{-b} = -\dfrac{-a}{b} = -\dfrac{a}{-b} = \dfrac{a}{b}$, $b \neq 0$.

20. $8 - 12 = 8 + (-12)$ is an example of the general definition of subtraction as addition of opposites: $a - b = a + (-b)$.

22. $5 \div (-6) = 5\left(\dfrac{1}{-6}\right)$ is a special case of division $a \div b = a\left(\dfrac{1}{b}\right)$ with $a = 5$ and $b = -6$ $\dfrac{a}{b} \div \dfrac{c}{d} = \dfrac{a}{b} \cdot \dfrac{d}{c}$ with $a = 5$, $b = 1$, $c = -6$ and $d = 1$.

24. $ab(c + d) = abc + abd$ follows from the distributive property $x(y + z) = xy + xz$ with $x = ab$, $y = c$, and $z = d$.

26. $(x + y) \cdot 0 = 0$ follows from the property of zero $a \cdot 0 = 0$ where $a = x + y$.

28. $\{x \mid x$ is an odd integer between -4 and $6\}$ is the set $\{-3, -1, 1, 3, 5\}$.

30. $\{x \mid x$ is a letter in "consensus"$\} = \{c, o, n, s, e, u\}$

32. $\{x \mid x$ is a month with 32 days$\} = \emptyset$. There are no 32 day months.

34. $S_1 = a$ has $2^1 = 2$ subsets; $S_2 = \{a, b\}$ has $2^2 = 4$ subsets; $S_3 = \{a, b, c\}$ has $2^3 = 8$ subsets; $S_4 = \{a, b, c, d\}$ has $2^4 = 16$ subsets. Generalizing, S_n with n terms will have 2^n subsets.

36. $(ab)(ba) = (ab)(ab)$ illustrates the commutative property $(\cdot)$ where $ba = ab$.

38. $s + (t + 2) = (s + t) + 2$ illustrates the associative property $(+)$.

40. $p(r - 1) + q(r - 1) = (p + q)(r - 1)$ illustrates the distributive property $xy + xz = x(y + z)$ where $r - 1 = x$, $p = y$, and $q = z$.

42. $\dfrac{-y}{-(1 - y)} = \dfrac{y}{1 - y}$ illustrates the property of negatives $\dfrac{a}{b} = \dfrac{-a}{-b}$ where $y = a$ and $1 - y = b$.

44. If $ab = 1$, does either a or b have to be 1? No, $\left(\dfrac{3}{5}\right)\left(\dfrac{5}{3}\right) = 1$ and neither $a = \dfrac{3}{5}$ or $b = \dfrac{5}{3}$ is 1.

46. (A) All integers are natural numbers is false since -1 is an integer but not a natural number.

(B) All rational numbers are real numbers is true.

(C) All natural numbers are rational numbers is true

since $1 = \frac{1}{1}$, $2 = \frac{2}{1}$, $3 = \frac{3}{1}$, … for the natural numbers.

48. $\sqrt{2}$ is an example of a real number that is not a rational number since $\sqrt{2}$ cannot be written as the ratio of two integers. π (pi) is also such a number. In fact, there are infinitely many such numbers.

50. $S = \left\{-\sqrt{5},\ -1,\ -\frac{1}{2},\ 2,\ \sqrt{7},\ 6,\ \frac{25}{3}\right\}$

(A) Natural numbers: $S_N = \{2,\ 6\}$

(B) Integers: $S_Z = \{-1,\ 2,\ 6\}$

(C) Rational numbers: $S_Q = \left\{-1,\ -\frac{1}{2},\ 2,\ 6,\ \frac{25}{3}\right\}$

52. (A) $\frac{13}{6} = 2.1666…$

$= 2.1\overline{6}$ repeating

(B) $\sqrt{21} = 4.582575695…$

non-repeating and non-terminating

(C) $\frac{7}{16} = 0.437500…$

$= 0.4375$ terminating

(D) $\frac{29}{111} = 0.261261261…$

$= 0.\overline{261}$ repeating

54. (A) $(a + b) + c = a + (b + c)$ is true, associative (+)

(B) $(a - b) - c = a - (b - c)$ is false, since
$(8 - 4) - 2 = 4 - 2$ and $8 - (4 - 2) = 8 - 2$
$= 2$ $= 6$
There is no associative property for subtraction

(C) $a(bc) = (ab)c$ is true, associative ($\cdot$)

(D) $(a \div b) \div c = a \div (b \div c)$ is false, since
$(8 \div 4) \div 2 = 2 \div 2$ and $8 \div (4 \div 2) = 8 \div 2$
$= 1$ $= 4$
There is no associative property for division.

56. $F = \{-2,\ 0,\ 2\};\ G = \{-1,\ 0,\ 1,\ 2\}$

(A) $\{x \mid x \in F$ or $x \in G\} = \{-2,\ -1,\ 0,\ 1,\ 2\}$

(B) $\{x \mid x \in F$ and $x \in G\} = \{0,\ 2\}$

58. Let $x = 0.181818…$, then $100x = 18.181818…$
$\underline{\ \ \ \ \ -\ x = -\ .181818…}$
$99x = 18$
$x = \frac{18}{99}$
$x = \frac{2}{11}$

60.

statement		reason
1. $(a + b) + (-a) = (-a) + (a + b)$		1. commutative (+)
2.	$= [(-a) + a] + b$	2. associative (+)
3.	$= 0 + b$	3. inverse (+)
4.	$= b$	4. identity (+)

Exercise 1-2

2. $2x^2 + x - 1$ is degree 2

4. $(2x^2 + x - 1) + (3x - 2) = 2x^2 + (1 + 3)x - 1 - 2$
$$= 2x^2 + 4x - 3$$

6. $(2x^2 + x - 1) - (3x - 2) = 2x^2 + x - 1 - 3x + 2$
$$= 2x^2 - 2x + 1$$

8. $(2x^2 + x - 1)(3x - 2) = 6x^3 - 4x^2 + 3x^2 - 2x - 3x + 2$
$$= 6x^3 - x^2 - 5x + 2$$

10. $2(u - 1) - (3u + 2) - 2(2u - 3) = 2u - 2 - 3u - 2 - 4u + 6$
$$= -5u + 2$$

12. $4a - 2a[5 - 3(a + 2)] = 4a - 2a[5 - 3a - 6]$
$$= 4a - 2a[-3a - 1]$$
$$= 4a + 6a^2 + 2a$$
$$= 6a^2 + 6a$$

14. $(a + b)(a - b) = a^2 - ab + ba - b^2$
$$= a^2 - b^2 \quad \text{[or use special product 1: } (a + b)(a - b) = a^2 - b^2]$$

16. $(3x - 5)(2x + 1) = 6x^2 + 3x - 10x - 5$
$$= 6x^2 - 7x - 5$$

18. $(2x - 3y)(x + 2y) = 2x^2 + 4xy - 3xy - 6y^2$
$$= 2x^2 + xy - 6y^2$$

20. $(3y + 2)(3y - 2) = (3y)^2 - (2)^2$
$$= 9y^2 - 4$$

22. $(3m + 7n)(2m - 5n) = 6m^2 - 15mn + 14mn - 35n^2$
$$= 6m^2 - mn - 35n^2$$

24. $(4m + 3n)(4m - 3n) = (4m)^2 - (3n)^2$
$$= 16m^2 - 9n^2$$

26. $(3u + 4v)^2 = (3u)^2 + 2(3u)(4v) + (4v)^2$
$$= 9u^2 + 24uv + 16v^2$$

28. $(a - b)(a^2 + ab + b^2) = a^3 + a^2b + ab^2 - a^2b - ab^2 - b^3$
$$= a^3 - b^3$$

30. $m - \{m - [m - (m - 1)]\} = m - \{m - [m - m + 1]\}$
$$= m - \{m - 1\}$$
$$= m - m + 1$$
$$= 1$$

32. $5b - 3\{-[2 - 4(2b - 1)] + 2(2 - 3b)\} = 5b - 3\{-[2 - 8b + 4] + 4 - 6b\}$
$$= 5b - 3\{-[6 - 8b] + 4 - 6b\}$$
$$= 5b - 3\{-6 + 8b + 4 - 6b\}$$
$$= 5b - 3\{2b - 2\}$$
$$= 5b - 6b + 6$$
$$= -b + 6$$

34. $(x^2 - 3xy + y^2)(x^2 + 3xy + y^2)$
$$= x^4 + 3x^3y + x^2y^2 - 3x^3y - 9x^2y^2 - 3xy^3 + x^2y^2 + 3xy^3 + y^4$$
$$= x^4 - 7x^2y^2 + y^4$$

36. $(n^2 + 4nm + m^2)(n^2 - 4nm + m^2)$
$$= n^4 - 4n^3m + n^2m^2 + 4n^3m - 16n^2m^2 + 4nm^3 + n^2m^2 - 4nm^3 + m^4$$
$$= n^4 - 14n^2m^2 + m^4$$

38. $(2a - b)^2 - (a + 2b)^2 = (4a^2 - 4ab + b^2) - (a^2 + 4ab + 4b^2)$
$$= 4a^2 - 4ab + b^2 - a^2 - 4ab - 4b^2$$
$$= 3a^2 - 8ab - 3b^2$$

40. $(y + 3)(y^2 - 3y + 1) + 8y - 1 = y^3 - 3y^2 + y + 3y^2 - 9y + 3 + 8y - 1$
$$= y^3 + 2$$

42. $(3a + 2b)^3 = (9a^2 + 12ab + 4b^2)(3a + 2b)$
$$= 27a^3 + 18a^2b + 36a^2b + 24ab^2 + 12ab^2 + 8b^3$$
$$= 27a^3 + 54a^2b + 36ab^2 + 8b^3$$

44. $(x + h)^2 - x^2 = x^2 + 2xh + h^2 - x^2$
$$= 2xh + h^2$$

46. $-4(x + h)^2 + 6(x + h) - (-4x^2 + 6x) = -4(x^2 + 2xh + h^2) + 6x + 6h + 4x^2 - 6x$
$$= -4x^2 - 8xh - 4h^2 + 6h + 4x^2$$
$$= -8xh - 4h^2 + 6h$$

48. $3(x + h)^2 + 5(x + h) + 7 - (3x^2 + 5x + 7)$
$$= 3(x^2 + 2xh + h^2) + 5x + 5h + 7 - 3x^2 - 5x - 7$$
$$= 3x^2 + 6xh + 3h^2 + 5h - 3x^2$$
$$= 6xh + 3h^2 + 5h$$

50. $(x + h)^3 + 3(x + h) - (x^3 + 3x) = (x + h)(x^2 + 2xh + h^2) + 3x + 3h - x^3 - 3x$
$$= x^3 + 2x^2h + xh^2 + x^2h + 2xh^2 + h^3 + 3h - x^3$$
$$= 3x^2h + 3xh^2 + h^3 + 3h$$

52. $(2x^2 - 4xy + y^2) + (3xy - y^2) - [(x^2 - 2xy - y^2) + (-x^2 + 3xy - 2y^2)]$
$$= 2x^2 - 4xy + y^2 + 3xy - y^2 - [x^2 - 2xy - y^2 - x^2 + 3xy - 2y^2]$$
$$= 2x^2 - xy - [xy - 3y^2]$$
$$= 2x^2 - xy - xy + 3y^2$$
$$= 2x^2 - 2xy + 3y^2$$

54. $(2x - 1)^3 - 2(2x - 1)^2 + 3(2x - 1) + 7$
$$= (4x^2 - 4x + 1)(2x - 1) - 2(4x^2 - 4x + 1) + 6x - 3 + 7$$
$$= 8x^3 - 4x^2 - 8x^2 + 4x + 2x - 1 - 8x^2 + 8x - 2 + 6x + 4$$
$$= 8x^3 - 20x^2 + 20x + 1$$

56. $2\{(x - 3)(x^2 - 2x + 1) - x[3 - x(x - 2)]\}$
$$= 2\{x^3 - 2x^2 + x - 3x^2 + 6x - 3 - x[3 - x^2 + 2x]\}$$
$$= 2\{x^3 - 5x^2 + 7x - 3 - 3x + x^3 - 2x^2\}$$
$$= 2\{2x^3 - 7x^2 + 4x - 3\}$$
$$= 4x^3 - 14x^2 + 8x - 6$$

58. Suppose $(a - b)^2 = a^2 - b^2$,
then $a^2 - 2ab + b^2 = a^2 - b^2$ For example, $(2 - 1)^2 = 1^2 = 1$
$2ab - 2b^2 = 0$ $2^2 - 1^2 = 4 - 1 = 3$
$b(a - b) = 0$ so $(2 - 1)^2 \neq 2^2 - 1^2$
$b = 0$ or $a - b = 0$
$a = b$

Therefore, unless $b = 0$ or $a = b$, $(a - b)^2 = a^2 - b^2$ will not be true.
In general, $(a - b)^2 \neq a^2 - b^2$.

60. Let $a_n x^n$ be the term of highest degree in the first polynomial and $a_m x^m$ be the term of highest degree in the second polynomial, then $a_n a_m x^n x^m = a_n a_m x^{n+m}$ will be the term with the highest degree in the product; thus, the product is of degree $m + n$.

62. Answer does not change. The product is still of degree $m + n = m + m = 2m$.

64.

$$A = \ell w$$
$$= (x + 8)x$$
$$= x^2 + 8x$$

66.
$$x = \text{number of quarters}$$
$$x + 4 = \text{number of dimes}$$
$$\text{Value} = 25x + 10(x + 4)$$
$$= 25x + 10x + 40$$
$$= 35x + 40$$

68.
$$V = (x + 4)^3 - x^3$$
$$= (x^2 + 8x + 16)(x + 4) - x^3$$
$$= x^3 + 4x^2 + 8x^2 + 32x + 16x + 64 - x^3$$
$$= 12x^2 + 48x + 64$$

Exercise 1-3

2. $6m^4 - 9m^3 - 3m^2 = 3m^2(2m^2 - 3m - 1)$

4. $8u^3v - 6u^2v^2 + 4uv^3 = 2uv(4u^2 - 3uv + 2v^2)$

6. $7m(2m - 3) + 5(2m - 3) = (2m - 3)(7m + 5)$

8. $a(3c + d) - 4b(3c + d) = (3c + d)(a - 4b)$

10. $2y^2 - 6y + 5y - 15 = 2y(y - 3) + 5(y - 3)$
$$= (y - 3)(2y + 5)$$

12. $5x^2 - 40x - x + 8 = 5x(x - 8) - (x - 8)$
$$= (x - 8)(5x - 1)$$

14. $3a^2 - 12ab - 2ab + 8b^2 = 3a(a - 4b) - 2b(a - 4b)$
$$= (a - 4b)(3a - 2b)$$

16. $3pr - 2qs - qr + 6ps = 3pr - qr + 6ps - 2qs$
$$= r(3p - q) + 2s(3p - q)$$
$$= (r + 2s)(3p - q)$$

18. $3y^2 - 8y - 3 = (3y + 1)(y - 3)$

20. $u^2 + 4uv - 12v^2 = (u + 6v)(u - 2v)$

22. $x^2 + 3xy - 10y^2 = (x + 5y)(x - 2y)$

24. $x^2 + 4y^2$ is prime relative to the integers.

26. $a^2b^2 - c^2 = (ab - c)(ab + c)$

28. $9x^2 - 4 = (3x - 2)(3x + 2)$

30. $3z^2 - 28z + 48$ is prime relative to the integers.

32. $2x^4 - 24x^3 + 40x^2 = 2x^2(x^2 - 12x + 20)$ **34.** $4xy^2 - 12xy + 9x = x(4y^2 - 12y + 9)$
$$= 2x^2(x - 10)(x - 2)$$
$$= x(2y - 3)^2$$

36. $6m^2 - mn - 12n^2 = (2m - 3n)(3m + 4n)$ **38.** $4u^3v - uv^3 = uv(4u^2 - v^2)$
$$= uv(2u - v)(2u + v)$$

40. $2x^3 - 2x^2 + 8x = 2x(x^2 - x + 4)$

42. $r^3 - t^3 = (r - t)(r^2 + rt + t^2)$ difference of cubes

44. $(x - 1)^3 + 3x(x - 1)^2 = (x - 1)^2[(x - 1) + 3x] = (x - 1)^2(4x - 1)$

46. $2(x - 3)(4x + 7)^2 + 8(x - 3)^2(4x + 7) = 2(x - 3)(4x + 7)[(4x + 7) + 4(x - 3)]$
$$= 2(x - 3)(4x + 7)(4x + 7 + 4x - 12)$$
$$= 2(x - 3)(4x + 7)(8x - 5)$$

48. $3x^4(x - 7)^2 + 4x^3(x - 7)^3 = x^3(x - 7)^2[3x + 4(x - 7)]$
$$= x^3(x - 7)^2(3x + 4x - 28)$$
$$= x^3(x - 7)^2(7x - 28)$$
$$= 7x^3(x - 7)^2(x - 4)$$

50. $4(x - 3)^3(x^2 + 2)^3 + 6x(x - 3)^4(x^2 + 2)^2$
$$= 2(x - 3)^3(x^2 + 2)^2[2(x^2 + 2) + 3x(x - 3)]$$
$$= 2(x - 3)^3(x^2 + 2)^2(2x^2 + 4 + 3x^2 - 9x)$$
$$= 2(x - 3)^3(x^2 + 2)^2(5x^2 - 9x + 4)$$
$$= 2(x - 3)^3(x^2 + 2)^2(5x - 4)(x - 1)$$

52. $(x + 2)^2 + 9$ is prime relative to the integers.

54. $15ac - 20ad + 3bc - 4bd = 5a(3c - 4d) + b(3c - 4d)$
$$= (5a + b)(3c - 4d)$$

56. $5u^2 + 4uv - v^2 = (5u - v)(u + v)$

58. $x^3 - x^2 - x + 1 = x^2(x - 1) - (x - 1)$
$$= (x^2 - 1)(x - 1)$$
$$= (x + 1)(x - 1)(x - 1)$$
$$= (x + 1)(x - 1)^2$$

60. $t^3 - 2t^2 + t - 2 = t^2(t - 2) + (t - 2)$
$$= (t^2 + 1)(t - 2)$$

62. $6(x - y)^2 + 23(x - y) - 4 = [(x - y) + 4][6(x - y) - 1]$
$$= (x - y + 4)(6x - 6y - 1)$$

64. $y^4 - 3y^2 - 4 = (y^2 - 4)(y^2 + 1)$
$$= (y - 2)(y + 2)(y^2 + 1)$$

66. $27a^2 + a^5b^3 = a^2(27 + a^3b^3)$
$$= a^2(3 + ab)(9 - 3ab + a^2b^2)$$

68. $y^2 - 2xy + x^2 - y + x = (y - x)^2 - (y - x)$
$$= (y - x)(y - x - 1)$$

70. $25(4x^2 - 12xy + 9y^2) - 9a^2b^2 = 25(2x - 3y)^2 - 9a^2b^2$
$$= [5(2x - 3y) + 3ab][5(2x - 3y) - 3ab]$$
$$= [10x - 15y + 3ab][10x - 15y - 3ab]$$

72. $a^4 + 2a^2b^2 + b^4 - a^2b^2 = (a^2 + b^2)^2 - a^2b^2$
$$= [(a^2 + b^2) - ab][(a^2 + b^2) + ab]$$
$$= (a^2 + b^2 - ab)(a^2 + b^2 + ab)$$

74. (A) Area $= 16 \cdot 9 - 4x^2 = 144 - 4x^2 = 4(36 - x^2) = 4(6 - x)(6 + x)$
(B) Volume $= (16 - 2x)(9 - 2x) \cdot x = 2x(8 - x)(9 - 2x) = 4x^3 - 50x^2 + 144x$

Exercise 1-4

2. $\dfrac{d^5}{3a} \div \left(\dfrac{d^2}{6a^2} \cdot \dfrac{a}{4d^3}\right) = \dfrac{d^5}{3a} \div \left(\dfrac{1}{24ad}\right)$

$\qquad\qquad\qquad = \dfrac{d^5}{3a} \cdot \dfrac{24ad}{1}$

$\qquad\qquad\qquad = 8d^6$

4. $\dfrac{x^2}{12} + \dfrac{x}{18} - \dfrac{1}{30} = \dfrac{15x^2}{180} + \dfrac{10x}{180} - \dfrac{6}{180}$

$\qquad\qquad\qquad\quad = \dfrac{15x^2 + 10x - 6}{180}$

6. $\dfrac{4m - 3}{18m^3} + \dfrac{3}{4m} - \dfrac{2m - 1}{6m^2} = \dfrac{2(4m - 3)}{36m^3} + \dfrac{9m^2(3)}{36m^3} - \dfrac{6m(2m - 1)}{36m^3}$

$\qquad\qquad\qquad\qquad\qquad = \dfrac{8m - 6 + 27m^2 - 12m^2 + 6m}{36m^3}$

$\qquad\qquad\qquad\qquad\qquad = \dfrac{15m^2 + 14m - 6}{36m^3}$

8. $\dfrac{3x^2 + x - 2}{3x^2 - 2x} \div (3x^2 + 5x + 2) = \dfrac{(3x - 2)(x + 1)}{x(3x - 2)} \cdot \dfrac{1}{(3x + 2)(x + 1)}$

$\qquad\qquad\qquad\qquad\qquad\qquad = \dfrac{1}{x(3x + 2)}$

10. $\dfrac{4y^2 - 4y + 1}{2y^2 + 5y - 3} \div \dfrac{2y^2 - 3y - 2}{2y^2 + 7y + 3} = \dfrac{(2y - 1)(2y - 1)}{(2y - 1)(y + 3)} \cdot \dfrac{(2y + 1)(y + 3)}{(2y + 1)(y - 2)}$

$\qquad\qquad\qquad\qquad\qquad\qquad = \dfrac{2y - 1}{y - 2}$

12. $\dfrac{x + 2}{x^2 - 1} - \dfrac{x - 2}{(x - 1)^2} = \dfrac{(x - 1)(x + 2)}{(x - 1)^2(x + 1)} - \dfrac{(x + 1)(x - 2)}{(x - 1)^2(x + 1)}$

$\qquad\qquad\qquad\qquad = \dfrac{x^2 + x - 2 - (x^2 - x - 2)}{(x - 1)^2(x + 1)}$

$\qquad\qquad\qquad\qquad = \dfrac{2x}{(x - 1)^2(x + 1)}$

14. $\dfrac{x + 1}{x - 1} + x = \dfrac{x + 1}{x - 1} + \dfrac{x(x - 1)}{x - 1}$

$\qquad\qquad\qquad = \dfrac{x + 1 + x^2 - x}{x - 1}$

$\qquad\qquad\qquad = \dfrac{x^2 + 1}{x - 1}$

16. $\dfrac{1}{a - 3} - \dfrac{2}{3 - a} = \dfrac{1}{a - 3} - \dfrac{-2}{a - 3}$

$\qquad\qquad\qquad = \dfrac{1 + 2}{a - 3}$

$\qquad\qquad\qquad = \dfrac{3}{a - 3}$

18. $\dfrac{4x}{x^2 - y^2} + \dfrac{3}{x + y} - \dfrac{2}{x - y} = \dfrac{4x}{(x + y)(x - y)} + \dfrac{3(x - y)}{(x + y)(x - y)} - \dfrac{2(x + y)}{(x + y)(x - y)}$

$\qquad\qquad\qquad\qquad\qquad\qquad = \dfrac{4x + 3x - 3y - 2x - 2y}{(x + y)(x - y)}$

$\qquad\qquad\qquad\qquad\qquad\qquad = \dfrac{5x - 5y}{(x + y)(x - y)}$

$\qquad\qquad\qquad\qquad\qquad\qquad = \dfrac{5(x - y)}{(x + y)(x - y)} = \dfrac{5}{x + y}$

20. $\dfrac{\dfrac{4}{x} - x}{\dfrac{2}{x} - 1} \cdot \dfrac{x}{x} = \dfrac{4 - x^2}{2 - x} = \dfrac{(2 - x)(2 + x)}{2 - x} = 2 + x$

22.
$$\frac{4x^4(x^2+3) - 3x^2(x^2+3)^2}{x^6} = \frac{x^2(x^2+3)[4x^2 - 3(x^2+3)]}{x^6}$$
$$= \frac{(x^2+3)(x^2-9)}{x^4}$$
$$= \frac{(x^2+3)(x+3)(x-3)}{x^4}$$

24.
$$\frac{2x(2x+3)^4 - 8x^2(2x+3)^3}{(2x+3)^8} = \frac{2x(2x+3)^3[(2x+3) - 4x]}{(2x+3)^8}$$
$$= \frac{2x(3-2x)}{(2x+3)^5}$$

26.
$$\frac{3x^2(x+1)^3 - 3(x^3+4)(x+1)^2}{(x+1)^6} = \frac{3(x+1)^2[x^2(x+1) - (x^3+4)]}{(x+1)^6}$$
$$= \frac{3[x^3 + x^2 - x^3 - 4]}{(x+1)^4}$$
$$= \frac{3(x^2-4)}{(x+1)^4}$$
$$= \frac{3(x+2)(x-2)}{(x+1)^4}$$

28.
$$\frac{x}{x^2-9x+18} + \frac{x-8}{x-6} + \frac{x+4}{x-3}$$
$$= \frac{x}{(x-6)(x-3)} + \frac{(x-8)(x-3)}{(x-6)(x-3)} + \frac{(x+4)(x-6)}{(x-3)(x-6)}$$
$$= \frac{x + x^2 - 11x + 24 + x^2 - 2x - 24}{(x-6)(x-3)}$$
$$= \frac{2x^2 - 12x}{(x-6)(x-3)}$$
$$= \frac{2x(x-6)}{(x-6)(x-3)}$$
$$= \frac{2x}{x-3}$$

30.
$$\frac{x+1}{x(1-x)} \cdot \frac{x^2-2x+1}{x^2-1} = \frac{x+1}{-x(x-1)} \cdot \frac{(x-1)(x-1)}{(x-1)(x+1)} = -\frac{1}{x}$$

32.
$$\frac{c+2}{5c-5} - \frac{c-2}{3c-3} + \frac{c}{1-c} = \frac{c+2}{5(c-1)} - \frac{c-2}{3(c-1)} - \frac{c}{c-1}$$
$$= \frac{3(c+2)}{15(c-1)} - \frac{5(c-2)}{15(c-1)} - \frac{15c}{15(c-1)}$$
$$= \frac{3c + 6 - 5c + 10 - 15c}{15(c-1)}$$
$$= \frac{-17c + 16}{15(c-1)}$$

34.
$$\left(\frac{x^3-y^3}{y^3} \cdot \frac{y}{x-y}\right) \div \frac{x^2+xy+y^2}{y^2} = \left(\frac{(x-y)(x^2+xy+y^2)}{y^3} \cdot \frac{y}{x-y}\right) \cdot \frac{y^2}{(x^2+xy+y^2)}$$
$$= 1$$

36.
$$\left(\frac{x^2-xy}{xy+y^2} \div \frac{x^2-y^2}{x^2+2xy+y^2}\right) \div \frac{x^2-2xy+y^2}{x^2y+xy^2} = \left(\frac{x(x-y)}{y(x+y)} \cdot \frac{(x+y)^2}{(x+y)(x-y)}\right) \cdot \left(\frac{xy(x+y)}{(x-y)^2}\right)$$
$$= \left(\frac{x}{y}\right)\left(\frac{xy(x+y)}{(x-y)^2}\right)$$
$$= \frac{x^2(x+y)}{(x-y)^2}$$

38. $\left(\dfrac{3}{x-2} - \dfrac{1}{x+1}\right) \div \dfrac{x+4}{x-2} = \dfrac{3(x+1) - (x-2)}{(x-2)(x+1)} \cdot \dfrac{x-2}{x+4}$

$\qquad\qquad\qquad\qquad\qquad\quad = \dfrac{3x+3 - x + 2}{x+1} \cdot \dfrac{1}{x+4}$

$\qquad\qquad\qquad\qquad\qquad\quad = \dfrac{2x+5}{(x+1)(x+4)}$

40. $\dfrac{\dfrac{x}{y} - 2 + \dfrac{y}{x}}{\dfrac{x}{y} - \dfrac{y}{x}} \cdot \dfrac{xy}{xy} = \dfrac{x^2 - 2xy + y^2}{x^2 - y^2}$

$\qquad\qquad\qquad\qquad = \dfrac{(x-y)^2}{(x-y)(x+y)}$

$\qquad\qquad\qquad\qquad = \dfrac{x-y}{x+y}$

42. $\dfrac{\dfrac{1}{(x+h)^2} - \dfrac{1}{x^2}}{h} \cdot \dfrac{x^2(x+h)^2}{x^2(x+h)^2} = \dfrac{x^2 - (x+h)^2}{hx^2(x+h)^2}$

$\qquad\qquad\qquad\qquad\qquad\quad = \dfrac{x^2 - x^2 - 2xh - h^2}{hx^2(x+h)^2}$

$\qquad\qquad\qquad\qquad\qquad\quad = \dfrac{-2xh - h^2}{hx^2(x+h)^2} = \dfrac{h(-2x - h)}{hx^2(x+h)^2}$

$\qquad\qquad\qquad\qquad\qquad\quad = \dfrac{-2x - h}{x^2(x+h)^2}$

44. $\dfrac{\dfrac{2x+2h+3}{x+h} - \dfrac{2x+3}{x}}{h} \cdot \dfrac{x(x+h)}{x(x+h)} = \dfrac{2x^2 + 2xh + 3x - (2x+3)(x+h)}{xh(x+h)}$

$\qquad\qquad\qquad\qquad\qquad\qquad\quad = \dfrac{2x^2 + 2xh + 3x - 2x^2 - 2xh - 3x - 3h}{xh(x+h)}$

$\qquad\qquad\qquad\qquad\qquad\qquad\quad = \dfrac{-3h}{xh(x+h)}$

$\qquad\qquad\qquad\qquad\qquad\qquad\quad = \dfrac{-3}{x(x+h)}$

46. (A) Solution shown is incorrect. The two terms "-3" were canceled incorrectly. Only factors can be canceled.

$\quad$ (B) $\dfrac{x^2 - 2x - 3}{x - 3} = \dfrac{(x-3)(x+1)}{(x-3)} = x + 1$

48. (A) Solution shown is incorrect. The term "+h" in the numerator was canceled incorrectly. Only factors can be canceled.

$\quad$ (B) $\dfrac{(x+h)^3 - x^3}{h} = \dfrac{x^3 + 3x^2h + 3xh^2 + h^3 - x^3}{h}$

$\qquad\qquad\qquad\quad = \dfrac{h(3x^2 + 3xh + h^2)}{h}$

$\qquad\qquad\qquad\quad = 3x^2 + 3xh + h^2$

50. (A) Solution shown is correct.

$\qquad \dfrac{2}{x-1} - \dfrac{x+3}{x^2-1} = \dfrac{2(x+1) - (x+3)}{(x-1)(x+1)} = \dfrac{2x+2 - x - 3}{(x-1)(x+1)}$

$\qquad\qquad\qquad\qquad = \dfrac{x-1}{(x-1)(x+1)} = \dfrac{1}{x+1}$

52. (A) Solution shown is incorrect. The two terms were combined incorrectly. The first term "x" must be built up as a fraction with a common denominator.

(B) $x + \dfrac{x - 2}{x^2 - 3x + 2} = \dfrac{x(x^2 - 3x + 2) + x - 2}{x^2 - 3x + 2}$

$\qquad\qquad\qquad\qquad = \dfrac{x(x - 2)(x - 1) + (x - 2)}{(x - 2)(x - 1)}$

$\qquad\qquad\qquad\qquad = \dfrac{(x - 2)(x(x - 1) + 1)}{(x - 2)(x - 1)}$

$\qquad\qquad\qquad\qquad = \dfrac{x^2 - x + 1}{x - 1}$

54. $\dfrac{\dfrac{s^2}{s - t} - s}{\dfrac{t^2}{s - t} + t} \cdot \dfrac{s - t}{s - t} = \dfrac{s^2 - s(s - t)}{t^2 + t(s - t)}$

$\qquad\qquad\qquad\qquad = \dfrac{s^2 - s^2 + st}{t^2 + st - t^2}$

$\qquad\qquad\qquad\qquad = 1$

56. $1 - \dfrac{1}{1 - \dfrac{1}{1 - \frac{1}{x} \cdot \frac{x}{x}}} = 1 - \dfrac{1}{1 - \frac{x}{x - 1}} \cdot \dfrac{x - 1}{x - 1}$

$\qquad\qquad\qquad\qquad = 1 - \dfrac{x - 1}{x - 1 - x}$

$\qquad\qquad\qquad\qquad = 1 - \dfrac{x - 1}{-1}$

$\qquad\qquad\qquad\qquad = 1 - \dfrac{1 - x}{1}$

$\qquad\qquad\qquad\qquad = 1 - 1 + x$

$\qquad\qquad\qquad\qquad = x$

58. $\dfrac{a}{b} + \dfrac{c}{b} = a\left(\dfrac{1}{b}\right) + c\left(\dfrac{1}{b}\right)$ definition of division

$\qquad\qquad = (a + c)\left(\dfrac{1}{b}\right)$ distributive

$\qquad\qquad = \dfrac{a + c}{b}$ definition of division

Exercise 1-5

2. $y^7 y^{-7} = y^{7 + (-7)} = y^0 = 1$

4. $(2a^3)(7a^4)(3a^9) = 42a^{3+4+9} = 42a^{16}$

6. $(3u^{-2}v^3)^{-2} = \dfrac{1}{(3u^{-2}v^3)^2} = \dfrac{1}{3^2(u^{-2})^2(v^3)^2} = \dfrac{1}{9u^{-4}v^6} = \dfrac{u^4}{9v^6}$

8. $\left(\dfrac{a^3 b^2}{2c^5}\right)^2 = \dfrac{(a^3)^2(b^2)^2}{2^2(c^5)^2} = \dfrac{a^6 b^4}{4c^{10}}$

10. $\dfrac{10^{-9} \cdot 10^{-12}}{10^{-17} \cdot 10^5} = \dfrac{10^{-9+(-12)}}{10^{-17+5}} = \dfrac{10^{-21}}{10^{-12}} = 10^{-21-(-12)} = 10^{-9} = \dfrac{1}{10^9}$

12. $\dfrac{20u^{-4}v^5}{4u^4 v^{-3}} = \dfrac{20v^5 v^3}{4u^4 u^4} = \dfrac{5v^8}{u^8}$

14. $\left(\dfrac{w^{-2}}{w^{-4}}\right)^{-2} = \dfrac{(w^{-2})^{-2}}{(w^{-4})^{-2}} = \dfrac{w^4}{w^8} = \dfrac{1}{w^4}$

16. $\dfrac{15 \times 10^{-8}}{5 \times 10^{-5}} = 3 \times 10^{-8-(-5)} = 3 \times 10^{-3} = \dfrac{3}{10^3}$

18. $3{,}670 = 3.67 \times 10^3$

20. $0.029 = 2.9 \times 10^{-2}$

22. $0.000\ 497 = 4.97 \times 10^{-4}$

24. $3 \times 10^{-3} = 0.003$

26. $8.63 \times 10^8 = 863{,}000{,}000$

28. $1.6 \times 10^{-7} = 0.000\ 000\ 16$

30. $\dfrac{32n^5n^{-8}}{24m^{-7}m^7} = \dfrac{4n^{-3}}{3m^0}$

$\qquad\qquad\quad = \dfrac{4}{3n^3}$

32. $\left(\dfrac{m^{-2}n^3}{m^4n^{-1}}\right)^2 = \left(\dfrac{n^4}{m^6}\right)^2$ simplify inside parentheses first

$\qquad\qquad\quad = \dfrac{n^8}{m^{12}}$

34. $\left(\dfrac{6mn^{-2}}{3m^{-1}n^2}\right)^{-3} = \left(\dfrac{2m^2}{n^4}\right)^{-3}$

$\qquad\qquad\qquad = \left(\dfrac{n^4}{2m^2}\right)^3$

$\qquad\qquad\qquad = \dfrac{n^{12}}{8m^6}$

36. $\left[\left(\dfrac{x^{-2}y^3t}{x^{-3}y^{-2}t^2}\right)^2\right]^{-1} = \left[\left(\dfrac{xy^5}{t}\right)^2\right]^{-1}$

$\qquad\qquad\qquad\qquad = \left[\dfrac{x^2y^{10}}{t^2}\right]^{-1}$

$\qquad\qquad\qquad\qquad = \dfrac{t^2}{x^2y^{10}}$

38. $(a^2 - b^2)^{-1} = \dfrac{1}{a^2 - b^2}$

40. $\dfrac{1 - x}{x^{-1} - 1} = \dfrac{1 - x}{\frac{1}{x} - 1} \cdot \dfrac{x}{x}$

$\qquad\qquad\quad = \dfrac{x(1 - x)}{(1 - x)}$

$\qquad\qquad\quad = x$

42. $\dfrac{u + v}{u^{-1} + v^{-1}} = \dfrac{u + v}{\frac{1}{u} + \frac{1}{v}} \cdot \dfrac{uv}{uv}$

$\qquad\qquad\quad = \dfrac{uv(u + v)}{v + u}$

$\qquad\qquad\quad = uv$

44. $-2(x^2 + 3x)^{-3}(2x + 3) = \dfrac{-2(2x + 3)}{(x^2 + 3x)^3}$

46. $2^{(3^2)} = 2^9 = 512,\ (2^3)^2 = 8^2 = 64$
On a calculator 2^3^2 = 64, (2^3)^2 = 64 and 2^(3^2) = 512

48. $a^{-n} \cdot a^n = a^n \cdot a^{-n} = a^{n + (-n)} = a = 1$. The definition of reciprocal gives $a^n \cdot \dfrac{1}{a^n} = 1$ and comparing with $a^n \cdot a^{-n} = 1$ helps motivate the definition $a^{-n} = \dfrac{1}{a^n}$.

50. $\dfrac{6x^3 + 9x}{3x^3} = \dfrac{6x^3}{3x^3} + \dfrac{9x}{3x^3}$

$\qquad\qquad\quad = 2 + 3x^{-2}$

52. $\dfrac{7x^5 - x^2}{4x^5} = \dfrac{7x^5}{4x^5} - \dfrac{x^2}{4x^5}$

$\qquad\qquad\quad = \dfrac{7}{4} - \dfrac{1}{4}x^{-3}$

54. $\dfrac{3x^4 - 4x^2 - 1}{4x^3} = \dfrac{3x^4}{4x^3} - \dfrac{4x^2}{4x^3} - \dfrac{1}{4x^3}$

$\qquad\qquad\qquad = \dfrac{3}{4}x - x^{-1} - \dfrac{1}{4}x^{-3}$

56. $\dfrac{(4,320)(0.000\,000\,000\,704)}{(835)(635,000,000,000)} = \dfrac{(4.32 \times 10^3)(7.04 \times 10^{-10})}{(8.35 \times 10^2)(6.35 \times 10^{11})}$

$\qquad\qquad\qquad\qquad\qquad\quad = 5.74 \times 10^{-21}$ using calculator

58. $\dfrac{0.000\,000\,007\,23}{(0.0933)(43,700,000,000)} = \dfrac{7.23 \times 10^{-9}}{(9.333 \times 10^{-2})(4.37 \times 10^{11})}$

$\qquad\qquad\qquad\qquad\qquad\quad = 1.77 \times 10^{-18}$ using calculator

60. $(-302)^7 = -2.2911 \times 10^{17}$

62. $(23.8)^{-8} = 9.7137 \times 10^{-12}$

64. $(0.000\,000\,000\,482)^{-4} = (4.82 \times 10^{-10})^{-4} = 1.8527 \times 10^{37}$

66. $\dfrac{4(x-3)^{-4}}{8(x-3)^{-2}} = \dfrac{1}{2(x-3)^2}$

68. $\dfrac{b^{-2} - c^{-2}}{b^{-3} - c^{-3}} = \dfrac{\dfrac{1}{b^2} - \dfrac{1}{c^2}}{\dfrac{1}{b^3} - \dfrac{1}{c^3}} \cdot \dfrac{b^3 c^3}{b^3 c^3}$

$\qquad = \dfrac{bc^3 - b^3 c}{c^3 - b^3}$

$\qquad = \dfrac{bc(c^2 - b^2)}{(c - b)(c^2 + bc + b^2)}$

$\qquad = \dfrac{bc(c - b)(c + b)}{(c - b)(c^2 + bc + b^2)}$

$\qquad = \dfrac{bc(c + b)}{c^2 + bc + b^2}$

70. $\left[\dfrac{u^{-2} - v^{-2}}{(u^{-1} - v^{-1})^2}\right]^{-1} = \left[\dfrac{\dfrac{1}{u^2} - \dfrac{1}{v^2}}{u^{-2} - 2u^{-1}v^{-1} + v^{-2}}\right]^{-1}$

$\qquad = \left[\dfrac{\dfrac{v^2 - u^2}{u^2 v^2}}{\dfrac{1}{u^2} - \dfrac{2}{uv} + \dfrac{1}{v^2}} \cdot \dfrac{u^2 v^2}{u^2 v^2}\right]^{-1}$

$\qquad = \left[\dfrac{v^2 - u^2}{v^2 - 2uv + u^2}\right]^{-1}$

$\qquad = \left[\dfrac{(v - u)(v + u)}{(v - u)(v - u)}\right]^{-1}$

$\qquad = \left[\dfrac{v + u}{v - u}\right]^{-1} = \dfrac{v - u}{v + u}$

72. weight in pounds = (weight per gram)(number of grams)

$\qquad = \dfrac{2.2 \times 10^{-3} \text{ lb}}{\text{gram}} \cdot 1.5 \times 10^{21} \text{ gram}$

$\qquad = 3.3 \times 10^{18} \text{ lb}$

74. distance = (rate)(time)

$\qquad = \left(1.86 \times 10^5 \dfrac{\text{mi}}{\text{sec}}\right)(10^{-10} \text{ sec})$

$\qquad = 1.86 \times 10^{-5} \text{ mi}$

$\qquad = 1.86 \times 10^{-5} \text{ mi} \left(\dfrac{5280 \text{ ft}}{\text{mi}}\right)$

$\qquad \approx 9.82 \times 10^{-2} \text{ ft}$

$\qquad \approx 9.82 \times 10^{-2} \text{ ft} \left(\dfrac{12 \text{ in}}{\text{ft}}\right)$

$\qquad \approx 1.18 \text{ in}$

76. GNP per person $= \dfrac{\text{GNP}}{\text{population}}$

$\qquad = \dfrac{8.87 \times 10^{12}}{2.74 \times 10^8}$

$\qquad \approx 3.24 \times 10^4$

$\qquad \approx \$32{,}400 \text{ per person}$

Exercise 1-6

2. $27^{1/3} = 3$

4. $8^{2/3} = (8^{1/3})^2 = (2)^2 = 4$

6. $64^{2/3} = (64^{1/3})^2 = (4)^2 = 16$

8. $(-64)^{2/3} = (-64^{1/3})^2 = (-4)^2 = 16$

10. $\left(\dfrac{25}{36}\right)^{3/2} = \left[\left(\dfrac{25}{36}\right)^{1/2}\right]^3 = \left(\dfrac{5}{6}\right)^3 = \dfrac{125}{216}$

12. $9^{-5/2} = \dfrac{1}{(9^{1/2})^5} = \dfrac{1}{3^5} = \dfrac{1}{243}$

14. $b^{2/5} b^{4/5} = b^{2/5 + 4/5} = b^{6/5}$

16. $d^{1/5} d^{-3/5} = d^{1/5 - 3/5} = d^{-2/5} = \dfrac{1}{d^{2/5}}$

18. $(v^{-3/4})^8 = v^{-6} = \dfrac{1}{v^6}$

20. $(27x^{-6}y^9)^{1/3} = 27^{1/3}(x^{-6})^{1/3}(y^9)^{1/3}$
$= 3x^{-2}y^3$
$= \dfrac{3y^3}{x^2}$

22. $\left(\dfrac{m^{-2/3}}{n^{-1/2}}\right)^{-6} = \dfrac{(m^{-2/3})^{(-6)}}{(n^{-1/2})^{(-6)}}$
$= \dfrac{m^4}{n^3}$

24. $\left(\dfrac{w^4}{9x^{-2}}\right)^{-1/2} = \dfrac{w^{4(-1/2)}}{9^{-1/2}(x^{-2})^{(-1/2)}}$
$= \dfrac{w^{-2}}{\frac{1}{9^{1/2}}x}$
$= \dfrac{\frac{1}{w^2}}{\frac{x}{3}} = \dfrac{1}{w^2} \cdot \dfrac{3}{x}$
$= \dfrac{3}{xw^2}$

26. $\left(\dfrac{25x^5y^{-1}}{16x^{-3}y^{-5}}\right)^{1/2} = \dfrac{25^{1/2}(x^5)^{(1/2)}(y^{-1})^{(1/2)}}{16^{1/2}(x^{-3})^{(1/2)}(y^{-5})^{(1/2)}}$
$= \dfrac{5x^{5/2}y^{-1/2}}{4x^{-3/2}y^{-5/2}}$
$= \dfrac{5}{4}x^{5/2-(-3/2)}y^{-1/2-(-5/2)}$
$= \dfrac{5}{4}x^{8/2}y^{4/2}$
$= \dfrac{5}{4}x^4y^2$

28. $\dfrac{6a^{3/4}}{15a^{-1/3}} = \dfrac{2}{5}a^{3/4-(-1/3)}$
$= \dfrac{2}{5}a^{13/12}$

30. $\left(\dfrac{x^{-1/3}y^{1/2}}{x^{-1/4}y^{1/3}}\right)^6 = (x^{-1/3-(-1/4)}y^{1/2-1/3})^6$
$= (x^{-1/12}y^{1/6})^6$
$= x^{-1/2}y^1$
$= \dfrac{y}{x^{1/2}}$

32. $3x^{3/4}(4x^{1/4} - 2x^8) = 12x^{3/4+1/4} - 6x^{3/4+8}$
$= 12x - 6x^{35/4}$

34. $(3u^{1/2} - v^{1/2})(u^{1/2} - 4v^{1/2}) = 3u^{1/2+1/2} - 12u^{1/2}v^{1/2} - v^{1/2}u^{1/2} + 4v^{1/2+1/2}$
$= 3u - 13u^{1/2}v^{1/2} + 4v$

36. $(5m^{1/2} + n^{1/2})(5m^{1/2} - n^{1/2}) = (5m^{1/2})^2 - (n^{1/2})^2$
$= 25m - n$

38. $(3x^{1/2} - y^{1/2})^2 = (3x^{1/2})^2 - 2(3x^{1/2})(y^{1/2}) + (y^{1/2})^2$
$= 9x - 6x^{1/2}y^{1/2} + y$

40. $22^{3/2} \approx 103.2$ using calculator

42. $827^{-3/8} \approx 0.08053$ using calculator

44. $37.09^{7/3} \approx 4588$ using calculator

46. $(491,300,000,000)^{7/4} = (4.913 \times 10^{11})^{1.75} \approx 2.883 \times 10^{20}$

48. For $x = 2$, $y = 3$: $(x^3 + y^3)^{1/3} = (2^3 + 3^3)^{1/3} = (8 + 27)^{1/3} = 35^{1/3} \approx 3.271$
while $(x + y) = 2 + 3 = 5$.

50. For $x = 2$, $y = 3$: $(x + y)^{-1/2} = (2 + 3)^{-1/2} = 5^{-1/2} = \dfrac{1}{\sqrt{5}} \approx 0.447$
while $\dfrac{1}{(x + y)^2} = \dfrac{1}{(2 + 3)^2} = \dfrac{1}{5^2} = \dfrac{1}{25} = 0.04$.

52. $\dfrac{x^{2/3} + 2}{2x^{1/3}} = \dfrac{x^{2/3}}{2x^{1/3}} + \dfrac{2}{2x^{1/3}} = \dfrac{1}{2}x^{1/3} + x^{-1/3}$

54. $\dfrac{2x^{3/4} + 3x^{1/3}}{3x} = \dfrac{2x^{3/4}}{3x} + \dfrac{3x^{1/3}}{3x}$
$= \dfrac{2}{3}x^{-1/4} + x^{-2/3}$

56. $\dfrac{2x^{1/3} - x^{1/2}}{4x^{1/2}} = \dfrac{2x^{1/3}}{4x^{1/2}} - \dfrac{x^{1/2}}{4x^{1/2}}$
$= \dfrac{1}{2}x^{-1/6} - \dfrac{1}{4}$

58. $(a^{n/2}b^{n/3})^{1/n} = (a^{n/2})^{1/n}(b^{n/3})^{1/n}$

$\qquad\qquad\qquad = a^{(n/2)(1/n)}b^{(n/3)(1/n)}$

$\qquad\qquad\qquad = a^{1/2}b^{1/3}$

60. $(a^{m/3}b^{n/2})^{-6} = (a^{m/3})^{-6}(b^{n/2})^{-6}$

$\qquad\qquad\qquad = a^{(m/3)(-6)}b^{(n/2)(-6)}$

$\qquad\qquad\qquad = a^{-2m}b^{-3n}$

$\qquad\qquad\qquad = \dfrac{1}{a^{2m}b^{3n}}$

62. (A) let $x = 2$, then $(x^2)^{1/2} = (2^2)^{1/2} = 4^{1/2} = 2 \neq -2$ which shows 2 is a real value of x such that $(x^2)^{1/2} \neq -x$

(B) let $x = -2$, then $(x^2)^{1/2} = ((-2)^2)^{1/2} = (4)^{1/2} = 2 = -(-2)$ which shows -2 is a real value of x such that $(x^2)^{1/2} = -x$

(C) $\quad (x^3)^{1/3} = -x$

$\qquad\qquad x = -x$

$\qquad\quad x^3 = (-x)^3$

$\qquad\quad x^3 = -x^3$

$\qquad 2x^3 = 0$

$\qquad\quad x = 0,$

which shows $(x^3)^{1/3} = -x$ only for $x = 0$

64. For $b \geq 0$, $(b^m)^{1/n} = (b^{1/n})^m$. for $b < 0$, both $(b^m)^{1/n}$ and $(b^{1/n})^m$ are not real. No, it is not possible for one to be real and the other not.

66. $\dfrac{(x-1)^{1/2} - x(\frac{1}{2})(x-1)^{-1/2}}{(x-1)} \cdot \dfrac{2(x-1)^{1/2}}{2(x-1)^{1/2}} = \dfrac{2(x-1) - x}{2(x-1)^{3/2}}$

$\qquad\qquad\qquad\qquad\qquad\qquad\qquad\qquad\quad = \dfrac{2x - 2 - x}{2(x-1)^{3/2}}$

$\qquad\qquad\qquad\qquad\qquad\qquad\qquad\qquad\quad = \dfrac{x - 2}{2(x-1)^{3/2}}$

68. $\dfrac{(x+2)^{2/3} - x(\frac{2}{3})(x+2)^{-1/3}}{(x+2)^{4/3}} \cdot \dfrac{3(x+2)^{1/3}}{3(x+2)^{1/3}} = \dfrac{3(x+2) - 2x}{3(x+2)^{5/3}}$

$\qquad\qquad\qquad\qquad\qquad\qquad\qquad\qquad\qquad = \dfrac{3x + 6 - 2x}{3(x+2)^{5/3}}$

$\qquad\qquad\qquad\qquad\qquad\qquad\qquad\qquad\qquad = \dfrac{x + 6}{3(x+2)^{5/3}}$

70. $N = 50x^{1/2}y^{1/2}$

$\qquad = 50(256)^{1/2}(144)^{1/2}$

$\qquad = 50(16)(12)$

$\qquad = 9600$ units

72. $d = 0.0212v^{7/3}$

$\qquad = 0.0212(50)^{7/3}$

$\qquad \approx 195$ ft

Exercise 1-7

2. $n^{4/5} = \sqrt[5]{n^4}$

4. $7y^{2/5} = 7\sqrt[5]{y^2}$

6. $(7x^2y)^{5/7} = \sqrt[7]{(7x^2y)^5}$

8. $x^{1/2} + y^{1/2} = \sqrt{x} + \sqrt{y}$

10. $\sqrt{c} = c^{1/2}$

12. $7m\sqrt[5]{n^2} = 7mn^{2/5}$

14. $\sqrt[9]{(3m^4n)^2} = (3m^4n)^{2/9}$

16. $\sqrt[3]{x+y} = (x+y)^{1/3}$

18. $\sqrt[3]{-27} = -3$ since $(-3)^3 = -27$

20. $\sqrt{16m^4y^8} = \sqrt{16}\sqrt{m^4}\sqrt{y^8} = (4^2)^{1/2}(m^4)^{1/2}(y^8)^{1/2}$

$\qquad\qquad\qquad\qquad\qquad\qquad\qquad\qquad\qquad = 4m^2y^4$

22. $\sqrt[5]{32a^{15}b^{10}} = 32^{1/5}(a^{15})^{1/5}(b^{10})^{1/5}$

$= 2a^3b^2$

24. $\sqrt{27m^2n^7} = \sqrt{9m^2n^6 \cdot 3n}$

$= 3mn^3\sqrt{3n}, \ m \geq 0$

26. $\sqrt[4]{2^4x^5y^8} = \sqrt[4]{2^4x^4y^8 \cdot x}$

$= 2xy^2\sqrt[4]{x}$

28. $\sqrt[10]{n^6} = n^{6/10}$

$= n^{3/5}$

$= \sqrt[5]{n^3}, \ n \geq 0$

30. $\sqrt{\sqrt[4]{5x}} = ((5x)^{1/4})^{1/2} \ (x \geq 0)$

$= (5x)^{1/8}$

$= \sqrt[8]{5x}$

32. $\sqrt{2x}\sqrt{8xy} = \sqrt{16x^2y} \ (x \geq 0, \ y \geq 0)$

$= 4x\sqrt{y}$

34. $\dfrac{1}{\sqrt{7}} = \dfrac{1}{\sqrt{7}} \cdot \dfrac{\sqrt{7}}{\sqrt{7}}$

$= \dfrac{\sqrt{7}}{7}$

36. $\dfrac{12y^2}{\sqrt{6y}} = \dfrac{12y^2}{\sqrt{6y}} \cdot \dfrac{\sqrt{6y}}{\sqrt{6y}}$

$= \dfrac{12y^2\sqrt{6y}}{6y}$

$= 2y\sqrt{6y}$

38. $\dfrac{4}{\sqrt{6}-2} = \dfrac{4}{\sqrt{6}-2} \cdot \dfrac{\sqrt{6}+2}{\sqrt{6}+2}$

$= \dfrac{4\sqrt{6}+8}{6-4}$

$= \dfrac{4\sqrt{6}+8}{2}$

$= \dfrac{2(2\sqrt{6}+4)}{2}$

$= 2\sqrt{6}+4$

40. $\dfrac{\sqrt{2}}{\sqrt{10}-2} = \dfrac{\sqrt{2}}{\sqrt{10}-2} \cdot \dfrac{\sqrt{10}+2}{\sqrt{10}+2}$

$= \dfrac{\sqrt{20}+2\sqrt{2}}{10-4}$

$= \dfrac{2\sqrt{5}+2\sqrt{2}}{6}$

$= \dfrac{2(\sqrt{5}+\sqrt{2})}{6}$

$= \dfrac{\sqrt{5}+\sqrt{2}}{3}$

42. $2a\sqrt[3]{8a^8b^{13}} = 2a\sqrt[3]{2^3a^6b^{12} \cdot a^2b}$

$= 2a \cdot 2a^2b^4\sqrt[3]{a^2b}$

$= 4a^3b^4\sqrt[3]{a^2b}$

44. $\dfrac{\sqrt[5]{32u^{12}v^8}}{uv} = \dfrac{\sqrt[5]{2^5u^{10}v^5 \cdot u^2v^3}}{uv}$

$= \dfrac{2u^2v\sqrt[5]{u^2v^3}}{uv}$

$= 2u\sqrt[5]{u^2v^3}$

46. $\sqrt[8]{3^6(u+v)^6} = 3^{6/8} \cdot (u+v)^{6/8}$

$= 3^{3/4}(u+v)^{3/4}$

$= \sqrt[4]{3^3(u+v)^3}$

48. $\sqrt{\sqrt[6]{x^8y^6}} = [(x^8y^6)^{1/6}]^{1/2}$

$= (x^8y^6)^{1/12}$

$= x^{8/12}y^{6/12}$

$= x^{4/6}y^{3/6}$

$= \sqrt[6]{x^4y^3}$

$= \sqrt[3]{x^2}\sqrt{y}$

50. $\sqrt[4]{4m^5n}\ \sqrt[4]{6m^3n^4} = \sqrt[4]{24m^8n^5}$

$$= \sqrt[4]{m^8n^4 \cdot 24n}$$

$$= m^2n\ \sqrt[4]{24n}$$

52. $\sqrt{x^2 + y^2}$ cannot be simplified further

54. $\dfrac{\sqrt{6}\ \sqrt{8c}}{\sqrt{18c}} = \dfrac{\sqrt{48x}}{3\sqrt{2c}} \cdot \dfrac{\sqrt{2c}}{\sqrt{2c}}$

$$= \dfrac{\sqrt{2^5c^2 \cdot 3}}{6c}$$

$$= \dfrac{4c\sqrt{6}}{6c}$$

$$= \dfrac{2\sqrt{6}}{3}$$

56. $\dfrac{8x^3y^5}{\sqrt[3]{4x^2y}} \cdot \dfrac{\sqrt[3]{2xy^2}}{\sqrt[3]{2xy^2}} = \dfrac{8x^3y^5\ \sqrt[3]{2xy^2}}{\sqrt[3]{8x^3y^3}}$

$$= \dfrac{8x^3y^5\ \sqrt[3]{2xy^2}}{2xy}$$

$$= 4x^2y^4\ \sqrt[3]{2xy^2}$$

58. $\sqrt[5]{\dfrac{4x^2}{16y^3}} = \sqrt[5]{\dfrac{x^2}{4y^3}}$

$$= \dfrac{\sqrt[5]{x^2}}{\sqrt[5]{4y^3}} \cdot \dfrac{\sqrt[5]{8y^2}}{\sqrt[5]{8y^2}}$$

$$= \dfrac{\sqrt[5]{8x^2y^2}}{2y}$$

60. $\dfrac{5\sqrt{x}}{3 - 2\sqrt{x}} \cdot \dfrac{3 + 2\sqrt{x}}{3 + 2\sqrt{x}} = \dfrac{15\sqrt{x} + 10x}{9 - 4x}$

62. $\dfrac{3\sqrt{2} - 2\sqrt{3}}{3\sqrt{3} - 2\sqrt{2}} \cdot \dfrac{3\sqrt{3} + 2\sqrt{2}}{3\sqrt{3} + 2\sqrt{2}} = \dfrac{9\sqrt{6} + 12 - 18 - 4\sqrt{6}}{27 - 8}$

$$= \dfrac{5\sqrt{6} - 6}{19}$$

64. $\dfrac{-y^2}{2 - \sqrt{y^2 + 4}} \cdot \dfrac{2 + \sqrt{y^2 + 4}}{2 + \sqrt{y^2 + 4}} = \dfrac{-2y^2 - y^2\ \sqrt{y^2 + 4}}{4 - (y^2 + 4)}$

$$= \dfrac{-2y^2 - y^2\ \sqrt{y^2 + 4}}{4 - y^2 - 4}$$

$$= \dfrac{-2y^2 - y^2\ \sqrt{y^2 + 4}}{-y^2}$$

$$= \dfrac{-y^2(2 + \sqrt{y^2 + 4})}{-y^2}$$

$$= 2 + \sqrt{y^2 + 4}$$

66. $\dfrac{\sqrt{x} - \sqrt{y}}{\sqrt{x} + \sqrt{y}} \cdot \dfrac{\sqrt{x} + \sqrt{y}}{\sqrt{x} + \sqrt{y}} = \dfrac{x - y}{x + 2\sqrt{xy} + y}$

68. $\dfrac{\sqrt{2 + h} + \sqrt{2}}{h} \cdot \dfrac{\sqrt{2 + h} - \sqrt{2}}{\sqrt{2 + h} - \sqrt{2}} = \dfrac{2 + h - 2}{h\sqrt{2 + h} - h\sqrt{2}}$

$$= \dfrac{h}{h\sqrt{2 + h} - h\sqrt{2}}$$

$$= \dfrac{1}{\sqrt{2 + h} - \sqrt{2}}$$

70. $\sqrt{419.763} = 20.49$ to four significant digits

72. $\sqrt[4]{0.098\ 553} = 0.5603$ to four significant digits

74. $\sqrt[7]{4.892 \times 10^{16}}$ = 242.2 to four significant digits

76. $\sqrt[3]{2 + \sqrt[3]{2}}$ = 1.483 to four significant digits

78. $\sqrt[3]{\sqrt[7]{500}}$ = 1.344 to four significant digits

$\sqrt[21]{500}$ = 1.344 to four significant digits

80. $\dfrac{1}{\sqrt[3]{2}}$ = 0.7937 to four significant digits

$\dfrac{\sqrt[3]{4}}{2}$ = 0.7937 to four significant digits

82. $\sqrt{x^2} = |x|$ from which $\sqrt{x^2} = x$ if and only if $|x| = x$ which is true for $x \geq 0$. Hence, $\sqrt{x^2} = x$ for $x \geq 0$.

84. $\sqrt[3]{x^3} = x$ from which $\sqrt[3]{x^3} = -x$ if and only if $x = -x$ which is true only for $x = 0$. Hence, $\sqrt[3]{x^3} = x$ for $x = 0$.

86. (A) $2\sqrt[3]{2 + \sqrt{5}}$ = 3.236067977...   (B) $\sqrt{8}$ = 2.828427125...

(C) $\sqrt{3} + \sqrt{7}$ = 4.377802119...   (D) $\sqrt{3 + \sqrt{8}} + \sqrt{3 - \sqrt{8}}$ = 2.828427125...

(E) $\sqrt{10 + \sqrt{84}}$ = 4.377802119...   (F) $1 + \sqrt{5}$ = 3.236067977...

(A) & (F), (B) & (D), and (C) & (E) have the same value on a calculator.

Let $x = 1 + \sqrt{5}$, then

$x^3 = 1 + 3 \cdot 1^2 \cdot \sqrt{5} + 3 \cdot 1 \cdot \sqrt{5}^2 + \sqrt{5}^3$

$x^3 = 1 + 3\sqrt{5} + 3 \cdot 5 + 5\sqrt{5}$

$x^3 = 16 + 8\sqrt{5} = 8(2 + \sqrt{5})$

$x = 2\sqrt[3]{2 + \sqrt{5}}$ which shows (A) & (F) are equal.

Let $x = \sqrt{3 + \sqrt{8}} + \sqrt{3 - \sqrt{8}} > 0$, then

$x^2 = 3 + \sqrt{8} + 2\sqrt{3 + \sqrt{8}} \sqrt{3 - \sqrt{8}} + 3 - \sqrt{8}$

$x^2 = 6 + 2\sqrt{3^2 - \sqrt{8}^2} = 6 + 2$

$x^2 = 8$

$x = \sqrt{8}$ since $x > 0$, which shows (B) & (D) are equal.

Let $x = \sqrt{3} + \sqrt{7} > 0$, then

$x^2 = 3 + 2\sqrt{3}\sqrt{7} + 7$

$x^2 = 10 + 2\sqrt{21} = 10 + \sqrt{4 \cdot 21}$

$x^2 = 10 + \sqrt{84}$

$x = \sqrt{10 + \sqrt{84}}$ since $x > 0$, which shows (C) & (E) are equal.

88.
$$\frac{1}{\sqrt[3]{m} + \sqrt[3]{n}} = \frac{1}{m^{1/3} + n^{1/3}}$$

$$= \frac{1}{m^{1/3} + n^{1/3}} \cdot \frac{m^{2/3} - m^{1/3}n^{1/3} + n^{2/3}}{m^{2/3} - m^{1/3}n^{1/3} + n^{2/3}}$$

$$= \frac{m^{2/3} - m^{1/3}n^{1/3} + n^{2/3}}{m - m^{2/3}n^{1/3} + m^{1/3}n^{2/3} + m^{2/3}n^{1/3} - m^{1/3}n^{2/3} + n}$$

$$= \frac{m^{2/3} - (mn)^{1/3} + n^{2/3}}{m + n}$$

$$= \frac{\sqrt[3]{m^2} - \sqrt[3]{mn} + \sqrt[3]{n^2}}{m + n}$$

90.
$$\frac{1}{\sqrt{x} + \sqrt{y} - \sqrt{z}} \cdot \frac{(\sqrt{x} + \sqrt{y}) + \sqrt{z}}{(\sqrt{x} + \sqrt{y}) + \sqrt{z}} = \frac{\sqrt{x} + \sqrt{y} + \sqrt{z}}{(\sqrt{x} + \sqrt{y})^2 - z}$$

$$= \frac{\sqrt{x} + \sqrt{y} + \sqrt{z}}{x + 2\sqrt{x}\sqrt{y} + y - z}$$

$$= \frac{\sqrt{x} + \sqrt{y} + \sqrt{z}}{(x + y - z) + 2\sqrt{x}\sqrt{y}} \cdot \frac{(x + y - z) - 2\sqrt{x}\sqrt{y}}{(x + y - z) - 2\sqrt{x}\sqrt{y}}$$

$$= \frac{(\sqrt{x} + \sqrt{y} + \sqrt{z})(x + y - z - 2\sqrt{x}\sqrt{y})}{(x + y - z)^2 - 4xy}$$

92.
$$\frac{\sqrt[3]{t} - \sqrt[3]{x}}{t - x} = \frac{t^{1/3} - x^{1/3}}{t - x} \cdot \frac{t^{2/3} + t^{1/3}x^{1/3} + x^{2/3}}{t^{2/3} + t^{1/3}x^{1/3} + x^{2/3}}$$

$$= \frac{t + t^{2/3}x^{1/3} + t^{1/3}x^{2/3} - t^{2/3}x^{1/3} - t^{1/3}x^{2/3} - x}{(t - x)(t^{2/3} + t^{1/3}x^{1/3} + x^{2/3})}$$

$$= \frac{t - x}{(t - x)(t^{2/3} + t^{1/3}x^{1/3} + x^{2/3})}$$

$$= \frac{1}{\sqrt[3]{t^2} + \sqrt[3]{t}\sqrt[3]{x} + \sqrt[3]{x^2}}$$

94.
$$\sqrt[m]{\sqrt[n]{x}} = \sqrt[m]{x^{1/n}}$$

$$= (x^{1/n})^{1/m}$$

$$= x^{1/mn}$$

$$= \sqrt[mn]{x}$$

96.
$$T = 2\pi\sqrt{\frac{L}{g}}$$

$$= 2\pi\sqrt{\frac{L}{g} \cdot \frac{g}{g}}$$

$$= 2\pi\sqrt{\frac{Lg}{g^2}}$$

$$= 2\pi\frac{\sqrt{Lg}}{\sqrt{g^2}}$$

$$= \frac{2\pi\sqrt{Lg}}{g}$$

CHAPTER 2

Exercise   2-1

2. $3(y - 4) + 2y = 18$
$3y - 12 + 2y = 18$
$5y - 12 = 18$
$5y = 30$
$y = 6$

4. $4 - 3(t + 2) + t = 5(t - 1) - 7t$
$4 - 3t - 6 + t = 5t - 5 - 7t$
$-2t - 2 = -2t - 5$
$-2 = -5$
No solution

6. $\dfrac{3b}{7} + \dfrac{2b - 5}{2} = -4$
$2(3b) + 7(2b - 5) = 14(-4)$
$6b + 14b - 35 = -56$
$20b - 35 = -56$
$20b = -21$
$b = -\dfrac{21}{20}$ or -1.05

8. $\dfrac{x}{5} + \dfrac{3x - 1}{2} = \dfrac{6x + 5}{4}$
$4x + 10(3x - 1) = 5(6x + 5)$
$4x + 30x - 10 = 30x + 25$
$34x - 10 = 30x + 25$
$4x = 35$
$x = \dfrac{35}{4}$ or 8.75

10. $0.1(w + 0.5) + 0.2w = 0.2(w - 0.4)$
$0.1w + 0.05 + 0.2w = 0.2w - 0.08$
$0.3w + 0.05 = 0.2w - 0.08$
$0.1w = -0.13$
$w = -1.3$

12. $0.35(u + 0.34) - 0.15u = 0.2u - 1.66$
$0.35u + 0.119 - 0.15u = 0.2u - 1.66$
$0.2u + 0.119 = 0.2u - 1.66$
$0.119 = -1.66$
No solution

14. $\dfrac{3 + w}{6w} = \dfrac{1}{2w} + \dfrac{4}{3}$
$\dfrac{3 + w}{6w} \cdot 6w = \dfrac{1}{2w} \cdot 6w + \dfrac{4}{3} \cdot 6w$
$3 + w = 3 + 8w$
$-7w = 0$
$w = 0$, restricted
value
No solution

16. $\dfrac{t}{t - 1} = \dfrac{2}{t - 1} + 2$
$\dfrac{t}{t - 1}(t - 1) = \dfrac{2}{t - 1}(t - 1) + 2(t - 1)$
$t = 2 + 2t - 2$
$-t = 0$
$t = 0$

18. $\dfrac{3(n - 2)}{5} + \dfrac{2n + 3}{6} = \dfrac{4n + 1}{9} + 2$
$\dfrac{3(n - 2)}{5} \cdot 90 + \dfrac{2n + 3}{6} \cdot 90 = \dfrac{4n + 1}{9} \cdot 90 + 2 \cdot 90$
$54(n - 2) + 15(2n + 3) = 10(4n + 1) + 180$
$54n - 108 + 30n + 45 = 40n + 10 + 180$
$84n - 63 = 40n + 190$
$44n = 253$
$n = \dfrac{253}{44} = \dfrac{23}{4} = 5.75$

20. $\dfrac{2x - 3}{x + 1} = 2 - \dfrac{3x - 1}{x + 1}$
$\dfrac{2x - 3}{x + 1}(x + 1) = 2(x + 1) - \dfrac{3x - 1}{x + 1}(x + 1)$
$2x - 3 = 2x + 2 - (3x - 1)$
$2x - 3 = -x + 3$
$3x = 6$
$x = 2$

22. $\dfrac{4y}{y-3} + 5 = \dfrac{12}{y-3}$

$\quad \dfrac{4y}{y-3}(y-3) + 5(y-3) = \dfrac{12}{y-3}(y-3)$

$\qquad\qquad\qquad 4y + 5y - 15 = 12$

$\qquad\qquad\qquad\qquad\; 9y - 15 = 12$

$\qquad\qquad\qquad\qquad\qquad 9y = 27$

$\qquad\qquad\qquad\qquad\qquad\;\; y = 3; \text{ restricted value} \quad \text{No solution}$

24. $\dfrac{1}{b-5} - \dfrac{10}{b^2 - 5b + 25} = \dfrac{1}{b+5}$ Multiply by $(b-5)(b^2 - 5b + 25)(b+5)$

$\quad (b^2 - 5b + 25)(b+5) - 10(b-5)(b+5) = (b-5)(b^2 - 5b + 25)$

$b^3 + 5b^2 - 5b^2 - 25b + 25b + 125 - 10b^2 + 250 = b^3 - 5b^2 + 25b - 5b^2 + 25b - 125$

$\qquad\qquad\qquad\qquad b^3 - 10b^2 + 375 = b^3 - 10b^2 + 50b - 125$

$\qquad\qquad\qquad\qquad\qquad\qquad\quad 500 = 50b$

$\qquad\qquad\qquad\qquad\qquad\qquad\quad\;\; b = 10$

26. $0.0512x + 0.125(x - 2) = 0.725x$

$\quad 0.0512x + 0.125x - 0.25 = 0.725x$

$\qquad\quad\; 0.1762x - 0.25 = 0.725x$

$\qquad\qquad\qquad\; -0.5488x = 0.25$

$\qquad\qquad\qquad\qquad\quad\; x = -0.456 \text{ three significant digits}$

28. $\dfrac{6.08}{x} + 4.49 = \dfrac{4.49x}{x+3}$

$\quad 6.08(x+3) + 4.49x(x+3) = 4.49x^2$

$6.08x + 18.24 + 4.49x^2 + 13.47x = 4.49x^2$

$\qquad\qquad\quad 19.55x + 18.24 = 0$

$\qquad\qquad\qquad\quad\; 19.55x = -18.24$

$\qquad\qquad\qquad\qquad\quad x = -0.933 \text{ three significant digits}$

30. $F = \dfrac{9}{5}C + 32$

$\quad \dfrac{9}{5}C = F - 32$

$\qquad C = \dfrac{5}{9}(F - 32)$

32. $\dfrac{1}{R} = \dfrac{1}{R_1} + \dfrac{1}{R_2}$

$\quad R_1 R_2 = RR_2 + RR_1$

$R_1 R_2 - RR_1 = RR_2$

$R_1(R_2 - R) = RR_2$

$\qquad R_1 = \dfrac{RR_2}{R_2 - R}$

34. $A = 2ab + 2ac + 2bc$

$\quad 2ac + 2bc = A - 2ab$

$\quad c(2a + 2b) = A - 2ab$

$\qquad\qquad c = \dfrac{A - 2ab}{2a + 2b}$

36. $x = \dfrac{3y + 2}{y - 3}$

$\quad x(y - 3) = 3y + 2$

$\quad xy - 3x = 3y + 2$

$\quad xy - 3y = 3x + 2$

$\quad y(x - 3) = 3x + 2$

$\qquad\quad y = \dfrac{3x + 2}{x - 3}$

38. $\dfrac{x^2 + 1}{x - 1} = \dfrac{x^2 + 4x - 3}{x - 1}$

$\quad x^2 + 1 = x^2 + 4x - 3$

$\qquad\quad 4 = 4x$

$\quad x = 1$ which gives division by zero in the original equation. *No solution* is the correct answer.

40. $\dfrac{x - \dfrac{1}{x}}{x + 1 - \dfrac{2}{x}} = 1$

$\quad x - \dfrac{1}{x} = x + 1 - \dfrac{2}{x}$

$\quad x^2 - 1 = x^2 + x - 2$

$\qquad x = 1, \text{ restricted value} \quad \text{No solution}$

42.
$$\frac{y}{1-y} = \left(\frac{x}{1-x}\right)^3$$

$$y = \left(\frac{x}{1-x}\right)^3 (1-y)$$

$$y = \left(\frac{x}{1-x}\right)^3 - \left(\frac{x}{1-x}\right)^3 y$$

$$y + \left(\frac{x}{1-x}\right)^3 y = \left(\frac{x}{1-x}\right)^3$$

$$y \left(1 + \left(\frac{x}{1-x}\right)^3\right) = \left(\frac{x}{1-x}\right)^3$$

$$y = \frac{\left(\frac{x}{1-x}\right)^3}{1 + \left(\frac{x}{1-x}\right)^3} \cdot \frac{(1-x)^3}{(1-x)^3}$$

$$y = \frac{x^3}{(1-x)^3 + x^3}$$

$$y = \frac{x^3}{1 - 3x + 3x^2 - x^3 + x^3}$$

$$y = \frac{x^3}{3x^2 - 3x + 1}$$

44. $m > n$ implies $m = n + p$ where $p > 0$

$m = n + p$	multiply both sides by $m - n$
$m(m - n) = (n + p)(m - n)$	remove parentheses
$m^2 - mn = mn + mp - n^2 - np$	subtract mp from both sides
$m^2 - mn - mp = mn - n^2 - np$	factor both sides
$m(m - n - p) = n(m - n - p)$	divide both sides by $m - n - p$
$m = n$	

Fallacy: last step, dividing both sides by $m - n - p$, is division by zero since $m = n + p$ or $m - n - p = 0$.

46. Let x = the number,
then $\frac{1}{2}x + 6 = \frac{2}{3}x$

$$\frac{2}{3}x - \frac{1}{2}x = 6$$

$$4x - 3x = 36$$

$$x = 36$$

48. If x = the first of three consecutive even integers

$x + 2$ = the second of three consecutive even integers

$x + 4$ = the third of three consecutive even integers

$$x + 2(x + 2) = 2(x + 4)$$

$$x + 2x + 4 = 2x + 8$$

$$3x + 4 = 2x + 8$$

$$x = 4$$

$$x + 2 = 6$$

$$x + 4 = 8$$

4, 6, and 8 are the integers.

50. $A = \ell w$ rectangle

$A = s^2$ square $A = 12^2 = 144$

$A = \ell w$

$144 = 24 \cdot w$

$w = \frac{144}{24}$

$w = 6$

The rectangle is 24m in length and 6m in width.

52.
$$P = a + b + c$$
$$P = 11 + \frac{1}{5}P + \frac{1}{4}P$$
$$20P = 220 + 4P + 5P$$
$$11P = 220$$
$$P = 20 \text{ cm}$$

54. cost + mark-up = price
$$c + 0.6c = 144$$
$$1.6c = 144$$
$$c = 90$$
The cost is \$90.

56. (A) earnings = base salary + commission
$$3170 = 1175 + 0.05x$$
$$0.05x = 1995$$
$$x = \$39,900 \text{ in sales}$$

(B)
$$2150 + 0.08(x - 7000) = 1175 + 0.05x$$
$$2150 + 0.08x - 560 = 1175 + 0.05x$$
$$0.03x = -415$$

$$x = -13,833.\overline{3} \text{ and since sales cannot be negative,}$$
earnings will never be the same. Take the
first payment method.

58. (A) $V = V_S + (0.03A)V_S = V_S(1 + 0.03A)$

(B) $V = 120(1 + 0.03(6.4))$
$V = 143$ mph

(C) $125 = V(1 + 0.03(8.5))$
$V = 99.6$ mph

(D) $155 = 135(1 + 0.03(A))$
$$1 + 0.03A = \frac{155}{135}$$
$$0.03A = \frac{155}{135} - 1$$
$$A = \frac{\frac{155}{135} - 1}{0.03}$$
$$A = 4.94$$
The mountain resort has an altitude of 4,940 ft.

60. $d = rt = 5000t$ underwater
$$d = 1100(t + 39) \text{ above water}$$
$$5000t = 1100(t + 39)$$
$$5000t = 1100t + 42,900$$
$$3900t = 42,900$$
$$t = 11$$
$$d = 5000(11)$$
$$d = 55,000 \text{ ft.}$$

62. $$\frac{\text{total number of marked trout}}{\text{total population}} = \frac{\text{number marked in sample}}{\text{number in sample}}$$
$$\frac{300}{x} = \frac{6}{180}$$
$$6x = 54,000$$
$$x = 9000 \text{ trout in lake}$$

64.

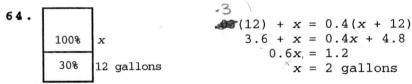

$$.3$$
$$\cancel{45}(12) + x = 0.4(x + 12)$$
$$3.6 + x = 0.4x + 4.8$$
$$0.6x = 1.2$$
$$x = 2 \text{ gallons}$$

Adding 2 gallons of pure hydrochloric acid to a 30% mixture will produce a 40% solution.

66.

0.3%	x
0.9%	120,000 gallons

$$0.8(x + 120,000) = 0.9(120,000) + 0.3x$$
$$0.8x + 96,000 = 108,000 + 0.3x$$
$$0.5x = 12,000$$
$$x = 24,000 \text{ gallons}$$

Adding 24,000 gallons of 0.3% sulfur solution to 120,000 gallons of 0.9% sulfur solution will produce a 0.8% solution.

68. $\frac{1}{8} \cdot 3 + \frac{1}{t} \cdot 3 = 1$

$$\frac{3}{t} = \frac{5}{8}$$

$$5t = 24$$

$$t = \frac{24}{5} \text{ hours for the}$$

second pump to fill the tank operating alone.

70. $d = 8 \cdot t_1$ for trip upstream (1)

$d = 12 \cdot t_2$ for return trip (2)

from (1) $t_1 = \frac{d}{8}$ and from (2) $t_2 = \frac{d}{12}$

and since $t_1 + t_2 = 5,$ $\frac{d}{8} + \frac{d}{12} = 5$

$$12d + 8d = 480$$

$$20d = 480$$

$$d = 24 \text{ miles}$$

from resort at turnaround

$t_1 = \frac{24}{8} = 3$ hr which gives 10:00 a.m. as turnaround time.

72. $\frac{10}{12} = \frac{220}{x}$

$$10x = 2640$$

$$x = 264 \text{ hertz}$$

for second note of minor chord

$$\frac{12}{15} = \frac{264}{x}$$

$$12x = 3960$$

$$x = 330 \text{ hertz}$$

for third note of minor chord

74. Equating the approach strength and avoidance strength gives

$$-\frac{1}{5}d + 70 = -\frac{4}{3}d + 230$$

$$\frac{4}{3}d - \frac{1}{5}d = 160$$

$$20d - 3d = 2400$$

$$17d = 2400$$

$$d \approx 141.2 \text{ cm}$$

76. Let x = total distance; then

$$x = \frac{1}{3}x + 10 + \frac{1}{6}x$$

$$6x = 2x + 60 + x$$

$$3x = 60$$

$$x = 20 \text{ miles}$$

Exercise 2-2

2. (1) $y = 5x - 8$

(2) $y = 2x + 4$

$$5x - 8 = 2x + 4$$

$$3x = 12$$

$$x = 4$$

(1) $y = 5(4) - 8 = 12$

$(4, 12)$

4. (1) $x + 3y = 1 \Rightarrow x = 1 - 3y$

(2) $2x + 7y = 4$

$$2(1 - 3y) + 7y = 4$$

$$2 - 6y + 7y = 4$$

$$y = 2$$

(1) $x = 1 - 3(2) = -5$

$(-5, 2)$

6. (1) $9x + 7y = 8$

$$7y = 8 - 9x$$

$$y = \frac{8 - 9x}{7}$$

(2) $-4x + 3y = 27$

$$-4x + 3\left(\frac{8 - 9x}{7}\right) = 27$$

$$-28x + 3(8 - 9x) = 189$$

$$-28x + 24 - 27x = 189$$

$$-55x = 165$$

$$x = -3$$

(1) $y = \frac{8 - 9x}{7} = \frac{8 - 9(-3)}{7}$

$$y = \frac{35}{7} = 5$$

$(-3, 5)$

8. (1) $2s - 9t = 22$

$$2s = 22 + 9t$$

$$s = \frac{22 + 9t}{2}$$

(2) $8s - 11t = 48$

$$8\left(\frac{22 + 9t}{2}\right) - 11t = 48$$

$$4(22 + 9t) - 11t = 48$$

$$88 + 36t - 11t = 48$$

$$25t = -40$$

$$t = \frac{40}{25} = -\frac{8}{5}$$

(1) $s = \frac{22 + 9(-8/5)}{2} \cdot \frac{5}{5}$

$$s = \frac{110 - 72}{10}$$

$$s = \frac{38}{10} = \frac{19}{5}$$

$\left(\frac{19}{5}, -\frac{8}{5}\right)$ or $(3.8, -1.6)$

10. (1) $12m - 11n = 2$

$$12m = 11n + 2$$

$$m = \frac{11n + 2}{12}$$

(2) $18m + 7n = 3$

$$18\left(\frac{11n + 2}{12}\right) + 7n = 3$$

$$18(11n + 2) + 84n = 36$$

$$198n + 36 + 84n = 36$$

$$282n = 0$$

$$n = 0$$

(1) $m = \dfrac{11(0) + 2}{12} = \dfrac{2}{12} = \dfrac{1}{6}$

$\left(\dfrac{1}{6},\ 0\right)$

12. (1) $y = 7.15x$

(2) $y = 13,860 + 3.85x$

$$7.15x = 13,860 + 3.85x$$

$$3.3x = 13,860$$

$$x = 4200$$

(1) $y = 7.15(4200) = 30,030$

$(4200,\ 30,030)$

14. (1) $0.8u - 0.2v = 0.3$

$$-0.2v = 0.3 - 0.8u$$

$$v = \frac{0.8u - 0.3}{0.2}$$

$$v = 4u - 1.5$$

(2) $0.4u - 0.9v = 0.71$

$$0.4u - 0.9(4u - 1.5) = 0.71$$

$$0.4u - 3.6u + 1.35 = 0.71$$

$$-3.2u = -0.64$$

$$u = 0.2$$

(1) $v = 4(0.2) - 1.5 = 0.8 - 1.5$

$$= -0.7$$

$(0.2,\ -0.7)$

16. (1) $\dfrac{3}{8}a - \dfrac{1}{2}b = 2$

$$3a - 4b = 16$$

$$3a = 16 + 4b$$

$$a = \frac{16 + 4b}{3}$$

(2) $\dfrac{9}{10}a + \dfrac{2}{5}b = 4$

$$9a + 4b = 40$$

$$9\left(\frac{16 + 4b}{3}\right) + 4b = 40$$

$$3(16 + 4b) + 4b = 40$$

$$48 + 12b + 4b = 40$$

$$16b = -8$$

$$b = -\frac{1}{2}$$

(1) $a = \dfrac{16 + 4(-1/2)}{3} = \dfrac{16 - 2}{3} = \dfrac{14}{3}$

$\left(\dfrac{14}{3},\ -\dfrac{1}{2}\right)$ or $(4.\overline{6},\ -0.5)$

18. (1) $x - 2y = -3 \Rightarrow x = 2y - 3$

(2) $-2x + 4y = 6$

(2) $-2(2y - 3) + 4y = 6$

$$-4y + 6 + 4y = 6$$

$$6 = 6$$

The system has an infinite number of solutions given by the set,
$\{(x,\ y) \mid x - 2y = -3\}$

20. (1) $x = -1 + 2p - q \Rightarrow q = -x + 2p - 1$

(2) $y = 4 - p + q$

(2) $y = 4 - p - x + 2p - 1$

$$y = 3 + p - x$$

$$p = y + x - 3$$

(1) $q = -x + 2(y + x - 3) - 1 = -x + 2y + 2x - 6 - 1$

$$q = 2y + x - 7$$

Check: (1) $-1 + 2(y + x - 3) - (2y + x - 7)$

$$-1 + 2y + 2x - 6 - 2y - x + 7 = x$$

(2) $4 - (y + x - 3) + 2y + x - 7$

$$4 - y - x + 3 + 2y + x - 7 = y$$

22. If $ad - bc = 0$, there may be no solutions or an infinite number of solutions.

24. (1) $d = (150 - 30) \cdot t_1 \Rightarrow t_1 = \dfrac{d}{120}$

(2) $d = (150 + 30) \cdot t_2 \Rightarrow t_2 = \dfrac{d}{180}$

(3) $t_1 + t_2 = 20$

$\dfrac{d}{120} + \dfrac{d}{180} = 20$

$\dfrac{3d + 2d}{360} = 20$

$5d = 7200$

$d = 1440$ miles

26. (1) $20 = (b + w) \cdot 2 \Rightarrow b + w = 10$

$\Rightarrow b = 10 - w$

(2) $20 = (b - w) \cdot 3$

(2) $20 = (10 - w - w) \cdot 3$

$20 = (10 - 2w) \cdot 3$

$20 = 30 - 6w$

$6w = 10$

$w = \dfrac{5}{3}$ mph

28. (1) $\dfrac{12}{24}x + \dfrac{18}{24}y = \dfrac{14}{24} \cdot 10$

(2) $x + y = 10 \Rightarrow y = 10 - x$

(1) $12x + 18(10 - x) = 140$

$12x + 180 - 18x = 140$

$-6x = -40$

$x = 6\dfrac{2}{3}$ grams of 12-carat gold

(2) $y = 10 - 6\dfrac{2}{3} = 3\dfrac{1}{3}$ grams of 18-carat gold

30. At break-even, cost = revenue

$3000 + 10x = 15x$

$5x = 3000$

$x = 600$ units

32. (1) $x + y = 20,000 \Rightarrow y = 20,000 - x$

(2) $0.08x + 0.12y = 0.11(20,000)$

$0.08x + 0.12(20,000 - x) = 2200$

$0.08x + 2400 - 0.12x = 2200$

$-0.04x = -200$

$x = 5000$

(1) $y = 20,000 - 5000$

$y = 1500$

Invest \$5000 at 8% and \$15,000 at 12%.

34. (1) $800G + 500S = 62,250$

$500S = 62,250 - 800G$

$S = 124.5 - 1.6G$

(2) $800G + 1000S = 76,500$

$800G + 1000(124.5 - 1.6G) = 76,500$

$800G + 124,500 - 1600G = 76,500$

$-800G = -48,000$

$G = 60$

(1) $S = 124.5 - 1.6(60) = 28.5$

60 hours at Green Bay and 28.5 hours at Sheboygan.

36. (1) $8A + 7B = 720 \Rightarrow B = \dfrac{720 - 8A}{7}$

(2) $4A + 7B = 500$

(2) $4A + 7 \cdot \dfrac{720 - 8A}{7} = 500$

$4A + 720 - 8A = 500$

$-4A = -220$

$A = 55$

(1) $B = \dfrac{720 - 8(55)}{7} = 40$

55 bags of brand A and 40 bags of brand B.

38. (A) supply: $p = aq + b$
$$1.4 = a(1075) + b$$
$$1.2 = a(575) + b$$
from which $a = 0.0004$ and $b = 0.97$. The supply equation is $p = 0.0004q + 0.97$.

(B) demand: $p = aq + b$
$$1.2 = a(980) + b$$
$$1.4 = a(580) + b$$
from which $a = -0.0005$ and $b = 1.69$. The demand equation is $p = -0.0005q + 1.69$.

(C) Solving (1) $p = 0.0004q + 0.97$
　　　　　　(2) $p = -0.0005q + 1.69$ gives
$p = \$1.29$, equilibrium price
$q = 800$ bushels, equilibrium quantity

40. (A) Solving (1) $240 = a + b \cdot 1^2$
　　　　　　(2) $192 = a + b \cdot 2^2$ gives
$a = 256$, $b = -16$

(B) $s = 256 - 16 \cdot t^2$
$s = 256 - 16 \cdot 0^2 = 256$ ft, height of building

(C) At impact $s = 0 = 256 - 16 \cdot t^2$
$$t^2 = 16$$
$$t = 4 \text{ sec to reach ground}$$

42. (1) $d = 1100(t + 6)$
(2) $d = 5000 \cdot t$
(1) $5000t = 1100(t + 6)$
$$5000t = 1100t + 6600$$
$$3900t = 6600$$
$$t = 1\tfrac{9}{13} \text{ sec, underwater}$$
$$t + 6 = 7\tfrac{9}{13} \text{ sec, above water}$$
$$d = 5000\left(1\tfrac{9}{13}\right) \approx 8462 \text{ feet}$$

Exercise 2-3

2. $(-4, 8)$; $-4 < x < 8$;

4. $(-3, 3]$; $-3 < x \le 3$;

6. $(-\infty, 7)$; $x < 7$;

8. $-5 \le x \le 5$; $[-5, 5]$;

10. $-4 \le x < 5$; $[-4, 5)$;

12. $x > 3$; $(3, \infty)$;

14. $[-5, 6]$; $-5 \le x \le 6$

16. $(1, \infty)$; $x > 1$

18. $4x + 8 \ge x - 1$
$$3x \ge -9$$
$$x \ge -3; \ [-3, \infty);$$

20. $2(x - 3) + 5 < 5 - x$
$$2x - 6 < -x$$
$$3x < 6$$
$$x < 2; \ (-\infty, 2);$$

22. $\dfrac{M}{-3} \le -2$
$$M \ge 6; \ [6, \infty);$$

24. $-7n \geq 21$
$n \leq -3;\ (-\infty, -3]$

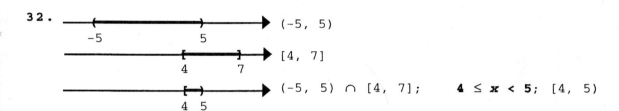

26. $2(1 - u) \geq 5u$
$2 - 2u \geq 5u$
$2 \geq 7u$
$\frac{2}{7} \geq u$

$u \leq \frac{2}{7};\ \left(-\infty,\ \frac{2}{7}\right];$

28. $\frac{y - 3}{4} - 1 > \frac{y}{2}$
$y - 3 - 4 > 2y$
$y - 7 > 2y$
$-y > 7$
$y < -7;\ (-\infty, -7);$

30. $2 \leq 3m - 7 < 14$
$9 \leq 3m < 21$
$3 \leq m < 7;\ [3, 7);$

32.
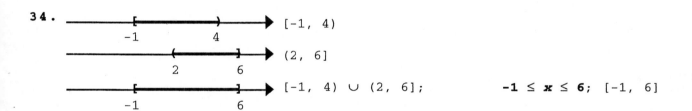
$(-5, 5)$
$[4, 7]$
$(-5, 5) \cap [4, 7];$ $\mathbf{4 \leq x < 5;}$ $[4, 5)$

34.
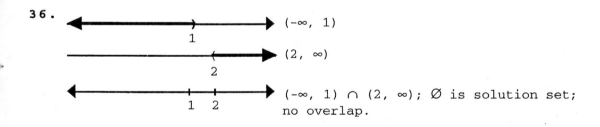
$[-1, 4)$
$(2, 6]$
$[-1, 4) \cup (2, 6];$ $\mathbf{-1 \leq x \leq 6;}$ $[-1, 6]$

36.
$(-\infty, 1)$
$(2, \infty)$
$(-\infty, 1) \cap (2, \infty);\ \emptyset$ is solution set;
no overlap.

38.
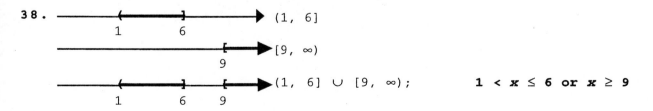
$(1, 6]$
$[9, \infty)$
$(1, 6] \cup [9, \infty);$ $\mathbf{1 < x \leq 6\ or\ x \geq 9}$

40.

$[2, 3]$

$(1, 5)$

$[2, 3] \cap (1, 5);$ $2 \leq x \leq 3; \; [2, 3]$

42.

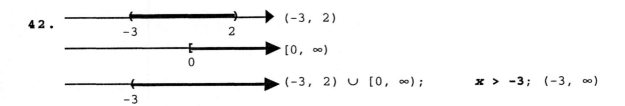

$(-3, 2)$

$[0, \infty)$

$(-3, 2) \cup [0, \infty);$ $x > -3; \; (-3, \infty)$

44.
$$\frac{p}{3} - \frac{p-2}{2} \leq \frac{p}{4} - 4$$
$$4p - 6(p - 2) \leq 3p - 48$$
$$4p - 6p + 12 \leq 3p - 48$$
$$-5p \leq -60$$
$$p \geq 12$$

$[12, \infty)$

46.
$$\frac{2}{3}(x + 7) - \frac{x}{4} > \frac{1}{2}(3 - x) + \frac{x}{6}$$
$$8(x + 7) - 3x > 6(3 - x) + 2x$$
$$8x + 56 - 3x > 18 - 6x + 2x$$
$$5x + 56 > 18 - 4x$$
$$9x > -38$$
$$x > -\frac{38}{9}$$
$$\text{or} \quad x > -4\frac{2}{9}$$

$(-4\frac{2}{9}, \infty)$

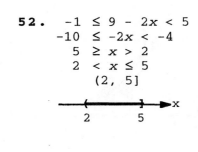

48. $-1 \leq \frac{2}{3}A + 5 \leq 11$
$$-3 \leq 2A + 15 \leq 33$$
$$-18 \leq 2A \leq 18$$
$$-9 \leq A \leq 9$$
$$[-9, 9]$$

50. $24 \leq \frac{2}{3}(x - 5) < 36$
$$72 \leq 2(x - 5) < 108$$
$$72 \leq 2x - 10 < 108$$
$$82 \leq 2x < 118$$
$$41 \leq x < 59$$
$$[41, 59)$$

52. $-1 \leq 9 - 2x < 5$
$$-10 \leq -2x < -4$$
$$5 \geq x > 2$$
$$2 < x \leq 5$$
$$(2, 5]$$

54. $15 \leq 7 - \frac{2}{5}x \leq 21$
$$8 \leq -\frac{2}{5}x \leq 14$$
$$40 \leq -2x \leq 70$$
$$-20 \geq x \geq -35$$
$$-35 \leq x \leq -20$$
$$[-35, -20]$$

56. $72.3x - 4.07 > 9.02(11.7x - 8.22)$
$$72.3x - 4.07 > 105.534x - 74.1444$$
$$-33.234x > -70.0744$$
$$x < 2.11 \text{ to two decimal places}$$

58. $-4.26 < 3.88 - 6.07x < 5.66$
$$-8.14 < -6.07x < 1.78$$
$$1.3410 > x > -0.2932$$
$$-0.29 < x < 1.34 \text{ to two decimal places}$$

60. $\sqrt{x + 5}$ represents a real number for $x + 5 \geq 0$ or $x \geq -5$

62. $\sqrt{7 - 2x}$ represents a real number for $7 - 2x \geq 0$

$$-2x \geq -7$$
$$x \leq \frac{7}{2}$$

64. $\dfrac{1}{\sqrt[4]{5 - 6x}}$ represents a real number for $5 - 6x > 0$

$$- 6x > -5$$
$$x < \frac{5}{6}$$

66. (A) for $abc > 0$ — Two of three numbers must be negative and one positive or all three must be positive.

(B) for $\dfrac{ab}{c} < 0$ — Two of three numbers must be positive and one negative or all three must be negative.

(C) for $\dfrac{a}{bc} > 0$ — Two of three numbers must be negative and one positive or all three must be positive.

(D) for $\dfrac{a^2}{bc} < 0$ — $a \neq 0$ and b and c must have opposite signs.

68. $p + q < p - q$ the following inequalities are equivalent

$$p + 2q < p$$
$$2q < 0$$
$$q < 0$$

which is true for all real p and negative q

70. $\dfrac{b}{a} > 1$ is equivalent to $b > a$ ($a > 0$ and $b > 0$) from which $0 > a - b$ or $a - b < 0$. $a - b$ is negative.

72.

$m > n$	where m and n are both positive
$mn > n^2$	multiply both sides by n
$mn - m^2 > n^2 - m^2$	subtract m^2 from both sides
$m(n - m) > (n + m)(n - m)$	factor
$m > n + m$	divide both sides by $n - m$
$0 > n$	which is a contradiction since $n > 0$

The error was dividing both sides by $n - m$ without reversing the inequality since $n - m$ is negative. [$m > n > 0$ or $0 > n - m$ or $n - m < 0$]

74.

$a < b$ means	$a - b$ is negative or
$a - b < 0$	add $0 = c - c$ to left hand side
$a - b + c - c < 0$	rearrange
$a - c - b + c < 0$	factor
$(a - c) - (b - c) < 0$	which means
$a - c < b - c$	

76. (A) $a < b$
$a - b < 0$ and for c positive

$$\frac{a - b}{c} < 0$$
$$\frac{a}{c} - \frac{b}{c} < 0$$
$$\frac{a}{c} < \frac{b}{c}$$

(B) for $c < 0$, $a < b$
$a - b < 0$

$$\frac{a - b}{c} > 0$$
$$\frac{a}{c} - \frac{b}{c} > 0$$
$$\frac{a}{c} > \frac{b}{c}$$

78.
$$-40 \leq T \leq 26$$
$$-40 \leq 70 - 0.0055h \leq 26$$
$$-110 \leq -0.0055h \leq -44$$
$$20{,}000 \geq h \geq 8000$$
$$8000 \leq h \leq 20{,}000$$
[8000 feet, 20,000 feet]

80. (A) To make a profit, revenue > cost

$$140x > 550,000 + 120x$$
$$20x > 550,000$$
$$x > 27,500$$

(B) To break-even, revenue = cost

$$140x = 550,000 + 120x$$
$$x = 27,500$$

(C) Answers may vary.

82. (A) Answers may vary.

(B) $140x > 660,000 + 120x$
$$20x > 660,000$$
$$x > 33,000$$

(C) $27,500p = 660,000 + 120(27,500)$
$$27,500p = 3,960,000$$
$$p = \$144, \text{ new price}$$

84. $80 \leq IQ \leq 140$

$$80 \leq \frac{MA}{CA}100 \leq 140$$

$$80 \leq \frac{MA}{12} \cdot 100 \leq 140$$

$$960 \leq 100MA \leq 1680$$

$$9.6 \leq MA \leq 16.8 \text{ or}$$
$$[9.6, 16.8]$$

86. Let B = benefit reduction and E = earnings.

$$13,000 \leq E \leq 16,000$$
$$13,000 - 8,880 \leq E - 8,880 \leq 16,000 - 8,880$$
$$4,120 \leq E - 8,880 \leq 7,120$$
$$\frac{1}{3}(4,120) \leq \frac{1}{3}(E - 8,880) \leq \frac{1}{3}(7,120)$$
$$1,373.33 \leq B \leq 2,373.33$$
$$\$1,373.33 \leq \text{Benefit reduction} \leq \$2,373.33$$

Exercise 2-4

2. $\left|-\dfrac{3}{4}\right| = -\left(-\dfrac{3}{4}\right)$

$$= \frac{3}{4}$$

4. $|(-2) - (-6)| = |-2 + 6|$
$$= |4|$$
$$= 4$$

6. $|\sqrt{7} - 2| = \sqrt{7} - 2$ since $\sqrt{7} > 2$ or $\sqrt{7} - 2 > 0$

8. $|2 - \sqrt{7}| = -(2 - \sqrt{7})$ since $2 < \sqrt{7}$ or $2 - \sqrt{7} < 0$
$$= -2 + \sqrt{7}$$
$$= \sqrt{7} - 2$$

10. $d(A, B) = |b - a|$
$$= |12 - 3|$$
$$= |9|$$
$$= 9$$

12. $d(A, B) = |b - a|$
$$= |-17 - (-9)|$$
$$= |-17 + 9|$$
$$= |-8|$$
$$= 8$$

14. $d(A, B) = |b - a|$
$$= |-4 - (-9)|$$
$$= |-4 + 9|$$
$$= |5|$$
$$= 5$$

16. $d(B, A) = |a - b|$
$$= |-9 - (-4)|$$
$$= |-9 + 4|$$
$$= |-5|$$
$$= 5$$

18. $d(D, C) = |c - d|$
$$= |5 - 8|$$
$$= |-3|$$
$$= 3$$

20. y is 3 units from 1; $|y - 1| = 3$

22. n is 7 units from -5; $|n - (-5)| = 7$
$$|n + 5| = 7$$

24. z is less than 8 units from -2; $|z - (-2)| < 8$
$$|z + 2| < 8$$

26. c is no greater than 7 units from -3; $|c - (-3)| \leq 7$

$$|c + 3| \leq 7$$

28. d is no more than 4 units from 5; $|d - 5| \leq 4$

30. $|t| \leq 5$

$-5 \leq t \leq 5$

$[-5, 5]$

32. $|x| \geq 5$

$x \leq -5$ or $x \geq 5$

34. $|t - 3| = 4$

$t - 3 = \pm 4$

$t = 3 \pm 4$

$t = 7$ or -1

36. $|t - 3| < 4$

$-4 < t - 3 < 4$

$-1 < t < 7$

$(-1, 7)$

38. $|t - 3| > 4$

$t - 3 < -4$ or $t - 3 > 4$

$t < -1$ or $t > 7$

$(-\infty, -1) \cup (7, \infty)$

40. $|x + 1| = 5$

$x + 1 = \pm 5$

$x = -1 \pm 5$

$x = -6$ or 4

42. $|x + 1| \leq 5$

$-5 \leq x + 1 \leq 5$

$-6 \leq x \leq 4$

$[-6, 4]$

44. $|x + 1| \geq 5$

$x + 1 \leq -5$ or $x + 1 \geq 5$

$x \leq -6$ or $x \geq 4$

$(-\infty, -6] \cup [4, \infty)$

46. $|5y + 2| \geq 8$

$5y + 2 \leq -8$ or $5y + 2 \geq 8$

$5y \leq -10$ $5y \geq 6$

$y \leq -2$ $y \geq \dfrac{6}{5}$

$y \geq 1.2$

$y \leq -2$ or $y \geq 1.2$; $(-\infty, -2] \cup [1.2, \infty)$

48. $|10 + 4s| < 6$

$-6 < 10 + 4s < 6$

$-16 < 4s < -4$

$-4 < s < -1$; $(-4, -1)$

50. $|4 - 5n| \leq 8$

$-8 \leq 4 - 5n \leq 8$

$-12 \leq -5n \leq 4$

$\dfrac{12}{5} \geq n \geq -\dfrac{4}{5}$

$-\dfrac{4}{5} \leq n \leq \dfrac{12}{5}$; $\left[-\dfrac{4}{5}, \dfrac{12}{5}\right]$

$-0.8 \leq n \leq 2.4$; $[-0.8, 2.4]$

52. $\left|\dfrac{1}{3}z + \dfrac{5}{6}\right| = 1$

$\dfrac{1}{3}z + \dfrac{5}{6} = \pm 1$

$\dfrac{1}{3}z = -\dfrac{5}{6} \pm 1$

$2z = -5 \pm 6$

$z = \dfrac{-5 \pm 6}{2}$

$z = -\dfrac{11}{2}, \dfrac{1}{2}$

$z = -5.5, 0.5$

54. $|0.5v - 2.5| > 1.6$

$0.5v - 2.5 < -1.6$ or $0.5v - 2.5 > 1.6$

$0.5v < 0.9$ $0.5v > 4.1$

$v < 1.8$ $v > 8.2$

$v < 1.8$ or $v > 8.2$; $(-\infty, 1.8) \cup (8.2, \infty)$

56. $\left|\dfrac{5}{9}(F - 32)\right| < 40$

$-40 < \dfrac{5}{9}(F - 32) < 40$

$-360 < 5(F - 32) < 360$

$-72 < F - 32 < 72$

$-40 < F < 104$

$(-40, 104)$

58.
$$\sqrt{m^2} > 3$$
$$|m| > 3$$
$$m < -3 \text{ or } m > 3$$
$$(-\infty, -3) \cup (3, \infty)$$

60.
$$\sqrt{(3 - 2x)^2} < 5$$
$$|3 - 2x| < 5$$
$$-5 < 3 - 2x < 5$$
$$-8 < -2x < 2$$
$$4 > x > -1$$
$$-1 < x < 4$$
$$(-1, 4)$$

62.
$$\sqrt{(3m + 5)^2} \geq 4$$
$$|3m + 5| \geq 4$$
$$3m + 5 \leq -4 \text{ or } 3m + 5 \geq 4$$
$$3m \leq -9 \qquad 3m \geq -1$$
$$m \leq -3 \quad \text{or} \quad m \geq -\frac{1}{3}$$
$$(-\infty, -3] \cup \left[-\frac{1}{3}, \infty\right)$$

64.
$$0 < |x - 5| < 0.01 \text{ is equivalent to}$$
$$0 < |x - 5| \qquad \text{and} \qquad |x - 5| < 0.01$$
$$|x - 5| > 0 \qquad\qquad\qquad -0.01 < x - 5 < 0.01$$
$$x - 5 < -0 \text{ or } x - 5 > 0 \qquad 4.99 < x < 5.01$$
$$x < 5 \qquad x > 5$$

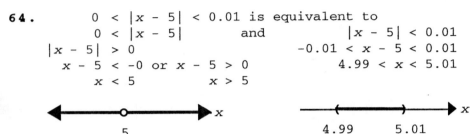

Since both must be true for $0 < |x - 5| < 0.01$ to be true, the graph of the solution is

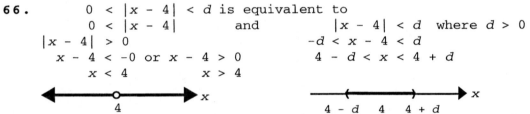

x ; $(4.99, 5) \cup (5, 5.01)$

66.
$$0 < |x - 4| < d \text{ is equivalent to}$$
$$0 < |x - 4| \qquad \text{and} \qquad |x - 4| < d \text{ where } d > 0$$
$$|x - 4| > 0 \qquad\qquad\qquad -d < x - 4 < d$$
$$x - 4 < -0 \text{ or } x - 4 > 0 \qquad 4 - d < x < 4 + d$$
$$x < 4 \qquad x > 4$$

Since both must be true for $0 < |x - 4| < d$ to be true, the graph of the solution is

x ; $(4 - d, 4) \cup (4, 4 + d)$

68. $|x + 4| = -(x + 4)$
Case 1: for $x + 4 \geq 0$, $|x + 4| = -(x + 4)$ becomes
$$x \geq -4 \qquad x + 4 = -x - 4$$
$$2x = -8$$
$$x = -4$$

Case 2: for $x + 4 < 0$, $|x + 4| = -(x + 4)$ becomes
$$x < -4 \qquad -(x + 4) = -(x + 4)$$
which is true for all x, but is restricted to $x \leq -4$

Summary: For both cases, $x \leq -4$. Graphically, $y_1 = |x + 4|$, $y_2 = -(x + 4)$ has the solution $x \leq -4$.

70. $|3x - 9| = 3x - 9$
Case 1: for $3x - 9 \geq 0$, $|3x - 9| = 3x - 9$
$$3x \geq 9 \qquad 3x - 9 = 3x - 9$$
$$x \geq 3 \quad \text{which is true for all } x, \text{ but is restricted to } x \geq 3.$$

Case 2: for $3x - 9 < 0$ $|3x - 9| = 3x - 9$
$$3x < 9 \qquad -(3x - 9) = 3x - 9$$
$$x < 3 \qquad -3x + 9 = 3x - 9$$
$$-6x = -18$$
$$x = 3 \quad \text{which is rejected since } x < 3.$$

Summary: For both cases, $x \geq 3$. Graphically, $y_1 = |3x - 9|$, $y_2 = 3x - 9$ has the solution $x \geq 3$.

72. $|7 - 2x| = 5 - x$

$7 - 2x = 5 - x$ or $7 - 2x = -(5 - x)$

$-x = -2$ $7 - 2x = -5 + x$

$x = 2$ $-3x = -12$

$x = 4$ $\{2, 4\}$

74. $|x| - |x - 5| = 5$

Case 1: $x \geq 0$, $x - 5 \geq 0$: $|x| - |x - 5| = 5$

$x \geq 5$ $x - (x - 5) = 5$

$5 = 5$, restricted to $x \geq 5$

Case 2: $x \geq 0$, $x - 5 < 0$: $|x| - |x - 5| = 5$

$x < 5$ $x - (-(x - 5)) = 5$

$x + x - 5 = 5$

$2x = 10$

$x = 5$

Case 3: $x < 0$, $x - 5 \geq 0$: These are mutually contradictory, so no solution

$x \geq 5$ is possible in this case.

Case 4: $x < 0$, $x - 5 < 0$: $|x| - |x - 5| = 5$

$x < 5$ $-x - (-(x - 5)) = 5$

$-x + x - 5 = 5$

$-5 = 5$, contradiction; no solution

Summary: The solution is $x \geq 5$.

76. $|3x + 1| + |3 - 2x| = 11$

Case 1: $3x + 1 \geq 0$ and $3 - 2x \geq 0$: $|3x + 1| + |3 - 2x| = 11$

$x \geq -\dfrac{1}{3}$ $x \leq \dfrac{3}{2}$ $3x + 1 + 3 - 2x = 11$

$x + 4 = 11$

$x = 7$, not a solution

since $x \leq \dfrac{3}{2}$.

Case 2: $3x + 1 \geq 0$ and $3 - 2x < 0$: $|3x + 1| + |3 - 2x| = 11$

$x \geq -\dfrac{1}{3}$ $x > \dfrac{3}{2}$ $3x + 1 + -(3 - 2x) = 11$

$3x + 1 - 3 + 2x = 11$

$5x - 2 = 11$

$5x = 13$

$x = \dfrac{13}{5}$, a solution since both
conditions are met

Case 3: $3x + 1 < 0$ and $3 - 2x \geq 0$: $|3x + 1| + |3 - 2x| = 11$

$x < -\dfrac{1}{3}$ $x \leq \dfrac{3}{2}$ $-(3x + 1) + (3 - 2x) = 11$

$-3x - 1 + 3 - 2x = 11$

$-5x + 2 = 11$

$-5x = 9$

$x = -\dfrac{9}{5}$, a solution since both
conditions are met

Case 4: $3x + 1 < 0$ and $3 - 2x < 0$: These are mutually contradictory, so

$x < -\dfrac{1}{3}$ $x > \dfrac{3}{2}$ no solution is possible in this case.

Summary: $x = -\dfrac{9}{5}$ (-1.8) or $x = \dfrac{13}{5}$ (2.6)

78. $\dfrac{|x - 1|}{x - 1} = \dfrac{x - 1}{x - 1} = 1$ for $x - 1 > 0$

$\dfrac{|x - 1|}{x - 1} = \dfrac{-(x - 1)}{x - 1} = -1$ for $x - 1 < 0$

$\dfrac{|x - 1|}{x - 1} = \pm 1$

80. *Case 1:* For $x \geq 0$, $|x|^2 = (x)^2 = x^2$

Case 2: For $x \leq 0$, $|x|^2 = (-x)^2 = (-x)(-x) = x^2$

82. Consider $d\left(m, \dfrac{m + n}{2}\right) = \left|\dfrac{m + n}{2} - m\right|$

$= \left|\dfrac{m + n - 2m}{2}\right|$

$= \left|\dfrac{n - m}{2}\right|$

$= \dfrac{|n - m|}{|2|}$ and since $m < n$ or $n - m > 0$

$d\left(m, \dfrac{m + n}{2}\right) = \dfrac{n - m}{2}$ $\qquad$ (1)

Now consider $d\left(\dfrac{m + n}{2}, n\right) = \left|n - \dfrac{m + n}{2}\right|$

$= \left|\dfrac{2n - m - n}{2}\right|$

$= \left|\dfrac{n - m}{2}\right|$

$= \dfrac{|n - m|}{|2|}$ and since $m < n$ or $n - m > 0$

$d\left(\dfrac{m + n}{2}, n\right) = \dfrac{n - m}{2}$ $\qquad$ (2)

Comparing (1) and (2) shows

$d\left(m, \dfrac{m + n}{2}\right) = d\left(\dfrac{m + n}{2}, n\right)$

84. $|m| = |n|$ if and only if $m = n$ or $m = -n$ may be proved by showing
(A) if $m = n$ or $m = -n$, then $|m| = |n|$ and
(B) if $|m| = |n|$, then $m = n$ or $m = -n$.

Proof of (A) involves showing two things:
(1) if $m = n$, then $|m| = |n|$ which follows immediately since equal numbers will have equal absolute values and
(2) if $m = -n$, then $|m| = |-n|$ so $|m| = |n|$.

Proof of (B) involves two cases:
Case 1: For $m \geq 0$, $|m| = |n|$ becomes

$m = |n|$

$m = \pm n$

which shows if $|m| = |n|$, then $m = n$ or $m = -n$.

Case 2: For $m < 0$, $|m| = |n|$ becomes
$$-m = |n|$$
$$m = -|n|$$
$$m = -(\pm n) \text{ or } m = \pm n$$
which shows if $|m| = |n|$, then $m = n$ or $m = -n$.

86. Prove that $|mn| = |m||n|$. There are four cases:
Case 1: $m \geq 0$, $n \geq 0$
$$|m| \cdot |n| = mn = |mn| \text{ since } mn \geq 0$$

Case 2: $m \geq 0$, $n < 0$
$$|m||n| = m(-n) = -(mn) = |mn| \text{ since } mn < 0$$

Case 3: $m < 0$, $n \geq 0$
$$|m| \cdot |n| = (-m)(n) = -(mn) = |mn| \text{ since } mn < 0$$

Case 4: $m < 0$, $n < 0$
$$|m| \cdot |n| = (-m)(-n) = mn = |mn| \text{ since } mn > 0$$

88. Prove $|m + n| \leq |m| + |n|$.
From problem 87
$$-|m| \leq m \leq |m|$$
$$\underline{-|n| \leq n \leq |n|} \qquad \text{adding}$$
$$-|m| - |n| \leq m + n \leq |m| + |n|$$
$$-(|m| + |n|) \leq m + n \leq (|m| + |n|)$$

which has the form $-p \leq x \leq p$ for $p > 0$ or equivalently $|x| \leq p$. Comparison gives $|m + n| \leq |m| + |n|$.

90. Suppose $a < b$. On the number line, then

The mid-point is $\dfrac{a + b}{2}$ so that $\dfrac{1}{2}$ distance between a and b

$$a = \frac{a + b}{2} - \frac{1}{2} \text{ distance between } a \text{ and } b$$
$$a = \frac{a + b}{2} - \frac{1}{2}|b - a| = \frac{1}{2}[a + b - |b - a|]$$
$$a = \frac{1}{2}[a + b - |a - b|]$$

92.
$$\left|\frac{x - m}{s}\right| < n$$
$$\left|\frac{x - 28.6}{6.5}\right| < 2$$
$$-2 < \frac{x - 28.6}{6.5} < 2$$
$$-13 < x - 28.6 < 13$$
$$15.6 < x < 41.6$$

94.
$$200 - 10 \leq T \leq 200 + 10$$
$$-10 \leq T - 200 \leq 10$$
$$|T - 200| \leq 10$$

96.
$$|V - 6.94| < 0.02$$
$$-0.02 < V - 6.94 < 0.02$$
$$6.92 < V < 6.96$$
$$(6.92, 6.96)$$

98.
$$3.65 \times 10^{-3} - 5 \times 10^{-6} \leq N \leq 3.65 \times 10^{-3} + 5 \times 10^{-6}$$
$$-5 \times 10^{-6} \leq N - 3.65 \times 10^{-3} \leq 5 \times 10^{-6}$$
$$|N - 3.65 \times 10^{-3}| \leq 5 \times 10^{-6}$$

Exercise 2-5

2. $(4 + i) + (5 + 3i) = 4 + i + 5 + 3i$
$\quad\quad\quad\quad\quad\quad\quad\quad\quad = 4 + 5 + i + 3i$
$\quad\quad\quad\quad\quad\quad\quad\quad\quad = 9 + 4i$

4. $(-1 + 2i) + (4 - 7i) = -1 + 2i + 4 - 7i$
$\quad\quad\quad\quad\quad\quad\quad\quad\quad\quad = -1 + 4 + 2i - 7i$
$\quad\quad\quad\quad\quad\quad\quad\quad\quad\quad = 3 - 5i$

6. $(3 + 7i) - (2 + 5i) = 3 + 7i - 2 - 5i$
$\quad\quad\quad\quad\quad\quad\quad\quad\quad = 3 - 2 + 7i - 5i$
$\quad\quad\quad\quad\quad\quad\quad\quad\quad = 1 + 2i$

8. $(-4 - 2i) - (1 + i) = -4 - 2i - 1 - i$
$\quad\quad\quad\quad\quad\quad\quad\quad\quad = -4 - 1 - 2i - i$
$\quad\quad\quad\quad\quad\quad\quad\quad\quad = -5 - 3i$

10. $(2i + 7) - 4i = 7 + 2i - 4i$
$\quad\quad\quad\quad\quad\quad\quad = 7 - 2i$

12. $(3i)(5i) = 15i^2 = -15$

14. $(-4i)(2 - 3i) = (-4i)(2) + (-4i)(-3i)$
$\quad\quad\quad\quad\quad\quad\quad\quad = -8i + 12i^2$
$\quad\quad\quad\quad\quad\quad\quad\quad = -12 - 8i$

16. $(2 - i)(-5 + 6i) = 2(-5 + 6i) - i(-5 + 6i)$
$\quad\quad\quad\quad\quad\quad\quad\quad\quad = -10 + 12i + 5i - 6i^2$
$\quad\quad\quad\quad\quad\quad\quad\quad\quad = -10 + 6 + 12i + 5i$
$\quad\quad\quad\quad\quad\quad\quad\quad\quad = -4 + 17i$

18. $(5 + 2i)(4 - 3i) = 5(4 - 3i) + 2i(4 - 3i)$
$\quad\quad\quad\quad\quad\quad\quad\quad\quad = 20 - 15i + 8i - 6i^2$
$\quad\quad\quad\quad\quad\quad\quad\quad\quad = 20 + 6 - 15i + 8i$
$\quad\quad\quad\quad\quad\quad\quad\quad\quad = 26 - 7i$

20. $(3 + 8i)(3 - 8i) = (3)^2 - (8i)^2$
$\quad\quad\quad\quad\quad\quad\quad\quad\quad = 9 - 64i^2$
$\quad\quad\quad\quad\quad\quad\quad\quad\quad = 9 + 64$
$\quad\quad\quad\quad\quad\quad\quad\quad\quad = 73 \text{ or } 73 + 0i$

22. $\dfrac{i}{3 + i} \cdot \dfrac{3 - i}{3 - i} = \dfrac{3i - i^2}{9 + 1}$
$\quad\quad\quad\quad\quad\quad\quad\quad = \dfrac{1 + 3i}{10}$
$\quad\quad\quad\quad\quad\quad\quad\quad = \dfrac{1}{10} + \dfrac{3}{10}i \quad \text{or} \quad 0.1 + 0.3i$

24. $\dfrac{3 - 5i}{2 - i} \cdot \dfrac{2 + i}{2 + i} = \dfrac{6 + 3i - 10i - 5i^2}{4 + 1}$
$\quad\quad\quad\quad\quad\quad\quad\quad = \dfrac{6 - 7i + 5}{5}$
$\quad\quad\quad\quad\quad\quad\quad\quad = \dfrac{11 - 7i}{5}$
$\quad\quad\quad\quad\quad\quad\quad\quad = \dfrac{11}{5} - \dfrac{7}{5}i \quad \text{or} \quad 2.2 - 1.4i$

26. $\dfrac{-5 + 10i}{3 + 4i} \cdot \dfrac{3 - 4i}{3 - 4i} = \dfrac{-15 + 20i + 30i - 40i^2}{9 - 16i^2}$
$\quad\quad\quad\quad\quad\quad\quad\quad\quad = \dfrac{-15 + 50i + 40}{9 + 16}$
$\quad\quad\quad\quad\quad\quad\quad\quad\quad = \dfrac{25 + 50i}{25}$
$\quad\quad\quad\quad\quad\quad\quad\quad\quad = \dfrac{25}{25} + \dfrac{50}{25}i$
$\quad\quad\quad\quad\quad\quad\quad\quad\quad = 1 + 2i$

28. $(3 - \sqrt{-4}) + (-8 + \sqrt{-25}) = (3 - i\sqrt{4}) + (-8 + i\sqrt{25})$
$\quad\quad\quad\quad\quad\quad\quad\quad\quad\quad\quad\quad = 3 - 2i - 8 + 5i$
$\quad\quad\quad\quad\quad\quad\quad\quad\quad\quad\quad\quad = -5 + 3i$

30. $(-2 - \sqrt{-36}) - (4 + \sqrt{-49}) = -2 - 6i - 4 - 7i$
$$= -6 - 13i$$

32. $(2 - \sqrt{-1})(5 + \sqrt{-9}) = (2 - i)(5 + 3i)$
$$= 10 + i - 3i^2$$
$$= 10 + i + 3$$
$$= 13 + i$$

34. $\dfrac{6 - \sqrt{-64}}{2} = \dfrac{6 - 8i}{2}$
$$= 3 - 4i$$

36. $\dfrac{1}{3 - \sqrt{-16}} = \dfrac{1}{3 - 4i} \cdot \dfrac{3 + 4i}{3 + 4i}$
$$= \dfrac{3 + 4i}{9 + 16}$$
$$= \dfrac{3}{25} + \dfrac{4}{25}i$$

38. $\dfrac{1}{3i} = \dfrac{1}{3i} \cdot \dfrac{i}{i}$
$$= \dfrac{i}{3i^2}$$
$$= -\dfrac{1}{3}i \quad \text{or} \quad 0 - \dfrac{1}{3}i$$

40. $\dfrac{2 - i}{3i} = \dfrac{2 - i}{3i} \cdot \dfrac{i}{i}$
$$= \dfrac{2i - i^2}{3i^2}$$
$$= \dfrac{2i + 1}{-3}$$
$$= -\dfrac{1}{3} - \dfrac{2}{3}i$$

42. $(2 - i)^2 + 3(2 - i) - 5 = 4 - 4i + i^2 + 6 - 3i - 5$
$$= 5 - 7i - 1$$
$$= 4 - 7i$$

44. $x = 1 + i:\ x^2 - 2x + 2 = (1 + i)^2 - 2(1 + i) + 2$
$$= 1 + 2i + i^2 - 2 - 2i + 2$$
$$= 1 + i^2$$
$$= 1 - 1$$
$$= 0 \text{ or } 0 + 0i$$

46. $i^{21} = i^{20} \cdot i$ $i^{43} = i^{40} \cdot i^3$ $i^{52} = (i^4)^{13}$
$\quad\ \ = (i^4)^5 \cdot i$ $\quad\ \ = (i^4)^{10} \cdot (-i)$ $\quad\ \ = (1)^{13}$
$\quad\ \ = (1)^5 \cdot i$ $\quad\ \ = (1)^{10} \cdot (-i)$ $\quad\ \ = 1$
$\quad\ \ = i$ $\quad\ \ = -i$

48. $3x + (y - 2)i = (5 - 2x) + (3y - 8)i$ equate real and imaginary parts
$\quad 3x = 5 - 2x \qquad y - 2 = 3y - 8$
$\quad 5x = 5 \qquad\qquad 2y = 6$
$\quad\ \ x = 1 \qquad\qquad\ \ y = 3$

50. $\sqrt{5 + x}$ is imaginary for $5 + x < 0$ or $x < -5$

52. $\sqrt{3 + 2x}$ is imaginary for $3 + 2x < 0$
$$2x < -3$$
$$x < -\dfrac{3}{2}$$

54. $(6.12 + 4.92i)(1.82 - 5.05i) = 11.1384 - 30.906i + 8.9544i - 24.846i^2$
$$= 11.1384 - 21.9516i + 24.846$$
$$= 35.9844 - 21.9516i$$
$$= 35.98 - 21.95i \text{ to two decimal places}$$

56. $\dfrac{7.66 + 3.33i}{4.72 - 2.68i} = \dfrac{7.66 + 3.33i}{4.72 - 2.68i} \cdot \dfrac{4.72 + 2.68i}{4.72 + 2.68i}$

$\qquad\qquad = \dfrac{36.1552 + 36.2464i + 8.9244i^2}{4.72^2 + 2.68^2}$

$\qquad\qquad = \dfrac{27.2308 + 36.2464i}{29.4608}$

$\qquad\qquad = 0.92 + 1.23i$ to two decimal places

58. $(a + bi) - (c + di) = a + bi - c - di$ $\qquad$ **60.** $(u - vi)(u + vi) = u^2 + v^2$
$\qquad\qquad = (a - c) + (b - d)i$ $\qquad\qquad\qquad\qquad$ or $(u^2 + v^2) + 0i$

62. $\dfrac{a + bi}{c + di} = \dfrac{a + bi}{c + di} \cdot \dfrac{c - di}{c - di}$ $\qquad$ **64.** $i^{4k+1} = i^{4k} \cdot i$

$\qquad\qquad = \dfrac{ac + (bc - ad)i - bdi^2}{c^2 + d^2}$ $\qquad\qquad\qquad = (i^4)^k \cdot i$

$\qquad\qquad\qquad\qquad\qquad\qquad\qquad\qquad\quad = (1)^k \cdot i$

$\qquad\qquad = \dfrac{(ac + bd) + (bc - ad)i}{c^2 + d^2}$ $\qquad\qquad\qquad = i$

$\qquad\qquad = \dfrac{ac + bd}{c^2 + d^2} + \dfrac{(bc - ad)}{c^2 + d^2}i$

66.

statement		reason
1. $(a + bi)(c + di)$	$= (ac - bd) + (ad + bc)i$	1. def. of multiplication
2.	$= (ca - db) + (da + cb)i$	2. commutative $(\cdot)$
3.	$= (c + di)(a + bi)$	3. def. of multiplication

68. $z + \bar{z} = (x + yi) + (x - iy)$ $\qquad$ **70.** $\bar{\bar{z}} = \overline{\overline{(x + yi)}} = \overline{(x - yi)} = (x + yi) = z$
$\qquad\qquad = x + yi + x - iy$
$\qquad\qquad = 2x$, a real number

72. $\overline{z - w} = \overline{(x + yi) - (u + vi)}$

$\qquad\quad = \overline{x - u + (y - v)i}$

$\qquad\quad = x - u - (y - v)i$

$\qquad\quad = x - yi - u + vi$

$\qquad\quad = (x - yi) - (u - vi)$

$\qquad\quad = \bar{z} - \bar{w}$

74. $\overline{\left(\dfrac{z}{w}\right)} = \overline{\left(\dfrac{x + yi}{u + vi}\right)} = \overline{\left(\dfrac{x + yi}{u + vi} \cdot \dfrac{u - vi}{u - vi}\right)}$

$\qquad\quad = \overline{\left(\dfrac{(xu + vy) + (yu - xv)i}{u^2 + v^2}\right)}$

$\qquad\quad = \overline{\left(\dfrac{xu + vy}{u^2 + v^2} + \dfrac{(yu - xv)}{u^2 + v^2}i\right)}$

$\qquad\quad = \dfrac{xu + vy}{u^2 + v^2} + \dfrac{xv - yu}{u^2 + v^2}i \qquad\qquad (1)$

$\dfrac{\bar{z}}{\bar{w}} = \dfrac{x - yi}{u - vi} \cdot \dfrac{u + vi}{u + vi}$

$\qquad = \dfrac{(xu + vy) + (xv - yu)i}{u^2 + v^2}$

$\qquad = \dfrac{xu + vy}{u^2 + v^2} = \dfrac{xv - yu}{u^2 + v^2}i \qquad\qquad (2)$

comparison of (1) and (2) shows $\overline{\left(\dfrac{z}{w}\right)} = \dfrac{\bar{z}}{\bar{w}}$

Exercise 2-6

2. $2y^2 + 5y = 3$
$\quad\quad 2y^2 + 5y - 3 = 0$
$\quad (2y - 1)(y + 3) = 0$
$\quad 2y - 1 = 0 \quad\quad y + 3 = 0$
$\quad\quad\quad 2y = 1 \quad\quad\quad\quad y = -3$
$\quad\quad\quad\quad y = \dfrac{1}{2}$

4. $3s^2 = -6s$
$\quad 3s^2 + 6s = 0$
$\quad 3s(s + 2) = 0$
$\quad 3s = 0 \quad\quad s + 2 = 0$
$\quad\quad s = 0 \quad\quad\quad s = -2$

6. $16x^2 + 9 = 24x$
$\quad\quad 16x^2 - 24x + 9 = 0$
$\quad\quad (4x - 3)(4x - 3) = 0$
$\quad\quad 4x - 3 = 0$
$\quad\quad\quad 4x = 3$
$\quad\quad\quad\quad x = \dfrac{3}{4} \text{ (double root)}$

8. $n^2 + 16 = 0$
$\quad\quad n^2 = -16$
$\quad\quad n = \pm\sqrt{-16}$
$\quad\quad n = \pm 4i$

10. $d^2 - 36 = 0$
$\quad\quad d^2 = 36$
$\quad\quad d = \pm 6$

12. $9x^2 - 25 = 0$
$\quad\quad 9x^2 = 25$
$\quad\quad x^2 = \dfrac{25}{9}$
$\quad\quad x = \pm\dfrac{5}{3}$

14. $16w^2 + 27 = 0$
$\quad\quad 16w^2 = -27$
$\quad\quad w^2 = -\dfrac{27}{16}$
$\quad\quad w = \pm\sqrt{-\dfrac{27}{16}}$
$\quad\quad w = \pm\dfrac{3\sqrt{3}}{4}i$

16. $(t - 2)^2 = -3$
$\quad\quad t - 2 = \pm\sqrt{-3}$
$\quad\quad t - 2 = \pm i\sqrt{3}$
$\quad\quad\quad t = 2 \pm i\sqrt{3}$
$\quad\quad\quad t = 2 \pm \sqrt{3}i$

18. $(m + 4)^2 = 1$
$\quad\quad m + 4 = \pm 1$
$\quad\quad\quad m = -4 \pm 1$
$\quad\quad\quad m = -5, \; -3$

20. $y^2 - 4y + 7 = 0; \quad a = 1, \; b = -4,$
$\quad\quad\quad\quad\quad\quad\quad\quad\quad c = 7$
$\quad y = \dfrac{4 \pm \sqrt{16 - 4(1)(7)}}{2(1)}$
$\quad\quad = \dfrac{4 \pm \sqrt{-12}}{2}$
$\quad\quad = \dfrac{4 \pm 2i\sqrt{3}}{2}$
$\quad\quad = \dfrac{2(2 \pm i\sqrt{3})}{2}$
$\quad\quad = 2 \pm i\sqrt{3}$

22. $y^2 - 4y + 1 = 0; \quad a = 1, \; b = -4,$
$\quad\quad\quad\quad\quad\quad\quad\quad\quad c = 1$
$\quad y = \dfrac{4 \pm \sqrt{16 - 4(1)(1)}}{2(1)}$
$\quad\quad = \dfrac{4 \pm \sqrt{12}}{2}$
$\quad\quad = \dfrac{4 \pm 2\sqrt{3}}{2}$
$\quad\quad = \dfrac{2(2 \pm \sqrt{3})}{2} = 2 \pm \sqrt{3}$

24. $9s^2 + 2 = 12s$
$\quad 9s^2 - 12s + 2 = 0; \quad a = 9, \; b = -12,$
$\quad\quad\quad\quad\quad\quad\quad\quad\quad\quad c = 2$
$\quad s = \dfrac{12 \pm \sqrt{144 - 4(9)(2)}}{2(9)}$
$\quad\quad = \dfrac{12 \pm \sqrt{72}}{18}$
$\quad\quad = \dfrac{12 \pm 6\sqrt{2}}{18}$
$\quad\quad = \dfrac{6(2 \pm \sqrt{2})}{18} = \dfrac{2 \pm \sqrt{2}}{3}$

26. $9s^2 + 7 = 12s$
$\quad 9s^2 - 12s + 7 = 0; \quad a = 9, \; b = -12,$
$\quad\quad\quad\quad\quad\quad\quad\quad\quad\quad c = 7$
$\quad s = \dfrac{12 \pm \sqrt{144 - 4(9)(7)}}{2(9)}$
$\quad\quad = \dfrac{12 \pm \sqrt{-108}}{18}$
$\quad\quad = \dfrac{12 \pm 6i\sqrt{3}}{18}$
$\quad\quad = \dfrac{6(2 \pm i\sqrt{3})}{18}$
$\quad\quad = \dfrac{2 \pm i\sqrt{3}}{3}$

28.
$$y^2 + 4y - 3 = 0$$
$$y^2 + 4y = 3$$
$$y^2 + 4y + \left(\frac{4}{2}\right)^2 = 3 + \left(\frac{4}{2}\right)^2$$
$$(y + 2)^2 = 7$$
$$y + 2 = \pm\sqrt{7}$$
$$y = -2 \pm \sqrt{7}$$

30.
$$2s^2 - 6s + 7 = 0$$
$$2s^2 - 6s = -7$$
$$s^2 - 3s = -\frac{7}{2}$$
$$s^2 - 3s + \left(\frac{3}{2}\right)^2 = -\frac{7}{2} + \left(\frac{3}{2}\right)^2$$
$$\left(s - \frac{3}{2}\right)^2 = -\frac{7}{2} + \frac{9}{4}$$
$$\left(s - \frac{3}{2}\right)^2 = -\frac{5}{4}$$
$$s - \frac{3}{2} = \pm\sqrt{\frac{-5}{4}}$$
$$s - \frac{3}{2} = \pm i\frac{\sqrt{5}}{2}$$
$$x = \frac{3}{2} \pm i\frac{\sqrt{5}}{2} = \frac{3 \pm i\sqrt{5}}{2}$$

32.
$$4v^2 + 16v + 23 = 0$$
$$v^2 + 4v + \frac{23}{4} = 0$$
$$v^2 + 4v = -\frac{23}{4}$$
$$v^2 + 4v + 4 = -\frac{23}{4} + 4$$
$$(v + 2)^2 = -\frac{23}{4} + \frac{16}{4}$$
$$(v + 2)^2 = -\frac{7}{4}$$
$$v + 2 = \pm\sqrt{-\frac{7}{4}}$$
$$v + 2 = \pm\frac{i\sqrt{7}}{2}$$
$$v = -2 \pm i\frac{\sqrt{7}}{2}$$
$$v = \frac{-4 \pm i\sqrt{7}}{2}$$

34.
$$3z^2 - 8z + 1 = 0$$
$$z^2 - \frac{8}{3}z + \frac{1}{3} = 0$$
$$z^2 - \frac{8}{3}z = -\frac{1}{3}$$
$$z^2 - \frac{8}{3}z + \frac{16}{9} = -\frac{1}{3} + \frac{16}{9}$$
$$\left(z - \frac{4}{3}\right)^2 = \frac{13}{9}$$
$$z - \frac{4}{3} = \pm\frac{\sqrt{13}}{3}$$
$$z = \frac{4}{3} \pm \frac{\sqrt{13}}{3} \quad \text{or} \quad \frac{4 \pm \sqrt{13}}{3}$$

36.
$$9x^2 + 9x = 4$$
$$9x^2 + 9x - 4 = 0$$
$$(3x + 4)(3x - 1) = 0$$
$$3x + 4 = 0, \quad 3x - 1 = 0$$
$$3x = -4 \qquad 3x = 1$$
$$x = -\frac{4}{3} \qquad x = \frac{1}{3}$$

38.
$$(3m + 2)^2 = -4$$
$$3m + 2 = \pm 2i$$
$$3m = -2 \pm 2i$$
$$m = -\frac{2}{3} \pm \frac{2}{3}i$$

40.
$$x^2 + 2x = 2$$
$$x^2 + 2x + 1 = 2 + 1$$
$$(x + 1)^2 = 3$$
$$x + 1 = \pm\sqrt{3}$$
$$x = -1 \pm \sqrt{3}$$

42.
$$8u^2 + 3u = 0$$
$$u(8u + 3) = 0$$
$$u = 0, \quad 8u + 3 = 0$$
$$8u = -3$$
$$u = -\frac{3}{8}$$
$$u = 0, \quad -\frac{3}{8}$$

44.
$$\frac{2}{u} = \frac{3}{u^2} + 1$$
$$2u = 3 + u^2$$
$$u^2 - 2u + 1 = -3 + 1$$
$$(u - 1)^2 = -2$$
$$u - 1 = \pm i\sqrt{2}$$
$$u = 1 \pm i\sqrt{2}$$

46.
$$\frac{1.2}{y - 1} + \frac{1.2}{y} = 1$$
$$1.2y + 1.2(y - 1) = y(y - 1)$$
$$1.2y + 1.2y - 1.2 = y^2 - y$$
$$y^2 - 3.4y + 1.2 = 0$$
$$(y - 3)(y - 0.4) = 0$$
$$y - 3 = 0, \quad y - 0.4 = 0$$
$$y = 3 \quad y = 0.4 = \frac{2}{5}$$

48.
$$\frac{3}{x - 1} - \frac{2}{x + 3} = \frac{4}{x - 2}$$
$$3(x + 3)(x - 2) - 2(x - 1)(x - 2) = 4(x - 1)(x + 3)$$
$$3(x^2 + x - 6) - 2(x^2 - 3x + 2) = 4(x^2 + 2x - 3)$$
$$3x^2 + 3x - 18 - 2x^2 + 6x - 4 = 4x^2 + 8x - 12$$
$$3x^2 - x + 10 = 0$$
$$x = \frac{-(-1) \pm \sqrt{(-1)^2 - 4(3)(10)}}{2(3)}$$
$$x = \frac{1 \pm \sqrt{-119}}{6}$$
$$x = \frac{1}{6} \pm \frac{\sqrt{119}}{6} i$$

50.
$$\frac{11}{x^2 - 4} + \frac{x + 3}{2 - x} = \frac{2x - 3}{x + 2}$$
$$\frac{11}{x^2 - 4} - \frac{x + 3}{x - 2} = \frac{2x - 3}{x + 2}$$
$$11 - (x + 3)(x + 2) = (2x - 3)(x - 2)$$
$$11 - (x^2 + 5x + 6) = 2x^2 - 7x + 6$$
$$11 - x^2 - 5x - 6 = 2x^2 - 7x + 6$$
$$3x^2 - 2x + 1 = 0$$
$$x = \frac{-(-2) \pm \sqrt{(-2)^2 - 4(3)(1)}}{2(3)}$$
$$x = \frac{2 \pm \sqrt{-8}}{6} = \frac{2 \pm 2\sqrt{2}i}{6}$$
$$x = \frac{1}{3} \pm \frac{\sqrt{2}}{3} i$$

52. $|12 + 7x| = x^2$ is equivalent to
$12 + 7x = \pm x^2$ therefore we must solve

$$12 + 7x = x^2 \qquad \text{and} \qquad 12 + 7x = -x^2$$
$$x^2 - 7x - 12 = 0 \qquad\qquad\qquad x^2 + 7x + 12 = 0$$
$$x = \frac{-(-7) \pm \sqrt{(-7)^2 - 4(1)(-12)}}{2(1)} \qquad (x + 4)(x + 3) = 0$$
$$x = \frac{7 \pm \sqrt{97}}{2} \qquad\qquad\qquad x + 4 = 0, \ x + 3 = 0$$
$$x = -4 \qquad x = -3$$

54.
$$a^2 + b^2 = c^2$$
$$a^2 = c^2 - b^2$$
$$a = \sqrt{c^2 - b^2}$$

56.
$$A = P(1 + r)^2$$
$$(1 + r)^2 = \frac{A}{P}$$
$$1 + r = \sqrt{\frac{A}{P}}$$
$$r = \sqrt{\frac{A}{P}} - 1$$

58. $0.61x^2 - 4.28x + 2.93 = 0$

$$x = \frac{-(-4.28) \pm \sqrt{(-4.28)^2 - 4(0.61)(2.93)}}{2(0.61)}$$

$$x \approx 6.25,\ 0.77$$

60. $5.13x^2 + 7.27x - 4.32 = 0$

$$x = \frac{-7.27 \pm \sqrt{(7.27)^2 - 4(5.13)(-4.32)}}{2(5.13)}$$

$$x \approx -1.87,\ 0.45$$

62. Solving $x^2 - 2x + c = 0$ with the quadratic formula gives $x = 1 \pm \sqrt{1 - c}$.
For $1 - c > 0 \Leftrightarrow c < 1$, two distinct real roots.
For $1 - c = 0 \Leftrightarrow c = 1$, one real root (a double root).
For $1 - c < 0 \Leftrightarrow c > 1$, two complex roots (conjugates).

64. $0.543x^2 - 0.182x + 0.00312 = 0$

$$b^2 - 4ac = (-0.182)^2 - 4(0.543)(0.00312)$$
$$= 0.02634736 > 0,\ \text{real solutions}$$

66. $0.543x^2 - 0.182x + 0.0312 = 0$

$$b^2 - 4ac = (-0.182)^2 - 4(0.543)(0.0312)$$
$$= -0.0346424 < 0,\ \text{no real solutions}$$

68. $2\sqrt{2}x + \sqrt{3} = \sqrt{3}x^2$

$$\sqrt{3}x^2 - 2\sqrt{2}x - \sqrt{3} = 0$$

$$x = \frac{-(-2\sqrt{2}) \pm \sqrt{(-2\sqrt{2})^2 - 4(\sqrt{3})(-\sqrt{3})}}{2\sqrt{3}}$$

$$x = \frac{2\sqrt{2} \pm \sqrt{8 + 12}}{2\sqrt{3}} = \frac{2\sqrt{2} \pm \sqrt{20}}{2\sqrt{3}}$$

$$x = \frac{2\sqrt{2} \pm 2\sqrt{5}}{2\sqrt{3}} = \frac{\sqrt{2} \pm \sqrt{5}}{\sqrt{3}} \cdot \frac{\sqrt{3}}{\sqrt{3}}$$

$$x = \frac{\sqrt{6} \pm \sqrt{15}}{3}$$

70.
$$x^2 = 2ix - 3$$
$$x^2 - 2ix + 3 = 0$$
$$(x - 3i)(x + i) = 0$$
$$x - 3i = 0,\ x + i = 0$$
$$x = 3i \qquad x = -i$$

72.
$$x^4 - 1 = 0$$
$$(x^2 - 1)(x^2 + 1) = 0$$
$$(x - 1)(x + 1)(x - i)(x + i) = 0$$
$$x - 1 = 0,\ x + 1 = 0,\ x - i = 0,\ x + i = 0$$
$$x = 1 \qquad x = -1 \qquad x = i \qquad x = -i$$

74. No. Complex roots to quadratics with real coefficients occur in conjugate pairs.

76. $r_1 + r_2 = \dfrac{-b + \sqrt{b^2 - 4ac}}{2a} + \dfrac{-b - \sqrt{b^2 - 4ac}}{2a}$

$= \dfrac{-b + \sqrt{b^2 - 4ac} - b - \sqrt{b^2 - 4ac}}{2a}$

$= \dfrac{-2b}{2a}$

$= -\dfrac{b}{a}$

78. The step following $(a - b)^2 = (b - a)^2$ which is
$$a - b = b - a \text{ is incorrect.}$$
If $A^2 = B^2$, it may or may not follow that $A = B$.

80.

$x + x = x^2$
$x^2 = 2x$
$x^2 - 2x = 0$
$x(x - 2) = 0$
$x = 0, \quad x - 2 = 0$
$\qquad\qquad x = 2$
$x = 0, 2$

82.

$x + \dfrac{1}{x} = \dfrac{10}{3}$
$3x^2 + 3 = 10x$
$3x^2 - 10x + 3 = 0$
$(3x - 1)(x - 3) = 0$
$3x - 1 = 0, \quad x - 3 = 0$
$3x = 1 \qquad\qquad x = 3$
$x = \dfrac{1}{3}$

84.

$A = 2, \; b = h + 3$
$A = \dfrac{1}{2} bh$
$2 = \dfrac{1}{2}(h + 3)h$
$4 = h^2 + 3h$
$0 = h^2 + 3h - 4$
$0 = (h + 4)(h - 1)$
$h = -4 \quad (\text{reject})$
$h = 1$
$b = h + 3 = 4$
The base is 4 feet,
the height is 1 foot.

86. If $p = \dfrac{75,000}{q} \Rightarrow q = \dfrac{75,000}{p}$

If $p = 0.0005q + 12.5 \Rightarrow q = 2000p - 25,000$

Equilibrium: $\dfrac{75,000}{p} = 2000p - 25,000$

$75,000 = 2000p^2 - 25,000p$

$2000p^2 - 25,000p - 75,000 = 0$

$2p^2 - 25p - 75 = 0$

$(2p + 5)(p - 15) = 0$

$p = -\dfrac{5}{2} \; (\text{reject}) \text{ or } p = 15$

The equilibrium price is \$15.

88. Upstream: $24 = (10 - r)t \Rightarrow t = \dfrac{24}{10 - r}$ (1)

Downstream: $24 = (10 + r)(t - 1) \Rightarrow t - 1 = \dfrac{24}{10 + r}$ (2)

Substituting (1) $\to$ (2): $\dfrac{24}{10 - r} - 1 = \dfrac{24}{10 + r}$

$24(10 + r) - 1(10 - r)(10 + r) = 24(10 - r)$

$240 + 24r - 100 + r^2 = 240 - 24r$

$r^2 + 48r - 100 = 0$

$(r + 50)(r - 2) = 0$

$r = -50, \text{ reject} \quad r = 2$

Rate of current is 2 mph.

90.

	d	r	t
Sm	$\dfrac{1}{5}$	$r + 1$	$t - \dfrac{1}{60}$
Lg	$\dfrac{1}{5}$	r	t

$$t - \frac{1}{60} = \frac{1}{5(r + 1)} \qquad (1)$$

$$t = \frac{1}{5r} \qquad (2)$$

Substitute $(2) \rightarrow (1)$: $\dfrac{1}{5r} - \dfrac{1}{60} = \dfrac{1}{5(r + 1)}$

$$12(r + 1) - r(r + 1) = 12r$$
$$12r + 12 - r^2 - r = 12r$$
$$r^2 + r - 12 = 0$$
$$(r + 4)(r - 3) = 0$$
$$r = -4, \text{ reject}; \qquad r = 3$$
$$r + 1 = 4$$

The small gear makes 4 rpm; the large gear makes 3 rpm.

92. (A) $y = 176t - 16t^2 = 0$
$$16t(11 - t) = 0$$
$$16t = 0, \quad 11 - t = 0$$
$$t = 0, \qquad t = 11$$
$t = 0$ when projectile leaves the ground
$t = 11$ sec. when projectile returns to ground

(B)
$$16 = 176t - 16t^2$$
$$16t^2 - 176t + 16 = 0$$
$$t^2 - 11t + 1 = 0$$
$$t = \frac{-(-11) \pm \sqrt{(-11)^2 - 4(1)(1)}}{2(1)}$$
$$t \approx 10.91 \text{ sec and } 0.09 \text{ sec}$$

94.

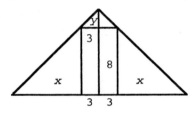

area $= \dfrac{1}{2}$ base·height

$$98 = \frac{1}{2}(6 + 2x)(8 + y) \qquad (1)$$

from similar triangles
$$\frac{y}{3} = \frac{y + 8}{x + 3} \qquad (2)$$
$$y(x + 3) = 3(y + 8)$$
$$yx + 3y = 3y + 24$$
$$x = \frac{24}{y}$$

substituting this result into (1) gives

$$98 = \frac{1}{2}\left(6 + 2 \cdot \frac{24}{y}\right)(8 + y)$$

$$196 = \left(6 + \frac{48}{y}\right)(8 + y)$$

$$196 = \left(\frac{6y + 48}{y}\right)(8 + y)$$

$$196y = (6y + 48)(8 + y)$$

$$196y = 6y^2 + 96y + 384$$

$$6y^2 - 100y + 384 = 0$$
$$(y - 6)(6y - 64) = 0$$
$$y - 6 = 0, \qquad\qquad 6y - 64 = 0$$
$$y = 6 \qquad\qquad\qquad 6y = 64$$
$$y = 10\tfrac{2}{3}$$

$$x = \frac{24}{y} = 4 \qquad\qquad x = \frac{24}{y} = 2.25$$
width $= 2x + 6 = 14$ ft. $\qquad$ width $= 2x + 6 = 10.5$ ft.
height $= y + 8 = 14$ ft. $\qquad$ height $= y + 8 = 18.67$ ft.

96. Let x = length of straightaways and
y = radius of semicircles, then

(1) $2x + 2\pi y = \dfrac{1}{4}$ mile = 1320 ft

$x + \pi y = 660$ and

(2) $\pi y^2 + 2yx = 100,000$

Solving (1) for x gives $x = 660 - \pi y$ and substitution of this result into (2) yields

$\pi y^2 + 2y(660 - \pi y) = 100,000$

$\pi y^2 + 1320y - 2\pi y^2 = 100,000$

$\pi y^2 - 1320y + 100,000 = 0$

which may be solved using the quadratic formula to give

$y = 321.0102612$ and

$y = 99.15878857$

$y = 321$ is rejected since it gives a negative value for x

$y = 99.158...$ gives $x = 660 - \pi y = 348.4834783$

Summary: straightaways: 348 ft

diameter = $2y$ = 198 ft to the nearest foot.

Exercise 2-7

2. $\sqrt{25} = \pm 5$ is false since
$\sqrt{25}$ is the principal square root
and $\sqrt{25} = 5$.

4. $(\sqrt{x - 1})^2 + 1 = x$ is true.

6. If $x^{1/3} = 8$, then $x = 2$ is false.
[If $x = 8 \Rightarrow 8^{1/3} = 2$]

8. $\sqrt{x - 4} = 2$
$x - 4 = 4$
$x = 8$

10. $\sqrt{4y + 1} = 5 - y$
$4y + 1 = 25 - 10y + y^2$
$0 = y^2 - 14y + 24$
$0 = (y - 12)(y - 2)$
$y = 12, 2$

Check $y = 2$: $\sqrt{8 + 1} \overset{?}{=} 5 - 2$
$3 = 3 \checkmark$

The solution is $y = 2$.

Check $y = 12$: $\sqrt{48 + 1} \overset{?}{=} 5 - 12$
$7 \neq -7$

12. $\sqrt{2w - 3} + w = 1$
$\sqrt{2w - 3} = 1 - w$
$2w - 3 = 1 - 2w + w^2$
$0 = w^2 - 4w + 4$
$0 = (w - 2)^2$
$w = 2$

Check $w = 2$: $\sqrt{4 - 3} + 2 \overset{?}{=} 1$
$1 + 2 \neq 1$

There is no solution.

14. $\sqrt{5t + 4} - 2\sqrt{t} = 1$
$\sqrt{5t + 4} = 2\sqrt{t} + 1$
$5t + 4 = 4t + 4\sqrt{t} + 1$
$t + 3 = 4\sqrt{t}$
$t^2 + 6t + 9 = 16t$
$t^2 - 10t + 9 = 0$
$(t - 9)(t - 1) = 0$
$t = 1, \; t = 9$

Check $t = 1$: $\sqrt{9} - 2\sqrt{1} \overset{?}{=} 1$
$3 - 2 = 1 \checkmark$

Check $t = 9$: $\sqrt{49} - 2\sqrt{9} \overset{?}{=} 1$
$7 - 6 = 1 \checkmark$

The solution is $t = 1, 9$.

16.
$$m^4 + 4m^2 - 12 = 0$$
$$(m^2)^2 + 4m^2 - 12 = 0$$
$$(m^2 + 6)(m^2 - 2) = 0$$
$$m^2 = -6 \qquad m^2 = 2$$
$$m = \pm\sqrt{-6} \qquad m = \pm\sqrt{2}$$
$$m = \pm i\sqrt{6}$$

18.
$$x = \sqrt{5x^2 + 9}$$
$$x^2 = 5x^2 + 9$$
$$0 = 4x^2 + 9$$
$$4x^2 = -9$$
$$x^2 = -\frac{9}{4}$$
$$x = \pm\sqrt{\frac{-9}{4}}$$
$$x = \pm\frac{3}{2}i$$

20. $3y^{2/3} + 2y^{1/3} - 8 = 0$

Let $u = y^{1/3}$:
$$3u^2 + 2u - 8 = 0$$
$$(3u - 4)(u + 2) = 0$$
$$u = \frac{4}{3} \qquad\qquad u = -2$$
$$y^{1/3} = \frac{4}{3} \qquad\qquad y^{1/3} = -2$$
$$(y^{1/3})^3 = \left(\frac{4}{3}\right)^3 \qquad (y^{1/3})^3 = (-2)^3$$
$$y = \frac{64}{27} \qquad\qquad y = -8$$

22. $(m^2 + 2m)^2 - 6(m^2 + 2m) = 16$

Let $u = m^2 + 2m$:
$$u^2 - 6u = 16$$
$$u^2 - 6u - 16 = 0$$
$$(u - 8)(u + 2) = 0$$
$$u = 8 \qquad\qquad u = -2$$
$$m^2 + 2m = 8 \qquad\qquad m^2 + 2m = -2$$
$$m^2 + 2m - 8 = 0 \qquad m^2 + 2m + 2 = 0$$
$$(m + 4)(m - 2) = 0 \qquad m = -1 \pm i$$
$$m = 2, -4$$

24. $\sqrt{2x - 1} - \sqrt{x - 5} = 3$
$$\sqrt{2x - 1} = \sqrt{x - 5} + 3$$
$$2x - 1 = x - 5 + 6\sqrt{x - 5} + 9$$
$$x - 5 = 6\sqrt{x - 5}$$
$$x^2 - 10x + 25 = 36(x - 5)$$
$$x^2 - 10x + 25 = 36x - 180$$
$$x^2 - 46x + 205 = 0$$
$$(x - 41)(x - 5) = 0$$
$$x = 5, 41$$

Check $x = 5$: $\sqrt{9} - \sqrt{0} \overset{?}{=} 3$
$$3 \overset{\surd}{=} 3$$

Check $x = 41$: $\sqrt{81} - \sqrt{36} \overset{?}{=} 3$
$$9 - 6 \overset{\surd}{=} 3$$

The solution is $x = 5, 41$.

26. $\sqrt{w + 7} = 2 + \sqrt{3 - w}$
$$w + 7 = 4 + 4\sqrt{3 - w} + 3 - w$$
$$2w = 4\sqrt{3 - w}$$
$$4w^2 = 16(3 - w)$$
$$4w^2 = 48 - 16w$$
$$4w^2 + 16w - 48 = 0$$
$$w^2 + 4w - 12 = 0$$
$$(w + 6)(w - 2) = 0$$
$$w = -6 \qquad w = 2$$

Check $w = -6$: $\sqrt{1} \overset{?}{=} 2 + \sqrt{9}$
$$1 \neq 2 + 3$$

Check $w = 2$: $\sqrt{9} \overset{?}{=} 2 + \sqrt{1}$
$$3 \overset{\surd}{=} 3$$

The solution is $w = 2$.

28. $\sqrt{3z + 1} + 2 = \sqrt{z - 1}$

$3z + 1 + 4\sqrt{3z + 1} + 4 = z - 1$

$2z + 6 = -4\sqrt{3z + 1}$

$z + 3 = -2\sqrt{3z + 1}$

$z^2 + 6z + 9 = 4(3z + 1)$

$z^2 + 6z + 9 = 12z + 4$

$z^2 - 6z + 5 = 0$

$(z - 5)(z - 1) = 0$

$z = 1, 5$

Check $z = 1$: $\sqrt{4} + 2 \overset{?}{=} \sqrt{0}$

$\qquad\qquad\qquad 4 \neq 0$

Check $z = 5$: $\sqrt{16} + 2 \overset{?}{=} \sqrt{4}$

$\qquad\qquad\qquad 6 \neq 2$

No solution.

30. $6x - \sqrt{4x^2 - 20x + 17} = 15$

$-\sqrt{4x^2 - 20x + 17} = 15 - 6x$

$4x^2 - 20x + 17 = 225 - 180x + 36x^2$

$32x^2 - 160x + 208 = 0$

$2x^2 - 10x + 13 = 0$

$x = \dfrac{10 \pm \sqrt{100 - 4(2)(13)}}{2(2)} = \dfrac{10 \pm 2i}{4}$

$x = \dfrac{5}{2} + \dfrac{1}{2}i$

32. $y^{-2} - 3y^{-1} + 4 = 0$

$\dfrac{1}{y^2} - 3\left(\dfrac{1}{y}\right) + 4 = 0$

$1 - 3y + 4y^2 = 0$

$4y^2 - 3y + 1 = 0$

$y = \dfrac{3 \pm \sqrt{9 - 4(4)(1)}}{2(4)}$

$y = \dfrac{3 \pm \sqrt{-7}}{8}$

$y = \dfrac{3}{8} \pm \dfrac{\sqrt{7}}{8}i$

34. $15t^{-4} - 23t^{-2} + 4 = 0$

$\dfrac{15}{t^4} - \dfrac{23}{t^2} + 4 = 0$

$15 - 23t^2 + 4t^4 = 0$

$4t^4 - 23t^2 + 15 = 0$

$(4t^2 - 3)(t^2 - 5) = 0$

$t^2 = \dfrac{3}{4} \qquad\qquad t^2 = 5$

$t = \pm\sqrt{\dfrac{3}{4}} \qquad\quad t = \pm\sqrt{5}$

$t = \dfrac{\pm\sqrt{3}}{2}$

36. $2z^{-1} - 3z^{-1/2} + 2 = 0$

Let $u = z^{-1/2}$:

$2u^2 - 3u + 2 = 0$

$u = \dfrac{3 \pm \sqrt{9 - 4(2)(2)}}{2(2)}$

$u = \dfrac{3 \pm \sqrt{-7}}{4}$

$u = \dfrac{3 \pm i\sqrt{7}}{4}$

$z^{-1/2} = \dfrac{3 + i\sqrt{7}}{4}$

$z^{-1} = \dfrac{9 + 6i\sqrt{7} - 7}{16}$

$z^{-1} = \dfrac{2 + 6i\sqrt{7}}{16}$

$z = \dfrac{16}{2 + 6i\sqrt{7}}$

$z = \dfrac{16}{2 + 6i\sqrt{7}} \cdot \dfrac{2 - 6i\sqrt{7}}{2 - 6i\sqrt{7}}$

$z = \dfrac{32 - 96i\sqrt{7}}{4 + 252}$

$z = \dfrac{32 - 96i\sqrt{7}}{256}$

$z = \dfrac{1 - 3i\sqrt{7}}{8}$

$z = \dfrac{1}{8} \pm \dfrac{3i\sqrt{7}}{8}$

$z^{-1/2} = \dfrac{3 - i\sqrt{7}}{4}$

$z^{-1} = \dfrac{9 - 6i\sqrt{7} - 7}{16}$

$z^{-1} = \dfrac{2 - 6i\sqrt{7}}{16}$

$z = \dfrac{16}{2 - 6i\sqrt{7}}$

$z = \dfrac{16}{2 - 6i\sqrt{7}} \cdot \dfrac{2 + 6i\sqrt{7}}{2 + 6i\sqrt{7}}$

$z = \dfrac{32 + 96i\sqrt{7}}{4 + 252}$

$z = \dfrac{32 + 96i\sqrt{7}}{256}$

$z = \dfrac{1 + 3i\sqrt{7}}{8}$

38. $4m + 8\sqrt{m} - 21 = 0$

Method I: $4m - 21 = -8\sqrt{m}$

$16m^2 - 168m + 441 = 64m$

$16m^2 - 232m + 441 = 0$

$(4m - 49)(4m - 9) = 0$

$m = \dfrac{49}{4} \qquad m = \dfrac{9}{4}$

Check $m = \dfrac{49}{4}$: $49 + 8\left(\dfrac{7}{2}\right) - 21 \overset{?}{=} 0$

$49 + 28 - 21 \neq 0$

$m = \dfrac{9}{4}$ or 2.25

Method II: Let $u = \sqrt{m}$

$4u^2 + 8u - 21 = 0$

$(2u + 7)(2u - 3) = 0$

$u = \dfrac{-7}{2} \qquad u = \dfrac{3}{2}$

$\sqrt{m} = -\dfrac{7}{2} \qquad \sqrt{m} = \dfrac{3}{2}$

reject $\qquad m = \dfrac{9}{4}$ or 2.25

Check $m = \dfrac{9}{4}$: $9 + 8\left(\dfrac{3}{2}\right) - 21 \overset{?}{=} 0$

$9 + 12 - 21 \overset{\checkmark}{=} 0$

40. $3w + 5\sqrt{w} = 12$

Method I: $3w - 12 = -5\sqrt{w}$

$9w^2 - 72w + 144 = 25w$

$9w^2 - 97w + 144 = 0$

$(9w - 16)(w - 9) = 0$

$w = \dfrac{16}{9} \qquad w = 9$

Check $w = \dfrac{16}{9}$: $3\left(\dfrac{16}{9}\right) + 5\left(\dfrac{4}{3}\right) \overset{?}{=} 12$

$\dfrac{16}{3} + \dfrac{20}{3} \overset{?}{=} 12$

$\dfrac{36}{3} \overset{\checkmark}{=} 12$

$w = \dfrac{16}{9}$

Method II: Let $u = \sqrt{w}$

$3u^2 + 5u = 12$

$3u^2 + 5u - 12 = 0$

$(3u - 4)(u + 3) = 0$

$u = \dfrac{4}{3} \qquad u = -3$

$\sqrt{w} = \dfrac{4}{3} \qquad \sqrt{w} = -3$

$w = \dfrac{16}{9} \qquad$ reject

Check $w = 9$: $27 + 15 \neq 12$

42. $\sqrt{1 + 3x} - \sqrt{2x - 1} = \sqrt{x + 2}$

$1 + 3x - 2\sqrt{1 + 3x} \cdot \sqrt{2x - 1} + 2x - 1 = x + 2$

$5x - 2\sqrt{(1 + 3x)(2x - 1)} = x + 2$

$4x - 2 = 2\sqrt{(1 + 3x)(2x - 1)}$

$2x - 1 = \sqrt{(1 + 3x)(2x - 1)}$

$4x^2 - 4x + 1 = (1 + 3x)(2x - 1)$

$4x^2 - 4x + 1 = 6x^2 - x - 1$

$2x^2 + 3x - 2 = 0$

$(2x - 1)(x + 2) = 0$

$x = \dfrac{1}{2} \qquad x = -2$

Check $x = \dfrac{1}{2}$:

$\sqrt{1 + \dfrac{3}{2}} - \sqrt{1 - 1} \overset{?}{=} \sqrt{\dfrac{1}{2} + 2}$

$\sqrt{\dfrac{5}{2}} \overset{\checkmark}{=} \sqrt{\dfrac{5}{2}}$

Check $x = -2$:

$\sqrt{1 - 6} - \sqrt{-4 - 1} \overset{?}{=} \sqrt{-2 + 2}$

$\sqrt{-5} - \sqrt{-5} \overset{?}{=} \sqrt{0}$

$0 \overset{\checkmark}{=} 0$

44. $2 + 4x^{-4} = 7x^{-2}$

$4x^{-4} - 7x^{-2} + 2 = 0$

Let $u = x^{-2}$:

$4u^2 - 7u + 2 = 0$

$u = \dfrac{7 \pm \sqrt{49 - 4(4)(2)}}{2(4)}$ $x^{-2} = \dfrac{7 \pm \sqrt{17}}{8}$

$u = \dfrac{7 \pm \sqrt{17}}{8}$ $\dfrac{1}{x^2} = \dfrac{7 \pm \sqrt{17}}{8}$

$x^2 = \dfrac{8}{7 \pm \sqrt{17}} \cdot \dfrac{7 \mp \sqrt{17}}{7 \mp \sqrt{17}} = \dfrac{56 \pm 8\sqrt{17}}{32} = \dfrac{7 \pm \sqrt{17}}{4}$

$x = \pm\sqrt{\dfrac{7 \pm \sqrt{17}}{4}}$ (4 roots)

46. $3\sqrt{x - 1} = 0.05x + 2.9$

$9(x - 1) = 0.0025x^2 + 0.29x + 8.41$

$9x - 9 = 0.0025x^2 + 0.29x + 8.41$

$0 = 0.0025x^2 - 8.71x + 17.41$

$x = \dfrac{8.71 \pm \sqrt{(-8.71)^2 - 4(0.0025)(17.41)}}{2(0.0025)}$

$x = \dfrac{8.71 \pm \sqrt{75.8641 - 0.1741}}{0.005}$

$x = \dfrac{8.71 \pm \sqrt{75.69}}{0.005}$

$x = \dfrac{8.71 \pm 8.7}{0.005}$

$x = \dfrac{8.71 + 8.7}{0.005} = 3482$

$x = \dfrac{8.71 - 8.7}{0.005} = 2$

48. $x^{-2/5} - 3x^{-1/5} + 1 = 0$

Let $u = x^{-1/5}$: $u^2 - 3u + 1 = 0$

$u = \dfrac{3 \pm \sqrt{9 - 4(1)(1)}}{2(1)}$

$u = \dfrac{3 \pm \sqrt{5}}{2}$

$u = \dfrac{3 + \sqrt{5}}{2}$ $u = \dfrac{3 - \sqrt{5}}{2}$

$\dfrac{1}{x^{1/5}} = \dfrac{3 + \sqrt{5}}{2}$ $\dfrac{1}{x^{1/5}} = \dfrac{3 - \sqrt{5}}{2}$

$x^{1/5} = \dfrac{2}{3 + \sqrt{5}} \cdot \dfrac{3 - \sqrt{5}}{3 - \sqrt{5}}$ $x^{1/5} = \dfrac{2}{3 - \sqrt{5}} \cdot \dfrac{3 + \sqrt{5}}{3 + \sqrt{5}}$

$x^{1/5} = \dfrac{6 - 2\sqrt{5}}{4} = \dfrac{3 - \sqrt{5}}{2}$ $x^{1/5} = \dfrac{6 + 2\sqrt{5}}{4} = \dfrac{3 + \sqrt{5}}{2}$

$x = \left(\dfrac{3 - \sqrt{5}}{2}\right)^5 \approx 0.008131$ $x = \left(\dfrac{3 + \sqrt{5}}{2}\right)^5 \approx 122.991869$

50. Let the dimensions of an individual box be x and y, then

(1) $x^2 + y^2 = 6^2$ using the Pythagorean Theorem and noting that the box diagonal is a radius = 6

(2) $xy = 15$

Solving (2) for y gives $y = \dfrac{15}{x}$ and substitution into (1) yields

$$x^2 + \left(\frac{15}{x}\right)^2 = 36$$

$$x^2 + \frac{225}{x^2} = 36$$

$$x^4 + 225 = 36x^2$$

$x^4 - 36x^2 + 225 = 0$ quadratic in x^2

$x^2 = 27.94987437$ or $x = 5.286764074$

$x^2 = 8.050125629$ or $x = 2.837274331$ using the quadratic formula

$y = \dfrac{15}{x} = \dfrac{15}{5.286764074} = 2.837274331$ or $y = \dfrac{15}{2.837274331} = 5.286764074$

To one decimal place the dimensions are 5.3 in by 2.8 in.

52.
$$\pi r \sqrt{r^2 + h^2} = S$$

$$\pi r \sqrt{r^2 + 10^2} = 125$$

$$\pi^2 r^2 (r^2 + 100) = 125^2$$

$\pi^2 r^4 + 100\pi^2 r^2 - 125^2 = 0$ which may be solved using the quadratic formula

$r^2 = 13.8994796$ and -113.8994796 (reject)

$r = 3.73$ cm to two decimal places.

Exercise 2-8

2.
$$x^2 + x < 12$$
$$x^2 + x - 12 < 0$$
$$(x + 4)(x - 3) < 0$$

zeros: $-4, 3$
test numbers: $-5, 0, 5$
      value: $8, -12, 18$
      signs: $+, -, +$

$x^2 + x - 12 < 0$ on $(-4, 3)$. $-4 < x < 3$.

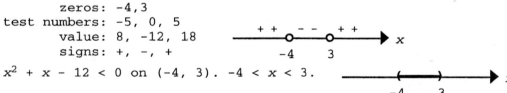

4.
$$x^2 + 7x + 10 > 0$$
$$(x + 5)(x + 2) > 0$$

zeros: $-5, -2$
test numbers: $-10, -3, 0$
      value: $40, -2, 10$
      sign: $+, -, +$

$x^2 + 7x + 10 > 0$ on $(-\infty, -5) \cup (-2, \infty)$.
$x < -5$ or $x > -2$.

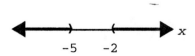

6. $x^2 + 6x \geq 0$
   $x(x + 6) \geq 0$

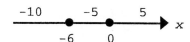

   zeros: 0, -6
   test numbers: -10, -5, 5
   value: 40, -5, 55
   sign: +, -, +

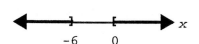

$x^2 + 6x \geq 0$ on $(-\infty, -6] \cup [0, \infty)$.
$x \leq -6$ or $x \geq 0$.

8. $x^2 \leq 4x$
   $x^2 - 4x \leq 0$
   $x(x - 4) \leq 0$

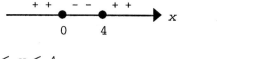

   zeros: 0, 4
   test numbers: -1, 2, 5
   value: 5, -4, 5
   sign: +, -, +

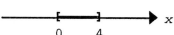

$x^2 - 4x \leq 0$ on $[0, 4]$. $0 \leq x \leq 4$.

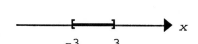

10. $x^2 \leq 9$
   $x^2 - 9 \leq 0$
   $(x + 3)(x - 3) \leq 0$

   zeros: -3, 3
   test numbers: -5, 0, 5
   value: 16, -9, 16
   sign: +, -, +

$x^2 - 9 \leq 0$ on $[-3, 3]$. $-3 \leq x \leq 3$.

12. $\dfrac{x + 3}{x - 1} \geq 0$; $x \neq 1$

   zeros: -3, 1
   test numbers: -5, 0, 5
   value: $\dfrac{1}{3}$, -3, 2
   sign: +, -, +

$\dfrac{x + 3}{x - 1} \geq$ on $(-\infty, -3] \cup (1, \infty)$.
$x \leq -3$ or $x > 1$.

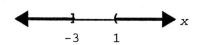

14. $\dfrac{3 - x}{x + 5} \leq 0$; $x \neq -5$

   zeros: 3, -5
   test numbers: -10, 0, 5
   value: -2.6, 0.6, -0.2
   sign: -, +, -

$\dfrac{3 - x}{x + 5} \leq 0$ on $(-\infty, -5) \cup [3, \infty)$.
$x < -5$ or $x \geq 3$.

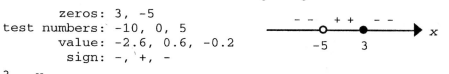

16. $\dfrac{x - 4}{x^2 + 2x} \leq 0$

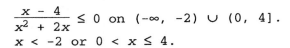

$\dfrac{x - 4}{x(x + 2)} \leq 0; \ x \neq -2, \ 0$

zeros: -2, 0, 4

test numbers: -5, -1, 2, 5

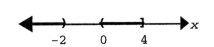

value: -0.6, 5, -0.25, $\dfrac{1}{35}$

sign: -, +, -, +

$\dfrac{x - 4}{x^2 + 2x} \leq 0$ on $(-\infty, -2) \cup (0, 4]$.

x < -2 or 0 < x ≤ 4.

18. $\dfrac{x^2 - x - 12}{x^2 + 4} \leq 0$

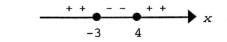

$\dfrac{(x - 4)(x + 3)}{x^2 + 4} \leq 0$

zeros: -3, 4

test numbers: -5, 0, 5

value: 0.62, -3, 0.28

sign: +, -, +

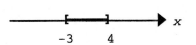

$\dfrac{x^2 - x - 12}{x^2 + 4} \leq 0$ on $[-3, 4]$.

-3 ≤ x ≤ 4.

20. $\dfrac{5}{x} > 3$

$\dfrac{5}{x} - 3 > 0$

$\dfrac{5 - 3x}{x} > 0$

zeros: 0, $\dfrac{5}{3}$

test numbers: -1, 1, 2

value: -8, 2, $-\dfrac{1}{2}$

sign: -, +, -

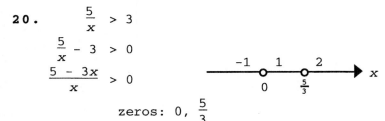

$\dfrac{5}{x} > 3$ on $\left(0, \ \dfrac{5}{3}\right)$.   0 < x < $\dfrac{5}{3}$.

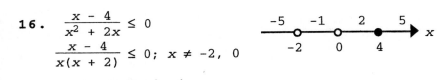

22.
$$\frac{5x - 8}{x - 5} \geq 2$$

$$\frac{5x - 8}{x - 5} - 2 \geq 0$$

$$\frac{5x - 8 - 2(x - 5)}{x - 5} \geq 0$$

$$\frac{5x - 8 - 2x + 10}{x - 5} \geq 0$$

$$\frac{3x + 2}{x - 5} \geq 0; \quad x \neq 5$$

zeros: $-\frac{2}{3}$, 5

test numbers: -1, 0, 10

value: $\frac{1}{6}$, -0.4, 6.4

sign: $+$, $-$, $+$

$$\frac{5x - 8}{x - 5} \geq 2 \text{ on } \left(-\infty, -\frac{2}{3}\right] \cup (5, \infty)$$

$x \leq -\frac{2}{3}$ or $x > 5$.

24.
$$\frac{3}{x - 3} \leq \frac{2}{x + 2}$$

$$\frac{3}{x - 3} - \frac{2}{x + 2} \leq 0$$

$$\frac{3(x + 2) - 2(x - 3)}{(x - 3)(x + 2)} \leq 0$$

$$\frac{3x + 6 - 2x + 6}{(x - 3)(x + 2)} \leq 0$$

$$\frac{x + 12}{(x - 3)(x + 2)} \leq 0; \quad x \neq -2, 3$$

zeros: -12, -2, 3

test numbers: -15, -10, 0, 5

value: -0.013, 0.019, -2, 1.21

sign: $-$, $+$, $-$, $+$

$$\frac{3}{x - 3} \leq \frac{2}{x + 2} \text{ on } (-\infty, -12] \cup (-2, 3).$$

$x \leq -12$ or $-2 < x < 3$.

26.
$$2x^3 + x^2 > 6x$$
$$2x^3 + x^2 - 6x > 0$$
$$x(2x^2 + x - 6) > 0$$
$$x(x + 2)(2x - 3) > 0$$

zeros: -2, 0, $\frac{3}{2}$

test numbers: -3, -1, 1, 2

value: -27, 5, -3, 8

sign: $-$, $+$, $-$, $+$

$2x^3 + x^2 > 6x$ on $(-2, 0) \cup \left(\frac{3}{2}, \infty\right)$.

$-2 < x < 0$ or $x > \frac{3}{2}$.

28. $\sqrt{4 - x^2}$ represents a real number for

$$4 - x^2 \geq 0 \text{ or}$$
$$x^2 \leq 4$$
$$x^2 - 4 \leq 0$$
$$(x + 2)(x - 2) \leq 0$$

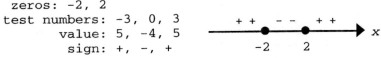

zeros: -2, 2
test numbers: -3, 0, 3
value: 5, -4, 5
sign: $+$, $-$, $+$

$\sqrt{4 - x^2}$ is a real number for $-2 \leq x \leq 2$. $[-2, 2]$

30. $\sqrt{3x^2 - 7x - 6}$ is a real number for

$$3x^2 - 7x - 6 \geq 0$$
$$(x - 3)(3x + 2) \geq 0$$

zeros: $-\dfrac{2}{3}$, 3
test numbers: -1, 0, 4
value: 4, -6, 14
sign: $+$, $-$, $+$

$\sqrt{3x^2 - 7x - 6}$ is real for $x \leq -\dfrac{2}{3}$ or $x \geq 3$.

32. $\sqrt{\dfrac{x - 1}{x + 3}}$ is real for $\dfrac{x - 1}{x + 3} \geq 0$; $x \neq -3$

zeros: -3, 1
test numbers: -4, 0, 2
value: 5, $-\dfrac{1}{3}$, 0.2
sign: $+$, $-$, $+$

$\sqrt{\dfrac{x - 1}{x + 3}}$ is real for $x < -3$ or $x \geq 1$.

34. $ax^2 + bx + c \leq 0$: For $a > 0$, the solution set is $[r_1, r_2]$.
For $a < 0$, the solution set is $(-\infty, r_1] \cup [r_2, \infty)$.

36. $ax^2 + bx + c < 0$: For $a > 0$, the solution set is $\varnothing$, the empty set.
For $a < 0$, the solution set is $(-\infty, r) \cup (r, \infty)$.

38. $x^2 < 0$ is a quadratic inequality whose solution set is the empty set.

40.
$$x^2 + 25 < 10x$$
$$x^2 - 10x + 25 < 0$$
$$(x - 5)^2 < 0.$$ LHS is positive for all x; RHS is negative; positive cannot be $<$ negative, therefore, no solution. $\varnothing$

42.
$$x^2 + 3 > 2x$$
$$x^2 - 2x + 3 > 0$$
$$x = \frac{-(-2) \pm \sqrt{(-2)^2 - 4(1)(3)}}{2(1)}$$
$$x = \frac{2 \pm \sqrt{-8}}{2}.$$ $x^2 - 2x + 3 = 0$ has no real roots. This implies $x^2 + 3 > 2x$ is true for all x or false for all x. To check, let $x = 0$, then $0^2 + 3 > 2(0)$ becomes $3 > 0$ which is true. Therefore, $x^2 + 3 > 2x$ for all x. $(-\infty, \infty)$

44.
$$2x + 2 > x^2$$
$$x^2 - 2x - 2 < 0$$
$$x = \frac{-(-2) \pm \sqrt{(-2)^2 - 4(1)(-2)}}{2(1)} = \frac{2 \pm \sqrt{12}}{2}$$
$$x = \frac{2 \pm 2\sqrt{3}}{2} = 1 \pm \sqrt{3}$$

zeros: $1 - \sqrt{3},\ 1 + \sqrt{3}$
test numbers: $-1,\ 0,\ 3$
value: $1,\ -2,\ 1$
sign: $+,\ -,\ +$

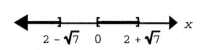

$2x + 2 > x^2$ on $(1 - \sqrt{3},\ 1 + \sqrt{3})$.
$1 - \sqrt{3} < x < 1 + \sqrt{3}$.

46.
$$x^3 \leq 4x^2 + 3x$$
$$x^3 - 4x^2 - 3x \leq 0$$
$$x(x^2 - 4x - 3) \leq 0$$
$$x = \frac{-(-4) \pm \sqrt{(-4)^2 - 4(1)(-3)}}{2(1)} = \frac{4 \pm \sqrt{28}}{2} = \frac{4 \pm 2\sqrt{7}}{2}$$
$$x = 2 \pm \sqrt{7}$$

zeros: $2 - \sqrt{7},\ 0,\ 2 + \sqrt{7}$
test numbers: $-1,\ -\frac{1}{2},\ 1,\ 5$
value: $-2,\ 0.375,\ -6,\ 10$
sign: $-,\ +,\ -,\ +$

$x^3 \leq 4x^2 + 3x$ on $(-\infty,\ 2 - \sqrt{7}] \cup [0,\ 2 + \sqrt{7}]$.
$x \leq 2 - \sqrt{7}$ or $0 \leq x \leq 2 + \sqrt{7}$.

48.
$$x^4 + 36 \geq 13x^2$$
$$x^4 - 13x^2 + 36 \geq 0$$
$$(x^2 - 9)(x^2 - 4) \geq 0$$
$$(x - 3)(x + 3)(x - 2)(x + 2) \geq 0$$

zeros: $-3,\ -2,\ 2,\ 3$
test numbers: $-4,\ -\frac{5}{2},\ 0,\ \frac{5}{2},\ 4$
value: $84,\ -6.1875,\ 36,\ -6.1875,\ 84$
sign: $+,\ -,\ +,\ -,\ +$

$x^4 + 36 \geq 13x^2$ on $(-\infty,\ -3] \cup [-2,\ 2] \cup [3,\ \infty)$.
$x \leq -3$ or $-2 \leq x \leq 2$ or $x \geq 3$.

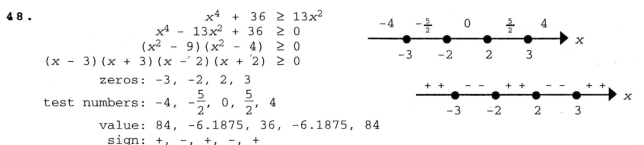

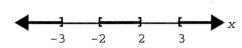

50. $\left|\dfrac{x + 1}{x}\right| > 2$ is equivalent to

(1) $\dfrac{x + 1}{x} < -2$ or $\dfrac{x + 1}{x} > 2$ (2)

(1) $\dfrac{x + 1}{x} < -2$ (2) $\dfrac{x + 1}{x} - 2 > 0$

$\dfrac{x + 1}{x} + 2 < 0$ $\dfrac{x + 1 - 2x}{x} > 0$

$\dfrac{x + 1 + 2x}{x} < 0$ $\dfrac{1 - x}{x} > 0$

$\dfrac{3x + 1}{x} < 0$ $-\dfrac{x - 1}{x} < 0$

(1)   zeros: $0,\ -\dfrac{1}{3}$

test numbers: $-2,\ -\dfrac{1}{4},\ 1$

value: $2.5,\ -1,\ 4$

sign: $+,\ -,\ +$

$\dfrac{3x + 1}{x} < 0$ on $\left(-\dfrac{1}{3},\ 0\right)$. $-\dfrac{1}{3} < x < 0$.

(2)   zeros: $0,\ 1$

test numbers: $-1,\ \dfrac{1}{2},\ 2$

value: $2,\ -1,\ \dfrac{1}{2}$

sign: $+,\ -,\ +$

$\dfrac{x - 1}{x} < 0$ on $(0,\ 1)$. $0 < x < 1$.

The union of (1) and (2) gives the solution $\left(-\dfrac{1}{3},\ 0\right) \cup (0,\ 1)$. $-\dfrac{1}{3} < x < 0$ or $0 < x < 1$.

52. (A) profit results when revenue > cost
$10p - p^2 > 27 - 2p$
$-p^2 + 12p - 27 > 0$
$p^2 - 12p + 27 < 0$
$(p - 9)(p - 3) < 0$

zeros: $3,\ 9$
test numbers: $2,\ 5,\ 10$
value: $7,\ -8,\ 7$
sign: $+,\ -,\ +$

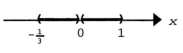

profit: $\$3 < p < \$9$. $(\$3,\ \$9)$

(B) loss results when revenue < cost
$10p - p^2 < 27 - 2p$
$-p^2 + 12p - 27 < 0$
$p^2 - 12p + 27 > 0$

from (A) the solution to this inequality is $p < 3$ or $p > 9$ but since $p < 0$ makes no sense (the price cannot be negative), p must be at least 0. The solution is $\$0 \le p < \$3$ or $p > \$9$. $[\$0,\ \$3) \cup (\$9,\ \infty)$

54. $d = 112t - 16t^2 > 0$

$\quad\quad 16t^2 - 112t < 0$

$\quad\quad 16t(t - 7) < 0$

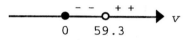

$\quad\quad\quad$ zeros: $0, 7$

test numbers: $-1, 1, 10$

$\quad\quad$ value: $128, -96, 480$

$\quad\quad\quad$ sign: $+, -, +$

Ball is above the ground for $0 < t < 7$.

56. $d = 0.044v^2 + 1.1v \quad$ stopping distance

$\quad\quad\quad 0.044v^2 + 1.1v < 220$

$0.044v^2 + 1.1v - 220 < 0$

Using the quadratic formula, the zeros are 59.3 and -84.3 which is rejected since $v \geq 0$ (cars do not have negative speed).

test numbers: $20, 80$

$\quad\quad$ value: $-180.4, 149.6$

$\quad\quad\quad$ sign: $-, +$

Stopping distance is less than 220 ft for $0 \leq v < 59.3$ mph.

58. $\quad\quad\quad\quad\quad \dfrac{0.12t}{t^2 + 2} \geq 0.04$

$\quad\quad\quad\quad\quad 0.12t \geq 0.04(t^2 + 2)$

$-0.04t^2 + 0.12t - 0.08 \geq 0$

$\quad 0.04t^2 - 0.12t + 0.08 \leq 0$

Using the quadratic formula, the zeros are 1 and 2.

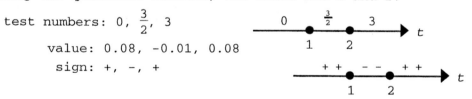

test numbers: $0, \dfrac{3}{2}, 3$

$\quad\quad$ value: $0.08, -0.01, 0.08$

$\quad\quad\quad$ sign: $+, -, +$

Concentration will be 0.04 mg/ml or greater for $1 \leq t \leq 2$ sec.

CHAPTER 3

Exercise 3-1

2. $\{(x, y) \mid x > 0, y > 0\}$: Quadrant I

4. $\{(x, y) \mid y = 0\}$: The x axis

6. $\{(x, y) \mid y < 0, x \neq 0\}$:
Quadrants III and IV

8. $\{(x, y) \mid x < 0, y > 0\}$: Quadrant II

10. $\{(x, y) \mid xy > 0\}$: Quadrants I and III

12. $y = \frac{1}{2}x + 1$

symmetry with respect to x axis? $-y = \frac{1}{2}x + 1$

$\qquad y = -\frac{1}{2}x - 1$ not equivalent

$\qquad$ no symmetry with respect to x axis.

symmetry with respect to y axis? $y = \frac{1}{2}(-x) + 1$

$\qquad y = -\frac{1}{2}x + 1$ not equivalent

$\qquad$ no symmetry with respect to y axis.

symmetry with respect to the origin? $-y = \frac{1}{2}(-x) + 1$

$\qquad y = \frac{1}{2}x - 1$ not equivalent

$\qquad$ no symmetry with respect to origin.

x	y
0	1
2	2
4	3

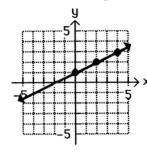

No symmetry

14. $y = 2x$

symmetry with respect to x axis? $\quad -y = 2x$
$\qquad y = -2x$ not equivalent
no symmetry with respect to x axis.

symmetry with respect to y axis? $\quad y = 2(-x)$
$\qquad y = -2x$ not equivalent
no symmetry with respect to y axis.

symmetry with respect to origin? $\quad -y = 2(-x)$
$\qquad y = 2x$ equivalent
yes, symmetry with respect to origin.

x	y
0	0
2	4
3	6

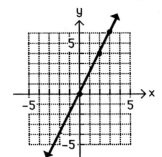

Symmetric with respect to the origin.

16. $|y| = -x$

symmetry with respect to x axis?

$|-y| = -x$
$|y| = -x$ equivalent
yes, symmetry with respect to x axis.

symmetry with respect to y axis?

$|y| = -(-x)$
$|y| = x$ not equivalent

no symmetry with respect to y axis.

symmetry with respect to origin?

$|-y| = -(-x)$
$|y| = x$ not equivalent

no symmetry with respect to origin.

x	y
0	0
-1	±1
-2	±2

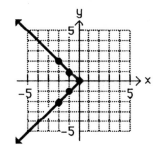

Symmetric with respect to the x axis.

18. $y = -x$

symmetry with respect to x axis?

$-y = -x$
$y = x$ not equivalent
no symmetry with respect to x axis.

symmetry with respect to y axis?

$y = -(-x)$
$y = x$ not equivalent
no symmetry with respect to y axis.

symmetry with respect to origin?

$-y = -(-x)$
$-y = x$
$y = -x$ equivalent
yes, symmetry with respect to origin.

x	y
0	0
-1	1
-2	2

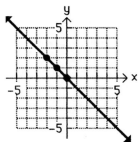

Symmetric with respect to the origin.

20. $(-6, 4)$, $(2, -1)$: $d = \sqrt{(-6 - 2)^2 + (4 - (-1))^2}$

$\quad = \sqrt{(-8)^2 + 5^2}$

$\quad = \sqrt{64 + 25}$

$\quad = \sqrt{89}$

22. $(2, -5)$, $(-3, 1)$: $d = \sqrt{(2 - (-3))^2 + (-5 - 1)^2}$

$\quad = \sqrt{5^2 + (-6)^2}$

$\quad = \sqrt{25 + 36}$

$\quad = \sqrt{61}$

24. $C(0, 0)$, $r = 6$: $(x - h)^2 + (y - k)^2 = r^2$

$\quad\quad\quad (x - 0)^2 + (y - 0)^2 = 6^2$

$\quad\quad\quad x^2 + y^2 = 36$

26. $C(-4, 2)$, $r = 5$: $(x - h)^2 + (y - k)^2 = r^2$
$(x - (-4))^2 + (y - 2)^2 = 5^2$
$(x + 4)^2 + (y - 2)^2 = 25$

28. $C(-1, -3)$, $r = \sqrt{5}$: $(x - h)^2 + (y - k)^2 = r^2$
$(x - (-1))^2 + (y - (-3))^2 = (\sqrt{5})^2$
$(x + 1)^2 + (y + 3)^2 = 5$

30. (A) $(-4, -4)$, (B) $(-1, 5)$, (C) $(-3, 1)$ and $(1, 1)$, (D) $(-2, 4)$ and $(0, 4)$

32. (A) 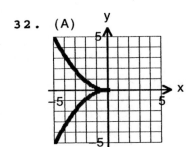   (B) 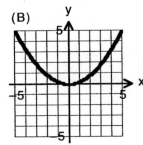   (C) 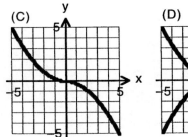   (D)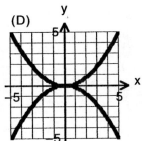

34. $y^2 = x - 2$
symmetry with respect to x axis?

$(-y)^2 = x - 2$
$y^2 = x - 2$ equivalent
yes, symmetry with respect to x axis.

symmetry with respect to y axis?

$y^2 = (-x) - 2$
$y^2 = -x - 2$ not equivalent
no symmetry with respect to y axis.

symmetry with respect to origin?

$(-y)^2 = (-x) - 2$
$y^2 = -x - 2$ not equivalent
no symmetry with respect to origin.

x	y
2	0
6	± 2

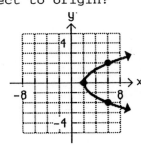

Symmetric with respect to the x axis.

36. $y + 2 = x^2$
symmetry with respect to x axis?

$-y + 2 = x^2$
$y - 2 = -x^2$ not equivalent
no symmetry with respect to x axis.

symmetry with respect to y axis?

$y + 2 = (-x)^2$
$y + 2 = x^2$ equivalent
yes, symmetry with respect to y axis.

symmetry with respect to origin?

$-y + 2 = (-x)^2$
$-y + 2 = x^2$ not equivalent
no symmetry with respect to origin.

x	y
0	-2
± 1	-1
± 2	2
± 3	7

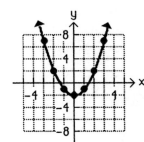

Symmetric with respect to the y axis.

38. $x^2 + 9y^2 = 9$. Since both variables are raised to even powers, graph has symmetry with respect to x axis, y axis, and origin.

x	y
0	± 1
± 3	0

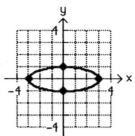

40. $4x^2 - y^2 = 1$. Since both variables are squared, graph has symmetry with respect to x axis, y axis, and origin.

x	y
$\pm\frac{1}{2}$	0
± 1	$\pm\sqrt{3}$
± 2	$\pm\sqrt{15}$
± 3	$\pm\sqrt{35}$

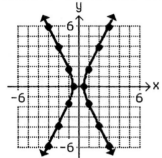

42. $y = x^4$. Symmetry with respect to y axis.

x	y
0	0
± 1	1
± 2	16

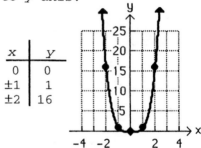

44. $x = 0.8y^2 - 3.5$. Symmetry with respect to x axis.

x	y
-3.5	0
0	$\pm\sqrt{\dfrac{35}{8}}$

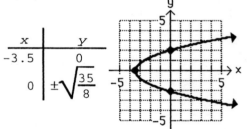

46. $y = \sqrt{100 - 4x^2}$. Symmetry with respect to y axis.

x	y
0	10
± 5	0

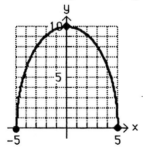

48. $y^{2/3} = x$

symmetry with respect to x axis? $(-y)^{2/3} = x$
$\qquad\qquad\qquad\qquad\qquad\quad y^{2/3} = x$ equivalent
yes, symmetry with respect to x axis.

symmetry with respect to y axis? $y^{2/3} = -x$ not equivalent
no symmetry with respect to y axis.

symmetry with respect to origin? $(-y)^{2/3} = -x$
$\qquad\qquad\qquad\qquad\qquad\quad y^{2/3} = -x$ not equivalent
no symmetry with respect to origin.

x	y
0	0
4	±8

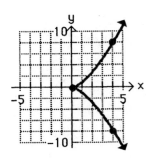

Symmetric with respect to the x axis.

50. $(-4, -1)$, $(0, 7)$, $(6, -6)$

$(-4, -1)$ to $(0, 7)$:
$$\begin{aligned} d &= \sqrt{(-4)^2 + (-1 - 7)^2} \\ &= \sqrt{16 + 64} \\ &= \sqrt{80} \end{aligned}$$

$(0, 7)$ to $(6, -6)$:
$$\begin{aligned} d &= \sqrt{6^2 + (7 + 6)^2} \\ &= \sqrt{36 + 169} \\ &= \sqrt{205} \end{aligned}$$

$(-4, -1)$ to $(6, -6)$:
$$\begin{aligned} d &= \sqrt{(-4 - 6)^2 + (-1 + 6)^2} \\ &= \sqrt{100 + 25} \\ &= \sqrt{125} \end{aligned}$$

$$a^2 + b^2 = c^2$$
$$(\sqrt{80})^2 + (\sqrt{125})^2 = (\sqrt{205})^2$$
$$80 + 125 = 205$$

$$\begin{aligned} \text{Area} &= \frac{1}{2}bh \\ &= \frac{1}{2}(\sqrt{80})(\sqrt{125}) \\ &= 50 \end{aligned}$$

$$\begin{aligned} \text{Perimeter} &= \sqrt{80} + \sqrt{125} + \sqrt{205} \\ &\approx 34.442433 \\ &\approx 34.44 \end{aligned}$$

52. $(x, 2)$ is 4 units from $(3, -3)$:
$$\begin{aligned} d &= \sqrt{(x_1 - x_2)^2 + (y_1 - y_2)^2} \\ 4 &= \sqrt{(x - 3)^2 + (2 - (-3))^2} \\ 16 &= (x - 3)^2 + 25 \\ -9 &= (x - 3)^2 \end{aligned}$$
There is no solution.

54. $(3, y)$ is 13 units from $(-9, 2)$:
$$\begin{aligned} d &= \sqrt{(x_1 - x_2)^2 + (y_1 - y_2)^2} \\ 13 &= \sqrt{(3 - (-9))^2 + (y - 2)^2} \\ 169 &= 144 + (y - 2)^2 \\ 25 &= (y - 2)^2 \\ \pm 5 &= y - 2 \\ y &= 2 + 5 = 7 \\ y &= 2 - 5 = -3 \end{aligned}$$

56. $(x - 5)^2 + (y + 7)^2 = 15$
$(x - 5)^2 + (y - (-7))^2 = (\sqrt{15})^2$
from which $(h, k) = (5, -7)$
and $r = \sqrt{15}$.

58.
$$x^2 + y^2 - 2x - 10y = 55$$
$$x^2 - 2x + 1 + y^2 - 10y + 25 = 55 + 26$$
$$(x - 1)^2 + (y - 5)^2 = 81 = 9^2$$
from which center = $(1, 5)$;
radius = 9

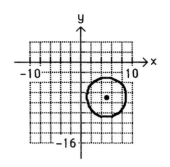

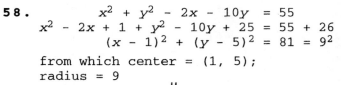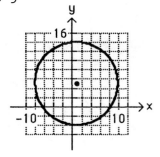

60. $x^2 + y^2 + 4x + 10y + 15 = 0$
$x^2 + 4x + 4 + y^2 + 10y + 25 = -15 + 4 + 25$
$(x + 2)^2 + (y + 5)^2 = 14$
$(x - (-2))^2 + (y - (-5))^2 = (\sqrt{14})^2$
from which center = $(-2, -5)$;
radius = $\sqrt{14}$

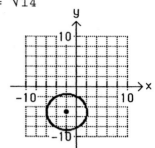

62. (A) and (B)

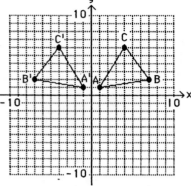

(C) Changing the sign of the x coordinate of all the points on the graph reflects the graph across the y axis.

64. (A) and (B)

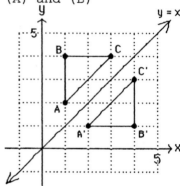

(C) Reversing the coordinates of each point on a graph reflects the graph across the $y = x$ line.

66. $x^2 + y^2 = 5$
$y^2 = 5 - x^2$
$y = \pm\sqrt{5 - x^2}$

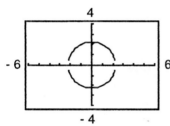

68. $(x - 2)^2 + (y - 1)^2 = 3$
$(y - 1)^2 = 3 - (x - 2)^2$
$y - 1 = \pm\sqrt{3 - (x - 2)^2}$
$y = 1 \pm\sqrt{3 - (x - 2)^2}$

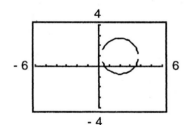

70. $y = 1 \pm\sqrt{1 - x^2}$
$y - 1 = \pm\sqrt{1 - x^2}$
$(y - 1)^2 = 1 - x^2$
$x^2 + (y - 1)^2 = 1$
center = $(0, 1)$
radius = 1

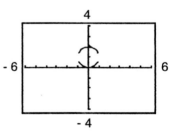

From the graph, choose one point on the lower half of the circle, $(0, 0)$, and check by substituting these values into the second equation.
$0 = 1 - \sqrt{1 - 0^2}$
$0 = 0$: checks

Choose one point on the upper half of the circle, $(0, 2)$, and check by substituting these values into the first equation.
$2 = 1 + \sqrt{1 - 0^2}$
$2 = 2$: checks

72.

$$y = -1 \pm\sqrt{4x - x^2}$$

$$y + 1 = \pm\sqrt{4x - x^2}$$

$$(y + 1)^2 = 4x - x^2$$

$$x^2 - 4x + (y + 1)^2 = 0$$

$$x^2 - 4x + 4 + (y + 1)^2 = 4$$

$$(x - 2)^2 + (y + 1)^2 = 2^2$$

center = (2, -1); radius = 2

Use the same method as in problem 70. On the lower half, test (2, -3).

$$-3 = -1 - \sqrt{4(2) - (2)^2}$$

-3 = -3: checks

On the upper half, test (2, 1).

$$1 = -1 + \sqrt{4(2) - (2)^2}$$

1 = 1: checks

74. $|y| = x^3$

symmetry with respect to *x* axis?

$|-y| = x^3$
$|y| = x^3$ equivalent
yes, symmetry with respect to *x* axis.

symmetry with respect to *y* axis?

$|y| = (-x)^3$
$|y| = -x^3$ not equivalent
no symmetry with respect to *y* axis.

symmetry with respect to origin?

$|-y| = (-x)^3$
$|y| = -x^3$ not equivalent
no symmetry with respect to origin.

x	y
0	0
1	±1
2	±8

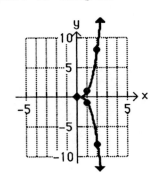

Symmetric with respect to the *x* axis.

76. $xy = -1$

symmetry with respect to *x* axis?

$x(-y) = -1$
$-xy = -1$
$xy = 1$ not equivalent
no symmetry with respect to *x* axis.

symmetry with respect to *y* axis?

$-x(y) = -1$
$xy = 1$ not equivalent
no symmetry with respect to *y* axis.

symmetry with respect to origin?

$(-x)(-y) = -1$
$xy = -1$ equivalent
yes, symmetry with respect to origin.

x	y
1	-1
-1	1

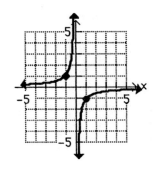

Symmetric with respect to the origin.

78. $y = x^2 - 6x$

symmetry with respect to x axis? $-y = x^2 - 6x$
$y = -x^2 + 6x$ not equivalent
no symmetry with respect to x axis.

symmetry with respect to y axis? $y = (-x)^2 - 6(-x)$
$y = x^2 + 6x$ not equivalent
no symmetry with respect to y axis.

symmetry with respect to origin? $-y = (-x)^2 - 6(-x)$
$-y = x^2 + 6x$
$y = -x^2 - 6x$ not equivalent
no symmetry with respect to origin.

x	y
0	0
3	-9
6	0

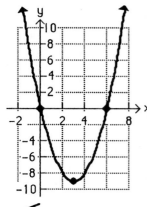

No symmetry

80.

$A(x_1, y_1)$, $B\left(\dfrac{x_1 + x_2}{2}, \dfrac{y_1 + y_2}{2}\right)$, $C(x_2, y_2)$

If B is the midpoint of $\overline{AC}$, then the distance from $\overline{AB}$ = the distance from $\overline{BC}$.

$$d_{AB} = \sqrt{\left(x_1 - \frac{x_1 + x_2}{2}\right)^2 + \left(y_1 - \frac{y_1 + y_2}{2}\right)^2}$$

$$= \sqrt{\left(\frac{2x_1 - x_1 - x_2}{2}\right)^2 + \left(\frac{2y_1 - y_1 - y_2}{2}\right)^2}$$

$$= \sqrt{\left(\frac{x_1 - x_2}{2}\right)^2 + \left(\frac{y_1 - y_2}{2}\right)^2}$$

$$d_{BC} = \sqrt{\left(\frac{x_1 + x_2}{2} - x_2\right)^2 + \left(\frac{y_1 + y_2}{2} - y_2\right)^2}$$

$$= \sqrt{\left(\frac{x_1 + x_2 - 2x_2}{2}\right)^2 + \left(\frac{y_1 + y_2 - 2y_2}{2}\right)^2}$$

$$= \sqrt{\left(\frac{x_1 - x_2}{2}\right)^2 + \left(\frac{y_1 - y_2}{2}\right)^2}$$

$$d_{AB} = d_{BC}$$

82.

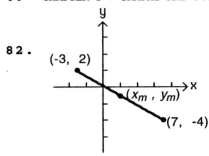

$$x_m = \frac{-3 + 7}{2} = 2$$

$$y_m = \frac{2 - 4}{2} = -1 \qquad \text{center} = (2, -1)$$

$$r = \sqrt{(2 - 7)^2 + (-1 - (-4))^2} = \sqrt{34}: \text{radius}$$

equation: $(x - 2)^2 + (y - (-1))^2 = (\sqrt{34})^2$

$$(x - 2)^2 + (y + 1)^2 = 34$$

84. $C(-5, 4)$ passes through $(2, -3)$.

$$(x - (-5))^2 + (y - 4)^2 = r^2$$
$$(x + 5)^2 + (y - 4)^2 = r^2$$
$(2, -3):$ $(2 + 5)^2 + (-3 - 4)^2 = r^2$
$$49 + 49 = r^2$$
Equation: $(x + 5)^2 + (y - 4)^2 = 98$

86. Yes. a, $b > 0$. Symmetric with respect to the y axis:

If (a, b) then $(-a, b)$
$(a, -b)$ then $(-a, -b)$

a, $b > 0$. Symmetric with respect to the origin:

If (a, b) then $(-a, -b)$
$(-a, b)$ then $(a, -b)$

which implies (a, b) then $(\pm a, \pm b)$, so symmetric with respect to the x axis, $(\pm a, b)$ then $(\pm a, -b)$, is included.

88. (A) The supply is 3000 cases when the price is $5.60.

(B) As the price increases from $5.60 to $5.80 the supply increases by about 300 cases.

(C) As the price decreases from $5.60 to $5.40 the supply decreases by about 400 cases.

(D) As price increases so does supply. As price decreases so does supply.

90. (A) The temperature at 7 p.m. is about 60°. (B) The lowest temperature is 44° at 5 a.m. (C) The temperature is 52° at about 9 a.m. and 10 p.m.

92. (A) $V = 4\sqrt{25 - x^2}$

(B) The speed of the ball is zero at the top and bottom of the oscillation and has a maximum speed of 4 at the rest position.

94.

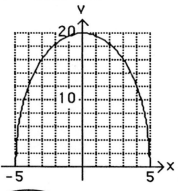

$$r^2 = (r - 4)^2 + 6^2$$
$$r^2 = r^2 - 8r + 16 + 36$$
$$8r = 52$$
$$r = 6.5 \text{ mm}$$

96. (A)

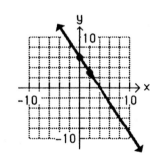

$$AT = 2TB$$
$$\sqrt{(x-0)^2 + (y-0)^2} = 2\sqrt{(x-36)^2 + (y-15)^2}$$
$$x^2 + y^2 = 4(x^2 - 72x + 36^2) + 4(y^2 - 30y + 15^2)$$
$$x^2 + y^2 = 4x^2 - 288x + 5184 + 4y^2 - 120y + 900$$
$$3x^2 - 288x + 3y^2 - 120y = -6084$$
$$x^2 - 96x + 1728 + y^2 - 40y + 300 = -2028$$
$$x^2 - 96x + 2304 + y^2 - 40y + 400 = -2028 + 2304 + 400$$
$$(x - 48)^2 + (y - 20)^2 = 676 = 26^2 \text{: circle}$$
$$\text{center} = (48, 20); \text{ radius } = 26$$

(B) On the circle, find y when $x = 0$:
$$(x - 48)^2 + (0 - 20)^2 = 676$$
$$(x - 48)^2 = 276$$
$$x - 48 = \pm 16.613$$
$$x = 64.6 \text{ miles or}$$
$$x = 31.4 \text{ miles}$$

Exercise 3-2

2. From the graph, x-intercept = 1
y-intercept = 1
slope = -1

$y = -x + 1$

4. From the graph, x-intercept = -1
y-intercept = -3
slope = -3

$y = -3x - 3$

6. From the graph, x-intercept = 4
y-intercept = -2
slope = $\frac{1}{2}$

$y = \frac{1}{2}x - 2$

8. $y = -\frac{3}{2}x + 6$

x	y
0	6
2	3

slope = $-\frac{3}{2}$

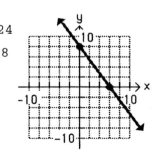

10. $y = \frac{2}{3}x - 3$

x	y
0	-3
3	-1

slope = $\frac{2}{3}$

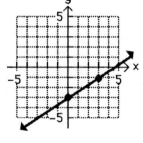

12. $4x + 3y = 24$
$3y = -4x + 24$
$y = -\frac{4}{3}x + 8$

x	y
0	8
6	0

slope = $-\frac{4}{3}$

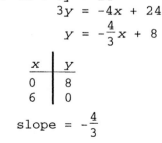

14. $6x - 7y = -49$
$7y = 6x + 49$
$y = \frac{6}{7}x + 7$

x	y
0	7
-7	1

slope = $\frac{6}{7}$

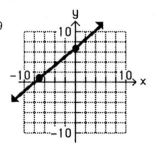

16. $\dfrac{y}{6} - \dfrac{x}{5} = 1$

$\dfrac{y}{6} = \dfrac{x}{5} + 1$

$y = \dfrac{6}{5}x + 6$

x	y
0	6
-5	0

slope = $\dfrac{6}{5}$

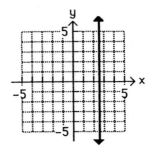

18. $y = -2$, horizontal line

slope = 0

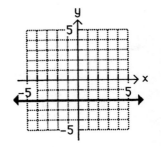

20. $x = 2.5$, vertical line undefined slope

22. $m = -1$, $b = 7$:

$y = mx + b$

$y = -x + 7$

$x + y = 7$

24. $m = \dfrac{5}{3}$, $b = 6$:

$y = mx + b$

$y = \dfrac{5}{3}x + 6$

$3y = 5x + 18$

$-5x + 3y = 18$

$5x - 3y = -18$

26. $(4, 0)$; $m = 3$:

$y - y_1 = m(x - x_1)$

$y - 0 = 3(x - 4)$

$y = 3x - 12$

28. $(2, -3)$; $m = -\dfrac{4}{5}$:

$y - y_1 = m(x - x_1)$

$y - (-3) = -\dfrac{4}{5}(x - 2)$

$y + 3 = -\dfrac{4}{5}x + \dfrac{8}{5}$

$y = -\dfrac{4}{5}x + \dfrac{8}{5} - \dfrac{15}{5}$

$y = -\dfrac{4}{5}x - \dfrac{7}{5}$

30. $(-1, 4)$; $(3, 2)$:

$m = \dfrac{4 - 2}{-1 - 3} = \dfrac{2}{-4} = -\dfrac{1}{2}$

$y - y_1 = m(x - x_1)$

$y - 4 = -\dfrac{1}{2}(x - (-1))$

$y - 4 = -\dfrac{1}{2}x - \dfrac{1}{2}$

$y = -\dfrac{1}{2}x - \dfrac{1}{2} + \dfrac{8}{2}$

$y = -\dfrac{1}{2}x + \dfrac{7}{2}$

32. $(0, 5)$; $(2, 5)$:

$m = \dfrac{5 - 5}{0 - 2} = 0$

Equation of the form $y = b$

$y = 5$

34. $(5, -4)$; $(5, 6)$:

$m = \dfrac{-4 - 6}{5 - 5}$; undefined slope

Equation of the form $x = a$

$x = 5$

36. $(-3, 2)$; parallel to $y = 4x - 5$:
$m = 4$; parallel slope $= 4$
$y - y_1 = m(x - x_1)$
$\;y - 2 = 4(x - (-3))$
$\;y - 2 = 4x + 12$
$4x - y = -14$

38. $(-2, 0)$; parallel to $-3x + 4y = 10$
$\qquad\qquad\qquad\quad 4y = 3x + 10$
$\qquad\qquad\qquad\quad y = \dfrac{3}{4}x + \dfrac{5}{2}$
$m = \dfrac{3}{4}$; parallel $m = \dfrac{3}{4}$
$y - y_1 = m(x - x_1)$
$\;y - 0 = \dfrac{3}{4}(x - (-2))$
$y = \dfrac{3}{4}x + \dfrac{3}{2}$
$4y = 3x + 6$
$3x - 4y = -6$

40. $(-2, -1)$; parallel to y axis:
Equation of the form $x = a$
$\quad x = -2$

42. $(-1, 3)$; perpendicular to
$y = -\dfrac{3}{5}x + 2$
$m = -\dfrac{3}{5}$; perpendicular slope $= \dfrac{5}{3}$
$\;y - y_1 = m(x - x_1)$
$\;y - 3 = \dfrac{5}{3}(x - (-1))$
$\;y - 3 = \dfrac{5}{3}x + \dfrac{5}{3}$
$3y - 9 = 5x + 5$
$5x - 3y = -14$

44. $(0, 3)$; perpendicular to $2x + y = 1$
$\qquad\qquad\qquad\qquad y = -2x + 1$
$m = -2$; perpendicular slope $= \dfrac{1}{2}$
$y - y_1 = m(x - x_1)$
$\;y - 3 = \dfrac{1}{2}(x - 0)$
$\;y - 3 = \dfrac{1}{2}x$
$2y - 6 = x$
$x - 2y = -6$

46. $(1, -7)$; perpendicular to y axis:
Equation of the form $y = b$
$\quad y = -7$

48. $A(-5, -2)$; $B(-3, 4)$; $C(6, 10)$;
$D(4, 4)$
$m_{AB} = \dfrac{-2 - 4}{-5 - (-3)} = \dfrac{-6}{-2} = 3$
$m_{BC} = \dfrac{4 - 10}{-3 - 6} = \dfrac{-6}{-9} = \dfrac{2}{3}$
$m_{CD} = \dfrac{10 - 4}{6 - 4} = \dfrac{6}{2} = 3$
$m_{AD} = \dfrac{-2 - 4}{-5 - 4} = \dfrac{-6}{-9} = \dfrac{2}{3}$
Since $AB \parallel CD$ and $BC \parallel AD$, but AB is not $\perp$ to BC, the figure is a parallelogram.

50. $A(-6, 3)$; $B(3, 7)$; $C(2, 4)$;
$D(-4, -1)$
$m_{AB} = \dfrac{3 - 7}{-6 - 3} = \dfrac{-4}{-9} = \dfrac{4}{9}$
$m_{BC} = \dfrac{7 - 4}{3 - 2} = \dfrac{3}{1} = 3$
$m_{CD} = \dfrac{4 - (-1)}{2 - (-4)} = \dfrac{5}{6}$
$m_{AD} = \dfrac{3 - (-1)}{-6 - (-4)} = \dfrac{4}{-2} = -2$
The figure is neither a trapezoid, parallelogram, nor a rectangle, since no two sides are parallel or perpendicular.

52. Let (x, y) be a point on the perpendicular bisector of the line segment joining $(-4, -3)$ and $(2, 4)$. Then the distance from (x, y) to $(-4, -3)$ is equal to the distance from (x, y) to $(2, 4)$.

$$\sqrt{(x + 4)^2 + (y + 3)^2} = \sqrt{(x - 2)^2 + (y - 4)^2}$$
$$(x + 4)^2 + (y + 3)^2 = (x - 2)^2 + (y - 4)^2$$
$$x^2 + 8x + 16 + y^2 + 6y + 9 = x^2 - 4x + 4 + y^2 - 8y + 16$$
$$8x + 16 + 6y + 9 = -4x + 4 - 8y + 16$$
$$8x + 6y + 25 = -4x - 8y + 20$$
$$12x + 14y = -5$$

Which is equivalent to $y = -\dfrac{6}{7}x - \dfrac{5}{14}$.

54.

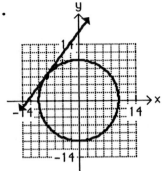
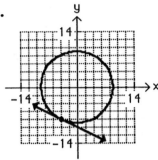

$x^2 + y^2 = 100$

m of line from $(0, 0)$ to $(-8, 6)$: $m = -\frac{6}{8}$

tangent line: $m = \frac{8}{6} = \frac{4}{3}$

$y - y_1 = m(x - x_1)$

$y - 6 = \frac{4}{3}(x - (-8))$

$y - 6 = \frac{4}{3}x + \frac{32}{3}$

$3y - 18 = 4x + 32$

$4x - 3y = -50$

56.

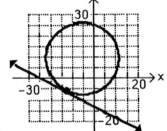

$x^2 + y^2 = 80$

m of line from $(0, 0)$ to $(-4, -8)$: $m = \frac{8}{4} = 2$

tangent line: $m = -\frac{1}{2}$

$y - y_1 = m(x - x_1)$

$y - (-8) = -\frac{1}{2}(x - (-4))$

$y + 8 = -\frac{1}{2}x - 2$

$2y + 16 = -x - 4$

$x + 2y = -20$

58. $(x + 5)^2 + (y - 9)^2 = 289$
center $= (-5, 9)$

m of line from $(-5, 9)$ to $(-13, -6)$:

$$m = \frac{9 - (-6)}{-5 - (-13)} = \frac{15}{8}$$

tangent line: $m = -\frac{8}{15}$

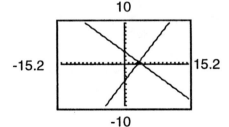

$y - y_1 = m(x - x_1)$

$y - (-6) = -\frac{8}{15}(x - (-13))$

$y + 6 = -\frac{8}{15}x - \frac{104}{15}$

$15y + 90 = -8x - 104$

$8x + 15y = -194$

60. (A) The graphs of $3x + 4y = 12$ and $4x - 3y = 12$ are

(B) The graphs of $2x + 3y = 12$ and $3x - 2y = 12$ are

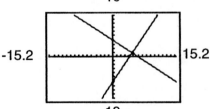

(C) The graphs of $Ax + By = C$ and $Bx - Ay = C$ are perpendicular lines.

(D) $Ax + By = C$ may be written $y = -\frac{A}{B}x + \frac{C}{B}$ and $Bx - Ay = C$ may be written $y = \frac{B}{A}x - \frac{C}{A}$. Multiplying the slopes gives $-\frac{A}{B} \cdot \frac{B}{A} = -1$ which shows the lines are perpendicular.

62. $y = |x + 2|$. This is graph of $y = |x|$ shifted 2 units to the left.

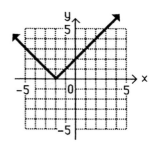

64. The graph of $y = -\frac{1}{2}|x| + 1$ is the graph of $y = |x|$ reflected in the x axis, shifted vertically upward one unit, and broadened by a factor of $\frac{1}{2}$.

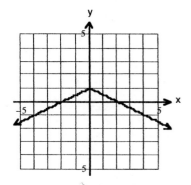

66.
$$4y^2 - 9x^2 = 0$$
$$4y^2 = 9x^2$$
$$2\sqrt{y^2} = 3\sqrt{x^2}$$
$$2|y| = 3|x|$$
$$|y| = \frac{3}{2}|x|$$

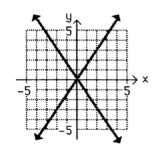

for $y \geq 0$, $x \geq 0$; $\quad y = \frac{3}{2}x$

$\quad y \leq 0$, $x \geq 0$; $\quad -y = \frac{3}{2}x$

$\quad y \geq 0$, $x \leq 0$; $\quad y = -\frac{3}{2}x$

$\quad y \leq 0$, $x \leq 0$; $\quad -y = -\frac{3}{2}x$

68. The graph of $y = mx + b$ is a straight line with slope m and y intercept of b. The graph of $y = m|x| + b$ is the same as the graph of $y = mx + b$ for $x \geq 0$. For $x < 0$, the graph of $y = m|x| + b$ is the same as the graph of $y = -mx + b$.

70. $(3, 0)$ and $(0, 5)$
$$m = \frac{0 - 5}{3 - 0} = -\frac{5}{3}$$
$$y - y_1 = m(x - x_1)$$
$$y - 0 = -\frac{5}{3}(x - 3)$$
$$y = -\frac{5}{3}x + 5$$
$$3y = -5x + 15$$
$$5x + 3y = 15$$

72.

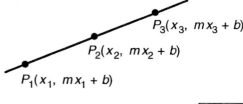

$$d(P_1, P_2) = \sqrt{(x_2 - x_1)^2 + (mx_2 + b - mx_1 - b)^2}$$
$$d(P_1, P_2) = \sqrt{(x_2 - x_1)^2 + m^2(x_2 - x_1)^2}$$
$$d(P_1, P_2) = (x_2 - x_1)\sqrt{1 + m^2}$$
$$\text{Similarly } d(P_2, P_3) = (x_3 - x_2)\sqrt{1 + m^2}$$
$$d(P_1, P_3) = (x_3 - x_1)\sqrt{1 + m^2}$$
$$d(P_1, P_2) + d(P_2, P_3) = (x_2 - x_1)\sqrt{1 + m^2} + (x_3 - x_2)\sqrt{1 + m^2}$$
$$= (x_3 - x_1)\sqrt{1 + m^2}$$
$$= d(P_1, P_3)$$

which shows that P_1, P_2, P_3 are collinear.

74. (A)

x	0	1	2	3	4	5
A	25	16	7	-2	-11	-20

$A = 25 - 9x$

(B) For every kilometer increase in altitude the air temperature decreases 9°C.

76. The charge is $15 for travel to site plus 70 cents for each minute it takes to do the installation.

78. (A)

x	0	1	2	3	4
net income	1.2	1.5	1.8	2.1	2.4
y	1.2	1.5	1.8	2.1	2.4

$y = 1.2 + 0.3x$

(B)
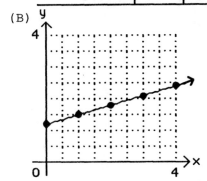

(C) In 1993 ($x = 5$) income $= 1.2 + 0.3(5)$
$= \$2.7$ billion.

In 2000 ($x = 12$) income $= 1.2 + 0.3(12)$
$= \$4.8$ billion.

(D) In 1988 the company's income was $1.2 billion and in 1992 the company's income was $2.4 billion, an increase $0.3 billion each year.

80. (A) $s = kw$
$2 = k \cdot 5$
$k = 0.4$
$s = 0.4w$

(B) $3.6 = 0.4w$
$w = 9$ lbs.

(C) slope $= 0.4$

82. (A)

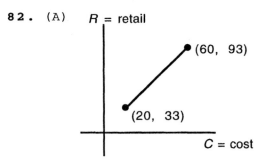

$m = \dfrac{93 - 33}{60 - 20} = 1.5$

$R - 33 = 1.5(C - 20)$
$R - 33 = 1.5C - 30$
$R = 1.5C + 3 \quad (C > 10)$

(B) $R = 1.5C + 3$
$240 = 1.5C + 3$
$1.5C = 237$
$C = \$158$

(C) slope $= 1.5$

84. (A) $T = 200 + 0.02(200)A$ where $A =$ altitude in thousands of feet.
$T = 4A + 200 \quad (A \geq 0)$

(B) $T = 4(6.5) + 200$
$T = 226$ mph

(C) slope $= 4$ which indicates that true air speed increases 4 mph for each one thousand foot increase in altitude.

86. (A)

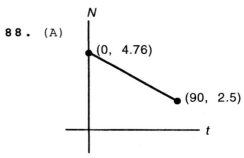

slope $= \dfrac{30 - 15}{33} = \dfrac{5}{11}$

$p - 15 = \dfrac{5}{11}(d - 0)$

$p = \dfrac{5}{11}d + 15$

where d is the depth 'below' the surface.

(B) $40 = \dfrac{5}{11}d + 15$

$d = 55$ ft.

88. (A)

slope $= \dfrac{4.76 - 2.5}{0 - 90} \approx -0.0251 \left(\text{or } \dfrac{113}{4500} \right)$

$N - 4.76 = -0.0251(t - 0)$

$N = -0.0251t + 4.76 \ (t \geq 0)$

(B) $N = -0.0251(100) + 4.76$

$N = 2.25$ people per household

Exercise 3-3

2. A function. Each domain value is associated with a unique (= one and only one) range value.

4. Not a function. The domain value −1 is associated with two range values.

6. A function. Each domain value is associated with a unique range value.

8. A function. No two ordered pairs have the same first term.
Domain = {−1, 0, 1, 2}; Range = {4, 3, 2, 1}

10. A function. No two ordered pairs have the same first term.
Domain = {−10, −5, 0, 5, 10}; Range = {0, 5, 10}

12. Not a function. The ordered pairs (1, 1) and (1, 2) as well as (2, 1) and (2, 2) and (3, 1) and (3, 2) have the same first term.

14. Vertical line test is passed, therefore a function.

16. Vertical line test is passed. A function.

18. Vertical line test failed. Not a function.

20. $g(t) \ 3 - 2t$
$g(6) = 3 - 2(6) = 3 - 12 = -9$

22. $F(m) = 2m^2 + 3m - 1$
$F(-3) = 2(-3)^2 + 3(-3) - 1$
$= 2(9) - 9 - 1$
$= 8$

24. $G(2) - g(-3)$ where $G(u) = u^2 + u - 2$, $g(t) = 3 - 2t$
$G(2) - g(-3) = (2^2 + 2 - 2) - (3 - 2(-3))$
$= 4 - 9$
$= -5$

26. $3G(-2) + 2F(-1)$ where $G(u) = u^2 + u - 2$, $F(m) = 2m^2 + 3m - 1$
$3G(-2) + 2F(-1) = 3[(-2)^2 + (-2) - 2] + 2[2(-1)^2 + 3(-1) - 1]$
$= 3[4 - 4] + 2[2 - 3 - 1]$
$= 3(0) + 2(-2)$
$= -4$

28. $g(t) = 3 - 2t$, $f(x) = 2x + 6$, $G(u) = u^2 + u - 2$

$$\frac{g(4) \cdot f(2)}{G(1)} = \frac{[3 - 2(4)] \cdot [2(2) + 6]}{1^2 + 1 - 2}$$

$$= \frac{[3 - 8] \cdot [4 + 6]}{0} \text{ is undefined}$$

30. $y = f(4) = -5$

32. $-2 = f(x) \Rightarrow x = -6, 1, 5$

34. $y^2 - x = 1$
$y^2 = x + 1$
$y = \pm\sqrt{x + 1}$
Not a function
$x = 3 \Rightarrow y = \pm 2$

36. $3x^2 + y^3 = 8$
$y^3 = 8 - 3x^2$
$y = \sqrt[3]{8 - 3x^2}$
A function whose domain is $(-\infty, \infty)$.

38. $x^3 + |y| = 6$
$|y| = 6 - x^3$
$y = 6 - x^3$ and $y = x^3 - 6$
Not a function
$x = 1 \Rightarrow y = 5, -5$

40. $xy = 1$
$y = \frac{1}{x}$
A function whose domain is $(-\infty, 0) \cup (0, \infty)$.

42. $x^2 + xy = 0$
$xy = -x^2$
$y = -\frac{x^2}{x}$
$y = -x, \ x \neq 0$
Not a function
$x = 0 \Rightarrow y$ is any real number

44. $g(t) = \sqrt[3]{5 - t}$
domain: all real numbers

46. $K(s) = \sqrt{-1 - s}$
$-1 - s \geq 0$
$-s \geq 1$
$s \leq -1$
domain: $s \leq -1$

48. $G(m) = \frac{1 - 2m}{m^2 + 3}$
$m^2 + 3 \neq 0$
domain: all real numbers

50. $K(v) = \frac{2v^2 - 9}{v^2 - v - 6}$
$v^2 - v - 6 = (v - 3)(v + 2)$
domain: all real numbers
except -2 and 3.

52. $J(z) = \sqrt{z^2 - 2z + 5}$
$z^2 - 2z + 5 \geq 0$

$$z = \frac{2 \pm \sqrt{4 - 20}}{2}$$

$$= \frac{2 \pm i\sqrt{15}}{2} \Rightarrow \text{No } x \text{ intercepts}$$

domain: all real numbers

54. $g(t) = \sqrt{\dfrac{t - 1}{5 - t}}$

$\dfrac{t - 1}{5 - t} \geq 0$; $t \neq 5$

$t = 0: \ -\dfrac{1}{5}$

$t = 2: \ \dfrac{1}{3}$

$t = 6: \ \dfrac{5}{-1}$

domain: $[1, 5)$

56. $G(z) = \sqrt{\dfrac{z^2 + 4z + 6}{z^2 + 4z + 3}}$

$\dfrac{z^2 + 4z + 6}{z^2 + 4z + 3} \geq 0$

$\dfrac{(z^2 + 4z + 6)}{(z + 3)(z + 1)} \geq 0$

numerator is always > 0

$z = -4 : 2$

$z = -2 : -2$

$z = 0 : 2$

$$\begin{array}{ccccccc} + & + & & - & - & & + & + \\ \hline & & \circ & & & \circ & & \end{array} \longrightarrow z$$

$-3 \qquad -1$

$(-\infty, -3) \cup (-1, \infty)$

domain: $z < -3$ or $z > -1$

58. $f(x) = -3x + 4$

60. $f(x) = -8x^3 + 3\sqrt{3}$

62. Function g multiplies the domain element by -2 and adds 7 to the result.

64. Function G multiplies 4 times the square root of the domain element and subtracts the square of the domain element from the result.

66. $K(r) = 7 - 4r$

$\dfrac{K(1 + h) - K(1)}{h} = \dfrac{7 - 4(1 + h) - (7 - 4(1))}{h}$

$= \dfrac{7 - 4 - 4h - 7 + 4}{h} = \dfrac{-4h}{h}$

$= -4$

68. $P(m) = 2m^2 + 3$

$\dfrac{P(2 + h) - P(2)}{h} = \dfrac{2(2 + h)^2 + 3 - (2(2)^2 + 3)}{h}$

$= \dfrac{2(4 + 4h + h^2) + 3 - 8 - 3}{h}$

$= \dfrac{8 + 8h + 2h^2 - 8}{h} = \dfrac{8h + 2h^2}{h}$

$= 8 + 2h$

70. $D(p) = -3p^2 - 4p + 9$

$\dfrac{D(-1 + h) - D(-1)}{h} = \dfrac{-3(-1 + h)^2 - 4(-1 + h) + 9 - (-3(-1)^2 - 4(-1) + 9)}{h}$

$= \dfrac{-3(1 - 2h + h^2) + 4 - 4h + 9 + 3 - 4 - 9}{h}$

$= \dfrac{-3 + 6h - 3h^2 - 4h + 3}{h}$

$= \dfrac{2h - 3h^2}{h}$

$= -3h + 2$

72. $g(w + h) = -4(w + h)^3 + 7(w + h) - 5$

$\qquad g(w) = -4w^3 + 7w - 5$

74. $s(z + h) = 3(z + h) + 9\sqrt{z + h} + 1$

$\qquad s(z) = 3z + 9\sqrt{z} + 1$

76. $f(x) = -5x + 2$

(A) $\dfrac{f(x + h) - f(x)}{h} = \dfrac{-5(x + h) + 2 - (-5x + 2)}{h}$

$= \dfrac{-5x - 5h + 2 + 5x - 2}{h} = \dfrac{-5h}{h}$

$= -5$

(B) $\dfrac{f(x) - f(a)}{x - a} = \dfrac{(-5x + 2) - (-5a + 2)}{x - a}$

$= \dfrac{-5x + 2 + 5a - 2}{x - a}$

$= \dfrac{-5x + 5a}{x - a}$

$= \dfrac{-5(x - a)}{(x - a)}$

$= -5$

78. $f(x) = 5 - 3x^2$

(A) $\dfrac{f(x + h) - f(x)}{h} = \dfrac{5 - 3(x + h)^2 - (5 - 3x^2)}{h}$

$= \dfrac{5 - 3(x^2 + 2xh + h^2) - 5 + 3x^2}{h}$

$= \dfrac{5 - 3x^2 - 6xh - 3h^2 - 5 + 3x^2}{h}$

$= \dfrac{-6xh - 3h^2}{h} = -6x - 3h$

(B) $\dfrac{f(x) - f(a)}{x - a} = \dfrac{5 - 3x^2 - (5 - 3a^2)}{x - a}$

$= \dfrac{5 - 3x^2 - 5 + 3a^2}{x - a}$

$= \dfrac{-3x^2 + 3a^2}{x - a}$

$= \dfrac{-3(x^2 - a^2)}{x - a}$

$= \dfrac{-3(x - a)(x + a)}{x - a}$

$= -3x - 3a$

80. $f(x) = 3x^2 - 5x - 9$

(A) $\dfrac{f(x + h) - f(x)}{h} = \dfrac{3(x + h)^2 - 5(x + h) - 9 - (3x^2 - 5x - 9)}{h}$

$= \dfrac{3(x^2 + 2xh + h^2) - 5x - 5h - 9 - 3x^2 + 5x + 9}{h}$

$= \dfrac{3x^2 + 6xh + 3h^2 - 5x - 5h - 9 - 3x^2 + 5x + 9}{h}$

$= \dfrac{6xh + 3h^2 - 5h}{h}$

$= 6x + 3h - 5$

(B) $\dfrac{f(x) - f(a)}{x - a} = \dfrac{3x^2 - 5x - 9 - (3a^2 - 5a - 9)}{x - a}$

$= \dfrac{3x^2 - 3a^2 - 5x + 5a}{x - a}$

$= \dfrac{3(x^2 - a^2) - 5(x - a)}{x - a}$

$= \dfrac{3(x - a)(x + a) - 5(x - a)}{x - a}$

$= 3(x + a) - 5$

$= 3x + 3a - 5$

82. $f(x) = x^2 - x^3$

(A) $\dfrac{f(x + h) - f(x)}{h} = \dfrac{(x + h)^2 - (x + h)^3 - (x^2 - x^3)}{h}$

$\quad = \dfrac{x^2 + 2xh + h^2 - (x^3 + 3hx^2 + 3h^2x + h^3) - x^2 + x^3}{h}$

$\quad = \dfrac{2xh + h^2 - 3hx^2 - 3h^2x - h^3}{h}$

$\quad = 2x + h - 3x^2 - 3hx - h^2$

(B) $\dfrac{f(x) - f(a)}{x - a} = \dfrac{x^2 - x^3 - (a^2 - a^3)}{x - a}$

$\quad = \dfrac{x^2 - a^2 - x^3 + a^3}{x - a}$

$\quad = \dfrac{(x - a)(x + a) - (x - a)(x^2 + ax + a^2)}{x - a}$

$\quad = x + a - (x^2 + ax + a^2)$

$\quad = x - x^2 - ax + a - a^2$

84. $P = 2\ell + 2w = 50 \Rightarrow \ell = \dfrac{50 - 2w}{2} = 25 - w$

$\quad A = \ell w = (25 - w)w$

$A(w) = -w^2 + 25w$

86.

$h^2 = b^2 + 4^2$
$b^2 = h^2 - 16$
$b(h) = \sqrt{h^2 - 16}$

domain: $h^2 - 16 > 0$
$(h - 4)(h + 4) > 0$, $h > 0$

$h > 4$

88. $C(x) = 68x + 3750$

90. $s(t) = 10t^2$

(A) $s(8) = 10(8)^2 = 640$
$\quad s(9) = 10(9)^2 = 810$
$\quad s(10) = 10(10)^2 = 1000$
$\quad s(11) = 10(11)^2 = 1210$

(B) $\dfrac{s(11 + h) - s(11)}{h} = \dfrac{10(11 + h)^2 - 10(11)^2}{h}$

$\quad = \dfrac{10(11^2 + 22h + h^2) - 10(11)^2}{h}$

$\quad = \dfrac{10(11)^2 + 220h + 10h^2 - 10(11)^2}{h}$

$\quad = \dfrac{220h + 10h^2}{h}$

$\quad = 220 + 10h$

(C) $220 + 10h \to 220$ as h tends to 0.
This is the speed of the automobile at the instant $t = 11$ sec.

92.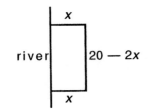

$A(x) = x(20 - 2x)$ where $0 < x < 10$.

94. Let y = length of rectangle.
A = area of semicircle + area of rectangle = 24

(1) $\qquad \frac{1}{8}\pi x^2 + xy = 24$

P = perimeter of semicircle + x + $2y$

(2) $P = \frac{1}{2}(\pi x) + x + 2y$

from (1) $y = \frac{24}{x} - \frac{\pi x}{8}$ which, upon substitution in (2), gives

$$P(x) = \frac{\pi x}{2} + x + 2\left(\frac{24}{x} - \frac{\pi x}{8}\right)$$

$$P(x) = \frac{\pi x}{2} + x + \frac{48}{x} - \frac{\pi x}{4}$$

$$P(x) = x + \frac{48}{x} + \frac{\pi x}{4}$$

$$P(x) = x\left(1 + \frac{\pi}{4}\right) + \frac{48}{x}$$

x	$P(x) = x\left(1 + \dfrac{\pi}{4}\right) + \dfrac{48}{x}$
4	19.1
5	18.5
6	18.7
7	19.4

96. $d^2 = h^2 + 10^2$

$d(h) = \sqrt{h^2 + 100}$

98. $d = vt$; for $d = 500 = vt \Rightarrow v = \dfrac{500}{t}$

cost = fuel cost + other costs

$= \dfrac{v^2}{5} + 400 \cdot t$

$C(t) = \dfrac{1}{5} \cdot \left(\dfrac{500}{t}\right)^2 + 400t$

$C(t) = \dfrac{50,000}{t^2} + 400t$

Exercise 3-4

2. (A) $(-5, 5]$
(B) $[-4, 4)$
(C) 0
(D) 0
(E) none
(F) $(-5, 5]$
(G) none
(H) none

4. (A) $(-\infty, \infty)$
(B) $(-\infty, 3]$
(C) 0, 4
(D) 0
(E) $(-\infty, 2]$
(F) $[2, \infty)$
(G) none
(H) none

6. (A) $(-\infty, -3) \cup (-3, \infty)$
(B) $(-\infty, -2) \cup (2, \infty)$
(C) none
(D) 2
(E) $(-\infty, -3) \cup [3, \infty)$
(F) none
(G) $(-3, 3]$
(H) $x = -3$

8.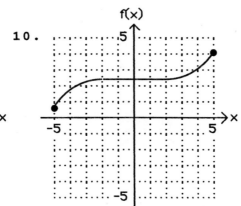

10.

12.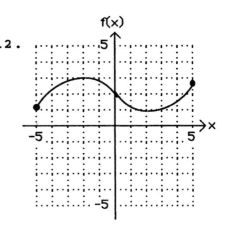

14.
$$f(x) = 3x - 3$$
$$3x - 3 = 0$$
$$x = 1 \ x \ \text{int}$$
$$f(0) = 3(0) - 3$$
$$f(0) = -3 \ y \ \text{int}$$
$$\text{slope} = 3$$

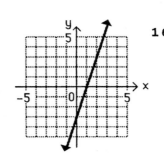

16.
$$f(x) = -\frac{3}{4}x + \frac{6}{5}$$
$$0 = -\frac{3}{4}x + \frac{6}{5}$$
$$x = \frac{8}{5} \ x \ \text{int}$$
$$f(0) = -\frac{3}{4}(0) + \frac{6}{5}$$
$$f(0) = \frac{6}{5} \ y \ \text{int}$$
$$\text{slope} = -\frac{3}{4}$$

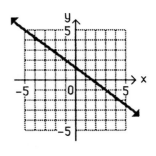

18.
$$f(-3) = -2 \Rightarrow (-3, -2) \qquad m = \frac{-2 - 4}{-3 - 5} = \frac{-6}{-8} = \frac{3}{4}$$
$$f(5) = 4 \Rightarrow (5, 4)$$
$$y - y_1 = m(x - x_1)$$
$$y - 4 = \frac{3}{4}(x - 5)$$
$$y - 4 = \frac{3}{4}x - \frac{15}{4}$$
$$y = \frac{3}{4}x - \frac{15}{4} + \frac{16}{4}$$
$$y = \frac{3}{4}x + \frac{1}{4}$$
$$f(x) = \frac{3}{4}x + \frac{1}{4}$$

20.
$$f(x) = \frac{1}{2}(x + 2)^2 - 4$$
$$\min f(x) = f(-2) = -4$$
$$\text{range} = [-4, \infty]$$
$$\text{axis:} \ x = -2$$
$$\text{vertex:} \ (-2, -4)$$

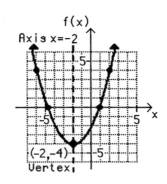

22. $f(x) = -(x - 2)^2 + 4$

$\max f(x) = f(2) = 4$

$\text{range} = (-\infty, 4]$

$\text{axis: } x = 2$

$\text{vertex: } (2, 4)$

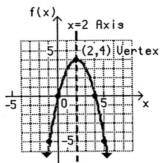

24. $f(x) = x^2 - 6x + 5$
$= x^2 - 6x + 9 - 9 + 5$
$= (x - 3)^2 - 4$
$\text{vertex} = (3, -4)$
$\text{axis: } x = 3$
$f(0) = 0^2 - 6(0) + 5, \ (0, 5) \ y \text{ int}$
$x^2 - 6x + 5 = 0$
$(x - 1)(x - 5) = 0$
$x = 1, \ x = 5$
$(1, 0), \ (5, 0) \ x \text{ int}$

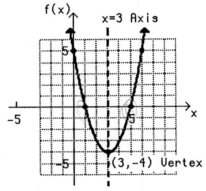

26. $f(x) = -x^2 + 2x + 8$
$= -(x^2 - 2x) + 8$
$= -(x^2 - 2x + 1 - 1) + 8$
$= -(x - 1)^2 + 9$
$\text{vertex} = (1, 9)$
$\text{axis: } x = 1$
$f(0) = -0^2 + 2(0) + 8 = 8, \ (0, 8) \ y \text{ int}$
$-x^2 + 2x + 8 = 0$
$x^2 - 2x - 8 = 0$
$(x - 4)(x + 2) = 0$
$x = 4, \ x = -2$
$(4, 0), \ (-2, 0) \ x \text{ int}$

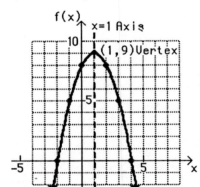

28. $f(x) = x^2 - 8x + 14$
$= x^2 - 8x + 16 - 16 + 14$
$= (x - 4)^2 - 2$
$\text{vertex} = (4, -2)$
$\text{axis: } x = 4$
$f \text{ is increasing on } [4, \infty)$
$f \text{ is decreasing on } (-\infty, 4]$

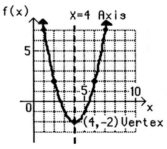

30. $f(x) = -x^2 - 10x - 24$
$= -(x^2 + 10x) - 24$
$= -(x^2 + 10x + 25 - 25) - 24$
$= -(x + 5)^2 + 1$
$\text{vertex} = (-5, 1)$
$\text{axis: } x = -5$
$f \text{ is increasing on } (-\infty, -5]$
$f \text{ is decreasing on } [-5, \infty)$

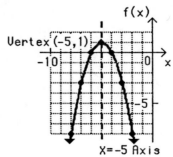

32. $f(x) = \begin{cases} x & \text{if } -2 \le x < 1 \\ -x + 2 & \text{if } 1 \le x \le 2 \end{cases}$

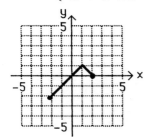

Domain: $[-2, 2]$; Range: $[-2, 1]$

34. $f(x) = \begin{cases} 1 & \text{if } -2 \le x < 2 \\ -3 & \text{if } 2 < x \le 5 \end{cases}$

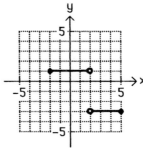

Domain: $[-2, 2) \cup (2, 5]$; Range: $\{-3, 1\}$
Discontinuous at $x = 2$

36. $f(x) = \begin{cases} -1 - x & \text{if } x \le 2 \\ 5 - x & \text{if } x > 2 \end{cases}$

Domain: all real numbers
Range: all real numbers
Discontinuous at $x = 2$

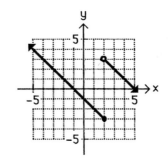

38. $h(x) = \begin{cases} -x^2 - 2 & \text{if } x < 0 \\ x^2 + 2 & \text{if } x > 0 \end{cases}$

Domain: $x \ne 0 \Leftrightarrow (-\infty, 0) \cup (0, \infty)$
Range: $(-\infty, -2) \cup (2, \infty)$
Discontinuous at $x = 0$

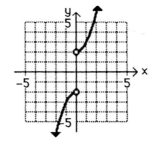

40. $f(x) = 2x^2 - 12x + 14$
$\qquad = 2(x^2 - 6x) + 14$
$\qquad = 2(x^2 - 6x + 9 - 9) + 14$
$\qquad = 2(x - 3)^2 - 4$
vertex = $(3, -4)$; min $f(x) = -4$
axis: $x = 3$
range: $[-4, \infty)$
$\qquad\qquad f(0) = 2(0)^2 - 12(0) + 14 = 14$ y-int
$2x^2 - 12x + 14 = 0$
$\quad x^2 - 6x + 7 = 0$ which may be solved using the
quadratic formula to obtain $x = 3 + \sqrt{2}$ and $x = 3 - \sqrt{2}$
for x intercepts, ($\approx 1.6, 4.4$).
f is increasing on $[3, \infty)$
f is decreasing on $(-\infty, 3]$

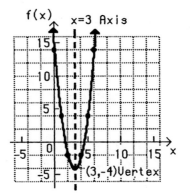

42. $f(x) = -\dfrac{1}{2}x^2 + 4x - 10$

$\qquad = -\dfrac{1}{2}(x^2 - 8x) - 10$

$\qquad = -\dfrac{1}{2}(x^2 - 8x + 16 - 16) - 10$

$\qquad = -\dfrac{1}{2}(x - 4)^2 - 2$

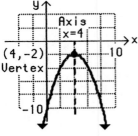

axis: $x = 4$
vertex $= (4, -2)$
max $f(x) = -2$
range: $(-\infty, -2]$

$\qquad f(0) = -\dfrac{1}{2}(0)^2 + 4(0) - 10 = -10$, y int

$b^2 - 4ac = 4^2 - 4\left(-\dfrac{1}{2}\right)(-10) = -4 \Rightarrow$ no x intercepts

f is increasing on $(-\infty, 4]$
f is decreasing on $[4, \infty)$

44. $f(x) = -4x^2 - 4x - 1$
$\qquad = -4(x^2 + x) - 1$

$\qquad = -4\left(x^2 + x + \dfrac{1}{4} - \dfrac{1}{4}\right) - 1$

$\qquad = -4\left(x + \dfrac{1}{2}\right)^2$

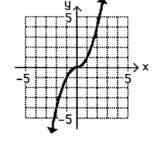

axis: $x = -\dfrac{1}{2}$

vertex $= \left(-\dfrac{1}{2},\ 0\right)$

max $f(x) = f\left(-\dfrac{1}{2}\right) = 0$

range: $(-\infty, 0]$
$\qquad f(0) = -4(0)^2 - 4(0) - 1 = -1$ y int
$-4x^2 - 4x - 1 = 0$
$\quad 4x^2 + 4x + 1 = 0$
$\qquad (2x + 1)^2 = 0$

$\qquad\qquad x = -\dfrac{1}{2}$ x int

f is increasing on $\left(-\infty, -\dfrac{1}{2}\right]$; f is decreasing on $\left[-\dfrac{1}{2}, \infty\right)$

46. $f(x) = x|x| = \begin{cases} x \cdot x = x^2 \text{ if } x \geq 0 \\ x(-x) = -x^2 \text{ if } x < 0 \end{cases}$

Domain: all real numbers
Range: all real numbers

48. $f(x) = x + 2\dfrac{|x + 1|}{x + 1}$

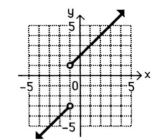

$$= \begin{cases} x + 2\dfrac{x + 1}{x + 1} = x + 2 & \text{for } x + 1 > 0 \text{ or } x > -1 \\ x + 2\dfrac{-(x + 1)}{x + 1} = x - 2 & \text{for } x + 1 < 0 \text{ or } x < -1 \end{cases}$$

Domain: $x \neq -1$ or $(-\infty, -1) \cup (-1, \infty)$
Range: $(-\infty, -3) \cup (1, \infty)$
Discontinuous at $x = -1$

50. $f(x) = |x| - |x - 3| = \begin{cases} -x - (-(x - 3)) = -3 & \text{for } x < 0 \\ x - (-(x - 3)) = 2x - 3 & \text{for } 0 \leq x < 3 \\ x - (x - 3) = 3 & \text{for } x \geq 3 \end{cases}$

Domain: all real numbers
Range: $[-3, 3]$
no discontinuity

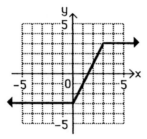

52. $f(x) = \left[\!\left[\dfrac{x}{3}\right]\!\right]$

$\left[\!\left[\dfrac{x}{3}\right]\!\right] = n$ where $n \quad\leq \dfrac{x}{3} < n + 1$ or

$\qquad\qquad\qquad 3n \quad\leq x < 3n + 3$

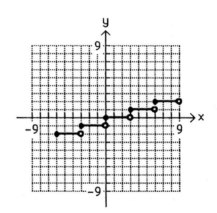

$$f(x) = \begin{cases} \vdots \\ n = -2 & -2 \text{ if } -6 \leq x < -3 \\ n = -1 & -1 \text{ if } -3 \leq x < 0 \\ n = 0 & 0 \text{ if } 0 \leq x < 3 \\ n = 1 & 1 \text{ if } 3 \leq x < 6 \\ n = 2 & 2 \text{ if } 6 \leq x < 9 \\ \vdots \end{cases}$$

Domain: all real numbers
Range: all integers
Discontinuous at all integers divisible by 3.

54. $f(x) = [\![2x]\!]$
$[\![2x]\!] = n$ where $n \leq 2x < n + 1$ or
$$\frac{n}{2} \leq x < \frac{n + 1}{2}$$

$$f(x) = \begin{cases} \quad\vdots \\ n = -2 \quad -2 \text{ if } -1 \leq x < -\dfrac{1}{2} \\ n = -1 \quad -1 \text{ if } -\dfrac{1}{2} \leq x < 0 \\ n = 0 \quad\;\; 0 \text{ if } 0 \leq x < \dfrac{1}{2} \\ n = 1 \quad\;\; 1 \text{ if } \dfrac{1}{2} \leq x < 1 \\ n = 2 \quad\;\; 2 \text{ if } 1 \leq x < \dfrac{3}{2} \\ \quad\vdots \end{cases}$$

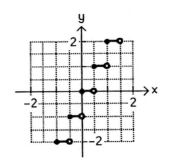

Domain: all real numbers
Range: all integers
Discontinuous at all rational numbers of the form $\dfrac{k}{2}$ where k is an integer.

56. $f(x) = [\![x]\!] - x$

$$f(x) = \begin{cases} \quad\vdots \\ n = -2 \quad -2 - x \text{ if } -2 \leq x < -1 \\ n = -1 \quad -1 - x \text{ if } -1 \leq x < 0 \\ n = 0 \quad\;\; 0 - x \text{ if } 0 \leq x < 1 \\ n = 1 \quad\;\; 1 - x \text{ if } 1 \leq x < 2 \\ n = 2 \quad\;\; 2 - x \text{ if } 2 \leq x < 3 \\ \quad\vdots \end{cases}$$

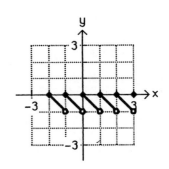

Domain: all real numbers
Range: (-1, 0]
Discontinuous at all integers.

58.   max $f(x) = f(-3) = -5 \Rightarrow$ vertex = (-3, -5) from which axis: $x = -3$ and
range: $(-\infty, -5]$. There are no x intercepts since max $f(x)$ is below x-axis.

60.   (A)

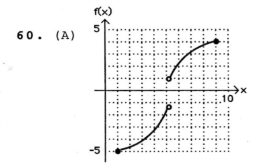

(B) Graph does not cross x
axis. Yes, it could
cross the x axis more
times. (at most one
time) No, it could not
cross the x axis fewer
times.

62. (A)

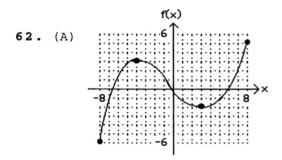

(B) The graph crosses the *x* axis three times. Yes, it could cross an infinite number of times. It could not cross fewer than three times.

64. $f(x) = 9 - x^2$; $(-2, 5)$, $(4, -7)$

$$m_{SL} = \frac{5 - (-7)}{-2 - 4} = -2$$

$$y - y_1 = m(x - x_1)$$

$$y - 5 = -2(x - (-2))$$

$$y - 5 = -2x - 4$$

$$y = -2x + 1$$

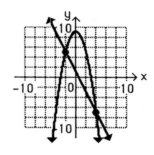

66. $f(x) = x^2 + 2x - 6$

(A) $f(2) = 2^2 + 2(2) - 6$

$\qquad = 4 + 4 - 6$

$\qquad = 2$

$f(2 + h) = (2 + h)^2 + 2(2 + h) - 6$

$\qquad = 4 + 4h + h^2 + 4 + 2h - 6$

$\qquad = h^2 + 6h + 2$

$$m_{SL} = \frac{f(2 + h) - f(2)}{(2 + h) - 2}$$

$$= \frac{h^2 + 6h + 2 - 2}{h}$$

$$= \frac{h^2 + 6h}{h}$$

$$= h + 6$$

(B)

h	1	0.1	0.01	0.001
m_{SL}	7	6.1	6.01	6.001

Slope seems to be approaching 6.

68. $f(x) = 3x + 1$, $g(x) = -0.5x - 4$

Graphs of *f* and *g*   Graph of *m*   Graph of *n*

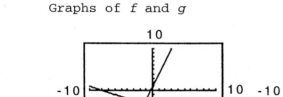

70. $f(x) = 0.15x^2 - 5$, $g(x) = 5 - 1.5|x|$

Graphs of f and g Graph of m Graph of n

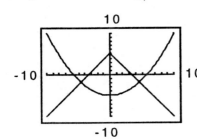 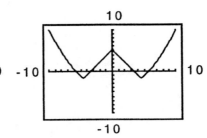 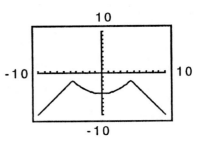

72. $f(x) = 8 + 1.5x - 0.4x^2$, $g(x) = -0.2x + 5$

Graphs of f and g Graph of m Graph of n

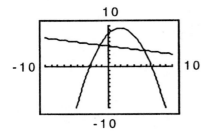 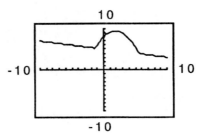 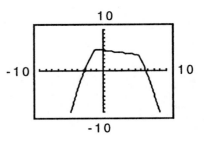

74. $n(x) = \min[f(x), g(x)]$

76. (A)

x	0	1	2	3	4
Production	4.7	4.1	3.5	3.7	5.0
$f(x)$	4.8	3.8	3.5	3.9	4.9

$f(x) = 0.33x^2 - 1.3x + 4.8$

(B)

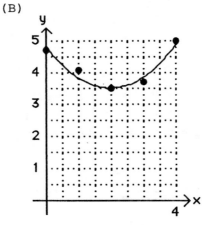

(C) 1994: $f(5) = 0.33(5)^2 - 1.3(5) + 4.8 \approx 6.55$ million vehicles
     1995: $f(6) = 0.33(6)^2 - 1.3(6) + 4.8 \approx 8.88$ million vehicles

(D) After decreasing from 4.7 million vehicles in 1989 to 3.5 million vehicles in 1991, production increased the next two years.

78. (A) $V = f(t) = \dfrac{20{,}000 - 2{,}000}{0 - 10}x + 20{,}000$

$\qquad\qquad f(t) = -1800t + 20{,}000$

(B) $f(4) = -1800(4) + 20{,}000 = \$12{,}800$
$\qquad f(8) = -1800(8) + 20{,}000 = \$5600$

(C) slope = -1800

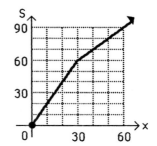

80. $S(x) = \begin{cases} 2x \text{ if } 0 \le x \le 30 \\ 2(30) + 1(x - 30) = x + 30 \text{ if } x > 30 \end{cases}$

No points of discontinuity.

$S(25) = 2(25) = 50$
$S(45) = 45 + 30 = 75$

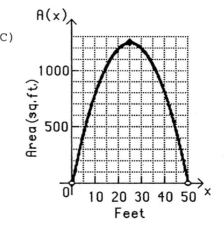

82.

$100 - 2x$

$x \qquad\qquad x$

existing fence

(A) $A(x) = x(100 - 2x)$
$\qquad\qquad = -2x^2 + 100x$

(B) $0 < x < 50$

(C)

(D) $A(x) = 100x - 2x^2$
$\qquad\quad = -2(x^2 - 50x)$
$\qquad\quad = -2(x^2 - 50x + 25^2 - 25^2)$
$\qquad\quad = -2(x - 25)^2 + 1250$
$\qquad x = 25$
$\quad 100 - 2(25) = 50$
$\quad 25$ ft. by 50 ft. will maximize area.

84. $f(x) = 100 \left[\!\left[0.5 + \dfrac{x}{100} \right]\!\right]$

x	40	-40	60	-60	740	750	7,551	-601	-649	-651
$f(x)$	0	0	100	-100	700	800	7,600	-600	-600	-700

$f(x)$ rounds to the nearest hundred.

86. $f(x) = \dfrac{1}{1000} \left[\!\left[0.5 + 1000x \right]\!\right]$ is a function that rounds real numbers to the nearest thousandth.

88. (A) $C(x) = \begin{cases} 4 & 0 < x \le 1 \\ 6 & 1 < x \le 2 \\ 8 & 2 < x \le 3 \\ 10 & 3 < x \le 4 \\ 12 & 4 < x \le 5 \\ 14 & 5 < x \le 6 \end{cases}$

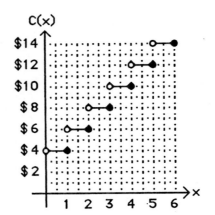

(B)   No, $f(x) = 4 + 2[\![x]\!] \neq C(x)$
for $x = 1, 2, 3, 4, 5, 6$.

90. Let x = number of \$1 increases. Then
price of room = $70 + 1x$ and
number of rooms rented = $400 - 4x$

Since each room costs \$10 to service, we need to maximize the profit function,
$P(x) = (70 + x - 10)(400 - 4x)$

$= (60 + x)(400 - 4x)$

$= -4x^2 + 160x + 24000$

$= -4(x^2 - 40x + 400 - 400) + 24000$

$= -4(x - 20)^2 + 8000$

$x = 20$ is the number of \$1 increases.

To maximize profits, charge $70 + 20 = \$90$ per room.
The number of rooms rented will be $400 - 4(20) = 320$.
The maximum profit will be $\$90 \cdot 320 - 320 \cdot \$10 = \$25,600$.

92. (A) $x - \dfrac{1}{100}x^2 = 0$

$x\left(1 - \dfrac{1}{100}x\right) = 0$

$x = 0$ at firing; $1 - \dfrac{1}{100}x = 0$

$x = 100$ at landing

Place the net 100 feet from the cannon.

(B) $f(x) = x - \dfrac{1}{100}x^2$

$= -\dfrac{1}{100}(x^2 - 100x)$

$= -\dfrac{1}{100}(x^2 - 100x + 50^2 - 50^2)$

$= -\dfrac{1}{100}(x - 50)^2 + 25$

$f(50) = 25$
max height above ground = $25 + 10 = 35$ ft

Exercise   3-5

2. $m(x) = -\sqrt[3]{x}$ has domain R and range R

4. $f(x) = -0.5|x|$ has domain R and range $y \le 0$

6. $G(x) = 4x^3$ has domain R and range R

8. $f(x) = 3x$, $g(x) = x - 2$
$(f + g)(x) = f(x) + g(x) = 3x + x - 2 = 4x - 2$
$(f - g)(x) = f(x) - g(x) = 3x - (x - 2) = 2x + 2$
$(fg)(x) = f(x)g(x) = 3x(x - 2) = 3x^2 - 6x$

$$\left(\frac{f}{g}\right)(x) = \frac{f(x)}{g(x)} = \frac{3x}{x - 2}$$

Domain $f + g$, $f - g$, fg: $(-\infty, \infty)$
Domain $\dfrac{f}{g}$: $(-\infty, 2) \cup (2, \infty)$

10. $f(x) = 3x$, $g(x) = x^2 + 4$
$(f + g)(x) = f(x) + g(x) = 3x + x^2 + 4 = x^2 + 3x + 4$
$(f - g)(x) = f(x) - g(x) = 3x - (x^2 + 4) = -x^2 + 3x - 4$
$(fg)(x) = f(x)g(x) = 3x(x^2 + 4) = 3x^3 + 12x$

$$\left(\frac{f}{g}\right)(x) = \frac{f(x)}{g(x)} = \frac{3x}{x^2 + 4}$$

Domain $f + g$, $f - g$, fg, $\dfrac{f}{g}$: $(-\infty, \infty)$

12. $f(x) = x^2 - 5x$; $g(x) = x^2 + 1$
$f \circ g = f[g(x)] = f(x^2 + 1) = (x^2 + 1)^2 - 5(x^2 + 1)$
$$= x^4 + 2x^2 + 1 - 5x^2 - 5$$
$$= x^4 - 3x^2 - 4$$
$g \circ f = g[f(x)] = g(x^2 - 5x) = (x^2 - 5x)^2 + 1$
$$= x^4 - 10x^3 + 25x^2 + 1$$

domain f, g, $f \circ g$ and $g \circ f$: $(-\infty, \infty)$

14. $f(x) = 4 - x^3$; $g(x) = 3x^{1/3}$ domain f: $(-\infty, \infty)$
$f \circ g = f[g(x)] = f(3x^{1/3})$ domain g: $(-\infty, \infty)$
$\qquad = 4 - (3x^{1/3})^3$ domain $f \circ g$: $(-\infty, \infty)$
$\qquad = 4 - 27x$ domain $g \circ f$: $(-\infty, \infty)$

$g \circ f = g[f(x)] = g(4 - x^3)$
$\qquad = 3(4 - x^3)^{1/3}$

16. $g(x) - 1$:
Vertical shift down
1 unit.

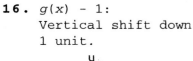
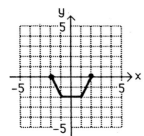

18. $f(x - 1)$: Horizontal
shift 1 unit right.

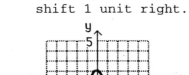
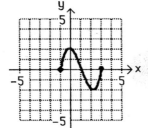

20. $-g(x)$: Reflection
about the x axis.

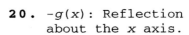
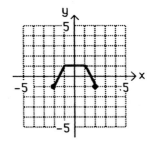

22. $\frac{1}{2} f(x)$: Vertical contraction.

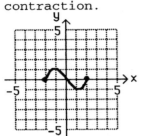

24. $h(x) = -|x - 4|$ is the graph of $f(x) = |x|$ reflected in the x axis and shifted right 4 units.

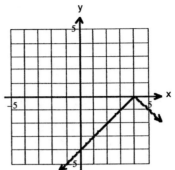

26. $m(x) = (x + 1)^2 + 3$ is the graph of $f(x) = x^2$ shifted left 1 unit and up 3 units.

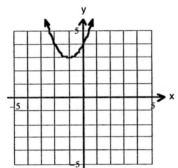

28. $g(x) = -2 + 3\sqrt[3]{x}$ is the graph of $f(x) = \sqrt[3]{x}$ expanded vertically by a factor of 3 and shifted down 2 units.

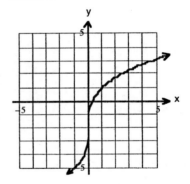

30. $f(x) = \sqrt{5 - x}$; $g(x) = \sqrt{x + 1}$ domain f: $(-\infty, 5]$; domain g: $[-1, \infty)$

$(f + g)(x) = f(x) + g(x) = \sqrt{5 - x} + \sqrt{x + 1}$

$(f - g)(x) = f(x) - g(x) = \sqrt{5 - x} - \sqrt{x + 1}$

$(fg)(x) = f(x) \cdot g(x) = \sqrt{5 - x} \cdot \sqrt{x + 1} = \sqrt{-x^2 + 4x + 5}$

$\left(\dfrac{f}{g}\right)(x) = \dfrac{f(x)}{g(x)} = \dfrac{\sqrt{5 - x}}{\sqrt{x + 1}} = \sqrt{\dfrac{5 - x}{x + 1}}$

domain $f + g$, $f - g$, fg: $(-\infty, 5] \cap [-1, \infty) = [-1, 5]$

domain $\dfrac{f}{g}$: $(-1, 5]$

32. $f(x) = 3\sqrt{x} + 6$; $g(x) = \sqrt{x} - 1$; domain f, g: $[0, \infty)$

$(f + g)(x) = f(x) + g(x) = 3\sqrt{x} + 6 + \sqrt{x} - 1 = 4\sqrt{x} + 5$

$(f - g)(x) = f(x) - g(x) = 3\sqrt{x} + 6 - \sqrt{x} + 1 = 2\sqrt{x} + 7$

$(fg)(x) = f(x) \cdot g(x) = (3\sqrt{x} + 6)(\sqrt{x} - 1)$

$\qquad\qquad = 3x - 3\sqrt{x} + 6\sqrt{x} - 6$

$\qquad\qquad = 3x + 3\sqrt{x} - 6$

$\left(\dfrac{f}{g}\right)(x) = \dfrac{f(x)}{g(x)} = \dfrac{3\sqrt{x} + 6}{\sqrt{x} - 1}$

domain $f + g$, $f - g$, fg: $[0, \infty)$

domain $\dfrac{f}{g}$: $[0, 1) \cup (1, \infty)$

34. $f(x) = \sqrt{x^2 + 3x - 10}$; $g(x) = \sqrt{x^2 - x - 12}$

domain f: $x^2 + 3x - 10 \geq 0 \Rightarrow (-\infty, -5] \cup [2, \infty)$

domain g: $x^2 - x - 12 \geq 0 \Rightarrow (-\infty, -3] \cup [4, \infty)$

$(f + g)(x) = \sqrt{x^2 + 3x - 10} + \sqrt{x^2 - x - 12}$

$(f - g)(x) = \sqrt{x^2 + 3x - 10} - \sqrt{x^2 - x - 12}$

$(fg)(x) = \sqrt{x^2 + 3x - 10} \cdot \sqrt{x^2 - x - 12} = \sqrt{x^4 + 2x^3 - 25x^2 - 26x + 120}$

$\left(\dfrac{f}{g}\right)(x) = \sqrt{(x^2 + 3x - 10)/(x^2 - x - 12)}$

domain $f + g$, $f - g$, fg: $(-\infty, -5] \cup [4, \infty)$

domain $\dfrac{f}{g}$: $(-\infty, -5] \cup (4, \infty)$

36. $f(x) = \sqrt{x + 1}$; $g(x) = x - 2$

domain f: $[-1, \infty)$; domain g: $(-\infty, \infty)$

$f \circ g = f[g(x)] = f(x - 2) = \sqrt{x - 2 + 1} = \sqrt{x - 1}$

domain $f \circ g$: $[1, \infty)$

$g \circ f = g[f(x)] = g(\sqrt{x + 1}) = \sqrt{x + 1} - 2$

domain $g \circ f$: $[-1, \infty)$

38. $f(x) = \dfrac{x}{x + 4}$; $g(x) = 2 - x$

domain f: $(-\infty, -4) \cup (-4, \infty)$; domain g: $(-\infty, \infty)$

$f \circ g = f[g(x)] = f(2 - x) = \dfrac{2 - x}{2 - x + 4} = \dfrac{2 - x}{6 - x}$

domain $f \circ g$: $(-\infty, 6) \cup (6, \infty)$

$g \circ f = g[f(x)] = g\left(\dfrac{x}{x + 4}\right) = 2 - \dfrac{x}{x + 4}$

$ = \dfrac{2(x + 4) - x}{x + 4}$

$ = \dfrac{2x + 8 - x}{x + 4}$

$ = \dfrac{x + 8}{x + 4}$

domain $g \circ f$: $(-\infty, -4) \cup (-4, \infty)$

40. $f(x) = \dfrac{x}{x - 4}$; $g(x) = |x + 3|$

domain f: $(-\infty, 4) \cup (4, \infty)$; domain g: $(-\infty, \infty)$

$f \circ g = f[g(x)] = f(|x + 3|) = \dfrac{|x + 3|}{|x + 3| - 4}$

for domain: $|x + 3| - 4 = 0 \Rightarrow x + 3 = 4$ and $x + 3 = -4$

$ x = 1 x = -7$

domain $f \circ g$: $(-\infty, -7) \cup (-7, 1) \cup (1, \infty)$

$g \circ f = g[f(x)] = g\left(\dfrac{x}{x - 4}\right) = \left|\dfrac{x}{x - 4} + 3\right| = \left|\dfrac{x + 3x - 12}{x - 4}\right|$

$ = \left|\dfrac{4x - 12}{x - 4}\right| = 4\left|\dfrac{x - 3}{x - 4}\right|$

domain $g \circ f$: $(-\infty, 4) \cup (4, \infty)$

42. $y = -(x - 2)^2 + 4$ is $y = x^2$ reflected across the x axis, shifted right 2 and up 4.

44. $y = -2 - \sqrt{x}$ is $y = \sqrt{x}$ reflected across the x axis and shifted down 2.

46. $y = (x - 3)^3 - 1$ is $y = x^3$ shifted right 3 and down 1.

48. $g(x) = \sqrt[3]{x - 3} - 2$ **50.** $g(x) = -|x + 1|$ **52.** $g(x) = -(x - 2)^2 - 4$

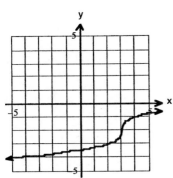   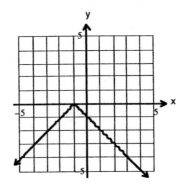   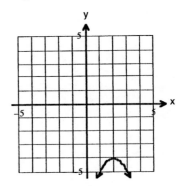

54. The basic function $y = \sqrt[3]{x}$ is shifted right 1 unit, up 2 units and is expanded vertically by a factor of 2: $y = 2\sqrt[3]{x - 1} + 2$.

56. $F1(x) = f(x) + k$ Vertical shift
$F2(x) = F1(-x) = f(-x) + k$ Reflected across the y axis

$G1(x) = f(-x)$ Reflected across y axis
$G2(x) = G1(x) + k = f(-x) + k$ Vertical shift

Since $F2 = G2$, order does not matter.

58. $F1(x) = f(x) + k$ Vertical shift
$F2(x) = cF1(x) = cf(x) + ck$ Expansion

$G1(x) = cf(x)$ Expansion
$G2(x) = G1(x) + k = cf(x) + k$ Vertical shift

Since $F2$ and $G2$ are different, order does matter.

60. Let $f(x) = x^7$ and $g(x) = 3 - 5x$, then $h(x) = f(g(x)) = f(3 - 5x) = (3 - 5x)^7$.

62. Let $f(x) = x^{1/2}$ and $g(x) = 3x - 11$, then $h(x) = f(g(x)) = f(3x - 11) = (3x - 11)^{1/2}$.

64. Let $g(x) = 5x + 3$ and $f(x) = x^6$, then $h(x) = g(f(x)) = g(x^6) = 5x^6 + 3$.

66. Let $g(x) = -2x + 1$ and $f(x) = x^{-1/2}$, then $h(x) = g(f(x)) = g(x^{-1/2}) = -2x^{-1/2} + 1 = -\dfrac{2}{\sqrt{x}} + 1$.

68. The given graph is the graph of $y = x^2$ with a vertical contraction of 0.25: $y = 0.25x^2$.

70. The given graph is the graph of $y = \sqrt[3]{x}$ reflected across the x axis with a vertical expansion of 2: $y = -2\sqrt[3]{x}$.

72. $f \circ g = g \circ f$ only when they both are equal to x. See problems 35 - 40 for examples where $f \circ g \neq g \circ f$.

74. If $g = 1$, then $fg = gf = f$ for all functions f.

76. $f(x) = x - 1,$ $\qquad\qquad\qquad g(x) = x - \dfrac{6}{x - 1}$

Domain f: $(-\infty, \infty)$ $\qquad\qquad$ Domain g: $(-\infty, 1) \cup (1, \infty)$

$(f + g)(x) = f(x) + g(x) = x - 1 + x - \dfrac{6}{x - 1} = 2x - 1 - \dfrac{6}{x - 1}$

$(f - g)(x) = f(x) - g(x) = x - 1 - \left(x - \dfrac{6}{x - 1}\right) = -1 + \dfrac{6}{x - 1}$

$(fg)(x) = f(x)g(x) = (x - 1)\left(x - \dfrac{6}{x - 1}\right) = x^2 - x - 6$

$\left(\dfrac{f}{g}\right)(x) = \dfrac{f(x)}{g(x)} = \dfrac{x - 1}{x - \frac{6}{x - 1}} = \dfrac{(x - 1)^2}{x^2 - x - 6} = \dfrac{(x - 1)^2}{(x - 3)(x + 2)}$

Domain $f + g$, $f - g$, fg: $(-\infty, 1) \cup (1, \infty)$

Domain $\dfrac{f}{g}$: $(-\infty, -2) \cup (-2, 1) \cup (1, 3) \cup (3, \infty)$

78. $f(x) = x + |x|,$ $\qquad\qquad\qquad g(x) = x - |x|$

Domain f: $(-\infty, \infty)$ $\qquad\qquad$ Domain g: $(-\infty, \infty)$

$(f + g)(x) = f(x) + g(x) = x + |x| + x - |x| = 2x$

$(f - g)(x) = f(x) - g(x) = x + |x| - (x - |x|) = 2|x|$

$(fg)(x) = f(x)g(x) = (x + |x|)(x - |x|) = x^2 - |x|^2 = 0$

$\left(\dfrac{f}{g}\right)(x) = \dfrac{f(x)}{g(x)} = \dfrac{x + |x|}{x - |x|} = 0$

if $x > 0$, $\dfrac{f(x)}{g(x)} = \dfrac{x + x}{x - x}$ which is undefined

if $x < 0$, $\dfrac{f(x)}{g(x)} = \dfrac{x - x}{x + x} = 0$, $x \neq 0$

Domain $f + g$, $f - g$, fg: $(-\infty, \infty)$

Domain $\dfrac{f}{g}$: $(-\infty, 0)$

80. $f(x) = \sqrt{x - 16}$; $g(x) = x^2$

$\qquad$ domain f: $x \geq 16$; domain g: $(-\infty, \infty)$

$f \circ g = f[g(x)] = f(x^2) = \sqrt{x^2 - 16}$

$\qquad$ domain $f \circ g$: $(-\infty, -4] \cup [4, \infty)$

$g \circ f = g[f(x)] = g(\sqrt{x - 16}) = (\sqrt{x - 16})^2 = x - 16$

$\qquad$ domain $g \circ f$: $[16, \infty)$

82. $f(x) = \dfrac{x + 2}{x - 4}$; $g(x) = \dfrac{x - 5}{x + 1}$

$\qquad$ domain f: $(-\infty, 4) \cup (4, \infty)$; domain g: $(-\infty, -1) \cup (-1, \infty)$

$f \circ g = f[g(x)] = f\left(\dfrac{x - 5}{x + 1}\right) = \dfrac{\frac{x - 5}{x + 1} + 2}{\frac{x - 5}{x + 1} - 4} = \dfrac{x - 5 + 2(x + 1)}{x - 5 - 4(x + 1)} = \dfrac{3x - 3}{-3x - 9}$

$\qquad\qquad\qquad\qquad\qquad = \dfrac{3(x - 1)}{-3(x + 3)} = -\dfrac{x - 1}{x + 3}$ or $\dfrac{1 - x}{x + 3}$

$\qquad$ domain $f \circ g$: $(-\infty, -3) \cup (-3, -1) \cup (-1, \infty)$

$$g \circ f = g[f(x)] = g\left(\frac{x+2}{x-4}\right) = \frac{\dfrac{x+2}{x-4} - 5}{\dfrac{x+2}{x-4} + 1} = \frac{x+2-5x+20}{x+2+x-4} = \frac{-4x+22}{2x-2}$$

$$= \frac{2(11-2x)}{2(x-1)} = \frac{11-2x}{x-1}$$

domain of $g \circ f$: $(-\infty, 1) \cup (1, 4) \cup (4, \infty)$

84. $f(x) = \sqrt{x^2 + 8}$; $g(x) = \sqrt{x^2 - 9}$

domain f: $x^2 + 8 \geq 0 \Rightarrow (-\infty, \infty)$

domain g: $x^2 - 9 \geq 0 \Rightarrow (-\infty, -3] \cup [3, \infty)$

$$f \circ g = f[g(x)] = f(\sqrt{x^2 - 9}) = \sqrt{(\sqrt{x^2 - 9})^2 + 8}$$

$$= \sqrt{x^2 - 9 + 8}$$

$$= \sqrt{x^2 - 1}$$

domain $f \circ g$: $x^2 - 1 \geq 0$ and $x^2 - 9 \geq 0 \Rightarrow (-\infty, -3] \cup [3, \infty)$

$$g \circ f = g[f(x)] = g(\sqrt{x^2 + 8}) = \sqrt{(\sqrt{x^2 + 8})^2 - 9}$$

$$= \sqrt{x^2 + 8 - 9}$$

$$= \sqrt{x^2 - 1}$$

domain $g \circ f$: $x^2 - 1 \geq 0 \Rightarrow (-\infty, -1] \cup [1, \infty)$

86. $P(x) = R(x) - C(x) = 50x - \dfrac{x^2}{100} - (20x + 40{,}000)$

$$P(x) = 50x - \frac{x^2}{100} - 20x - 40{,}000$$

$$= 30x - \frac{x^2}{100} - 40{,}000$$

$P(p) = 30(5000 - 100p) - \dfrac{(5000 - 100p)^2}{100} - 40{,}000$ which simplifies to

$$P(p) = -100p^2 + 7000p - 140{,}000$$

88. $y = 2C - \dfrac{2}{C}x^2$ **90.** $V(t) = \dfrac{1}{C^2}(t + 6C)^2$ **92.** (A) From similar triangles, $\dfrac{w}{h} = \dfrac{4}{2}$

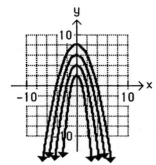

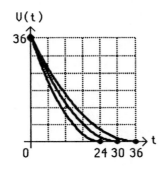

from which
$$w = w(h) = 2h$$

(B) $V = 3wh$
$$V = 3(2h)h$$
$$V(h) = 6h^2$$

(C) $V = 6h^2$
$$V(t) = 6(2 - 0.2\sqrt{t})^2$$

Exercise 3-6

2. $\{(-1, 0), (0, 1), (1, -1), (2, 1)\}$ is not a one-to-one function because 2 ordered pairs, $(0, 1)$ and $(2, 1)$, have the same second term.

4. $\{(5, 4), (4, 3), (3, 2), (2, 1)\}$ is a one-to-one function because no two ordered pairs have the same second term.

6.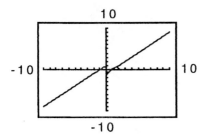

−2 ⟶ −3

−1 ⟶

0 ⟶ 7

1 ⟶

2 ⟶ 9

Not one-to-one because two range values, −3 and 9, are paired with more than one domain value.

8.

domain		range
1	→	5
2	→	3
3	→	1
4	→	2
5	→	4

One-to-one, each range value is paired with only one domain value.

10. Not one-to-one; since graph fails the horizontal line test.

12. One-to-one; passes the horizontal line test.

14. Not one-to-one; fails the horizontal line test.

16. One-to-one; passes the horizontal line test.

18. $G(x) = -\frac{1}{3}x + 1$; linear function which passes the horizontal line test and is therefore one-to-one.

If $(a, f(a))$ and $(b, f(b))$ are 2 points on $G(x)$, then if

$$f(a) = f(b)$$
$$-\frac{1}{3}a + 1 = -\frac{1}{3}b + 1$$
$$-\frac{1}{3}a = -\frac{1}{3}b$$
$$a = b$$

20. $K(x) = \sqrt{4 - x}$

$$f(a) = f(b)$$
$$\sqrt{4 - a} = \sqrt{4 - b}$$
$$4 - a = 4 - b$$
$$a = b$$

K is one-to-one.

22. $N(x) = x^2 - 1$

$$f(a) = f(b)$$
$$a^2 - 1 = b^2 - 1$$
$$a^2 = b^2$$
$$a = \pm b; \ N \text{ is not one-to-one}$$

24. $f(x) = \dfrac{x^2 - |x|}{x}$

Not one-to-one, fails HLT

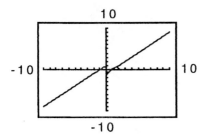

26. $f(x) = \dfrac{|x|^3 + |x|}{x}$

One-to-one, passes HLT

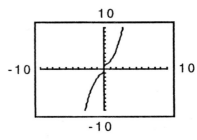

28. $f(x) = \dfrac{1 - x^2}{|x + 1|}$

Not one-to-one, fails HLT

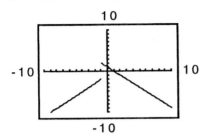

30. $f(x) = \dfrac{4x - x^3}{|x^2 - 4|}$

One-to-one, passes HLT

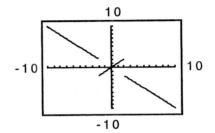

32. From graph D_f: $-2 \le x \le 5$; R_f: $-4 \le y \le 3$

from which $D_{f^{-1}}$: $-4 \le x \le 3$; $R_{f^{-1}}$: $-2 \le y \le 5$

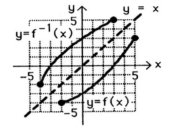

34. From graph D_f: $0 \le x \le 5$; R_f: $-5 \le y \le 5$

from which $D_{f^{-1}}$: $-5 \le x \le 5$; $R_{f^{-1}}$: $0 \le y \le 5$

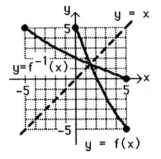

36. $f(x) = -\dfrac{1}{2}x + 2$; $g(x) = -2x + 4$

$f(g(x)) = f(-2x + 4) = -\dfrac{1}{2}(-2x + 4) + 2$

$\qquad\qquad\qquad = x - 2 + 2 = x$

$g(f(x)) = g\left(-\dfrac{1}{2}x + 2\right) = -2\left(-\dfrac{1}{2}x + 2\right) + 4$

$\qquad\qquad\qquad = x - 4 + 4 = x$

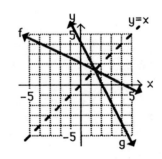

38. $f(x) = \sqrt{x + 2}$; $g(x) = x^2 - 2 \ (x \ge 0)$

$f(g(x)) = f(x^2 - 2) = \sqrt{x^2 - 2 + 2} = \sqrt{x^2} = |x| = x$

$g(f(x)) = g(\sqrt{x + 2}) = (\sqrt{x + 2})^2 - 2 = x + 2 - 2 = x$

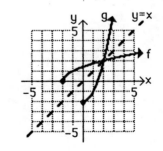

40. $f(x) = 6 - x^2 \ (x \leq 0), \ g(x) = -\sqrt{6 - x}$

$f(g(x)) = f(-\sqrt{6 - x}) = 6 - (-\sqrt{6 - x})^2 = 6 - (6 - x)$

$\qquad\qquad\qquad\qquad\qquad\qquad\qquad = 6 - 6 + x = x$

$g(f(x)) = g(6 - x^2) = -\sqrt{6 - (6 - x^2)} = -\sqrt{6 - 6 + x^2} = -\sqrt{x^2}$

$\qquad\qquad\qquad\qquad\qquad\qquad\qquad = -|x| = -(-x) = x$

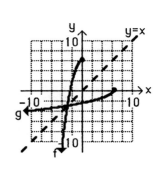

42. $f(x) = 4x;$ D, R: $(-\infty, \infty)$

$\qquad\qquad 4x = y$

$\qquad x = f^{-1}(y) = \dfrac{1}{4} y$

$\qquad y = f^{-1}(x) = \dfrac{1}{4} x;$ D, R: $(-\infty, \infty)$

44. $f(x) = 0.25x + 2.25;$ D, R: $(-\infty, \infty)$

$\qquad 0.25x + 2.25 = y$

$\qquad\qquad 0.25x = y - 2.25$

$\qquad x = f^{-1}(y) = \dfrac{y - 2.25}{0.25}$

$\qquad\qquad\qquad = 4(y - 2.25) = 4y - 9$

$\qquad y = f^{-1}(x) = 4x - 9;$ D, R: $(-\infty, \infty)$

46. $f(x) = 7 - 8x;$ D, R: $(-\infty, \infty)$

$\qquad\qquad 7 - 8x = y$

$\qquad\qquad -8x = y - 7$

$\qquad x = f^{-1}(y) = \dfrac{y - 7}{-8} = -\dfrac{1}{8} y + \dfrac{7}{8}$

$\qquad y = f^{-1}(x) = -\dfrac{1}{8} x + \dfrac{7}{8};$

$\qquad\qquad\qquad\qquad$ D, R: $(-\infty, \infty)$

48. $f(x) = 5 + \dfrac{4}{x};$ D: $x \neq 0,$ R: $y \neq 5$

$\qquad\qquad 5 + \dfrac{4}{x} = y$

$\qquad\qquad\qquad \dfrac{4}{x} = y - 5$

$\qquad\qquad xy - 5x = 4$

$\qquad\qquad x(y - 5) = 4$

$\qquad x = f^{-1}(y) = \dfrac{4}{y - 5}$

$\qquad y = f^{-1}(x) = \dfrac{4}{x - 5};$

$\qquad\qquad\qquad\qquad$ D: $x \neq 5,$ R: $y \neq 0$

50. $f(x) = \dfrac{4x}{2 - x};$ D: $x \neq 2,$ R: $y \neq -4$

$\qquad\qquad \dfrac{4x}{2 - x} = y$

$\qquad\qquad 4x = 2y - xy$

$\qquad\qquad 4x + xy = 2y$

$\qquad\qquad x(4 + y) = 2y$

$\qquad x = f^{-1}(y) = \dfrac{2y}{4 + y}$

$\qquad y = f^{-1}(x) = \dfrac{2x}{4 + x};$

$\qquad\qquad\qquad\qquad$ D: $x \neq -4,$ R: $y \neq 2$

52. $f(x) = \dfrac{x - 0.2}{x + 0.5};$ D: $x \neq -0.5,$ R: $y \neq 1$

$\qquad\qquad \dfrac{x - 0.2}{x + 0.5} = y$

$\qquad\qquad x - 0.2 = xy + 0.5y$

$\qquad\qquad x - xy = 0.5y + 0.2$

$\qquad\qquad x(1 - y) = 0.5y + 0.2$

$\qquad x = f^{-1}(y) = \dfrac{0.5y + 0.2}{1 - y}$

$\qquad y = f^{-1}(x) = \dfrac{0.5x + 0.2}{1 - x};$

$\qquad\qquad\qquad\qquad$ D: $x \neq 1,$ R: $y \neq -0.5$

54. $f(x) = 2x^5 + 9$; D, R: $(-\infty, \infty)$

$$2x^5 + 9 = y$$
$$2x^5 = y - 9$$
$$x^5 = \frac{y - 9}{2}$$
$$x = f^{-1}(y) = \sqrt[5]{\frac{y - 9}{2}}$$
$$y = f^{-1}(x) = \sqrt[5]{\frac{x - 9}{2}}$$

D, R: $(-\infty, \infty)$

56. $f(x) = -1 + \sqrt[3]{4 - 5x}$; D, R: $(-\infty, \infty)$

$$-1 + \sqrt[3]{4 - 5x} = y$$
$$\sqrt[3]{4 - 5x} = y + 1$$
$$4 - 5x = (y + 1)^3$$
$$-5x = (y + 1)^3 - 4$$
$$x = f^{-1}(y) = \frac{4 - (y + 1)^3}{5}$$
$$\text{or } \frac{4}{5} - \frac{1}{5}(y + 1)^3$$
$$y = f^{-1}(x) = \frac{4}{5} - \frac{1}{5}(x + 1)^3;$$

D, R: $(-\infty, \infty)$

58. $f(x) = 3\sqrt{x - 4}$; D: $x \geq 4$, R: $y \geq 0$

$$3\sqrt{x - 4} = y$$
$$\sqrt{x - 4} = \frac{y}{3}$$
$$x - 4 = \frac{y^2}{9}$$
$$x = f^{-1}(y) = \frac{1}{9}y^2 + 4$$
$$y = f^{-1}(x) = \frac{1}{9}x^2 + 4;$$

D: $x \geq 0$, R: $y \geq 4$

60. $f(x) = 4 - \sqrt{x + 5}$; D: $[-5, \infty)$; R: $(-\infty, 4]$

$$4 - \sqrt{x + 5} = y$$
$$-\sqrt{x + 5} = y - 4$$
$$\sqrt{x + 5} = 4 - y$$
$$x + 5 = (4 - y)^2 = 16 - 8y + y^2$$
$$x = f^{-1}(y) = y^2 - 8y + 11$$
$$y = f^{-1}(x) = x^2 - 8x + 11;$$

D: $(-\infty, 4]$, R: $[-5, \infty)$

62. No, a constant function fails the horizontal line test and is not a one-to-one function; therefore, it cannot have an inverse.

64. $f(x) = 3 - (x - 5)^2$;

D: $x \leq 5$, R: $y \leq 3$

$$3 - (x - 5)^2 = y$$
$$-(x - 5)^2 = y - 3$$
$$(x - 5)^2 = 3 - y$$
$$x - 5 = \pm\sqrt{3 - y}$$
$$x = f^{-1}(y) = 5 \pm \sqrt{3 - y}$$
$$y = f^{-1}(x) = 5 - \sqrt{3 - x};$$

D: $x \leq 3$, R: $y \leq 5$

66. $f(x) = x^2 + 8x + 7$; D: $x \geq -4$, R: $y \geq -9$

$$x^2 + 8x + 7 = y$$
$$x^2 + 8x + (7 - y) = 0$$
$$x = \frac{-8 \pm \sqrt{64 - 4(7 - y)}}{2}$$
$$x = \frac{-8 \pm \sqrt{36 + 4y}}{2}$$
$$x = \frac{-8 \pm 2\sqrt{9 + y}}{2}$$
$$x = f^{-1}(y) = -4 \pm \sqrt{9 + y}$$
$$y = f^{-1}(x) = \sqrt{9 + x} - 4;$$

D: $x \geq -9$, R: $y \geq -4$

68. $f(x) = \sqrt{9 - x^2}$; D: [0, 3], R: [0, 3]

$$\sqrt{9 - x^2} = y$$
$$9 - x^2 = y^2$$
$$-x^2 = y^2 - 9$$
$$x^2 = 9 - y^2$$
$$x = f^{-1}(y) = \pm\sqrt{9 - y^2}$$
$$y = f^{-1}(x) = \sqrt{9 - x^2};\ D: [0, 3],\ R: [0, 3]$$

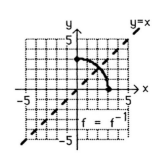

70. $f(x) = -\sqrt{9 - x^2}$; D: [-3, 0], R: [-3, 0]

$$-\sqrt{9 - x^2} = y$$
$$\sqrt{9 - x^2} = -y$$
$$9 - x^2 = y^2$$
$$-x^2 = y^2 - 9$$
$$x^2 = 9 - y^2$$
$$x = f^{-1}(y) = \pm\sqrt{9 - y^2}$$
$$y = f^{-1}(x) = -\sqrt{9 - y^2};\ D, R: [-3, 0]$$

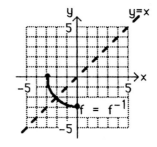

72. $f(x) = 1 - \sqrt{1 - x^2}$; D, R: [0, 1]

$$1 - \sqrt{1 - x^2} = y$$
$$-\sqrt{1 - x^2} = y - 1$$
$$\sqrt{1 - x^2} = 1 - y$$
$$1 - x^2 = y^2 - 2y + 1$$
$$-x^2 = y^2 - 2y$$
$$x^2 = -y^2 + 2y$$
$$x = f^{-1}(y) = \pm\sqrt{-y^2 + 2y}$$
$$y = f^{-1}(x) = \sqrt{2x - x^2};\ D, R: [0, 1]$$

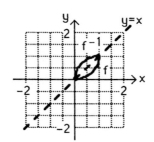

74. $f(x) = 1 + \sqrt{1 - x^2}$; D: [-1, 0], R: [1, 2]

$$1 + \sqrt{1 - x^2} = y$$
$$\sqrt{1 - x^2} = y - 1$$
$$1 - x^2 = y^2 - 2y + 1$$
$$-x^2 = y^2 - 2y$$
$$x^2 = 2y - y^2$$
$$x = f^{-1}(y) = \pm\sqrt{2y - y^2}$$
$$y = f^{-1}(x) = -\sqrt{2x - x^2};\ D: [1, 2],\ R: [-1, 0]$$

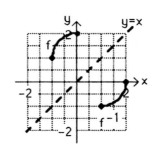

76. $f(x) = \sqrt{a^2 - x^2}$, $a > 0$, $0 \le x \le a$, $0 \le y \le a$

$$\sqrt{a^2 - x^2} = y$$
$$a^2 - x^2 = y^2$$
$$-x^2 = y^2 - a^2$$
$$x^2 = a^2 - y^2$$
$$x = f^{-1}(y) = \pm\sqrt{a^2 - y^2}$$
$$y = f^{-1}(x) = \sqrt{a^2 - x^2};\ D: [0, a],\ R: [0, a]$$

78. The graph of a function that is its own inverse is symmetric with respect to the line $y = x$.

80. Let $P = (a, b)$, $Q = \left(\dfrac{a + b}{2}, \dfrac{a + b}{2}\right)$ and $R = (b, a)$, then

$$PQ = \sqrt{\left(a - \dfrac{a + b}{2}\right)^2 + \left(b - \dfrac{a + b}{2}\right)^2} = \sqrt{\left(\dfrac{a - b}{2}\right)^2 + \left(\dfrac{b - a}{2}\right)^2}$$

$$QR = \sqrt{\left(\dfrac{a + b}{2} - b\right)^2 + \left(\dfrac{a + b}{2} - a\right)^2} = \sqrt{\left(\dfrac{a - b}{2}\right)^2 + \left(\dfrac{b - a}{2}\right)^2}$$

which shows $\left(\dfrac{a + b}{2}, \dfrac{a + b}{2}\right)$ bisects line segment from (a, b) to (b, a).

82. $f(x) = (1 + x)^2$
$$(1 + x)^2 = y$$
$$1 + x = \pm\sqrt{y}$$
$$x = f^{-1}(y) = \pm\sqrt{y} - 1$$
$$y = f^{-1}(x) = \pm\sqrt{x} - 1$$

(A) $x \leq -1 \Rightarrow y \geq 0$
  $f^{-1}(x) = -\sqrt{x} - 1$;
  D: $[0, \infty)$, R: $(-\infty, -1]$

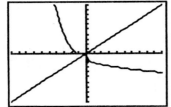

standard window

(B) $x \geq -1 \Rightarrow y \geq 0$
  $f^{-1}(x) = \sqrt{x} - 1$;
  D: $[0, \infty)$, R: $[-1, \infty)$

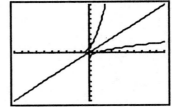

standard window

84. $f(x) = \sqrt{6x - x^2}$
$$\sqrt{6x - x^2} = y$$
$$6x - x^2 = y^2$$
$$-x^2 + 6x - y^2 = 0$$

$$x = \dfrac{-6 \pm \sqrt{36 - 4y^2}}{-2}$$
$$= \dfrac{6 \pm 2\sqrt{9 - y^2}}{2}$$
$$= 3 \pm \sqrt{9 - y^2}$$
$$f^{-1}(x) = 3 \pm \sqrt{9 - x^2}$$

(A) $0 \leq x \leq 3 \Rightarrow 0 \leq y \leq 3$
  $f^{-1}(x) = 3 - \sqrt{9 - x^2}$;
  D: $[0, 3]$, R: $[0, 3]$

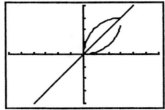

(B) $3 \leq x \leq 6 \Rightarrow 0 \leq y \leq 3$
  $f^{-1}(x) = 3 + \sqrt{9 - x^2}$;
  D: $[0, 3]$, R: $[3, 6]$

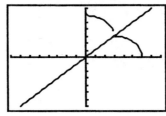

CHAPTER 4

Exercise 4-1

2. $g(x) = -ax^4$ is graph (a).   **4.** $k(x) = -ax^5$ is graph (b).

6. $f(x)$ could be a third degree polynomial.   **8.** $g(x)$ in not a polynomial.

10.
$$
\begin{array}{r}
a - 2 \\
a + 2\,\overline{)\,a^2 + 0a + 4} \\
\underline{a^2 + 2a} \\
-2a + 4 \\
\underline{-2a - 4} \\
8
\end{array}
\qquad R = 8
$$

12.
$$
\begin{array}{r}
b - 3 \\
b - 3\,\overline{)\,b^2 - 6b + 9} \\
\underline{b^2 - 3b} \\
-3b + 9 \\
\underline{-3b + 9} \\
0
\end{array}
\qquad R = 0
$$

14.
$$
\begin{array}{r}
-x^2 + 4 \\
x - 2\,\overline{)\,-x^3 + 2x^2 + 4x - 8} \\
\underline{-x^3 + 2x^2} \\
0 + 4x - 8 \\
\underline{4x - 8} \\
0
\end{array}
\qquad R = 0
$$

16.
$$
\begin{array}{r}
4y^2 + 3y + 1 \\
2y - 3\,\overline{)\,8y^3 - 6y^2 - 7y + 3} \\
\underline{8y^3 - 12y^2} \\
6y^2 - 7y \\
\underline{6y^2 - 9y} \\
2y + 3 \\
\underline{2y - 3} \\
6
\end{array}
\qquad R = 6
$$

18.
$$
\begin{array}{r|rrr}
 & 1 & -2 & -1 \\
 & & 4 & 8 \\
\hline
4 & 1 & 2 & 7
\end{array}
\quad \text{from which}
$$
$$
(x^2 - 2x - 1) \div (x - 4)
$$
$$
= x + 2 + \frac{7}{x - 4}
$$

20.
$$
\begin{array}{r|rrr}
 & 4 & 18 & 4 \\
 & & -20 & 10 \\
\hline
-5 & 4 & -2 & 14
\end{array}
\quad \text{from which}
$$
$$
(4x^2 + 18x + 4) \div (x + 5)
$$
$$
= 4x - 2 + \frac{14}{x + 5}
$$

22.
$$
\begin{array}{r|rrrr}
 & 3 & -4 & -7 & 9 \\
 & & 6 & 4 & -6 \\
\hline
2 & 3 & 2 & -3 & 3
\end{array}
\quad \text{from which}
$$
$$
(3x^3 - 4x^2 - 7x + 9) \div (x - 2)
$$
$$
= 3x^2 + 2x - 3 + \frac{3}{x - 2}
$$

24.
$$
\begin{array}{r|rrr}
 & 3 & -4 & 2 \\
 & & 6 & 4 \\
\hline
2 & 3 & 2 & 6
\end{array}
\quad P(2) = 6
$$

26.
$$
\begin{array}{r|rrrr}
 & 5 & 14 & 3 & 10 \\
 & & -15 & 3 & -18 \\
\hline
-3 & 5 & -1 & 6 & -8
\end{array}
\quad P(-3) = -8
$$

28.
$$
\begin{array}{r|rrrrr}
 & 3 & 18 & 1 & 4 & -7 \\
 & & -18 & 0 & -6 & 12 \\
\hline
-6 & 3 & 0 & 1 & -2 & 5
\end{array}
\quad P(-6) = 5
$$

30.
$$
\begin{array}{r|rrrrr}
 & 3 & 0 & 0 & -2 & -5 \\
 & & -3 & 3 & -3 & 5 \\
\hline
-1 & 3 & -3 & 3 & -5 & 0
\end{array}
$$
$$
3x^3 - 3x^2 + 3x - 5; \; R = 0
$$

32.
$$
\begin{array}{r|rrrrrr}
 & 1 & 0 & 0 & 0 & 0 & -32 \\
 & & 2 & 4 & 8 & 16 & 32 \\
\hline
2 & 1 & 2 & 4 & 8 & 16 & 0
\end{array}
$$
$$
x^4 + 2x^3 + 4x^2 + 8x + 16; \; R = 0
$$

34.
$$
\begin{array}{r|rrrrr}
 & 2 & 6 & -4 & -5 & 7 \\
 & & -6 & 0 & 12 & -21 \\
\hline
-3 & 2 & 0 & -4 & 7 & -14
\end{array}
$$
$$
2x^3 - 4x + 7; \; R = -14
$$

36.
$$
\begin{array}{r|rrrrrrr}
 & 1 & 6 & 2 & 12 & 0 & -3 & -18 \\
 & & -6 & 0 & -12 & 0 & 0 & 18 \\
\hline
-6 & 1 & 0 & 2 & 0 & 0 & -3 & 0
\end{array}
$$
$$
x^5 + 2x^3 - 3; \; R = 0
$$

38.

```
     2      5      0      5      8
           -1     -2      1     -3
 _____
-½ | 2      4     -2      6      5
```

$2x^3 + 4x^2 - 2x + 6;\ R = 5$

40.

```
     4    -11     18     -5      4
            3     -6      9      3
 _____
¾ | 4     -8     12      4      7
```

$4x^3 - 8x^2 + 12x + 4;\ R = 7$

42.

```
       3      0     -4       5         8
            -2.4   1.92    1.664    -5.3312
 _____
-0.8 | 3   -2.4   -2.08    6.664     2.6688
```

$3x^3 - 2.4x^2 - 2.08x + 6.664;\ R = 2.6688$

44.

```
        10     -4      0      2      4      -1
                4      0      0     0.8    1.92
 _____
0.4 | 10       0      0      2     4.8     0.92
```

$10x^4 + 2x + 4.8;\ R = 0.92$

46. $P(x) = x^3 + 2x^2 - 5x - 6,\ -4 \le x \le 3$

```
      1       2      -5      -6
             -4       8     -12
 _____
-4  | 1      -2       3     -18
       P(-4) = -18
```

```
      1       2      -5      -6
             -2       0      10
 _____
-2  | 1       0      -5       4
       P(-2) = 4
```

```
      1       2      -5      -6
              1       3      -2
 _____
1   | 1       3      -2      -8
       P(1) = -8
```

```
      1       2      -5      -6
              3      15      30
 _____
3   | 1       5      10      24
       P(3) = 24                    ; P(0) = -6
```

3 x intercepts
2 turning points
left behavior: $\to -\infty$
right behavior: $\to +\infty$

```
      1       2      -5      -6
             -3       3       6
 _____
-3  | 1      -1      -2       0
       P(-3) = 0
```

```
      1       2      -5      -6
             -1      -1       6
 _____
-1  | 1       1      -6       0
       P(-1) = 0
```

```
      1       2      -5      -6
              2       8       6
 _____
2   | 1       4       3       0
       P(2) = 0
```

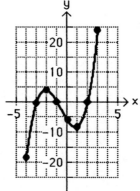

48. $P(x) = x^3 - 2x^2 - 5x + 6,\ -3 \le x \le 4$

```
      1      -2      -5       6
             -3      15     -30
 _____
-3  | 1      -5      10     -24
       P(-3) = -24
```

```
      1      -2      -5       6
             -1       3       2
 _____
-1  | 1      -3      -2       8
       P(-1) = 8
```

```
      1      -2      -5       6
             -2       8      -6
 _____
-2  | 1      -4       3       0
       P(-2) = 0
```

```
      1      -2      -5       6
              1      -1      -6
 _____
1   | 1      -1      -6       0
       P(1) = 0
```

```
    1         -2        -5         6              1         -2        -5         6
              2          0       -10                        3          3        -6
  2│1          0        -5        -4            3│1          1        -2         0
```

$P(2) = -4$ $P(3) = 0$

```
    1         -2        -5         6
              4          8        12
  4│1          2          3        18
```

$P(4) = 18$; $P(0) = 6$

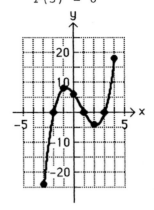

3 x intercepts
2 turning points
left behavior: $\rightarrow -\infty$
right behavior: $\rightarrow +\infty$

50. $P(x) = -x^3 - x + 4, \ -2 \leq x \leq 2$

```
    -1         0        -1         4              -1         0        -1         4
               2        -4        10                         1        -1         2
 -2│-1         2        -5        14           -1│-1         1        -2         6
```

$P(-2) = 14$ $P(-1) = 6$

```
    -1         0        -1         4              -1         0        -1         4
              -1        -1        -2                        -2        -4       -10
  1│-1        -1        -2         2            2│-1        -2        -5        -6
```

$P(1) = 2$ $P(2) = -6$
$P(0) = 4$

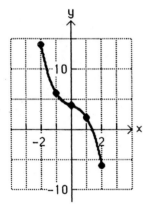

1 x intercept
0 turning points
left behavior: $\rightarrow +\infty$
right behavior: $\rightarrow -\infty$

52. $P(x) = -x^3 + x^2 + 4x + 6, \ -3 \leq x \leq 4$

```
    -1         1         4         6              -1         1         4         6
               3       -12        24                         2        -6         4
 -3│-1         4        -8        30           -2│-1         3        -2        10
```

$P(-3) = 30$ $P(-2) = 10$

```
    -1         1         4         6              -1         1         4         6
               1        -2        -2                        -1         0         4
 -1│-1         2         2         4            1│-1         0         4        10
```

$P(-1) = 4$ $P(1) = 10$

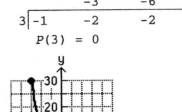

$$
\begin{array}{r}
-1 \qquad 1 \qquad 4 \qquad 6 \\
-2 \qquad -2 \qquad 4 \\
\hline
2|-1 \qquad -1 \qquad 2 \qquad 10
\end{array}
$$

$P(2) = 10$

$$
\begin{array}{r}
-1 \qquad 1 \qquad 4 \qquad 6 \\
-4 \qquad -12 \qquad -32 \\
\hline
4|-1 \qquad -3 \qquad -8 \qquad -26
\end{array}
$$

$P(4) = -26$; $P(0) = 6$

1 x intercept
2 turning points
left behavior: $\to +\infty$
right behavior: $\to -\infty$

$$
\begin{array}{r}
-1 \qquad 1 \qquad 4 \qquad 6 \\
-3 \qquad -6 \qquad -6 \\
\hline
3|-1 \qquad -2 \qquad -2 \qquad 0
\end{array}
$$

$P(3) = 0$

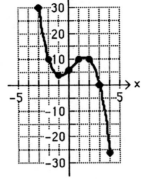

54. $P(x) = x^4 + 1$ is a 4th degree polynomial with no x intercepts.

56. There are no 4th degree polynomials with zero turning points.

58.

$$
\begin{array}{r}
x^2 + 2x + 1; \ R = 0 \\
x^2 - 4 \overline{\smash{)}\, x^4 + 2x^3 - 3x^2 - 8x - 4} \\
\underline{x^4 - 4x^2} \\
2x^3 + x^2 - 8x - 4 \\
\underline{2x^3 - 8x} \\
x^2 - 4 \\
\underline{x^2 - 4} \\
0
\end{array}
$$

60.

$$
\begin{array}{r}
x^2 - 3x + 2; \ R = 2x - 1 \\
x^2 - 4x + 1 \overline{\smash{)}\, x^4 - 7x^3 + 15x^2 - 9x + 1} \\
\underline{x^4 - 4x^3 + x^2} \\
-3x^3 + 14x^2 - 9x + 1 \\
\underline{-3x^3 + 12x^2 - 3x} \\
2x^2 - 6x + 1 \\
\underline{2x^2 - 8x + 2} \\
2x - 1
\end{array}
$$

62.

$$
\begin{array}{r}
1 \qquad 2 \qquad -2 \qquad 2 \qquad -3 \\
0 - i \quad -1 - 2i \quad -2 + 3i \quad 3 \\
\hline
-i|1 \quad 2 - i \quad -3 - 2i \quad 0 + 3i \quad 0
\end{array}
$$
from which

$(x^4 + 2x^3 - 2x^2 + 2x - 3) \div (x + i) = x^3 + (2 - i)x^2 + (-3 - 2i)x + 3i; \ R = 0$

64. $P(x) = x^2 - 4ix - 13$

(A) $P(5 + 6i)$:
$$
\begin{array}{r}
1 \qquad\qquad -4i \qquad -13 \\
5 + 6i \qquad 13 + 40i \\
\hline
5 + 6i|1 \quad 5 + 2i \qquad \boxed{40i}
\end{array}
$$

(B) $P(1 + 2i)$:
$$
\begin{array}{r}
1 \qquad\qquad -4i \qquad -13 \\
1 + 2i \qquad 5 \\
\hline
1 + 2i|1 \quad 1 - 2i \qquad \boxed{-8}
\end{array}
$$

(C) $P(3 + 2i)$:
$$
\begin{array}{r}
1 \qquad\qquad -4i \qquad -13 \\
3 + 2i \qquad 13 \\
\hline
3 + 2i|1 \quad 3 - 2i \qquad \boxed{0}
\end{array}
$$

(D) $P(-3 + 2i)$:
$$
\begin{array}{r}
1 \qquad\qquad -4i \qquad -13 \\
-3 + 2i \qquad 13 \\
\hline
-3 + 2i|1 \quad -3 - 2i \qquad \boxed{0}
\end{array}
$$

66.

x	$P(x)$
-3	0
-2	-24
-1	-16
0	-6
1	0
2	20

$P(x) = x^4 + x^3 - 3x^2 + 7x - 6$

number of x intercepts: 2

number of turning points: 1

left behavior → ∞

right behavior → ∞

68.

x	$P(x)$
-2	2
-1	7
0	10
1	-1
2	-14
3	7

$P(x) = x^4 - 8x^2 - 4x + 10$

number of x intercepts: 2

number of turning points: 3

left behavior → ∞

right behavior → ∞

70.

x	$P(x)$
-4	5
-3	8
-2	-7
-1	-10
0	5
1	20
2	-7

$P(x) = -x^4 - 5x^3 + x^2 + 20x + 5$

number of x intercepts: 4

number of turning points: 3

left behavior → -∞

right behavior → -∞

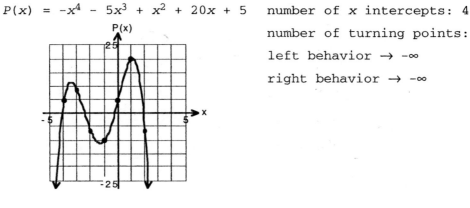

72.

x	$P(x)$
-3	-19
-2	16
-1	-13
0	-10
1	1
2	-4

$P(x) = x^5 - 9x^3 + 4x^2 + 15x - 10$

number of x intercepts: 5

number of turning points: 4

left behavior → -∞

right behavior → ∞

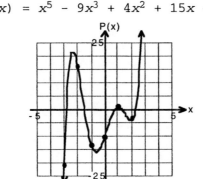

74. (A) Using synthetic division to divide $P(x) = a_3x^3 + a_2x^2 + a_1x + a_0$
by $x - r$ gives

$$
\begin{array}{c|cccc}
 & a_3 & a_2 & a_1 & a_0 \\
 & & a_3r & a_2r + a_3r^2 & a_1r + a_2r^2 + a_3r^3 \\
\hline
r & a_3 & a_2 + a_3r & a_1 + a_2r + a_3r^2 & a_0 + a_1r + a_2r^2 + a_3r^3
\end{array}
$$

$a_3x^2 + (a_2 + a_3r)x + a_1 + a_2r + a_3r^2$ is the quotient and $a_0 + a_1r + a_2r^2 + a_3r^3$
is the remainder.

Using the long-division algorithm gives

$$
\require{enclose}
\begin{array}{r}
a_3x^2 + (a_2 + a_3r)x + (a_1 + a_2r + a_3r^2) \\
x - r \enclose{longdiv}{a_3x^3 + a_2x^2 + a_1x + a_0} \\
\end{array}
$$

$$
\begin{array}{l}
\underline{a_3x^3 - a_3rx^2} \\
\quad (a_2 + a_3r)x^2 + a_1x + a_0 \\
\quad \underline{(a_2 + a_3r)x^2 - (a_2 + a_3r)rx} \\
\qquad (a_1 + a_2r + a_3r^2)x + a_0 \\
\qquad \underline{(a_1 + a_2r + a_3r^2)x - (a_1 + a_2r + a_3r^2)r} \\
\qquad\qquad a_0 + (a_1 + a_2r + a_3r^2)r
\end{array}
$$

from which $a_3x^2 + (a_2 + a_3r)x + (a_1 + a_2r + a_3r^2)$ is the quotient and
$a_0 + (a_1r + a_2r^2 + a_3r^3)$ is the remainder.

Summary: both methods give the same results.

(B) $P(r) = a_3r^3 + a_2r^2 + a_1r + a_0 = $ remainder

76.
$$
\begin{aligned}
P(x) &= 3x^4 + x^3 - 10x^2 + 5x - 2 \\
&= (3x + 1)x^3 - 10x^2 + 5x - 2 \\
&= [(3x + 1)x - 10]x^2 + 5x - 2 \\
&= \{[(3x + 1)x - 10]x + 5\}x - 2 \\
P(-2) &= -12 \\
P(1.3) &= -1.6347
\end{aligned}
$$

Exercise 4-2

2. $P(x) = (x + 6)^2(x - 5)^3$ degree of $P(x) = 2 + 3 = 5$

Zeros	multiplicity
-6	2
5	3

4. $P(x) = 2(x + 4)^3(x - 3)^3(x - 4)$ degree of $P(x) = 3 + 2 + 1 = 6$

Zeros	multiplicity
-4	3
3	2
4	1

6. $P(x) = (x - (-4))^2(x - 0)(x - 2)^3$ degree of $P(x) = 2 + 1 + 3 = 6$
$P(x) = x(x + 4)^2(x - 2)^3$

8. $P(x) = (x - 1)^3(x - (-3 + \sqrt{2}))(x - (-3 - \sqrt{2}))$ degree of $P(x) = 3 + 1 + 1 = 5$
$P(x) = (x - 1)^3(x + 3 - \sqrt{2})(x + 3 + \sqrt{2})$

10. $P(x) = (x - 2i)^2(x - (-2i))^2(x - 2)^3$ degee of $P(x) = 2 + 2 + 3 = 7$
$P(x) = (x - 2i)^2(x + 2i)^2(x - 2)^3$

12. Zeros of $P(x)$: -2, -1, 1, 3 all of multiplicity 1.
$P(x) = (x + 2)(x + 1)(x - 1)(x - 3)$, degree 4

14. Zeros of $P(x)$: -3 (multiplicity 1), 1 (multiplicity 2).
$P(x) = (x + 3)(x - 1)^2$, degree 3

16. Zeros of $P(x)$: -2 (multiplicity 2), 0 (multiplicity 1), 2 (multiplicity 2).
$P(x) = (x + 2)^2 \cdot x \cdot (x - 2)^2$, degree 5

18. $P(x) = x^{23} - 1$; $x + 1$
$P(-1) = (-1)^{23} - 1 = -2$; $x + 1$ is not a factor of $P(x)$

20. $P(x) = 3x^3 - 5x^2 - 4x + 6$; $x - 1$
$P(1) = 3(1)^3 - 5(1)^2 - 4(1) + 6$
$\qquad = 3 - 5 - 4 + 6$
$\qquad = 0 \qquad\qquad$; $x - 1$ is a factor of $P(x)$

22. $P(x) = x^3 + 5x^2 - 8x + 14$
factors of b: ± 1, ± 2, ± 7, ± 14
factors of c: ± 1
possible rational zeros: ± 1, ± 2, ± 7, ± 14

24. $P(x) = 3x^3 - 2x^2 - 4x + 2$
factors of b: ± 1, ± 2
factors of c: ± 1, ± 3
possible rational zeros: ± 1, ± 2, $\pm \dfrac{1}{3}$, $\pm \dfrac{2}{3}$

26. $P(x) = 10x^3 + 2x^2 - 7x - 9$
factors of b: ± 1, ± 3, ± 9
factors of c: ± 1, ± 2, ± 5, ± 10
possible rational zeros: ± 1, ± 3, ± 9, $\pm \dfrac{1}{2}$, $\pm \dfrac{3}{2}$, $\pm \dfrac{9}{2}$, $\pm \dfrac{1}{5}$, $\pm \dfrac{3}{5}$, $\pm \dfrac{9}{5}$, $\pm \dfrac{1}{10}$, $\pm \dfrac{3}{10}$, $\pm \dfrac{9}{10}$

28. $P(x) = x^3 - 4x^2 - 3x + 18$;
3 a double zero

$$
\begin{array}{r|rrrr}
 & 1 & -4 & -3 & 18 \\
 &   & 3 & -3 & -18 \\
\hline
3 & 1 & -1 & -6 & 0 \\
 &   & 3 & 6 & \\
\hline
3 & 1 & 2 & 0 & \Rightarrow x + 2
\end{array}
$$

$P(x) = (x - 3)(x - 3)(x + 2)$

30. $P(x) = x^4 + 2x^2 + 1$;
i is a double zero

$$
\begin{array}{r|rrrrr}
 & 1 & 0 & 2 & 0 & 1 \\
 &   & i & -1 & i & -1 \\
\hline
i & 1 & i & 1 & i & 0 \\
 &   & i & -2 & -i & \\
\hline
i & 1 & 2i & -1 & 0 & \Rightarrow x^2 + 2ix - 1
\end{array}
$$

$x = \dfrac{-2i \pm \sqrt{4i^2 - 4(-1)}}{2}$

$\quad = \dfrac{-2i \pm \sqrt{0}}{2} = -i$ (double zero)

$P(x) = (x - i)(x - i)(x + i)(x + i)$

32. $P(x) = 3x^3 - 10x^2 + 31x + 26;$ $-\dfrac{2}{3}$ is a zero

$$
\begin{array}{r}
\phantom{-\frac{2}{3}} \quad 3 \quad -10 \quad 31 \quad 26 \\
\phantom{-\frac{2}{3}3} \quad -2 \quad 8 \quad -26 \\
\hline
-\dfrac{2}{3} \Big| 3 \quad -12 \quad 39 \quad 0
\end{array} \Rightarrow 3x^2 - 12x + 39
$$

$P(x) = \left(x + \dfrac{2}{3}\right)(3x^2 - 12x + 39)$

$P(x) = 3\left(x + \dfrac{2}{3}\right)(x^2 - 4x + 13)$

$x = \dfrac{4 \pm \sqrt{16 - 4(13)}}{2}$

$ = \dfrac{4 \pm \sqrt{-36}}{2}$

$ = \dfrac{4 \pm 6i}{2} = 2 \pm 3i$

$P(x) = 3\left(x + \dfrac{2}{3}\right)(x - (2 + 3i))(x - (2 - 3i))$

$P(x) = (3x + 2)(x - 2 - 3i)(x - 2 + 3i)$

34. $2x^3 - 7x^2 - 6x - 1 = 0$ possible rational zeros: ± 1, $\pm\dfrac{1}{2}$

$$
\begin{array}{r}
 \quad 2 \quad -7 \quad -6 \quad -1 \\
 \quad -1 \quad 4 \quad 1 \\
\hline
-0.5 \Big| 2 \quad -8 \quad -2 \quad 0
\end{array}
$$

$P(-.5) = 0$ is the only rational zero $\Rightarrow$ $(x + .5)$ is a factor

$(x + 0.5)(2x^2 - 8x - 2) = 0$

$x = \dfrac{8 \pm \sqrt{64 - 4(2)(-2)}}{4} = \dfrac{8 \pm \sqrt{80}}{4} = \dfrac{8 \pm 4\sqrt{5}}{4} = 2 \pm \sqrt{5}$

Roots: -0.5, $2 \pm \sqrt{5}$

36. $x^4 - 11x^2 + 12x + 4 = 0$ possible rational zeros: ± 1, ± 2, ± 4

$$
\begin{array}{r}
 \quad 1 \quad 0 \quad -11 \quad 12 \quad 4 \\
 \quad 2 \quad 4 \quad -14 \quad -4 \\
\hline
2 \Big| 1 \quad 2 \quad -7 \quad -2 \quad 0
\end{array}
$$

$$
\begin{array}{r}
 \quad 2 \quad 8 \quad 2 \\
\hline
2 \Big| 1 \quad 4 \quad 1 \quad 0 \quad \text{2 is a double root}
\end{array}
$$

$(x - 2)^2(x^2 + 4x + 1) = 0$

$x = \dfrac{-4 \pm \sqrt{16 - 4}}{2} = \dfrac{-4 \pm 2\sqrt{3}}{2} = -2 \pm \sqrt{3}$

Roots: 2 (multiplicity 2), $-2 \pm \sqrt{3}$

38. $x^4 - 2x^3 + 9x^2 + 2x - 10 = 0$ possible rational zeros: ± 1, ± 2, ± 5, ± 10

$$
\begin{array}{r}
1 \quad -2 \quad\ \ 9 \quad\ \ 2 \quad -10 \\
\underline{-1 \quad\ \ 3 \quad -12 \quad\ \ 10} \\
-1|\ 1 \quad -3 \quad\ 12 \quad -10 \quad\ \ 0
\end{array}
$$

$$
\begin{array}{r}
1 \quad -2 \quad\ \ 10 \\
\underline{} \\
1|\ 1 \quad -2 \quad\ \ 10 \quad\ \ 0
\end{array}
$$

$(x + 1)(x - 1)(x^2 - 2x + 10) = 0$

$$x = \frac{2 \pm \sqrt{4 - 40}}{2} = \frac{2 \pm 6i}{2} = 1 \pm 3i$$

Roots: -1, 1, $1 + 3i$, $1 - 3i$

40. $3x^5 + 10x^4 + 4x^3 - 20x^2 - 7x + 10 = 0$

possible rational zeros: ± 1, ± 2, ± 5, ± 10, $\pm\frac{1}{3}$, $\pm\frac{2}{3}$, $\pm\frac{5}{3}$, $\pm\frac{10}{3}$

$$
\begin{array}{r}
3 \quad\ 10 \quad\ \ 4 \quad -20 \quad -7 \quad\ \ 10 \\
\underline{-3 \quad\ -7 \quad\ \ 3 \quad\ \ 17 \quad -10} \\
-1|\ 3 \quad\ \ 7 \quad -3 \quad -17 \quad\ 10 \quad\ \ 0
\end{array}
$$

$$
\begin{array}{r}
3 \quad\ 10 \quad\ \ 7 \quad -10 \\
\underline{} \\
1|\ 3 \quad\ 10 \quad\ \ 7 \quad -10 \quad\ \ 0
\end{array}
$$

$$
\begin{array}{r}
2 \quad\ \ 8 \quad\ \ 10 \\
\underline{} \\
\tfrac{2}{3}|\ 3 \quad\ 12 \quad\ 15 \quad\ \ 0
\end{array}
$$

$(x + 1)(x - 1)\left(x - \frac{2}{3}\right)(3x^2 + 12x + 15) = 0$

$$3x^2 + 12x + 15 = 0$$
$$x^2 + 4x + 5 = 0$$

$$x = \frac{-4 \pm \sqrt{16 - 20}}{2} = \frac{-4 \pm 2i}{2} = -2 \pm i$$

Roots: -1, 1, $\frac{2}{3}$, $-2 + i$, $-2 - i$

42. $P(x) = x^3 - 4x^2 - 9x + 36$

possible rational zeros: ± 1, ± 2, ± 3, ± 4, ± 6, ± 9, ± 12, ± 18, ± 36

$$
\begin{array}{r}
1 \quad -4 \quad -9 \quad\ \ 36 \\
\underline{-3 \quad\ 21 \quad -36} \\
-3|\ 1 \quad -7 \quad\ 12 \quad\ \ 0
\end{array}
$$

$$
\begin{array}{r}
3 \quad -12 \\
\underline{} \\
3|\ 1 \quad -4 \quad\ \ 0 \quad \Rightarrow x - 4 = 0,\ x = 4
\end{array}
$$

Zeros: -3, 3, 4

44. $P(x) = x^4 - 4.1x^3 + 0.1x^2 + 1.2x$

$$= \frac{1}{10}(10x^4 - 41x^3 + x^2 + 12x)$$

$$= \frac{1}{10}x(10x^3 - 41x^2 + x + 12) \Rightarrow x = 0$$

possible rational zeros: ± 1, ± 2, ± 3, ± 4, ± 6, ± 12, $\pm\frac{1}{2}$, $\pm\frac{3}{2}$, $\pm\frac{1}{5}$, $\pm\frac{2}{5}$, $\pm\frac{3}{5}$, $\pm\frac{4}{5}$,

$\pm\frac{6}{5}$, $\pm\frac{12}{5}$, $\pm\frac{1}{10}$, $\pm\frac{3}{10}$

$$\begin{array}{r} 10 \quad -41 \quad 1 \quad 12 \\ 40 \quad -4 \quad -12 \\ \hline 4\,|\,10 \quad -1 \quad -3 \quad 0 \end{array} \quad \Rightarrow \quad x = 4$$

$10x^2 - x - 3 = 0$

$$x = \frac{1 \pm \sqrt{1 - 4(-30)}}{20} = \frac{1 \pm \sqrt{121}}{20} = \frac{1 \pm 11}{20}$$

$$x = -\frac{1}{2}, \frac{3}{5}$$

zeros: $0, \ 4, \ -\dfrac{1}{2}, \ \dfrac{3}{5}$ or $0, \ 4, \ -0.5, \ 0.6$

46. $P(x) = x^4 + 9x^3 + 23x^2 + 8x - 16$ possible rational zeros: $\pm 1, \ \pm 2, \ \pm 4, \ \pm 8, \ \pm 16$

$$\begin{array}{r} 1 \quad 9 \quad 23 \quad 8 \quad -16 \\ -4 \quad -20 \quad -12 \quad 16 \\ \hline -4\,|\,1 \quad 5 \quad 3 \quad -4 \quad 0 \\ -4 \quad -4 \quad 4 \\ \hline -4\,|\,1 \quad 1 \quad -1 \quad 0 \end{array}$$

$x^2 + x - 1 = 0$

$$x = \frac{-1 \pm \sqrt{1 + 4}}{2} = \frac{-1 \pm \sqrt{5}}{2}$$

zeros: -4 (multiplicity 2), $-\dfrac{1}{2} \pm \dfrac{\sqrt{5}}{2}$

48. $P(x) = 4x^5 - 18x^4 + 24x^3 - 7x^2 - 4x + 4$

possible rational zeros: $\pm 1, \ \pm 2, \ \pm 4, \ \pm\dfrac{1}{2}, \ \pm\dfrac{1}{4}$

$$\begin{array}{r} 4 \quad -18 \quad 24 \quad -7 \quad -4 \quad 4 \\ 8 \quad -20 \quad 8 \quad 2 \quad -4 \\ \hline 2\,|\,4 \quad -10 \quad 4 \quad 1 \quad -2 \quad 0 \\ 8 \quad -4 \quad 0 \quad 2 \\ \hline 2\,|\,4 \quad -2 \quad 0 \quad 1 \quad 0 \\ -2 \quad 2 \quad -1 \\ \hline -\frac{1}{2}\,|\,4 \quad -4 \quad 2 \quad 0 \end{array}$$

$4x^2 - 4x + 2 = 0$
$2x^2 - 2x + 1 = 0$

$$x = \frac{2 \pm \sqrt{4 - 8}}{4} = \frac{2 \pm 2i}{4} = \frac{1}{2} \pm \frac{1}{2}i$$

zeros: $-\dfrac{1}{2}, \ 2$ (multiplicity 2), $\dfrac{1}{2} \pm \dfrac{1}{2}i$

50. $P(x) = 6x^3 - 11x^2 - 4x + 4$

possible rational zeros: $\pm 1, \ \pm 2, \ \pm 4, \ \pm\dfrac{1}{2}, \ \pm\dfrac{1}{3}, \ \pm\dfrac{2}{3}, \ \pm\dfrac{4}{3}, \ \pm\dfrac{1}{6}$

$$\begin{array}{r} 6 \quad -11 \quad -4 \quad 4 \\ 12 \quad 2 \quad -4 \\ \hline 2\,|\,6 \quad 1 \quad -2 \quad 0 \end{array} \quad \Rightarrow \quad (x - 2) \text{ is a factor}$$

$6x^2 + x - 2 = 0$
$(3x + 2)(2x - 1) = 0$
$P(x) = (x - 2)(3x + 2)(2x - 1)$

52. $P(x) = x^3 - 4x^2 + 2x + 4$ possible rational zeros: ± 1, ± 2, ± 4

$$
\begin{array}{r|rrrr}
 & 1 & -4 & 2 & 4 \\
 & & 2 & -4 & -4 \\
\hline
2 & 1 & -2 & -2 & 0
\end{array}
\quad \Rightarrow \quad (x - 2) \text{ is a factor}
$$

$x^2 - 2x - 2 = 0$

$$x = \frac{2 \pm \sqrt{4 + 8}}{2} = \frac{2 \pm 2\sqrt{3}}{2} = 1 \pm \sqrt{3}$$

$P(x) = (x - 2)(x - (1 + \sqrt{3}))(x - (1 - \sqrt{3}))$

54. $P(x) = 4x^4 + 16x^3 + 7x^2 - 18x - 9$

possible rational zeros: ± 1, ± 3, ± 9, $\pm \frac{1}{4}$, $\pm \frac{3}{4}$, $\pm \frac{9}{4}$, $\pm \frac{1}{2}$, $\pm \frac{3}{2}$, $\pm \frac{9}{2}$

$$
\begin{array}{r|rrrrr}
 & 4 & 16 & 7 & -18 & -9 \\
 & & -12 & -12 & 15 & 9 \\
\hline
-3 & 4 & 4 & -5 & -3 & 0
\end{array}
\quad \Rightarrow \quad (x + 3) \text{ is a factor}
$$

$$
\begin{array}{r|rrrr}
 & 4 & 8 & 3 \\
\hline
1 & 4 & 8 & 3 & 0
\end{array}
\quad \Rightarrow \quad (x - 1) \text{ is a factor}
$$

$4x^2 + 8x + 3 = 0$

$(2x + 1)(2x + 3) = 0$

$P(x) = (x + 3)(x - 1)(2x + 1)(2x + 3)$

56. $x^2 > 2x + 1$

$x^2 - 2x - 1 > 0$; $x = \dfrac{-(-2) \pm \sqrt{(-2)^2 - 4(1)(-1)}}{2(1)} = 1 \pm \sqrt{2}$

$(x - (1 + \sqrt{2}))(x - (1 - \sqrt{2})) > 0$

$P(-1) = 2$ $P(0) = -1$ $P(3) = 2$

$x < 1 - \sqrt{2}$ or $x > 1 + \sqrt{2}$; $(-\infty, 1 - \sqrt{2}) \cup (1 + \sqrt{2}, \infty)$

58. $9x + 9 \leq x^3 + x^2$
$x^3 + x^2 - 9x - 9 \geq 0$
$(x - 3)(x + 1)(x + 3) \geq 0$

$P(-4) = -21$, $P(-2) = 5$, $P(2) = -15$, $P(4) = 35$
$-3 \leq x \leq -1$ or $x \geq 3$; $[-3, -1] \cup [3, \infty)$

60. $5x^3 - 3x^2 < 10x - 6$

$5x^3 - 3x^2 - 10x + 6 < 0$; Possible rational zeros: ± 1, $\pm \frac{1}{5}$, ± 2, $\pm \frac{2}{5}$, ± 3, $\pm \frac{3}{5}$, ± 6, $\pm \frac{6}{5}$

$\frac{3}{5}$ is a zero. From synthetic division,

$$\left(x - \frac{3}{5}\right)(5x^2 - 10) < 0$$

$$\left(x - \frac{3}{5}\right)(x^2 - 2) < 0$$

$\left(x - \frac{3}{5}\right)(x - \sqrt{2})(x + \sqrt{2}) < 0$

$P(-2) = -26$, $P(0) = 6$, $P(1) = -2$, $P(2) = 20$

$x < -\sqrt{2}$ or $\frac{3}{5} < x < \sqrt{2}$; $(-\infty, -\sqrt{2}) \cup \left(\frac{3}{5}, \sqrt{2}\right)$

62. $[x - (5 + 2i)][x - (5 - 2i)] = x^2 - (5 - 2i)x - (5 + 2i)x + (5 + 2i)(5 - 2i)$
$$= x^2 - 5x + 2ix - 5x - 2ix + 25 - 4i^2$$
$$= x^2 - 10x + 29$$

64. $(x - bi)(x + bi) = x^2 - b^2i^2 = x^2 + b^2$

66. $P(x) = x^3 + 2x^2 - 3x - 10$; $-2 + i$ is one zero $\Rightarrow$ $-2 - i$ is also a zero.

```
           1      2        -3        -10
                -2 + i   -1 - 2i      10
   -2 + i │ 1   0 + i    -4 - 2i       0

                -2 - i    4 + 2i
   -2 - i │ 1    -2         0      ⇒   x - 2 = 0   or   x = 2
```

zeros: $-2 + i$, $-2 - i$, 2

68. $P(x) = x^3 - 5x^2 + 4x - 20$; $2i$ is one zero $\Rightarrow$ $-2i$ is also a zero.

```
         1    -5         4          -20
            0 + 2i    -4 - 10i       20
    2i │ 1  -5 + 2i    0 - 10i        0

            0 - 2i     0 + 10i
   -2i │ 1    -5          0       ⇒   x - 5 = 0   or   x = 5
```

zeros: $-2i$, $2i$, 5

70. $P(x) = x^4 - 6x^3 + 19x^2 - 42x + 10$; $1 - 3i$ is one zero $\Rightarrow$ $1 + 3i$ is also a zero.

```
          1     -6          19         -42         10
               1 - 3i    -14 + 12i    41 - 3i     -10
  1 - 3i │ 1   -5 - 3i    5 + 12i     -1 - 3i       0

               1 + 3i    -4 - 12i     1 + 3i
  1 + 3i │ 1    -4           1           0
```

$x^2 - 4x + 1 = 0$
$$x = \frac{4 \pm \sqrt{16 - 4}}{2} = \frac{4 \pm 2\sqrt{3}}{2} = 2 \pm \sqrt{3}$$

zeros: $1 - 3i$, $1 + 3i$, $2 + \sqrt{3}$, $2 - \sqrt{3}$

72.
$$\frac{7}{2x^3 - x^2 - 8x + 4} \leq 0$$

$$\frac{7}{(x - 2)(x + 2)(2x - 1)} \leq 0$$

```
                  -2         ½          2
        - - - - +  + + + + +  - - - - - -  + + + + +
    ─────────○───────────○───────────○──────────────▶ x
   test number  -3       0        1         3
   value        -1/5     7/4     -8/3      0.28
```

$x < -2$ or $\dfrac{1}{2} < x < 2$

$(-\infty, -2) \cup \left(\dfrac{1}{2}, 2\right)$

74.
$$\frac{x^2 + 4x - 21}{x^3 + 7x^2 + 7x - 15} \geq 0$$
$$\frac{(x - 3)(x + 7)}{(x + 5)(x + 3)(x - 1)} \geq 0$$

test number	-8	-6	-4	0	2	4
value	-0.08	0.42857	-4.2	1.4	-0.257	0.058

$-7 \leq x < -5$ or $-3 < x < 1$ or $x \geq 3$
$[-7, -5) \cup (-3, 1) \cup [3, \infty)$

76. $P(x) = 2x^3 - 9x^2 - 2x + 30$. From the graph there are three real zeros, one between -2 and -1, one between 2 and 3 and one between 3 and 4. $\frac{5}{2}$ is a possible rational zero between 2 and 3 and $P\left(\frac{5}{2}\right) = 0 \Rightarrow \frac{5}{2}$ is a zero. Synthetic division by $\frac{5}{2}$ gives $P(x) = \left(x - \frac{5}{2}\right)(2x^2 - 4x - 12)$.

$2x^2 - 4x - 12$ is a quadratic with zeros of $1 \pm \sqrt{7}$.
zeros: $\frac{5}{2}$, $1 \pm \sqrt{7}$

78. $P(x) = 6x^4 + 35x^3 + 2x^2 - 233x - 360$. From the graph there are two real zeros, one between -4 and -5 and one between 2 and 3. From the list of possible rational zeros, $-\frac{9}{2}$ and $\frac{8}{3}$ are in these intervals. $P\left(-\frac{9}{2}\right) = 0$ and $P\left(\frac{8}{3}\right) = 0$, $-\frac{9}{2}$ and $\frac{8}{3}$ are zeros. Synthetic division by these zeros gives the factorization $P(x) = \left(x - \frac{8}{3}\right)\left(x + \frac{9}{2}\right)(6x^2 + 24x + 30)$. Zeros of the quadratic are $-2 \pm i$.
zeros: $\frac{8}{3}$, $-\frac{9}{2}$, $-2 \pm i$

80. $P(x) = x^5 - 6x^4 + 6x^3 + 28x^2 - 72x + 48$. From the graph (after several zoom ins), 2 appears to be a zero as well as another root between 2 and 3, and a third between -2 and -3.
$P(2) = 0$, 2 is a zero. Synthethic division by 2 gives
$P(x) = (x - 2)(x^4 - 4x^3 - 2x^2 + 24x - 24)$; a second time gives
$P(x) = (x - 2)(x - 2)(x^3 - 2x^2 - 6x + 12)$ and a third yields
$P(x) = (x - 2)(x - 2)(x - 2)(x^2 - 6)$ from which
zeros: 2(triple zero), $\pm\sqrt{6}$.

82. (A) $x^3 - 8 = 0$ is degree 3 $\Rightarrow$ there are 3 cube roots of 8.
(B) $x^3 - 8 = (x - 2)(x^2 + 2x + 4) = 0$.

Solving $x^2 + 2x + 4 = 0$ with the quadratic formula gives $-1 \pm i\sqrt{3}$ as the other two cube roots of 8.

84. If P is a polynomial function with real coefficients of degree n, with n even, then the maximum number of times the graph of $y = P(x)$ can cross the x axis is n with all roots real and the minimum number is 0 with all roots complex.

86. Let $H(x) = P(x) - Q(x)$, then deg $H \leq n$ which means H can have at most n zeros. But since $P(x) = Q(x)$ for more than n values of x, $H(x) = 0$ for more than n values ($\Rightarrow$ H has more than n zeros). This is a contradiction unless $H(x) = 0 \Rightarrow P(x) - Q(x) = 0$ or $P(x) = Q(x)$.

88. Let x = number of feet each dimension is increased. Then
$$(1 + x)(1 + x)(2 + x) = 6(1)(1)(2)$$
$$x^3 + 4x^2 + 5x + 2 = 12$$
$$x^3 + 4x^2 + 5x - 10 = 0$$
$$(x - 1)(x^2 + 5x + 10) = 0 \qquad x^2 + 5x + 10 \text{ has no real solutions.}$$
Increase each dimension by 1 foot.

90. Let x = the dimension of the side of the square to be cut out. Then
$$(10 - 2x)(8 - 2x)(x) = 48 \qquad x = 4 \text{ since } 8 - 2x = 0$$
$$4x^3 - 36x^2 + 80x = 48$$
$$4x^3 - 36x^2 + 80x - 48 = 0$$
$$x^3 - 9x^2 + 20x - 12 = 0$$
$$(x - 1)(x - 2)(x - 6) = 0 \Rightarrow x = 1, 2, 6 \text{ (delete)}$$
The squares can be 1 ft by 1 ft or 2 ft by 2 ft.

Exercise 4-3

Note: For the synthetic division tables in this section, enter the coefficients of $P(x) \to L_1$ and use the SYNDIV program.

2. There is at least one x-intercept in each of the intervals $(-8, -2)$, $(2, 4)$, and $(4, 9)$.

4. There is at least one x-intercept in each of the intervals $(-1, 0)$, $(0, 2)$, and $(2, 5)$.

6. $P(x) = x^3 - 12x^2 + 44x - 49$; $\{1, -12, 44, -49\} \to L_1$, program SYNDIV:

	1	-12	44	-49
2	1	-10	24	-1
3	1	-9	17	2
4	1	-8	12	-1
6	1	-6	8	-1
7	1	-5	9	14

The last column, $P(x)$, changes sign for the following intervals: $(2, 3)$, $(3, 4)$ and $(6,7)$, so there are zeros in each of these intervals.

8. $P(x) = x^3 + x^2 - 4x - 3$

	1	1	-4	-3
-3	1	-2	2	-9
-2	1	-1	-2	1
-1	1	0	-4	1
0	1	1	-4	-3
1	1	2	-2	-5
2	1	3	2	1
3	1	4	8	21

The last column, $P(x)$, changes signs, so there are zeros in each of the intervals: $(-3, -2)$, $(-1, 0)$, and $(1, 2)$.

10. $P(x) = x^3 - 4x^2 + 4$

		1	-4	0	4
	-2	1	-6	12	-20
Lower bound:	-1	1	-5	5	-1
	0	1	-4	0	4
	1	1	-3	-3	1
	2	1	-2	-4	-4
	3	1	-1	-3	-5
Upper bound:	4	1	0	0	4

12. $P(x) = x^4 - 4x^3 + 6x^2 - 4x - 7$

		1	-4	6	-4	-7
	-2	1	-6	18	-40	73
Lower bound:	-1	1	-5	11	-15	8
	0	1	-4	6	-4	-7
	1	1	-3	3	-1	-8
	2	1	-2	2	0	-7
	3	1	-1	3	5	8
Upper bound:	4	1	0	6	20	73

14. $P(x) = x^5 - 3x^4 + 3x^2 + 2x - 1$

		1	-3	0	3	2	-1
Lower bound:	-1	1	-4	4	-1	3	-4
	0	1	-3	0	3	2	-1
	1	1	-2	-2	1	3	2
	2	1	-1	-2	-1	0	-1
Upper bound:	3	1	0	0	3	11	32

16. $P(x) = x^3 + x^2 - 4x - 1$

(A)

		1	1	-4	-1
LB:	-3	1	-2	2	-7
	-2	1	-1	-2	3
	-1	1	0	-4	3
	0	1	1	-4	-1
	1	1	2	-2	-3
UB:	2	1	3	2	3

Real zeros in $(-3, -2)$, $(-1, 0)$ and $(1, 2)$.

(B)
```
RIGHT BOUND: 2
            (1 2)
          (1.5 2)
        (1.5 1.75)
      (1.625 1.75)
    (1.6875 1.75)
  (1.6875 1.71875)
```

Using the BISECT program,
5 additional intervals.
$x \approx 1.7$

18. $P(x) = x^3 - 3x^2 - x - 2$

(A)

		1	-3	-1	-2
	-2	1	-5	9	-20
LB:	-1	1	-4	3	-5
	0	1	-3	-1	-2
	1	1	-2	-3	-5
	2	1	-1	-3	-8
	3	1	0	-1	-5
UB:	4	1	1	3	10

Real zeros in $(3, 4)$.

(B)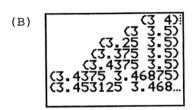

Using the BISECT program,
6 additional intervals.
$x \approx 3.5$

20. $P(x) = x^4 - x^3 - 9x^2 + 9x + 4$

(A)

		1	-1	-9	9	4
	-4	1	-5	11	-35	144
LB:	-3	1	-4	3	0	4
	-2	1	-3	-3	15	-26
	-1	1	-2	-7	16	-12
	0	1	-1	-9	9	4
	1	1	0	-9	0	4
	2	1	1	-7	-5	-6
	3	1	2	-3	0	4
UB:	4	1	3	3	21	88

Real zeros in $(-3, -2)$, $(-1, 0)$, $(1, 2)$, and $(2, 3)$.

(B)
```
        (2 3)
      (2.5 3)
     (2.75 3)
   (2.75 2.875)
  (2.8125 2.875)
 (2.84375 2.875)
(2.859375 2.875)
```

Using the BISECT program,
6 additional intervals.
$x \approx 2.9$

22. $P(x) = x^4 - 3x^3 - x^2 + 3x + 3$

(A)

		1	-3	-1	3	3
LB:	-1	1	-4	3	0	3
	0	1	-3	-1	3	3
	1	1	-2	-3	0	3
	2	1	-1	-3	-3	-3
	3	1	0	-1	0	3
UB:	4	1	1	3	15	63

Real zeros in $(1, 2)$ and $(2, 3)$.

(B)
```
        (2.5 3)
       (2.75 3)
    (2.75 2.875)
   (2.8125 2.875)
  (2.84375 2.875)
 (2.84375 2.8593...)
(2.8515625 2.85...)
```

Using the BISECT program,
7 additional intervals.
$x \approx 2.9$

24. $P(x) = x^3 + 3x^2 + 4x + 5$

(A)

		1	3	4	5
LB:	-3	1	0	4	-7
	-2	1	1	2	1
	-1	1	2	2	3
	0	1	3	4	5
UB:	1	1	4	8	13

Real zeros in $(-3, -2)$.

(B) Use either the BISECT program or locate the zero on the graph of
$P(x)$: $x \approx -2.21$.

26. $P(x) = x^4 - x^3 - 8x^2 - 12x - 25$

(A)

		1	-1	-8	-12	-25
LB:	-3	1	-4	4	-24	47
	-2	1	-3	-2	-8	-9
	-1	1	-2	-6	-6	-19
	0	1	-1	-8	-12	-25
	1	1	0	-8	-20	-45
	2	1	1	-6	-24	-73
	3	1	2	-2	-18	-79
	4	1	3	4	4	-9
UB:	5	1	4	12	48	215

(B) Use either the BISECT program or locate the zeros on the graph of $P(x)$: $x \approx -2.29, 4.07$.

28. $P(x) = x^5 - x^4 - 2x^2 - 4x - 5$

(A)

		1	-1	0	-2	-4	-5
LB:	-1	1	-2	2	-4	0	-5
	0	1	-1	0	-2	-4	-5
	1	1	0	0	-2	-6	-11
	2	1	1	2	2	0	-5
UB:	3	1	2	6	16	44	127

(B) Use either the BISECT program or locate the zero on the graph of $P(x)$: $x \approx 2.12$.

30. $P(x) = x^5 - 2x^4 - 6x^2 - 9x + 10$

(A)

		1	-2	0	-6	-9	10
LB:	-2	1	-4	8	-22	35	-60
	-1	1	-3	3	-9	0	10
	0	1	-2	0	-6	-9	10
	1	1	-1	-1	-7	-16	-6
	2	1	0	0	-6	-21	-32
UB:	3	1	1	3	3	0	10

(B) Use either the BISECT program or locate the zeros on the graph of $P(x)$: $x \approx -1.35, 0.72, 2.92$.

32. $P(x) = x^5 - 2x^4 - 7x^3 + 8x^2 + 12x - 5$

(A)

	1	-2	-7	8	12	-5	
1	1	-1	-8	0	12	7	
2	1	0	-7	-6	0	-5	
3	1	1	-4	-4	0	-5	
4	1	2	1	12	60	235	4 is an upper bound
-1	1	-3	-4	12	0	-5	
-2	1	-4	1	6	0	-5	
-3	1	-5	8	-16	60	-185	-3 is a lower bound

4 and -3 are the smallest positive integer and largest negative integer that, by Theorem 2, are upper and lower bounds, respectively, for the real zeros of $P(x)$.

There are real zeros in $(-2, -1)$, $(0, 1)$, $(1, 2)$, and $(3, 4)$.

(B) Using bisection the largest real zero of $P(x)$ is 3.07 to two places.

34. $P(x) = x^5 - 9x^3 + 4x^2 + 12x - 15$

(A)

	1	0	-9	4	12	-15
1	1	1	-8	-4	8	-7
2	1	2	-5	-6	0	-15
3	1	3	0	4	24	57
-1	1	-1	-8	12	0	-15
-2	1	-2	-5	14	-16	17
-3	1	-3	0	4	0	-15
-4	1	-4	7	-24	108	-447

3 is an upper bound

-4 is a lower bound

3 and -4 are the smallest positive integer and largest negative integer that, by Theorem 2, are upper and lower bounds, respectively, for the real zeros of $P(x)$.

There are real zeros in $(-3, -2)$, $(-2, -1)$, and $(2, 3)$.

(B) Using bisection the largest real zero of $P(x)$, to two decimal places, is 2.55.

36. $P(x) = x^3 - 37x^2 + 70x - 20$

(A)

	1	-37	70	-20
10	1	-27	-200	-2020
20	1	-17	-270	-5420
30	1	-7	-140	-4220
40	1	3	190	7580
-10	1	-47	540	-5420

40 and -10 are the smallest positive integer multiple of 10 and largest negative integer multiple of 10 that, by Theorem 2, are upper and lower bounds, respectively, for the real zeros of $P(x)$.

(B) 0.35, 1.63, and 35.02 are the real zeros to two places.

38. $P(x) = x^4 - 12x^3 - 425x^2 + 7000$

(A)

	1	-12	-425	0	7,000
10	1	-2	-445	-4450	-37,500
20	1	8	-265	-5300	-99,000
30	1	18	115	3450	110,500
-10	1	-22	-205	2050	-13,500
-20	1	-32	215	-4300	93,000

30 is an upper bound

-20 is a lower bound

30 and -20 are the smallest positive integer multiple of 10 and largest negative integer multiple of 10 that, by Theorem 2, are upper and lower bounds, respectively, for the real zeros of $P(x)$.

(B) -14.70, -4.46, 3.92, and 27.25 are the real zeros of $P(x)$ to two decimal places.

40. $P(x) = x^4 - 5x^3 - 50x^2 - 500x + 7000$

(A)

	1	-5	-50	-500	7,000
10	1	5	0	-500	2,000
20	1	15	250	4500	97,000
-10	1	-15	100	-1500	22,000

20 is an upper bound

-10 is a lower bound

20 and -10 are the smallest positive integer multiple of 10 and largest negative integer multiple of 10 that, by Theorem 2, are upper and lower bounds, respectively, for the real zeros of $P(x)$.

(B) There are no real zeros.

42. $P(x) = 9x^4 + 120x^3 - 3083x^2 - 25,674x - 48,400$

(A)

	9	120	-3083	-25,674	-48,400	
10	9	210	-983	-35,504	-403,440	
20	9	300	2917	32,666	604,920	20 is an upper bound
-10	9	30	-3383	8,156	-129,960	
-20	9	-60	-1883	11,986	-288,120	
-30	9	-150	1417	-68,184	1,997,120	-30 is a lower bound

20 and -30 are the smallest positive integer multiple of 10 and largest negative integer multiple of 10 that, by Theorem 2, are upper and lower bounds, respectively, for the real zeros of $P(x)$.

(B) -23.22, -3.67 (double zero), and 17.22 are the real zeros of $P(x)$ to two decimal places.

44. $P(x) = 0.1x^5 + 0.7x^4 - 18.775x^3 - 340x^2 - 1645x - 2450$

(A)

	0.1	0.7	-18.775	-340	-1645	-2,450	
10	0.1	1.7	-1.775	-357.75	-5222.5	-54,675	
20	0.1	2.7	35.225	364.5	5645	110,450	20 is an upper bound
-10	0.1	-0.3	-15.775	-182.25	177.5	-4,225	
-20	0.1	-1.3	7.225	-484.5	8045	-163,350	-20 is a lower bound

20 and -20 are the smallest positive integer multiple of 10 and largest negative integer multiple of 10 that, by Theorem 2, are upper and lower bounds, respectively, for the real zeros of $P(x)$.

(B) -3.50 (double zero) and 17.69 are the real zeros of $P(x)$ to two decimal places.

46. $y = x^2$; all points 1 unit away from (2, 1).

$$d = \sqrt{(x - x_1)^2 + (y - y_1)^2}$$
$$1 = \sqrt{(x - 2)^2 + (y - 1)^2}$$
$$1 = (x - 2)^2 + (x^2 - 1)^2$$
$$1 = x^2 - 4x + 4 + x^4 - 2x^2 + 1$$
$$0 = x^4 - x^2 - 4x + 4$$

Graph $y_1 = x^4 - x^2 - 4x + 4$. The zeros are at $x = 1$ and $x = 1.315$. The points are (1, 1) and (1.3, 1.7).

48. $\ell = \dfrac{40 - 3x}{2}$, $w = 20 - 2x$, $h = x$

$V = \ell wh$

$V(x) = (20 - 1.5x)(20 - 2x)x$

$x(400 - 40x - 30x + 3x^2) = 500$

$3x^3 - 70x^2 + 400x - 500 = 0$

Graph $y_1 = 3x^3 - 70x^2 + 400x - 500$. The zeros are at $x \approx 1.741$ and $x \approx 6.234$. The values of x that would result in a box with a volume of 50 cubic inches are 1.7 inches and 6.2 inches.

50. $V = x^2y = 2$

$$y = \frac{2}{x^2}$$

tape = 20.5 ft - 6 inches = 20.5 ft - .5 ft = 20 ft.
length of tape = $(4x) + (2x + 2y) + (2x + 2y) = 20$

$$8x + 4y = 20$$

$$8x + 4\left(\frac{2}{x^2}\right) = 20$$

$$8x^3 + 8 = 20x^2$$

$$8x^3 - 20x^2 + 8 = 0$$

Graph $y_1 = 8x^3 - 20x^2 + 8$. The zeros are at $x \approx -0.57$ (discard), 0.758 (0.8), and 2.313 (2.3).

at $x = 0.758$, $y = \dfrac{2}{(0.758)^2} = 3.481 \approx 3.5$

at $x = 2.313$, $y = \dfrac{2}{(2.313)^2} = 0.374 \approx 0.4$

The dimensions are 0.8 × 0.8 × 3.5 feet or 2.3 × 2.3 × 0.4 feet.

Exercise 4-4

2. $k(x) = \dfrac{4 - 2x}{x + 2}$ **4.** $f(x) = \dfrac{2x - 4}{x + 2}$

6. $g(x) = \dfrac{3x + 6}{x - 1}$

Domain: all x except 1 or $(-\infty, 1) \cup (1, \infty)$

$3x + 6 = 0$

$\quad 3x = -6$

$\quad\quad x = -2$, x intercept

8. $k(x) = \dfrac{x^2 - 36}{x^2 - 25}$

Domain: all x except ± 5 or $(-\infty, -5) \cup (-5, 5) \cup (5, \infty)$

$x^2 - 36 = 0$

$\quad\; x^2 = 36$

$\quad\; x = \pm 6$, x intercepts

10. $s(x) = \dfrac{x^2 + x - 12}{x^2 + x - 6} = \dfrac{(x + 4)(x - 3)}{(x + 3)(x - 2)}$

Domain: all x except -3 and 2 or $(-\infty, -3) \cup (-3, 2) \cup (2, \infty)$

$(x + 4)(x - 3) = 0$

x intercepts: -4, 3

12. $G(x) = \dfrac{x^2}{x^2 + 16}$

Domain: all real numbers

$(x^2 + 16 = 0 \implies x^2 = -16$ which never happens$)$

x intercept: 0

14. $h(x) = \dfrac{3x}{x + 5}$

vertical asymptote: $d(x) = 0$ at $x = -5$

horizontal asymptote: $y = 3$, $n(x)$ and $d(x)$ have same degree

$(y = \dfrac{3}{1} = 3)$

16. $r(x) = \dfrac{5x^2 - 7x}{2x^2 - 50}$

vertical asymptote: $2x^2 - 50 = 0$

$\quad\quad\quad\quad\quad\quad 2x^2 = 50$

$\quad\quad\quad\quad\quad\quad\; x^2 = 25$

$\quad\quad\quad\quad\quad\quad\quad x = \pm 5$

horizontal asymptote: $y = \dfrac{5}{2}$ since $n(x)$ and $d(x)$ have same degree

18. $q(x) = \dfrac{5x^4}{2x^2 + 3x - 2} = \dfrac{5x^4}{(2x - 1)(x + 2)}$

vertical asymptote: $x = \dfrac{1}{2}$ and $x = -2$

deg $n(x) = 4 >$ deg $d(x) \implies$ no horizontal asymptote

20. $g(x) = \dfrac{3x}{x^4 + 2x^2 + 1}$

no vertical asymptote since $x^4 + 2x^2 + 1 > 0$ for all x

horizontal asymptote: $y = 0$, deg $n(x) <$ deg $d(x)$

22. $g(x) = \dfrac{1}{x + 3} = \dfrac{n(x)}{d(x)}$

$n(x)$ has no zeros: no x intercept

$g(0) = \dfrac{1}{3}$: y intercept

$d(x) = x + 3 = 0$
   $x = -3$: vertical asymptote

deg $n(x)$ < deg $d(x)$ $\Rightarrow$ horizontal asymptote: x axis

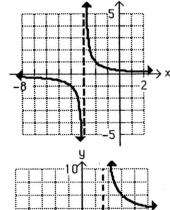

24. $f(x) = \dfrac{3x}{x - 3} = \dfrac{n(x)}{d(x)}$

$n(x) = 3x = 0$
   $x = 0$: x intercept

$f(0) = \dfrac{3(0)}{0 - 3} = 0$: y intercept

$d(x) = x - 3 = 0$
   $x = 3$: vertical asymptote

deg $n(x)$ = deg $d(x)$ $\Rightarrow$ horizontal asymptote: $y = \dfrac{a_1}{b_1} = 3$

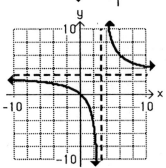

26. $p(x) = \dfrac{3x}{4x + 4} = \dfrac{n(x)}{d(x)}$

$n(x) = 3x = 0$
   $x = 0$: x intercept

$f(0) = \dfrac{3(0)}{4(0) + 4} = 0$: y intercept

$d(x) = 4x + 4 = 0$
       $x = -1$: vertical asymptote

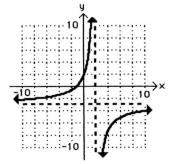

deg $n(x)$ = deg $d(x)$: $y = \dfrac{a_1}{b_1} = \dfrac{3}{4}$ horizontal asymptote

28. $f(x) = \dfrac{3x + 3}{2 - x} = \dfrac{n(x)}{d(x)}$

$n(x) = 3x + 3 = 0$
       $x = -1$: x intercept

$f(0) = 1.5$: y intercept

$d(x) = 2 - x = 0$
       $x = 2$: vertical asymptote

deg $n(x)$ = deg $d(x)$: horizontal asymptote: $y = -3$

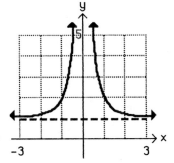

30. $f(x) = \dfrac{x^2 + 1}{x^2} = \dfrac{n(x)}{d(x)}$

$n(x) = x^2 + 1 = 0$ has no real solutions;
no x intercepts

$f(0) = 1/0$ is undefined; no y intercept

$d(x) = x^2 = 0$
       $x = 0$: vertical asymptote

deg $n(x)$ = deg $d(x)$ $\Rightarrow$ $y = 1$: horizontal asymptote

32. $g(x) = \dfrac{6}{x^2 - x - 6} = \dfrac{n(x)}{d(x)} = \dfrac{6}{(x - 3)(x + 2)}$

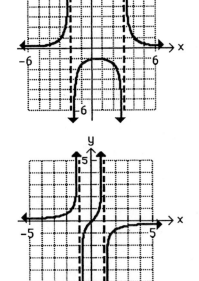

$n(x) = 6 = 0$ has no real solutions $\Rightarrow$ no x intercepts

$f(0) = -1$: y intercept

$d(x) = 0$ for $x = 3$, $x = -2$: vertical asymptotes

deg $n(x) <$ deg $d(x) \Rightarrow y = 0$ (x-axis): vertical asymptote

34. $p(x) = \dfrac{x}{1 - x^2} = \dfrac{n(x)}{d(x)} = \dfrac{x}{(1 - x)(1 + x)}$

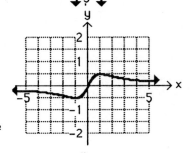

$n(x) = x = 0$: x intercept

$p(0) = 0$: y intercept

$d(x) = 0$ for $x = \pm 1$: vertical asymptotes

deg $n(x) <$ deg $d(x) \Rightarrow y = 0$ (x axis): horizontal asymptote

36. $f(x) = \dfrac{x}{x^2 + 1} = \dfrac{n(x)}{d(x)}$

$n(x) = x = 0$: x intercept

$f(0) = 0$: y intercept

$d(x) = 0$ has no real solutions $\Rightarrow$ no vertical asymptotes

deg $n(x) <$ deg $d(x) \Rightarrow y = 0$: horizontal asymptote

38. $f(x) = \dfrac{7x^2}{(2x - 3)^2} = \dfrac{7x^2}{4x^2 - 12x + 9} = \dfrac{n(x)}{d(x)}$

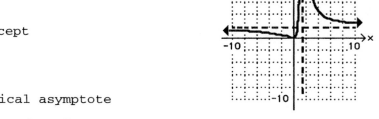

$n(x) = 7x^2 = 0$

$\qquad x = 0$: x intercept

$f(0) = 0$: y intercept

$d(x) = (2x - 3)^2 = 0$

$\qquad\qquad x = \dfrac{3}{2}$: vertical asymptote

deg $n(x) =$ deg $d(x) \Rightarrow y = \dfrac{a_2}{b_2} = \dfrac{7}{4}$: horizontal asymptote

40. $f(x) = \dfrac{x^2 + 6x + 8}{x^2 - x - 2} = \dfrac{(x + 2)(x + 4)}{(x - 2)(x + 1)} = \dfrac{n(x)}{d(x)}$

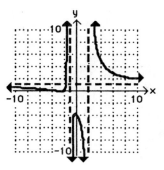

$n(x) = 0 \Rightarrow x = -2, -4$: x intercepts

$f(0) = -4$: y intercept

$d(x) = 0 \Rightarrow x = 2$, $x = -1$: vertical asymptotes

deg $n(x) =$ deg $d(x) \Rightarrow y = 1$: horizontal asymptote

42. The maximum number of vertical asymptotes is 2, as in $f(x) = \dfrac{x^2}{x^2 - 1}$, and the minimum number is 0, as in $f(x) = \dfrac{x^2}{x^2 + 1}$.

44. $g(x) = \dfrac{3x^2}{x + 2} = \dfrac{n(x)}{d(x)}$

$d(x) = x + 2 = 0$
  $x = -2$: vertical asymptote

$$
\begin{array}{r}
3x - 6 \\
x + 2 \overline{\smash{\big)}\ 3x^2} \\
\underline{3x^2 + 6x} \\
-6x \\
\underline{-6x - 12} \\
12
\end{array}
$$

$\Rightarrow g(x) = 3x - 6 + \dfrac{12}{x + 2}$
from which
   $y = 3x - 6$ is an oblique asymptote

46. $q(x) = \dfrac{x^5}{x^3 - 8} = \dfrac{n(x)}{d(x)}$

$d(x) = x^3 - 8 = 0$
      $x = 2$: vertical asymptote

deg $n(x) >$ deg $d(x) \Rightarrow$ no horizontal asymptotes
deg $n(x) >$ deg $d(x) + 1 \Rightarrow$ no oblique asymptotes

48. $s(x) = \dfrac{-3x^2 + 5x + 9}{x} = \dfrac{n(x)}{d(x)}$

$d(x) = x = 0$: vertical asymptote

$\dfrac{-3x^2 + 5x + 9}{x} = -3x + 5 + \dfrac{9}{x}$ from which
      $y = -3x + 5$: oblique asymptote

50. $f(x) = \dfrac{2x}{\sqrt{x^2 - 1}} \to 2$ as $x \to \infty$

$f(x) = \dfrac{2x}{\sqrt{x^2 - 1}} \to -2$ as $x \to -\infty$

$y = \pm 2$ are horizontal asymptotes

52. $f(x) = \dfrac{3\sqrt{x^2 + 1}}{x - 1} \to 3$ as $x \to \infty$

$f(x) = \dfrac{3\sqrt{x^2 + 1}}{x - 1} \to -3$ as $x \to -\infty$

$y = \pm 3$ are horizontal asymptotes

54. $g(x) = \dfrac{x^2 - 1}{x} = \dfrac{n(x)}{d(x)}$

$n(x) = x^2 - 1 = 0$
      $x = \pm 1$: x intercepts

$g(0) = \dfrac{-1}{0}$ undefined: no y intercept

$d(x) = x = 0$: vertical asymptote

$g(x) = x - \dfrac{1}{x} \Rightarrow y = x$: oblique asymptote

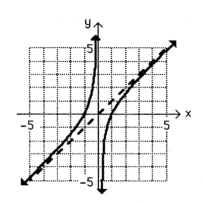

56. $h(x) = \dfrac{x^2 + x - 2}{2x - 4} = \dfrac{n(x)}{d(x)} = \dfrac{(x - 1)(x + 2)}{2(x - 2)}$

$n(x) = (x - 1)(x + 2) = 0$

$\qquad\qquad x = 1, -2$: x intercepts

$h(0) = \dfrac{1}{2}$: y intercept

$d(x) = 2(x - 2) = 0$

$\qquad\qquad x = 2$: vertical asymptote

$$2x - 4 \overline{\smash{\big)}\ x^2 + x - 2} \qquad \overset{\tfrac{1}{2}x + \tfrac{3}{2}}{}$$

$$\underline{x^2 - 2x}$$
$$\qquad 3x - 2$$
$$\qquad \underline{3x - 6}$$
$$\qquad\qquad 4$$

$\Rightarrow h(x) = \dfrac{1}{2}x + \dfrac{3}{2} + \dfrac{4}{2x - 4}$

from which

$y = \dfrac{1}{2}x + \dfrac{3}{2}$: oblique asymptote

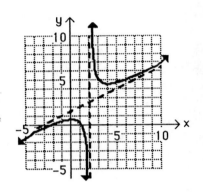

58. $G(x) = \dfrac{x^4 + 1}{x^3} = \dfrac{n(x)}{d(x)}$

$n(x) = x^4 + 1 = 0$ has no real solutions $\Rightarrow$ no x intercepts

$G(0) = \dfrac{1}{0}$ undefined $\Rightarrow$ no y intercepts

$d(x) = x^3 = 0$

$\qquad x = 0$ vertical asymptote

$G(x) = x + \dfrac{1}{x^3}$ from which $y = x$: oblique asymptote

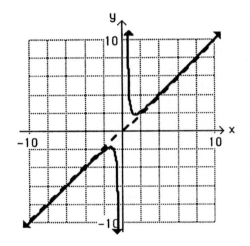

60. $f(x) = \dfrac{x^5}{x^2 + 1}$

$$x^2 + 1 \overline{\smash{\big)}\ x^5} \qquad \overset{x^3 - x}{}$$
$$\underline{x^5 + x^3}$$
$$\qquad -x^3$$
$$\qquad \underline{-x^3 - x}$$
$$\qquad\qquad +x$$

$f(x) = p(x) + \dfrac{q(x)}{d(x)}$

$f(x) = \dfrac{x^5}{x^2 + 1} = x^3 - x + \dfrac{x}{x^2 + 1} \Rightarrow p(x) = x^3 - x$

As $x \to \infty$, both $f(x)$ and $p(x) \to \infty$. As $x \to -\infty$, both $f(x)$ and $p(x) \to -\infty$. They have the same end behavior. $[f(x) - p(x)] \to 0$ as $x \to \pm\infty$

62. $f(x) = \dfrac{x^5}{x^3 - 1}$

$$x^3 - 1\overline{\smash{\big)}\,x^5} \quad\begin{array}{r} x^2 \\ \hline \end{array}$$

$$\underline{x^5 - x^2}$$
$$x^2$$

$f(x) = p(x) + \dfrac{q(x)}{d(x)}$

$f(x) = \dfrac{x^5}{x^2 + 1} = x^2 + \dfrac{x^2}{x^3 - 1} \Rightarrow p(x) = x^2$

As $x \to \infty$, both $f(x)$ and $p(x) \to \infty$. As $x \to -\infty$, both $f(x)$ and $p(x) \to -\infty$.
They have the same end behavior. $[f(x) - p(x)] \to 0$ as $x \to \pm\infty$

64. $g(x) = \dfrac{x^2 - 1}{x + 1} = \dfrac{(x - 1)(x + 1)}{(x + 1)} = x - 1$ for $x \neq -1$

   Domain: $x \neq -1$ or $(-\infty, -1) \cup (-1, \infty)$

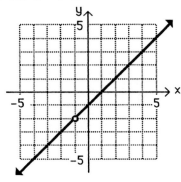

66. $s(x) = \dfrac{x - 1}{x^2 - 1} = \dfrac{x - 1}{(x - 1)(x + 1)} = \dfrac{1}{x + 1}$, $x \neq \pm 1$

   Domain: $x \neq \pm 1$ or $(-\infty, -1) \cup (-1, 1) \cup (1, \infty)$

   $s(x) = \dfrac{1}{x + 1} = \dfrac{n(x)}{d(x)}$

   $n(x) = 1 = 0$, no real roots $\Rightarrow$ no x intercepts
   $s(0) = 1$: y intercept
   $d(x) = x + 1 = 0$
      $x = -1$ vertical asymptote

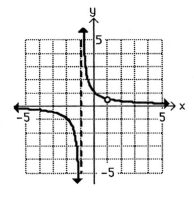

68. $S(w) = \dfrac{26 + 0.06w}{w}$, $w \geq 5$

   Domain: $S(w)$ is defined at all values given ($w \geq 5$).
   $y = 0.06$ is the horizontal asymptote.

$$S(w) = \dfrac{26}{w} + 0.06 \to 0.06 \text{ as } w \to \infty.$$

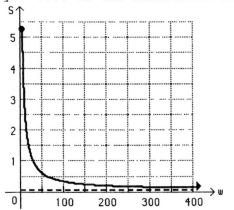

70. $f(x) = \dfrac{50(x + 1)}{x + 5} = \dfrac{50x + 50}{x + 5}$ $x \geq 0$

$f(0) = 10$

$y = 50$ is horizontal asymptote

$f(x) \to 50$ as $x \to \infty$

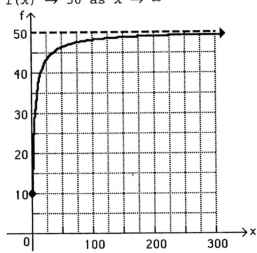

72. (A) $\overline{C}(x) = \dfrac{C(x)}{x} = \dfrac{\frac{1}{5}x^2 + 2x + 2000}{x}$

$\qquad = \dfrac{1}{5}x + 2 + \dfrac{2000}{x}$

$y = \dfrac{1}{5}x + 2$: oblique asymptote

(B) Use the minimum routine on your calculator.

The average cost per unit will be minimal at a production level of 100.

(C)

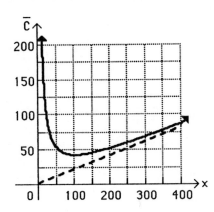

74.

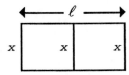

(A) area = $x \cdot \ell = 225$

$\qquad \ell = \dfrac{225}{x}$

$L = 3x + 2\ell = 3x + \dfrac{450}{x}$

$L(x) = 3x + \dfrac{450}{x} \Rightarrow L = 3x$: oblique asymptote

(B) Domain of $L(x)$: $x > 0$ or $(0, \infty)$, although one could argue about the width required for a dog.

(C) Graph $L(x)$; use the minimum routine to obtain the local minimum point:

(12.247, 73.485) $(5\sqrt{6}, 30\sqrt{6})$

$\ell = \dfrac{225}{x} = \dfrac{225}{12.247} \approx 18.372 \quad \left(\dfrac{15\sqrt{6}}{2}\right)$

Dimensions of $x = 12.247$ ft by $\ell = 18.372$ ft will require the least amount of fencing, 73.485 ft.

(D)

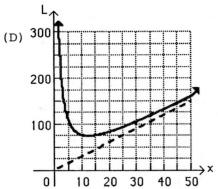

Exercise 4-5

2. $3x + 18 = A(x - 1) + B(x + 2)$

$\quad x = 1: 3 + 18 = A(0) + B(3)$

$\qquad\qquad\quad 21 = 3B \qquad\qquad \Rightarrow \boldsymbol{B = 7}$

$\quad x = -2: -6 + 18 = A(-3) + B(0)$

$\qquad\qquad\quad 12 = -3A \qquad\qquad \Rightarrow \boldsymbol{A = -4}$

4. $-32x - 13 = A(4x - 7) + B(2x + 8)$

$x = \dfrac{7}{4}:\quad -32\left(\dfrac{7}{4}\right) - 13 = A(0) + B\left(2\left(\dfrac{7}{4}\right) + 8\right)$

$-56 - 13 = B\left(\dfrac{7}{2} + 8\right)$

$-69 = \dfrac{23}{2}B$

$-138 = 23B \qquad\qquad \Rightarrow \boldsymbol{B = -6}$

$x = -4:\quad -32(-4) - 13 = A(-16 - 7) + B(0)$

$128 - 13 = -23A \qquad \Rightarrow \boldsymbol{A = -5}$

6. $\dfrac{x^2 + 5x - 12}{(x + 1)(x - 3)^2} = \dfrac{A}{x + 1} + \dfrac{B}{x - 3} + \dfrac{C}{(x - 3)^2}$

$x^2 + 5x - 12 = A(x - 3)^2 + B(x + 1)(x - 3) + C(x + 1)$

$x = 3:\ 9 + 15 - 12 = A(0) + B(0) + C(4)$

$12 = 4C \Rightarrow \boldsymbol{C = 3}$

$x = -1:\ 1 - 5 - 12 = A(-4)^2 + B(0) + C(0)$

$-16 = 16A \Rightarrow \boldsymbol{A = -1}$

$x = 0,\ A = -1,\ C = 3:\ -12 = -1(-3)^2 + B(1)(-3) + 3(1)$

$-12 = -9 - 3B + 3$

$-6 = -3B \Rightarrow \boldsymbol{B = 2}$

8. $\dfrac{3x^2 - 2x - 16}{x(x^2 + 4)} = \dfrac{A}{x} + \dfrac{Bx + C}{x^2 + 4}$

$3x^2 - 2x - 16 = A(x^2 + 4) + (Bx + C)x$

$= Ax^2 + 4A + Bx^2 + Cx$

x^2 terms: $3x^2 = Ax^2 + Bx^2 \Rightarrow 3 = A + B$ (1)

x terms: $-2x = Cx \Rightarrow \boldsymbol{C = -2}$

constants: $-16 = 4A \Rightarrow \boldsymbol{A = -4}$

$A = -4 \rightarrow$ (1): $3 = -4 + B \Rightarrow \boldsymbol{B = 7}$

10. $\dfrac{4x^2 - 2x + 13}{(x^2 - x + 4)^2} = \dfrac{Ax + B}{x^2 - x + 4} + \dfrac{Cx + D}{(x^2 - x + 4)^2}$

$4x^2 - 2x + 13 = (Ax + B)(x^2 - x + 4) + Cx + D$

$= Ax^3 - Ax^2 + 4Ax + Bx^2 - Bx + 4B + Cx + D$

x^3 terms: $0 = Ax^3 \Rightarrow \boldsymbol{A = 0}$

x^2 terms, $A = 0$: $4x^2 = 0x^2 + Bx^2 \Rightarrow \boldsymbol{B = 4}$

x terms, $A = 0,\ B = 4$: $-2x = 4Ax - Bx + Cx$

$-2 = -4 + C \Rightarrow \boldsymbol{C = 2}$

constants, $B = 4$: $13 = 4B + D$

$13 = 16 + D \Rightarrow \boldsymbol{D = -3}$

12. $\dfrac{4x - 43}{x^2 + 3x - 10} = \dfrac{A}{x + 5} + \dfrac{B}{x - 2}$

$4x - 43 = A(x - 2) + B(x + 5)$

$x = 2:\ 8 - 43 = A(0) + B(7)$

$-35 = 7B \qquad \Rightarrow \boldsymbol{B = -5}$

$x = -5:\ -20 - 43 = A(-7) + B(0)$

$-63 = -7A \Rightarrow \boldsymbol{A = 9} \qquad \dfrac{4x - 43}{x^2 + 3x - 10} = \dfrac{9}{x + 5} - \dfrac{5}{x - 2}$

14. $\dfrac{x - 27}{10x^2 - 13x - 3} = \dfrac{A}{5x + 1} + \dfrac{B}{2x - 3}$

$x - 27 = A(2x - 3) + B(5x + 1)$

$x = \dfrac{3}{2}:\quad \dfrac{3}{2} - 27 = A(0) + B\left(\dfrac{15}{2} + 1\right)$

$\qquad\qquad 3 - 54 = 17B \Rightarrow \boldsymbol{B = -3}$

$x = -\dfrac{1}{5}:\quad -\dfrac{1}{5} - 27 = A\left(-\dfrac{2}{5} - 3\right) + B(0)$

$\qquad\qquad -1 - 135 = -17A \Rightarrow \boldsymbol{A = 8}$
$\qquad\qquad\qquad \dfrac{x - 27}{10x^2 - 13x - 3} = \dfrac{8}{5x + 1} - \dfrac{3}{2x - 3}$

16. $\dfrac{7x - 8}{9x^3 - 12x^2 + 4x} = \dfrac{7x - 8}{x(9x^2 - 12x + 4)} = \dfrac{7x - 8}{x(3x - 2)^2}$

$\dfrac{7x - 8}{9x^3 - 12x^2 + 4x} = \dfrac{A}{x} + \dfrac{B}{3x - 2} + \dfrac{C}{(3x - 2)^2}$

$\qquad 7x - 8 = A(3x - 2)^2 + Bx(3x - 2) + Cx$

$x = 0:\quad -8 = A(4) + B(0) + C(0) \Rightarrow \boldsymbol{A = -2}$

$x = \dfrac{2}{3}:\quad \dfrac{14}{3} - 8 = A(0) + B(0) + C\left(\dfrac{2}{3}\right)$

$\qquad\qquad -\dfrac{10}{3} = \dfrac{2}{3}C \Rightarrow \boldsymbol{C = -5}$

$x = 1,\ A = -2,\ C = -5:\ 7 - 8 = -2(1)^2 + B(1) + (-5)(1)$

$\qquad\qquad\qquad -1 = -2 + B - 5 \Rightarrow \boldsymbol{B = 6}$

$\dfrac{7x - 8}{9x^3 - 12x^2 + 4x} = \dfrac{-2}{x} + \dfrac{6}{3x - 2} - \dfrac{5}{(3x - 2)^2}$

18. $\dfrac{9x^2 + 14}{x^3 + x^2 + 2x} = \dfrac{9x^2 + 14}{x(x^2 + x + 2)} = \dfrac{A}{X} + \dfrac{Bx + C}{x^2 + x + 2}$

$\qquad 9x^2 + 14 = A(x^2 + x + 2) + (Bx + C)x$

$\qquad 9x^2 + 14 = Ax^2 + Ax + 2A + Bx^2 + Cx$

x^2 terms: $9x^2 = Ax^2 + Bx^2 \Rightarrow 9 = A + B \qquad (1)$

x terms: $\quad 0x = Ax + Cx \Rightarrow 0 = A + C \qquad (2)$

constants: $14 = 2A \Rightarrow \boldsymbol{A = 7}$

$\qquad A = 7 \rightarrow (1): 9 = 7 + B \Rightarrow \boldsymbol{B = 2}$

$\qquad A = 7 \rightarrow (2): 0 = 7 + C \Rightarrow \boldsymbol{C = -7}$

$\dfrac{9x^2 + 14}{x^3 + x^2 + 2x} = \dfrac{7}{x} + \dfrac{2x - 7}{x^2 + x + 2}$

20. $\dfrac{2x^3 - x^2 + 11x}{x^4 + 8x^2 + 16} = \dfrac{2x^3 - x^2 + 11x}{(x^2 + 4)^2} = \dfrac{Ax + B}{x^2 + 4} + \dfrac{Cx + D}{(x^2 + 4)^2}$

$2x^3 - x^2 + 11x = (Ax + B)(x^2 + 4) + Cx + D$

$2x^3 - x^2 + 11x = Ax^3 + 4Ax + Bx^2 + 4B + Cx + D$

x^3 terms: $2x^3 = Ax^3 \Rightarrow \boldsymbol{A = 2}$

x^2 terms: $-x^2 = Bx^2 \Rightarrow \boldsymbol{B = -1}$

x terms: $\quad 11x = 4Ax + Cx$

$\qquad\qquad 11 = 8 + C \Rightarrow \boldsymbol{C = 3}$

constants: $\quad 0 = 4B + D$

$\qquad\qquad 0 = -4 + D \Rightarrow \boldsymbol{D = 4}$

$\dfrac{2x^3 - x^2 + 11x}{x^4 + 8x^2 + 16} = \dfrac{2x - 1}{x^2 + 4} + \dfrac{3x + 4}{(x^2 + 4)^2}$

22. $\dfrac{5x^2 - 8x + 12}{x^3 - x^2 - 4} = \dfrac{A}{x - 2} + \dfrac{Bx + C}{x^2 + x + 2}$

$5x^2 - 8x + 12 = A(x^2 + x + 2) + (Bx + C)(x - 2)$

$5x^2 - 8x + 12 = Ax^2 + Ax + 2A + Bx^2 - 2Bx + Cx - 2C$

$x = 2:\ 20 - 16 + 12 = A(4 + 2 + 2) + 0$

$$16 = 8A \Rightarrow \boldsymbol{A = 2}$$

x^2 terms: $5x^2 = Ax^2 + Bx^2 \Rightarrow 5 = A + B \Rightarrow \boldsymbol{B = 3}$

x terms: $-8x = Ax - 2Bx + Cx \Rightarrow -8 = 2 - 6 + C \Rightarrow \boldsymbol{C = -4}$

$\dfrac{5x^2 - 8x + 12}{x^3 - x^2 - 4} = \dfrac{2}{x - 2} + \dfrac{3x - 4}{x^2 + x + 2}$

24. $\dfrac{2x^5 + 2x^4 - 6x^3}{x^4 + 4x + 3}$

$$
\begin{array}{r}
2x + 2 \\
x^4 + 4x + 3\,\overline{\big)\,2x^5 + 2x^4 - 6x^3 } \\
\underline{2x^5 + 8x^2 + 6x} \\
2x^4 - 6x^3 - 8x^2 - 6x \\
\underline{2x^4 + 8x + 6} \\
-6x^3 - 8x^2 - 14x - 6
\end{array}
$$

$\dfrac{2x^5 + 2x^4 - 6x^3}{x^4 + 4x + 3} = 2x + 2 + \dfrac{-6x^3 - 8x^2 - 14x - 6}{x^4 + 4x + 3}$

$\dfrac{-6x^3 - 8x^2 - 14x - 6}{(x + 1)^2(x^2 - 2x + 3)} = \dfrac{A}{x + 1} + \dfrac{B}{(x + 1)^2} + \dfrac{Cx + D}{x^2 - 2x + 3}$

(#1): $-6x^3 - 8x^2 - 14x - 6$
$\qquad = A(x + 1)(x^2 - 2x + 3) + B(x^2 - 2x + 3) + (Cx + D)(x + 1)^2$

(#2): $-6x^3 - 8x^2 - 14x - 6$
$\qquad = Ax^3 - Ax^2 + Ax + 3A + Bx^2 - 2Bx + 3B + Cx^3 + 2Cx^2 + Cx + Dx^2 + 2Dx + D$

$x = -1 \to$ #1: $6 - 8 + 14 - 6 = A(0) + B(1 + 2 + 3) + C(0)$

$$6 = 6B \Rightarrow \boldsymbol{B = 1}$$

(#2): x^3 terms: $-6 = A + C$ (#3)

$\qquad\quad x^2$ terms: $-8 = -A + B + 2C + D$

$\qquad\qquad\qquad\qquad -9 = -A + 2C + D$ (#4)

$\qquad\quad x$ terms: $-14 = A - 2B + C + 2D$

$\qquad\qquad\qquad\quad -12 = A + C + 2D$ (#5)

$\qquad\text{constants:}\ -6 = 3A + 3B + D$

$\qquad\qquad\qquad\qquad -9 = 3A + D$ (#6)

(#4) $+ (-2)\cdot$(#5): $-9 = -A + 2C + D$
$$\underline{\qquad\qquad\qquad\quad 24 = -2A - 2C - 4D}$$
$$15 = -3A - 3D \quad (\#7)$$

(#6) $+$ (#7): $-9 = 3A + D$
$$\underline{\qquad\qquad\quad 15 = -3A - 3D}$$
$$6 = -2D \Rightarrow \boldsymbol{D = -3}$$

$D = -3 \Rightarrow$ (#6): $-9 = 3A - 3 \Rightarrow \boldsymbol{A = -2}$

$A = -2 \Rightarrow$ (#3): $-6 = -2 + C \Rightarrow \boldsymbol{C = -4}$

$\dfrac{2x^5 + 2x^4 - 6x^3}{x^4 + 4x + 3} = 2x + 2 + \dfrac{-2}{x + 1} + \dfrac{1}{(x + 1)^2} + \dfrac{-4x - 3}{x^2 - 2x + 3}$

$\qquad\qquad\qquad\quad = 2x + 2 - \dfrac{2}{x + 1} + \dfrac{1}{(x + 1)^2} - \dfrac{4x + 3}{x^2 - 2x + 3}$

26. $\dfrac{x^5 + 2x^4 + 3x^2 - 14x}{x^4 - x^2 - 4x - 4} = x + 2 + \dfrac{x^3 + 9x^2 - 2x + 8}{x^4 - x^2 - 4x - 4}$

$$
\begin{array}{r}
x + 2 \\
x^4 - x^2 - 4x - 4\overline{\smash{\big)}\,x^5 + 2x^4 + 0x^3 + 3x^2 - 14x} \\
\underline{x^5 \qquad\quad - x^3 - 4x^2 - 4x} \\
2x^4 + x^3 + 7x^2 - 10x \\
\underline{2x^4 \qquad\quad - 2x^2 - 8x - 8} \\
x^3 + 9x^2 - 2x - 8
\end{array}
$$

$\dfrac{x^3 + 9x^2 - 2x + 8}{(x - 2)(x + 1)(x^2 + x + 2)} = \dfrac{A}{x - 2} + \dfrac{B}{x + 1} + \dfrac{Cx + D}{x^2 + x + 2}$

(#1): $x^3 + 9x^2 - 2x + 8$
$\qquad = A(x + 1)(x^2 + x + 2) + B(x - 2)(x^2 + x + 2) + (Cx + D)(x - 2)(x + 1)$

(#2): $x^3 + 9x^2 - 2x + 8$
$\qquad = Ax^3 + 2Ax^2 + 3Ax + 2A + Bx^3 - Bx^2 - 4B + Cx^3 - Cx^2 - 2Cx + Dx^2 - Dx - 2D$

$x = 2 \Rightarrow$ (#1): $\quad 8 + 36 - 4 + 8 = A(3)(8) + B(0) + (Cx + D)(0)$
$\qquad\qquad\qquad\qquad\qquad\quad 48 = 24A \Rightarrow \textbf{\textit{A} = 2}$

$x = -1 \Rightarrow$ (#1): $\quad -1 + 9 + 2 + 8 = A(0) + B(-3)(2) + (Cx + D)(0)$
$\qquad\qquad\qquad\qquad\qquad\quad 18 = -6B \Rightarrow \textbf{\textit{B} = -3}$

x^3 terms (#2): $\quad 1 = A + B + C \Rightarrow 1 = 2 - 3 + C \Rightarrow \textbf{\textit{C} = 2}$

x^2 terms (#2): $\quad 9 = 2A - B - C + D \Rightarrow 9 = 4 + 3 - 2 + D \Rightarrow \textbf{\textit{D} = 4}$.

$\dfrac{x^5 + 2x^4 + 3x^2 - 14x}{x^4 - x^2 - 4x - 4} = x + 2 + \dfrac{2}{x - 2} - \dfrac{3}{x + 1} + \dfrac{2x + 4}{x^2 + x + 2}$

28. $\dfrac{1}{x(x + a)^2} = \dfrac{A}{x} + \dfrac{B}{x + a} + \dfrac{C}{(x + a)^2}, \quad a \neq 0$

$\qquad\qquad 1 = A(x + a)^2 + Bx(x + a) + Cx$

$x = 0: \quad 1 = A(a^2) + B(0) + C(0) \Rightarrow \textbf{\textit{A}} = \dfrac{1}{a^2}$

$x = -a: \quad 1 = A(0) + B(0) + C(-a) \Rightarrow \textbf{\textit{C}} = -\dfrac{1}{a}$

$\qquad\qquad 1 = Ax^2 + 2Aax + Aa^2 + Bx^2 + Bxa + Cx$

x^2 terms: $\quad 0 = A + B = \dfrac{1}{a^2} + B \Rightarrow \textbf{\textit{B}} = -\dfrac{1}{a^2}$

$\dfrac{1}{x(x + a)^2} = \dfrac{\frac{1}{a^2}}{x} + \dfrac{\frac{-1}{a^2}}{x + a} + \dfrac{\frac{-1}{a}}{(x + a)^2}$

$\qquad\qquad = \dfrac{1}{a^2 x} - \dfrac{1}{a^2(x + a)} - \dfrac{1}{a(x + a)^2}$

30. $\dfrac{x}{(x - a)(x - b)} = \dfrac{A}{x - a} + \dfrac{B}{x - b}$, $a \neq b$

$\qquad x = A(x - b) + B(x - a)$

$x = a: \ a = A(a - b) + B(0) \ \Rightarrow \ \boldsymbol{A = \dfrac{a}{a - b}}$

$x = b: \ b = A(0) + B(b - a) \ \Rightarrow \ \boldsymbol{B} = \dfrac{b}{b - a} = \boldsymbol{\dfrac{-b}{a - b}}$

$\dfrac{x}{(x - a)(x - b)} = \dfrac{\dfrac{a}{a - b}}{x - a} + \dfrac{\dfrac{-b}{a - b}}{x - b}$

$\qquad\qquad\qquad = \dfrac{a}{(a - b)(x - a)} - \dfrac{b}{(a - b)(x - b)}$

CHAPTER 5

Exercise 5-1

2. $y = 5^x$; $[-2, 2]$

x	y
-2	0.04
-1	0.2
0	1
1	5
2	25

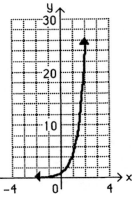

4. $y = \left(\dfrac{1}{5}\right)^x = 5^{-x}$; $[-2, 2]$

x	y
-2	25
-1	5
0	1
1	0.2
2	0.04

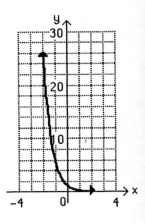

6. $f(x) = -5^x$; $[-2, 2]$

x	$f(x)$
-2	-0.04
-1	-0.2
0	-1
1	-5
2	-25

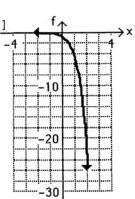

8. $f(x) = 4(5^x)$; $[-2, 2]$

x	$f(x)$
-2	0.16
-1	0.8
0	4
1	20
2	100

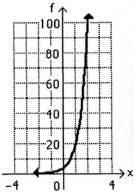

10. $y = 5^{x+2} + 4$; $[-4, 0]$

x	y
-4	4.04
-3	4.2
-2	5
-1	9
0	29

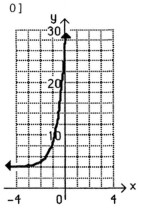

12. $5^{2x-3} \, 5^{6-4x} = 5^{2x-3+6-4x}$
$$= 5^{-2x+3} \text{ or } 5^{3-2x}$$

14. $\dfrac{7^{-3y-x}}{7^{-4x-6y}} = 7^{-3y-x-(-4x-6y)}$
$$= 7^{3x+3y}$$

16. $(x^3)^4 = x^{12}$

18. $2^{x^3} \, 2^{x^2} = 2^{x^3+x^2}$

20. $\left(\dfrac{3^{2x}}{7^{3y}}\right)^2 = \dfrac{3^{4x}}{7^{6y}}$

22. $\left(\dfrac{a^{-4}b^3c^2}{a^{-6}b^2c^{-1}}\right)^3 = (a^{-4-(-6)} \, b^{3-2} \, c^{2-(-1)})^3$
$$= (a^2 b^1 c^3)^3$$
$$= a^6 b^3 c^9$$

24.
$$4^{4x+1} = 4^{2x-2}$$
$$4x + 1 = 2x - 2$$
$$2x = -3$$
$$x = -\frac{3}{2} = -1.5$$

26.
$$5^{x^2-5} = 5^{3x+5}$$
$$x^2 - 5 = 3x + 5$$
$$x^2 - 3x - 10 = 0$$
$$(x - 5)(x + 2) = 0$$
$$x = -2, 5$$

28.
$$(2x - 1)^5 = -32$$
$$(2x - 1)^5 = (-2)^5$$
$$2x - 1 = -2$$
$$2x = -1$$
$$x = -\frac{1}{2} = -0.5$$

30.
$$4^{5x+1} = 16^{2x-1}$$
$$4^{5x+1} = (4^2)^{2x-1}$$
$$5x + 1 = 2(2x - 1)$$
$$5x + 1 = 4x - 2$$
$$x = -3$$

32.
$$100^{2x+4} = 1000^{x+4}$$
$$(10^2)^{2x+4} = (10^3)^{x+4}$$
$$2(2x + 4) = 3(x + 4)$$
$$4x + 8 = 3x + 12$$
$$x = 4$$

34.
$$3^{x^2} = 9^{x+4}$$
$$3^{x^2} = (3^2)^{x+4}$$
$$x^2 = 2x + 8$$
$$x^2 - 2x - 8 = 0$$
$$(x - 4)(x + 2) = 0$$
$$x = -2, 4$$

36. 2 and -2 are real numbers such that $2 \neq -2$ but $2^4 = (-2)^4$. The third exponential function property requires a, b both positive.

38. $f(t) = 2^{t/10}$

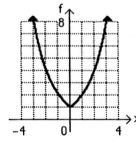

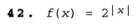

t	$f(t)$
-30	$\frac{1}{8}$
-20	$\frac{1}{4}$
-10	$\frac{1}{2}$
0	1
10	2
20	4
30	8

40. $y = 7(2^{-2x})$

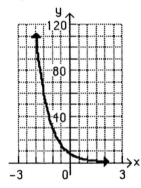

x	y
-1	28
0	7
1	1.75
2	0.4375

42. $f(x) = 2^{|x|}$

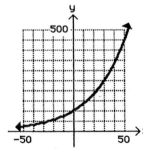

x	$f(x)$
-3	8
-2	4
-1	2
0	1
1	2
2	4
3	8

44. $y = 100(1.03)^x$

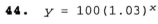

x	y
-50	22.8
-20	55
0	100
30	243

46. $y = 3^{-x^2}$

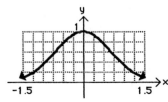

x	y
±1.5	0.08
±1	0.33
0	1

48. $(3^x - 3^{-x})(3^x + 3^{-x}) = 3^{2x} + 3^0 - 3^0 - 3^{-2x}$
$$= 3^{2x} + 1 - 1 - 3^{-2x}$$
$$= 3^{2x} - 3^{-2x}$$

50. $(3^x - 3^{-x})^2 + (3^x + 3^{-x})^2 = 3^{2x} - 2 \cdot 3^{x-x} + 3^{-2x} + 3^{2x} + 2 \cdot 3^{x-x} + 3^{-2x}$
$$= 2(3^{2x}) + 2(3^{-2x})$$

52. $h(x) = x(2^x)$

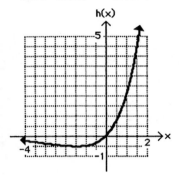

x	hx
-4	-0.25
-2	-0.5
0	0
1	2
1.5	4.2

54. $g(x) = \dfrac{3^x + 3^{-x}}{2}$

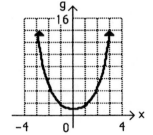

x	$g(x)$
± 3	13.5
± 1	1.7
0	1

56. $f(x) = 4 + 2^{-x}$

(A) No real zeros.

(B) $f(x) \to 4$ as $x \to \infty$, $f(x) \to \infty$ as $x \to -\infty$. $y = 4$ is an horizontal asymptote.

58. $f(x) = 8 - x^2 + 2^{-x}$

(A) 2.85

(B) $f(x) \to \infty$ as $x \to -\infty$, $f(x) \to -\infty$ as $x \to \infty$. No horizontal asymptotes.

60. $P = P_0 2^{t/d}$
$$= 100 \ 2^{t/(1/2)}$$
$$= 100 \ 2^{2t}$$

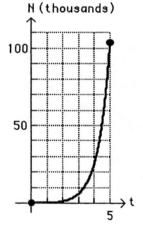

62. $P = P_0 2^{t/d}$
$$= 30{,}000{,}000 \ 2^{t/19}$$

(A) $P(10) = 30{,}000{,}000 \ 2^{10/19} \approx 43{,}000{,}000$

(B) $P(30) = 30{,}000{,}000 \ 2^{30/19} \approx 90{,}000{,}000$

64. $A = A_0 \left(\dfrac{1}{2}\right)^{t/h}$
$$= 12 \left(\dfrac{1}{2}\right)^{t/6}$$

(A) $A(3) = 12 \left(\dfrac{1}{2}\right)^{3/6} \approx 8.49$ mg

(B) $A(24) = 12 \left(\dfrac{1}{2}\right)^{24/6} \approx 0.750$ mg

66. $A = P\left(1 + \dfrac{r}{n}\right)^{nt}$

$\quad = 2500\left(1 + \dfrac{0.07}{4}\right)^{4t}$

(A) $A\left(\dfrac{3}{4}\right) = 2500\left(1 + \dfrac{0.07}{4}\right)^{4(3/4)} \approx \$2633.56$

(B) $A(15) = 2500\left(1 + \dfrac{0.07}{4}\right)^{4(15)} \approx \$7079.54$

68. $A = P\left(1 + \dfrac{r}{n}\right)^{nt}$

$\quad 15{,}000 = P\left(1 + \dfrac{0.0975}{52}\right)^{52(5)}$

$\quad\quad P \approx \$9217$

70. $5000\left(1 + \dfrac{r}{365}\right)^{365} \geq 5000\left(1 + \dfrac{0.13}{2}\right)^{2}$

$\quad\quad \left(1 + \dfrac{r}{365}\right) \geq \left(1 + \dfrac{0.13}{2}\right)^{2/365}$

$\quad\quad\quad r \geq 0.125973313$, about 12.6%

Exercise 5-2

2. $y = -e^{-x}$; $[-3, 3]$

x	y
-3	-20.09
-2	-7.39
-1	-2.72
0	-1.00
1	-0.37
2	-0.14
3	-0.05

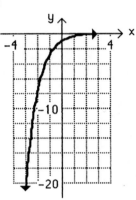

4. $y = 100e^{0.1x}$; $[-5, 5]$

x	y
-5	60.65
-4	67.03
-3	74.08
-2	81.87
-1	90.48
0	100
1	110.52
2	122.14
3	134.99
4	149.18
5	164.87

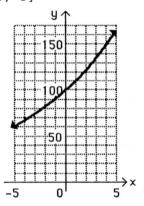

6. $g(t) = 10e^{-0.2t}$; $[-5, 5]$

t	$g(t)$
-5	27.18
-4	22.26
-3	18.22
-2	14.92
-1	12.21
0	10
1	8.19
2	6.70
3	5.49
4	4.49
5	3.68

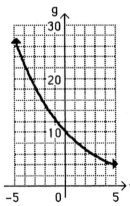

8. $(e^{-x})^4 = e^{-4x}$

10. $e^{-4x}e^{6x} = e^{-4x+6x} = e^{2x}$

12. $\dfrac{e^{4-3x}}{e^{2-5x}} = e^{4-3x-(2-5x)}$

$\quad\quad = e^{4-3x-2+5x} = e^{2x+2}$

14. (A) $\left(1 + \dfrac{1}{m}\right)$ is not constant and b is.   (B) e.

16. $y = -3 + e^{1+x}$

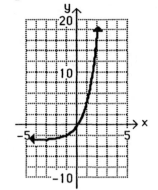

x	y
-4	-3
-1	-2
0	-e
1	4.4

18. $y = e^{|x|}$

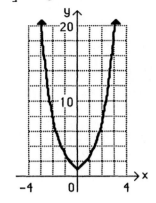

x	y
±3	20
±2	7.4
±1	e
0	1

20. $C(x) = \dfrac{e^x + e^{-x}}{2}$

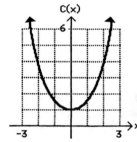

x	y
±2	3.8
±1	1.5
0	1

22. $N = \dfrac{100}{1 + e^{-t}}$

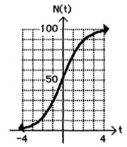

x	y
-3	4.7
-1	26.9
0	50
1	73.1
3	95.3

24. $\dfrac{5x^4 e^{5x} - 4x^3 e^{5x}}{x^8} = \dfrac{x^3 e^{5x}(5x - 4)}{x^8} = \dfrac{e^{5x}(5x - 4)}{x^5}$

26. $e^x(e^{-x} + 1) - e^{-x}(e^x + 1) = e^{x-x} + e^x - e^{-x+x} - e^{-x}$
$$= e^0 + e^x - e^0 - e^{-x}$$
$$= e^x - e^{-x}$$

28. $\dfrac{e^x(e^x + e^{-x}) - (e^x - e^{-x})e^x}{e^{2x}} = \dfrac{e^{2x} + e^{x-x} - e^{2x} + e^{-x+x}}{e^{2x}}$

$$= \dfrac{e^0 + e^0}{e^{2x}}$$

$$= \dfrac{2}{e^{2x}}$$

30. $(x - 3)e^x = 0 \Rightarrow x - 3 = 0$, $e^x = 0$, no solution, $e^x > 0$
$$x = 3$$

32. $3xe^{-x} + x^2 e^{-x} = 0 \Rightarrow e^{-x}(3x + x^2) = 0$; $e^{-x} > 0$
$x^2 + 3x = 0$
$x(x + 3) = 0$
$x = 0$, $x = -3$

34. $g(x) = \dfrac{1}{\sqrt{\pi}} e^{-x^2/2}$

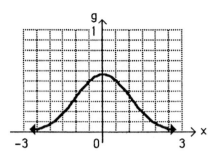

36. $f(s) = (1 + s)^{1/s}$

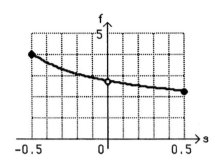

38. $f(x) = e^x$;

$P_2(x) = 1 + x + \dfrac{1}{2}x^2 + \dfrac{1}{6}x^3$

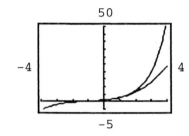

40. $f(x) = e^x$;

$P_4(x) = 1 + x + \dfrac{1}{2}x^2 + \dfrac{1}{6}x^3 + \dfrac{1}{24}x^4 + \dfrac{1}{120}x^5$

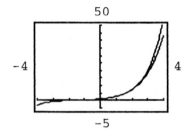

42. $g_1(x) = xe^x$: as $x \to \infty$, $g_1(x) \to \infty$; as $x \to -\infty$, $g_1(x) \to 0$;
horizontal asymptote: $y = 0$

$g_2(x) = x^2 e^x$: as $x \to \infty$, $g_2(x) \to \infty$; as $x \to -\infty$, $g_2(x) \to 0$;
horizontal asymptote: $y = 0$

$g_3(x) = x^3 e^x$: as $x \to \infty$, $g_3(x) \to \infty$; as $x \to -\infty$, $g_3(x) \to 0$;
horizontal asymptote: $y = 0$

$g_n(x) = x^n e^x$: as $x \to \infty$, $g_n(x) \to \infty$; as $x \to -\infty$, $g_n(x) \to 0$;
horizontal asymptote: $y = 0$

44. $P = P_0 e^{kt}$
   $P = 100 e^{0.023t}$
$P(8) = 100 e^{0.023(8)}$
$P(8) \approx 120$ million

46. 1996, $t = 0$:
   G: 84 million, -0.15%
   E: 64 million, 1.9%
   $P_G = 84 e^{-0.0015t}$;
   $P_E = 64 e^{0.019t}$
   Graph P_G and P_E; $t \approx 13.3$

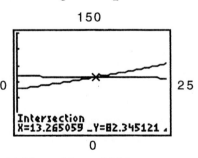

1996 + 13 = 2009

48. $P = 14.7 e^{-0.21h}$

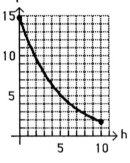

50. $I = I_0 e^{-0.23d}$: $I/I_0 = e^{-0.23d}$
   (A) for $d = 10$: $I/I_0 = e^{-0.23(10)} = 0.10 = 10\%$
   (B) for $d = 20$: $I/I_0 = e^{-0.23(20)} = 0.01 = 1\%$

52. $A = Pe^{rt}$, $P = \$7500$, $r = 8.35°$
(A) $A(5.5) = 7500e^{0.0835(5.5)} = \$11,871.65$
(B) $A(12) = 7500e^{0.0835(12)} = \$20,427.93$

54. $A = P\left(1 + \dfrac{r}{n}\right)^{nt}$

Alamo: $A = 10,000\left(1 + \dfrac{0.0825}{4}\right)^{4(1)} = \$10,850.88$

Lamar: $A = Pe^{rt} = 10,000e^{0.0805(1)} = \$10,838.29$

56. $P = P_0e^{rt}$
$50,000 = P_0e^{(0.10*5.5)}$

$P_0 = \dfrac{50,000}{e^{0.55}}$

$P_0 = \$28,847.49$

58. 1996, $t = 0$; $P = 28$ million, $r = 19\%$
(A) 2000, $t = 4$: $A = 28e^{(0.19 \times 4)} \approx 59.87$ million
(B) 2004, $t = 8$: $A = 28e^{(0.19 \times 8)} \approx 128.02$ million

60. $N(t) = 2(1 - e^{-0.037t})$: N tends to 2 as t increases without bound

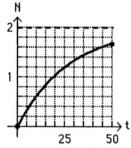

62. $T = T_m + (T_0 - T_m)e^{-kt}$; $T_0 = 72°F$, $T_m = 40°F$, $k = 0.4$, $t = 5$
$T = 40 + (72 - 40)e^{-0.4(5)}$
$T = 40 + 32e^{-0.4(5)}$
$T \approx 44°F$

64. $q(t) = 0.000\,008(1 - e^{-2t})$: max charge = 0.000 008 coulombs

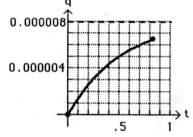

66. $N(t) = \dfrac{200}{4 + 21e^{-0.1t}}$: $N_{max} = 50$ computers

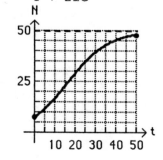

68. $y = \dfrac{e^{0.4x} + e^{-0.4x}}{2(0.4)}$

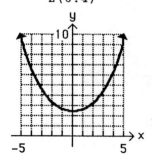

Exercise 5-3

2. $\log_6 216 = 3 \Leftrightarrow 216 = 6^3$

4. $\log_{10} 0.000001 = -6 \Leftrightarrow 0.000001 = 10^{-6}$

6. $\log_{16} 2 = \frac{1}{4} \Leftrightarrow 2 = 16^{1/4}$

8. $\log_{1/5} 25 = -2 \Leftrightarrow 25 = \left(\frac{1}{5}\right)^{-2}$

10. $10,000,000 = 10^7 \Leftrightarrow \log_{10} 10,000,000 = 7$

12. $64 = 16^{3/2} \Leftrightarrow \log_{16} 64 = \frac{3}{2}$

14. $32^{-2/5} = \frac{1}{4} \Leftrightarrow \log_{32}\left(\frac{1}{4}\right) = -\frac{2}{5}$

16. $11 = \sqrt{121}$
$11 = 121^{1/2} \Leftrightarrow \log_{121} 11 = \frac{1}{2}$

18. $\log_5 1 = m \Rightarrow 5^m = 1$
$m = 0$
so $\log_5 1 = 0$

20. $\log_{0.2} 0.2 = m \Rightarrow 0.2^m = 0.2$
$m = 1$
so $\log_{0.2} 0.2 = 1$

22. $\log_2 64 = m \Rightarrow 2^m = 64$
$2^6 = 64$
$m = 6$
so $\log_2 64 = 6$

24. $\log_5 \sqrt[3]{5} = \frac{1}{3} \log_5 5 = \frac{1}{3}(1) = \frac{1}{3}$

26. $\log_{10} 0.0001 = \log_{10} 10^{-4} = -4 \log_{10} 10 = -4$

28. $10^{\log_{10} \sqrt{x}} = \sqrt{x} \qquad [b^{\log_b x} = x]$

30. $e^{-2 \log_e (x+1)} = e^{\log_e (x+1)^{-2}}$
$= (x + 1)^{-2} \text{ or } \frac{1}{(x + 1)^2}$
$[b^{\log_b x} = x]$

32. $\log_3 x = 2$
$x = 3^2 = 9$

34. $\log_4 x = -3$
$x = 4^{-3} = \frac{1}{4^3} = \frac{1}{64}$

36. $\log_4 64 = y$
$4^y = 64$
$y = 3$

38. $\log_8 x = \frac{2}{3}$
$x = 8^{2/3}$
$x = 4$

40. $\log_{1/3} 81 = y$
$\left(\frac{1}{3}\right)^y = 81$
$3^y = \frac{1}{81}$
$3^y = \frac{1}{3^4} = 3^{-4}$
$y = -4$

42. $\log_b 8 = 0.5$
$b^{0.5} = 8$
$(b^{0.5})^2 = 8^2$
$b = 64$

44. $\log_b 1000 = -3$
$b^{-3} = 1000 = 10^3$
$b^{-3} = \left(\frac{1}{10}\right)^{-3}$
$b = \frac{1}{10} \text{ or } 0.1$

46. $\log_b x^{2/3} y^{4/3} = \log_b x^{2/3} + \log_b y^{4/3}$
$= \frac{2}{3} \log_b x + \frac{4}{3} \log_b y$

48. $\log_b \frac{v^7}{u^8} = \log_b v^7 - \log_b u^8$
$= 7 \log_b v - 8 \log_b u$

50. $\log_b \frac{mnp}{q} = \log_b m + \log_b n + \log_b p - \log_b q$

52. $\log_b \frac{1}{a^3} = \log_b a^{-3} = -3 \log_b a$

54. $\log_b \sqrt[4]{c^4 + d^4} = \log_b (c^4 + d^4)^{1/4}$
$= \frac{1}{4} \log_b (c^4 + d^4)$

56. $\log_b \frac{u^3 v^4}{\sqrt{w}} = \log_b u^3 + \log_b v^4 - \log_b \sqrt{w}$
$= 3 \log_b u + 4 \log_b v - \frac{1}{2} \log_b w$

58. $\log_b \sqrt[4]{\left(\dfrac{\sqrt{x}}{y^2 z^3}\right)^3} = \dfrac{1}{4} \log_b \left(\dfrac{x^{1/2}}{y^2 z^3}\right)^3$

$\qquad\qquad\qquad = \dfrac{1}{4} \log_b \dfrac{x^{3/2}}{y^6 z^9}$

$\qquad\qquad\qquad = \dfrac{1}{4} [\log_b x^{3/2} - \log_b y^6 - \log_b z^9]$

$\qquad\qquad\qquad = \dfrac{1}{4} \left[\dfrac{3}{2} \log_b x - 6 \log_b y - 9 \log_b z\right]$

$\qquad\qquad\qquad = \dfrac{3}{8} \log_b x - \dfrac{3}{2} \log_b y - \dfrac{9}{4} \log_b z$

60. $\log_b m - \dfrac{1}{2} \log_b n = \log_b m - \log_b n^{1/2} = \log_b \dfrac{m}{n^{1/2}}$

$\qquad\qquad\qquad\qquad\qquad\qquad\qquad = \log_b \dfrac{m}{\sqrt{n}}$

62. $\log_b w + \log_b x - \log_b y = \log_b wx - \log_b y$

$\qquad\qquad\qquad\qquad\qquad = \log_b \dfrac{wx}{y}$

64. $\dfrac{1}{3} \log_b w - 3 \log_b x - 5 \log_b y = \log_b w^{1/3} - \log_b x^3 - \log_b y^5$

$\qquad\qquad\qquad\qquad\qquad = \log_b \dfrac{w^{1/3}}{x^3} - \log_b y^5$

$\qquad\qquad\qquad\qquad\qquad = \log_b \dfrac{\sqrt[3]{w}}{x^3 y^5}$

66. $7 \left(4 \log_b m + \dfrac{1}{3} \log_b n\right) = 7 (\log_b m^4 + \log_b n^{1/3})$

$\qquad\qquad\qquad\qquad = 7 (\log_b (m^4 \sqrt[3]{n}))$

$\qquad\qquad\qquad\qquad = \log_b (m^4 \sqrt[3]{n})^7$

68. $\dfrac{1}{3} (4 \log_b x - 2 \log_b y) = \dfrac{1}{3} (\log_b x^4 - \log_b y^2)$

$\qquad\qquad\qquad\qquad = \dfrac{1}{3} \left(\log_b \dfrac{x^4}{y^2}\right) = \log_b \left(\dfrac{x^4}{y^2}\right)^{1/3}$

$\qquad\qquad\qquad\qquad = \log_b \sqrt[3]{\dfrac{x^4}{y^2}}$

70. $\log_b [(5x - 4)^3 (3x + 2)^4] = \log_b (5x - 4)^3 + \log_b (3x + 2)^4$

$\qquad\qquad\qquad\qquad = 3 \log_b (5x - 4) + 4 \log_b (3x + 2)$

72. $\log_b \dfrac{(x - 3)^5}{(5 + x)^3} = \log_b (x - 3)^5 - \log_b (5 + x)^3$

$\qquad\qquad\qquad = 5 \log_b (x - 3) - 3 \log_b (5 + x)$

74. $\log_b \dfrac{\sqrt{x - 1}}{x^3} = \log_b \sqrt{x - 1} - \log_b x^3$

$\qquad\qquad\qquad = \dfrac{1}{2} \log_b (x - 1) - 3 \log_b x$

76. $\log_b(x^5 + 5x^4 - 14x^3) = \log_b[x^3(x + 7)(x - 2)]$
$$= 3 \log_b x + \log_b (x + 7) + \log_b (x - 2)$$

78. $\log_{10} (5 - x) = 3 \log_{10} 2$
$\log_{10} (5 - x) = \log_{10} 2^3$
$5 - x = 2^3$
$5 - x = 8$
$-3 = x$

80. $\log_{10} (x^2 - 2x - 2) = 2 \log_{10} (x - 2)$
$\log_{10} (x^2 - 2x - 2) = \log_{10} (x - 2)^2$
$x^2 - 2x - 2 = (x - 2)^2$
$x^2 - 2x - 2 = x^2 - 4x + 4$
$2x = 6$
$x = 3$

82. $\log_7 4x - \log_7 (x + 1) = \frac{1}{2} \log_7 4$
$\log_7 \dfrac{4x}{x + 1} = \log_7 4^{1/2}$
$\dfrac{4x}{x + 1} = \sqrt{4} = 2$
$4x = 2(x + 1)$
$2x = 2$
$x = 1$

84. $\log_4 x + \log_4 (x + 2) = \frac{1}{2} \log_4 9$
$\log_4 [x(x + 2)] = \log_4 9^{1/2}$
$x(x + 2) = 3$
$x^2 + 2x - 3 = 0$
$(x + 3)(x - 1) = 0$
$x = -3 \text{ (reject)}, \quad x = 1$

86. $\frac{3}{2} \log_b 4 - \frac{2}{3} \log_b 8 + 2 \log_b 2 = \log_b x$
$\log_b 4^{3/2} - \log_b 8^{2/3} + \log_b 2^2 = \log_b x$
$\log_b 8 - \log_b 4 + \log_b 4 = \log_b x$
$\log_b 8 = \log_b x$
$x = 8$

88. $\log_b 12 = \log_b 2^2(3)$
$= 2 \log_b 2 + \log_b 3$
$= 2(0.69) + 1.10$
$= 2.48$

90. $\log_b \frac{5}{3} = \log_b 5 - \log_b 3$
$= 1.61 - 1.10$
$= 0.51$

92. $\log_b 16 = \log_b 2^4 = 4 \log_b 2 = 4(0.69) = 2.76$

94. $\log_b \sqrt{3} = \frac{1}{2} \log_b 3 = \frac{1}{2} (1.10) = 0.55$

96. $\log_b \sqrt[3]{1.5} = \frac{1}{3} \log_b \frac{3}{2} = \frac{1}{3} [\log_b 3 - \log_b 2]$
$= \frac{1}{3} [1.10 - 0.69]$
$= 0.137$

98. $y = \log_2 (x + 3)$

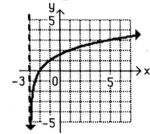

100. $y = \log_2 x + 3$

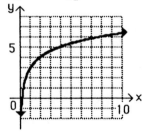

102. (A) $f = \left\{ (x, y) \mid y = \left(\dfrac{1}{3}\right)^{x} = 3^{-x} \right\}$

Graph f, f^{-1} and $y = x$:

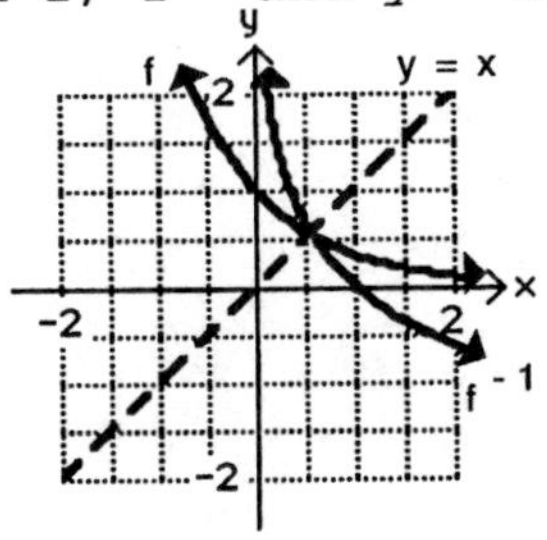

(B) Domain of f: $(-\infty, \infty)$
Range of f: $(0, \infty)$
Domain of f^{-1}: $(0, \infty)$
Range of f^{-1}: $(-\infty, \infty)$

(C) If $y = 3^{-x}$ then

$-x = \log_3 y$
$x = -\log_3 y$
$f^{-1}(x) = -\log_3 x$

or

If $y = \left(\dfrac{1}{3}\right)^{x}$ then

$x = \log_{1/3} y$
$f^{-1}(x) = \log_{1/3} x$

104. $g(x) = 3^{2x-3} - 2$
$y = 3^{2x-3} - 2$
$y + 2 = 3^{2x-3}$
$2x - 3 = \log_3(y + 2)$
$2x = \log_3(y + 2) + 3$
$x = \dfrac{1}{2}[\log_3(y + 2) + 3]$
$g^{-1}(x) = \dfrac{1}{2}[\log_3(x + 2) + 3]$

106. $f(x) = 2 + \log_e(5x - 3)$
$y = 2 + \log_e(5x - 3)$
$y - 2 = \log_e(5x - 3)$
$5x - 3 = e^{y-2}$
$5x = e^{y-2} + 3$
$x = \dfrac{1}{5}(e^{y-2} + 3)$
$f^{-1}(x) = \dfrac{1}{5}(e^{x-2} + 3)$

108. The graph of $y = 2^{|x|}$ has the shape of a parabola opening upward. The reflection is not a function since y is not one-to-one.

110. $\log_e x - \log_e C + kt = 0$

$\log_e\left(\dfrac{x}{C}\right) + kt = 0$

$\log_e\left(\dfrac{x}{C}\right) = -kt$

$e^{-kt} = \dfrac{x}{C}$

$x = Ce^{-kt}$

112. $\log_b m^p = \log_b (\underbrace{m \cdot m \cdot m \cdot \ldots \cdot m}_{p \text{ factors}})$

$= \underbrace{\log_b m + \log_b m + \ldots + \log_b m}_{p \text{ terms}}$

$= p \log_b m$

Exercise 5-4

2. $\log 0.000539 \approx -3.2684$ **4.** $\log 120{,}564 \approx 5.0812$ **6.** $\ln 0.023\ 198 \approx -3.7637$

8. ln 132.43 ≈ 4.8861

10. ln x = -0.2985

   $x = e^{-0.2985}$

   $x ≈ 0.7419$

12. ln x = 6.8236

   $x = e^{6.8236}$

   $x ≈ 919.3$

14. log x = -2.6123

   $x = 10^{-2.6123}$

   $x ≈ 0.002\ 442$

16. log x = 2.5017

   $x = 10^{2.5017}$

   $x ≈ 317.5$

18. $\log \dfrac{3.215}{2.569} ≈ 0.097$

20. $\dfrac{\ln 0.5545}{\ln 0.0545} ≈ 0.203$

22. $\dfrac{\log 0.7}{0.005} ≈ -30.980$

24. $\dfrac{\ln 300}{\ln 3} ≈ 5.192$

26. $x = \ln(4.3931 \times 10^{-11})$

   $x ≈ -23.848$

28. $x = \log(5.1212 \times 10^{14})$

   $x ≈ 14.709$

30. ln x = 14.561094

   $x = e^{14.561094}$

   $x ≈ 2,107,700$ or 2.1077×10^6

32. log x = -15.599943

   $x = 10^{-15.599943}$

   $x ≈ 2.5122 \times 10^{-16}$

34. $y = -\ln x$

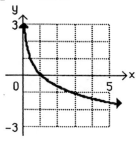

36. $y = \ln |x|$

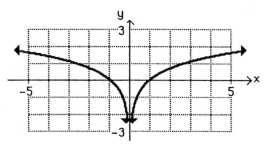

38. $y = 2 \ln x + 2$

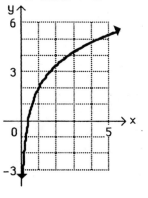

40. $y = 4 \ln(x - 3)$

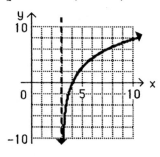

42. $\log \dfrac{1}{2}$ = -0.3010 < 0, thus when 3 > 2 is multiplied on both sides by $\log \dfrac{1}{2}$ (a negative number) the order of the inequality should be reversed:

$3 \log \dfrac{1}{2} < 2 \log \dfrac{1}{2}$ rather than $3 \log \dfrac{1}{2} > 2 \log \dfrac{1}{2}$ as shown.

44. (A) ln 1000 ≈ 6.9   ln(ln(1000)) ≈ 1.9

   ln 10,000 ≈ 9.2   ln(ln(10,000)) ≈ 2.2

   an increase of 2.3   an increase of 0.3

(B) ln(ln(x)) has domain (1, ∞) and range (-∞, ∞)

(C) Answers may vary. See graph.

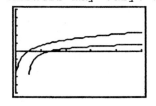

46.

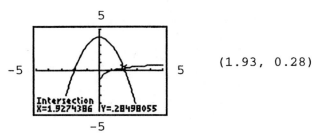

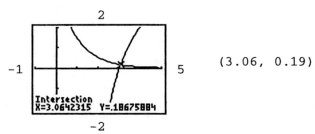

$(1.93, 0.28)$

48.

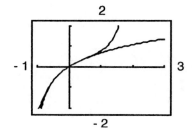

$(3.06, 0.19)$

50. $g(x) = \ln(1 + x)$

$P_2(x) = x - \dfrac{1}{2}x^2 + \dfrac{1}{3}x^3$

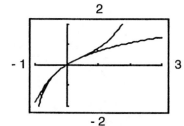

52. $g(x) = \ln(1 + x)$

$P_4(x) = x - \dfrac{1}{2}x^2 + \dfrac{1}{3}x^3 - \dfrac{1}{4}x^4 + \dfrac{1}{5}x^5$

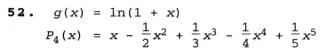

54. (A) $D = 10 \log \dfrac{I}{I_0} = 10 \log \dfrac{3.2 \times 10^{-6}}{10^{-12}} \approx 65$ decibels

(B) $D = 10 \log \dfrac{I}{I_0} = 10 \log \dfrac{8.3 \times 10^2}{10^{-12}} \approx 150$ decibels

56. $D_2 - D_1 = 10 \log \dfrac{10{,}000 I_1}{I_0} - 10 \log \dfrac{I_1}{I_0}$

$= 10[\log 10{,}000 I_1 - \log I_0] - 10[\log I_1 - \log I_0]$

$= 10[\log 10{,}000 I_1 - \log I_1 - \log I_0 + \log I_0]$

$= 10[\log 10{,}000 I_1 - \log I_1]$

$= 10\left[\log \dfrac{10{,}000\ I_1}{I_1}\right]$

$= 10[4]$

$= 40$ decibels

58. $M = \dfrac{2}{3} \log \dfrac{E}{E_0} = \dfrac{2}{3} \log \dfrac{7.08 \times 10^{16}}{10^{4.4}} \approx 8.3$

60. $5.6 = \frac{2}{3} \log \frac{E_1}{E_0} \Rightarrow \log E_1 - \log E_0 = \frac{5.6(3)}{2}$

$8.6 = \frac{2}{3} \log \frac{E_2}{E_0} \Rightarrow \underline{\log E_2 - \log E_0 = \frac{8.6(3)}{2}} \quad \text{subtract}$

$\qquad\qquad\qquad\qquad\qquad \log E_1 - \log E_2 = -4.5$

$\log \frac{E_1}{E_2} = -4.5$

$\quad \frac{E_1}{E_2} = 10^{-4.5}$

$\quad E_2 = 10^{4.5} E_1 \approx 32{,}000 E_1 \,; \quad \text{Approximately 32,000 times as powerful}$

62. $v = c \ln \frac{w_t}{w_b} = 5.2 \ln 6.2 \approx 9.49 \frac{\text{km}}{\text{sec}}$

64. (A) $\text{pH} = -\log [H^+] = -\log (2.83 \times 10^{-7}) \approx 6.5$ acidic
(B) $\text{pH} = -\log [H^+] = -\log (3.78 \times 10^{-6}) \approx 5.4$ acidic

66. $5.7 = -\log[H^+] \Rightarrow 10^{-5.7} = H^+ = 2.0 \times 10^{-6}$ moles per liter

Exercise 5-5

2. $e^x = 9.62$
$x = \ln 9.62$
$x \approx 2.26$

4. $10^{-x} = 1.25$
$-x = \log 1.25$
$x = -\log 1.25$
$x \approx -0.0969$

6. $e^{1-3x} = 9.62$
$1 - 3x = \ln 9.62$
$-3x = \ln 9.62 - 1$
$x = -\dfrac{\ln 9.62 - 1}{3}$
$x \approx -0.421$

8. $10^{4x-1} = 5000$
$4x - 1 = \log 5000$
$4x = \log 5000 + 1$
$x = \dfrac{\log 5000 + 1}{4}$
$x \approx 1.17$

10. $2^x = 0.0525$
$\ln 2^x = \ln 0.0525$
$x \ln 2 = \ln 0.0525$
$x = \dfrac{\ln 0.0525}{\ln 2}$
$x \approx -4.25$

12. $4^{-x} = 0.0001$
$\log 4^{-x} = \log 0.0001$
$-x \log 4 = \log 10^{-4}$
$-x = \dfrac{-4}{\log 4}$
$x = \dfrac{4}{\log 4}$
$x \approx 6.64$

14. $\ln x + \ln 4 = 1$
$\ln(4x) = 1$
$4x = e^1$
$x = \dfrac{1}{4} e$

16. $\log 8 - \log x = 2$
$\log \dfrac{8}{x} = 2$
$\dfrac{8}{x} = 10^2$
$x = \dfrac{8}{10^2}$
$x = \dfrac{2}{25} \quad \text{or} \quad 0.08$

18. $\log(x + 5) + \log(x - 10) = 3$
$\log[(x + 5)(x - 10)] = 3$
$(x + 5)(x - 10) = 10^3$
$x^2 - 5x - 50 = 1000$
$x^2 - 5x - 1050 = 0$
$(x - 35)(x + 30) = 0$
$x = 35, \quad x = -30 \text{ (reject)}$

20. $3 = 1.001^{12x}$
$\ln 3 = \ln 1.001^{12x}$
$\ln 3 = 12x \ln 1.001$
$x = \dfrac{\ln 3}{12 \ln 1.001}$
$x \approx 91.6$

22. $e^{25x} = 1.25$
$25x = \ln 1.25$
$x = \dfrac{\ln 1.25}{25}$
$x \approx 0.00893$

24. $1000 = 46 e^{-0.4x}$
$\dfrac{1000}{46} = e^{-0.4x}$
$-0.4x = \ln \dfrac{1000}{46}$
$x = \dfrac{\ln \dfrac{1000}{46}}{-0.4}$
$x \approx -7.70$

26.
$$e^{-0.2x^2} = 0.5$$
$$-0.2x^2 = \ln 0.5$$
$$x^2 = \frac{\ln 0.5}{-0.2}$$
$$x = \pm\sqrt{\frac{\ln 0.5}{-0.2}}$$
$$x \approx 1.86, -1.86$$

28.
$$\log(6x + 5) - \log 3 = \log 2 - \log x$$
$$\log\frac{6x + 5}{3} = \log\frac{2}{x}$$
$$\frac{6x + 5}{3} = \frac{2}{x}$$
$$6x^2 + 5x = 6$$
$$6x^2 + 5x - 6 = 0$$
$$(3x - 2)(2x + 3) = 0$$
$$x = \frac{2}{3}, \quad x = -\frac{3}{2} \text{ reject}$$

30.
$$\ln(x + 1) = \ln(3x + 1) - \ln x$$
$$\ln(x + 1) = \ln\frac{3x + 1}{x}$$
$$x + 1 = \frac{3x + 1}{x}$$
$$x^2 + x = 3x + 1$$

$$x^2 - 2x - 1 = 0$$
$$x = \frac{2 \pm \sqrt{8}}{2} = \frac{2 \pm 2\sqrt{2}}{2}$$
$$x = 1 \pm \sqrt{2}$$
$1 - \sqrt{2}$ must be rejected
$$x = 1 + \sqrt{2}$$

32.
$$1 - \log(x - 2) = \log(3x + 1)$$
$$1 = \log(3x + 1) + \log(x - 2)$$
$$1 = \log(3x + 1)(x - 2)$$
$$(3x + 1)(x - 2) = 10^1$$
$$3x^2 - 5x - 2 = 10$$
$$3x^2 - 5x - 12 = 0$$
$$(x - 3)(3x + 4) = 0$$
$$x = 3, \quad x = -\frac{4}{3} \text{ reject}$$

34.
$$(\log x)^3 = \log x^4$$
$$(\log x)^3 = 4 \log x$$
$$(\log x)^3 - 4 \log x = 0$$
$$\log x[(\log x)^2 - 4] = 0$$
$$\log x = 0, \quad (\log x)^2 - 4 = 0$$
$$x = 1 \qquad (\log x)^2 = 4$$
$$\log x = \pm 2$$
$$x = 100, \frac{1}{100}$$

36.
$$\log(\log x) = 1$$
$$\log x = 10$$
$$x = 10^{10}$$

38.
$$3^{\log x} = 3x$$
$$\log 3^{\log x} = \log 3x$$
$$\log x \log 3 = \log 3 + \log x$$
$$\log x \log 3 - \log x = \log 3$$
$$\log x(\log 3 - 1) = \log 3$$
$$\log x = \frac{\log 3}{\log 3 - 1}$$
$$x = 10^{(\log 3)/(\log 3 - 1)}$$

40. (A)
$$\ln(\ln x) + \ln x = 2$$
$$\ln[(\ln x)(x)] = 2$$
$$x \ln x = e^2$$
$$\ln x = \frac{e^2}{x}$$

It is difficult to isolate the x's.

(B)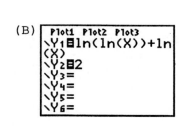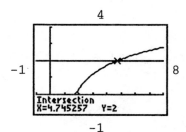

There is one solution.

42. (A) $e^{x/4} = 5 \log x + 4 \ln x$

logs of different bases are used.

(B)

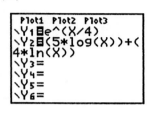 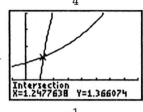 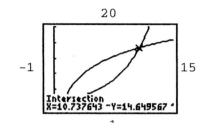

$x \approx 1.248, \ 10.738$

44. $\log_4 23 = \dfrac{\ln 23}{\ln 4}$

≈ 2.2618

46. $\log_2 0.005439 = \dfrac{\ln 0.005439}{\ln 2}$

≈ -7.5224

48. $\log_{12} 435.62 = \dfrac{\ln 435.62}{\ln 12}$

≈ 2.4455

50. $A = P\left(1 + \dfrac{r}{n}\right)^{nt}$ for t

$\dfrac{A}{P} = \left(1 + \dfrac{r}{n}\right)^{nt}$

$\ln \dfrac{A}{P} = \ln\left(1 + \dfrac{r}{n}\right)^{nt}$

$\ln \dfrac{A}{P} = nt \ln\left(1 + \dfrac{r}{n}\right)$

$t = \dfrac{\ln \frac{A}{P}}{n \ln(1 + \frac{r}{n})}$

52. $t = \dfrac{-1}{k}(\ln A - \ln A_0)$ for A

$-kt = \ln A - \ln A_0$

$-kt = \ln \dfrac{A}{A_0}$

$e^{-kt} = \dfrac{A}{A_0}$

$A = A_0 e^{-kt}$

54. $L = 8.8 + 5.1 \log D$ for D

$\log D = \dfrac{L - 8.8}{5.1}$

$D = 10^{(L-8.8)/5.1}$

56. $S = R\left[\dfrac{(1 + i)^n - 1}{i}\right]$ for n

$\dfrac{Si}{R} + 1 = (1 + i)^n$

$\ln\left(\dfrac{Si}{R} + 1\right) = n \ln(1 + i)$

$n = \dfrac{\ln(\frac{Si}{R} + 1)}{\ln(1 + i)}$

58. $y = \dfrac{e^x - e^{-x}}{2}$

$2y = e^x - \dfrac{1}{e^x}$

$2ye^x = e^{2x} - 1$

$e^{2x} - 2ye^x - 1 = 0$ which is quadratic in e^x with solutions

$e^x = y \pm \sqrt{y^2 + 1}$, reject $y - \sqrt{y^2 + 1}$ since $e^x > 0$

$e^x = y + \sqrt{y^2 + 1}$

$x = \ln[y + \sqrt{y^2 + 1}]$

60. $y = \dfrac{e^x + e^{-x}}{e^x - e^{-x}} \cdot \dfrac{e^x}{e^x} = \dfrac{e^{2x} + 1}{e^{2x} - 1}$

$$y(e^{2x} - 1) = e^{2x} + 1$$
$$ye^{2x} - y = e^{2x} + 1$$
$$ye^{2x} - e^{2x} = y + 1$$
$$e^{2x}(y - 1) = y + 1$$
$$e^{2x} = \frac{y + 1}{y - 1}$$
$$2x = \ln\frac{y + 1}{y - 1}$$
$$x = \frac{1}{2}\ln\frac{y + 1}{y - 1}$$

62. $y = \log_3(4 + x) - 5$

$$y = \frac{\ln(4 + x)}{\ln 3} - 5$$

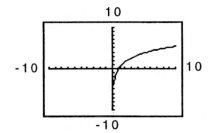

64. $y = \log_3 x + \log_2 x$

$$y = \frac{\ln x}{\ln 3} + \frac{\ln x}{\ln 2}$$

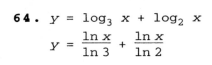

66. $3^{-x} - 3x = 0$
Graph $y = 3^{-x} - 3x$. The x-intercept (zero) is at $x = 0.25$ to 2 decimal places.

68. $x2^x - 1 = 0$
Graph $y = x2^x - 1$. The x-intercept (zero) is at $x = 0.64$ to 2 decimal places.

70. $xe^{2x} - 1 = 0$
Graph $y = xe^{2x} - 1$. The x-intercept (zero) is at $x = 0.43$ to 2 decimal places.

72. $e^{-x} - 2x = 0$
Graph $y = e^{-x} - 2x$. The x-intercept (zero) is at $x = 0.35$ to 2 decimal places.

74. $\ln x + x^2 = 0$
Graph $y = \ln x + x^2$. The x-intercept (zero) is at $x = 0.65$ to 2 decimal places.

76. $\ln x + x = 0$
Graph $y = \ln x + x$. The x-intercept (zero) is at $x = 0.57$ to 2 decimal places.

78. $A = P\left[1 + \dfrac{r}{m}\right]^n$

$$4P = P\left[1 + \frac{0.2}{1}\right]^n$$
$$4 = [1.2]^n$$
$$\ln 4 = \ln 1.2^n$$
$$n = \frac{\ln 4}{\ln 1.2}$$
$$n \approx 7.6$$

8 yrs. to nearest year

80. $A = Pe^{rt}$

$$8000 = 5000e^{0.09t}$$
$$1.6 = e^{0.09t}$$
$$\ln 1.6 = 0.09t$$
$$t = \frac{\ln 1.6}{0.09} \approx 5.22 \text{ years}$$

82. (A) $L = 8.8 + 5.1 \log D$
$L = 8.8 + 5.1 \log 6$
$L \approx 12.8$

(B) $20.6 = 8.8 + 5.1 \log D$
$11.8 = 5.1 \log D$
$\dfrac{11.8}{5.1} = \log D$
$D = 10^{11.8/5.1} \approx 205.93$
$D \approx 206$ in.

84. $P = P_0 e^{rt}$
$1.7 \times 10^{14} = 4 \times 10^9 e^{0.02t}$
$e^{0.02t} = 42,500$
$0.02t = \ln 42,500$
$t = \dfrac{\ln 42,500}{0.02}$
$t = 533$ years to nearest year

86. $A = A_0 e^{-0.000124t}$
$\dfrac{A_0}{2} = A_0 e^{-0.000124t}$
$e^{-0.000124t} = 0.5$
$-0.000124t = \ln 0.5$
$t = \dfrac{\ln 0.5}{-0.000124}$
$t = 5590$ years to 3 significant digits

88. $N = 2(1 - e^{-0.037t})$
$2(0.8) = 2(1 - e^{-0.037t})$
$1 - e^{-0.037t} = 0.8$
$e^{-0.037t} = 0.2$
$-0.037t = \ln 0.2$
$t = \dfrac{\ln 0.2}{-0.037}$
$t = 43$ days to nearest day

90. $I = I_0 e^{-kd}$
$\dfrac{I_0}{2} = I_0 e^{-k(14.3)}$
$e^{-14.3k} = 0.5$
$-14.3k = \ln 0.5$
$k = \dfrac{\ln 0.5}{-14.3}$
$k \approx 0.0485$

Photic zone $\approx 1\%$ of I_0:
$I = I_0 e^{-0.0485d}$
$0.01I_0 = I_0 e^{-0.0485d}$
$\ln 0.01 = -0.0485d$
$d = \dfrac{\ln 0.01}{-0.0485}$
$d \approx 95.0$ feet

92. $N = \dfrac{200}{4 + 21e^{-0.1t}}$

$40 = \dfrac{200}{4 + 21e^{-0.1t}}$

$40(4 + 21e^{-0.1t}) = 200$

$160 + 840e^{-0.1t} = 200$

$840e^{-0.1t} = 40$

$e^{-0.1t} = \dfrac{40}{840}$

$-0.1t = \ln \dfrac{40}{840}$

$t = \dfrac{\ln \dfrac{40}{840}}{-0.1} = 30$ days to the nearest day

CHAPTER 6
Exercise 6-1

2. $\frac{1}{5}$ rotation $= \frac{1}{5}(360°)$
$\qquad = 72°$

4. $\frac{7}{6}$ rotations $= \frac{7}{6}(360°)$
$\qquad = 420°$

6. $\theta = \frac{s}{r} = \frac{16}{8}$
$\quad \theta = 2$

8. $\theta = \frac{s}{r} = \frac{27}{18}$
$\quad \theta = 1.5$

10. $\frac{1}{6}$ rotation $= \frac{1}{6}(2\pi)$
$\qquad = \frac{\pi}{3}$

12. $\frac{11}{8}$ rotations $= \frac{11}{8}(2\pi)$
$\qquad = \frac{11\pi}{4}$

14. $60°\left(\frac{\pi}{180°}\right) = \frac{\pi}{3}$

$120°\left(\frac{\pi}{180°}\right) = \frac{2\pi}{3}$

$180°\left(\frac{\pi}{180°}\right) = \pi$

$240°\left(\frac{\pi}{180°}\right) = \frac{4\pi}{3}$

$300°\left(\frac{\pi}{180°}\right) = \frac{5\pi}{3}$

$360°\left(\frac{\pi}{180°}\right) = 2\pi$

16. $-90°\left(\frac{\pi}{180°}\right) = -\frac{\pi}{2}$

$-180°\left(\frac{\pi}{180°}\right) = -\pi$

$-270°\left(\frac{\pi}{180°}\right) = -\frac{3\pi}{2}$

$-360°\left(\frac{\pi}{180°}\right) = -2\pi$

18. $\frac{\pi}{6} \cdot \frac{180°}{\pi} = 30°$

$\frac{\pi}{3} \cdot \frac{180°}{\pi} = 60°$

$\frac{\pi}{2} \cdot \frac{180°}{\pi} = 90°$

$\frac{2\pi}{3} \cdot \frac{180°}{\pi} = 120°$

$\frac{5\pi}{6} \cdot \frac{180°}{\pi} = 150°$

$\pi \cdot \frac{180°}{\pi} = 180°$

20. $-\frac{\pi}{4} \cdot \frac{180°}{\pi} = -45°$

$-\frac{\pi}{2} \cdot \frac{180°}{\pi} = -90°$

$-\frac{3\pi}{4} \cdot \frac{180°}{\pi} = -135°$

$-\pi \cdot \frac{180°}{\pi} = -180°$

22. True. For example, if two angles are complementary, their sum is 90°. If two positive numbers have a sum of 90°, each number must be less than 90°.

24. True. For example, to be in standard position means that the vertex is at the origin and the initial side is along the positive x axis. Hence, if two angles, in standard position have the same measure, the terminal side will be the same amount of rotation in the same direction from the initial side. Thus, they are coterminal.

26. False. For example, $\theta = 180°$ is a Quadrantal angle which is not a right angle.

28. $14°18'37" = 14° + \frac{18}{60} + \frac{37}{3600}$
$\qquad = 14.310°$

30. $184°31'7" = 184 + \frac{31}{60} + \frac{7}{3600}$
$\qquad = 184.519°$

32. $49.715° = 49°(0.715 \cdot 60)'$
$\qquad = 49°42.9'$
$\qquad = 49°42'(0.9 \cdot 60)"$
$\qquad = 49°42'54"$

```
49.715▶DMS
        49°42'54"
```

34. $156.808° = 156°(0.808 \cdot 60)'$
$\qquad = 156°48.48'$
$\qquad = 156°48'(0.48 \cdot 60)"$
$\qquad = 156°48'29"$

```
156.808▶DMS
         156°48'28.8"
```

36. $\theta_{rad} = \dfrac{\pi \text{ rad}}{180°} \ \theta_{deg} = \dfrac{\pi}{180}(79) = 1.379$ **38.** $48°55'12'' = 48° + \dfrac{55}{60} + \dfrac{12}{3600} = 48.92°$

$$\theta_{rad} = \dfrac{\pi \text{ rad}}{180°} \ \theta_{deg} = \dfrac{\pi}{180}(48.92) = 0.854$$

40. $\theta_{deg} = \dfrac{180°}{\pi \text{ rad}} \ \theta_{rad} = \dfrac{180}{\pi}(0.64) = 36.67°$

42. $\theta_{deg} = \dfrac{180°}{\pi \text{ rad}} \ \theta_{rad} = \dfrac{180}{\pi}(-2.65) = -151.83°$

44. $90° < 97° < 180°$, Quadrant II

46. $-4.75 + 2\pi \approx 1.53 \rightarrow -4.75$ is coterminal with 1.53

$0 < 1.53 < 1.57 \approx \dfrac{\pi}{2}$, 1.53 is in Quadrant I $\rightarrow -4.75$ is in Quadrant I

48. $\dfrac{8\pi}{3} - 2\pi = \dfrac{2\pi}{3} \rightarrow \dfrac{8\pi}{3}$ is coterminal with $\dfrac{2\pi}{3}$

$\dfrac{\pi}{2} < \dfrac{2\pi}{3} < \pi$, $\dfrac{2\pi}{3}$ is in Quadrant II $\rightarrow \dfrac{8\pi}{3}$ is in Quadrant II

50. $\dfrac{11\pi}{5} - 2\pi = \dfrac{\pi}{5} \rightarrow \dfrac{11\pi}{5}$ is coterminal with $\dfrac{\pi}{5}$

$0 < \dfrac{\pi}{5} < \dfrac{\pi}{2}$, $\dfrac{\pi}{5}$ is in Quadrant I $\rightarrow \dfrac{11\pi}{5}$ is in Quadrant I

52. $-630° + 2(360°) = 90° \rightarrow -630°$ is coterminal with $90° \rightarrow$ Quadrantal angle

54. $24.14 - 3(2\pi) \approx 5.29 \rightarrow 24.14$ is coterminal with 5.29

$\dfrac{3\pi}{2} \approx 4.71 < 5.29 < 6.28 \approx 2\pi$, 5.29 is in Quadrant IV $\rightarrow 24.14$ is in Quadrant IV

56. $120°$ is in Quadrant II, $240°$ is in Quadrant III. Not coterminal.

58. $840° - 2(360°) = 120°$. Coterminal.

60. $\theta_{deg} = \dfrac{180°}{\pi \text{ rad}} \ \theta_{rad} = \dfrac{180}{\pi}\left(-\dfrac{8\pi}{3}\right) = -480°$

$-480° + 2(360°) = 240°$; $120°$ is in Quadrant II, $240°$ is in

Quadrant III $\rightarrow -\dfrac{8\pi}{3}$ is in Quadrant III. Not coterminal.

62. $\dfrac{5\pi}{4} - 2\pi = -\dfrac{3\pi}{4}$. Coterminal.   **64.** $-\dfrac{19\pi}{4} + 2(2\pi) = -\dfrac{3\pi}{4}$. Coterminal.

66. $\theta_{rad} = \dfrac{\pi \text{ rad}}{180°} \ \theta_{deg} = \dfrac{\pi}{180}(855) = \dfrac{19\pi}{4}$

$\dfrac{19\pi}{4} - 3(2\pi) = -\dfrac{5\pi}{4}$; $-\dfrac{3\pi}{4}$ is in Quadrant III,

$-\dfrac{5\pi}{4}$ is in Quadrant II $\rightarrow 855°$ is in Quadrant II.

Not coterminal.

68. $7°12' = 7\dfrac{12}{60}° = 7.2°$

$\dfrac{s}{C} = \dfrac{\theta}{360°}$

$\dfrac{500}{C} = \dfrac{7.2°}{360°}$

$C = 25{,}000$ miles

70. Using the formula for circumference, set $2\pi r$ equal to the result from Problem 67. Solve for the radius r. For the surface area, use this radius in the formula $SA = 4\pi r^2$. For volume use this radius in the formula $V = \dfrac{4}{3}\pi r^3$.

72. At 1:30 the minute hand points straight down, which is an angle of π from 12:00, and the hour hand has made $\frac{1.5}{12} = \frac{1}{8}$ revolutions from 12:00; therefore the angle between the hands $= \pi - \frac{\pi}{4} = \frac{3\pi}{4}$.

74. $s = 4$ ft $= 48$ in

$r = \frac{d}{2} = \frac{6}{2} = 3$ in

$\theta = \frac{s}{r} = \frac{48}{3} = 16$ rad

76. $\left(\frac{9}{24} \text{ rev}\right)\left(\frac{2\pi}{1 \text{ rev}}\right) = \frac{3\pi}{4} \approx 2.36$ rad

78. The arc which both tires rotate through will be the same.

$s = \theta_{\text{front}} r_{\text{front}} = 15 \cdot 40 = 600$ cm

$\theta_{\text{back}} = \frac{s}{r_{\text{back}}} = \frac{600}{60} = 10$ rad

80. $s = r\theta = 381,000(0.0092)$

$s \approx 3500$ km

82. $8° \cdot \frac{\pi}{180°} \approx .1396$ rad

$s = \theta r$

$= 0.1396(500)$

≈ 70 feet

Exercise 6-2

2. $\sin(90° - \theta) = \frac{\text{Opp}}{\text{Hyp}} = \frac{a}{c}$

$\cos(90° - \theta) = \frac{\text{Adj}}{\text{Hyp}} = \frac{b}{c}$

$\sin(90° - \theta) = \frac{\text{Opp}}{\text{Adj}} = \frac{a}{b}$

$\csc(90° - \theta) = \frac{\text{Hyp}}{\text{Opp}} = \frac{c}{a}$

$\sec(90° - \theta) = \frac{\text{Hyp}}{\text{Adj}} = \frac{c}{b}$

$\cot(90° - \theta) = \frac{\text{Adj}}{\text{Opp}} = \frac{b}{a}$

4. $\cos 46.18 = 0.6924$

6. $\csc 1°13' = \frac{1}{\sin 1°13'} = 47.10$

8. $\sec 15.92° = \frac{1}{\cos 15.92°} = 1.040$

10. $\tan 24°29' = 0.4554$

12. $\cos^{-1} 0.5277 = 58.15°$

14. $\sin^{-1} 0.0317 = 1.82°$

16. $\tan^{-1} 4.296 = 76.90°$

18. $\tan^{-1} 1.359 = 53°40'$

20. $\cos^{-1} 0.0128 = 89°20'$

22. $\sin^{-1} 0.4862 = 29°10'$

24. $\alpha = 90° - \beta = 90° - 33.7° = 56.3°$

$\sin 33.7 = \frac{\text{Opp}}{\text{Hyp}} = \frac{22.4}{c} \Rightarrow c = \frac{22.4}{\sin 33.7} = 40.4$

$\tan 33.7 = \frac{\text{Opp}}{\text{Adj}} = \frac{22.4}{a} \Rightarrow a = \frac{22.4}{\tan 33.7} = 33.6$

26. $\alpha = 90° - \beta = 90° - 62°30' = 27°30'$

$\sin 62°30' = \frac{\text{Opp}}{\text{Hyp}} = \frac{b}{42.5} \Rightarrow c = 42.5 \sin 62°30' = 37.7$

$\cos 62°30' = \frac{\text{Adj}}{\text{Hyp}} = \frac{a}{42.5} \Rightarrow a = 42.5 \cos 62°30' = 19.6$

28. $\beta = 90° - \alpha = 90° - 54° = 36°$

$\cos 54° = \frac{\text{Adj}}{\text{Hyp}} = \frac{b}{4.3} \Rightarrow b = 4.3 \cos 54° = 2.5$

$\sin 54° = \frac{\text{Opp}}{\text{Hyp}} = \frac{a}{4.3} \Rightarrow a = 4.3 \sin 54° = 3.5$

30. $\beta = 90° - \alpha = 90° - 35.73° = 54.27°$

$\tan 35.73° = \dfrac{\text{Opp}}{\text{Adj}} = \dfrac{a}{6.482} \Rightarrow a = 6.482 \tan 35.73° = 4.663$

$\cos 35.73° = \dfrac{\text{Adj}}{\text{Hyp}} = \dfrac{6.482}{c} \Rightarrow c = \dfrac{6.482}{\cos 35.73°} = 7.985$

32. $a^2 + b^2 = c^2 \Rightarrow a = \sqrt{c^2 - b^2} = \sqrt{165^2 - 50^2} = 157$

$\cos \alpha = \dfrac{\text{Adj}}{\text{Hyp}} = \dfrac{50}{165} \Rightarrow \alpha = \cos^{-1} \dfrac{50}{165} = 72.4° = 72°20'$

$\beta = 90° - \alpha = 90° - 72°20' = 27°40'$

34. False: $20° < 70°$; $\cos 20° \approx 0.940 > 0.342 \approx \cos 70°$

36. False: $20° < 70°$; $\cot 20° \approx 2.75 > 0.364 \approx \cot 70°$

38. False: $35° < 55°$; $\csc 35° \approx 1.74 > 1.22 \approx \csc 55°$

40. (A) Using ΔOAD; $\sin \theta = \dfrac{\text{Opp}}{\text{Hyp}} = \dfrac{AD}{1} = AD$

(B) Using ΔODC; $\tan \theta = \dfrac{\text{Opp}}{\text{Adj}} = \dfrac{DC}{1} = DC$

(C) $\theta + \angle EOD = 90°$; $\angle EOD + \angle OED = 90° \Rightarrow \angle OED = \theta$

Using ΔOED; $\csc \theta = \csc(\angle OED) = \dfrac{\text{Hyp}}{\text{Opp}} = \dfrac{OE}{1} = OE$

42. (A) As $\theta \to 90°$, opposite $\to 1$, $\sin \theta = \dfrac{\text{Opp}}{\text{Hyp}} \to 1$

(B) As $\theta \to 90°$, opposite $\to 1$, adjacent $\to 0$, $\tan \theta = \dfrac{\text{Opp}}{\text{Adj}} \to \infty$

(C) As $\theta \to 90°$, $\sin \theta \to 1$, $\csc \theta = \dfrac{1}{\sin \theta} \to 1$

44. (A) As $\theta \to 0°$, adjacent $\to 1$, $\cos \theta = \dfrac{\text{Adj}}{\text{Hyp}} \to 1$

(B) As $\theta \to 0°$, opposite $\to 0$, adjacent $\to 1$, $\cot \theta = \dfrac{\text{Adj}}{\text{Opp}} \to \infty$

(C) As $\theta \to 0°$, $\cos \theta \to 1$, $\sec \theta = \dfrac{1}{\cos \theta} \to 1$

46. $\cot \beta = \dfrac{x}{h} \Rightarrow x = h \cot \beta$

$\cot \alpha = \dfrac{d - x}{h} \Rightarrow x = d - h \cot \alpha$

$h \cot \beta = d - h \cot \alpha$

$d = h \cot \beta + h \cot \alpha$

$d = h(\cot \beta + \cot \alpha)$

$h = \dfrac{d}{\cot \beta + \cot \alpha}$

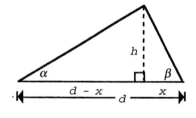

48.

$\tan 32.2° = \dfrac{h}{500}$

$h = 500 \tan 32.2° = 315$ m

50.

$\sin 15°30' = \dfrac{8}{315t} \Rightarrow t = \dfrac{8}{315 \sin 15°30'} = 0.095$ hr

$0.095 \text{ hr} \cdot \left(\dfrac{60 \text{ min}}{1 \text{ hr}}\right) = 6$ min

52. 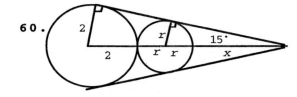 $\tan 32' = \dfrac{D}{93,000,000} \Rightarrow D = 93,000,000 \cdot \tan 32' = 870,000$ mi

54. Finding the central angle of one side, $\dfrac{360°}{9} = 40°$. Drop a perpendicular from the center to a side. This will divide the central angle and the side in half.

$\sin 20° = \dfrac{\frac{d}{2}}{4.06} \Rightarrow d = 2 \cdot 4.06 \sin 20° \approx 2.78$ in.

56. $g = \dfrac{v}{t \sin \theta} = \dfrac{9 \frac{ft}{sec}}{(4 \text{ sec}) \sin 4°}$

$g = 32.3 \dfrac{ft}{sec^2}$

58. (A) Cost = C = cost along shore + cost underwater
$\qquad\qquad C = 20,000(20 - 4 \tan \theta) + 30,000(4 \sec \theta)$
$\qquad\quad C(\theta) = 120,000 \sec \theta - 80,000 \tan \theta + 400,000$
(B)

θ	$C(\theta) = 120,000 \sec \theta - 80,000 \tan \theta + 400,000$
10°	\$507,745
20°	\$498,584
30°	\$492,376
40°	\$489,521
50°	\$491,347

60.

(1) $\sin 15° = \dfrac{r}{r + x} \Rightarrow r + x = \dfrac{r}{\sin 15°}$

(2) $\sin 15° = \dfrac{2}{2 + r + r + x} = \dfrac{2}{2 + r + \frac{r}{\sin 15°}}$

$2 + r + \dfrac{r}{\sin 15°} = \dfrac{2}{\sin 15°}$

$2 \sin 15° + r \sin 15° + r = 2$

$r \sin 15° + r = 2 - 2 \sin 15°$

$r(\sin 15° + 1) = 2 - 2 \sin 15°$

$r = \dfrac{2 - 2 \sin 15°}{\sin 15° + 1} = 1.2$ in

Exercise 6-3

2. $(8, 6) \Rightarrow r = \sqrt{8^2 + 6^2} = 10$

$\sin \theta = \dfrac{6}{10} = \dfrac{3}{5}$

$\cos \theta = \dfrac{8}{10} = \dfrac{4}{5}$

$\tan \theta = \dfrac{6}{8} = \dfrac{3}{4}$

$\sec \theta = \dfrac{5}{4}$

$\csc \theta = \dfrac{5}{3}$

$\cot \theta = \dfrac{4}{3}$

4. $(-4, -3) \Rightarrow r = \sqrt{(-4)^2 + (-3)^2} = 5$

$\sin \theta = \dfrac{-3}{5}$

$\cos \theta = \dfrac{-4}{5}$

$\tan \theta = \dfrac{-3}{-4} = \dfrac{3}{4}$

$\sec \theta = -\dfrac{5}{4}$

$\csc \theta = -\dfrac{5}{3}$

$\cot \theta = \dfrac{4}{3}$

6. $(1, -2) \Rightarrow r = \sqrt{1^2 + (-2)^2} = \sqrt{5}$

$\sin \theta = \dfrac{-2}{\sqrt{5}}$

$\cos \theta = \dfrac{1}{\sqrt{5}}$

$\tan \theta = \dfrac{-2}{1} = -2$

$\sec \theta = \sqrt{5}$

$\csc \theta = -\dfrac{\sqrt{5}}{2}$

$\cot \theta = -\dfrac{1}{2}$

8. $(3, b) \Rightarrow b = \sqrt{5^2 - 3^2} = 4$ $\sin \theta = \dfrac{4}{5}$

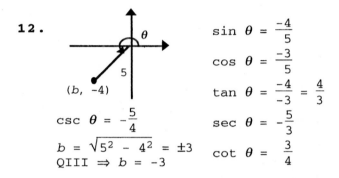

$\cos \theta = \dfrac{3}{5}$

$\tan \theta = \dfrac{4}{3}$

$\sec \theta = \dfrac{5}{3}$

$\csc \theta = \dfrac{5}{4}$

$\cot \theta = \dfrac{3}{4}$

10.

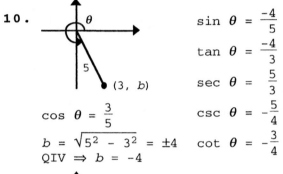

$\cos \theta = \dfrac{3}{5}$

$b = \sqrt{5^2 - 3^2} = \pm 4$
QIV $\Rightarrow b = -4$

$\sin \theta = \dfrac{-4}{5}$

$\tan \theta = \dfrac{-4}{3}$

$\sec \theta = \dfrac{5}{3}$

$\csc \theta = -\dfrac{5}{4}$

$\cot \theta = -\dfrac{3}{4}$

12.

$\csc \theta = -\dfrac{5}{4}$

$b = \sqrt{5^2 - 4^2} = \pm 3$
QIII $\Rightarrow b = -3$

$\sin \theta = \dfrac{-4}{5}$

$\cos \theta = \dfrac{-3}{5}$

$\tan \theta = \dfrac{-4}{-3} = \dfrac{4}{3}$

$\sec \theta = -\dfrac{5}{3}$

$\cot \theta = \dfrac{3}{4}$

14.

$\csc \theta = -\dfrac{5}{4}$

$b = \sqrt{5^2 - 4^2} = \pm 3$
QIV $\Rightarrow b = 3$

$\sin \theta = \dfrac{-4}{5}$

$\cos \theta = \dfrac{3}{5}$

$\tan \theta = \dfrac{-4}{3}$

$\sec \theta = \dfrac{5}{3}$

$\cot \theta = -\dfrac{3}{4}$

16. In degree mode, $\tan 21° = 0.3839.$

18. In radian mode,
$\csc(-11) = \dfrac{1}{\sin(-11)} = 1.000.$

20. In degree mode, $\sin 14°27' = 0.2495.$

22. In degree mode,
$\sec(-93°53') = \dfrac{1}{\cos(-93°53')} = -14.77.$

24. In radian mode,
$\cot 25.1 = \dfrac{1}{\tan 25.1} = -30.53.$

26. In radian mode,
$\cos(-4.61) = -0.1022.$

28. $(1, 1) \Rightarrow r = \sqrt{1^2 + 1^2} = \sqrt{2}$

$\sin \theta = \dfrac{1}{\sqrt{2}}$

$\cos \theta = \dfrac{1}{\sqrt{2}}$

$\tan \theta = \dfrac{1}{1} = 1$

$\csc \theta = \sqrt{2}$

$\sec \theta = \sqrt{2}$

$\cot \theta = 1$

30. $(1, -\sqrt{3}) \Rightarrow r = \sqrt{1^2 + (-\sqrt{3})^2} = 2$

$\sin \theta = \dfrac{-\sqrt{3}}{2}$

$\cos \theta = \dfrac{1}{2}$

$\tan \theta = \dfrac{-\sqrt{3}}{1} = -\sqrt{3}$

$\csc \theta = -\dfrac{2}{\sqrt{3}}$

$\sec \theta = 2$

$\cot \theta = -\dfrac{1}{\sqrt{3}}$

32. $(\sqrt{2}, -\sqrt{2}) \Rightarrow r = \sqrt{(\sqrt{2})^2 + (-\sqrt{2})^2} = 2$

$\sin \theta = \dfrac{-\sqrt{2}}{2}$

$\cos \theta = \dfrac{\sqrt{2}}{2}$

$\tan \theta = \dfrac{-\sqrt{2}}{\sqrt{2}} = -1$

$\csc \theta = -\dfrac{2}{\sqrt{2}}$

$\sec \theta = \dfrac{2}{\sqrt{2}}$

$\cot \theta = -1$

34. I and III quadrants, since $\tan \theta = b/a$ and a and b are either both positive or both negative in these quadrants.

36. I and II quadrants, since $\sin \theta = b/r$ and b is positive only in these quadrants (r is always positive).

38. II and III quadrants, since $\cos \theta = a/r$ and a is negative only in these quadrants (r is always positive).

40. II and III quadrants, since $\sec \theta = r/a$ and a is negative only in these quadrants (r is always positive).

42. I and III quadrants, since $\cot \theta = a/b$ and a and b are either both positive or both negative in these quadrants.

44. I and IV quadrants, since $\sec \theta = r/a$ and a is positive only in these quadrants (r is always positive).

46.

$\sin \theta = -\dfrac{2}{3}$

$3^2 = (-2)^2 + a^2$

$a = -\sqrt{5}$

$\cos \theta = \dfrac{-\sqrt{5}}{3}$

$\tan \theta = \dfrac{-2}{-\sqrt{5}} = \dfrac{2}{\sqrt{5}}$

$\csc \theta = -\dfrac{3}{2}$

$\sec \theta = -\dfrac{3}{\sqrt{5}}$

$\cot \theta = \dfrac{\sqrt{5}}{2}$

48.

$\sin \theta = -\dfrac{2}{3}$

$a = \sqrt{5}$ (see #46)

$\cos \theta = \dfrac{\sqrt{5}}{3}$

$\tan \theta = \dfrac{-2}{\sqrt{5}}$

$\csc \theta = -\dfrac{3}{2}$

$\sec \theta = \dfrac{3}{\sqrt{5}}$

$\cot \theta = -\dfrac{\sqrt{5}}{2}$

50.

$\sec \theta = \sqrt{3}$

$(\sqrt{3})^2 = 1^2 + b^2$

$b = -\sqrt{2}$

$\sin \theta = \dfrac{-\sqrt{2}}{\sqrt{3}}$

$\cos \theta = \dfrac{1}{\sqrt{3}}$

$\tan \theta = \dfrac{-\sqrt{2}}{1} = -\sqrt{2}$

$\csc \theta = -\dfrac{\sqrt{3}}{\sqrt{2}}$

$\cot \theta = -\dfrac{1}{\sqrt{2}}$

52. The formula for the area of a triangle is $A = \frac{1}{2}bh$ where $b = a = 1$. The height of the triangle is the unmarked side which can be found by $\tan \theta = \frac{h}{a} = h$. The area is then $A = \frac{1}{2} \cdot 1 \cdot \tan \theta = \frac{1}{2} \tan \theta$.

54. When the terminal side lies along the horizontal axis, the y-coordinate is $0 \Rightarrow$ division by 0 will occur for cotangent $\left(\cot \theta = \frac{x}{y} \right)$ and cosecant $\left(\csc \theta = \frac{r}{y} \right)$ which are, therefore, not defined.

56. (A) $\theta = \frac{s}{r} = \frac{8}{2} = 4$ radians

(B) $\sin \theta = \frac{b}{2}$ $\qquad\qquad \cos \theta = \frac{a}{2}$

$2(\sin 4) = b$ $\qquad\qquad a = 2 \cos 4$

$\qquad b = -1.514$ $\qquad\qquad a = -1.307$

$P(a, b) = (-1.307, -1.514)$

58.

$\tan \theta = \frac{5}{12} \Rightarrow \theta = \tan^{-1}\left(\frac{5}{12} \right) = 0.39479$ rad

$s = \theta r = 0.39479 \text{ rad} \cdot 13 = 5.13$ units

(12, 5) s θ

$r = \sqrt{12^2 + 5^2} = 13$

60. (A) $I = k \cos \theta = 0.940k$ for $\theta = 20°$

$\qquad\qquad\qquad = 0.643k$ for $\theta = 50°$

$\qquad\qquad\qquad = 0$ $\qquad$ for $\theta = 90°$

(B) $I_v = k \cos 0° = k$

$0.8 I_v = 0.8k = k \cos \theta \Rightarrow \cos \theta = 0.8 \Rightarrow \theta = \cos^{-1}(0.8)$

$\qquad\qquad\qquad\qquad\qquad\qquad\qquad\quad \theta = 36.9°$

62. $y = \sin(6\pi t) + \sqrt{16 - (\cos 6\pi t)^2}$

$\quad = \sin(6\pi(0.2)) + \sqrt{16 - (\cos(6\pi(0.2)))^2}$

$\quad = 3.33$ inches

64. Divide the polygon into n triangles with base b equal to one side of the polygon. The radius $r = 1$ drawn to the endpoints of the polygon side will form an isosceles triangle. The included angle between the two equal sides is the central angle, $\alpha = \frac{360°}{n}$. Drop a perpendicular from the center to the side, bisecting the angle and the base (see the drawing). This is the height h.

For the right tirangle with sides h, $\frac{b}{2}$, $r = 1$ and angle $\frac{180°}{n}$:

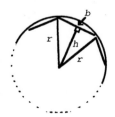

h: $\cos \frac{180°}{n} = \frac{h}{r} \Rightarrow h = r \cos \frac{180°}{n} = \cos \frac{180°}{n}$

$\frac{b}{2}$: $\sin \frac{180°}{n} = \frac{b/2}{r} \Rightarrow \frac{b}{2} = r \sin \frac{180°}{n} = \sin \frac{180°}{n}$

Area:

Right triangle: $A_R = \frac{1}{2} bh = \frac{1}{2} \sin \frac{180°}{n} \cos \frac{180°}{n}$

Isosceles triangle: $A_I = 2A_R = \sin \frac{180°}{n} \cos \frac{180°}{n}$

Polygon: n isosceles triangle: $A_P = n \sin \frac{180°}{n} \cos \frac{180°}{n}$

$\qquad\qquad\qquad\qquad\qquad = n \cos \frac{180°}{n} \sin \frac{180°}{n}$

(A)

n	$A = n \cos \dfrac{180°}{n} \sin \dfrac{180°}{n}$
8	2.82843
100	3.13953
1000	3.14157
10,000	3.14159

(B) A seems to approach π as $n \to \infty$. The area of a circle with radius $1 = \pi(1)^2 = \pi$.

66. (A) $m_1 = \tan \theta_1 = \tan 5.34° = 0.09$
$m_2 = \tan \theta_2 = \tan 92.4° = -23.86$

(B) $y - y_1 = m(x - x_1)$
$y - (-4) = \tan 106°(x - 6)$
$y + 4 = x \tan 106° - 6 \tan 106°$
$y + 4 = -3.49x + 20.92$
$y = -3.49x + 16.92$

Exercise 6-4

2. $\alpha = 180° - 135°$
$= 45°$

4. $\alpha = \theta = \dfrac{\pi}{4}$

6. $-\dfrac{5\pi}{4}$ coterminal with $\dfrac{3\pi}{4}$
$\alpha = \pi - \dfrac{3\pi}{4} = \dfrac{\pi}{4}$

8. $\cos 0° = 1$

10. $\sin 45° = \dfrac{1}{\sqrt{2}} = \dfrac{\sqrt{2}}{2}$

12. $\cos \dfrac{\pi}{3} = \dfrac{1}{2}$

14. $\sin 90° = 1$

16. $\cot 30° = \sqrt{3}$

18. $\sin \dfrac{\pi}{4} = \dfrac{\sqrt{2}}{2}$

20. $\cot \dfrac{\pi}{2} = 0$

22. $\sec 0 = 1$

24. $\cot 0$ is not defined

26. $\tan\left(-\dfrac{\pi}{4}\right) = -1$

28. $\sin(-30°) = -\dfrac{1}{2}$

30. $\sec\left(-\dfrac{\pi}{4}\right) = \sqrt{2}$

32. $\alpha = 210° - 180° = 30°$, Quadrant III
$\sin 210° = -\sin 30° = -\dfrac{1}{2}$

34. $\alpha = 225° - 180° = 45°$, Quadrant III
$\cot 225° = \cot 45° = \dfrac{1}{\tan 45°} = \dfrac{1}{1} = 1$

36. $\alpha = \dfrac{\pi}{3}$, Quadrant IV
$\cos\left(-\dfrac{\pi}{3}\right) = \cos \dfrac{\pi}{3} = \dfrac{1}{2}$

38. $\alpha = \dfrac{\pi}{3}$, Quadrant III
$\csc\left(-\dfrac{2\pi}{3}\right) = -\csc \dfrac{\pi}{3} = -\dfrac{2}{\sqrt{3}}$

40. $\alpha = 390° - 360° = 30°$, Quadrant I
$\tan 390° = \tan 30° = \dfrac{1}{\sqrt{3}}$

42. $\alpha = -450° + 360° = -90°$, Quadrantal angle
$\sec(-450°) = \sec(-90°) = \dfrac{-1}{0}$, Not defined

44. $\alpha = \dfrac{4\pi}{3} - \pi = \dfrac{\pi}{3}$, Quadrant III
$\cot\left(\dfrac{4\pi}{3}\right) = \cot \dfrac{\pi}{3} = \dfrac{1}{\sqrt{3}}$

46. $\alpha = \dfrac{\pi}{3}$, Quadrant IV
$\cos\left(-\dfrac{7\pi}{3}\right) = \cos \dfrac{\pi}{3} = \dfrac{1}{2}$

48. $690° = 690° - 720° = -30°$, Quadrant IV
$\sin 690° = \sin(-30°) = -\sin 30° = -\dfrac{1}{2}$

50. $90°$ and $270°$, since $\sec \theta = r/a$ and $a = 0$ at $\theta = 90°$ and $270°$

52. $0°$ and $180°$, since $\cot \theta = a/b$ and $b = 0$ at $\theta = 0°$ and $180°$

54. Defined for all θ, since $\sin \theta = b/r$ and r is never zero.

56. $\pi/2$ and $3\pi/2$, since $\tan x = \tan(x \text{ rad}) = b/a$ and $a = 0$ at $x = \pi/2$ and $3\pi/2$.

58. 0 and π, since $\csc x = \csc(x \text{ rad}) = r/b$ and $b = 0$ at $x = 0$ and π.

60. Defined for all x, since $\cos x = \cos(x \text{ rad}) = a/r$ and r is never zero.

62. $\cos \theta = -\dfrac{\sqrt{3}}{2}$

$\alpha = 30°$ in Quadrant II $\Rightarrow \theta = 150°$

64. $\csc \theta = -2$

$\alpha = 30°$ in Quadrant III $\Rightarrow \theta = 210°$

66. $\cot \theta = -1$

$\alpha = 45°$ in Quadrant II $\Rightarrow \theta = 135°$

68. $\cos x = -1$

Quadrantal angle $\Rightarrow x = \pi$

70. $\tan x = -1$

$\alpha = \dfrac{\pi}{4}$ in Quadrant II $\Rightarrow x = \dfrac{3\pi}{4}$

72. $\csc x = -\sqrt{2}$

$\alpha = \dfrac{\pi}{4}$ in Quadrant III $\Rightarrow x = \dfrac{5\pi}{4}$

74. $\cot \theta = -\dfrac{1}{\sqrt{3}}$

$\alpha = 60°$ in Quadrants II and IV
$\Rightarrow \theta = 120°,\ 300°$

76. $\tan \theta = 1$

$\alpha = \dfrac{\pi}{4}$ in Quadrants II and III

$\Rightarrow \theta = \dfrac{3\pi}{4},\ \dfrac{5\pi}{4}$

78. Divide the polygon into triangles with one side equal to the side of the polygon, and two legs from the center to endpoints of the side. The included angle of these is the central angle, $\alpha = \dfrac{360°}{n}$. The radius of the circle forms a perpendicular from the center to the side, bisecting the angle and the side and is the height of the new triangle. Using the triangle formed by the radius, one of the legs, and half the side, give the trigonometric identity, $\tan \dfrac{\alpha}{2} = \dfrac{\ell/2}{r}$ where ℓ is the length of a side of the polygon. Solving for ℓ, $\ell = 2r \tan \dfrac{\alpha}{2}$ to find the whole base of the larger triangle. Since there are n of these triangles, the area is

$$A = n\left(\frac{1}{2} bh\right) = n\,\frac{1}{2}\,r\ell = n\,\frac{1}{2}\,r\left(2r \tan \frac{\alpha}{2}\right) = nr^2 \tan \frac{360°/n}{2} = nr^2 \tan \frac{180°}{n}$$

$$= nr^2 \tan \frac{\pi}{n}.$$

80. Inscribed: $A = nr^2 \cos \dfrac{\pi}{n} \sin \dfrac{\pi}{n} = 6 \cdot 4^2 \cos \dfrac{\pi}{6} \sin \dfrac{\pi}{6} \approx 41.57 \text{ in}^2$

Circumscribed: $A = nr^2 \tan \dfrac{\pi}{n} = 6 \cdot 4^2 \tan \dfrac{\pi}{6} \approx 55.43 \text{ in}^2$

82. Inscribed: $A = nr^2 \cos \dfrac{\pi}{n} \sin \dfrac{\pi}{n} = 12 \cdot 5^2 \cos \dfrac{\pi}{12} \sin \dfrac{\pi}{12} \approx 75 \text{ m}^2$

Circumscribed: $A = nr^2 \tan \dfrac{\pi}{n} = 12 \cdot 5^2 \tan \dfrac{\pi}{12} \approx 80.38 \text{ m}^2$

84. (A) $\sin \dfrac{\pi}{6} = \dfrac{y}{1}$ $\qquad \cos \dfrac{\pi}{6} = \dfrac{x}{1}$ $\qquad$ (B) $\sin \dfrac{\pi}{4} = \dfrac{y}{1}$ $\qquad \cos \dfrac{\pi}{4} = \dfrac{x}{1}$

$\qquad\quad \dfrac{1}{2} = \dfrac{y}{1}$ $\qquad\quad \dfrac{\sqrt{3}}{2} = x$ $\qquad\qquad\quad \dfrac{\sqrt{2}}{2} = y$ $\qquad\quad \dfrac{\sqrt{2}}{2} = x$

$\qquad\quad y = \dfrac{1}{2}$ $\qquad\qquad x = \dfrac{\sqrt{3}}{2}$ $\qquad\qquad\quad y = \dfrac{\sqrt{2}}{2}$ $\qquad\quad x = \dfrac{\sqrt{2}}{2}$

86. (A) $\sin \dfrac{\pi}{3} = \dfrac{x}{6}$ $\qquad \cos \dfrac{\pi}{3} = \dfrac{y}{6}$ $\qquad$ (B) $\sin \dfrac{\pi}{4} = \dfrac{8}{x}$ $\qquad \tan \dfrac{\pi}{4} = \dfrac{8}{y}$

$\qquad\quad \dfrac{\sqrt{3}}{2} = \dfrac{x}{6}$ $\qquad\quad \dfrac{1}{2} = \dfrac{y}{6}$ $\qquad\qquad\quad \dfrac{\sqrt{2}}{2} = \dfrac{8}{x}$ $\qquad\quad 1 = \dfrac{8}{y}$

$\qquad\quad x = 3\sqrt{3}$ $\qquad\qquad y = 3$ $\qquad\qquad\quad x = \dfrac{16}{\sqrt{2}}$ $\qquad\qquad y = 8$

$\qquad\qquad\qquad\qquad\qquad\qquad\qquad\qquad\qquad\qquad\quad = 8\sqrt{2}$

$\qquad$ (C) $\sin \dfrac{\pi}{6} = \dfrac{y}{5}$ $\qquad \cos \dfrac{\pi}{6} = \dfrac{x}{5}$

$\qquad\qquad \dfrac{1}{2} = \dfrac{y}{5}$ $\qquad\quad \dfrac{\sqrt{3}}{2} = \dfrac{x}{5}$

$\qquad\qquad y = \dfrac{5}{2}$ $\qquad\qquad x = \dfrac{5\sqrt{3}}{2}$

Exercise 6-5

2. (A) $\dfrac{1}{2}c = \dfrac{1}{2}(2\pi)$ $\qquad$ (B) $\dfrac{1}{12}c = \dfrac{1}{12}(2\pi)$ $\qquad$ (C) $\dfrac{3}{4}c = \dfrac{3}{4}(2\pi)$

$\qquad\quad = \pi$ $\qquad\qquad\qquad = \dfrac{\pi}{6}$ $\qquad\qquad\qquad = \dfrac{3\pi}{2}$

4. (A) $P(\cos x, \sin x) = \left(\cos \dfrac{\pi}{2}, \sin \dfrac{\pi}{2}\right) = (0, 1)$

$\qquad$ (B) $P(\cos x, \sin x) = \left(\cos \dfrac{-3\pi}{2}, \sin \dfrac{-3\pi}{2}\right) = (0, 1)$

$\qquad$ (C) $P(\cos x, \sin x) = \left(\cos \dfrac{5\pi}{2}, \sin \dfrac{5\pi}{2}\right) = (0, 1)$

$\qquad$ (D) $P(\cos x, \sin x) = (\cos -4\pi, \sin -4\pi) = (1, 0)$

$\qquad$ (E) $P(\cos x, \sin x) = (\cos -5\pi, \sin -5\pi) = (-1, 0)$

$\qquad$ (F) $P(\cos x, \sin x) = (\cos 3\pi, \sin 3\pi) = (-1, 0)$

6. (A) for x in $\left[0, \dfrac{\pi}{2}\right]$, $\sin x$ increases from 0 to 1

$\qquad$ (B) for x in $\left[\dfrac{\pi}{2}, \pi\right]$, $\sin x$ decreases from 1 to 0

$\qquad$ (C) for x in $\left[\pi, \dfrac{3\pi}{2}\right]$, $\sin x$ decreases from 0 to -1

$\qquad$ (D) for x in $\left[\dfrac{3\pi}{2}, 2\pi\right]$, $\sin x$ increases from -1 to 0

$\qquad$ (E) for x in $\left[2\pi, \dfrac{5\pi}{2}\right]$, $\sin x$ increases from 0 to 1

8. (A) for x in $\left[0, \dfrac{-\pi}{2}\right]$, cos x decreases from 1 to 0

    (B) for x in $\left[\dfrac{-\pi}{2}, -\pi\right]$, cos x decreases from 0 to -1

    (C) for x in $\left[-\pi, \dfrac{-3\pi}{2}\right]$, cos x increases from -1 to 0

    (D) for x in $\left[\dfrac{-3\pi}{2}, -2\pi\right]$, cos x increases from 0 to 1

    (E) for x in $\left[-2\pi, \dfrac{-5\pi}{2}\right]$, cos x decreases from 1 to 0

10. for $0 \le x \le 4\pi$, cos x = 1 for $x = 0,\ 2\pi,\ 4\pi$

12. for $0 \le x \le 4\pi$, cot x = -1 for $x = \dfrac{3\pi}{4},\ \dfrac{7\pi}{4},\ \dfrac{11\pi}{4},\ \dfrac{15\pi}{4}$

14. for $0 \le x \le 4\pi$, csc x = -1 for $x = \dfrac{3\pi}{2},\ \dfrac{7\pi}{2}$

16. for $-2\pi \le x \le 2\pi$, cos $x = -\dfrac{1}{\sqrt{2}}$ for $x = \dfrac{-5\pi}{4},\ \dfrac{-3\pi}{4},\ \dfrac{3\pi}{4},\ \dfrac{5\pi}{4}$

18. for $-2\pi \le x \le 2\pi$, cot x = 0 for $x = \dfrac{-3\pi}{2},\ \dfrac{-\pi}{2},\ \dfrac{\pi}{2},\ \dfrac{3\pi}{2}$

20. for $-2\pi \le x \le 2\pi$, tan x is not defined for $x = -\dfrac{3\pi}{2},\ -\dfrac{\pi}{2},\ \dfrac{\pi}{2},\ \dfrac{3\pi}{2}$

22. for $-2\pi \le x \le 2\pi$, csc x is not defined for $x = -2\pi,\ -\pi,\ 0,\ \pi,\ 2\pi$

24. sec$(-45) = \dfrac{1}{\cos(-45)} = 1.904$ **26.** cos$(-0.2639) = 0.9654$

28. cot$(-0.0051) = \dfrac{1}{\tan(-0.0051)} = -196.1$

30. Since we have a unit circle, the radius = 1. cos 5.27 = 0.529 = $\dfrac{a}{r} = \dfrac{a}{1} = a$ and

    sin 5.27 = -0.849 = $\dfrac{b}{r} = \dfrac{b}{1} = b$. Thus, the coordinates are (0.529, -0.849).

    Since $a > 0$ and $b < 0$, p is in Quadrant IV.

32. Since we have a unit circle, the radius = 1. cos 105.08 = -0.163 = $\dfrac{a}{r} = \dfrac{a}{1} = a$

    and sin 105.08 = 0.987 = $\dfrac{b}{r} = \dfrac{b}{1} = b$. Thus, the coordinates are (-0.163, 0.987).

    Since $a < 0$ and $b > 0$, p is in Quadrant II.

34. $\sin \dfrac{3\pi}{4}$: $\alpha = \dfrac{\pi}{4}$ in Quadrant II   **36.** $\tan \dfrac{7\pi}{4}$: $\alpha = \dfrac{\pi}{4}$ in Quadrant IV

    $\sin \dfrac{3\pi}{4} = \sin \dfrac{\pi}{4} = \dfrac{\sqrt{2}}{2}$ $\tan \dfrac{7\pi}{4} = -\tan \dfrac{\pi}{4} = -1$

38. $\sec\left(-\dfrac{2\pi}{3}\right)$: $\alpha = \dfrac{\pi}{3}$ in Quadrant III

    $\sec\left(-\dfrac{2\pi}{3}\right) = -\sec \dfrac{\pi}{3} = -\dfrac{1}{\cos \pi/3} = -2$

40. $\sin x = \sin(x \pm k(2\pi))$ because x and $x \pm k(2\pi)$ are coterminal.
If $\sin x = -0.1377$, then
$\sin(x + 2\pi) = \sin(x - 2\pi) = \sin(x + 50\pi) = \sin(x - 66\pi) = -0.1377$.

42. (A) $\sin(-x) = -\sin x$ (B) $\sin(-(-22.9)) = -\sin(-22.9) = -0.789$
       $\sin(-1) = -\sin 1 = -0.841$

     (C) $\sin(-37°) = -\sin 37° = -0.602$ (D) $\sin(-(-432.5°)) = -\sin(-432.5°) = 0.954$

44. $\cos^2 x = 1 - \sin^2 x$
     (A) $\cos^2 5 = 1 - \sin^2 5 = 0.080$ (B) $\cos^2(-70.5) = 1 - \sin^2(-70.5) = 0.034$
     (C) $\cos^2 66° = 1 - \sin^2 66° = 0.165$ (D) $\cos^2(-432.5°) = 1 - \sin^2(-432.5°) = 0.090$

46. (A) (4) $\tan x = \dfrac{\sin x}{\cos x}$ (B) (9) $\sin^2 x + \cos^2 x = 1$ (C) (2) $\sec x = \dfrac{1}{\cos x}$

48. $\cot x \sec x = \dfrac{\cos x}{\sin x} \cdot \dfrac{1}{\cos x} = \dfrac{1}{\sin x} = \csc x$

50. $\csc x \sin x = \dfrac{1}{\sin x} \cdot \sin x = 1$

52. $\dfrac{\cos^2 x}{1 - \cos^2 x} = \dfrac{\cos^2 x}{\sin^2 x} = \left(\dfrac{\cos x}{\sin x}\right)^2 = \cot^2 x$

54. $\sin(-x)\sec(-x) = -\sin x \cdot \dfrac{1}{\cos(-x)} = -\dfrac{\sin x}{\cos x} = -\tan x$

56. $\sec x = \dfrac{1}{\cos x}$. Since cosine has a period of 2π, secant will also have a period of 2π.

58. For example, as $x \to \infty$, either $P(x) \to \infty$ or $P(x) \to -\infty$. This means that as x increases or decreases, $P(x)$ will either be larger or smaller than all earlier values, so it can't repeat itself.

60. True. For example, since the two functions are periodic with the same period, as they go through each period, the same point in the period will be input into each function at the same time, resulting in the same output. So fg and $\dfrac{f}{g}$ will also be periodic.

62. False; for example if $f(x) = \sin x$ (periodic) and $g(x) = x^2$, then $(f \circ g)(x) = \sin(x^2)$ which is not periodic.

64. $\cot(-x) = \dfrac{\cos(-x)}{\sin(-x)} = \dfrac{\cos x}{-\sin x} = -\cot x \Rightarrow$ cotangent is symmetric with respect to origin.

66. $\sec(-x) = \dfrac{1}{\cos(-x)} = \dfrac{1}{\cos x} = \sec x \Rightarrow$ secant is symmetric with respect to y axis.

68.

x	0.05	0.15	0.25	0.35	0.45
$1 - x^2/2$	0.9988	0.9888	0.9688	0.9388	0.8988
$\cos x$	0.9988	0.9888	0.9689	0.9394	0.9004

70. $a_1 = 1$
$a_2 = a_1 + \cos a_1 = 1.540302$
$a_3 = a_2 + \cos a_2 = 1.570792$
$a_4 = a_3 + \cos a_3 = 1.570796$
$a_5 = a_4 + \cos a_4 = 1.570796$

$\dfrac{\pi}{2} = 1.570796$

Exercise 6-6

2.

function	period
cosine	2π
tangent	π
secant	2π

4. (A) The graph of $y = \sin x$ deviates 1 unit from the x axis.
(B) The graph of $y = \cot x$ deviates indefinitely far from the x axis.
(C) The graph of $y = \sec x$ deviates indefinitely far from the x axis.

6. (A) $y = \cos x$: $[-2\pi,\ 2\pi]$
x-intercepts: $-\dfrac{3\pi}{2},\ \dfrac{-\pi}{2},\ \dfrac{\pi}{2},\ \dfrac{3\pi}{2}$

(B) $y = \tan x$: $[-2\pi,\ 2\pi]$
x-intercepts: $-2\pi,\ -\pi,\ 0,\ \pi,\ 2\pi$

(C) $y = \sec x$: $[-2\pi,\ 2\pi]$
x-intercepts: none

8. $y = \tan x$ and $y = \sec x$ are undefined at $x = \dfrac{\pi}{2}$.

10. vertical asymptotes: (A) $y = \sin x$: none   (B) $y = \cot x$: $-2\pi,\ -\pi,\ 0,\ \pi,\ 2\pi$
(C) $y = \sec x$: $-\dfrac{3\pi}{2},\ -\dfrac{\pi}{2},\ \dfrac{\pi}{2},\ \dfrac{3\pi}{2}$

12. (A) $y = \sin x$

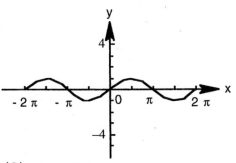

(B) $y = \cot x$

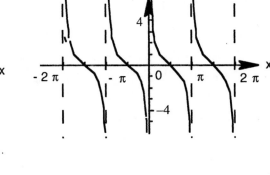

(C) $y = \sec x$

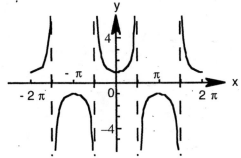

14. (A) Shifting $y = \sec x$, $\frac{\pi}{2}$ to the right produces $y = \csc x$.

(B) Shifting $y = \sec x$, $\frac{\pi}{2}$ to left and a reflection in the x axis produces

$y = \csc x$. $\left[y = -\sec\left(x + \frac{\pi}{2}\right) \right]$

16. (A)

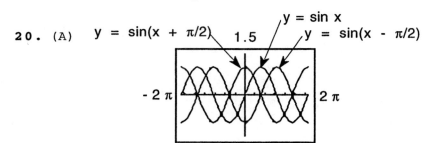

3

$y = -3 \sin x$

-2π $\qquad$ 2π

$y = \sin x$

$y = 2 \sin x$

-3

(B) The x-intercepts do not change.

(C) The graphs deviated 1, 2, and 3 units from the x axis.

(D) The amount of deviation from the x axis appears to be $|A|$.

18. (A)

2

$y = \cos x$

$-\pi$ $\qquad$ π

$y = \cos 2x$

$y = \cos 3x$

-2

(B) 1, 2, and 3

(C) For $y = \cos nx$, n a postive integer, n periods would appear in this viewing window.

20. (A)

$y = \sin(x + \pi/2)$

$y = \sin x$

1.5

$y = \sin(x - \pi/2)$

-2π $\qquad$ 2π

-1.5

(B) The graph of $y = \sin(x + C)$ is shifted C units to the left for $C > 0$ and $|C|$ units to the right for $C < 0$.

22. True. Since the graph of f is periodic, the graph of h is the same graph shifted horizontally 5 units left.

24. True. Since the graph of f is periodic, the graph of k is the same graph reflected about the x axis and shifted vertically 5 units up.

26. In all three cases the calculator gives a division by zero error.

(A) $\csc \pi = \dfrac{1}{\sin \pi} = \dfrac{1}{0}$ (B) $\tan \dfrac{\pi}{2} = \dfrac{1}{0}$ (C) $\cot 0 = \dfrac{1}{0}$

28. $h(x) = \tan x$, $g(x) = x$

```
WINDOW
Xmin=-1
Xmax=1
Xscl=.2
Ymin=-1
Ymax=1
Yscl=.2
Xres=1
```

1

-1 $\qquad$ 1

-1

(A) For x close to zero the two graphs are almost identical.

(B)

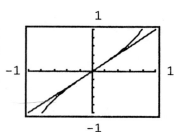

X	Y1	Y2
-.3	-.3093	-.3
-.2	-.2027	-.2
-.1	-.1003	-.1
0	0	0
.1	.10033	.1
.2	.20271	.2
.3	.30934	.3

X=-.3

Exercise 6-7

2. $y = \frac{1}{4} \cos x, \quad -2\pi \leq x \leq 2\pi$

Amplitude $= \frac{1}{4}$

Period $= \frac{2\pi}{1} = 2\pi$

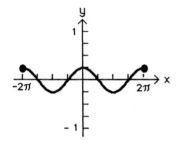

4. $y = -2 \sin x, \quad -2\pi \leq x \leq 2\pi$

Amplitude $= |-2| = 2$

Period $= \frac{2\pi}{1} = 2\pi$

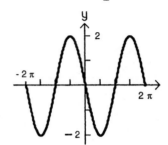

6. $y = \cos 2x, \quad -\pi \leq x \leq \pi$

Amplitude $= 1$

Period $= \frac{2\pi}{2} = \pi$

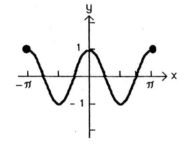

8. $y = \sin\left(\frac{x}{3}\right), \quad -6\pi \leq x \leq 6\pi$

Amplitude $= 1$

Period $= \frac{2\pi}{\frac{1}{3}} = 6\pi$

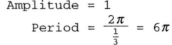
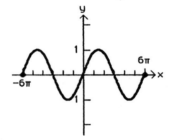

10. $y = \cos(\pi x), \quad -2 \leq x \leq 2$

Amplitude $= 1$

Period $= \frac{2\pi}{\pi} = 2$

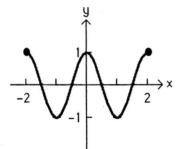

12. $y = 2 \sin 4x, \quad -\pi \leq x \leq \pi$

Amplitude $= 2$

Period $= \frac{2\pi}{4} = \frac{\pi}{2}$

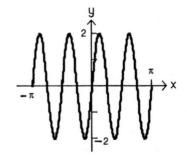

14. $y = -\dfrac{1}{3} \cos 2\pi x, \quad -2 \le x \le 2$

Amplitude $= \dfrac{1}{3}$

Period $= \dfrac{2\pi}{2\pi} = 1$

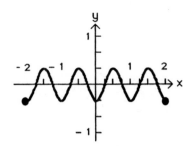

16. $y = -\dfrac{1}{4} \sin\left(\dfrac{x}{2}\right), \quad -4\pi \le x \le 4\pi$

Amplitude $= \dfrac{1}{4}$

Period $= \dfrac{2\pi}{\frac{1}{2}} = 4\pi$

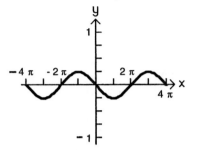

18. $y = 3 + 3 \cos\left(\dfrac{\pi x}{2}\right), \quad -4 \le x \le 4$

Amplitude $= 3$

Period $= \dfrac{2\pi}{\frac{\pi}{2}} = 4$

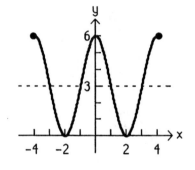

20. $y = 3 - 2 \sin\left(\dfrac{x}{2}\right), \quad -4\pi \le x \le 4\pi$

Amplitude $= 2$

Period $= \dfrac{2\pi}{\frac{1}{2}} = 4\pi$

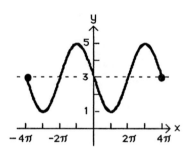

22. From the graph,

amplitude $= \dfrac{1}{4}$ and period $= 8\pi \Rightarrow \dfrac{2\pi}{b} = 8\pi \Rightarrow b = \dfrac{1}{4} \Rightarrow y = \dfrac{1}{4} \sin\left(\dfrac{x}{4}\right), \quad -4\pi \le x \le 8\pi$

24. From the graph,

amplitude $= \dfrac{1}{2}$ and period $= 4 \Rightarrow \dfrac{2\pi}{b} = 4 \Rightarrow b = \dfrac{\pi}{2} \Rightarrow y = -\dfrac{1}{2} \sin\left(\dfrac{\pi x}{2}\right), \quad -2 \le x \le 4$

26. From the graph,

amplitude $= 0.1$ and period $= \dfrac{\pi}{4} \Rightarrow \dfrac{2\pi}{b} = \dfrac{\pi}{4} \Rightarrow b = 8 \Rightarrow y = 0.1 \cos 8x, \quad -\dfrac{\pi}{8} \le x \le \dfrac{\pi}{4}$

28. From the graph,

amplitude $= 1$ and period $= \dfrac{1}{2} \Rightarrow \dfrac{2\pi}{b} = \dfrac{1}{2} \Rightarrow b = 4\pi \Rightarrow y = -\cos(4\pi x), \quad -0.25 \le x \le 0.5$

30.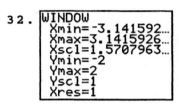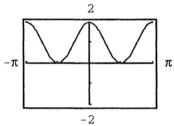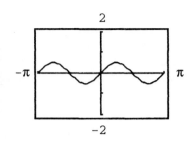

$y = \dfrac{1}{2}\,\sin(2x)$

32.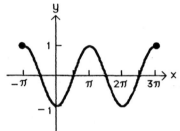

$y = 1 + \cos(2x)$

34. $y = \cos(x - \pi), \quad -\pi \le x \le 3\pi$

$\qquad$ Amplitude = 1

$\qquad\qquad$ Period = $\dfrac{2\pi}{1} = 2\pi$

$\qquad$ Phase Shift = $-\dfrac{-\pi}{1} = \pi$

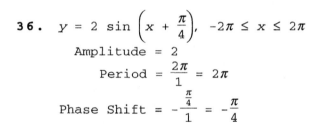

36. $y = 2\,\sin\left(x + \dfrac{\pi}{4}\right), \quad -2\pi \le x \le 2\pi$

$\qquad$ Amplitude = 2

$\qquad\qquad$ Period = $\dfrac{2\pi}{1} = 2\pi$

$\qquad$ Phase Shift = $-\dfrac{\frac{\pi}{4}}{1} = -\dfrac{\pi}{4}$

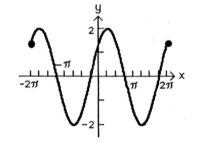

38. $y = \cos\left[2\pi\left(x - \dfrac{1}{2}\right)\right], \quad -1 \le x \le 2$

$\qquad$ Amplitude = 1

$\qquad\qquad$ Period = $\dfrac{2\pi}{2\pi} = 1$

$\qquad$ Phase Shift = $-\dfrac{-\pi}{2\pi} = \dfrac{1}{2}$

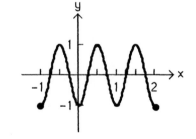

40. $y = 2\,\sin\left(\pi x - \dfrac{\pi}{4}\right), \quad -1 \le x \le 3$

$\qquad$ Amplitude = 2

$\qquad\qquad$ Period = $\dfrac{2\pi}{\pi} = 2$

$\qquad$ Phase Shift = $-\dfrac{-\frac{\pi}{4}}{\pi} = \dfrac{1}{4}$

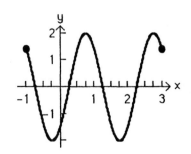

42. $y = 1 + \cos(x - \pi)$, $-\pi \le x \le 3\pi$

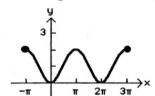

Amplitude = 1
period = 2π
phase shift = π
vertical shift = 1

44. $y = -1 - 2\cos(4x + \pi)$, $-\pi \le x \le \pi$

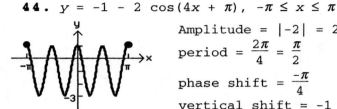

Amplitude = $|-2| = 2$

period = $\dfrac{2\pi}{4} = \dfrac{\pi}{2}$

phase shift = $\dfrac{-\pi}{4}$

vertical shift = -1

46. From the graph, amplitude = 4 and period = $4 = \dfrac{2\pi}{B} \Rightarrow B = \dfrac{\pi}{2}$

Phase Shift = $-\dfrac{C}{B} = -1 \Rightarrow B = C = \dfrac{\pi}{2}$.

$y = 4\sin\left(\dfrac{\pi}{2}x + \dfrac{\pi}{2}\right)$, $-1 \le x \le 3$

48. From graph, amplitude = $\dfrac{1}{2}$ and period = $8\pi \Rightarrow \dfrac{2\pi}{B} = 8\pi \Rightarrow B = \dfrac{1}{4}$

Phase Shift = $-\dfrac{C}{B} = -\pi \Rightarrow \dfrac{C}{\frac{1}{4}} = \pi \Rightarrow C = \dfrac{\pi}{4}$

$y = -\dfrac{1}{2}\cos\left(\dfrac{x}{4} + \dfrac{\pi}{4}\right)$, $-3\pi \le x \le 5\pi$

50. The period is $5 \Rightarrow \dfrac{2\pi}{b} = 5 \Rightarrow B = \dfrac{2\pi}{5}$.

The phase shift is $2 \Rightarrow -\dfrac{C}{B} = 2 \Rightarrow -\dfrac{C}{\frac{2\pi}{5}} = 2 \Rightarrow C = -\dfrac{4\pi}{5}$.

Both of these values are unambiguous. The amplitude, however, could result from either $|8| = 8$ or $|-8| = 8$. Thus, there are two possible equations:

$y = 8\cos\left(\dfrac{2\pi x}{5} - \dfrac{4\pi}{5}\right)$ and $y = -8\cos\left(\dfrac{2\pi x}{5} - \dfrac{4\pi}{5}\right)$

52. $y = 5.4\sin\left[\dfrac{\pi}{2.5}(t - 1)\right]$, $0 \le t \le 6$

Amplitude = 5.4

Period = $\dfrac{2\pi}{\frac{\pi}{2.5}} = 5$

Phase Shift = $-\dfrac{-\frac{\pi}{2.5}}{\frac{\pi}{2.5}} = 1$

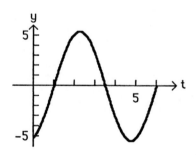

54. $y = 25\cos[5\pi(t - 0.1)]$, $0 \le t \le 2$

Amplitude = 25

Period = $\dfrac{2\pi}{5\pi} = \dfrac{2}{5}$

Phase Shift = $-\dfrac{-0.5\pi}{5\pi} = 0.1$

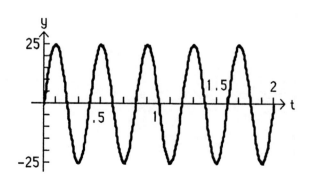

56.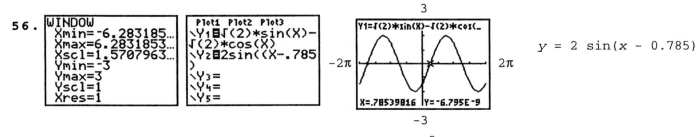

$y = 2 \sin(x - 0.785)$

58.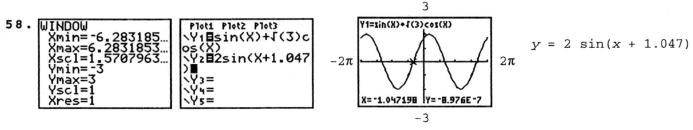

$y = 2 \sin(x + 1.047)$

60.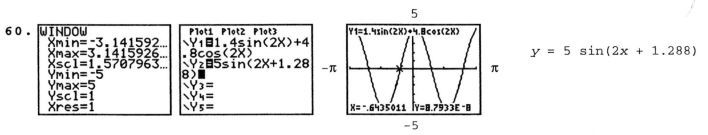

$y = 5 \sin(2x + 1.288)$

62. True. For example, in order to be a simple harmonic, a function can be written in the form

$f(x) = A \sin(Bx + C)$ or $f(x) = A \cos(Bx + C)$. For $h(x)$, we would then have either

$h(x) = A \sin(B(x + 3) + C) = A \sin(Bx + 3B + C) = A \sin(Bx + (3B + C))$ or
$h(x) = A \cos(B(x + 3) + C) = A \cos(Bx + 3B + C) = A \cos(Bx + (3B + C))$.
Both of these are still in the form of a simple harmonic.

64. False. For example, in order to be a simple harmonic, a function can be written in the form $f(x) = A \sin(Bx + C)$ or $f(x) = A \cos(Bx + C)$. For $h(x)$, we would then have either $h(x) = 3 - A \sin(Bx + C)$ or $h(x) = 3 - A \cos(Bx + C)$. Since there is no way to combine the 3 into the amplitude nor into the parenthesis, $h(x)$ cannot be written in the form of a simple harmonic.

66. The amplitude is decreasing.   **68.** The amplitude is increasing.

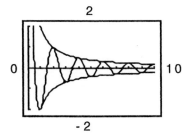

Example: car shock absorber.

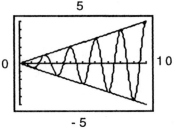

Example: swing bridge in high wind.

70.

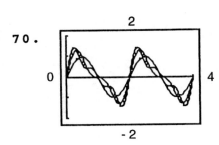

72. $I = 30 \sin 120t$

$$A = 30, \quad P = \frac{2\pi}{120} = \frac{\pi}{60}, \quad f = \frac{1}{\frac{\pi}{60}} = \frac{60}{\pi}$$

74. $A = 110$,

$$P = \frac{1}{60} = \frac{2\pi}{B} \Rightarrow B = 120\pi$$

$$E = 110 \cos(120\pi t)$$

76.

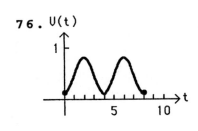

$A = 0.37$

$$P = \frac{2\pi}{\frac{\pi}{2}} = 4$$

The graph shows the volume of air in the lungs t seconds after exhaling.

78. $I = 30 \cos(120\pi t - \pi), \quad 0 \le t \le \frac{3}{60}$

$$A = 30, \quad P = \frac{2\pi}{120\pi} = \frac{1}{60}, \quad PS = -\frac{-\pi}{120\pi} = \frac{1}{120}$$

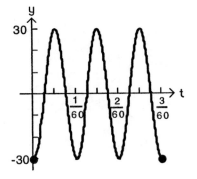

80. $\theta = \frac{\pi}{2} + 6\pi t$

$$y = 3 \sin \theta = 3 \sin\left(6\pi t + \frac{\pi}{2}\right)$$

$$y = 3 \sin\left(6\pi t + \frac{\pi}{2}\right), \quad 0 \le t \le 1$$

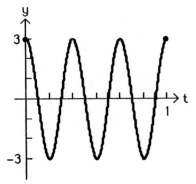

82. (A)

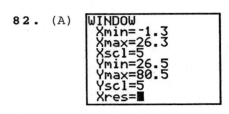

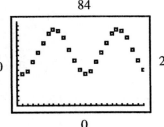

$$A = \frac{\max y - \min y}{2} = \frac{76 - 31}{2} = 22.5$$

The period was $12 \Rightarrow B = \frac{2\pi}{P} = \frac{2\pi}{12} = \frac{\pi}{6}$.

$k = \min y + A = 31 + 22.5 = 53.5$

Estimate phase shift to be $4.0 \Rightarrow -\frac{C}{B} = 4.0 \Rightarrow C = -4.0 \cdot \frac{\pi}{6} \approx 2.1$

(B) $y = 53.5 + 22.5 \sin(\pi x/6 - 2.1)$

```
Plot1 Plot2 Plot3
\Y1⊟53.5+22.5sin
(πX/6-2.1)
\Y2=■
\Y3=
\Y4=
\Y5=
\Y6=
```

(C)

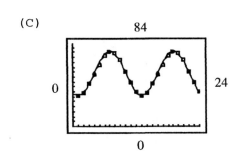

Exercise 6-8

2. $y = 3 \tan 2x$, $-\pi < x < \pi$

period $= \dfrac{\pi}{B} = \dfrac{\pi}{2}$

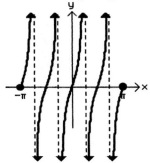

4. $y = -\dfrac{1}{2} \cot(2\pi x)$, $0 < x < 1$

period $= \dfrac{\pi}{2\pi} = \dfrac{1}{2}$

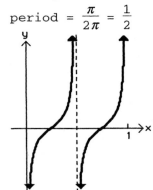

6. $y = \sec \pi x$, $-1.5 \le x \le 3.5$

period $= \dfrac{2\pi}{\pi} = 2$

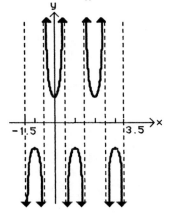

8. $y = 2 \csc\left(\dfrac{x}{2}\right)$, $0 < x < 8\pi$

period $= \dfrac{2\pi}{\frac{1}{2}} = 4\pi$

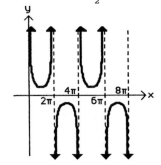

10. $y = \tan\left(x - \dfrac{\pi}{2}\right)$, $-\pi < x < \pi$

period $= \dfrac{\pi}{1} = \pi$

phase shift $= -\dfrac{-\dfrac{\pi}{2}}{1} = \dfrac{\pi}{2}$

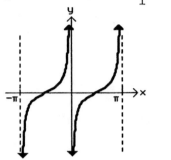

12. $y = \cot(2x - \pi)$, $-\dfrac{\pi}{2} \le x \le \dfrac{\pi}{2}$, has

period $= \dfrac{\pi}{2}$ and phase shift $= \dfrac{\pi}{2}$.

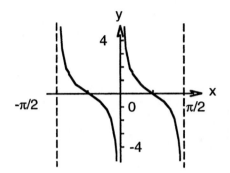

14. $y = \csc\left(\pi x - \dfrac{\pi}{2}\right)$, $-1 < x < 1$, has

period $= \dfrac{2\pi}{\pi} = 2$ and phase shift $= \dfrac{1}{2}$.

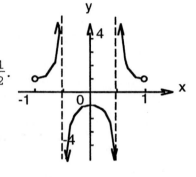

16. True. For example, since there is no phase shift and the periods are the same, these graphs will intersect whenever $x = \dfrac{1}{2} + k$ where k is any integer.

18. False. For example, if $x = 1$, then $y = 7 \tan(3\pi x + 2) = 7 \tan(3\pi + 2) \approx -15.3$.

20. $y = 2 \csc 2x$

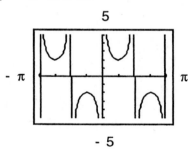

22. $y = \tan\left(\dfrac{x}{2}\right)$

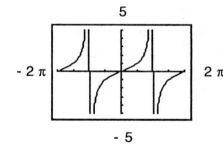

24. $y = -3 \cot(\pi x - \pi)$, $-2 < x < 2$

period $= \dfrac{\pi}{\pi} = 1$

phase shift $= -\dfrac{-\pi}{\pi} = 1$

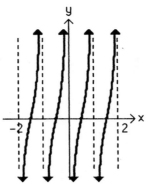

26. $y = 2 \sec\left(\pi x - \dfrac{\pi}{2}\right)$, $-1 < x < 3$

period $= \dfrac{2\pi}{\pi} = 2$

phase shift $= -\dfrac{-\frac{\pi}{2}}{\pi} = \dfrac{1}{2}$

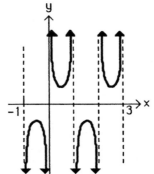

28.

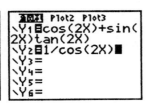

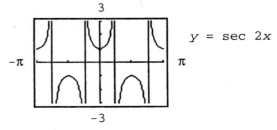

$y = \sec 2x$

30.

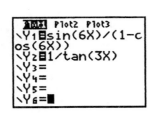

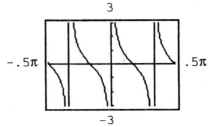

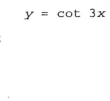

$y = \cot 3x$

32. (A) Using the triangle formed by the beacon, N and P,

$\tan \theta = \dfrac{a}{20} \Rightarrow a = 20 \tan\left(\dfrac{\pi t}{2}\right)$

(B)

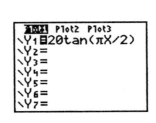

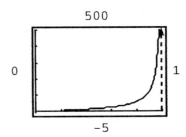

(C) Initially the distance from N is zero. The distance then begins to increase at an ever increasing rate.

Exercise 6-9

2. $\sin^{-1} 0 = 0$

4. $\arccos \dfrac{\sqrt{3}}{2} = \dfrac{\pi}{6}$

6. $\tan^{-1} 1 = \dfrac{\pi}{4}$

8. $\cos^{-1}\left(\dfrac{1}{2}\right) = \dfrac{\pi}{3}$

10. $\arctan\left(\dfrac{1}{\sqrt{3}}\right) = \dfrac{\pi}{6}$

12. $\tan^{-1} 0 = 0$

14. $\arcsin 0.5625 = 0.5974$ **16.** $\arccos 0.0127 = 1.558$ **18.** $\tan^{-1} 8.529 = 1.454$

20. $\arcsin(-\sqrt{3})$ is undefined **22.** $\cos^{-1}\left(-\dfrac{\sqrt{2}}{2}\right) = \dfrac{3\pi}{4}$ **24.** $\tan^{-1}\left(\dfrac{-1}{\sqrt{3}}\right) = -\dfrac{\pi}{6}$

26. $\sin(\sin^{-1}(-0.6)) = -0.6$ **28.** $\tan\left(\cos^{-1}\dfrac{1}{2}\right) = \sqrt{3}$ **30.** $\sec(\sin^{-1}(-0.0399)) = 1.001$

32. $\sqrt{2} + \tan^{-1}\sqrt[3]{5} = 2.456$ **34.** $\cos^{-1}\left(-\dfrac{1}{2}\right) = 120°$ **36.** $\arctan(-1) = -45°$

38. $\sin^{-1}(-1) = -90°$ **40.** $\tan^{-1}(12.4304) = 85.40°$ **42.** $\arccos(-0.9206) = 157.01°$

44. $\cos^{-1}[\cos(-0.5)] = 0.5$ which does not illustrate $\cos^{-1}(\cos x) = x$ because -0.5 is not in the range of $\cos^{-1}$.

46.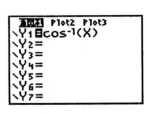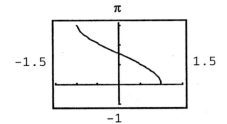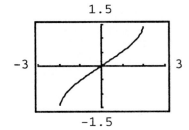

48. 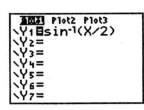

50.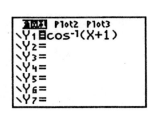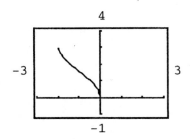

52.

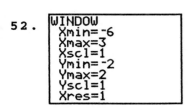
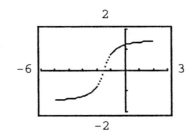
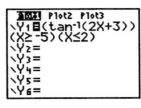

54. (A)

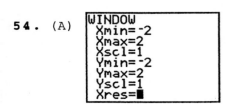
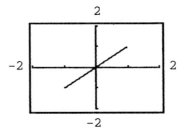

(B) The graph is the same. The domain of the inverse sine is the inverval $[-1, 1]$.

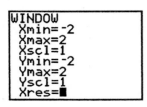

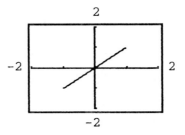

56. $x = 0$. For example, we are looking for an angle such that $\sin \theta = \tan \theta$. Since $\sin \theta = \dfrac{b}{r}$ and $\tan \theta = \dfrac{b}{a}$, we need $x = \dfrac{b}{r} = \dfrac{b}{a}$. r is the length of the hypotenuse of a right triangle, while a and b are legs in the same triangle. Thus, the only time $a = r$ is when $b = 0$ which implies $x = 0$.

58. $x = \pm 1$. For example, we need $x = \dfrac{1}{x}$. Solving provides $x^2 = 1$ and $x = \pm 1$.

60. for $-1 < x < 0$, $\dfrac{\pi}{2} < \cos^{-1} x < \pi$

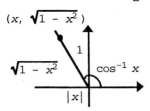

$\sin(\cos^{-1} x) = \sqrt{1 - x^2}$

for $0 < x < 1$, $\quad 0 < \cos^{-1} < \dfrac{\pi}{2}$

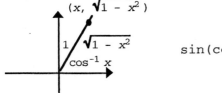

$\sin(\cos^{-1} x) = \sqrt{1 - x^2}$

$\sin(\cos^{-1} x) = \sqrt{1 - x^2}$ in both cases.

62. for $-1 < x < 1$ $\quad -\dfrac{\pi}{2} < \sin^{-1} x < 0$

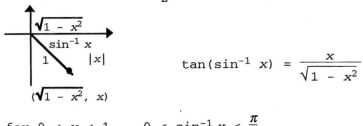

$$\tan(\sin^{-1} x) = \dfrac{x}{\sqrt{1 - x^2}}$$

for $0 < x < 1,$ $\quad 0 < \sin^{-1} x < \dfrac{\pi}{2}$

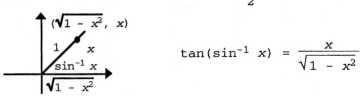

$$\tan(\sin^{-1} x) = \dfrac{x}{\sqrt{1 - x^2}}$$

$\tan(\sin^{-1} x) = \dfrac{x}{\sqrt{1 - x^2}}$ in both cases.

64. $y = 3 + 5 \sin(x - 1) : f$
$x = 3 + 5 \sin(y - 1) : f^{-1}$
$5 \sin(y - 1) = x - 3$

$$\sin(y - 1) = \dfrac{x - 3}{5}$$

$$y - 1 = \sin^{-1} \dfrac{x - 3}{5}$$

$$y = 1 + \sin^{-1} \dfrac{x - 3}{5}$$

$f^{-1}(x) = 1 + \sin^{-1} \dfrac{x - 3}{5}$ for $-1 \le \dfrac{x - 3}{5} \le 1$

$$-5 \le x - 3 \le 5$$
$$2 \le x \le 8$$

66. (A)

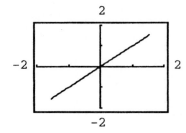

(B) A "saw-tooth" graph results.

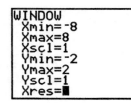

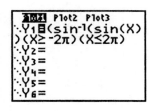

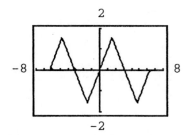

The domain of the sine function is R and the range of the sine function is $-1 \le y \le 1$ which is the domain of the inverse sine function which means the graph of $y = \sin^{-1}(\sin x)$ has domain R and range $-\dfrac{\pi}{2} \le y \le \dfrac{\pi}{2}$. However, the graph only coincides with the graph of $y = x$ for $-\dfrac{\pi}{2} \le x \le \dfrac{\pi}{2}$.

68. $\theta = 2 \tan^{-1} \dfrac{21.634}{x} = 2 \tan^{-1} \dfrac{21.634}{17} = 103.68°$

$\theta = 2 \tan^{-1} \dfrac{21.634}{x} = 2 \tan^{-1} \dfrac{21.634}{70} = 34.35°$

70. (A)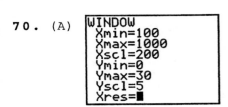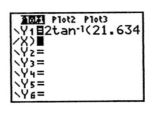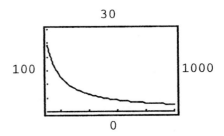

(B) 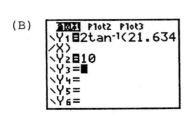 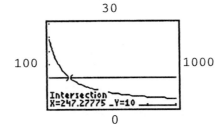   focal length = 247.28 mm

72. $L = \pi D + (d - D)\theta + 2C \sin \theta$

$= \pi D + (d - D)\cos^{-1}\left(\dfrac{D - d}{2C}\right) + 2C \sin\left(\cos^{-1}\dfrac{D - d}{2C}\right)$

$= \pi(6) + (4 - 6)\cos^{-1}\left(\dfrac{6 - 4}{2(10)}\right) + 2(10)\sin\left(\cos^{-1}\dfrac{6 - 4}{2(10)}\right)$

$= 35.81$ inches

74. (A)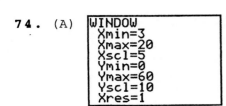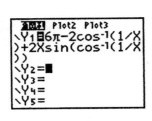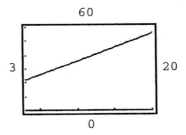

(B)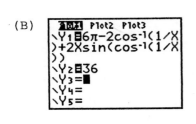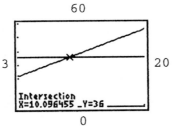

Distance between centers = 10.10 in.

76. $d = 2r \tan^{-1} \dfrac{x}{r}$

$= 2(50)\tan^{-1} \dfrac{25}{50}$

$= 46.36$ feet

CHAPTER 7

Exercise 7-1

2. Verify: $\cos \theta \csc \theta = \cot \theta$

$$\cos \theta \csc \theta = \cos \theta \cdot \frac{1}{\sin \theta}$$

$$= \frac{\cos \theta}{\sin \theta}$$

$$= \cot \theta$$

4. Verify: $\tan \theta \csc \theta \cos \theta = 1$

$$\tan \theta \csc \theta \cos \theta = \frac{\sin \theta}{\cos \theta} \cdot \frac{1}{\sin \theta} \cdot \cos \theta$$

$$= 1$$

6. Verify: $\cot(-x)\tan(x) = -1$

$$\cot(-x)\tan(x) = \frac{\cos(-x)}{\sin(-x)} \cdot \frac{\sin x}{\cos x}$$

$$= \frac{\cos x}{-\sin x} \cdot \frac{\sin x}{\cos x}$$

$$= -1$$

8. Verify: $\tan \alpha = \frac{\cos \alpha \sec \alpha}{\cot \alpha}$

$$\frac{\cos \alpha \sec \alpha}{\cot \alpha} = \frac{\cos \alpha \cdot \frac{1}{\cos \alpha}}{\frac{\cos \alpha}{\sin \alpha}}$$

$$= \frac{1}{\frac{\cos \alpha}{\sin \alpha}}$$

$$= \frac{\sin \alpha}{\cos \alpha}$$

$$= \tan \alpha$$

10. Verify: $\tan u + 1 = \sec u(\sin u + \cos u)$

$$\sec u(\sin u + \cos u) = \frac{1}{\cos u}(\sin u + \cos u)$$

$$= \frac{\sin u}{\cos u} + \frac{\cos u}{\cos u}$$

$$= \tan u + 1$$

12. Verify: $\frac{\cos^2 x - \sin^2 x}{\sin x \cos x} = \cot x - \tan x$

$$\frac{\cos^2 x - \sin^2 x}{\sin x \cos x} = \frac{\cos^2 x}{\sin x \cos x} - \frac{\sin^2 x}{\sin x \cos x}$$

$$= \frac{\cos x}{\sin x} - \frac{\sin x}{\cos x}$$

$$= \cot x - \tan x$$

14. Verify: $\frac{\cos^2 t}{\sin t} + \sin t = \csc t$

$$\frac{\cos^2 t}{\sin t} + \sin t = \frac{\cos^2 t + \sin^2 t}{\sin t}$$

$$= \frac{1}{\sin t}$$

$$= \csc t$$

16. Verify: $\frac{\sin u}{1 - \cos^2 u} = \csc u$

$$\frac{\sin u}{1 - \cos^2 u} = \frac{\sin u}{\sin^2 u}$$

$$= \frac{1}{\sin u}$$

$$= \csc u$$

18. Verify: $(1 - \sin t)(1 + \sin t) = \cos^2 t$

$$
\begin{aligned}
(1 - \sin t)(1 + \sin t) &= 1 - \sin t + \sin t - \sin^2 t \\
&= 1 - \sin^2 t \\
&= \cos^2 t
\end{aligned}
$$

20. Verify: $(\sin x + \cos x)^2 = 1 + 2 \sin x \cos x$

$$
\begin{aligned}
(\sin x + \cos x)^2 &= \sin^2 x + 2 \sin x \cos x + \cos^2 x \\
&= \sin^2 x + \cos^2 x + 2 \sin x \cos x \\
&= 1 + 2 \sin x \cos x
\end{aligned}
$$

22. Verify: $(\csc t - 1)(\csc t + 1) = \cot^2 t$

$$
\begin{aligned}
(\csc t - 1)(\csc t + 1) &= \csc^2 t - \csc t + \csc t - 1 \\
&= \csc^2 t - 1 \\
&= 1 + \cot^2 t - 1 \\
&= \cot^2 t
\end{aligned}
$$

24. Verify: $\sec^2 u - \tan^2 u = 1$

$$
\begin{aligned}
\sec^2 u - \tan^2 u &= 1 + \tan^2 u - \tan^2 u \\
&= 1
\end{aligned}
$$

26. $-\pi \le x \le \pi$

(A) $y = \sec^2 x$

Graph $y_1 = \dfrac{1}{(\cos x)^2}$

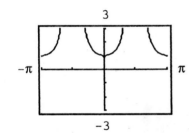

(B) $y = \tan^2 x$

Graph $y_1 = (\tan x)^2$

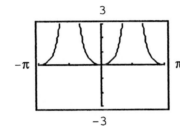

(C) $y = \sec^2 x - \tan^2 x$

Graph $y_1 = \dfrac{1}{(\cos x)^2} - (\tan x)^2$

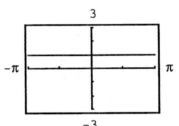

28. $-\pi \le x \le \pi$

(A) $y = \dfrac{\sin x}{\cos x \cdot \tan x}$

Graph $y_1 = \dfrac{\sin x}{\cos x \cdot \tan x}$

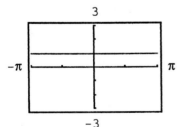

(B) $y = 1$

Graph $y_1 = 1$

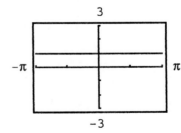

30. Yes. If the domain is $(-\infty, -2) \cup (-2, \infty)$, then
$$\frac{x^2 - 4}{x + 2} = \frac{(x + 2)(x - 2)}{x + 2} = x - 2 \text{ is an identity.}$$

32. No. Let $x = -2$:
$$\sqrt{x^2 + 2x + 1} = \sqrt{4 - 4 + 1} = 1$$
$$x + 1 = -2 + 1 = -1$$

34. No. Let $x = 0$:
$$\sin^2 0 - \cos^2 0 = 0 - 1 = -1 \text{ which does not equal } 1$$

36. No. Let $x = \pi$:
$$\sin^3 \pi + \cos^3 \pi = 0^3 + (-1)^3 = -1 \text{ which does not equal } 1$$

38. Verify: $\dfrac{1 - \cos^2 y}{(1 - \sin y)(1 + \sin y)} = \tan^2 y$

$$\frac{1 - \cos^2 y}{(1 - \sin y)(1 + \sin y)} = \frac{\sin^2 y}{1 - \sin^2 y}$$

$$= \frac{\sin^2 y}{\cos^2 y}$$

$$= \left(\frac{\sin y}{\cos y}\right)^2$$

$$= \tan^2 y$$

40. Verify: $\sin \theta + \cos \theta = \dfrac{\tan \theta + 1}{\sec \theta}$

$$\frac{\tan \theta + 1}{\sec \theta} = \frac{\frac{\sin \theta}{\cos \theta} + 1}{\frac{1}{\cos \theta}} \cdot \frac{\cos \theta}{\cos \theta}$$

$$= \sin \theta + \cos \theta$$

42. Verify: $1 - \sin y = \dfrac{\cos^2 y}{1 + \sin y}$

$$\frac{\cos^2 y}{1 + \sin y} = \frac{\cos^2 y}{1 + \sin y} \cdot \frac{1 - \sin y}{1 - \sin y}$$

$$= \frac{(1 - \sin^2 y)(1 - \sin y)}{(1 - \sin^2 y)}$$

$$= 1 - \sin y$$

44. Verify: $\sec^2 x + \csc^2 x = \sec^2 x \csc^2 x$

$$\sec^2 x + \csc^2 x = \frac{1}{\cos^2 x} + \frac{1}{\sin^2 x}$$

$$= \frac{\sin^2 x + \cos^2 x}{\sin^2 x \cos^2 x}$$

$$= \frac{1}{\cos^2 x \sin^2 x}$$

$$= \frac{1}{\cos^2 x} \cdot \frac{1}{\sin^2 x}$$

$$= \sec^2 x \csc^2 x$$

46. Verify: $\dfrac{1 + \sec \theta}{\sin \theta + \tan \theta} = \csc \theta$

$$\dfrac{1 + \sec \theta}{\sin \theta + \tan \theta} = \dfrac{1 + \frac{1}{\cos \theta}}{\sin \theta + \frac{\sin \theta}{\cos \theta}} \cdot \dfrac{\cos \theta}{\cos \theta}$$

$$= \dfrac{\cos \theta + 1}{\sin \theta \cos \theta + \sin \theta}$$

$$= \dfrac{\cos \theta + 1}{\sin \theta(\cos \theta + 1)}$$

$$= \dfrac{1}{\sin \theta}$$

$$= \csc \theta$$

48. Verify: $\ln(\cot x) = \ln(\cos x) - \ln(\sin x)$

$$\ln(\cos x) - \ln(\sin x) = \ln\!\left(\dfrac{\cos x}{\sin x}\right)$$

$$= \ln(\cot x)$$

50. Verify: $\ln(\csc x) = -\ln(\sin x)$

$$-\ln(\sin x) = -\ln\!\left(\dfrac{1}{\csc x}\right)$$

$$= -(\ln 1 - \ln(\csc x))$$

$$= -(0 - \ln(\csc x))$$

$$= \ln(\csc x)$$

52. Verify: $\dfrac{1 - \csc y}{1 + \csc y} = \dfrac{\sin y - 1}{\sin y + 1}$

$$\dfrac{1 - \csc y}{1 + \csc y} = \dfrac{1 - \frac{1}{\sin y}}{1 + \frac{1}{\sin y}} \cdot \dfrac{\sin y}{\sin y}$$

$$= \dfrac{\sin y - 1}{\sin y + 1}$$

54. Verify: $\sin^4 x + 2 \sin^2 x \cos^2 x + \cos^4 x = 1$

$$\sin^4 x + 2 \sin^2 x \cos^2 x + \cos^4 x = (\sin^2 x + \cos^2 x)^2$$

$$= 1^2$$

$$= 1$$

56. Verify: $\dfrac{\sin^2 t + 4 \sin t + 3}{\cos^2 t} = \dfrac{3 + \sin t}{1 - \sin t}$

$$\dfrac{\sin^2 t + 4 \sin t + 3}{\cos^2 t} = \dfrac{(\sin t + 1)(\sin t + 3)}{1 - \sin^2 t}$$

$$= \dfrac{(1 + \sin t)(3 + \sin t)}{(1 + \sin t)(1 - \sin t)}$$

$$= \dfrac{3 + \sin t}{1 - \sin t}$$

58. Verify: $\dfrac{\cos^3 u + \sin^3 u}{\cos u + \sin u} = 1 - \sin u \cos u$

$$\dfrac{\cos^3 u + \sin^3 u}{\cos u + \sin u} = \dfrac{(\cos u + \sin u)(\cos^2 u - \cos u \sin u + \sin^2 u)}{(\cos u + \sin u)}$$

$$= \cos^2 u + \sin^2 u - \cos u \sin u$$

$$= 1 - \sin u \cos u$$

60. Verify: $(\cot u - \csc u)^2 = \dfrac{1 - \cos u}{1 + \cos u}$

$$(\cot u - \csc u)^2 = \left(\frac{\cos u}{\sin u} - \frac{1}{\sin u}\right)^2$$

$$= \left(\frac{\cos u - 1}{\sin u}\right)^2$$

$$= \frac{(\cos u - 1)^2}{\sin^2 u}$$

$$= \frac{(\cos u - 1)(\cos u - 1)}{1 - \cos^2 u}$$

$$= \frac{-(1 - \cos u)(\cos u - 1)}{(1 - \cos u)(1 + \cos u)}$$

$$= \frac{-\cos u + 1}{1 + \cos u}$$

$$= \frac{1 - \cos u}{1 + \cos u}$$

62. Verify: $\dfrac{\sec^4 x - 1}{\tan^2 x} = 2 + \tan^2 x$

$$\frac{\sec^4 x - 1}{\tan^2 x} = \frac{(\sec^2 x - 1)(\sec^2 x + 1)}{\tan^2 x}$$

$$= \frac{(1 + \tan^2 x - 1)(1 + \tan^2 x + 1)}{\tan^2 x}$$

$$= \frac{\tan^2 x(2 + \tan^2 x)}{\tan^2 x}$$

$$= 2 + \tan^2 x$$

64. Verify: $\dfrac{\sin x}{1 - \cos x} = \dfrac{1 + \cos x}{\sin x}$

$$\frac{1 + \cos x}{\sin x} = \frac{1 + \cos x}{\sin x} \cdot \frac{1 - \cos x}{1 - \cos x}$$

$$= \frac{1 - \cos^2 x}{\sin x(1 - \cos x)}$$

$$= \frac{\sin^2 x}{\sin x(1 - \cos x)}$$

$$= \frac{\sin x}{1 - \cos x}$$

66. As the graph shows, $\dfrac{\cos(-x)}{\sin x \cot(-x)} = 1$ is not an identity since the left hand side is -1 for all x for which it is defined.

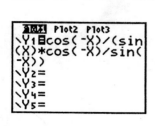 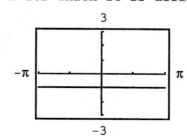

68. As the graph shows, $\dfrac{\cos x}{\sin(-x)\cot(-x)} = 1$ appears to be an identity.

$$\frac{\cos x}{\sin(-x)\cot(-x)} = \frac{\cos x}{-\sin x \cdot \dfrac{\cos(-x)}{\sin(-x)}}$$

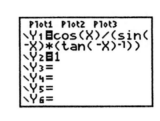

$$= \frac{\cos x}{-\sin x \cdot \dfrac{\cos x}{-\sin x}}$$

$$= 1$$

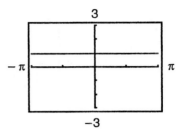

70. As the graphs show, $\dfrac{1 - \tan^2 x}{1 - \cot^2 x} = \tan^2 x$ does not appear to be an identity.

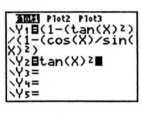

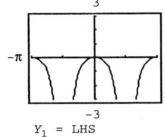

$Y_1 = \text{LHS}$

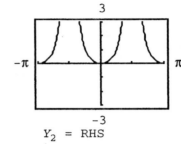

$Y_2 = \text{RHS}$

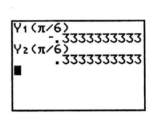

The last screen shows a value of x for which both sides are defined but not equal.

72. As the graph shows, $\dfrac{\tan^2 x - 1}{1 - \cot^2 x} = \tan^2 x$ appears to be an identity.

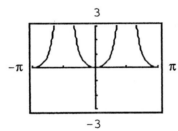

$$\frac{\tan^2 x - 1}{1 - \cot^2 x} = \frac{\dfrac{\sin^2 x}{\cos^2 x} - 1}{1 - \dfrac{\cos^2 x}{\sin^2 x}}$$

$$= \frac{\dfrac{\sin^2 x - \cos^2 x}{\cos^2 x}}{\dfrac{\sin^2 x - \cos^2 x}{\sin^2 x}}$$

$$= \frac{1}{\cos^2 x} \cdot \frac{\sin^2 x}{1}$$

$$= \tan^2 x$$

74. As the graph shows, $\dfrac{\cos x}{1 - \sin x} + \dfrac{\cos x}{1 + \sin x} = 2\sec x$ appears to be an identity.

$$\frac{\cos x}{1 - \sin x} + \frac{\cos x}{1 + \sin x}$$

$$= \frac{\cos x(1 + \sin x) + \cos x(1 - \sin x)}{(1 - \sin x)(1 + \sin x)}$$

$$= \frac{\cos x + \cos x \sin x + \cos x - \cos x \sin x}{1 - \sin^2 x}$$

$$= \frac{2\cos x}{\cos^2 x}$$

$$= \frac{2}{\cos x}$$

$$= 2\sec x$$

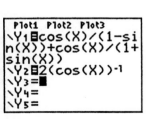

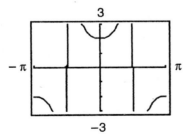

76. As the graphs show, $\dfrac{\cos x}{\sin x + 1} - \dfrac{\cos x}{\sin x - 1} = 2 \csc x$ does not appear to be an identity.

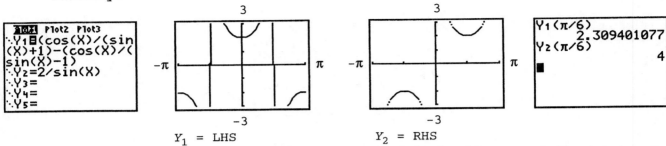

Y_1 = LHS Y_2 = RHS

The last screen shows a value of x for which both sides are defined but not equal.

78. Verify: $\dfrac{3 \cos^2 z + 5 \sin z - 5}{\cos^2 z} = \dfrac{3 \sin z - 2}{1 + \sin z}$

$$\dfrac{3 \cos^2 z + 5 \sin z - 5}{\cos^2 z} = \dfrac{3(1 - \sin^2 z) - 5(1 - \sin z)}{1 - \sin^2 z}$$

$$= \dfrac{(1 - \sin z)[3(1 + \sin z) - 5]}{(1 - \sin z)(1 + \sin z)}$$

$$= \dfrac{3(1 + \sin z) - 5}{1 + \sin z}$$

$$= \dfrac{3 + 3 \sin z - 5}{1 + \sin z}$$

$$= \dfrac{3 \sin z - 2}{1 + \sin z}$$

80. Verify: $\dfrac{\sin x \cos y + \cos x \sin y}{\cos x \cos y - \sin x \sin y} = \dfrac{\tan x + \tan y}{1 - \tan x \tan y}$

$$\dfrac{\tan x + \tan y}{1 - \tan x \tan y} = \dfrac{\frac{\sin x}{\cos x} + \frac{\sin y}{\cos y}}{1 - \frac{\sin x}{\cos x} \cdot \frac{\sin y}{\cos y}} \cdot \dfrac{\cos x \cos y}{\cos x \cos y}$$

$$= \dfrac{\sin x \cos y + \cos x \sin y}{\cos x \cos y - \sin x \sin y}$$

82. Verify: $\dfrac{\cot \alpha + \cot \beta}{\cot \alpha \cot \beta - 1} = \dfrac{\tan \alpha + \tan \beta}{1 - \tan \alpha \tan \beta}$

$$\dfrac{\tan \alpha + \tan \beta}{1 - \tan \alpha \tan \beta} = \dfrac{\frac{1}{\cot \alpha} + \frac{1}{\cot \beta}}{1 - \frac{1}{\cot \alpha} \cdot \frac{1}{\cot \beta}} \cdot \dfrac{\cot \alpha \cot \beta}{\cot \alpha \cot \beta}$$

$$= \dfrac{\cot \beta + \cot \alpha}{\cot \alpha \cot \beta - 1}$$

$$= \dfrac{\cot \alpha + \cot \beta}{\cot \alpha \cot \beta - 1}$$

84.

```
Plot1 Plot2 Plot3
\Y1■(1+sin(X))/(
2cos(X))-cos(X)/
(2+2sin(X))
\Y2■tan(X)
\Y3=
\Y4=
\Y5=
```

$$f(x) = \frac{1 + \sin x}{2 \cos x} - \frac{\cos x}{2 + 2 \sin x} = \frac{1 + \sin x}{2 \cos x} - \frac{\cos x}{2(1 + \sin x)}$$

$$= \frac{1}{2} \cdot \left[\frac{1 + \sin x}{\cos x} - \frac{\cos x}{1 + \sin x} \right]$$

$$= \frac{1}{2} \cdot \left[\frac{(1 + \sin x)^2 - \cos^2 x}{\cos x(1 + \sin x)} \right]$$

$$= \frac{1}{2} \cdot \left[\frac{1 + 2 \sin x + \sin^2 x - \cos^2 x}{\cos x(1 + \sin x)} \right]$$

$$= \frac{1}{2} \cdot \left[\frac{1 + 2 \sin x + \sin^2 x - (1 - \sin^2 x)}{\cos x(1 + \sin x)} \right]$$

$$= \frac{1}{2} \cdot \left[\frac{2 \sin x + 2 \sin^2 x}{\cos x(1 + \sin x)} \right]$$

$$= \frac{1}{2} \cdot \left[\frac{2 \sin x(1 + \sin x)}{\cos x(1 + \sin x)} \right]$$

$$= \tan x$$

86.

```
Plot1 Plot2 Plot3
\Y1■(tan(X)sin(X
))/(1-cos(X))
\Y2■1+(cos(X)⁻¹)
\Y3=
\Y4=
\Y5=
\Y6=
```

$$f(x) = \frac{\tan x \sin x}{1 - \cos x} = \frac{\frac{\sin x}{\cos x} \cdot \sin x}{1 - \cos x}$$

$$= \frac{\sin^2 x}{\cos x(1 - \cos x)}$$

$$= \frac{1 - \cos^2 x}{\cos x(1 - \cos x)}$$

$$= \frac{(1 - \cos x)(1 + \cos x)}{\cos x(1 - \cos x)}$$

$$= \frac{1 + \cos x}{\cos x}$$

$$= \frac{1}{\cos x} + 1$$

$$= 1 + \sec x$$

88.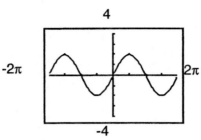

$$f(x) = \frac{3 \sin x - 2 \sin x \cos x}{1 - \cos x} - \frac{1 + \cos x}{\sin x}$$

$$= \frac{\sin x(3 \sin x - 2 \sin x \cos x) - (1 + \cos x)(1 - \cos x)}{\sin x(1 - \cos x)}$$

$$= \frac{3 \sin^2 x - 2 \sin^2 x \cos x - (1 - \cos^2 x)}{\sin x(1 - \cos x)}$$

$$= \frac{3 \sin^2 x - 2 \sin^2 x \cos x - \sin^2 x}{\sin x(1 - \cos x)}$$

$$= \frac{2 \sin^2 x(1 - \cos x)}{\sin x(1 - \cos x)}$$

$$= 2 \sin x$$

90. $\sqrt{1 - \sin^2 x} = \cos x$; $\sqrt{1 - \sin^2 x} \geq 0 \Rightarrow \cos x \geq 0 \Rightarrow x$ must be in quadrants I or IV.

92. $\sqrt{1 - \sin^2 x} = -\cos x$. $\sqrt{1 - \sin^2 x} \geq 0 \Rightarrow -\cos x \geq 0$

$\cos x \leq 0 \Rightarrow x$ in quadrants II or III.

94. $\sqrt{1 - \cos^2 x} = |\sin x|$. Both sides $\geq 0 \Rightarrow x$ in all quadrants.

96. $\dfrac{\sin x}{\sqrt{1 - \sin^2 x}} = -\tan x$. $\sqrt{1 - \sin^2 x} \geq 0 \Rightarrow$ identity when $\sin x$ and $\tan x$ have opposite signs $\Rightarrow x$ in quadrants II or III.

98. $\sqrt{a^2 - u^2} = \sqrt{a^2 - a^2 \cos^2 x} = \sqrt{a^2(1 - \cos^2 x)}$

$\quad = a\sqrt{\sin^2 x}$ and since for $0 < x < \pi$, $\sqrt{\sin^2 x} = \sin x$

$\quad = a \sin x$

100. $\sqrt{a^2 + u^2} = \sqrt{a^2 + a^2 \cot^2 x} = \sqrt{a^2(1 + \cot^2 x)}$

$\quad = a\sqrt{\csc^2 x}$ and since for $0 < x < \dfrac{\pi}{2}$, $\sqrt{\csc^2 x} = \csc x$

$\quad = a \csc x$

Exercise 7-2

2. Yes. $\cos(x - 2\pi) = \cos x \cos 2\pi + \sin x \sin 2\pi$

$\qquad\qquad\qquad = (\cos x)(1) + (\sin x)(0)$

$\qquad\qquad\qquad = \cos x$

4. Yes. $\sin(x - \pi) = \sin x \cos \pi - \cos x \sin \pi$

$\qquad\qquad\qquad = (\sin x)(-1) - (\cos x)(0)$

$\qquad\qquad\qquad = -\sin x$

6. No. $\tan(\pi - x) = \dfrac{\tan \pi - \tan x}{1 + \tan \pi \tan x}$

$\qquad\qquad = \dfrac{0 - \tan x}{1 + (0)\tan x}$

$\qquad\qquad = -\tan x \Rightarrow \tan(\pi - x) \neq \tan x$

8. Yes. $\sec(2\pi - x) = \dfrac{1}{\cos(2\pi - x)}$

$\qquad\qquad\quad = \dfrac{1}{\cos 2\pi \cos x - \sin 2\pi \sin x}$

$\qquad\qquad\quad = \dfrac{1}{(1)\cos x - (0)\sin x}$

$\qquad\qquad\quad = \dfrac{1}{\cos x}$

$\qquad\qquad\quad = \sec x$

10. Yes. $\tan(x + k\pi) = \dfrac{\tan x + \tan k\pi}{1 - \tan x \tan k\pi}$

$\qquad\qquad\quad = \dfrac{\tan x + 0}{1 - \tan x(0)}$

$\qquad\qquad\quad = \tan x$

12. Verify: $\tan\left(\dfrac{\pi}{2} - x\right) = \cot x$

$\qquad \tan\left(\dfrac{\pi}{2} - x\right) = \dfrac{\sin\left(\frac{\pi}{2} - x\right)}{\cos\left(\frac{\pi}{2} - x\right)}$

$\qquad\qquad\qquad = \dfrac{\cos x}{\sin x}$

$\qquad\qquad\qquad = \cot x$

14. Verify: $\sec\left(\dfrac{\pi}{2} - x\right) = \csc x$

$\qquad \sec\left(\dfrac{\pi}{2} - x\right) = \dfrac{1}{\cos\left(\frac{\pi}{2} - x\right)}$

$\qquad\qquad\qquad = \dfrac{1}{\sin x}$

$\qquad\qquad\qquad = \csc x$

16. $\sin(x + 30°) = \sin x \cos 30° + \cos x \sin 30°$

$\qquad\qquad\quad = \sin x \cdot \dfrac{\sqrt{3}}{2} + \cos x \cdot \dfrac{1}{2}$

$\qquad\qquad\quad = \dfrac{\sqrt{3} \sin x + \cos x}{2}$

18. $\cos(\pi - x) = \cos \pi \cos x + \sin \pi \sin x$

$\qquad\qquad\quad = (-1)\cos x + (0)\sin x$

$\qquad\qquad\quad = -\cos x$

20. $\tan(x - 45°) = \dfrac{\tan x - \tan 45°}{1 + \tan x \tan 45°}$

$\qquad\qquad\quad = \dfrac{\tan x - 1}{1 + (\tan x)(1)}$

$\qquad\qquad\quad = \dfrac{\tan x - 1}{1 + \tan x}$

22. $\sin 75° \cos 15° - \cos 75° \sin 15° = \sin(75° - 15°)$

$\qquad\qquad\qquad\qquad\qquad\qquad = \sin 60°$

$\qquad\qquad\qquad\qquad\qquad\qquad = \dfrac{\sqrt{3}}{2}$

24. $\dfrac{\tan 35° + \tan 25°}{1 - \tan 35° \tan 25°} = \tan(35° + 25°)$

$\qquad\qquad\qquad\qquad = \tan 60°$

$\qquad\qquad\qquad\qquad = \sqrt{3}$

26. $\cos 15° = \cos(45° - 30°) = \cos 45° \cos 30° + \sin 45° \sin 30°$

$\qquad\qquad\qquad\qquad\qquad = \dfrac{\sqrt{2}}{2} \cdot \dfrac{\sqrt{3}}{2} + \dfrac{\sqrt{2}}{2} \cdot \dfrac{1}{2}$

$\qquad\qquad\qquad\qquad\qquad = \dfrac{\sqrt{2} \cdot \sqrt{3} + \sqrt{2}}{4}$

$\qquad\qquad\qquad\qquad\qquad = \dfrac{\sqrt{2}}{4} (\sqrt{3} + 1)$

28. $\sin\left(-\dfrac{\pi}{12}\right) = \sin\left(\dfrac{\pi}{6} - \dfrac{\pi}{4}\right) = \sin \dfrac{\pi}{6} \cos \dfrac{\pi}{4} - \cos \dfrac{\pi}{6} \sin \dfrac{\pi}{4}$

$\qquad\qquad\qquad\qquad\qquad = \dfrac{1}{2} \cdot \dfrac{\sqrt{2}}{2} - \dfrac{\sqrt{3}}{2} \cdot \dfrac{\sqrt{2}}{2}$

$\qquad\qquad\qquad\qquad\qquad = \dfrac{\sqrt{2} - \sqrt{3} \cdot \sqrt{2}}{4}$

$\qquad\qquad\qquad\qquad\qquad = \dfrac{\sqrt{2}}{4} (1 - \sqrt{3})$

30. $\sin x = \dfrac{2}{3}$ (QII), $\cos y = -\dfrac{1}{4}$ (QIII).

Angle x: $a = -\sqrt{3^2 - 2^2} = -\sqrt{5} \Rightarrow \cos x = -\dfrac{\sqrt{5}}{3}$

Angle y: $b = -\sqrt{4^2 - (-1)^2} = -\sqrt{15} \Rightarrow \sin y = -\dfrac{\sqrt{15}}{4}$

$\sin(x - y) = \sin x \cos y - \sin y \cos x$

$\qquad\qquad = \dfrac{2}{3} \cdot \left(-\dfrac{1}{4}\right) - \dfrac{-\sqrt{15}}{4} \cdot \dfrac{-\sqrt{5}}{3}$

$\qquad\qquad = \dfrac{-2 - 5\sqrt{3}}{12}$

$\tan x = -\dfrac{2}{\sqrt{5}}$, $\tan y = \sqrt{15}$

$\tan(x + y) = \dfrac{\tan x + \tan y}{1 - \tan x \tan y} = \dfrac{-\dfrac{2}{\sqrt{5}} + \sqrt{15}}{1 - \dfrac{-2}{\sqrt{5}} \cdot \sqrt{15}} \cdot \dfrac{\sqrt{5}}{\sqrt{5}} = \dfrac{-2 + 5\sqrt{3}}{\sqrt{5} + 2\sqrt{15}}$

32. $\cos x = -\dfrac{1}{3}$ (QII), $\tan y = \dfrac{1}{2}$ (QIII)

Angle x: $b = \sqrt{3^2 - (-1)^2} = \sqrt{8}$

$\sin x = \dfrac{\sqrt{8}}{3}$, $\tan x = -\sqrt{8}$

Angle y: $c = \sqrt{(-2)^2 + (-1)^2} = \sqrt{5}$

$\cos y = \dfrac{-2}{\sqrt{5}}$, $\sin y = \dfrac{-1}{\sqrt{5}}$

$\sin(x - y) = \sin x \cos y - \sin y \cos x$

$= \dfrac{\sqrt{8}}{3} \cdot \dfrac{-2}{\sqrt{5}} - \dfrac{-1}{\sqrt{5}} \cdot \dfrac{-1}{3} = \dfrac{-4\sqrt{2} - 1}{3\sqrt{5}}$

$\tan(x + y) = \dfrac{\tan x + \tan y}{1 - \tan x \tan y} = \dfrac{-\sqrt{8} + \frac{1}{2}}{1 - (-\sqrt{8})(\frac{1}{2})} \cdot \dfrac{2}{2} = \dfrac{1 - 4\sqrt{2}}{2 + 2\sqrt{2}}$

34. Verify: $\sin 2x = \sin(x + x)$

$\sin(x + x) = \sin x \cos x + \cos x \sin x$

$= 2 \sin x \cos x$

36. Verify: $\cot(x - y) = \dfrac{\cot x \cot y + 1}{\cot y - \cot x}$

$\cot(x - y) = \dfrac{\cos(x - y)}{\sin(x - y)}$

$= \dfrac{\cos x \cos y + \sin x \sin y}{\sin x \cos y - \sin y \cos x} \cdot \dfrac{\frac{1}{\sin x \sin y}}{\frac{1}{\sin x \sin y}}$

$= \dfrac{\cot x \cot y + 1}{\cot y - \cot x}$

38. Verify: $\cot 2x = \dfrac{\cot^2 x - 1}{2 \cot x}$

$\cot 2x = \cot(x + x)$

$= \dfrac{\cos(x + x)}{\sin(x + x)}$

$= \dfrac{\cos x \cos x - \sin x \sin x}{\sin x \cos x + \sin x \cos x}$

$= \dfrac{\cos^2 x - \sin^2 x}{2 \sin x \cos x} \cdot \dfrac{\frac{1}{\sin^2 x}}{\frac{1}{\sin^2 x}}$

$= \dfrac{\cot^2 x - 1}{2 \cot x}$

40. Verify: $\dfrac{\sin(u + v)}{\sin(u - v)} = \dfrac{\tan u + \tan v}{\tan u - \tan v}$

$\dfrac{\sin(u + v)}{\sin(u - v)} = \dfrac{\sin u \cos v + \sin v \cos u}{\sin u \cos v - \sin v \cos u} \cdot \dfrac{\frac{1}{\cos u \cos v}}{\frac{1}{\cos u \cos v}}$

$= \dfrac{\tan u + \tan v}{\tan u - \tan v}$

42. Verify: $\tan x - \tan y = \dfrac{\sin(x - y)}{\cos x \cos y}$

$$\dfrac{\sin(x - y)}{\cos x \cos y} = \dfrac{\sin x \cos y - \sin y \cos x}{\cos x \cos y}$$

$$= \dfrac{\sin x \cos y}{\cos x \cos y} - \dfrac{\sin y \cos x}{\cos x \cos y}$$

$$= \tan x - \tan y$$

44. Verify: $\tan(x + y) = \dfrac{\cot x + \cot y}{\cot x \cot y - 1}$

$$\tan(x + y) = \dfrac{\tan x + \tan y}{1 - \tan x \tan y} \cdot \dfrac{\frac{1}{\tan x \tan y}}{\frac{1}{\tan x \tan y}}$$

$$= \dfrac{\frac{1}{\tan y} + \frac{1}{\tan x}}{\frac{1}{\tan x \tan y} - 1}$$

$$= \dfrac{\cot y + \cot x}{\cot x \cot y - 1}$$

$$= \dfrac{\cot x + \cot y}{\cot x \cot y - 1}$$

46. Verify: $\dfrac{\sin(x + h) - \sin x}{h} = \sin x\left(\dfrac{\cos h - 1}{h}\right) + \cos x\left(\dfrac{\sin h}{h}\right)$

$$\dfrac{\sin(x + h) - \sin x}{h} = \dfrac{\sin x \cos h + \sin h \cos x - \sin x}{h}$$

$$= \dfrac{\sin x(\cos h - 1) + \sin h \cos x}{h}$$

$$= \sin x\left(\dfrac{\cos h - 1}{h}\right) + \cos x\left(\dfrac{\sin h}{h}\right)$$

48. $x = 3.042, \; y = 2.384$

$$\begin{aligned}
\sin(x - y) &= \sin(3.042 - 2.384) \\
&= \sin(0.658) \\
&\approx 0.6115
\end{aligned}$$

$$\begin{aligned}
\sin(x - y) &= \sin x \cos y - \sin y \cos x \\
&= \sin 3.042 \cos 2.384 - \sin 2.384 \cos 3.042 \\
&\approx 0.6115
\end{aligned}$$

$$\begin{aligned}
\tan(x + y) &= \tan(3.042 + 2.384) \\
&= \tan 5.426 \\
&\approx -1.155
\end{aligned}$$

$$\begin{aligned}
\tan(x + y) &= \dfrac{\tan x + \tan y}{1 - \tan x \tan y} \\
&= \dfrac{\tan 3.042 + \tan 2.384}{1 - \tan 3.042 \tan 2.384} \\
&\approx -1.155
\end{aligned}$$

50. $x = 128.3°$, $y = 25.62°$

$$\sin(x - y) = \sin(128.3° - 25.62°)$$
$$= \sin(102.68°)$$
$$\approx 0.9756$$

$$\sin x \cos y - \sin y \cos x = \sin 128.3° \cos 25.62° - \sin 25.62° \cos 128.3°$$
$$\approx 0.9756$$

$$\tan(x + y) = \tan(128.3° + 25.62°)$$
$$= \tan(153.92°)$$
$$\approx -0.4895$$

$$\frac{\tan x + \tan y}{1 - \tan x \tan y} = \frac{\tan 128.3° + \tan 25.62°}{1 - \tan 128.3° \tan 25.62°}$$
$$\approx -0.4895$$

52. Evaluate each side for a particular set of values of x and y for which each side is defined. If the left side is not equal to the right side, then the equation is not an identity. For example, for $x = 2$ and $y = 1$, both sides are defined, but are not equal.

54. $y = \sin\left(x - \dfrac{\pi}{3}\right) = \sin x \cos \dfrac{\pi}{3} - \sin \dfrac{\pi}{3} \cos x = \dfrac{1}{2} \sin x - \dfrac{\sqrt{3}}{2} \cos x$

$y_1 = \sin(x - \pi/3)$

$y_2 = \dfrac{1}{2} \sin x - \dfrac{\sqrt{3}}{2} \cos x$

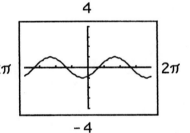

56. $y = \cos\left(x + \dfrac{5\pi}{6}\right) = \cos x \cos\left(\dfrac{5\pi}{6}\right) - \sin x \sin \dfrac{5\pi}{6} = -\dfrac{\sqrt{3}}{2} \cos x - \dfrac{1}{2} \sin x$

$y_1 = \cos(x + 5\pi/6)$

$y_2 = -\dfrac{\sqrt{3}}{2} \cos x - \dfrac{1}{2} \sin x$

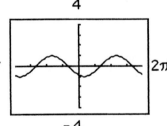

58. $y = \tan\left(x - \dfrac{\pi}{4}\right) = \dfrac{\tan x - \tan \frac{\pi}{4}}{1 + \tan x \tan \frac{\pi}{4}} = \dfrac{\tan x - 1}{1 + \tan x}$

$y_1 = \tan(x - \pi/4)$

$y_2 = \dfrac{\tan x - 1}{1 + \tan x}$

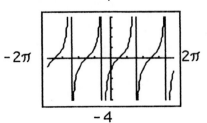

60. $\cos\left[\sin^{-1}\left(-\dfrac{3}{5}\right) + \cos^{-1}\left(\dfrac{4}{5}\right)\right]$

$$= \cos\left[\sin^{-1}\left(-\dfrac{3}{5}\right)\right]\cos\left[\cos^{-1}\left(\dfrac{4}{5}\right)\right] - \sin\left[\sin^{-1}\left(-\dfrac{3}{5}\right)\right]\sin\left[\cos^{-1}\left(\dfrac{4}{5}\right)\right]$$

$$= \left(\dfrac{4}{5}\right)\left(\dfrac{4}{5}\right) - \left(-\dfrac{3}{5}\right)\left(\dfrac{3}{5}\right)$$

$$= \dfrac{16}{25} + \dfrac{9}{25}$$

$$= 1$$

62. $\cos\left[\arccos\left(-\dfrac{\sqrt{3}}{2}\right) - \arcsin\left(-\dfrac{1}{2}\right)\right]$

$$= \cos\left(\arccos\left(-\dfrac{\sqrt{3}}{2}\right)\right)\cos\left(\arcsin\left(-\dfrac{1}{2}\right)\right) + \sin\left(\arccos\left(-\dfrac{\sqrt{3}}{2}\right)\right)\sin\left(\arcsin\left(-\dfrac{1}{2}\right)\right)$$

$$= \left(-\dfrac{\sqrt{3}}{2}\right)\left(\dfrac{\sqrt{3}}{2}\right) + \left(\dfrac{1}{2}\right)\left(-\dfrac{1}{2}\right)$$

$$= -\dfrac{3}{4} - \dfrac{1}{4}$$

$$= -1$$

64. Angle x: $b = x$, $c = 1$, $a = \sqrt{1 - x^2}$
Angle y: $a = y$, $c = 1$, $b = \sqrt{1 - y^2}$
$\cos(\sin^{-1} x - \cos^{-1} y) = \cos(\sin^{-1} x)\cos(\cos^{-1} y) + \sin(\sin^{-1} x)\sin(\cos^{-1} y)$

$$= \sqrt{1 - x^2} \cdot y + x \cdot \sqrt{1 - y^2}$$

$$= y\sqrt{1 - x^2} + x\sqrt{1 - y^2}$$

66. Verify: $\sin(x + y + z) = \sin x \cos y \cos z + \cos x \sin y \cos z$
$\qquad\qquad\qquad\qquad + \cos x \cos y \sin z - \sin x \sin y \sin z$
$\sin(x + y + z) = \sin((x + y) + z)$
$\qquad\qquad\quad = \sin(x + y)\cos z + \sin z \cos(x + y)$
$\qquad\qquad\quad = \cos z[\sin x \cos y + \sin y \cos x]$
$\qquad\qquad\qquad + \sin z[\cos x \cos y - \sin x \sin y]$
$\qquad\qquad\quad = \sin x \cos y \cos z + \cos x \sin y \cos z$
$\qquad\qquad\qquad + \cos x \cos y \sin z - \sin x \sin y \sin z$

68. $y = \sin 0.8x \cos 0.3x - \cos 0.8x \sin 0.3x = \sin((0.8 - 0.3)x) = \sin(0.5x)$

$Y_1 = \sin 0.8x \cos 0.3x - \cos 0.8x \sin 0.3x$

$Y_2 = \sin 0.5x$

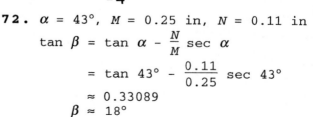

70. $y = 3x + 1$ and $y = \dfrac{1}{2}x - 1$

$$\tan(\theta_2 - \theta_1) = \dfrac{m_2 - m_1}{1 + m_1 m_2}$$

$$\tan(\theta_2 - \theta_1) = \dfrac{3 - \dfrac{1}{2}}{1 + 3\left(\dfrac{1}{2}\right)} \cdot \dfrac{2}{2} = \dfrac{6 - 1}{2 + 3} = 1$$

$$\theta_2 - \theta_1 = 45°$$

72. $\alpha = 43°$, $M = 0.25$ in, $N = 0.11$ in

$$\tan \beta = \tan \alpha - \dfrac{N}{M}\sec \alpha$$

$$= \tan 43° - \dfrac{0.11}{0.25}\sec 43°$$

$$\approx 0.33089$$

$$\beta \approx 18°$$

Exercise 7-3

2. Verify: $\sin 2x = 2 \sin x \cos x$ for $x = 45°$

$$\sin 2x = \sin(2 \cdot 45°) = \sin 90° = 1$$

$$2 \sin x \cos x = 2 \sin 45° \cos 45° = 2 \cdot \frac{\sqrt{2}}{2} \cdot \frac{\sqrt{2}}{2} = 1$$

4. Verify: $\tan 2x = \dfrac{2 \tan x}{1 - \tan^2 x}$ for $x = \dfrac{\pi}{6}$

$$\tan 2x = \tan\left(2 \cdot \frac{\pi}{6}\right) = \tan \frac{\pi}{3} = \sqrt{3}$$

$$\frac{2 \tan x}{1 - \tan^2 x} = \frac{2 \tan \frac{\pi}{6}}{1 - \tan^2 \frac{\pi}{6}} = \frac{2 \left(\frac{1}{\sqrt{3}}\right)}{1 - \left(\frac{1}{\sqrt{3}}\right)^2} = \frac{\frac{2}{\sqrt{3}}}{1 - \frac{1}{3}} \cdot \frac{3\sqrt{3}}{3\sqrt{3}} = \frac{6}{3\sqrt{3} - \sqrt{3}} \cdot \frac{\sqrt{3}}{\sqrt{3}} = \frac{6\sqrt{3}}{6} = \sqrt{3}$$

6. Verify: $\cos \dfrac{x}{2} = \pm\sqrt{\dfrac{1 + \cos x}{2}}$, $x = \dfrac{\pi}{2}$

$\dfrac{x}{2} = \dfrac{\pi}{4}$, Quad I: sign of $\cos \dfrac{x}{2}$ is +.

$$\cos \frac{x}{2} = \cos \frac{\frac{\pi}{2}}{2} = \cos \frac{\pi}{4} = \frac{1}{\sqrt{2}} = \frac{\sqrt{2}}{2}$$

$$\sqrt{\frac{1 + \cos x}{2}} = \sqrt{\frac{1 + \cos \frac{\pi}{2}}{2}}$$
$$= \sqrt{\frac{1 + 0}{2}}$$
$$= \frac{1}{\sqrt{2}} = \frac{\sqrt{2}}{2}$$

8. $\sin 165° = \sin \dfrac{330°}{2}$, Quadrant II, $\sin \theta$ is positive

$$\sin \frac{330°}{2} = \sqrt{\frac{1 - \cos 330°}{2}}$$
$$= \sqrt{\frac{1 - \sqrt{3}/2}{2} \cdot \frac{2}{2}}$$
$$= \sqrt{\frac{2 - \sqrt{3}}{4}}$$
$$= \frac{\sqrt{2 - \sqrt{3}}}{2}$$

10. $\tan 157.5° = \tan \dfrac{315°}{2}$

$$= \frac{1 - \cos 315°}{\sin 315°}$$

$$= \frac{1 - \frac{\sqrt{2}}{2}}{-\frac{\sqrt{2}}{2}} \cdot \frac{2}{2}$$

$$= \frac{2 - \sqrt{2}}{-\sqrt{2}} \cdot \frac{\sqrt{2}}{\sqrt{2}}$$

$$= \frac{2\sqrt{2} - 2}{-2}$$

$$= 1 - \sqrt{2}$$

12. $y_1 = \sin 2x$
$y_2 = 2 \sin x \cos x$

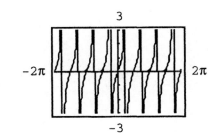

14. $y_1 = \tan 2x$
$y_2 = \dfrac{2 \tan x}{1 - \tan^2 x}$

16. Verify: $\sin 2x = (\tan x)(1 + \cos 2x)$

$$(\tan x)(1 + \cos 2x) = \frac{\sin x}{\cos x}(1 + 2\cos^2 x - 1)$$
$$= \frac{\sin x}{\cos x}(2\cos^2 x)$$
$$= 2\sin x \cos x$$
$$= \sin 2x$$

18. Verify: $\cos^2 x = \frac{1}{2}(\cos 2x + 1)$

$$\frac{1}{2}(\cos 2x + 1) = \frac{1}{2}(2\cos^2 x - 1 + 1)$$
$$= \frac{1}{2}(2\cos^2 x)$$
$$= \cos^2 x$$

20. Verify: $1 + \sin 2t = (\sin t + \cos t)^2$

$$1 + \sin 2t = 1 + 2\sin t \cos t$$
$$= \sin^2 t + \cos^2 t + 2\sin t \cos t$$
$$= \sin^2 t + 2\sin t \cos t + \cos^2 t$$
$$= (\sin t + \cos t)^2$$

22. Verify: $\cos^2 \frac{x}{2} = \frac{1 + \cos x}{2}$

$$\cos^2 \frac{x}{2} = \left(\pm\sqrt{\frac{1 + \cos x}{2}}\,\right)^2$$
$$= \frac{1 + \cos x}{2}$$

24. Verify: $\cot \frac{\theta}{2} = \frac{1 + \cos \theta}{\sin \theta}$

$$\cot \frac{\theta}{2} = \frac{1}{\tan \frac{\theta}{2}} = \frac{1}{\frac{\sin \theta}{1 + \cos \theta}} = \frac{1 + \cos \theta}{\sin \theta}$$

26. Verify: $\dfrac{\cos 2u}{1 - \sin 2u} = \dfrac{1 + \tan u}{1 - \tan u}$

$$\frac{\cos 2u}{1 - \sin 2u} = \frac{\cos^2 u - \sin^2 u}{1 - 2\sin u \cos u}$$
$$= \frac{(\cos u - \sin u)(\cos u + \sin u)}{\cos^2 u - 2\sin u \cos u + \sin^2 u}$$
$$= \frac{(\cos u - \sin u)(\cos u + \sin u)}{(\cos u - \sin u)^2}$$
$$= \frac{\cos u + \sin u}{\cos u - \sin u} \cdot \frac{\frac{1}{\cos u}}{\frac{1}{\cos u}}$$
$$= \frac{1 + \tan u}{1 - \tan u}$$

28. Verify: $\sec 2x = \dfrac{\sec^2 x}{2 - \sec^2 x}$

$$\sec 2x = \frac{1}{\cos 2x}$$

$$= \frac{1}{2 \cos^2 x - 1} \cdot \frac{\frac{1}{\cos^2 x}}{\frac{1}{\cos^2 x}}$$

$$= \frac{\frac{1}{\cos^2 x}}{2 - \frac{1}{\cos^2 x}}$$

$$= \frac{\sec^2 x}{2 - \sec^2 x}$$

30. $\sin 4x = 4 \sin x \cos x$ is not an identity.

Let $x = \dfrac{3\pi}{4}$: $\sin\left[4\left(\dfrac{3\pi}{4}\right)\right] = \sin(3\pi) = 0$

$$4 \sin \frac{3\pi}{4} \cos \frac{3\pi}{4} = 4 \cdot \frac{\sqrt{2}}{2} \cdot \frac{-\sqrt{2}}{2} = -2$$

32. $\tan 6x = \dfrac{6 \tan x}{1 - \tan^2 x}$ is not an identity.

Let $x = \dfrac{\pi}{3}$: $\tan\left(6\left(\dfrac{\pi}{3}\right)\right) = \tan(2\pi) = 0$

$$\frac{6 \tan \frac{\pi}{3}}{1 - \left(\tan \frac{\pi}{3}\right)^2} = \frac{6 \cdot \sqrt{3}}{1 - (\sqrt{3})^2} = \frac{6\sqrt{3}}{1 - 3} = \frac{6\sqrt{3}}{-2} = -3\sqrt{3}$$

34. $2 \csc 2x = \sec x \csc x$ is an identity.

$$2 \csc 2x = \frac{2}{\sin 2x} = \frac{2}{2 \sin x \cos x} = \frac{1}{\cos x \sin x} = \sec x \csc x$$

36. $\cos x = -\dfrac{4}{5}, \ \dfrac{\pi}{2} < x < \pi$

$a = -4, \ r = 5, \ b = 3$

$\sin 2x = 2 \sin x \cos x = 2 \cdot \dfrac{3}{5} \cdot \left(-\dfrac{4}{5}\right) = -\dfrac{24}{25}$

$\cos 2x = 1 - 2 \sin^2 x = 1 - 2\left(\dfrac{3}{5}\right)^2 = 1 - \dfrac{18}{25} = \dfrac{7}{25}$

$\tan 2x = \dfrac{2 \tan x}{1 - \tan^2 x} = \dfrac{2\left(-\frac{3}{4}\right)}{1 - \left(-\frac{3}{4}\right)^2} = \dfrac{-\frac{6}{4}}{1 - \frac{9}{16}} \cdot \dfrac{16}{16} = \dfrac{-24}{16 - 9} = -\dfrac{24}{7}$

38. $\cot x = -\dfrac{5}{12}, \quad -\dfrac{\pi}{2} < x < 0$

$a = 5, \quad b = -12, \quad r = 13$

$\sin 2x = 2 \sin x \cos x = 2 \cdot \dfrac{-12}{13} \cdot \dfrac{5}{13} = -\dfrac{120}{169}$

$\cos 2x = 1 - 2 \sin^2 x = 1 - 2\left(-\dfrac{12}{13}\right)^2 = 1 - \dfrac{288}{169} = -\dfrac{119}{169}$

$\tan 2x = \dfrac{2 \tan x}{1 - \tan^2 x} = \dfrac{2\left(-\frac{12}{5}\right)}{1 - \left(-\frac{12}{5}\right)^2} = \dfrac{-\frac{24}{5}}{1 - \frac{144}{25}} \cdot \dfrac{25}{25} = \dfrac{-120}{25 - 144} = \dfrac{120}{119}$

40. $\cos x = -\dfrac{1}{4}, \quad \pi < x < \dfrac{3\pi}{2}$

$a = -1, \quad r = 4, \quad b = -\sqrt{15}$

$\dfrac{\pi}{2} < \dfrac{x}{2} < \dfrac{3\pi}{4} \quad$ (QII)

$\sin \dfrac{x}{2} = \pm\sqrt{\dfrac{1 - \cos x}{2}} = \sqrt{\dfrac{1 - \frac{-1}{4}}{2}} = \sqrt{\dfrac{4 + 1}{8}} = \dfrac{\sqrt{5}}{2\sqrt{2}} \cdot \dfrac{\sqrt{2}}{\sqrt{2}} = \dfrac{\sqrt{10}}{4}$

$\cos \dfrac{x}{2} = \pm\sqrt{\dfrac{1 + \cos x}{2}} = -\sqrt{\dfrac{1 + \frac{-1}{4}}{2}} = -\sqrt{\dfrac{4 - 1}{8}} = \dfrac{-\sqrt{3}}{2\sqrt{2}} \cdot \dfrac{\sqrt{2}}{\sqrt{2}} = \dfrac{-\sqrt{6}}{4}$

$\tan \dfrac{x}{2} = \dfrac{1 - \cos x}{\sin x} = \dfrac{1 - \frac{-1}{4}}{\frac{-\sqrt{15}}{4}} = \dfrac{4 + 1}{-\sqrt{15}} \cdot \dfrac{\sqrt{15}}{\sqrt{15}} = \dfrac{-5\sqrt{15}}{15} = -\dfrac{\sqrt{15}}{3}$

42. $\tan x = \dfrac{3}{4}, \quad -\pi < x < -\dfrac{\pi}{2}$

$a = -4, \quad b = -3, \quad r = 5, \quad -\dfrac{\pi}{2} < \dfrac{x}{2} < -\dfrac{\pi}{4} \quad$ (QIV)

$\sin \dfrac{x}{2} = \pm\sqrt{\dfrac{1 - \cos x}{2}} = -\sqrt{\dfrac{1 - \frac{-4}{5}}{2}} = -\sqrt{\dfrac{5 + 4}{10}} = -\dfrac{3}{\sqrt{10}} \cdot \dfrac{\sqrt{10}}{\sqrt{10}} = \dfrac{-3\sqrt{10}}{10}$

$\cos \dfrac{x}{2} = \pm\sqrt{\dfrac{1 + \cos x}{2}} = \sqrt{\dfrac{1 + \frac{-4}{5}}{2}} = \sqrt{\dfrac{5 - 4}{10}} = \dfrac{1}{\sqrt{10}} \cdot \dfrac{\sqrt{10}}{\sqrt{10}} = \dfrac{\sqrt{10}}{10}$

$\tan \dfrac{x}{2} = \dfrac{1 - \cos x}{\sin x} = \dfrac{1 - \frac{-4}{5}}{\frac{-3}{5}} = \dfrac{5 + 4}{-3} = \dfrac{9}{-3} = -3$

44. Find the exact values of $\sin \theta$ and $\cos \theta$, given $\sec 2\theta = -\dfrac{5}{4}$, $0° < \theta < 90°$.

(A) $0° < \theta < 90° \Rightarrow 0° < 2\theta < 180°$ and since $\sec 2\theta = \dfrac{-5}{4} < 0$, 2θ is in QII.

(B) $\sec 2\theta = \dfrac{-5}{4} \Rightarrow \cos 2\theta = \dfrac{-4}{5}$

$\sin 2\theta = \sqrt{1 - \cos^2 2\theta} = \sqrt{1 - (\tfrac{-4}{5})^2} = \sqrt{1 - \dfrac{16}{25}} = \sqrt{\dfrac{9}{25}} = \dfrac{3}{5}$

(C) $\sin \theta = \pm\sqrt{\dfrac{1 - \cos 2\theta}{2}}$

$\cos \theta = \pm\sqrt{\dfrac{1 + \cos 2\theta}{2}}$

(D) & (E) θ is a quadrant I angle, so

$\sin \theta = \sqrt{\dfrac{1 - \cos 2\theta}{2}} = \sqrt{\dfrac{1 - \tfrac{-4}{5}}{2}} = \sqrt{\dfrac{5 + 4}{10}} = \dfrac{3}{\sqrt{10}} \cdot \dfrac{\sqrt{10}}{\sqrt{10}} = \dfrac{3\sqrt{10}}{10}$

$\cos \theta = \sqrt{\dfrac{1 + \cos 2\theta}{2}} = \sqrt{\dfrac{1 + \tfrac{-4}{5}}{2}} = \sqrt{\dfrac{5 - 4}{10}} = \dfrac{1}{\sqrt{10}} \cdot \dfrac{\sqrt{10}}{\sqrt{10}} = \dfrac{\sqrt{10}}{10}$

46. $x = 72.358°$
(A) $\tan 2x = \tan(2 \cdot 72.358°) = \tan 144.716° \approx -0.70762$

$\tan 2x = \dfrac{2 \tan x}{1 - \tan^2 x} = \dfrac{2 \tan 72.358°}{1 - \tan^2 72.358°} \approx -0.70762$

(B) $\cos \dfrac{x}{2} = \cos \dfrac{72.358°}{2} = \cos 36.179° \approx 0.80718$

$\cos \dfrac{x}{2} = \sqrt{\dfrac{1 + \cos x}{2}} = \sqrt{\dfrac{1 + \cos 72.358°}{2}} \approx 0.80718$

48. $x = 4$
(A) $\tan 2x = \tan(2 \cdot 4) = \tan 8 \approx -6.7997$

$\tan 2x = \dfrac{2 \tan x}{1 - \tan^2 x} = \dfrac{2 \tan 4}{1 - \tan^2 4} \approx -6.7997$

(B) $\cos \dfrac{x}{2} = \cos \dfrac{4}{2} = \cos 2 \approx -0.41615$

$\cos \dfrac{x}{2} = -\sqrt{\dfrac{1 + \cos x}{2}} = -\sqrt{\dfrac{1 + \cos 4}{2}} \approx -0.41615$ (Quadrant III)

50. $Y_1 = \cos \dfrac{x}{2}$

$Y_2 = -\sqrt{\dfrac{1 + \cos x}{2}}$

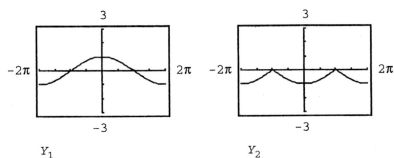

Y_1 Y_2

Y_1 and Y_2 are identities on the intervals $[-2\pi, -\pi]$ and $[\pi, 2\pi]$.

52. $Y_1 = \sin \dfrac{x}{2}$

$Y_2 = \sqrt{\dfrac{1 - \cos x}{2}}$

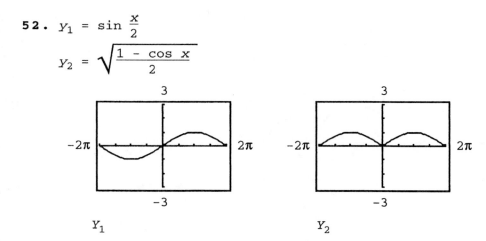

Y_1

Y_2

Y_1 and Y_2 are identities on the interval $[0, 2\pi]$.

54. Verify: $\sin 3x = 3 \sin x - 4 \sin^3 x$

$$\sin 3x = \sin(2x + x) = \sin 2x \cos x + \sin x \cos 2x$$
$$= 2 \sin x \cos x \cos x + \sin x(1 - 2 \sin^2 x)$$
$$= 2 \sin x \cos^2 x + \sin x - 2 \sin^3 x$$
$$= 2 \sin x(1 - \sin^2 x) + \sin x - 2 \sin^3 x$$
$$= 2 \sin x - 2 \sin^3 x + \sin x - 2 \sin^3 x$$
$$= 3 \sin x - 4 \sin^3 x$$

56. Verify: $\sin 4x = (\cos x)(4 \sin x - 8 \sin^3 x)$

$$\sin 4x = \sin(2x + 2x)$$
$$= \sin 2x \cos 2x + \sin 2x \cos 2x$$
$$= 2 \sin 2x \cos 2x$$
$$= 2(2 \sin x \cos x)(1 - 2 \sin^2 x)$$
$$= \cos x(4 \sin x)(1 - 2 \sin^2 x)$$
$$= (\cos x)(4 \sin x - 8 \sin^3 x)$$

58. Use $\sin 2\theta = 2 \sin \theta \cos \theta$

$$\sin\left[2 \cos^{-1} \frac{3}{5}\right] = 2 \sin\left(\cos^{-1} \frac{3}{5}\right)\cos\left(\cos^{-1} \frac{3}{5}\right)$$
$$= 2 \cdot \frac{4}{5} \cdot \frac{3}{5}$$
$$= \frac{24}{25}$$

60. Use $\tan 2\theta = \dfrac{2 \tan \theta}{1 - \tan^2 \theta}$

$$\tan\left[2 \tan^{-1}\left(-\frac{3}{4}\right)\right] = \frac{2 \tan(\tan^{-1}(-\frac{3}{4}))}{1 - \tan^2(\tan^{-1}(-\frac{3}{4}))}$$
$$= \frac{2(-\frac{3}{4})}{1 - (-\frac{3}{4})^2} \cdot \frac{16}{16}$$
$$= \frac{-24}{16 - 9}$$
$$= -\frac{24}{7}$$

62. Use $\sin \frac{\theta}{2} = \pm\sqrt{\frac{1 - \cos \theta}{2}}$, QIV

$$\sin\left[\frac{1}{2} \tan^{-1}\left(-\frac{4}{3}\right)\right] = -\sqrt{\frac{1 - \cos\left(\tan^{-1}\left(-\frac{4}{3}\right)\right)}{2}}$$

$$= -\sqrt{\frac{1 - \frac{3}{5}}{2}}$$

$$= -\sqrt{\frac{5 - 3}{10}}$$

$$= -\frac{\sqrt{2}}{\sqrt{10}} \cdot \frac{\sqrt{10}}{\sqrt{10}}$$

$$= \frac{-2\sqrt{5}}{10}$$

$$= -\frac{\sqrt{5}}{5}$$

64. $f(x) = \csc x + \cot x = \dfrac{1}{\sin x} + \dfrac{\cos x}{\sin x}$

$$= \frac{1 + \cos x}{\sin x}$$

$$= \frac{1}{\frac{\sin x}{1 + \cos x}}$$

$$= \frac{1}{\tan \frac{x}{2}}$$

$$= \cot \frac{x}{2}$$

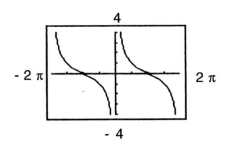

66. $f(x) = \dfrac{1 + 2 \cos 2x}{1 + 2 \cos x} = \dfrac{1 + 2(2 \cos^2 x - 1)}{1 + 2 \cos x}$

$$= \frac{1 + 4 \cos^2 x - 2}{1 + 2 \cos x}$$

$$= \frac{4 \cos^2 x - 1}{1 + 2 \cos x}$$

$$= \frac{(2 \cos x + 1)(2 \cos x - 1)}{(1 + 2 \cos x)}$$

$$= -1 + 2 \cos x$$

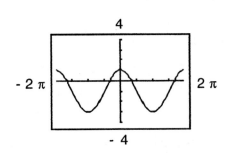

68. $f(x) = \dfrac{\cot x}{1 + \cos 2x} = \dfrac{\frac{\cos x}{\sin x}}{1 + (2 \cos^2 x - 1)}$

$$= \frac{\frac{\cos x}{\sin x}}{2 \cos^2 x}$$

$$= \frac{\cos x}{\sin x} \cdot \frac{1}{2 \cos^2 x}$$

$$= \frac{1}{2 \sin x \cos x}$$

$$= \frac{1}{\sin 2x}$$

$$= \csc 2x$$

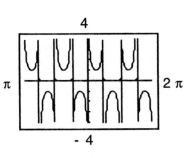

70. $\tan 2\theta = \dfrac{2 \tan \theta}{1 - \tan^2 \theta}$, $\tan \theta = \dfrac{2}{x}$, $\tan 2\theta = \dfrac{6}{x}$

$$\frac{6}{x} = \frac{2 \cdot \frac{2}{x}}{1 - \left(\frac{2}{x}\right)^2} \cdot \frac{x^2}{x^2}$$

$$\frac{6}{x} = \frac{4x}{x^2 - 4}$$

$$6x^2 - 24 = 4x^2$$

$$x^2 = 12$$

$$x = 2\sqrt{3} \approx 3.464 \text{ ft.}$$

$$\tan \theta = \frac{2}{x} = \frac{2}{2\sqrt{3}} = \frac{1}{\sqrt{3}}$$

$$\theta = 30.000°$$

72.

$$AM = \sqrt{s^2 + \left(\frac{s}{2}\right)^2} = \sqrt{\frac{5s^2}{4}} = \frac{\sqrt{5} \cdot s}{2}$$

$$MN = \sqrt{\left(\frac{s}{2}\right)^2 + \left(\frac{s}{2}\right)^2} = \sqrt{\frac{s^2}{2}} = \frac{\sqrt{2} \cdot s}{2}$$

$$\sin \frac{\theta}{2} = \frac{\frac{MN}{2}}{AM} = \frac{\frac{\sqrt{2} \cdot s}{4}}{\frac{\sqrt{5} \cdot s}{2}} = \frac{\sqrt{2}}{2\sqrt{5}} = \sqrt{\frac{1 - \cos \theta}{2}}$$

$$\frac{1 - \cos \theta}{2} = \frac{2}{20} = \frac{1}{10}$$

$$1 - \cos \theta = \frac{2}{10} = \frac{1}{5}$$

$$\cos \theta = \frac{4}{5}$$

Exercise 7-4

2. $\cos x \cos y = \dfrac{1}{2}[\cos(x + y) + \cos(x - y)]$

$$\cos 7A \cos 5A = \frac{1}{2}[\cos(7A + 5A) + \cos(7A - 5A)]$$

$$= \frac{1}{2}(\cos 12A + \cos 2A)$$

$$= \frac{1}{2}\cos 12A + \frac{1}{2}\cos 2A$$

4. $\cos x \sin y = \dfrac{1}{2}[\sin(x + y) - \sin(x - y)]$

$$\cos 2\theta \sin 3\theta = \frac{1}{2}[\sin(2\theta + 3\theta) - \sin(2\theta - 3\theta)]$$

$$= \frac{1}{2}[\sin 5\theta - \sin(-\theta)]$$

$$= \frac{1}{2}[\sin 5\theta + \sin \theta]$$

$$= \frac{1}{2}\sin 5\theta + \frac{1}{2}\sin \theta$$

6. $\cos x + \cos y = 2 \cos \dfrac{x + y}{2} \cos \dfrac{x - y}{2}$

$$\cos 7\theta + \cos 5\theta = 2 \cos \frac{7\theta + 5\theta}{2} \cos \frac{7\theta - 5\theta}{2}$$

$$= 2 \cos 6\theta \cos \theta$$

8. $\sin x - \sin y = 2 \cos \dfrac{x + y}{2} \sin \dfrac{x - y}{2}$

$$\sin u - \sin 5u = 2 \cos \dfrac{u + 5u}{2} \sin \dfrac{u - 5u}{2}$$

$$= 2 \cos 3u \sin(-2u)$$

$$= -2 \cos 3u \sin 2u$$

10. $\cos x \sin y = \dfrac{1}{2}[\sin(x + y) - \sin(x - y)]$

$$\cos 105° \sin 165° = \dfrac{1}{2}[\sin(105° + 165°) - \sin(105° - 165°)]$$

$$= \dfrac{1}{2}[\sin 270° - \sin(-60°)]$$

$$= \dfrac{1}{2}\left(-1 - \left(-\dfrac{\sqrt{3}}{2}\right)\right)$$

$$= \dfrac{1}{2}\left(\dfrac{-2 + \sqrt{3}}{2}\right)$$

$$= \dfrac{\sqrt{3} - 2}{4}$$

12. $\sin x \cos y = \dfrac{1}{2}[\sin(x + y) + \sin(x - y)]$

$$\sin 82.5° \cos 37.5° = \dfrac{1}{2}[\sin(82.5° + 37.5°) + \sin(82.5° - 37.5°)]$$

$$= \dfrac{1}{2}[\sin 120° + \sin 45°]$$

$$= \dfrac{1}{2}\left[\dfrac{\sqrt{3}}{2} + \dfrac{\sqrt{2}}{2}\right]$$

$$= \dfrac{\sqrt{3} + \sqrt{2}}{4}$$

14. $\cos x + \cos y = 2 \cos \dfrac{x + y}{2} \cos \dfrac{x - y}{2}$

$$\cos 75° + \cos 15° = 2 \cos \dfrac{75° + 15°}{2} \cos \dfrac{75° - 15°}{2}$$

$$= 2 \cos 45° \cos 30°$$

$$= 2\left(\dfrac{\sqrt{2}}{2}\right)\left(\dfrac{\sqrt{3}}{2}\right)$$

$$= \dfrac{\sqrt{6}}{2}$$

16. $\sin x + \sin y = 2 \sin \dfrac{x + y}{2} \cos \dfrac{x - y}{2}$

$$\sin 285° + \sin 195° = 2 \sin \dfrac{285° + 195°}{2} \cos \dfrac{285° - 195°}{2}$$

$$= 2 \sin 240° \cos 45°$$

$$= 2\left(-\dfrac{\sqrt{3}}{2}\right)\left(\dfrac{\sqrt{2}}{2}\right)$$

$$= -\dfrac{\sqrt{6}}{2}$$

18. Verify: $\sin x \sin y = \frac{1}{2}[\cos(x - y) - \cos(x + y)]$

$$\frac{1}{2}[\cos(x - y) - \cos(x + y)] = \frac{1}{2}[\cos x \cos y + \sin x \sin y$$
$$- (\cos x \cos y - \sin x \sin y)]$$
$$= \frac{1}{2}[2 \sin x \sin y]$$
$$= \sin x \sin y$$

20. Start with the product-sum identity

$$\cos u \cos v = \frac{1}{2}[\cos(u + v) + \cos(u - v)]$$

Let
$x = u + v$
$y = u - v$

Solving this system gives $u = \dfrac{x + y}{2}, \ v = \dfrac{x - y}{2}.$

Substituting into the product-sum identity,

$$\cos \frac{x + y}{2} \cos \frac{x - y}{2} = \frac{1}{2}[\cos x + \cos y]$$

or

$$\cos x + \cos y = 2 \cos \frac{x + y}{2} \sin \frac{x - y}{2}$$

22. Verify: $\dfrac{\cos t - \cos 3t}{\sin t + \sin 3t} = \tan t$

$$\frac{\cos t - \cos 3t}{\sin t + \sin 3t} = \frac{-2 \sin \frac{t + 3t}{2} \sin \frac{t - 3t}{2}}{2 \sin \frac{t + 3t}{2} \cos \frac{t - 3t}{2}} \qquad \text{Sum-product Identities}$$

$$= \frac{-\sin 2t \sin(-t)}{\sin 2t \cos(-t)} \qquad \text{Algebra}$$

$$= \frac{\sin 2t \sin t}{\sin 2t \cos t} \qquad \text{Identities for negatives}$$

$$= \frac{\sin t}{\cos t} \qquad \text{Algebra}$$

$$= \tan t \qquad \text{Quotient Identity}$$

24. Verify: $\dfrac{\sin x + \sin y}{\cos x + \cos y} = \tan \dfrac{x + y}{2}$

$$\frac{\sin x + \sin y}{\cos x + \cos y} = \frac{2 \sin \frac{x + y}{2} \cos \frac{x - y}{2}}{2 \cos \frac{x + y}{2} \cos \frac{x - y}{2}} \qquad \text{Sum-product Identities}$$

$$= \frac{\sin \frac{x + y}{2}}{\cos \frac{x + y}{2}} \qquad \text{Algebra}$$

$$= \tan \frac{x + y}{2} \qquad \text{Quotient Identity}$$

26. $(\sin 2x + \sin 2y)\tan(x - y) = \cos 2x - \cos 2y$ is not an identity.

Let $x = 90°$, $y = 30°$:

$$(\sin(2 \cdot 90°) + \sin(2 \cdot 30°))\tan(90° - 30°) = (\sin 180° + \sin 60°)\tan 60°$$

$$= \left(0 + \frac{\sqrt{3}}{2}\right)(\sqrt{3})$$

$$= \frac{3}{2}$$

$$\cos(2 \cdot 90°) - \cos(2 \cdot 30°) = \cos 180° - \cos 60°$$

$$= -1 - \frac{1}{2}$$

$$= -\frac{3}{2}$$

28. $\sin 2x = \sin(x + y)\cos(x - y) + \cos(x + y)\sin(x - y)$ is an identity.

$$\sin(x + y)\cos(x - y) + \cos(x + y)\sin(x - y) = \sin[(x + y) + (x - y)]$$

$$= \sin(x + y + x - y)$$

$$= \sin 2x$$

30. $\sec x \sec y[\cos(x + y) + \cos(x - y)] = 2$ is an identity

$$\sec x \sec y[\cos(x + y) + \cos(x - y)]$$

$$= \sec x \sec y[\cos x \cos y - \sin x \sin y + \cos x \cos y + \sin x \sin y]$$

$$= \sec x \sec y[2 \cos x \cos y]$$

$$= \frac{1}{\cos x \cos y} \cdot 2 \cos x \cos y$$

$$= 2$$

32. $x = 50.137°$, $y = 18.044°$

(A) $\cos 50.137° \sin 18.044° \approx 0.19853$

$$\frac{1}{2}[\sin(50.137° + 18.044°) - \sin(50.137° - 18.044°)]$$

$$= \frac{1}{2}[\sin 68.181 - \sin 32.093] \approx 0.19853$$

(B) $\cos 50.137° + \cos 18.044° \approx 1.5918$

$$2 \cos \frac{50.137° + 18.044°}{2} \cos \frac{50.137° - 18.044°}{2}$$

$$= 2 \cos 34.0905 \cos 16.0465 \approx 1.5918$$

34. $x = 0.03917$, $y = 0.61052$

(A) $\cos 0.03917 \sin 0.61052 \approx 0.57285$

$$\frac{1}{2}[\sin(0.03917 + 0.61052) - \sin(0.03917 - 0.61052)]$$

$$= \frac{1}{2}[\sin 0.64969 - \sin(-0.57135) \approx 0.57285$$

(B) $\cos 0.039817 + \cos 0.61052 \approx 1.8186$

$$2 \cos \frac{0.03917 + 0.61052}{2} \cos \frac{0.03917 - 0.61052}{2}$$

$$= 2 \cos 0.324845 \cos(-0.285675) \approx 1.8186$$

36. $y = \cos 3x + \cos x = 2 \cos\left(\dfrac{3x + x}{2}\right)\cos\left(\dfrac{3x - x}{2}\right) = 2 \cos 2x \cos x$

$y_1 = \cos 3x + \cos x$
$y_2 = 2 \cos 2x \cos x$

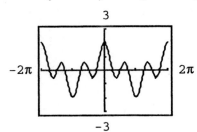

38. $y = \sin 2.1x - \sin 0.5x = 2 \cos \dfrac{2.1x + 0.5x}{2} \sin \dfrac{2.1x - 0.5x}{2}$

$\qquad\qquad = 2 \cos 1.3x \sin 0.8x$

$y_1 = \sin 2.1x - \sin 0.5x$
$y_2 = 2 \cos 1.3x \sin 0.8x$

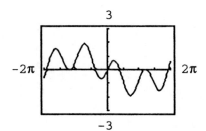

40. $y = \cos 5x \cos 3x = \dfrac{1}{2}[\cos(5x + 3x) + \cos(5x - 3x)] = \dfrac{1}{2}[\cos 8x + \cos 2x]$

$y_1 = \cos 5x + \cos 3x$
$y_2 = \dfrac{1}{2}[\cos 8x + \cos 2x]$

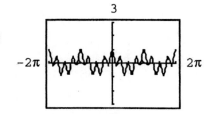

42. $y = \cos 1.9x \sin 0.5x = \dfrac{1}{2}[\sin(1.9x + 0.5x) - \sin(1.9x - 0.5x)]$

$\qquad\qquad\qquad = \dfrac{1}{2}[\sin 2.4x - \sin 1.4x]$

$y_1 = \cos 1.9x \sin 0.5x$
$y_2 = \dfrac{1}{2}[\sin 2.4x - \sin 1.4x]$

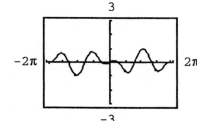

44. Verify: $\sin x \sin y \sin z = \frac{1}{4} [\sin(x + y - z) + \sin(y + z - x)$
$$+ \sin(z + x - y) - \sin(x + y + z)]$$

$\sin x \sin y \sin z = \sin x \left\{ \frac{1}{2} [\cos(y - z) - \cos(y + z)] \right\}$ Product-Sum Identity

$$= \frac{1}{2} \sin x \cos(y - z) - \frac{1}{2} \sin x \cos(y + z)$$ Algebra

$$= \frac{1}{2} \left\{ \frac{1}{2} [\sin(x + y - z) + \sin(x - \{y - z\})] \right\}$$ Product—Sum Identity
$$- \frac{1}{2} \left\{ \frac{1}{2} [\sin(x + y + z) + \sin(x - \{y + z\})] \right\}$$

$$= \frac{1}{4} \sin(x + y - z) + \frac{1}{4} \sin(x - y + z)$$
$$- \frac{1}{4} \sin(x + y + z) - \frac{1}{4} \sin(x - y - z)$$ Algebra

$$= \frac{1}{4} [\sin(x + y - z) - \sin(x - y - z)$$
$$+ \sin(z + x - y) - \sin(x + y + z)]$$ Algebra

$$= \frac{1}{4} [\sin(x + y - z) + \sin\{-(x - y - z)\}$$
$$+ \sin(z + x - y) - \sin(x + y + z)]$$ Identity for negatives

$$= \frac{1}{4} [\sin(x + y - z) + \sin(y + z - x)$$
$$+ \sin(z + x - y) - \sin(x + y + z)]$$ Algebra

46. (A)

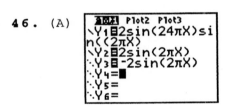
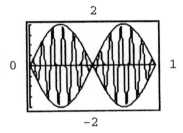

(B) $Y_1 = 2 \sin(24\pi x) \sin(2\pi x)$

$$= 2 \cdot \frac{1}{2} [\cos(24\pi x - 2\pi x) - \cos(24\pi x + 2\pi x)]$$

$$= \cos(22\pi x) - \cos(26\pi x). \text{ Graph is the same as part A.}$$

48. (A)

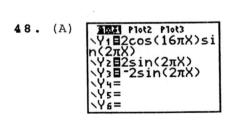
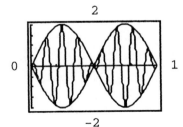

(B) $Y_1 = 2 \cos(16\pi x) \sin(2\pi x)$

$$= 2 \cdot \frac{1}{2} [\sin(16\pi x + 2\pi x) - \sin(16\pi x - 2\pi x)]$$

$$= \sin(18\pi x) - \sin(14\pi x). \text{ Graph is the same as part A.}$$

50. (A) $0.25 \cos(256\pi t) - 0.25 \cos(288\pi t)$

$$= 0.25[\cos(256\pi t) - \cos(288\pi t)]$$

$$= 0.25\left[-2 \sin\left(\frac{256\pi t + 288\pi t}{2}\right) \sin\left(\frac{256\pi t - 288\pi t}{2}\right)\right]$$

$$= -\frac{1}{2} \sin(272\pi t) \sin(-16\pi t)$$

$$= \frac{1}{2} \sin(272\pi t) \sin(16\pi t)$$

(B) $y = 0.25 \cos(256\pi t)$ $y = -0.25 \cos(288\pi t)$

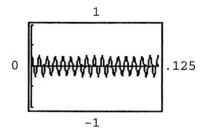   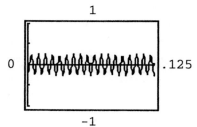

$y = 0.25 \cos(256\pi t) - 0.25 \cos(288\pi t)$ $y = 0.5 \sin(16\pi t) \sin(272\pi t)$

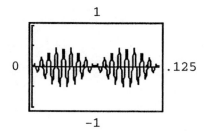   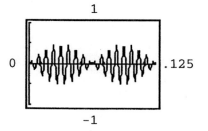

Exercise 7-5

2. $2 \cos x + 1 = 0$, $0 \leq x < 2\pi$

$$2 \cos x = -1$$

$$\cos x = -\frac{1}{2}$$

$$x = \frac{2\pi}{3}, \frac{4\pi}{3}$$

4. $2 \cos x + 1 = 0$, all real x

$$2 \cos x = -1$$

$$\cos x = -\frac{1}{2}$$

$$x = \frac{2\pi}{3} + 2k\pi, \frac{4\pi}{3} + 2k\pi,$$

$$k \text{ any integer}$$

6. $\sqrt{3} \tan x + 1 = 0$, $0 \leq x < \pi$

$$\sqrt{3} \tan x = -1$$

$$\tan x = \frac{-1}{\sqrt{3}}$$

$$x = \frac{5\pi}{6}$$

8. $\sqrt{3} \tan x + 1 = 0$, all real x

$$\sqrt{3} \tan x = -1$$

$$\tan x = \frac{-1}{\sqrt{3}}$$

$$x = \frac{5\pi}{6} + k\pi,$$

$$k \text{ any integer}$$

10. $\sqrt{2} \sin \theta - 1 = 0$, $0° \leq \theta < 360°$

$$\sqrt{2} \sin \theta = 1$$

$$\sin \theta = \frac{1}{\sqrt{2}}$$

$$\theta = 45°, 135°$$

12. $5 \cos x - 2 = 0$, $0 \leq x < 2\pi$

$$5 \cos x = 2$$

$$\cos x = \frac{2}{5}$$

$$x \approx 1.1593, 5.1239$$

14. $4 \tan \theta + 15 = 0, \quad 0° \le \theta < 180°$

$$4 \tan \theta = -15$$

$$\tan \theta = \frac{-15}{4}$$

$$\theta = \tan^{-1}\left(-\frac{15}{4}\right)$$

$$= -75.0686°$$

$$\theta \approx 104.9314°$$

For correct domain, $\theta = 180° - 75.0686°$

16. $5.0118 \sin x - 3.1105 = 0$, all real x

$$5.0118 \sin x = 3.1105$$

$$\sin x = \frac{3.1105}{5.0118}$$

$$x = \sin^{-1}\left(\frac{3.1105}{5.0118}\right)$$

$x \approx 0.6696$; QII: $x = \pi - 0.6696 \approx 2.4720$

$x \approx 0.6696 + 2k\pi,\ 2.4720 + 2k\pi,\ k$ any integer

18.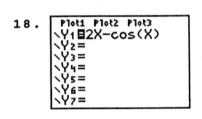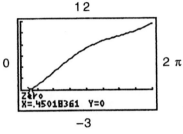

$x \approx 0.4502$

20.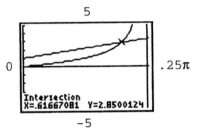

$x \approx 0.6167$

22. $\cos^2 \theta = \frac{1}{2} \cdot \sin 2\theta$, all θ

$$\cos^2 \theta = \frac{1}{2} \cdot 2 \sin \theta \cos \theta$$

$$\cos^2 \theta - \sin \theta \cos \theta = 0$$

$$\cos \theta \cdot (\cos \theta - \sin \theta) = 0$$

$\cos \theta = 0$ or $\cos \theta - \sin \theta = 0$

$\theta = 90° + k \cdot 180°$ $\qquad\qquad \cos \theta = \sin \theta$

$$\frac{\cos \theta}{\sin \theta} = 1$$

$$\tan \theta = 1$$

$$\theta = 45° + k \cdot 180°, \ k \text{ any integer}$$

24. $\cos x = \cot x$, $0 \le x < 2\pi$

$\cos x = \dfrac{\cos x}{\sin x}$

$\sin x \cos x - \cos x = 0$

$\cos x(\sin x - 1) = 0$

$\cos x = 0 \qquad\qquad \sin x - 1 = 0$

$\qquad x = \dfrac{\pi}{2}, \dfrac{3\pi}{2} \qquad\qquad \sin x = 1$

$\qquad\qquad\qquad\qquad\qquad x = \dfrac{\pi}{2}$

26. $\sin^2 \theta + 2 \cos \theta = -2$, $0° \le \theta < 360°$

$1 - \cos^2 \theta + 2 \cos \theta + 2 = 0$

$\cos^2 \theta - 2 \cos \theta - 3 = 0$

$(\cos \theta + 1)(\cos \theta - 3) = 0$

$\cos \theta + 1 = 0 \quad$ or $\quad \cos \theta - 3 = 0$

$\cos \theta = -1 \qquad\qquad \cos \theta = 3$, no solution

$\theta = 180°$

28. $\cos 2\theta + \sin^2 \theta = 0$, $0° \le \theta < 360°$

$1 - 2 \sin^2 \theta + \sin^2 \theta = 0$

$-\sin^2 \theta = -1$

$\sin^2 \theta = 1$

$\sin \theta = \pm 1$

$\theta = 90°,\ 270°$

30. $4 \cos^2 2x - 4 \cos 2x + 1 = 0$, $0 \le x < 2\pi \Leftrightarrow 0 \le 2x < 4\pi$

$(2 \cos 2x - 1)^2 = 0$

$\cos 2x = \dfrac{1}{2}$

$2x = \dfrac{\pi}{3}, \dfrac{5\pi}{3}, \dfrac{7\pi}{3}, \dfrac{11\pi}{3}$

$x = \dfrac{\pi}{6}, \dfrac{5\pi}{6}, \dfrac{7\pi}{6}, \dfrac{11\pi}{6}$

32. $4 \cos^2 \theta = 7 \cos \theta + 2$, $0° \le \theta \le 180°$

$4 \cos^2 \theta - 7 \cos \theta - 2 = 0$

$(4 \cos \theta + 1)(\cos \theta - 2) = 0$

$4 \cos \theta + 1 = 0 \quad$ or $\quad \cos \theta - 2 = 0$

$4 \cos \theta = -1 \qquad\qquad \cos \theta = 2$, no solution

$\cos \theta = \dfrac{-1}{4}$

$\theta = \cos^{-1}(-0.25)$

$\theta \approx 104.5°$

34. $8 \sin^2 x + 10 \sin x = 3$, $0 \le x \le \dfrac{\pi}{2}$

$8 \sin^2 x + 10 \sin x - 3 = 0$

$(4 \sin x - 1)(2 \sin x + 3) = 0$

$4 \sin x - 1 = 0 \quad$ or $\quad 2 \sin x + 3 = 0$

$4 \sin x = 1 \qquad\qquad 2 \sin x = -3$

$\sin x = \dfrac{1}{4} \qquad\qquad \sin x = \dfrac{-3}{2}$, no solution

$x = \sin^{-1}(0.25)$

$x \approx 0.2527$

36. $\cos 2x + 10 \cos x = 5$, $0 \le x < 2\pi$
$$2 \cos^2 x - 1 + 10 \cos x - 5 = 0$$
$$2 \cos^2 x + 10 \cos x - 6 = 0$$
$$\cos x = \frac{-10 \pm \sqrt{10^2 - 4(2)(-6)}}{2(2)} = \frac{-10 \pm 2\sqrt{37}}{4} = \frac{-5 \pm \sqrt{37}}{2}$$
$$\cos x = \frac{-5 + \sqrt{37}}{2} = 0.5413812651... \quad \text{or} \quad \cos x = \frac{-5 - \sqrt{37}}{2} = -5.54138265...$$
$$x \approx 0.9987,\ 5.284\ (2\pi - 0.9987) \qquad\qquad \text{no solution}$$

38. $2 \sec^2 x = \tan^2 x + 1$ has no solutions.
$\tan^2 x + 1 = \sec^2 x$ which implies $2 \sec^2 x = \sec^2 x$
$\sec^2 x \ne 0$, so divide each side by sec x: $2 = 1$

This statement is never true, so there are no solutions to the original equation.

40. $\pi \cos x + 2x = \pi$ has 3 solutions.

The graph of $\pi \cos x + 2x$ is an increasing graph with the repeated shape of a cubic equation. Any line can intersect this graph at most 3 times.

The solutions are $x = 0, \dfrac{\pi}{2}, \pi$.

42. $(\cot x - \tan x) \tan 2x = 2$ is an identity, so there are infinitely many solutions.
$$(\cot x - \tan x) \tan 2x = (\cot x - \tan x) \frac{2}{\cot x - \tan x} = 2$$

44. $y_1 = \cos 2x + 10 \cos x$
$y_2 = 5$

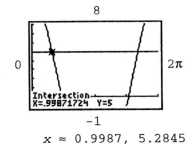
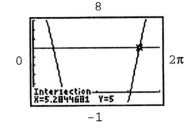

$$x \approx 0.9987,\ 5.2845$$

46. $y_1 = \cos^2 x$
$y_2 = 3 - 5 \cos x$

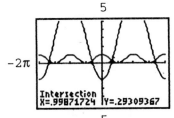
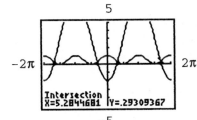

$$x \approx 0.9987 + 2k\pi,\ 5.2845 + 2k\pi,\ k \text{ any integer}$$

48. $y_1 = 2 \sin(x - 2)$
$y_2 = 3 - x^2$

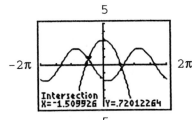
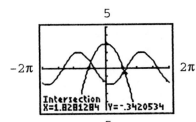

$$2 \sin(x - 2) < 3 - x^2 \text{ on } (-1.5099,\ 1.8281)$$

50. $y_1 = \sin(3 - 2x)$
$y_2 = 1 - 0.4x$

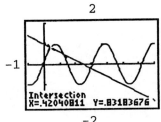 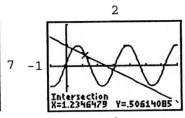 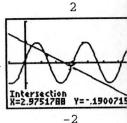

$\sin(3 - 2x) \geq 1 - 0.4x$ on $[0.4204, 1.2346]$, $[2.9752, \infty)$

52. $y_1 = e^{-\sin x}$
$y_2 = 3 - x$

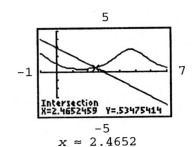

$x \approx 2.4652$

54. Evaluating $\cos^{-1}(-0.7334)$ gives a unique number, ≈ 2.3941, the value of the inverse cosine function at -0.7334, while solving $\cos x = -0.7334$ involves finding an infinite number of x values whose cosine is -0.7334 by adding $2\pi k$, k any integer, to each solution in one period of $\cos x$.

56. $\sin x + \cos x = 1$, $0 \leq x < 2\pi$
$\sin^2 x + 2 \sin x \cos x + \cos^2 x = 1$
$1 + 2 \sin x \cos x = 1$
$\sin x \cos x = 0$

$\sin x = 0$ or $\cos x = 0$

$x = 0, \pi$ $\qquad x = \dfrac{\pi}{2}, \dfrac{3\pi}{2}$

$\sin 0 + \cos 0 = 1$ $\qquad \sin \dfrac{\pi}{2} + \cos \dfrac{\pi}{2} = 1$

$\sin \pi + \cos \pi = -1$ (extraneous) $\quad \sin \dfrac{3\pi}{2} + \cos \dfrac{3\pi}{2} = -1$ (extraneous)

$x = 0, \dfrac{\pi}{2}$ are the solutions

58. $\sec x + \tan x = 1$, $0 \leq x < 2\pi$
$\sec x = 1 - \tan x$
$\sec^2 x = 1 - 2 \tan x + \tan^2 x$
$\sec^2 x = \sec^2 x - 2 \tan x$
$0 = -2 \tan x$
$\tan x = 0$
$x = 0, \pi$
$\sec 0 + \tan 0 = 1$
$\sec \pi + \tan \pi = -1$ (extraneous)
$x = 0$ is the solution

60. $2 \cos\left(\dfrac{1}{x}\right) = 950x - 4$, $0.006 < x < 0.007$

$y_1 = 2 \cos\left(\dfrac{1}{x}\right)$

$y_2 = 950x - 4$

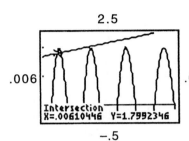

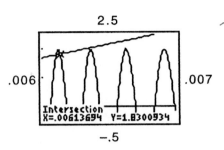

$x \approx 0.006104, 0.006137$

62. $g(x) = \cos\left(\dfrac{1}{x}\right)$ for $x > 0$

$y_1 = \cos\left(\dfrac{1}{x}\right)$

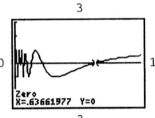

(A) 0.6366 is the largest zero. As $x \to \infty$, $\dfrac{1}{x} \to 0 \Rightarrow \cos\left(\dfrac{1}{x}\right) \to 1$ so $y = 1$ is a horizontal asymptote for the graph of g.

(B) Infinitely many zeros exist between 0 and b, for any b, however small. The exploration graphs suggest this conclusion, which is reinforced by the following reasoning: Note that for each interval $(0, b]$, however small, as x tends to zero through positive numbers, $1/x$ increases without bound, and as $1/x$ increases without bound, $\cos(1/x)$ will cross the x axis an unlimited number of times. The function g does not have a smallest zero, because, between 0 and b, no matter how small b is, there is always an unlimited number of zeros.

64. $I = 30 \sin(120\pi t)$, $I = 25$ amps

$25 = 30 \sin(120\pi t)$

$\sin(120\pi t) = \dfrac{25}{30}$

$120\pi t = \sin^{-1}\left(\dfrac{25}{30}\right)$

$t = \dfrac{1}{120\pi} \cdot \sin^{-1}\left(\dfrac{5}{6}\right)$

$t \approx 0.002613$ seconds

66. $I_L = I_E \cdot \cos^2\theta$, $I_L = 70\% \ I_E$

$0.7 I_E = I_E \cdot \cos^2\theta$

$0.7 = \cos^2\theta$

$\cos\theta = \pm\sqrt{0.7}$

$\theta = \cos^{-1}(\pm\sqrt{0.7})$

$\theta \approx 33.21°, 146.79°, 213.21°, 326.79°$

Smallest positive θ: 33.21°

68. $r = \dfrac{3.44 \times 10^7}{1 - 0.206 \cos\theta}$

$3.78 \times 10^7 = \dfrac{3.44 \times 10^7}{1 - 0.206 \cos\theta}$

$3.78 \times 10^7 - 7{,}786{,}800 \cos\theta = 3.44 \times 10^7$

$-7{,}786{,}800 \cos\theta = -3{,}400{,}000$

$\cos\theta \approx 0.436636359$

$\theta = \cos^{-1}(0.436636359)$

$\theta \approx 64.1°, 296°$

Smallest positive θ: 64.1°

70. $Y_1 = 40$

$Y_2 = \frac{1}{2} \cdot 10^2 (x - \sin x)$

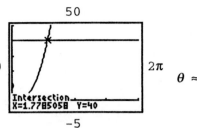

$\theta \approx 1.779$ rad

72. (A) $\sin \theta = \dfrac{a}{R} = \dfrac{5.4}{R}$ $\cos \theta = \dfrac{x}{R}$

$R = \dfrac{5.4}{\sin \theta}$ $x = R \cos \theta$

$R = x + b$

$\dfrac{5.4}{\sin \theta} = R \cos \theta + 2.4$

$\dfrac{5.4}{\sin \theta} = \dfrac{5.4 \cos \theta}{\sin \theta} + 2.4$

Graphing each side of the equation and finding the intersection gives $\theta \approx 0.83644866$.

$R = \dfrac{5.4}{\sin 0.83644866} \approx 7.274999994$

$L = R(2\theta)$

$L \approx 7.274999994(2 \cdot 0.83644866)$

$L \approx 12.1703$ mm to 4 decimal places

(B) Increase a to 5.5 mm:

$L = R(2\theta)$

$\theta = \dfrac{L}{2R}$

$\theta \approx \dfrac{12.17032799}{\dfrac{2(5.5)}{\sin \theta}}$

Graphing each side of the equation and finding the intersection gives $\theta \approx 0.77096792$.

$R \approx \dfrac{5.5}{\sin 0.770967922} \approx 7.892888691$

$x = R \cos \theta$

$x \approx 7.892888691 \cos 0.77096792 \approx 5.661068098$

$b = R - x$

$b \approx 7.892888691 - 5.661068098$

$b \approx 2.2318$ mm to 4 decimal places

74. $r = 2 \sin \theta, \ 0° \leq \theta \leq 360°$

$r = 2(1 - \sin \theta)$

$2 \sin \theta = 2(1 - \sin \theta)$

$4 \sin \theta = 2$

$\sin \theta = \dfrac{1}{2}, \ r = 2\left(\dfrac{1}{2}\right) = 1$

$\theta = 30°, \ 150° \Rightarrow (1, 30°), (1, 150°)$

76. $xy = -2$

$(u \cos \theta - v \sin \theta)(u \sin \theta + v \cos \theta) = -2$

$u^2 \sin \theta \cos \theta + uv \cos^2 \theta - uv \sin^2 \theta - v^2 \sin \theta \cos \theta = -2$

coefficient of uv term = 0:

$$\cos^2 \theta - \sin^2 \theta = 0$$
$$1 - \sin^2 \theta - \sin^2 \theta = 0$$
$$2 \sin^2 \theta = 1$$
$$\sin^2 \theta = \frac{1}{2}$$
$$\sin \theta = \pm\frac{1}{\sqrt{2}}$$
$$\theta = 45°, \ 135°, \ 225°, \ 315°$$

smallest positive $\theta = 45°$

CHAPTER 8

Note: Answers have been rounded to the number of significant digits given in Table 1; an = sign has been used rather than ≈.

Exercise 8-1

2. $\gamma = 180° - (41° + 33°)$

$\gamma = 106°$

$\dfrac{a}{\sin \alpha} = \dfrac{c}{\sin \gamma}$

$\dfrac{a}{\sin 41°} = \dfrac{21}{\sin 106°}$

$a = 14$ cm

$\dfrac{b}{\sin \beta} = \dfrac{c}{\sin \gamma}$

$\dfrac{b}{\sin 33°} = \dfrac{21}{\sin 106°}$

$b = 12$ cm

4. $\alpha = 180° - (43° + 36°)$

$\alpha = 101°$

$\dfrac{a}{\sin \alpha} = \dfrac{c}{\sin \gamma}$

$\dfrac{92}{\sin 101°} = \dfrac{c}{\sin 36°}$

$c = 55$ mm

$\dfrac{b}{\sin \beta} = \dfrac{a}{\sin \alpha}$

$\dfrac{b}{\sin 43°} = \dfrac{92}{\sin 101°}$

$b = 64$ mm

6. $\beta = 180° - (52° + 105°)$

$\beta = 23°$

$\dfrac{a}{\sin \alpha} = \dfrac{c}{\sin \gamma}$

$\dfrac{a}{\sin 52°} = \dfrac{47}{\sin 105°}$

$a = 38$ m

$\dfrac{b}{\sin \beta} = \dfrac{c}{\sin \gamma}$

$\dfrac{b}{\sin 23°} = \dfrac{47}{\sin 105°}$

$b = 19$ m

8. $\alpha = 180° - (83° + 77°)$

$\alpha = 20°$

$\dfrac{b}{\sin \beta} = \dfrac{c}{\sin \gamma}$

$\dfrac{b}{\sin 83°} = \dfrac{25}{\sin 77°}$

$b = 25$ mi

$\dfrac{a}{\sin \alpha} = \dfrac{c}{\sin \gamma}$

$\dfrac{a}{\sin 20°} = \dfrac{25}{\sin 77°}$

$a = 8.8$ mi

10. $a = 6$ in, $b = 5$ in, $\alpha = 30°$
SSA:
α is acute, $a > b \Rightarrow 1$ triangle; case (d)

12. $a = 2$ ft, $b = 5$ ft, $\alpha = 30°$
SSA:

$h = b \sin \alpha = 5 \sin 30° = \dfrac{5}{2} > 2 \Rightarrow 0$ triangles; case (a)

14. $a = 3$ in, $b = 4$ in, $\alpha = 45°$
SSA:

$h = b \sin \alpha = 4 \sin 45° = 2\sqrt{2} \approx 2.83$
$h < a < b \Rightarrow 2$ triangles; case (c)

16. $a = 6$ ft, $b = 4$ ft, $\alpha = 120°$
SSA:
α is obtuse, $a > b \Rightarrow 1$ triangle; case (f)

18. $a = 7$ in, $b = 8$ in, $\alpha = 60°$
SSA:

$h = b \sin \alpha = 8 \sin 60° = 4\sqrt{3} \approx 6.9$
$h < a < b \Rightarrow 2$ triangles; case (c)

20. $a = 12$ ft, $b = 13$ ft, $\alpha = 90°$
SSA:
α is a right angle with hypotenuse a, thus a must be the longest side.
Since $a < b \Rightarrow 0$ triangles; none of the cases.

22. $\beta = 27.5°$, $\gamma = 54.5°$, $a = 9.27$ inches

$\alpha = 180° - (27.5° + 54.5°)$

$\alpha = 98.0°$

$\dfrac{a}{\sin \alpha} = \dfrac{b}{\sin \beta}$

$\dfrac{9.27}{\sin 98°} = \dfrac{b}{\sin 27.5°}$

$b = 4.32$ in

$\dfrac{c}{\sin \gamma} = \dfrac{a}{\sin \alpha}$

$\dfrac{c}{\sin 54.5°} = \dfrac{9.27}{\sin 98°}$

$c = 7.62$ in

24. $\alpha = 122.7°$, $\beta = 34.4°$, $b = 18.3$ km

$\gamma = 180° - (122.7° + 34.4°)$

$\gamma = 22.9°$

$\dfrac{a}{\sin \alpha} = \dfrac{b}{\sin \beta}$

$\dfrac{a}{\sin 122.7°} = \dfrac{18.3}{\sin 34.4°}$

$a = 27.3$ km

$\dfrac{c}{\sin \gamma} = \dfrac{b}{\sin \beta}$

$\dfrac{c}{\sin 22.9°} = \dfrac{18.3}{\sin 34.4°}$

$c = 12.6$ km

26. $\alpha = 26.3°$, $a = 14.7$ inches, $b = 35.2$ inches

$\dfrac{a}{\sin \alpha} = \dfrac{b}{\sin \beta}$

$\dfrac{14.7}{\sin 26.3°} = \dfrac{35.2}{\sin \beta}$

$\sin \beta = 1.0609596 > 1 \Rightarrow$ No solution

28. $\alpha = 27.3°$, $a = 135$ cm, $b = 244$ cm

SSA, α is acute:

$h = b \sin \alpha = 244 \sin 27.3° = 112$

$h < a < b \Rightarrow 2$ triangles

Triangle 1:

$\dfrac{a}{\sin \alpha} = \dfrac{b}{\sin \beta_1}$

$\dfrac{135}{\sin 27.3°} = \dfrac{244}{\sin \beta_1}$

$\beta_1 = 56.0°$

$\gamma_1 = 180 - (27.3° + 56.0°) = 96.7°$

$\dfrac{a}{\sin \alpha} = \dfrac{c_1}{\sin \gamma_1}$

$\dfrac{135}{\sin 27.3°} = \dfrac{c_1}{\sin 96.7°}$

$c_1 = 292$ cm

Triangle 2:

$\beta_2 = 180° - \beta_1 = 180° - 96.7° = 124.0°$

$\gamma_2 = 180° - (27.3° + 124.0°) = 28.7°$

$\dfrac{a}{\sin \alpha} = \dfrac{c_2}{\sin \gamma_2}$

$\dfrac{135}{\sin 27.3°} = \dfrac{c_2}{\sin 28.7°}$

$c_2 = 141$ cm

30. $\alpha = 137.3°$, $a = 13.9$ m, $b = 19.1$ m

$\dfrac{a}{\sin \alpha} = \dfrac{b}{\sin \beta}$

$\dfrac{13.9}{\sin 137.3°} = \dfrac{19.1}{\sin \beta} \Rightarrow \beta = 68.73°$

$\beta + \alpha = 206.03° > 180°$

No solution

32. $\beta = 33°50'$, $a = 673$ m, $b = 1240$ m

$$\frac{b}{\sin \beta} = \frac{a}{\sin \alpha} \qquad\qquad \frac{b}{\sin \beta} = \frac{c}{\sin \gamma}$$

$$\frac{1240}{\sin 33°50'} = \frac{673}{\sin \alpha} \qquad\qquad \frac{1240}{\sin 33°50'} = \frac{c}{\sin 128°30'}$$

$$\alpha = 17°40' \qquad\qquad c = 1740 \text{ m}$$

$$\gamma = 180° - (33°50' + 17°40')$$

$$\gamma = 128°30'$$

34. $\alpha = 37.3°$, $b = 42.8$ cm

$k = 42.8 \sin 37.3° = 25.9$ is k such that $0 < a < k$ gives no solution; $a = k$ gives one solution; $k < a < b$ gives two solutions.

36. From the law of sines $\dfrac{a}{\sin \alpha} = \dfrac{c}{\sin \gamma} \Rightarrow \dfrac{a}{c} = \dfrac{\sin \alpha}{\sin \gamma}$ $\qquad$ (1)

$\qquad\qquad\qquad$ and $\dfrac{b}{\sin \beta} = \dfrac{c}{\sin \gamma} \Rightarrow \dfrac{b}{c} = \dfrac{\sin \beta}{\sin \gamma}$ $\qquad$ (2)

$\dfrac{a + b}{c} = \dfrac{\sin \alpha + \sin \beta}{\sin \gamma}$ $\qquad$ adding (1) and (2)

$\qquad = \dfrac{2 \sin \frac{\alpha + \beta}{2} \cos \frac{\alpha - \beta}{2}}{2 \sin \frac{\gamma}{2} \cos \frac{\gamma}{2}}$ $\qquad$ but $\sin \dfrac{\alpha + \beta}{2} = \sin \dfrac{1}{2}(180 - \gamma)$

$\qquad = \dfrac{\sin \frac{\alpha + \beta}{2} \cos \frac{\alpha - \beta}{2}}{\sin \frac{\gamma}{2} \sin \frac{\alpha + \beta}{2}}$ $\qquad\qquad = \sin\left(90 - \dfrac{\gamma}{2}\right)$

$\qquad\qquad\qquad\qquad\qquad\qquad\qquad\qquad = \cos \dfrac{\gamma}{2}$

$\dfrac{a + b}{c} = \dfrac{\cos \frac{\alpha - \beta}{2}}{\sin \frac{\gamma}{2}}$ $\qquad$ (3)

similarly, subtracting (1) and (2)

$\dfrac{a - b}{c} = \dfrac{\sin \alpha - \sin \beta}{\sin \gamma} = \dfrac{2 \cos \frac{\alpha + \beta}{2} \sin \frac{\alpha - \beta}{2}}{\sin \gamma}$

$\qquad = \dfrac{2 \cos \frac{\alpha + \beta}{2} \sin \frac{\alpha - \beta}{2}}{2 \sin \frac{\gamma}{2} \cos \frac{\gamma}{2}}$ $\qquad$ but $\cos \dfrac{\alpha + \beta}{2} = \cos \dfrac{1}{2}(180 - \gamma)$

$\qquad = \dfrac{\sin \frac{\gamma}{2} \sin \frac{\alpha - \beta}{2}}{\sin \frac{\gamma}{2} \cos \frac{\gamma}{2}}$ $\qquad\qquad = \cos\left(90 - \dfrac{\gamma}{2}\right)$

$\qquad\qquad\qquad\qquad\qquad\qquad\qquad\qquad = \sin \dfrac{\gamma}{2}$

$\dfrac{a - b}{c} = \dfrac{\sin \frac{\alpha - \beta}{2}}{\cos \frac{\gamma}{2}}$ $\qquad$ (4)

dividing (4) by (3)

$$\frac{\frac{a-b}{c}}{\frac{a+b}{c}} = \frac{\frac{\sin\frac{\alpha-\beta}{2}}{\cos\frac{\gamma}{2}}}{\frac{\cos\frac{\alpha-\beta}{2}}{\sin\frac{\gamma}{2}}}$$

$$\frac{a-b}{c} \cdot \frac{c}{a+b} = \frac{\sin\frac{\alpha-\beta}{2}}{\cos\frac{\gamma}{2}} \cdot \frac{\sin\frac{\gamma}{2}}{\cos\frac{\alpha-\beta}{2}}$$

$$\frac{a-b}{a+b} = \tan\frac{\alpha-\beta}{2}\ \tan\frac{\gamma}{2}\ \text{but}\ \tan\frac{\gamma}{2} = \cot\frac{\alpha+\beta}{2}$$

$$= \tan\frac{\alpha-\beta}{2} \cdot \frac{1}{\tan\frac{\alpha+\beta}{2}}$$

$$\frac{a-b}{a+b} = \frac{\tan\frac{\alpha-\beta}{2}}{\tan\frac{\alpha+\beta}{2}}$$

(B) from 1, $a = 41$ $\alpha = 73°$
              $b = 20$ $\beta = 28°$

$$\frac{\tan\frac{73°-28°}{2}}{\tan\frac{73°+28°}{2}} = 0.3415$$

$$\frac{41-20}{41+20} = 0.3443$$

Answers vary slightly due to rounding.

38.

$$\frac{b}{\sin 53°} = \frac{a}{\sin 28°30'} = \frac{10}{\sin 98°30'}$$

$$b = 8.08\ \text{miles from } A$$
$$a = 4.82\ \text{miles from } B$$

40.

$$\tan 43°5' = \frac{h}{x}$$

$$x = \frac{h}{\tan 43°5'}$$

$$\tan 38° = \frac{h}{2000+x} = \frac{h}{2000 + \frac{h}{\tan 43°5'}}$$

$$2000\ \tan 38° + h\left(\frac{\tan 38°}{\tan 43°5'}\right) = h$$

$$h\left(1 - \frac{\tan 38°}{\tan 43°5'}\right) = 2000\ \tan 38°$$

$$h = \frac{2000\ \tan 38°}{1 - \frac{\tan 38°}{\tan 43°5'}}$$

$$h \approx 9492.39$$

The distance above sea level = $5000 + h = 14{,}490$ feet to 4 significant digits.

42. $\dfrac{6.3}{\sin\alpha} = \dfrac{1.7}{\sin 11°} = \dfrac{c}{\sin\gamma}$

$\alpha = 45° \Rightarrow \gamma = 124° \Rightarrow c = 7.4''$

$\alpha = 135° \Rightarrow \gamma = 34° \Rightarrow c = 5.0''$

44. $\sin(SEV) = \dfrac{1.085 \times 10^8}{1.495 \times 10^8}$

$SEV = 46.5°$

46.

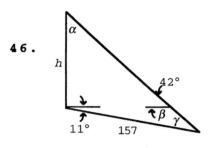

$$\alpha + 42° = 90°$$
$$\alpha = 48°$$
$$\beta + 42° = 180°$$
$$\beta = 138°$$

$$11° + \beta + \gamma = 180°$$
$$11° + 138° + \gamma = 180°$$
$$\gamma = 31°$$

$$\frac{h}{\sin \gamma} = \frac{157}{\sin \alpha}$$

$$\frac{h}{\sin 31°} = \frac{157}{\sin 48°}$$

$h = 109$ ft, to the nearest foot

48.

$$\frac{180° - 63.2°}{2} = 58.4°$$

$$\frac{10.2}{\sin 63.2} = \frac{R}{\sin 58.4°}$$

$$R = 9.73 \text{ mm to 3 significant digits}$$

$$s = R \cdot 63.2° \cdot \frac{\pi}{180°} = 10.7 \text{ mm to 3 significant digits}$$

50. Let x be the length of the side in the horizontal triangle that is also in the vertical triangle with angle γ.

In the horizontal triangle

$$\frac{x}{\sin \alpha} = \frac{d}{\sin(180° - (\alpha + \beta))}$$

$$x = d \sin \alpha \csc(\alpha + \beta)$$

In the vertical triangle

$$\tan \gamma = \frac{h}{x}$$

$$h = x \tan \alpha$$

$$= d \sin \alpha \csc(\alpha + \beta) \tan \gamma$$

$$\sin(180° - (\alpha + \beta))$$
$$= \sin 180° \cos(\alpha + \beta) - \cos 180° \sin(\alpha + \beta)$$
$$= 0 \cdot \cos(\alpha + \beta) - (-1) \sin(\alpha + \beta)$$
$$= \sin(\alpha + \beta)$$
$$= \frac{1}{\csc(\alpha + \beta)}$$

Exercise 8-2

2. A triangle can have at most one obtuse angle. Since $\alpha = 93.5°$ is obtuse both γ and β must be acute. [$\beta + \gamma = 180° - 93.5° = 86.5°$; thus both β and γ are less than 90°.]

4. $\beta = 57.3°$, $a = 6.08$ cm, $c = 5.25$ cm
$$a^2 + c^2 - 2ac \cos \beta = b^2$$
$$6.08^2 + 5.25^2 - 2(6.08)(5.25)\cos 57.3° = b^2 \Rightarrow b = 5.48 \text{ cm}$$

Solve for smallest angle:
$$\frac{5.25}{\sin \gamma} = \frac{5.48}{\sin 57.3°}$$
$$\gamma = 53.7°$$

$$\frac{6.08}{\sin \alpha} = \frac{5.48}{\sin 57.3°} \text{ or } \alpha = 180° - (57.3° + 53.7°)$$
$$\alpha = 69.0°$$

6. $\alpha = 135°50'$, $b = 8.44$ in, $c = 20.3$ in

$b^2 + c^2 - 2bc \cos \alpha = a^2$

$8.44^2 + 20.3^2 - 2(8.44)(20.3)\cos 135°50' = a^2 \Rightarrow a = 27.0$ in

Solve for smallest angle:

$$\frac{27}{\sin 135°50'} = \frac{8.44}{\sin \beta} \qquad \frac{20.3}{\sin \gamma} = \frac{27}{\sin 135°50'} \quad \text{or } \gamma = 180° - (135°50 + 12°30')$$
$$\beta = 12°30' \qquad\qquad \gamma = 31°40'$$

8. If $a = 12.5$ cm, $b = 25.3$ cm, $c = 10.7$ cm, then sides a and c are not long enough to construct a triangle: $a + c < b$

10. $a = 10.5$ mi, $b = 20.7$ mi, $c = 12.2$ mi

Solve for the largest angle:

$$b^2 = a^2 + c^2 - 2ac \cos \beta \qquad\qquad \frac{20.7}{\sin 131.4} = \frac{12.2}{\sin \gamma} \Rightarrow \gamma = 26.2°$$

$$20.7^2 = 10.5^2 + 12.2^2 - 2(10.5)(12.2)\cos \beta \qquad \alpha = 180° - (131.4° + 26.2°) = 22.4°$$

$$\cos \beta \approx -0.6612021858$$
$$\beta = 131.4°$$

12. $a = 31.5$ m, $b = 29.4$ m, $c = 33.7$ m

Solving for the largest angle:

$$c^2 = a^2 + b^2 - 2ab \cos \gamma$$
$$33.7^2 = 31.5^2 + 29.4^2 - 2(31.5)(29.4)\cos \gamma$$
$$\cos \gamma \approx 0.389223626$$
$$\gamma = 67.1°$$
$$\frac{33.7}{\sin 67.1°} = \frac{31.5}{\sin \alpha} \Rightarrow \alpha = 59.4°$$
$$\beta = 180° - (67.1° + 59.4°) = 53.5°$$

14. $\alpha + \gamma = 79.4° + 102.3° = 181.7° > 180° \Rightarrow$ no solution

16. $\alpha = 19.1°$, $a = 16.4$ yd, $b = 28.2$ yd

$$c^2 = a^2 + b^2 - 2ab \cos \gamma$$
$$= 16.4^2 + 28.2^2 - 2(16.4)(28.2)\cos 19.1°$$
$$c = 13.8 \text{ yd}$$

Solve for the smallest angle:

$$\frac{c}{\sin \gamma} = \frac{a}{\sin \alpha}$$
$$\frac{13.8}{\sin 19.1°} = \frac{16.4}{\sin \alpha}$$
$$\alpha = 22.9° \qquad\qquad \beta = 180° - (19.1° + 22.9°) = 138.0°$$

18. If $a = 86$ in, $b = 32$ in, $c = 53$ in, then sides b and c are not long enough to construct a triangle: $b + c < a$. Therefore, no solution.

20. $\gamma = 66.4°$, $b = 25.5$ m, $c = 25.5$ m

$$b = c \Rightarrow \gamma = \beta = 66.4°$$
$$\alpha = 180° - (\gamma + \beta) = 180° - (2(66.4°)) = 47.2°$$
$$\frac{25.5}{\sin 66.4°} = \frac{a}{\sin 47.2°}$$
$$a = 20.4 \text{ m}$$

22. $a = 10.5$ cm, $b = 5.23$ cm, $c = 8.66$ cm

Angle opposite longest side:

$$a^2 = b^2 + c^2 - 2bc \cos \alpha$$

$$10.5^2 = 5.23^2 + 8.66^2 - 2(5.23)(8.66)\cos \alpha$$

$$\alpha = 95.0°$$

$$\frac{10.5}{\sin 95.0°} = \frac{5.23}{\sin \beta}$$

$$\beta = 29.7°$$

$$\gamma = 180° - (\alpha + \beta) = 180° - (95° + 29.7°)$$

$$\gamma = 55.3°$$

24. $\alpha = 46.7°$, $a = 18.1$ m, $b = 22.6$ m

$$\frac{a}{\sin \alpha} = \frac{b}{\sin \beta}$$

$$\frac{18.1}{\sin 46.7} = \frac{22.6}{\sin \beta} \Rightarrow \beta = 65.3° \text{ or } \beta' = 114.7°$$

$$\beta = 65.3° \Rightarrow \gamma = 180° - (65.3° + 46.7°) = 68.0°$$

$$\beta' = 114.7° \Rightarrow \gamma' = 180° - (114.7° + 46.7°) = 18.6°$$

$$\frac{18.1}{\sin 46.7°} = \frac{c}{\sin 68.0°} = \frac{c'}{\sin 18.6°}$$

$$c = 23.1 \text{ m}$$

$$c' = 7.93 \text{ m}$$

Triangle I: $\beta = 65.3°$, $\gamma = 68.0°$, $c = 23.1$ m
Triangle II: $\beta = 114.7°$, $\gamma = 18.6°$, $c = 7.93$ m

26. $\gamma = 47.9°$, $b = 35.2$ in, $c = 25.5$ in

$$\frac{c}{\sin \gamma} = \frac{b}{\sin \beta}$$

$$\frac{25.5}{\sin 47.9°} = \frac{35.2}{\sin \beta}$$

$$\sin \beta = 1.0242176 \Rightarrow \text{No solution}$$

28. Given $c^2 = a^2 + b^2$:

$$c^2 = a^2 + b^2 - 2ab \cos \gamma \quad \text{law of cosines}$$

$$a^2 + b^2 = a^2 + b^2 - 2ab \cos \gamma \quad \text{substitution}$$

$$-2ab \cos \gamma = 0$$

$$\cos \gamma = 0$$

$$\gamma = 90°$$

30.

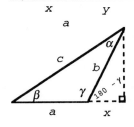

$a = x + y$: $\cos \beta = \dfrac{x}{c} \Rightarrow x = c \cos \beta$

: $\cos \gamma = \dfrac{y}{b} \Rightarrow y = b \cos \gamma$

$a = c \cos \beta + b \cos \gamma$

$\cos \beta = \dfrac{a + x}{c}$ $\cos(180 - \gamma) = \dfrac{x}{b}$

$a + x = c \cos \beta$ $-\cos \gamma = \dfrac{x}{b}$

$a = c \cos \beta - x$ $x = -b \cos \gamma$

$a = c \cos \beta - (-b \cos \gamma)$

$a = c \cos \beta + b \cos \gamma$

32. Form an isosceles triangle with two radii of the circle and one side of the inscribed polygon. The central angle, $\alpha = \dfrac{360°}{n}$. Drop a perpendicular bisector from the center to the side to form a right triangle with hypotenuse r, side $\dfrac{d}{2}$ opposite angle $\dfrac{180°}{n}$.

$\sin \dfrac{180°}{n} = \dfrac{d/2}{r}$

$r \sin \dfrac{180°}{n} = \dfrac{d}{2}$

$d = 2r \sin \dfrac{180°}{n}$

34. $AB = \sqrt{85^2 + 73^2 - 2(85)(73) \cos 110°} \approx 130$ m

36. $c = \sqrt{8^2 + 3^2 - 2(8)(3)\cos(144°50')} \approx 10.6$ ft

38. After 2 hours, Plane A has traveled 800 miles, Plane B 1000 miles. The angle between them is 45°.

$c = \sqrt{1000^2 + 800^2 - 2(1000)(800)\cos 45°} \approx 713$ mi

40. The angle at the center is $\dfrac{360°}{9} = 40°$. An isosceles triangle is formed, so the other two angles are $70° \left(\dfrac{180° - 40°}{2} \right)$. Let x be the chord formed in the circle. Using the law of sines to solve,

$\dfrac{7.09}{\sin 70°} = \dfrac{x}{\sin 40°}$

$x \approx 4.849846$

The perimeter, to 3 significiant digits, is $9x = 43.6$ cm.

42. $OA = \sqrt{3^2 + 4^2} = 5$ $AB^2 = OA^2 + OB^2 - 2(OA)(OB)\cos \theta$

$OB = \sqrt{5^2 + 1^2} = \sqrt{26}$ $(\sqrt{5})^2 = 5^2 + (\sqrt{26})^2 - 2(5)(\sqrt{26})\cos \theta$

$AB = \sqrt{(4 - 5)^2 + (3 - 1)^2} = \sqrt{5}$ $\theta \approx 0.446$ radian

44. The sides of the triangle have lengths of 5 + 2 = 7, 8 + 2 = 10, and 8 + 5 = 13. Find angle γ first (angle opposite longest side):

$$13^2 = 10^2 + 7^2 - 2(10)(7) \cos \gamma$$

$$\gamma \approx 98.2132 \approx 98°10'$$

Angle α: $\dfrac{13}{\sin 98°10} = \dfrac{7}{\sin \alpha}$

$$\alpha \approx 32.20845 \approx 32°10'$$

Angle β: $\beta = 180° - (\alpha + \gamma) \approx 180° - (98°10' + 32°10') \approx 49°40'$

46. $AB = \sqrt{4.3^2 + 8.1^2} = \sqrt{84.1}$

$AC = \sqrt{8.1^2 + 2.8^2} = \sqrt{73.45}$

$BC = \sqrt{4.3^2 + 2.8^2} = \sqrt{26.33}$

$$(AB)^2 = (AC)^2 + (CB)^2 - 2(AC)(BC) \cos(ACB)$$

$$84.1 = 73.45 + 26.33 - 2\sqrt{73.45}\sqrt{26.33} \cos(ACB)$$

Angle $ACB = 80°$

48. $(CS)^2 = R^2 + (ST)^2 - 2(R)(ST) \cos 122.4°$

$(CS)^2 = 3964^2 + 1034^2 - 2(3964)(1034) \cos 122.4°$

$CS \approx 4602$

height = $CS - R \approx 4602 - 3964 \approx 638$ miles

Exercise 8-3

2. $|\boldsymbol{u} + \boldsymbol{v}| = \sqrt{|\boldsymbol{u}|^2 + |\boldsymbol{v}|^2} = \sqrt{216^2 + 63^2} = 225$ mph

$\tan \theta = \dfrac{|\boldsymbol{v}|}{|\boldsymbol{u}|} = \dfrac{63}{216} \Rightarrow \theta = 16°$

4. $|\boldsymbol{u} + \boldsymbol{v}| = \sqrt{|\boldsymbol{u}|^2 + |\boldsymbol{v}|^2} = \sqrt{78^2 + 45^2} = 90$ kg

$\tan \theta = \dfrac{|\boldsymbol{v}|}{|\boldsymbol{u}|} = \dfrac{45}{78} \Rightarrow \theta = 30°$

6. $|\boldsymbol{u}| = |\boldsymbol{u} + \boldsymbol{v}| \cos \theta = 48 \cos 45° = 34$ lb. to 2 significant digits

$|\boldsymbol{v}| = |\boldsymbol{u} + \boldsymbol{v}| \sin \theta = 48 \sin 45° = 34$ lb. to 2 significant digits

8. $|\boldsymbol{u}| = |\boldsymbol{u} + \boldsymbol{v}| \cos \theta = 75 \cos 81° = 12$ mph to 2 significant digits

$|\boldsymbol{v}| = |\boldsymbol{u} + \boldsymbol{v}| \sin \theta = 75 \sin 81° = 74$ mph to 2 significant digits

10. $|\boldsymbol{u} + \boldsymbol{v}| = \sqrt{|\boldsymbol{u}|^2 + |\boldsymbol{v}|^2 - 2|\boldsymbol{u}||\boldsymbol{v}| \cos(180° - \theta)}$ $\dfrac{190}{\sin 136°} = \dfrac{84}{\sin \alpha}$

$\qquad = \sqrt{120^2 + 84^2 - 2(120)(84) \cos(180° - 44°)}$ $\alpha = 18°$

$\qquad = 190$ gm

12. $|\boldsymbol{u} + \boldsymbol{v}| = \sqrt{|\boldsymbol{u}|^2 + |\boldsymbol{v}|^2 - 2|\boldsymbol{u}||\boldsymbol{v}| \cos(180° - \theta)}$ $\dfrac{2.0}{\sin \alpha} = \dfrac{9.1}{\sin 116°}$

$\qquad = \sqrt{8.0^2 + 2.0^2 - 2(8.0)(2.0) \cos(180° - 64°)}$ $\alpha = 11°$

$\qquad = 9.1$ knots

14. $\dfrac{33}{\sin 137°} = \dfrac{|\boldsymbol{v}|}{\sin 17°} \Rightarrow |\boldsymbol{v}| = 14$ kg; $\dfrac{|\boldsymbol{u}|}{\sin 26°} = \dfrac{33}{\sin 137°} \Rightarrow |\boldsymbol{u}| = 21$ kg

16. $\dfrac{437}{\sin 129.5°} = \dfrac{|\boldsymbol{u}|}{\sin 32.7°} = \dfrac{|\boldsymbol{v}|}{\sin 17.8°} \Rightarrow |\boldsymbol{u}| = 306$ mph and $|\boldsymbol{v}| = 173$ mph

18. True. Since the zero vector has arbitrary direction, it can be parallel (or perpendicular) to any vector.

20. True. Equal vectors have the same magnitude and direction.

22. False. Vector $\mathbf{v}_1$ has an initial point at the origin and a terminal point at $(1, 0)$. Vector $\mathbf{v}_2$ has an initial point at the origin and a terminal point at $(0, 1)$.

24. False. Let $\mathbf{v}$ be the zero vector. Then $|\mathbf{u} + \mathbf{v}| = |\mathbf{u}|$.

26. $|\overline{v}| = \sqrt{15^2 + 3.9^2 - 2(15)(3.9)\cos(25° + 45°)} \approx 14$ mph

$\dfrac{3.9}{\sin\theta} = \dfrac{14}{\sin(70°)} \Rightarrow \theta = 15°$

heading $= 25° + 15° = 40°$

14 mph at 40°

28.

46

255 θ

$\sqrt{255^2 - 46^2} = 251$

$\sin\theta = \dfrac{46}{255}$

$\theta = 10.4°$

251 mph at 349.6° (360° - 10.4°)

30. $R = \sqrt{3600^2 + 2900^2 - 2(3600)(2900)\cos 149°} = 6300$

$\dfrac{6300}{\sin 149°} = \dfrac{2900}{\sin\alpha} \Rightarrow \alpha = 13.71°$

The third angle: $180° - (149° + 14°) = 17°$

direction $= 161° + 17° = 178°$

6300 kg @ 178°

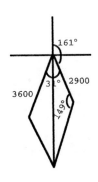

32. (A) parallel force $= 2500 \sin 15° = 650$ lb
     (B) force perpendicular $= 2500 \cos 15° = 2400$ lb

34. Left: $41 \sin 31° = 21$; Right: $31 \sin 41° = 20$
     $21 > 20 \Rightarrow$ slide left

Exercise 8-4

2. $\overrightarrow{AB} = \langle 0 - 5, 0 - 3 \rangle = \langle -5, -3 \rangle$ **4.** $\overrightarrow{AB} = \langle 6 - 0, 0 - (-5) \rangle = \langle 6, 5 \rangle$

6. $\overrightarrow{AB} = \langle 9 - (-6), 1 - (-3) \rangle = \langle 15, 4 \rangle$ **8.** $|\langle 0, 32 \rangle| = \sqrt{0^2 + 32^2} = 32$

10. $|\langle -48, -20 \rangle| = \sqrt{(-48)^2 + (-20)^2} = 52$ **12.** $|\langle 836, 123 \rangle| = \sqrt{836^2 + 123^2} = 845$

14. (A) $\mathbf{u} + \mathbf{v} = \langle -1, \ 2 \rangle + \langle 3, \ -2 \rangle = \langle -1 + 3, \ 2 + (-2) \rangle = \langle 2, \ 0 \rangle$

(B) $\mathbf{u} - \mathbf{v} = \langle -1, \ 2 \rangle - \langle 3, \ -2 \rangle = \langle -1 - 3, \ 2 - (-2) \rangle = \langle -4, \ 4 \rangle$

(C) $2\mathbf{u} - \mathbf{v} + 3\mathbf{w} = 2\langle -1, \ 2 \rangle - \langle 3, \ -2 \rangle + 3\langle 0, \ -2 \rangle = \langle -2 - 3 + 0, \ 4 + 2 - 6 \rangle = \langle -5, \ 0 \rangle$

16. (A) $\mathbf{u} + \mathbf{v} = \langle -3, \ 2 \rangle + \langle -2, \ 2 \rangle = \langle -3 + (-2), \ 2 + 2 \rangle = \langle -5, \ 4 \rangle$

(B) $\mathbf{u} - \mathbf{v} = \langle -3, \ 2 \rangle - \langle -2, \ 2 \rangle = \langle -3 - (-2), \ 2 - 2 \rangle = \langle -1, \ 0 \rangle$

(C) $2\mathbf{u} - \mathbf{v} + 3\mathbf{w} = 2\langle -3, \ 2 \rangle - \langle -2, \ 2 \rangle + 3\langle -3, \ 0 \rangle = \langle -6 + 2 - 9, \ 4 - 2 + 0 \rangle = \langle -13, \ 2 \rangle$

18. $\mathbf{v} = \langle 0, \ 14 \rangle = 14\langle 0, \ 1 \rangle = 14\mathbf{j}$

20. $\mathbf{v} = \langle -5, \ -18 \rangle = \langle -5, \ 0 \rangle + \langle 0, \ -18 \rangle$
$$= -5\langle 1, \ 0 \rangle - 18\langle 0, \ 1 \rangle$$
$$= -5\mathbf{i} - 18\mathbf{j}$$

22. $\overrightarrow{AB} = \langle 0 - (-2), \ 2 - (-1) \rangle = \langle 2, \ 3 \rangle = \langle 2, \ 0 \rangle + \langle 0, \ 3 \rangle$
$$= 2\langle 1, \ 0 \rangle + 3\langle 0, \ 1 \rangle = 2\mathbf{i} + 3\mathbf{j}$$

24. $\mathbf{u} - \mathbf{v} = 3\mathbf{i} - 2\mathbf{j} - (2\mathbf{i} + 4\mathbf{j}) = 3\mathbf{i} - 2\mathbf{j} - 2\mathbf{i} - 4\mathbf{j} = \mathbf{i} - 6\mathbf{j}$

26. $3\mathbf{u} + 2\mathbf{v} = 3(3\mathbf{i} - 2\mathbf{j}) + 2(2\mathbf{i} + 4\mathbf{j}) = 9\mathbf{i} - 6\mathbf{j} + 4\mathbf{i} + 8\mathbf{j} = 13\mathbf{i} + 2\mathbf{j}$

28. $\mathbf{u} - 3\mathbf{v} + 2\mathbf{w} = 3\mathbf{i} - 2\mathbf{j} - 3(2\mathbf{i} + 4\mathbf{j}) + 2(2\mathbf{i}) = 3\mathbf{i} - 2\mathbf{j} - 6\mathbf{i} - 12\mathbf{j} + 4\mathbf{i}$
$$= \mathbf{i} - 14\mathbf{j}$$

30. $\mathbf{u} = \dfrac{\langle 2, \ 1 \rangle}{|\langle 2, \ 1 \rangle|} = \dfrac{\langle 2, \ 1 \rangle}{\sqrt{2^2 + 1^2}} = \dfrac{\langle 2, \ 1 \rangle}{\sqrt{5}} = \left\langle \dfrac{2}{\sqrt{5}}, \ \dfrac{1}{\sqrt{5}} \right\rangle$

32. $\mathbf{u} = \dfrac{\langle -7, \ -24 \rangle}{|\langle -7, \ -24 \rangle|} = \dfrac{\langle -7, \ -24 \rangle}{\sqrt{(-7)^2 + (-24)^2}} = \dfrac{\langle -7, \ -24 \rangle}{25} = \left\langle -\dfrac{7}{25}, \ -\dfrac{24}{25} \right\rangle$

34. True. Two vectors which are scalar multiples mean that they have the same direction, but possibly different magnitudes.

36. False. Let $\mathbf{u} = \left\langle \dfrac{1}{\sqrt{2}}, \ \dfrac{1}{\sqrt{2}} \right\rangle$, the unit vector in the direction of $\langle 1, \ 1 \rangle$, and $k = -3$. Then $k\mathbf{u} = \left\langle -\dfrac{3}{\sqrt{2}}, \ -\dfrac{3}{\sqrt{2}} \right\rangle$ and

$$|k\mathbf{u}| = \sqrt{\left(-\dfrac{3}{\sqrt{2}} \right)^2 + \left(-\dfrac{3}{\sqrt{2}} \right)^2} = 3.$$

38. $\mathbf{u} + \mathbf{v} = \langle a, \ b \rangle + \langle c, \ d \rangle$
$$= \langle a + c, \ b + d \rangle$$
$$= \langle c + a, \ d + b \rangle$$
$$= \langle c, \ d \rangle + \langle a, \ b \rangle = \mathbf{v} + \mathbf{u}$$

40. $\mathbf{u} + (-\mathbf{u}) = \langle a, \ b \rangle + (-\langle a, \ b \rangle)$
$$= \langle a, \ b \rangle + \langle -a, \ -b \rangle$$
$$= \langle a + (-a), \ b + (-b) \rangle$$
$$= \langle 0, \ 0 \rangle$$
$$= \mathbf{0}$$

46. Let the left tension be represented by T_L and the right tension by T_R. Then

$T_L \sin 4.2° + T_R \sin 5.3° = 112$

$T_L \cos 4.2° = T_R \cos 5.3°$

Solving the second equation for T_L:

$T_L = T_R \dfrac{\cos 5.3°}{\cos 4.2°}$

Substituting: $\dfrac{T_R(\cos 5.3°)(\sin 4.2°)}{\cos 4.2°} + T_R \sin 5.3° = 112$

Graph $y1 = \dfrac{x(\cos 5.3°)(\sin 4.2°)}{\cos 4.2°} + x \sin 5.3°$ and $y2 = 112$.

$T_R \approx 677$ lb, $T_L \approx 676$ lb.

48. Let the left tension be represented by T_L and the right tension by T_R. Then

$T_L \sin 45° + T_R \sin 20° = 500$

$T_L \cos 45° = T_R \cos 20°$

Solving the second equation for T_L: $T_L = \dfrac{T_R \cos 20°}{\cos 45°}$

Substituting: $\dfrac{T_R(\cos 20°)(\sin 45°)}{\cos 45°} + T_R \sin 20° = 500$

Graph $y1 = \dfrac{x(\cos 20°)(\sin 45°)}{\cos 45°} + x \sin 20°$ and $y2 = 500$.

$T_R \approx 390$ lb, $T_L \approx 518$ lb

50. Angle $ABC = 30°$

$BC \sin 30° = 1000 \Rightarrow BC = 2000$ kg, tension

$BC \cos 30° = AB \Rightarrow AB = 2000 \cos 30° \approx 1730$ kg, compression

52. Angle ABC: $\cos(ABC) = \dfrac{5}{6} \Rightarrow ABC \approx 33.557°$ (Answers may vary due to rounding.)

$AB \sin 33.557° = 5000$

$AB \approx 9050$ kg, compression

$BC = AB \cos 33.557° \approx 9050 \cos 33.557° \approx 7540$ kg, tension

Exercise   8-5

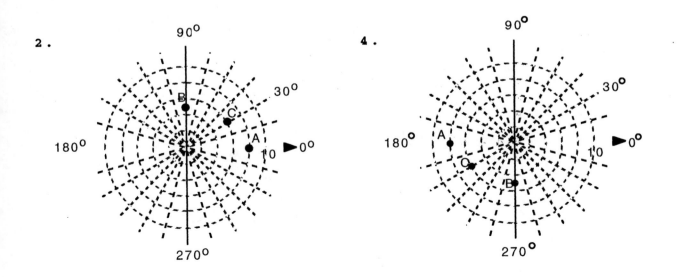

6.

8.

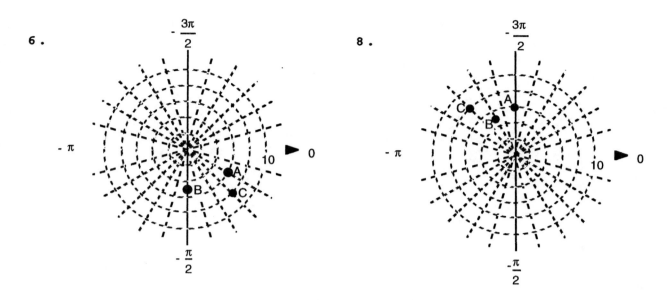

10. (-6, -210°): The polar axis is rotated 210° clockwise (negative direction) and the point is located 6 units from the pole along the negative polar axis. (-6, 150°): The polar axis is rotated 150° counterclockwise (positive direction) and the point is located 6 units from the pole along the negative polar axis. (6, 330°): The polar axis is rotated 330° counterclockwise (positive direction) and the point is located 6 units along the positive polar axis.

12.

θ	$10\cos\theta$
0	10
$\pi/6$	$5\sqrt{3}$
$\pi/4$	$5\sqrt{2}$
$\pi/3$	5
$\pi/2$	0
$2\pi/3$	-5
$3\pi/4$	$-5\sqrt{2}$
$5\pi/6$	$-5\sqrt{3}$
π	-10

14. $r = 5$

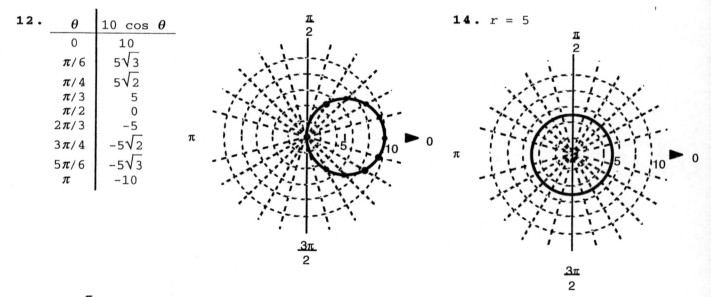

16. $\theta = \dfrac{\pi}{6}$

18. $(r, \theta) = \left(7, \dfrac{2\pi}{3}\right)$

$x = r \cos \theta = 7 \cos \dfrac{2\pi}{3} = 7\left(-\dfrac{1}{2}\right) = -3.500$

$y = r \sin \theta = 7 \sin \dfrac{2\pi}{3} = 7\left(\dfrac{\sqrt{3}}{2}\right) \approx 6.062$

```
P▸Rx(7,2π/3)
                -3.5
P▸Ry(7,2π/3)
         6.062177826
```
$(-3.500, \ 6.062)$

20. $(r, \theta) = \left(3, -\dfrac{3\pi}{7}\right)$

$x = r \cos \theta = 3 \cos\left(-\dfrac{3\pi}{7}\right) \approx 0.668$

$y = r \sin \theta = 3 \sin\left(-\dfrac{3\pi}{7}\right) \approx -2.925$

```
P▸Rx(3,-3π/7)
         .6675628019
P▸Ry(3,-3π/7)
        -2.924783737
■
```
$(0.668, \ -2.925)$

22. $(r, \theta) = (-9.028, -0.663)$
$x = r \cos \theta = -9.028 \cos(-0.663) \approx -7.115$
$y = r \sin \theta = -9.028 \sin(-0.663) \approx 5.557$

```
P▸Rx(-9.028,-.66
3)
        -7.11541214
P▸Ry(-9.028,-.66
3)
         5.556590149
■
```
$(-7.115, \ 5.557)$

24. $(x, y) = (0, -5)$, negative y axis

$r = \sqrt{x^2 + y^2} = \sqrt{0^2 + (-5)^2} = 5$

$\tan \theta = \dfrac{y}{x} = \dfrac{-5}{0}$ is undefined

$\theta = -90°$

```
R▸Pr(0,-5)
                  5
R▸Pθ(0,-5)
                -90
```
$(5, \ -90°)$

26. $(x, y) = (1, -\sqrt{3})$, QIV

$r = \sqrt{x^2 + y^2} = \sqrt{1^2 + (-\sqrt{3})^2} = 2$

$\tan \theta = \dfrac{y}{x} = -\dfrac{\sqrt{3}}{1}, \quad \theta = -60°$

```
R▸Pr(1,-√(3))
                  2
R▸Pθ(1,-√(3))
                -60
```
$(2, \ -60°)$

28. $(x, y) = (-4.26, 31.1)$, QII

$r = \sqrt{x^2 + y^2} = \sqrt{(-4.26)^2 + (31.1)^2} \approx 31.4$

$\tan \theta = \dfrac{y}{x} = \dfrac{31.1}{4.26} \approx 82.2°$ reference angle

QII: $180° - 82.2° = 97.8°$

```
R▸Pr(-4.26,31.1)
         31.39040618
R▸Pθ(-4.26,31.1)
         97.79969244
```
$(31.4, \ 97.8°)$

30.

θ varies from	cos θ varies from	4 cos θ varies from
0 to π/2	1 to 0	4 to 0
π/2 to π	0 to -1	0 to -4
π to 3π/2	-1 to 0	-4 to 0
3π/2 to 2π	0 to 1	0 to 4

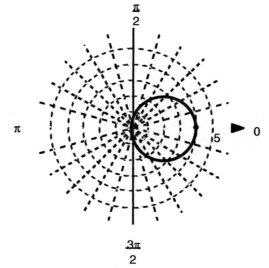

32.

θ varies from	2θ varies from	cos 2θ varies from	8 cos 2θ varies from
0 to π/4	0 to π/2	1 to 0	8 to 0
π/4 to π/2	π/2 to π	0 to -1	0 to -8
π/2 to 3π/4	π to 3π/2	-1 to 0	-8 to 0
3π/4 to π	3π/2 to 2π	0 to 1	0 to 8
π to 5π/4	2π to 5π/2	1 to 0	8 to 0
5π/4 to 3π/2	5π/2 to 3π	0 to -1	0 to -8
3π/2 to 7π/4	3π to 7π/2	-1 to 0	-8 to 0
7π/4 to 2π	7π/2 to 4π	0 to 1	0 to 8

34.

θ varies from	3θ varies from	sin 3θ varies from	6 sin 3θ varies from
0 to π/6	0 to π/2	0 to 1	0 to 6
π/6 to π/3	π/2 to π	1 to 0	6 to 0
π/3 to π/2	π to 3π/2	0 to -1	0 to -6
π/2 to 2π/3	3π/2 to 2π	-1 to 0	-6 to 0
2π/3 to 5π/6	2π to 5π/2	0 to 1	0 to 6
5π/6 to π	5π/2 to 3π	1 to 0	6 to 0
π to 7π/6	3π to 7π/2	0 to -1	0 to -6
7π/6 to 5π/3	7π/2 to 5π	-1 to 0	-6 to 0
⋮	⋮	⋮	⋮

36.

θ varies from	cos θ varies from	3 cos θ varies from	3 + 3 cos θ varies from
0 to π/2	1 to 0	3 to 0	6 to 3
π/2 to π	0 to -1	0 to -3	3 to 0
π to 3π/2	-1 to 0	-3 to 0	0 to 3
3π/2 to 2π	0 to 1	0 to 3	3 to 6

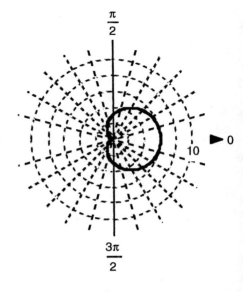

38.

θ varies from	cos θ varies from	4 cos θ varies from	2 + 4 cos θ varies from
0 to π/2	1 to 0	4 to 0	6 to 2
π/2 to π	0 to -1	0 to -4	2 to -2
π to 3π/2	-1 to 0	-4 to 0	-2 to 2
3π/2 to 2π	0 to 1	0 to 4	2 to 6

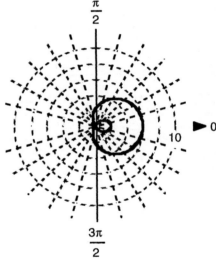

40. $r = 2 + 2 \cos \theta$ $r = 4 + 2 \cos \theta$ $r = 2 + 4 \cos \theta$

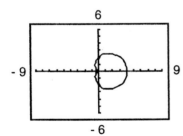
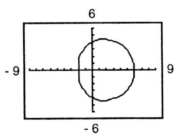
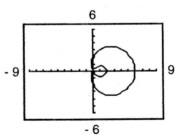

42. (A) $r = 4 \cos \theta$ $\qquad$ $r = 4 \cos 3\theta$ $\qquad$ $r = 4 \cos 5\theta$

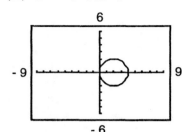 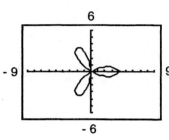 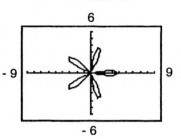

(B) 7 leaves in $r = 4 \cos 7\theta$

(C) n leaves in $r = a \cos(n\theta)$
$\quad$ $a > 0$ and n odd

44. (A) $r = 4 \cos 2\theta$ $\qquad$ $r = 4 \cos 4\theta$ $\qquad$ $r = 4 \cos 6\theta$

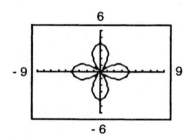 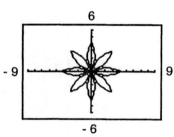 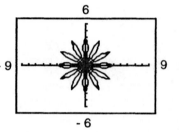

(B) 16 leaves in $r = 4 \cos 8\theta$

(C) $2n$ leaves in $r = a \cos n\theta$
$\quad$ $a > 0$ and n even

46. $x + y = 0$
$r \cos \theta \; r \sin \theta = 0$

$\dfrac{1}{r \cos \theta}(r \cos \theta + r \sin \theta) = 0 \left(\dfrac{1}{r \cos \theta} \right)$

$\dfrac{r \cos \theta}{r \cos \theta} + \dfrac{r \sin \theta}{r \cos \theta} = 0$

$1 + \tan \theta = 0$

$\tan \theta = -1 \quad$ or $\quad \theta = \dfrac{3\pi}{4}$; line

48. $x^2 + y^2 + 8x = 0$
$r^2 + 8r \cos \theta = 0$
$r(r + 8 \cos \theta) = 0$
$\quad r + 8 \cos \theta = 0$
$r = -8 \cos \theta$; circle

50. $x^2 - y^2 = 1$

$(r \cos \theta)^2 - (r \sin \theta)^2 = 1$

$r^2(\cos^2 \theta - \sin^2 \theta) = 1$

$r^2 \cos 2\theta = 1$

$r^2 = \dfrac{1}{\cos 2\theta}$

$r^2 = \sec 2\theta$; hyperbola

52. $\theta + \dfrac{\pi}{3} = 0$

$\tan^{-1} \dfrac{y}{x} + \dfrac{\pi}{3} = 0$

$\tan^{-1} \dfrac{y}{x} = -\dfrac{\pi}{3}$

$\dfrac{y}{x} = \tan\left(-\dfrac{\pi}{3}\right)$

$\dfrac{y}{x} = -\sqrt{3}$

$y = -x\sqrt{3}$; line

54.
$$r + 5 \sin \theta = 0$$
$$r(r + 5 \sin \theta) = r \cdot 0$$
$$r^2 + 5r \sin \theta = 0$$
$$x^2 + y^2 + 5y = 0$$
$$x^2 + y^2 = -5y \; ; \; \text{circle}$$

56.
$$r(1 + \cos \theta) = 1$$
$$r + r \cos \theta = 1$$
$$\sqrt{x^2 + y^2} + x = 1$$
$$\sqrt{x^2 + y^2} = 1 - x$$
$$x^2 + y^2 = 1 - 2x + x^2$$
$$y^2 = 1 - 2x \; ; \; \text{parabola}$$

58.

n	$r = 1 + 2 \cos(n\theta)$
1	1 small petal inside 1 large petal
2	2 small petals between 2 large petals
3	3 small petals inside 3 large petals
4	4 small petals between 4 large petals

$r = 1 + 2 \cos(n\theta)$ will have n large and n small petals. For n odd, the small petals are within the large petals. For n even, the small petals are between the large petals.

60. $r = 2 \cos \theta$ (1)
$r = 2 \sin \theta$ (2)
$0 \le \theta \le \pi$
Divide (2) by (1):
$$1 = \frac{2 \sin \theta}{2 \cos \theta} = \tan \theta$$
$$\theta = \frac{\pi}{4} \Rightarrow r = \sqrt{2}$$
$$\left(\sqrt{2}, \frac{\pi}{4}\right)$$
[Note: (0, 0) is not a solution to this system even though the graphs cross at the origin.]

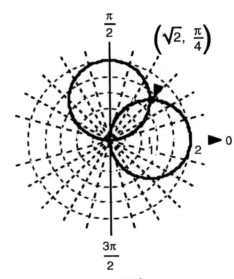

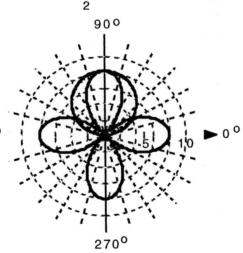

62. (1) $r = 8 \sin \theta$
(2) $r = 8 \cos 2\theta$
    $0° \le \theta \le 360°$
$$\sin \theta = \cos 2\theta = 1 - 2 \sin^2 \theta$$
$$2 \sin^2 \theta + \sin \theta - 1 = 0$$
$$(2 \sin \theta - 1)(\sin \theta + 1) = 0$$

$2 \sin \theta - 1 = 0$	$\sin \theta + 1 = 0$
$\sin \theta = \frac{1}{2}$	$\sin \theta = -1$
$\theta = 30°, 150°$	$\theta = 270°$
$r = 4, 4$	$r = -8$

$(4, 30°), (4, 150°), (-8, 270°)$
[Note: (0, 0) is not a solution to this system even though the graphs cross at the origin.]

64. $P_1(2, 30°)$ and $P_2(3, 60°)$
$$d = \sqrt{(r_1)^2 + (r_2)^2 - 2r_1 r_2 \cos(\theta_2 - \theta_1)}$$
$$d = \sqrt{2^2 + 3^2 - 2(2)(3)\cos(60° - 30°)}$$
$$d = \sqrt{13 - 12 \cos 30°}$$
$$d \approx 1.615$$

66. at 45°: $9k$, at 90°: $14k$, at 120°: $13k$, at 150°: $11k$

68. (A) $e = 0.6$: $r = \dfrac{8}{1 - 0.6 \cos \theta}$ (B) $e = 1$: $r = \dfrac{8}{1 - \cos \theta}$

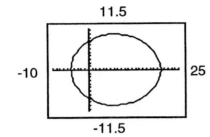

ellipse

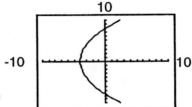

parabola

(C) $e = 2$: $r = \dfrac{8}{1 - 2 \cos \theta}$

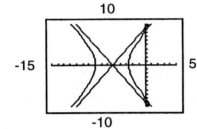

hyperbola

Exercise 8-6

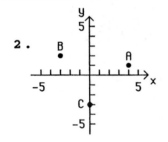

2.

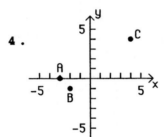

4.

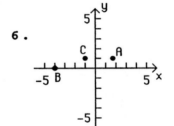

6.

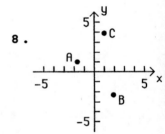

8.

10. (A) $-1 + i\sqrt{3}$

A sketch shows that $-1 + i\sqrt{3}$ is associated with $\theta = 120°$, $r = 2$

$-1 + i\sqrt{3} = 2(\cos 120° + i \sin 120°) = 2e^{120°i}$

(B) $-3i$

A sketch shows that $\theta = -90°$, $r = 3$

$-3i = 3(\cos(-90°) + i \sin(-90°)) = 3e^{(-90°)i}$

(C) $-7 - 4i$

$\gamma = \sqrt{(-7)^2 + (-4)^2} = \sqrt{65} \approx 8.06$

$\theta = -180° + \tan^{-1}\left(\dfrac{4}{7}\right) \approx -150.26°$

```
-1+i√(3)
          2e^(120i)
-3i
          3e^(-90i)
-7-4i
8.06e^(-150.26i)
```

$-7 - 4i \approx 8.06(\cos(-150.26°) + i \sin(-150.26°)) \approx 8.06e^{(-150.26°)i}$

12. (A) $\sqrt{3} - i$

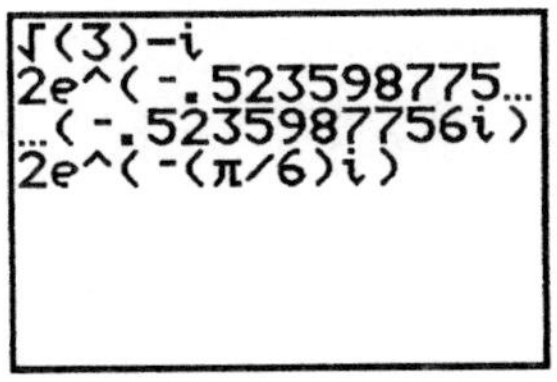

A sketch shows that $\theta = -\dfrac{\pi}{6}$, $r = 2$

$$\sqrt{3} - i = 2\left(\cos\left(-\frac{\pi}{6}\right)\right) + i\sin\left(-\frac{\pi}{6}\right) = 2e^{-(\pi/6)i}$$

(B) $-2 + 2i$

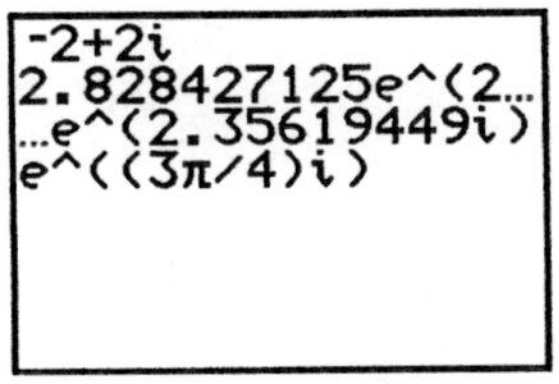

A sketch shows that $\theta = \dfrac{3\pi}{4}$, $r = \sqrt{8} = 2\sqrt{2}$

$$-2 + 2i = 2\sqrt{2}\left(\cos\frac{3\pi}{4} + i\sin\frac{3\pi}{4}\right) = 2\sqrt{2}e^{(3\pi/4)i}$$

(C) $6 - 5i$

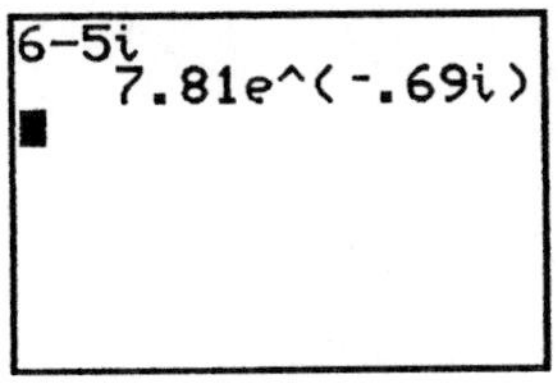

$r = \sqrt{6^2 + (-5)^2} = \sqrt{61} \approx 7.81$

$\theta = \tan^{-1}\left(-\dfrac{5}{6}\right) \approx -0.69$

$6 - 5i \approx 7.81(\cos(-0.69) + i\sin(-0.69)) \approx 7.81e^{-0.69i}$

14. (A) $2e^{30°i} = 2(\cos 30° + i\sin 30°)$ $\qquad 30° = \dfrac{\pi}{6}$

$\qquad\qquad = 2\left(\dfrac{\sqrt{3}}{2} + \dfrac{1}{2}i\right)$

$\qquad\qquad = \sqrt{3} + i$

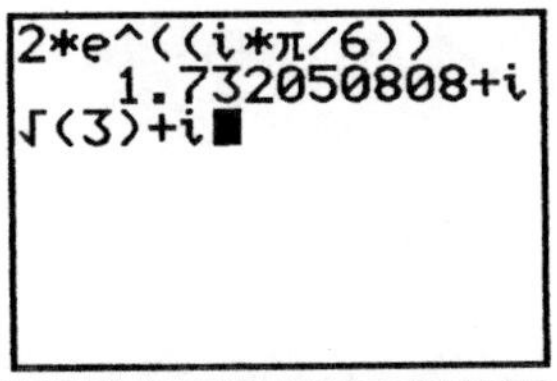

(B) $\sqrt{2}e^{(-3\pi/4)i} = \sqrt{2}\left(\cos\left(-\dfrac{3\pi}{4}\right) + i\sin\left(-\dfrac{3\pi}{4}\right)\right)$

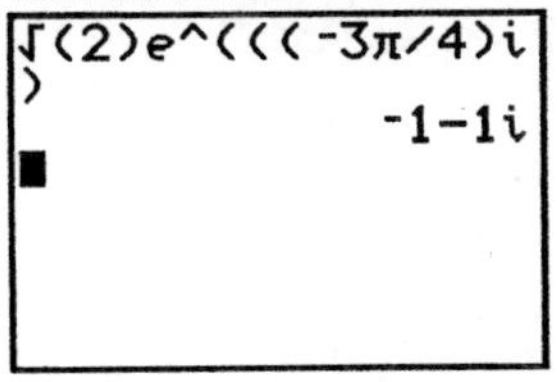

$\qquad\qquad\qquad = \sqrt{2}\left(-\dfrac{\sqrt{2}}{2} + i\left(-\dfrac{\sqrt{2}}{2}\right)\right)$

$\qquad\qquad\qquad = -1 - i$

(C) $5.71e^{(-0.48)i} = 5.71(\cos(-0.48) + i\sin(-0.48))$

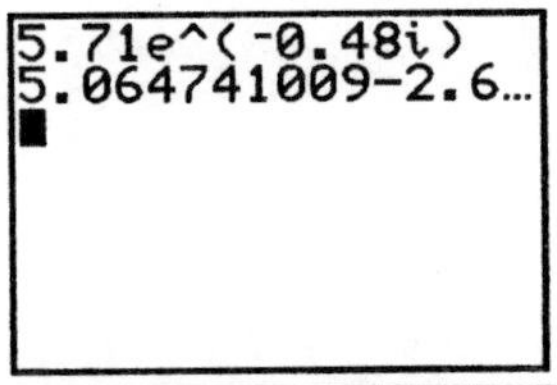

$\qquad\qquad\qquad \approx 5.06 - 2.64i$

16. (A) $\sqrt{3}e^{(-\pi/2)i} = \sqrt{3}\left(\cos\left(-\dfrac{\pi}{2}\right) + i\sin\left(-\dfrac{\pi}{2}\right)\right)$

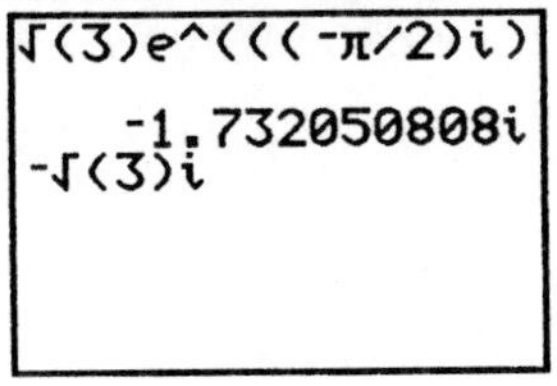

$\qquad\qquad\qquad = \sqrt{3}(0 - i)$

$\qquad\qquad\qquad = -i\sqrt{3}$

(B) $\sqrt{2}e^{135°i} = \sqrt{2}(\cos 135° + i\sin 135°)$ $\qquad 135° = \dfrac{3\pi}{4}$

$\qquad\qquad\qquad = \sqrt{2}\left(-\dfrac{\sqrt{2}}{2} + i\dfrac{\sqrt{2}}{2}\right)$

$\qquad\qquad\qquad = -1 + i$

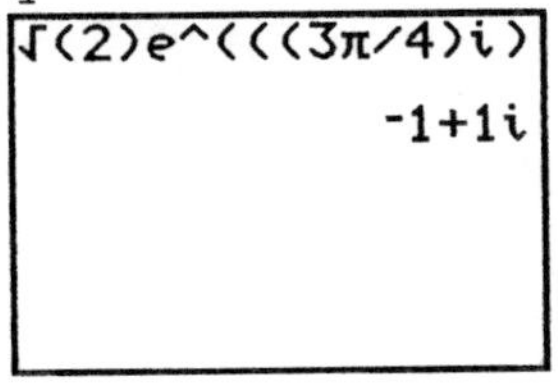

(C) $6.83e^{(-108.82°)i} = 6.83(\cos(-108.82°) + i\sin(-108.82°))$

$\qquad\qquad\qquad \approx 6.83(-0.322596 + i(-0.9465367))$

$\qquad\qquad\qquad \approx -2.20 - 6.46i$

$\qquad\qquad\qquad\qquad -108.82° = -1.899267292$

```
6.83e^(-1.899267
292i)
 -2.203331489-6.…
```

18. $z_1 z_2 = r_1 e^{i\theta_1} \cdot r_2 e^{i\theta_2} = r_1 r_2 e^{i(\theta_1 + \theta_2)}$ $\qquad \dfrac{z_1}{z_2} = \dfrac{r_1 e^{i\theta_1}}{r_2 e^{i\theta_2}} = \dfrac{r_1}{r_2} e^{i(\theta_1 - \theta_2)}$

$\quad z_1 z_2 = 6e^{132°i} \cdot 3e^{93°i} = 18e^{225°i}$ $\qquad \dfrac{z_1}{z_2} = \dfrac{6e^{132°i}}{3e^{93°i}} = 2e^{39°i}$

20. $z_1 z_2 = r_1 e^{i\theta_1} \cdot r_2 e^{i\theta_2} = r_1 r_2 e^{i(\theta_1 + \theta_2)}$ $\qquad \dfrac{z_1}{z_2} = \dfrac{r_1 e^{i\theta_1}}{r_2 e^{i\theta_2}} = \dfrac{r_1}{r_2} e^{i(\theta_1 - \theta_2)}$

$\quad z_1 z_2 = 3e^{67°i} \cdot 2e^{97°i} = 6e^{164°i}$ $\qquad \dfrac{z_1}{z_2} = \dfrac{3e^{67°i}}{2e^{97°i}} = 1.5e^{(-30°)i}$

22. $z_1 z_2 = r_1 e^{i\theta_1} \cdot r_2 e^{i\theta_2} = r_1 r_2 e^{i(\theta_1 + \theta_2)}$

$\quad z_1 z_2 = 7.11e^{0.79i} \cdot 2.66e^{1.07i} = 18.9126e^{1.86i} \approx 18.91e^{1.86i}$

$\dfrac{z_1}{z_2} = \dfrac{r_1 e^{i\theta_1}}{r_2 e^{i\theta_2}} = \dfrac{r_1}{r_2} e^{i(\theta_1 - \theta_2)}$

$\dfrac{z_1}{z_2} = \dfrac{7.11e^{0.79i}}{2.66e^{1.07i}} \approx 2.67e^{(-0.28)i}$

24. $(\sqrt{3} + i)^2 = 3 + 2i\sqrt{3} + i^2$

$\qquad\qquad\quad = 3 + 2i\sqrt{3} - 1$

$\qquad\qquad\quad = 2 + 2i\sqrt{3}$

$\quad \sqrt{3} + i: r = 2, \theta = 30° \Rightarrow 2e^{30°i}$

$\quad (2e^{30°i})^2 = 2e^{30°i} \cdot 2e^{30°i} = 4e^{60°i}$

26. $(\sqrt{3} + i\sqrt{3})(1 + i\sqrt{3}) = \sqrt{3} + 3i + i\sqrt{3} + 3i^2$

$\qquad\qquad\qquad\qquad\quad = \sqrt{3} + (3 + \sqrt{3})i - 3$

$\qquad\qquad\qquad\qquad\quad = \sqrt{3} - 3 + (3 + \sqrt{3})i$

$\quad (\sqrt{3} + i\sqrt{3}): r = \sqrt{6}, \theta = 45° \Rightarrow \sqrt{6}e^{45°i}$

$\quad (1 + i\sqrt{3}): r = 2, \theta = 60° \Rightarrow 2e^{60°i}$

$\quad (\sqrt{6}e^{45°i})(2e^{60°i}) = 2\sqrt{6}e^{105°i}$

28. $\dfrac{1 - i\sqrt{3}}{\sqrt{3} + i} \cdot \dfrac{\sqrt{3} - i}{\sqrt{3} - i} = \dfrac{\sqrt{3} - i - 3i + i^2\sqrt{3}}{3 - i^2}$

$\qquad\qquad\qquad\quad = \dfrac{\sqrt{3} - 4i - \sqrt{3}}{3 + 1}$

$\qquad\qquad\qquad\quad = \dfrac{-4i}{4} = -i$

$\quad 1 - i\sqrt{3}: r = 2, \theta = -60° \Rightarrow 2e^{-60°i}$

$\quad \sqrt{3} + i: r = 2, \theta = 30° \Rightarrow 2e^{30°i}$

$\dfrac{2e^{-60°i}}{2e^{30°i}} = e^{-90°i}$

30. The product of z with its conjugate is the square of the modulus of z.

32. $(r^{1/2}e^{(\theta/2)i})^2 = (r^{1/2})^2 e^{(2 \cdot (\theta/2)i)} = re^{i\theta}$

34.
$$\frac{z_1}{z_2} = \frac{r_1(\cos\theta_1 + i\sin\theta_1)}{r_2(\cos\theta_2 + i\sin\theta_2)}$$

$$= \frac{r_1}{r_2} \cdot \frac{\cos\theta_1 + i\sin\theta_1}{\cos\theta_2 + i\sin\theta_2} \cdot \frac{\cos\theta_2 - i\sin\theta_2}{\cos\theta_2 - i\sin\theta_2}$$

$$= \frac{r_1}{r_2} \cdot \frac{\cos\theta_1\cos\theta_2 - i\cos\theta_1\sin\theta_2 + i\cos\theta_2\sin\theta_1 - i^2\sin\theta_1\sin\theta_2}{\cos^2\theta_2 - i^2\sin^2\theta_2}$$

$$= \frac{r_1}{r_2} \cdot \frac{(\cos\theta_1\cos\theta_2 + \sin\theta_1\sin\theta_2) + i(\cos\theta_2\sin\theta_1 - \cos\theta_1\sin\theta_2)}{1}$$

$$= \frac{r_1}{r_2} \cdot [\cos(\theta_1 - \theta_2) + i\sin(\theta_1 - \theta_2)]$$

$$= \frac{r_1}{r_2} e^{i(\theta_1 - \theta_2)}$$

36. (A) $8e^{0°i} = 8(\cos 0° + i\sin 0°)$
$$= 8(1 + 0i)$$
$$= 8 + 0i$$
$$6e^{30°i} = 6(\cos 30° + i\sin 30°)$$
$$= 6\left(\frac{\sqrt{3}}{2} + \frac{1}{2}i\right)$$
$$= 3\sqrt{3} + 3i$$
$$(8 + 0i) + (3\sqrt{3} + 3i) = (8 + 3\sqrt{3}) + 3i$$

(B) $(8 + 3\sqrt{3}) + 3i$: $r = \sqrt{(8 + 3\sqrt{3})^2 + 3^2}$ $\tan\theta = \frac{3}{8 + 3\sqrt{3}}$
$$= \sqrt{100 + 48\sqrt{3}}$$ $\theta \approx 12.8°$
$$\approx 13.5$$

$(8 + 3\sqrt{3}) + 3i \approx 13.5e^{12.8°i}$

(C) $13.5e^{12.8°i}$ has magnitude 13.5 lb with direction 12.8°.

Exercise 8-7

2. $z^n = r^n e^{n\theta i}$
$$(\sqrt{2}e^{15°i})^5 = (\sqrt{2})^5 e^{5(15°i)}$$
$$= 4\sqrt{2}e^{75°i}$$

4. $(1 + i)$: $r = \sqrt{2}$, $\theta = 45° \Rightarrow \sqrt{2}e^{45°i}$
$$z^n = r^n e^{n\theta i}$$
$$(1 + i)^{12} = (\sqrt{2}e^{45°i})^{12}$$
$$= (\sqrt{2})^{12} e^{12(45°i)}$$
$$= 64e^{180°i}$$

6. $(1 - i\sqrt{3})$: $r = 2$, $\theta = -60° \Rightarrow 2e^{-60°i}$
$z^n = r^n e^{n\theta i}$
$(1 - i\sqrt{3})^8 = (2e^{-60°i})^8$
$\qquad\qquad = 256e^{-480°i}$
$\qquad\qquad = 256e^{-120°i}$

8. $(-1 + i)$: $r = \sqrt{2}$, $\theta = 135° \Rightarrow \sqrt{2}e^{135°i}$
$z^n = r^n e^{n\theta i}$
$(\sqrt{2}e^{135°i})^4 = (\sqrt{2})^4 e^{(4 \cdot 135°)i}$
$\qquad\qquad = 4e^{540°i}$
$\qquad\qquad = 4(\cos 180° + i \sin 180°)$
$\qquad\qquad = 4(-1 + 0i)$
$\qquad\qquad = -4$

10. $(-\sqrt{3} + i)$: $r = 2$, $\theta = 150° \Rightarrow 2e^{150°i}$
$z^n = r^n e^{n\theta i}$
$(2e^{150°i})^5 = 2^5 e^{(5 \cdot 150°)i}$
$\qquad\qquad = 32e^{750°i}$
$\qquad\qquad = 32e^{30°i}$
$\qquad\qquad = 32(\cos 30° + i \sin 30°)$
$\qquad\qquad = 32\left(\dfrac{\sqrt{3}}{2} + \dfrac{1}{2} i\right)$
$\qquad\qquad = 16\sqrt{3} + 16i$

12. $\left(-\dfrac{1}{2} - \dfrac{\sqrt{3}}{2}\right)$: $r = 1$, $\theta = 240° \Rightarrow 1e^{240°i}$
$z^n = r^n e^{n\theta i}$
$(1e^{240°i})^3 = 1^3 e^{(3 \cdot 240°)i}$
$\qquad\qquad = 1e^{720°i}$
$\qquad\qquad = 1e^{0°i}$
$\qquad\qquad = \cos 0° + i \sin 0°$
$\qquad\qquad = 1$

14. $z^{1/n} = r^{1/n} e^{[(\theta/n) + ((360°k)/n)]i}$
$(8e^{45°i})^{1/3} = 8^{1/3} e^{[(45°/3) + ((360°k)/3)]i}$
$\qquad\qquad = 2e^{(15° + 120°k)i}$
$\quad w_1 = 2e^{15°i}$
$\quad w_2 = 2e^{(15° + 120°)i} = 2e^{135°i}$
$\quad w_3 = 2e^{(15° + 240°)i} = 2e^{255°i}$

16. $z^{1/n} = r^{1/n} e^{[(\theta/n) + ((360°k)/n)]i}$
$(16e^{90°i})^{1/4} = 16^{1/4} e^{[(90°/4) + ((360°k)/4)]i}$
$\qquad\qquad = 2e^{(22.5° + 90°k)i}$
$\quad w_1 = 2e^{22.5°i}$
$\quad w_2 = 2e^{112.5°i}$
$\quad w_3 = 2e^{202.5°i}$
$\quad w_4 = 2e^{292.5°i}$

18. $(-1 + i)$: $r = \sqrt{2}$, $\theta = 135° \Rightarrow \sqrt{2}e^{135°i}$
$z^{1/n} = r^{1/n} e^{[(\theta/n) + ((360°k)/n)]i}$
$(\sqrt{2}e^{135°i})^{1/3} = (2^{1/2})^{1/3} e^{[(135°/3) + ((360°k)/3)]i}$
$\qquad\qquad = 2^{1/6} e^{(45° + 120°k)i}$
$\quad w_1 = 2^{1/6} e^{45°i}$
$\quad w_2 = 2^{1/6} e^{165°i}$
$\quad w_3 = 2^{1/6} e^{285°i}$

20. $z = 1 = 1e^{0°i}$
$z^{1/n} = r^{1/n} e^{[(\theta/n) + ((360°k)/n)]i}$
$(1e^{0°i})^{1/4} = 1^{1/4} e^{[0° + ((360°k)/4)]i}$
$\qquad\qquad = 1e^{90°ki}$
$w_1 = 1e^{0°i}$
$w_2 = 1e^{90°i}$
$w_3 = 1e^{180°i}$
$w_4 = 1e^{270°i}$

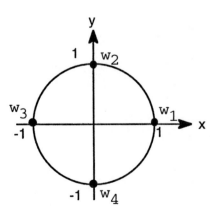

22. $z = -8 = 8e^{180°i}$

$z^{1/n} = r^{1/n}e^{[(\theta/n) + ((360°k)/n)]i}$

$(8e^{180°i})^{1/3} = 8^{1/3}e^{[(180°/3) + ((360°k)/3)]i}$

$\qquad = 2e^{(60° + 120°k)i}$

$w_1 = 2e^{60°i}$

$w_2 = 2e^{180°i}$

$w_3 = 2e^{300°i}$

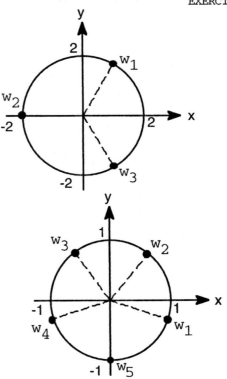

24. $z = -i = e^{-90°i}$

$z^{1/n} = r^{1/n}e^{[(\theta/n) + ((360°k)/n)]i}$

$(1e^{-90°})^{1/5} = 1^{1/5}e^{[(-90°/5) + ((360°k)/5)]i}$

$\qquad = 1e^{(-18° + 72°k)i}$

$w_1 = 1e^{(-18°)i}$

$w_2 = 1e^{54°i}$

$w_3 = 1e^{126°i}$

$w_4 = 1e^{198°i}$

$w_5 = 1e^{270°i}$

26. False. For example, let $w = 1 + i$, $w^3 = -2 + 2i$

$\qquad\qquad\qquad \overline{w} = 1 - i,\ \overline{w}^3 = -2 - 2i$

28. True. Let x be a fourth root of 1, then $x^4 = 1$

$\qquad\qquad\qquad\qquad\qquad\qquad\qquad (x^4)^3 = 1^3$

$\qquad\qquad\qquad\qquad\qquad\qquad\qquad\quad x^{12} = 1$

Hence x is a twelfth root of 1.

30. (A) $x^3 + 8 = 0$

$\qquad (-2)^3 + 8 = 0$

$\qquad -8 + 8 = 0$, -2 is a root of $x^3 + 8 = 0$

$x^3 + 8 = 0$ is degree 3 so there are two more roots.

(B)

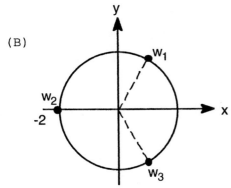

$\dfrac{360°}{3} = 120°$ is the spacing between roots

From problem 22, $w_1 = 2e^{60°i} = 1 + \sqrt{3}\,i$,

$w_2 = 2e^{180°i} = 1 - \sqrt{3}\,i$

(C) $(1 + \sqrt{3}\,i)^3 + 8 = [1 + 3(\sqrt{3}i) + 3(\sqrt{3}i)^2 + (\sqrt{3}i)^3] + 8$

$\qquad\qquad\qquad\quad = [1 + 3\sqrt{3}i - 9 - 3\sqrt{3}i] + 8$

$\qquad\qquad\qquad\quad = -8 + 8$

$\qquad\qquad\qquad\quad = 0$

(D) In the same manner, $(1 - \sqrt{3}\,i)^3 + 8 = -8 + 8 = 0$

32. $x_3 - 64 = 0$

$\qquad x_3 = 64$

$\qquad x = 64^{1/3} = (64e^{0°i})^{1/3}$

$\qquad z^{1/n} = r^{1/n}e^{[(\theta/n) + ((360°k)/n)]i}$

$(64e^{0°i})^{1/3} = 64^{1/3}e^{[(0°/3) + ((360°k)/3)]i}$

$\qquad\qquad = 4e^{120°ki}$

$x_1 = 4e^{0°i} = 4$

$x_2 = 4e^{120°i} = 4(\cos 120° + i \sin 120°) = 4\left(-\dfrac{1}{2} + \dfrac{\sqrt{3}}{2}i\right) = -2 + 2\sqrt{3}\,i$

$x_3 = 4e^{240°i} = 4(\cos 240° + i \sin 240°) = 4\left(-\dfrac{1}{2} - \dfrac{\sqrt{3}}{2}i\right) = -2 - 2\sqrt{3}\,i$

34. $x^3 + 27 = 0$

$\qquad x^3 = -27$

$\qquad x = (-27)^{1/3} = 27e^{180°i}$

$\qquad z^{1/n} = r^{1/n}e^{[(\theta/n) + ((360°k)/n)]i}$

$(27e^{180°i})^{1/3} = 27^{1/3}e^{[(180°/3) + ((360°k)/n)]i}$

$\qquad\qquad = 3e^{(60° + 120°k)i}$

$x_1 = 3e^{60°i} = 3(\cos 60° + i \sin 60°) = 3\left(\dfrac{1}{2} + \dfrac{\sqrt{3}}{2}i\right) = \dfrac{3}{2} + \dfrac{3\sqrt{3}}{2}i$

$x_2 = 3e^{180°i} = 3(\cos 180° + i \sin 180°) = 3(-1 + 0i) = -3$

$x_3 = 3e^{300°i} = 3(\cos 300° + i \sin 300°) = 3\left(\dfrac{1}{2} - \dfrac{\sqrt{3}}{2}i\right) = \dfrac{3}{2} - \dfrac{3\sqrt{3}}{2}i$

36. $z = 25i,\ n = 2$

$25i:\ r = 25,\ \theta = 90° \Rightarrow 25e^{90°i}$

$z^{1/n} = r^{1/n}e^{[(\theta/n + (360°k/n)]i}$

$(25e^{90°i})^{1/2} = 25^{1/2}e^{[(90°/2) + (360°k/2)]i}$

$\qquad\qquad = 5e^{(45° + 180°k)i}$

$w_1 = 5e^{45°i} = 5(\cos 45° + i \sin 45°) = 5\left(\dfrac{\sqrt{2}}{2} + \dfrac{\sqrt{2}}{2}i\right) = \dfrac{5\sqrt{2}}{2} + \dfrac{5\sqrt{2}}{2}i$

$w_2 = 5e^{225°i} = 5(\cos 225° + i \sin 225°) = 5\left(-\dfrac{\sqrt{2}}{2} - \dfrac{\sqrt{2}}{2}i\right) = -\dfrac{5\sqrt{2}}{2} - \dfrac{5\sqrt{2}}{2}i$

38. $z = -64i,\ n = 3$

$-64i:\ r = 64,\ \theta = 270°$

$z^{1/n} = r^{1/n}e^{[(\theta/n + (360°k/n)]i}$

$(64e^{270°i})^{1/3} = 64^{1/3}e^{[270°/3 + 360°k/3]i}$

$\qquad\qquad = 4e^{90° + 120i}$

$w_1 = 4e^{90°} = 4(\cos 90° + i \sin 90°) = 4(0 + 1i) = 4i$

$w_2 = 4e^{210°} = 4(\cos 210° + i \sin 210°) = 4\left(-\dfrac{\sqrt{3}}{2} - \dfrac{1}{2}i\right) = -2\sqrt{3} - 2i$

$w_3 = 4e^{330°} = 4(\cos 330° + i \sin 330°) = 4\left(\dfrac{\sqrt{3}}{2} - \dfrac{1}{2}i\right) = 2\sqrt{3} - 2i$

40. For $k = 0$, $r^{1/n}e^{(\theta/n + (k\cdot360°)/n)i} = r^{1/n}e^{(\theta/n)i}$

For $k = n$, $r^{1/n}e^{(\theta/n + (k\cdot360°)/n)i} = r^{1/n}e^{(\theta/n + 360°)i} = r^{1/n}e^{(\theta/n)i}$

42. $x^6 + 1 = 0$

$\quad\quad x^6 = -1$

$\quad\quad x = (-1)^{1/6} = 1e^{180°i}$

$\quad z^{1/n} = r^{1/n}e^{[(\theta/n) + ((360°k)/n)]i}$

$(1e^{180°i})^{1/6} = 1^{1/6}e^{[(180°/6) + ((360°k)/6)]i}$

$\quad\quad\quad = 1e^{(30° + 60°k)i}$

$x_1 = 1e^{30°i}$

$x_2 = 1e^{90°i}$

$x_3 = 1e^{150°i}$

$x_4 = 1e^{210°i}$

$x_5 = 1e^{270°i}$

$x_6 = 1e^{330°i}$

44. $x^3 - i = 0$

$\quad\quad x^3 = i$

$\quad\quad x = i^{1/3} = 1e^{90°i}$

$\quad z^{1/n} = r^{1/n}e^{[(\theta/n) + ((360°k)/n)]i}$

$(1e^{90°i})^{1/3} = 1^{1/3}e^{[(90°/3) + ((360°k)/3)]i}$

$\quad\quad\quad = 1e^{(30° + 120°k)i}$

$x_1 = 1e^{30°i}$

$x_2 = 1e^{150°i}$

$x_3 = 1e^{270°i}$

46. $P(x) = x^6 - 1$; find $x = 1^{1/6} = (1e^{0°i})^{1/6}$ and write as factors.

$z^{1/n} = r^{1/n}e^{[(\theta/n) + ((360°k)/n)]i}$

$(1e^{0°i})^{1/6} = 1^{1/6}e^{[(0°/6) + ((360°k)/6)]i}$

$\quad\quad\quad = 1e^{60°ki}$

$x_1 = e^{0°i} = 1$

$x_2 = e^{60°i} = \dfrac{1}{2} + \dfrac{\sqrt{3}}{2}i$

$x_3 = e^{120°i} = -\dfrac{1}{2} + \dfrac{\sqrt{3}}{2}i$

$x_4 = e^{180°i} = -1$

$x_5 = e^{240°i} = -\dfrac{1}{2} - \dfrac{\sqrt{3}}{2}i$

$x_6 = e^{300°i} = \dfrac{1}{2} - \dfrac{\sqrt{3}}{2}i$

$P(x) = x^6 + 1 = (x - 1)(x + 1)\left(x - \left(\dfrac{1}{2} + \dfrac{\sqrt{3}}{2}i\right)\right)\left(x - \left(-\dfrac{1}{2} - \dfrac{\sqrt{3}}{2}i\right)\right)$

$\quad\quad\quad \cdot\left(x - \left(-\dfrac{1}{2} + \dfrac{\sqrt{3}}{2}i\right)\right)\left(x - \left(\dfrac{1}{2} - \dfrac{\sqrt{3}}{2}i\right)\right)$

CHAPTER 9

Exercise 9-1

2. A, $(2, 1)$

4. C, infinitely many solutions: for any real number s, $x = s$, $y = 2s - 5$.

6. $x - y = 2$ $x + y = 4$

x	y
0	-2
2	0

x	y
0	4
4	0

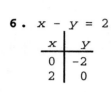
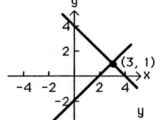

8. $3x - y = 2$ $x + 2y = 10$

x	y
0	-2
3	7

x	y
0	5
4	3

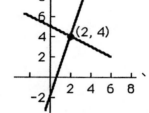

10. $m + 2n = 4$ $2m + 4n = -8$

m	n
0	2
4	0

m	n
0	-2
-4	0

parallel lines;
no solution

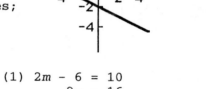

12. (1) $2m - n = 10$
(2) $m - 2n = -4$

(1) $2m - n = 10$
$-2 \times$ (2) $\underline{-2m + 4n = 8}$
$3n = 18$
$n = 6$

(1) $2m - 6 = 10$
$2m = 16$
$m = 8$

$(8, 6)$

14. (1) $5x + 2y = 1$
(2) $2x - 3y = -11$

$3 \times$ (1) $15x + 6y = 3$
$2 \times$ (2) $\underline{4x - 6y = -22}$
$19x = -19$
$x = -1$

$5x + 2y = 1$
$5(-1) + 2y = 1$
$2y = 6$
$y = 3$ $(-1, 3)$

16. B is 3×3. D is 2×1.

18. D is a column matrix.

20. One additional row would make matrix A square.

22. $a_{21} = 4$, $a_{13} = 0$

24. $a_{11} = 3$, $a_{22} = 1$

26. $\begin{bmatrix} 1 & -3 & | & 2 \\ 4 & -6 & | & -8 \end{bmatrix}$ $\frac{1}{2}R_2 \rightarrow R_2$ $\begin{bmatrix} 1 & -3 & | & 2 \\ 2 & -3 & | & -4 \end{bmatrix}$

28. $\begin{bmatrix} 1 & -3 & | & 2 \\ 4 & -6 & | & -8 \end{bmatrix}$ $-2R_1 \rightarrow R_1$ $\begin{bmatrix} -2 & 6 & | & -4 \\ 4 & -6 & | & -8 \end{bmatrix}$

30. $\begin{bmatrix} 1 & -3 & | & 2 \\ 4 & -6 & | & -8 \end{bmatrix}$ $-1R_2 \rightarrow R_2$ $\begin{bmatrix} 1 & -3 & | & 2 \\ -4 & 6 & | & 8 \end{bmatrix}$

32. $\begin{bmatrix} 1 & -3 & | & 2 \\ 4 & -6 & | & -8 \end{bmatrix}$ $(-\frac{1}{2}R_2) + R_1 \rightarrow R_1$ $\begin{bmatrix} -1 & 0 & | & 6 \\ 4 & -6 & | & -8 \end{bmatrix}$

34. $\begin{bmatrix} 1 & -3 & | & 2 \\ 4 & -6 & | & -8 \end{bmatrix}$ $\quad (-3)R_1 + R_2 \rightarrow R_2 \begin{bmatrix} 1 & -3 & | & 2 \\ 1 & 3 & | & -14 \end{bmatrix}$

36. $\begin{bmatrix} 1 & -3 & | & 2 \\ 4 & -6 & | & -8 \end{bmatrix}$ $\quad 1R_1 + R_2 \rightarrow R_2 \begin{bmatrix} 1 & -3 & | & 2 \\ 5 & -9 & | & -6 \end{bmatrix}$

38. $\begin{bmatrix} 1 & 1 & | & 5 \\ 1 & -1 & | & -3 \end{bmatrix}$ $\quad (-1)R_1 + R_2 \rightarrow R_2 \begin{bmatrix} 1 & 1 & | & 5 \\ 0 & -2 & | & -8 \end{bmatrix}$

$\qquad x_1 + x_2 = 5 \qquad\qquad\qquad\qquad x_1 + x_2 = 5$
$\qquad x_1 - x_2 = -3 \qquad\qquad\qquad\qquad\;\; -2x_2 = -8$

$\qquad (-\tfrac{1}{2})R_2 \rightarrow R_2 \begin{bmatrix} 1 & 1 & | & 5 \\ 0 & 1 & | & 4 \end{bmatrix}$ $\quad (-1)R_2 + R_1 \rightarrow R_1 \begin{bmatrix} 1 & 0 & | & 1 \\ 0 & 1 & | & 4 \end{bmatrix}$

$\qquad\qquad x_1 + x_2 = 5 \qquad\qquad\qquad\qquad x_1 \quad= 1$
$\qquad\qquad\quad\; x_2 = 4 \qquad\qquad\qquad\qquad\quad x_2 = 4$

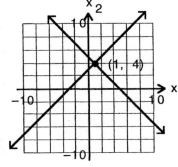 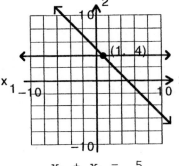 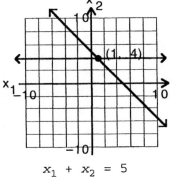 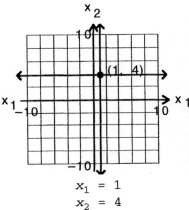

$\qquad x_1 + x_2 = 5 \qquad\;\; x_1 + x_2 = 5 \qquad\;\; x_1 + x_2 = 5 \qquad\qquad x_1 = 1$
$\qquad x_1 - x_2 = -3 \qquad\quad -2x_2 = -8 \qquad\qquad\;\; x_2 = 4 \qquad\qquad x_2 = 4$

Each pair of lines intersects at the same point.

40. $x_1 - 3x_2 = -5$
$\quad\; -3x_1 - x_2 = 5$

$\qquad \begin{bmatrix} 1 & -3 & | & -5 \\ -3 & -1 & | & 5 \end{bmatrix}$ $\quad 3R_1 + R_2 \rightarrow R_2 \begin{bmatrix} 1 & -3 & | & -5 \\ 0 & -10 & | & -10 \end{bmatrix}$

$\qquad \begin{bmatrix} 1 & -3 & | & -5 \\ 0 & -10 & | & -10 \end{bmatrix}$ $\quad -\tfrac{1}{10}R_2 \rightarrow R_2 \begin{bmatrix} 1 & -3 & | & -5 \\ 0 & 1 & | & 1 \end{bmatrix}$

$\qquad \begin{bmatrix} 1 & -3 & | & -5 \\ 0 & 1 & | & 1 \end{bmatrix}$ $\quad 3R_2 + R_1 \rightarrow R_1 \begin{bmatrix} 1 & 0 & | & -2 \\ 0 & 1 & | & 1 \end{bmatrix}$ $\quad \begin{array}{l} x_1 = -2 \\ x_2 = 1 \end{array}$

42. $2x_1 + x_2 = 0$
$\qquad x_1 - 2x_2 = -5$

$\qquad \begin{bmatrix} 2 & 1 & | & 0 \\ 1 & -2 & | & -5 \end{bmatrix}$ $\quad R_1 \leftrightarrow R_2 \begin{bmatrix} 1 & -2 & | & -5 \\ 2 & 1 & | & 0 \end{bmatrix}$

$\qquad \begin{bmatrix} 1 & -2 & | & -5 \\ 2 & 1 & | & 0 \end{bmatrix}$ $\quad -2R_1 + R_2 \rightarrow R_2 \begin{bmatrix} 1 & -2 & | & -5 \\ 0 & 5 & | & 10 \end{bmatrix}$

$\qquad \begin{bmatrix} 1 & -2 & | & -5 \\ 0 & 5 & | & 10 \end{bmatrix}$ $\quad \tfrac{1}{5}R_2 \rightarrow R_2 \begin{bmatrix} 1 & -2 & | & -5 \\ 0 & 1 & | & 2 \end{bmatrix}$

$\qquad \begin{bmatrix} 1 & -2 & | & -5 \\ 0 & 1 & | & 2 \end{bmatrix}$ $\quad 2R_2 + R_1 \rightarrow R_1 \begin{bmatrix} 1 & 0 & | & -1 \\ 0 & 1 & | & 2 \end{bmatrix}$ $\quad \begin{array}{l} x_1 = -1 \\ x_2 = 2 \end{array}$

44. $2x_1 - 3x_2 = -2$
$-4x_1 + 6x_2 = 7$

$$\begin{bmatrix} 2 & -3 & | & -2 \\ -4 & 6 & | & 7 \end{bmatrix} \quad \tfrac{1}{2}R_1 \to R_1 \begin{bmatrix} 1 & -\tfrac{3}{2} & | & -1 \\ -4 & 6 & | & 7 \end{bmatrix}$$

$$\begin{bmatrix} 1 & -\tfrac{3}{2} & | & -1 \\ -4 & 6 & | & 7 \end{bmatrix} \quad 4R_1 + R_2 \to R_2 \begin{bmatrix} 1 & -1.5 & | & -1 \\ 0 & 0 & | & 3 \end{bmatrix} \text{ no solution}$$

46. $3x_1 - x_2 = -5$
$x_1 + 3x_2 = 5$

$$\begin{bmatrix} 3 & -1 & | & -5 \\ 1 & 3 & | & 5 \end{bmatrix} \quad R_2 \leftrightarrow R_1 \begin{bmatrix} 1 & 3 & | & 5 \\ 3 & -1 & | & -5 \end{bmatrix}$$

$$\begin{bmatrix} 1 & 3 & | & 5 \\ 3 & -1 & | & -5 \end{bmatrix} \quad -3R_1 + R_2 \to R_2 \begin{bmatrix} 1 & 3 & | & 5 \\ 0 & -10 & | & -20 \end{bmatrix}$$

$$\begin{bmatrix} 1 & 3 & | & 5 \\ 0 & -10 & | & -20 \end{bmatrix} \quad -\tfrac{1}{10}R_2 \to R_2 \begin{bmatrix} 1 & 3 & | & 5 \\ 0 & 1 & | & 2 \end{bmatrix}$$

$$\begin{bmatrix} 1 & 3 & | & 5 \\ 0 & 1 & | & 2 \end{bmatrix} \quad -3R_2 + R_1 \to R_1 \begin{bmatrix} 1 & 0 & | & -1 \\ 0 & 1 & | & 2 \end{bmatrix} \quad \begin{matrix} x_1 = -1 \\ x_2 = 2 \end{matrix}$$

48. $2x_1 - 4x_2 = -2$
$-3x_1 + 6x_2 = 3$

$$\begin{bmatrix} 2 & -4 & | & -2 \\ -3 & 6 & | & 3 \end{bmatrix} \quad \tfrac{1}{2}R_1 \to R_1 \begin{bmatrix} 1 & -2 & | & -1 \\ -3 & 6 & | & 3 \end{bmatrix}$$

$$\begin{bmatrix} 1 & -2 & | & -1 \\ -3 & 6 & | & 3 \end{bmatrix} \quad 3R_1 + R_2 \to R_2 \begin{bmatrix} 1 & -2 & | & -1 \\ 0 & 0 & | & 0 \end{bmatrix}$$

infinitely many solutions: $x_2 = s$, $x_1 = 2s - 1$ for any real number s

50. $-6x_1 + 2x_2 = 4$
$3x_1 - x_2 = -2$

$$\begin{bmatrix} -6 & 2 & | & 4 \\ 3 & -1 & | & -2 \end{bmatrix} \quad -\tfrac{1}{6}R_1 \to R_1 \begin{bmatrix} 1 & -\tfrac{1}{3} & | & -\tfrac{2}{3} \\ 3 & -1 & | & -2 \end{bmatrix}$$

$$\begin{bmatrix} 1 & -\tfrac{1}{3} & | & -\tfrac{2}{3} \\ 3 & -1 & | & -2 \end{bmatrix} \quad -3R_1 + R_2 \to R_2 \begin{bmatrix} 1 & -\tfrac{1}{3} & | & -\tfrac{2}{3} \\ 0 & 0 & | & 0 \end{bmatrix}$$

infinitely many solutions: $x_2 = s$, $x_1 = \tfrac{1}{3}s - \tfrac{2}{3}$ for any real number s

52. $7x - 3y = 20$
$5x + 2y = 8$

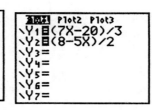 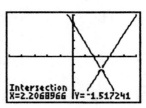

$(2.21, -1.52)$

54. $5.4x + 4.2y = -12.9$
$3.7x + 6.4y = -4.5$

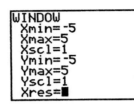

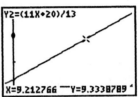

$(-3.35, 1.23)$

56. (A) $5x - 6y = -10$ $55x - 66y = -110$ $5x - 6(10) = -10$
$11x - 13y = -20$ $\underline{-55x + 65y = 100}$ $5x = 50$
$-y = -10$ $x = 10$
$y = 10$

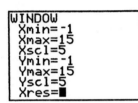

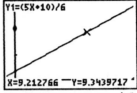

Graphs appear identical but trace shows slight difference.

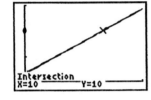

Graphical solution agrees with elimination by addition.

(B) $5x - 6y = -10$ $-10x + 12y = 20$ $5x - 6(0) = -10$
$10x - 13y = -20$ $\underline{10x - 13y = -20}$ $x = -2$
$-y = 0$
$y = 0$

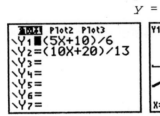

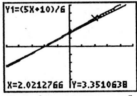

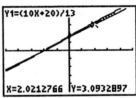

Graphs appear slightly different as trace shows.

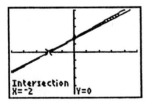

Graphical solution agrees with elimination by addition.

(C) $2[(5x - 6y) = -10] \rightarrow 10x - 12y = -20$. The system is dependent. The lines coincide giving infinitely many solutions.

58.

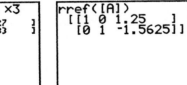

$x_1 = 1.25$
$x_2 = -1.5625$

60.

```
MATRIX[A] 2 ×3
[ 5.7   -8.55  -35.91 ]
[ 4.5    5.73   76.17 ]
```

```
rref([A])
  [[1 0 6.2625]
   [0 1 8.375 ]]
```

$x_1 = 6.2625$
$x_2 = 8.375$

62.

$$N + D = 89 \quad (1)$$
$$0.05N + 0.1D = 6.05 \quad (2)$$

$-5 \cdot (1):\ -5N - 5D = -445$

$100 \cdot (2):\ \underline{5N + 10D = 605}$

$$5D = 160$$
$$D = 32$$

$(1):\ N + 32 = 89$

$N = 57$

$N = 57$ nickels
$D = 32$ dimes

64. $0.146x + 0.098y = 0.11(T)$
$\quad\quad\quad x + y = T$

where T = total amount invested, x = amount invested in fund A, and y = amount invested in fund B.

$0.146x + 0.098y = 0.11(x + y)$
$$0.036x = 0.012y$$
$$x = \frac{1}{3}y$$

$$\frac{1}{3}y + y = T$$

$$y = \frac{3}{4}T, \text{ invest 75\% in fund } B$$

$$x = \frac{1}{4}T, \text{ invest 25\% in fund } A$$

66. $x + y = 80 \quad\quad\quad (1)$
$0.4x + 0.7y = 0.49(80) \quad (2)$

where x = amount of 40% alcohol and y = amount of 70% alcohol.

$-4 \cdot (1):\ -4x - 4y = -320$

$10 \cdot (2):\ \underline{4x + 7y = 392}$

$$3y = 72$$
$$y = 24$$

$(1):\ x + 24 = 80$

$x = 56$

Use 56 liters of 40% solution and 24 liters of 70% solution.

68.

	A	B	Total
Nitrogen	9	8	770
Phosphoric Acid	5	6	490

(1) $9A + 8B = 770$

(2) $5A + 6B = 490$

$3 \cdot (1):\ 27A + 24B = 2310$

$-4 \cdot (2):\ \underline{-20A - 24B = -1960}$

$$7A = 350$$
$$A = 50$$

(1) $9(50) + 8B = 770$

$$8B = 320$$
$$B = 40$$

Use 50 bags of brand A and 40 bags of brand B.

70. (A) $x + 4y = 29.95$ (1)   where x = base price and y = surcharge/lb.
$x + 19y = 59.20$ (2)

(2) − (1): $15y = 29.95$ (1): $x + 4(1.95) = 29.95$
$y = \$1.95$ $x = 22.15$

Base price = \$22.15, surcharge = \$1.95 per additional pound.

(B) For United in problem 69:
$x + 4y = 27.75$
$x + 19y = 64.50$ which gives $x = \$17.95$, base price and
$y = \$2.45$, surcharge.

United cost = $17.95 + 2.45p$
Federated cost = $22.15 + 1.95p$ where p = weight over 1 lb.
$y_1 = 17.95 + 2.45x$ and
$y_2 = 22.15 + 1.95x$ intersect at (8.4, 38.53). Packages of 8.4 lb cost \$38.53
with both carriers. Ship packages weighing more than 9 pounds with Federated
and all others with United Express.

72. (A) $50(132) = 6600$ lb of Columbian
$40(132) = 5280$ lb of Brazilian

$\dfrac{6}{16}$ lb of Columbian + $\dfrac{10}{16}$ lb of Brazilian = $\dfrac{16}{16}$ lb of mild

6 lb of Columbian + 10 lb of Brazilian = 16 lb of mild
and multiplying both sides by $528 = \dfrac{5280}{10}$ (since Brazilian is 62.5% of mix) gives

3168 lb of Columbian + 5280 lb of Brazilian = 8448 lb of mild.
(6600 − 3168) = 3432 lb of Columbian left over.

(B) $\dfrac{12}{16}$ lb of Columbian + $\dfrac{4}{16}$ lb of Brazilian = $\dfrac{16}{16}$ lb of robust

12 lb of Columbian + 4 lb of Brazilian = 16 lb of robust
and multiplying both sides by $550 = \dfrac{6600}{12}$ (since Columbian is 75% of mix) gives

6600 lb of Columbian + 2200 lb of Brazilian = 8800 lb of robust
(5280 − 2200) = 3080 lb of Brazilian left over.

Exercise 9-2

2. $\begin{bmatrix} 1 & 0 & | & 5 \\ 0 & 1 & | & -3 \end{bmatrix}$ Reduced form.

4. $\begin{bmatrix} 1 & -1 & 4 & | & 0 \\ 0 & 0 & 0 & | & 0 \\ 0 & 0 & 0 & | & 1 \end{bmatrix}$ Not reduced form; the 2nd and 3rd rows need to be interchanged.

6. $\begin{bmatrix} 1 & -2 & 4 & | & 1 \\ 0 & 0 & 1 & | & -3 \\ 0 & 0 & 0 & | & 0 \end{bmatrix}$ Not reduced form; the 4 in row 1 should be 0.

8. $\begin{bmatrix} 0 & 0 & 1 & | & 0 \\ 0 & 0 & 0 & | & 0 \end{bmatrix}$ Reduced form

10. $\begin{bmatrix} 1 & 0 & 0 & 0 & | & -2 \\ 0 & 1 & 0 & 0 & | & 0 \\ 0 & 0 & 1 & 0 & | & 1 \\ 0 & 0 & 0 & 1 & | & 3 \end{bmatrix} \Rightarrow$ $\begin{aligned} x_1 &= -2 \\ x_2 &= 0 \\ x_3 &= 1 \\ x_4 &= 3 \end{aligned}$

12. $\begin{bmatrix} 1 & -2 & 0 & | & -3 \\ 0 & 0 & 1 & | & 5 \\ 0 & 0 & 0 & | & 0 \end{bmatrix} \Rightarrow$ $\begin{aligned} x_1 - 2x_2 \quad &= -3 \\ x_3 &= 5 \end{aligned}$: system

infinite solutions

Let $x_2 = t$ any real number
then $x_1 = 2t - 3$
$x_2 = t$
$x_3 = 5$

14. $\begin{bmatrix} 1 & 0 & | & 5 \\ 0 & 1 & | & -3 \\ 0 & 0 & | & 0 \end{bmatrix} \Rightarrow$ $\begin{aligned} x_1 &= 5 \\ x_2 &= -3 \end{aligned}$

16. $\begin{bmatrix} 1 & 0 & -2 & 3 & | & 4 \\ 0 & 1 & -1 & 2 & | & -1 \end{bmatrix}$ $\begin{aligned} x_1 - 2x_3 + 3x_4 &= 4 \\ x_2 - x_3 + 2x_4 &= -1 \end{aligned}$: system

$x_1 = 2s - 3t + 4$
$x_2 = s - 2t - 1$
$x_3 = s$
$x_4 = t$
s and t = any real number

18. $\begin{bmatrix} 1 & 3 & | & 1 \\ 0 & 2 & | & -4 \end{bmatrix}$ $\frac{1}{2}R_2 \rightarrow R_2$ $\begin{bmatrix} 1 & 3 & | & 1 \\ 0 & 1 & | & -2 \end{bmatrix}$

$\begin{bmatrix} 1 & 3 & | & 1 \\ 0 & 1 & | & -2 \end{bmatrix}$ $-3R_2 + R_1 \rightarrow R_1$ $\begin{bmatrix} 1 & 0 & | & 7 \\ 0 & 1 & | & -2 \end{bmatrix}$

20. $\begin{bmatrix} 1 & 0 & 4 & | & 0 \\ 0 & 1 & -3 & | & -1 \\ 0 & 0 & -2 & | & 2 \end{bmatrix}$ $-\frac{1}{2}R_3 \rightarrow R_3$ $\begin{bmatrix} 1 & 0 & 4 & | & 0 \\ 0 & 1 & -3 & | & -1 \\ 0 & 0 & 1 & | & -1 \end{bmatrix}$

$\begin{bmatrix} 1 & 0 & 4 & | & 0 \\ 0 & 1 & -3 & | & -1 \\ 0 & 0 & 1 & | & -1 \end{bmatrix}$ $\begin{aligned} 3R_3 + R_2 \rightarrow R_2 \\ \\ -4R_3 + R_1 \rightarrow R_1 \end{aligned}$ $\begin{bmatrix} 1 & 0 & 0 & | & 4 \\ 0 & 1 & 0 & | & -4 \\ 0 & 0 & 1 & | & -1 \end{bmatrix}$

22. $\begin{bmatrix} 0 & -2 & 8 & | & 1 \\ 2 & -2 & 6 & | & -4 \\ 0 & -1 & 4 & | & \frac{1}{2} \end{bmatrix}$ $\quad R_2 \to R_1 \begin{bmatrix} 2 & -2 & 6 & | & -4 \\ 0 & -2 & 8 & | & 1 \\ 0 & -1 & 4 & | & \frac{1}{2} \end{bmatrix}$

$\begin{bmatrix} 2 & -2 & 6 & | & -4 \\ 0 & -2 & 8 & | & 1 \\ 0 & -1 & 4 & | & \frac{1}{2} \end{bmatrix}$ $\quad \frac{1}{2}R_1 \to R_1 \begin{bmatrix} 1 & -1 & 3 & | & -2 \\ 0 & -2 & 8 & | & 1 \\ 0 & -1 & 4 & | & \frac{1}{2} \end{bmatrix}$

$\begin{bmatrix} 1 & -1 & 3 & | & -2 \\ 0 & -2 & 8 & | & 1 \\ 0 & -1 & 4 & | & \frac{1}{2} \end{bmatrix}$ $\quad -\frac{1}{2}R_2 \to R_2 \begin{bmatrix} 1 & -1 & 3 & | & -2 \\ 0 & 1 & -4 & | & -\frac{1}{2} \\ 0 & -1 & 4 & | & \frac{1}{2} \end{bmatrix}$

$\begin{bmatrix} 1 & -1 & 3 & | & -2 \\ 0 & 1 & -4 & | & -\frac{1}{2} \\ 0 & -1 & 4 & | & \frac{1}{2} \end{bmatrix}$ $\quad \begin{matrix} 1R_2 + R_1 \to R_1 \\ \\ 1R_2 + R_3 \to R_3 \end{matrix} \begin{bmatrix} 1 & 0 & -1 & | & -\frac{5}{2} \\ 0 & 1 & -4 & | & -\frac{1}{2} \\ 0 & 0 & 0 & | & 0 \end{bmatrix}$

24. $\begin{bmatrix} 3 & 5 & -1 & | & -7 \\ 1 & 1 & 1 & | & -1 \\ 2 & 0 & 11 & | & 7 \end{bmatrix}$ $\quad R_1 \to R_2 \begin{bmatrix} 1 & 1 & 1 & | & -1 \\ 3 & 5 & -1 & | & -7 \\ 2 & 0 & 11 & | & 7 \end{bmatrix}$

$\begin{bmatrix} 1 & 1 & 1 & | & -1 \\ 3 & 5 & -1 & | & -7 \\ 2 & 0 & 11 & | & 7 \end{bmatrix}$ $\quad \begin{matrix} -3R_1 + R_2 \to R_2 \\ \\ -2R_1 + R_3 \to R_3 \end{matrix} \begin{bmatrix} 1 & 1 & 1 & | & -1 \\ 0 & 2 & -4 & | & -4 \\ 0 & -2 & 9 & | & 9 \end{bmatrix}$

$\begin{bmatrix} 1 & 1 & 1 & | & -1 \\ 0 & 2 & -4 & | & -4 \\ 0 & -2 & 9 & | & 9 \end{bmatrix}$ $\quad \frac{1}{2}R_2 \to R_2 \begin{bmatrix} 1 & 1 & 1 & | & -1 \\ 0 & 1 & -2 & | & -2 \\ 0 & -2 & 9 & | & 9 \end{bmatrix}$

$\begin{bmatrix} 1 & 1 & 1 & | & -1 \\ 0 & 1 & -2 & | & -2 \\ 0 & -2 & 9 & | & 9 \end{bmatrix}$ $\quad \begin{matrix} -1R_2 + R_1 \to R_1 \\ \\ 2R_2 + R_3 \to R_3 \end{matrix} \begin{bmatrix} 1 & 0 & 3 & | & 1 \\ 0 & 1 & -2 & | & -2 \\ 0 & 0 & 5 & | & 5 \end{bmatrix}$

$\begin{bmatrix} 1 & 0 & 3 & | & 1 \\ 0 & 1 & -2 & | & -2 \\ 0 & 0 & 5 & | & 5 \end{bmatrix}$ $\quad \frac{1}{5}R_3 \to R_3 \begin{bmatrix} 1 & 0 & 3 & | & 1 \\ 0 & 1 & -2 & | & -2 \\ 0 & 0 & 1 & | & 1 \end{bmatrix}$

$\begin{bmatrix} 1 & 0 & 3 & | & 1 \\ 0 & 1 & -2 & | & -2 \\ 0 & 0 & 1 & | & 1 \end{bmatrix}$ $\quad \begin{matrix} -3R_3 + R_1 \to R_1 \\ \\ 2R_3 + R_2 \to R_2 \end{matrix} \begin{bmatrix} 1 & 0 & 0 & | & -2 \\ 0 & 1 & 0 & | & 0 \\ 0 & 0 & 1 & | & 1 \end{bmatrix}$ $\quad \begin{matrix} x_1 = -2 \\ x_2 = 0 \\ x_3 = 1 \end{matrix}$

26. $\begin{bmatrix} 2 & 7 & 15 & | & -12 \\ 4 & 7 & 13 & | & -10 \\ 3 & 6 & 12 & | & -9 \end{bmatrix} \to \begin{bmatrix} 1 & 0 & 0 & | & 1 \\ 0 & 1 & 0 & | & -2 \\ 0 & 0 & 1 & | & 0 \end{bmatrix}$ $\quad \begin{matrix} x_1 = 1 \\ x_2 = -2 \\ x_3 = 0 \end{matrix}$

using $\frac{1}{2}R_1 \to R_1$; $-4R_1 + R_2 \to R_2$; $-3R_1 + R_3 \to R_3$; $-\frac{1}{7}R_2 \to R_2$; $-\frac{7}{2}R_2 + R_1 \to R_1$; $\frac{9}{2}R_2 + R_3 \to R_3$;

$\frac{7}{3}R_3 \to R_3$; $-\frac{17}{7}R_3 + R_2 \to R_2$; $1R_3 + R_1 \to R_1$

28. $\begin{bmatrix} 2 & 4 & -6 & | & 10 \\ 3 & 3 & -3 & | & 6 \end{bmatrix} \rightarrow \begin{bmatrix} 1 & 0 & 1 & | & -1 \\ 0 & 1 & -2 & | & 3 \end{bmatrix}$

using $\frac{1}{2}R_1 \rightarrow R_1$; $-3R_1 + R_2 \rightarrow R_2$; $-\frac{1}{3}R_2 \rightarrow R_2$; $-2R_2 + R_1 \rightarrow R_1$

from which $x_1 + x_3 = -1$

$x_2 - 2x_3 = 3$ and letting $x_3 = t$

$x_1 = -t - 1$

$x_2 = 3 + 2t$, t any real number

30. rref $\begin{bmatrix} 2 & -1 & | & 0 \\ 3 & 2 & | & 7 \\ 1 & -1 & | & -2 \end{bmatrix} \rightarrow \begin{bmatrix} 1 & 0 & | & 0 \\ 0 & 1 & | & 0 \\ 0 & 0 & | & 1 \end{bmatrix}$, no solution

32. $\begin{bmatrix} 3 & 7 & -1 & | & 11 \\ 1 & 2 & -1 & | & 3 \\ 2 & 4 & -2 & | & 10 \end{bmatrix} \rightarrow \begin{bmatrix} 1 & 0 & -5 & | & -1 \\ 0 & 1 & 2 & | & 2 \\ 0 & 0 & 0 & | & 4 \end{bmatrix}$

using $R_1 \rightarrow R_2$; $-3R_1 + R_2 \rightarrow R_2$; $-2R_1 + R_3 \rightarrow R_3$; $-2R_2 + R_1 \rightarrow R_1$

from which, no solution

34. $\begin{bmatrix} 2 & 5 & 4 & | & -7 \\ -4 & -5 & 2 & | & 9 \\ -2 & -1 & 4 & | & 3 \end{bmatrix} \rightarrow \begin{bmatrix} 1 & 0 & -3 & | & -1 \\ 0 & 1 & 2 & | & -1 \\ 0 & 0 & 0 & | & 0 \end{bmatrix}$

from which $x_1 - 3x_3 = -1$

$x_2 + 2x_3 = -1$; let $x_3 = t$

$x_1 = 3t - 1$, $x_2 = -2t - 1$, t any real number

36. $\begin{bmatrix} 2 & 8 & -6 & | & 4 \\ -3 & -12 & 9 & | & -6 \end{bmatrix} \rightarrow \begin{bmatrix} 1 & 4 & -3 & | & 2 \\ 0 & 0 & 0 & | & 0 \end{bmatrix}$

using $\frac{1}{2}R_1 \rightarrow R_1$; $3R_1 + R_2 \rightarrow R_2$

from which $x_1 + 4x_2 - 3x_3 = 2$, let $x_2 = s$ and $x_3 = t$

$x_1 = -4s + 3t + 2$, s, t any real numbers

38. rref $\begin{bmatrix} 4 & -2 & 2 & | & 5 \\ -6 & 3 & -3 & | & -2 \\ 10 & -5 & 9 & | & 4 \end{bmatrix} = \begin{bmatrix} 1 & -\frac{1}{2} & 0 & | & 0 \\ 0 & 0 & 1 & | & 0 \\ 0 & 0 & 0 & | & 1 \end{bmatrix}$ no solution

40. rref $\begin{bmatrix} -4 & 8 & 10 & | & -6 \\ 6 & -12 & -15 & | & 9 \\ -8 & 14 & 19 & | & -8 \end{bmatrix} = \begin{bmatrix} 1 & 0 & -\frac{3}{2} & | & -\frac{5}{2} \\ 0 & 1 & \frac{1}{2} & | & -2 \\ 0 & 0 & 0 & | & 0 \end{bmatrix}$

$x_1 - \frac{3}{2}x_3 = -\frac{5}{2}$ let $x_3 = t$, any real number

$x_2 + \frac{1}{2}x_3 = -2$

$x_1 = \frac{3}{2}t - \frac{5}{2}$

$x_2 = -\frac{1}{2}t - 2$

$x_3 = t$

or $x_1 = 1.5t - 2.5$

$x_2 = -0.5t - 2$

$x_3 = t$

42. $\text{rref}\begin{bmatrix} 4 & -2 & 3 & 3 \\ 3 & -1 & -2 & -10 \\ 2 & 4 & -1 & -1 \end{bmatrix} = \begin{bmatrix} 1 & 0 & 0 & -1 \\ 0 & 1 & 0 & 1 \\ 0 & 0 & 1 & 3 \end{bmatrix}$ $\begin{array}{l} x_1 = -1 \\ x_2 = 1 \\ x_3 = 3 \end{array}$

44. (A) $\begin{bmatrix} 1 & 0 & m & a \\ 0 & 1 & n & b \\ 0 & 0 & 0 & 0 \end{bmatrix}, \begin{bmatrix} 1 & m & 0 & a \\ 0 & 0 & 1 & b \\ 0 & 0 & 0 & 0 \end{bmatrix}$

(B) $\begin{bmatrix} 1 & 0 & m & 0 \\ 0 & 1 & n & 0 \\ 0 & 0 & 0 & 1 \end{bmatrix}, \begin{bmatrix} 1 & m & n & 0 \\ 0 & 0 & 0 & 1 \\ 0 & 0 & 0 & 0 \end{bmatrix}$

46. $\text{rref}\begin{bmatrix} 2 & 4 & 5 & 4 & 8 \\ 1 & 2 & 2 & 1 & 3 \end{bmatrix} = \begin{bmatrix} 1 & 2 & 0 & -3 & -1 \\ 0 & 0 & 1 & 2 & 2 \end{bmatrix}$

$\begin{array}{l} x_1 + 2x_2 - 3x_4 = -1 \\ \quad\quad x_3 + 2x_4 = 2 \end{array}$ let $x_2 = s$, $x_4 = t$ any real numbers.

$\begin{array}{l} x_1 = -2s + 3t - 1 \\ x_2 = s \\ x_3 = -2t + 2 \\ x_4 = t \end{array}$

48. $\text{rref}\begin{bmatrix} 1 & 1 & 4 & 1 & 1.3 \\ -1 & 1 & -1 & 0 & 1.1 \\ 2 & 0 & 1 & 3 & -4.4 \\ 2 & 5 & 11 & 3 & 5.6 \end{bmatrix} = \begin{bmatrix} 1 & 0 & 0 & 0 & -1.2 \\ 0 & 1 & 0 & 0 & 0.6 \\ 0 & 0 & 1 & 0 & 0.7 \\ 0 & 0 & 0 & 1 & -0.9 \end{bmatrix}$ $\begin{array}{l} x_1 = -1.2 \\ x_2 = 0.6 \\ x_3 = 0.7 \\ x_4 = -0.9 \end{array}$

50. $\text{rref}\begin{bmatrix} 1 & -3 & 1 & 1 & 2 & 2 \\ -1 & 5 & 2 & 2 & -2 & 0 \\ 2 & -6 & 2 & 2 & 4 & 4 \\ -1 & 3 & -1 & 0 & -1 & -3 \end{bmatrix} = \begin{bmatrix} 1 & 0 & 5.5 & 0 & -3.5 & 10.5 \\ 0 & 1 & 1.5 & 0 & -1.5 & 2.5 \\ 0 & 0 & 0 & 1 & 1 & -1 \\ 0 & 0 & 0 & 0 & 0 & 0 \end{bmatrix}$

$\begin{array}{l} x_1 + 5.5x_3 - 3.5x_5 = 10.5 \\ x_2 + 1.5x_3 - 1.5x_5 = 2.5 \\ \quad\quad\quad\quad x_4 + x_5 = -1 \end{array}$ let $x_3 = s$, $x_5 = t$ any real numbers

$\begin{array}{l} x_1 = -5.5s + 3.5t + 10.5 \\ x_2 = -1.5s + 1.5t + 2.5 \\ x_3 = s \\ x_4 = -t - 1 \\ x_5 = t \end{array}$

52. $\begin{array}{l} N + D + Q = 32 \\ 0.05N + 0.1D + 0.25Q = 6.8 \end{array}$ $\Rightarrow \begin{bmatrix} 1 & 1 & 1 & | & 32 \\ 0.05 & 0.1 & 0.25 & | & 6.8 \end{bmatrix}$ which

reduces to $\begin{bmatrix} 1 & 0 & -3 & | & -72 \\ 0 & 1 & 4 & | & 104 \end{bmatrix}$ $\Rightarrow \begin{array}{l} N - 3Q = -72 \\ D + 4Q = 104 \end{array}$

If $Q = t = 24, 25, 26$ then $N = 3t - 72$ and $D = 104 - 4t$

If $Q = 26$
$\quad D = 104 - 4(26) = 0$
$\quad N = 3(26) - 72 = 6$

If $Q = 25$
$\quad D = 104 - 4(25) = 4$
$\quad N = 3(25) - 72 = 3$

If $Q = 24$
$\quad D = 104 - 4(24) = 8$
$\quad N = 3(24) - 72 = 0$

54. $500x_1 + 500x_2 + 1500x_3 = 12,000$

$0.1(500)x_1 + 0.2(500)x_2 + 0.5(1500)x_3 = 12,000(0.3)$

$$\text{rref}\begin{bmatrix} 500 & 500 & 1500 & | & 12,000 \\ 50 & 100 & 750 & | & 3,600 \end{bmatrix} \rightarrow \begin{bmatrix} 1 & 0 & -9 & | & -24 \\ 0 & 1 & 12 & | & 48 \end{bmatrix}$$

Let $x_3 = t$; then $x_1 = 9t - 24 \Rightarrow t \geq 3$

$\qquad\qquad\qquad\qquad x_2 = -12t + 48 \Rightarrow t \leq 4$

If $t = 3$: $x_1 = 9(3) - 24 = 3$

$\qquad\qquad x_2 = 48 - 12(3) = 12$ (10%: 3 cc, 20%: 12 cc, 50%: 3 cc)

If $t = 4$: $x_1 = 9(4) - 24 = 12$

$\qquad\qquad x_2 = 48 - 12(4) = 0$ (10%: 12 cc, 20%: 0 cc, 50%: 4 cc)

56. $y = a + bx + cx^2$

$(1, 3) \Rightarrow 3 = a + b + c$

$(2, 2) \Rightarrow 2 = a + 2b + 4c \Rightarrow \text{rref}\begin{bmatrix} 1 & 1 & 1 & | & 3 \\ 1 & 2 & 4 & | & 2 \\ 1 & 3 & 9 & | & 5 \end{bmatrix} \rightarrow \begin{bmatrix} 1 & 0 & 0 & | & 8 \\ 0 & 1 & 0 & | & -7 \\ 0 & 0 & 1 & | & 2 \end{bmatrix}$

$(3, 5) \Rightarrow 5 = a + 3b + 9c$

$a = 8$, $b = -7$, $c = 2$

$y = 8 - 7x + 2x^2$

58. $\qquad\qquad\qquad x^2 + y^2 + ax + by + c = 0$

$(-4, 1): (-4)^2 + (1)^2 - 4a + b + c = 0 \Rightarrow -4a + b + c = -17$

$(-1, 2): (-1)^2 + (2)^2 - a + 2b + c = 0 \Rightarrow -a + 2b + c = -5$

$(3, -6): (3)^2 + (-6)^2 + 3a - 6b + c = 0 \Rightarrow 3a - 6b + c = -45$

$$\text{rref}\begin{bmatrix} -4 & 1 & 1 & | & -17 \\ -1 & 2 & 1 & | & -5 \\ 3 & -6 & 1 & | & -45 \end{bmatrix} \rightarrow \begin{bmatrix} 1 & 0 & 0 & | & 2 \\ 0 & 1 & 0 & | & 6 \\ 0 & 0 & 1 & | & -15 \end{bmatrix} \quad \begin{matrix} a = 2 \\ b = 6 \\ c = -15 \end{matrix}$$

$\qquad\qquad x^2 + y^2 + 2x + 6y - 15 = 0$

60. $0.5x + y + 1.5z = 350$

$0.6x + 0.9y + 1.2z = 330 \qquad \Rightarrow \quad \begin{bmatrix} 0.5 & 1 & 1.5 & | & 350 \\ 0.6 & 0.9 & 1.2 & | & 330 \\ 0.2 & 0.3 & 0.5 & | & 115 \end{bmatrix}$ which

$0.2x + 0.3y + 0.5z = 115$

reduces to $\begin{bmatrix} 1 & 0 & 0 & | & 150 \\ 0 & 1 & 0 & | & 200 \\ 0 & 0 & 1 & | & 50 \end{bmatrix}$ 150 one-person boats
200 two-person boats
50 four-person boats

62. $\begin{bmatrix} 0.5 & 1 & 1.5 & | & 350 \\ 0.6 & 0.9 & 1.2 & | & 330 \end{bmatrix} \rightarrow \begin{bmatrix} 1 & 0 & -1 & | & 100 \\ 0 & 1 & 2 & | & 300 \end{bmatrix}$

$x = 100 + t$ one-person

$y = 300 - 2t$ two-person

$z = t$ four-person $\quad 0 \leq t \leq 150$, t = integer

64. $\begin{bmatrix} 0.5 & 1 & | & 350 \\ 0.6 & 0.9 & | & 330 \\ 0.2 & 0.3 & | & 115 \end{bmatrix} \rightarrow \begin{bmatrix} 1 & 0 & | & 100 \\ 0 & 1 & | & 300 \\ 0 & 0 & | & 5 \end{bmatrix} \Rightarrow$ no solution

No production schedule will use all work hours in all departments.

66. $\text{rref}\begin{bmatrix} 30 & 10 & 20 & | & 400 \\ 10 & 10 & 20 & | & 160 \\ 10 & 30 & 20 & | & 240 \end{bmatrix} \rightarrow \begin{bmatrix} 1 & 0 & 0 & | & 12 \\ 0 & 1 & 0 & | & 4 \\ 0 & 0 & 1 & | & 0 \end{bmatrix}$ 12 oz. food A
4 oz. food B
0 oz. food C

68. rref $\begin{bmatrix} 30 & 10 & | & 400 \\ 10 & 10 & | & 160 \\ 10 & 30 & | & 240 \end{bmatrix} \rightarrow \begin{bmatrix} 1 & 0 & 12 \\ 0 & 1 & 4 \\ 0 & 0 & 0 \end{bmatrix}$　　12 oz. food A
　　　　　　　　　　　　　　　　　　　　　　　　4 oz. food B

70. $\begin{bmatrix} 30 & 10 & 20 & | & 400 \\ 10 & 10 & 20 & | & 160 \end{bmatrix} \rightarrow \begin{bmatrix} 1 & 0 & 0 & | & 12 \\ 0 & 1 & 2 & | & 4 \end{bmatrix}$　　$\begin{array}{l} 12 \text{ oz. food } A \\ 4 - 2t \text{ oz. of food } B \\ t \text{ oz. of food } C \text{ where } 0 \le t \le 2 \end{array}$

72. $\begin{bmatrix} 30 & 20 & | & 650 \\ 10 & 20 & | & 350 \end{bmatrix} \rightarrow \begin{bmatrix} 1 & 0 & | & 15 \\ 0 & 1 & | & 10 \end{bmatrix}$　$\begin{array}{l} 15 \text{ hours company } A \\ 10 \text{ hours company } B \end{array}$

Exercise 9-3

2. (1) $x^2 + y^2 = 25$　　　　(2) $\rightarrow$ (1)　$x^2 + (-4)^2 = 25 \Rightarrow x^2 = 9,\ x = \pm 3$
　　(2) 　　　$y = -4$
　　(3, -4), (-3, -4)

4. (1) $y^2 = 2x$

　　(2) 　$x = y - \dfrac{1}{2}$

　　(2) $\rightarrow$ (1): $y^2 = 2\left(y - \dfrac{1}{2}\right)$　　　　$y = 1 \rightarrow$ (2) $x = 1 - \dfrac{1}{2}$

　　　　　　　$y^2 = 2y - 1$　　　　　　　　　　　$x = \dfrac{1}{2}$

　　　　　　　$y^2 - 2y + 1 = 0$
　　　　　　　$(y - 1)^2 = 0$
　　　　　　　　$y = 1$　　　　$\left(\dfrac{1}{2},\ 1\right)$

6. (1) $x^2 + 4y^2 = 32$　　(2) $\rightarrow$ (1): $(-2y^2) + 4y^2 = 32$　　$y = 2 \rightarrow$ (2):　$x + 4 = 0$
　　(2)　$x + 2y = 0$　　　　　　　　$8y^2 = 32$　　　　　　　　　　　　$x = -4$
　　　　　$x = -2y$　　　　　　　　　$y^2 = 4$　　　$y = -2 \rightarrow$ (2):　$x - 4 = 0$
　　　　　　　　　　　　　　　　　　　$y = \pm 2$　　　　　　　　　　　$x = 4$
　　　　　　　　　(-4, 2), (4, -2)

8. (1) $x^2 = 2y$　　　(2) $\rightarrow$ (1): $x^2 = 2(3x - 2)$　　$x = 3 + \sqrt{5} \rightarrow$ (2): $y = 3(3 + \sqrt{5}) - 2$
　　(2) $3x = y + 2$　　　　　$x^2 = 6x - 4$　　　　　　　　　　　　$y = 9 + 3\sqrt{5} - 2$
　　　　$y = 3x - 2$　　　　　$x^2 - 6x + 4 = 0$　　　　　　　　　　$y = 7 + 3\sqrt{5}$
　　　　　　　　　　Using the quadratic formula,　　$x = 3 - \sqrt{5} \rightarrow$ (2): $y = 3(3 - \sqrt{5}) - 2$
　　　　　　　　　　　$x = 3 \pm \sqrt{5}$　　　　　　　　　　　　　$y = 9 - 3\sqrt{5} - 2$
　　　　　　　　　　　　　　　　　　　　　　　　　　　　　$y = 7 - 3\sqrt{5}$
　　　　　　　($3 + \sqrt{5}$, $7 + 3\sqrt{5}$), ($3 - \sqrt{5}$, $7 - 3\sqrt{5}$)

10. (1) $x^2 - y^2 = 3$　　$x = 2 \rightarrow$ (1): $2^2 - y^2 = 3$　　$x = -2 \rightarrow$ (1): $(-2)^2 - y^2 = 3$
　　　(2) $\dfrac{x^2 + y^2 = 5}{}$　　　　　　　$y^2 = 1$　　　　　　　　　　$y^2 = 1$
　　　　　　$2x^2 = 8$　　　　　　　$y = \pm 1$　　　　　　　　　$y = \pm 1$
　　　　　　　$x^2 = 4$
　　　　　　　$x = \pm 2$　　　(2, 1), (2, -1), (-2, 1), (-2, -1)

12. (1) $x^2 - 2y^2 = 1$　　$y = 2 \rightarrow$ (1): $x^2 - 8 = 1$　　$y = -2 \rightarrow$ (1): $x^2 - 8 = 1$
　　　(2) $x^2 + 4y^2 = 25$　　　　　　$x^2 = 9$　　　　　　　　　　$x = 9$
　　　(1) $-$ (2): $-6y^2 = -24$　　　　$x = \pm 3$　　　　　　　　　$x = \pm 3$
　　　　　　　$y^2 = 4$
　　　　　　　$y = \pm 2$　　　(3, 2), (-3, 2), (3, -2), (-3, -2)

14. (1) $xy - 6 = 0$ (2) → (1): $(y + 4)y - 6 = 0$ $y = -2 \pm \sqrt{10}$ → (2): $x = -2 \pm \sqrt{10} + 4$
    (2) $x - y = 4$ $y^2 + 4y - 6 = 0$ $x = 2 \pm \sqrt{10}$
    $x = y + 4$ Using the quadratic formula,
    $y = -2 \pm \sqrt{10}$

$(2 + \sqrt{10}, -2 + \sqrt{10})$, $(2 - \sqrt{10}, -2 - \sqrt{10})$

16. (1) $2x^2 + y^2 = 18$ (2) → (1): $2\left(\dfrac{4}{y}\right)^2 + y^2 = 18$ y → (2): $x = \dfrac{4}{4} = 1$
    (2) $xy = 4$
    $x = \dfrac{4}{y}$ $\dfrac{32}{y^2} + y^2 = 18$ $x = \dfrac{4}{-4} = -1$
    $32 + y^4 = 18y^2$ $x = \dfrac{4}{\sqrt{2}} \cdot \dfrac{\sqrt{2}}{\sqrt{2}} = \dfrac{4\sqrt{2}}{2} = 2\sqrt{2}$
    $y^4 - 18y^2 + 32 = 0$
    $(y^2 - 16)(y^2 - 2) = 0$
    $y^2 = 16, \ y^2 = 2$ $x = \dfrac{4}{-\sqrt{2}} = -2\sqrt{2}$
    $y = \pm 4, \ \ y = \pm\sqrt{2}$

$(1, 4)$, $(-1, -4)$, $(2\sqrt{2}, \sqrt{2})$, $(-2\sqrt{2}, -\sqrt{2})$

18. (1) $2x^2 - 3y^2 = 10$ (1): $2x^2 - 3y^2 = 10$ y → (2): $x^2 + 4(2i)^2 = -17$
    (2) $x^2 + 4y^2 = -17$ $-2 \cdot$ (2): $\underline{-2x^2 - 8y^2 = 34}$ $x^2 - 16 = -17$
    $-11y^2 = 44$ $x^2 = -1$
    $y^2 = -4$ $x = \pm i$
    $y = \pm 2i$ $x^2 + 4(-2i)^2 = -17$
    $x = \pm i$

$(i, 2i)$, $(i, -2i)$, $(-i, 2i)$, $(-i, -2i)$

20. (1) $x^2 + y^2 = 20$ (2) → (1): $y + y^2 = 20$ $y = -5$ → (2): $x^2 = -5$
    (2) $x^2 = y$ $y^2 + y - 20 = 0$ $x = \pm\sqrt{5}i$
    $(y + 5)(y - 4) = 0$ $y = 4$ → (2): $x^2 = 4$
    $y = -5, \ 4$ $x = \pm 2$

$(\sqrt{5}i, -5)$, $(-\sqrt{5}i, -5)$, $(2, 4)$, $(-2, 4)$

22. (1) $x^2 + y^2 = 16$ (2) → (1): $x^2 + (4 - x) = 16$ $x = 4$ → (2): $y^2 = 4 - 4 = 0$
    (2) $y^2 = 4 - x$ $x^2 - x - 12 = 0$ $x = -3$ → (2): $y^2 = 4 + 3 = 7$
    $(x - 4)(x + 3) = 0$ $y = \pm\sqrt{7}$
    $x = 4, -3$

$(4, 0)$, $(-3, \sqrt{7})$, $(-3, -\sqrt{7})$

24. (1) $y^2 = 5x^2 + 1$ (2) → (1): $\left(\dfrac{2}{x}\right)^2 = 5x^2 + 1$ $x = \dfrac{2}{\sqrt{5}}$ → (2): $y = \dfrac{2}{\frac{2}{\sqrt{5}}} = \sqrt{5}$
    (2) $xy = 2$
    $y = \dfrac{2}{x}$ $\dfrac{4}{x^2} = 5x^2 + 1$
    $4 = 5x^4 + x^2$ $x = -\dfrac{2}{\sqrt{5}}$ → (2): $y = \dfrac{2}{-\frac{2}{\sqrt{5}}} = -\sqrt{5}$
    $5x^4 + x^2 - 4 = 0$
    $(5x^2 - 4)(x^2 + 1) = 0$
    $x^2 = \dfrac{4}{5}, \ \ x^2 = -1$ $x = i$ → (2): $y = \dfrac{2}{i} = -2i$
    $x = \pm\dfrac{2}{\sqrt{5}}, \ x = \pm i$ $x = -i$ → (2): $y = \dfrac{2}{-i} = 2i$

$\left(\dfrac{2\sqrt{5}}{5}, \sqrt{5}\right)$, $\left(-\dfrac{2\sqrt{5}}{\sqrt{5}}, -\sqrt{5}\right)$, $(i, -2i)$, $(-i, 2i)$

26. (1) $y = 5x - x^2$
(2) $y = x + 3$
$$\Rightarrow$$
$5x - x^2 = x + 3$
$x^2 - 4x + 3 = 0$
$x = 3, \quad x = 1$
$y = 6 \quad y = 4$

$(1, 4), (3, 6)$

28. (1) $y = x^2 + 2x$
(2) $y = 3x$
$$\Rightarrow$$
$x^2 + 2x = 3x$
$x^2 - x = 0$
$x = 1, \quad x = 0$
$y = 3 \quad y = 0$

$(1, 3), (0, 0)$

30. (1) $y = x^2 + 2x + 3$
(2) $y = 2x + 4$
$$\Rightarrow$$
$x^2 + 2x + 3 = 2x + 4$
$x^2 = 1$
$x = 1, \quad x = -1$
$y = 6 \quad y = 2$

$(1, 6), (-1, 2)$

32. (1) $y = x^2 - 4x - 10$
(2) $y = 14 - 2x - x^2$
$$\Rightarrow$$
$x^2 - 4x - 10 = 14 - 2x - x^2$
$2x^2 - 2x - 24 = 0$
$x^2 - x - 12 = 0$
$(x - 4)(x + 3) = 0$
$x = 4, \quad x = -3$
$y = -10 \quad y = 11$

$(4, -10), (-3, 11)$

34. Write $3x + 4y = b$ as $y = -\frac{3}{4}x + \frac{b}{4}$. The lines in this family intersecting the circle at one point are tangent to the circle and perpendicular to the radius drawn to the point of tangency. If (x_0, y_0) is the point of tangency on the circle, then $x_0{}^2, + y_0{}^2 = 25$ and $y_0 = \frac{4}{3}x_0$ ($y = \frac{4}{3}x$ is the equation of the line through origin perpendicular to $3x + 4y = b$) which may be solved to give $(x_0, y_0) = (3, 4)$ or $(-3, -4)$. The b values of the tangent lines are $4 = -\frac{3}{4} \cdot 3 + \frac{b}{4} \Rightarrow b = 25$ and $-4 = -\frac{3}{4} \cdot -3 + \frac{b}{4} \Rightarrow b = -25$.

The tangent line equations are $y = -\frac{3}{4}x + \frac{25}{4}$ and $y = -\frac{3}{4}x - \frac{25}{4}$.

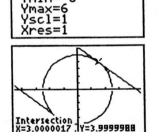

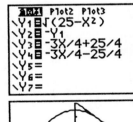

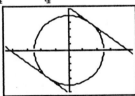

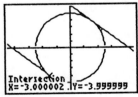

36. (1) $2x + 3y + xy = 16$

(2) $xy - 5 = 0$

$\qquad y = \dfrac{5}{x}$

(2) $\rightarrow$ (1): $2x + 3\left(\dfrac{5}{x}\right) + x\left(\dfrac{5}{x}\right) = 16$

$\qquad 2x^2 + 15 + 5x = 16x$

$\qquad 2x^2 - 11x + 15 = 0$

$\qquad (2x - 5)(x - 3) = 0$

$\qquad x = 3, \qquad x = \dfrac{5}{2}$

$\qquad y = \dfrac{5}{3} \qquad y = 2$

$\left(3, \dfrac{5}{3}\right), \left(\dfrac{5}{2}, 2\right)$

38. (1) $x^2 + xy - y^2 = -5$

(2) $y - x = 3$

$\qquad y = x + 3$

(2) $\rightarrow$ (1): $x^2 + x(x + 3) - (x + 3)^2 = -5$

$\qquad x^2 + x^2 + 3x - x^2 - 6x - 9 = -5$

$\qquad x^2 - 3x - 4 = 0$

$\qquad (x - 4)(x + 1) = 0$

$\qquad x = 4, \quad x = -1$

$\qquad y = x + 3 = 7 \qquad y = x + 3 = 2$

$(4, 7), (-1, 2)$

40. (1) $x^2 + 2xy + y^2 = 36$

(2) $\qquad x^2 - xy = 0$

(2): $x^2 - xy = 0$

$\qquad x(x - y) = 0$

$\qquad x = 0, \; x = y$

$x = 0 \rightarrow$ (1): $0 + 0 + y^2 = 36$

$\qquad y = \pm 6$

$x = y \rightarrow$ (1): $y^2 + 2y^2 + y^2 = 36$

$\qquad 4y^2 = 36$

$\qquad y^2 = 9$

$\qquad y = \pm 3$

$(0, 6), (0, -6), (3, 3), (-3, -3)$

42. (1) $x^2 - 2xy + 2y^2 = 16$

(2) $x^2 - y^2 = 0$

$\qquad (x - y)(x + y) = 0$

$\qquad x = y, \; x = -y$

$x = y \rightarrow$ (1): $y^2 - 2y^2 + 2y^2 = 16$

$\qquad y^2 = 16$

$\qquad y = \pm 4$

$x = -y \rightarrow$ (1): $y^2 + 2y^2 + 2y^2 = 16$

$\qquad 5y^2 = 16$

$\qquad y^2 = \dfrac{16}{5}$

$\qquad y = \pm\dfrac{4}{\sqrt{5}} = \pm\dfrac{4\sqrt{5}}{5}$

$(4, 4), (-4, -4), \left(\dfrac{4\sqrt{5}}{5}, -\dfrac{4\sqrt{5}}{5}\right), \left(-\dfrac{4\sqrt{5}}{5}, \dfrac{4\sqrt{5}}{5}\right)$

44. Write $-x^2 + 4xy + y^2 = 2$ as $y^2 + 4xy - x^2 - 2 = 0$ with solutions

$$y = \frac{-4x \pm \sqrt{16x^2 + 4(x^2 + 2)}}{2}.$$

Write $8x^2 - 2xy + y^2 = 9$ as $y^2 - 2xy + 8x^2 - 9 = 0$ with solutions

$$y = \frac{2x \pm \sqrt{4x^2 - 4(8x^2 - 9)}}{2}.$$

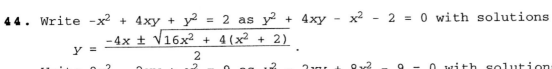

```
WINDOW
 Xmin=-2
 Xmax=2
 Xscl=1
 Ymin=-3
 Ymax=3
 Yscl=1
 Xres=1
```

```
Plot1 Plot2 Plot3
\Y1■-4X+√(16X²+
4(X²+2)))/2
\Y2■(-4X-√(16X²+
4(X²+2)))/2
\Y3■(2X+√(4X²-4(
8X²-9)))/2
\Y4■(2X-√(4X²-4(
```

```
WINDOW
 Xmin=-.8829787…
 Xmax=.11702127…
 Xscl=1
 Ymin=1.6693548…
 Ymax=3.1693548…
 Yscl=1
 Xres=1
```

```
Intersection
X=-.3871749  Y=2.4325182
```

QII (−0.39, 2.43)

```
WINDOW
 Xmin=■606382979
 Xmax=1.6063829…
 Xscl=1
 Ymin=-.0725806…
 Ymax=1.4274193…
 Yscl=1
 Xres=1
```

```
Intersection
X=1.1191043  Y=.63615606
```

QI (1.12, 0.64)

```
WINDOW
 Xmin=■1.606382…
 Xmax=-.6063829…
 Xscl=1
 Ymin=-1.233870…
 Ymax=.266129032
 Yscl=1
 Xres=1
```

```
Intersection
X=-1.119104  Y=-.6361561
```

QIII (−1.12, −0.64)

```
WINDOW
 Xmin=-.1170212…
 Xmax=.882978723
 Xscl=1
 Ymin=-3.169354…
 Ymax=-1.669354…
 Yscl=1
 Xres=■
```

```
Intersection
X=.38717493  Y=-2.432518
```

QIV (0.39, −2.43)

46. Write $5x^2 + 4xy + y^2 = 4$ as $y^2 + 4xy + 5x^2 - 4 = 0$ with solutions

$$y = -2x \pm \sqrt{4 - x^2}.$$

Write $4x^2 - 2xy + y^2 = 16$ as $y^2 - 2xy + 4x^2 - 16 = 0$ with solutions

$$y = x \pm \sqrt{16 - 3x^2}.$$

```
WINDOW
 Xmin=-5
 Xmax=5
 Xscl=1
 Ymin=-5
 Ymax=5
 Yscl=1■
 Xres=1
```

```
Plot1 Plot2 Plot3
\Y1■-2X+√(4-X²)
\Y2■-2X-√(4-X²)
\Y3■X+√(16-3X²)
\Y4■X-√(16-3X²)
\Y5=
\Y6=
\Y7=
```

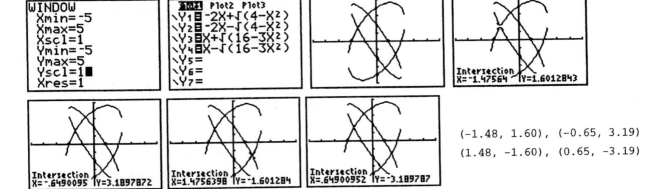

```
Intersection
X=-1.47564  Y=1.6012843
```

```
Intersection
X=-.6490095  Y=3.1897872
```

```
Intersection
X=1.4756398  Y=-1.6012B4
```

```
Intersection
X=.64900952  Y=-3.189787
```

(−1.48, 1.60), (−0.65, 3.19)

(1.48, −1.60), (0.65, −3.19)

48. Write $2x^2 + 2xy + y^2 = 12$ as $y^2 + 2xy + 2x^2 - 12 = 0$ with solutions
$y = -x \pm \sqrt{12 - x^2}$.

Write $4x^2 - 4xy + y^2 + x + 2y = 9$ as $y^2 + (2 - 4x)y + 4x^2 + x - 9 = 0$ with solutions $y = 2x - 1 \pm \sqrt{10 - 5x}$.

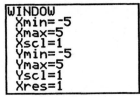

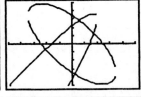
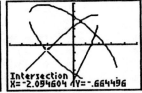

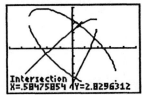
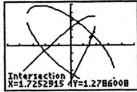

$(-2.09, -0.66), (0.58, 2.83)$
$(1.73, 1.28), (0.18, -3.64)$

50. (1) $x - y = 1$ (2) → (1): $x - \dfrac{1}{x} = 1$ $x = \dfrac{1 + \sqrt{5}}{2}$ → (2): $y = \dfrac{2}{1 + \sqrt{5}}$

(2) $xy = 1$ $x^2 - x - 1 = 0$ $y = \dfrac{-1 + \sqrt{5}}{2}$

$y = \dfrac{1}{x}$ Using the quadratic formula

$x = \dfrac{1 \pm \sqrt{5}}{2}$ $x = \dfrac{1 - \sqrt{5}}{2}$ → (2): $y = \dfrac{2}{1 - \sqrt{5}}$

$y = \dfrac{-1 - \sqrt{5}}{2}$

$\left(\dfrac{1 + \sqrt{5}}{2}, \dfrac{-1 + \sqrt{5}}{2}\right), \left(\dfrac{1 - \sqrt{5}}{2}, \dfrac{-1 - \sqrt{5}}{2}\right)$

52. (1) $2\ell + 2w = 36$ (2) → (1): $\ell + \dfrac{32}{\ell} = 18$

$\ell + w = 18$ $\ell^2 + 32 = 18\ell$

(2) $\ell w = 32$ $\ell^2 - 18\ell + 32 = 0$

$w = \dfrac{32}{\ell}$ $(\ell - 16)(\ell - 2) = 0$

$\ell = 16, \quad \ell = 2$

$w = 2, \quad w = 16$

The rectangle is 2 meters by 16 meters.

54. Let (x, y) be a point on circle in QI. $\Rightarrow x^2 + y^2 = \left(\dfrac{6.5}{2}\right)^2$

$A = (2x)(2y) = 15 \Rightarrow xy = \dfrac{15}{4}$

(1) $x^2 + y^2 = \dfrac{42.25}{4}$ (2) → (1): $x^2 + \left(\dfrac{15}{4x}\right)^2 = \dfrac{42.25}{4}$

(2) $y = \dfrac{15}{4x}$ $x^2 + \dfrac{225}{16x^2} = \dfrac{42.25}{4}$

$16x^4 + 225 = 169x^2$

$16x^4 - 169x^2 + 225 = 0$

$x^2 = 9 \qquad x^2 = \dfrac{25}{16}$

$x = 3 \qquad x = 1.25$

$y = 1.25 \qquad y = 3$

dimensions: $2x = 6$ in by $2y = 2.5$ in

56.
$$xy = 768 \rightarrow y = \frac{768}{x}$$

$$(x - 12)(y - 12)(6) = 1440$$

$$(x - 12)\left(\frac{768}{x} - 12\right)(6) = 1440 \Rightarrow 12x^2 - 672x + 9216 = 0$$

$x = 32$	x	$= 24$
$y = 24$	y	$= 32$

original dimensions: 24 in by 32 in

58. A: $210 = r \cdot t \rightarrow r = \frac{210}{t}$

B: $210 = (r + 10)\left(t - \frac{1}{2}\right)$

$$210 = \left(\frac{210}{t} + 10\right)\left(t - \frac{1}{2}\right) \Rightarrow 10t^2 - 5t - 105 = 0$$

$$(2t - 7)(5t + 15) = 0$$

$$t = 3.5 \qquad t = -3 \text{ reject}$$

B overtakes A at 3:30 PM $(12 + 3.5)$

Exercise 9-4

2. $3x + 4y < 12$

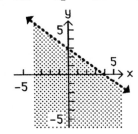

4. $3y - 2x \geq 24$

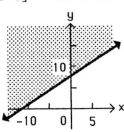

6. $y \geq \frac{1}{3}x - 2$

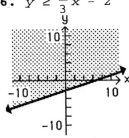

8. $x > -5$

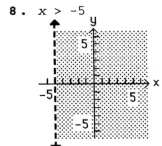

10. $-1 < x \leq 3$

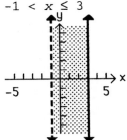

12. $x + 2y \geq 8$
$3x - 2y \leq 0$ $\Rightarrow$ II

14. $x + 2y \leq 8$
$3x - 2y \leq 0$ $\Rightarrow$ III

16. $x \leq 4$
$y \geq 2$

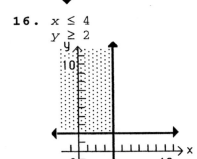

18. $3x + 4y \leq 12$
$y \geq -3$

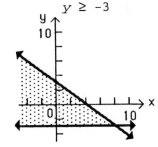

20. $2x + 5y \leq 20$
$x - 5y \leq -5$

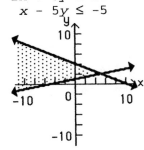

22. $x + 3y \leq 18$
$2x + y \leq 16 \implies$ III
$x \geq 0$
$y \geq 0$

Corner Points:
(0, 6), (0, 0), (8, 0), (6, 4)

24. $x + 3y \geq 18$
$2x + y \leq 16 \implies$ II
$x \geq 0$
$y \geq 0$

Corner Points:
(6, 4), (0, 6), (0, 16)

26. $4x + 3y \leq 12$
$x \geq 0$
$y \geq 0$

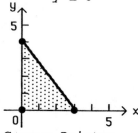

Corner Points:
(0, 0), (0, 4), (3, 0); bounded

28. $5x + 6y \geq 30$
$x \geq 0$
$y \geq 0$

Corner Points:
(0, 5), (6, 0); unbounded

30. $x + 2y \leq 10$
$3x + y \leq 15$
$x \geq 0$
$y \geq 0$

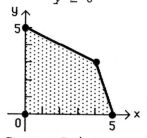

Corner Points:
(0, 0), (0, 5), (4, 3), (5, 0);
bounded

32. $x + 2y \geq 8$
$2x + y \geq 10$
$x \geq 0$
$y \geq 0$

Corner Points:
(8, 0), (4, 2), (0, 10); unbounded

34. $3x + y \leq 21$
$x + y \leq 9$
$x + 3y \leq 21$
$x \geq 0$
$y \geq 0$

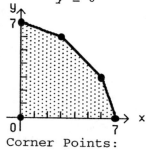

Corner Points:
(0, 0), (0, 7), (3, 6), (6, 3),
(7, 0); bounded

36. $3x + y \geq 30$
$x + y \geq 16$
$x + 3y \geq 24$
$x \geq 0$
$y \geq 0$

Corner Points:
(0, 30), (7, 9), (12, 4), (24, 0);
unbounded

38. $4x + y \leq 32$
$x + 3y \leq 30$
$5x + 4y \geq 51$

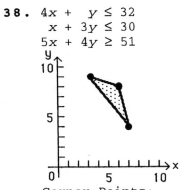

Corner Points:
  $(3, 9)$, $(6, 8)$, $(7, 4)$; bounded

40. $3x + 4y \leq 48$
$x + 2y \geq 24$
$y \leq 9$

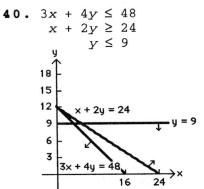

The feasible region is empty.

42. $3x - y \geq 1$
$-x + 5y \geq 9$
$x + y \leq 9$
$y \leq 5$

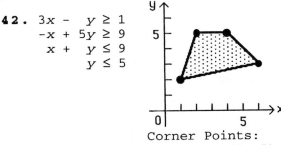

Corner Points:
  $(1, 2)$, $(2, 5)$, $(4, 5)$, $(6, 3)$; bounded

44.

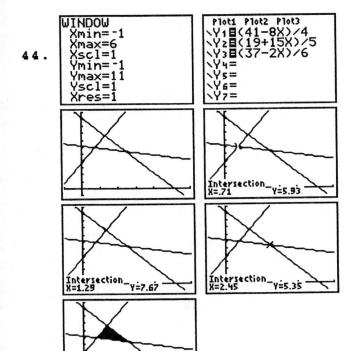

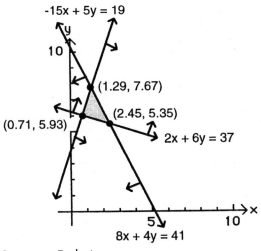

Corner Points:
  $(0.71, 5.93)$, $(1.29, 7.67)$,
  $(2.45, 5.35)$; bounded

46.

	assembly	finishing
x table	8	2
y chair	2	1
	≤ 400	≤ 120

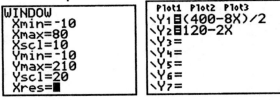

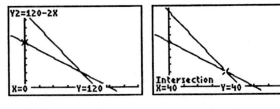

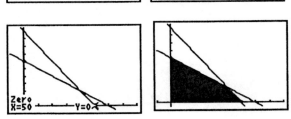

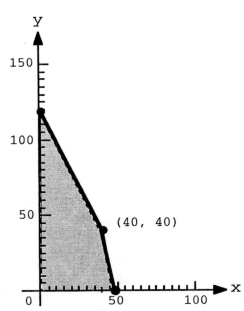

Corner Points:
(0, 0), (0, 120), (40, 40), (50, 0)

48.

	assembly	finishing	profit = $P = 50x + 15y$
x table	8	2	50
y chair	2	1	15
	≤ 400	≤ 120	

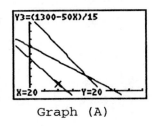

Graph (A)

(A) Graphing $50x + 15y = 1300$ above gives Graph (A) for $x = 20$, and $y = 20$. Any other production mix on this line will also result in a profit of \$1300. The slope of the profit line is $-\dfrac{50}{15}$ and the y intercept is $\dfrac{P}{15}$, $y = -\dfrac{50}{15}x + \dfrac{P}{15}$, which means all profit lines have the same slope. All production schedules in the feasible region that are on the graph of $50x + 15y = 1300$ will result in a profit of \$1300.

(B) The profit line that has the largest y intercept and still passes through the region of feasible solutions will produce the maximum profit.

(C) If a profit of \$1950 is desired then Graph (C) shows how the profit line passes through the region of feasible solutions. A production mix of 30 chairs and 30 tables is shown but any other production mix on this line will also produce a profit of \$1950. The idea is to increase the y intercept, thus increasing the profit, of the line while keeping the slope the same and making sure the line passes through at least one point in the region of feasible solutions.

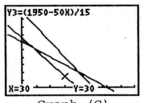

Graph (C)

50.

food	M	N		
calcium	30	10	$\geq$ 360	$30x + 10y \geq 360$
iron	10	10	$\geq$ 160	$10x + 10y \geq 160$
vit. A	10	30	$\geq$ 240	$10x + 30y \geq 240$

$$x \geq 0, \ y \geq 0$$

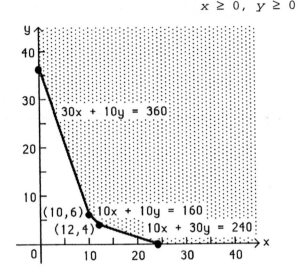

52.

animal	mouse	rat	
box A	10	20	$\leq$ 800
box B	20	10	$\leq$ 640

$$10x + 20y \leq 800$$
$$20x + 10y \leq 640$$
$$x \geq 0, \ y \geq 0$$

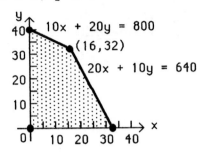

Exercise 9-5

2.

Corner points (x, y)	Objective function $z = 4x + y$
(0, 0)	0
(0, 12)	12
(7, 9)	37
(10, 0)	40

$z_{max} = 40$ at $(10, 0)$

4.

Corner points (x, y)	Objective function $z = 9x + 3y$
(0, 0)	0
(0, 12)	36
(7, 9)	90
(10, 0)	90

$z_{max} = 90$ at $(7, 9)$ and $(10, 0)$; multiple optimal solutions

6.

Corner points (x, y)	Objective function $z = 7x + 9y$
(0, 8)	72
(0, 12)	108
(12, 0)	84
(4, 3)	55

$z_{min} = 55$ at $(4, 3)$

8.

Corner points (x, y)	Objective function $z = 5x + 4y$
(0, 8)	32
(0, 12)	48
(12, 0)	60
(4, 3)	32

$z_{min} = 32$ at $(0, 8)$ and $(4, 3)$; multiple optimal solutions

10. $2x + y \leq 12 \quad \Rightarrow \quad y \leq -2x + 12$

$\qquad x + 3y \leq 21 \quad \Rightarrow \quad y \leq -\frac{1}{3}x + 7$

$\qquad x, \ y \geq 0$

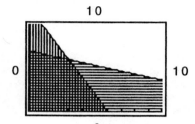

Corner points $(x, \ y)$	Objective function $z = 4x + 5y$
(0, 0)	0
(0, 7)	35
(3, 6)	42
(6, 0)	24

$z_{max} = 42$ at $(3, 6)$

12. $4x + 3y \geq 24 \quad \Rightarrow \quad y \geq -\frac{4}{3}x + 8$

$\qquad 4x + y \leq 16 \quad \Rightarrow \quad y \leq -4x + 16$

$\qquad x, \ y \geq 0$

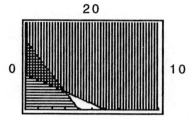

Corner points $(x, \ y)$	Objective function $z = 2x + y$
(0, 8)	8
(0, 16)	16
(3, 4)	10

$z_{min} = 8$ at $(0, 8)$

14. $3x + y \leq 24 \quad \Rightarrow \quad y \leq -3x + 24$

$\qquad x + y \leq 10 \quad \Rightarrow \quad y \leq -x + 10$

$\qquad x + 3y \leq 24 \quad \Rightarrow \quad y \leq -\frac{1}{3}x + 8$

$\qquad x, \ y \geq 0$

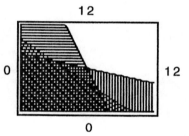

Corner points $(x, \ y)$	Objective function $z = 5x + 3y$
(0, 0)	0
(0, 8)	24
(3, 7)	36
(7, 3)	44
(8, 0)	40

$z_{max} = 44$ at $(7, 3)$

16. $2x + 3y \geq 30 \quad \Rightarrow \quad y \geq -\frac{2}{3}x + 10$

$\qquad 3x + 2y \geq 30 \quad \Rightarrow \quad y \geq -\frac{3}{2}x + 15$

$\qquad x + y \leq 15 \quad \Rightarrow \quad y \leq -x + 15$

$\qquad x, \ y \geq 0$

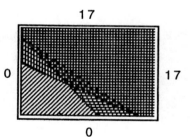

Corner points $(x, \ y)$	Objective function $z = x + 2y$
(0, 15)	30
(6, 6)	18
(15, 0)	15

$z_{min} = 15$ at $(15, 0)$

18. $x + 2y \geq 100 \implies y \geq -\frac{1}{2}x + 50$

$2x - y \leq 0 \implies y \geq 2x$

$2x + y \leq 200 \implies y \leq -2x + 200$

$x, y \geq 0$

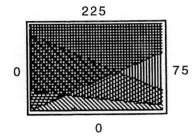

225

0   75

0

Corner points (x, y)	Objective function $z = 15x + 30y$
(0, 50)	1500
(0, 200)	6000
(50, 100)	3750
(20, 40)	1500

$z_{max} = 6000$ at (0, 200)

$z_{min} = 1500$ at (0, 50) and (20, 40); multiple optimal solutions

20. $2x + 3y \geq 120 \implies y \geq -\frac{2}{3}x + 40$

$3x + 2y \leq 360 \implies y \leq -\frac{3}{2}x + 180$

$x \leq 80$

$y \leq 120$

$x, y \geq 0$

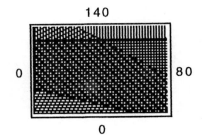

140

0   80

0

Corner points (x, y)	Objective function $z = 25x + 30y$
(0, 40)	1200
(0, 120)	3600
(40, 120)	4600
(80, 60)	3800
(80, 0)	2000
(60, 0)	1500

$z_{min} = 1200$ at (0, 40)

$z_{max} = 4600$ at (40, 120)

22. $245x + 452y \leq 4,181 \implies y \leq \frac{-245x + 4,181}{452}$

$290x + 379y \leq 3,888 \implies y \leq \frac{-290x + 3,888}{379}$

$390x + 299y \leq 4,407 \implies y \leq \frac{-390x + 4,407}{299}$

$x, y \geq 0$

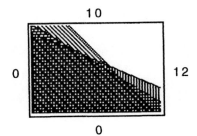

10

0   12

0

Corner points (x, y)	Objective function $P = 300x + 460y$
(0, 0)	0
(0, 9.25)	4255
(4.52, 6.8)	4484
(8.31, 3.9)	4287
(11.3, 0)	3390

$P_{max} = 4484$ at (4.52, 6.8)

24.
$$x + y \geq 4$$
$$x + 2y \geq 6$$
$$2x + 3y \leq 12$$
$$x, y \geq 0$$

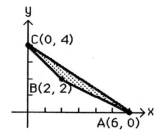

Corner points (x, y)	Objective function $z = ax + by$
$A = (6, 0)$	$6a$
$B = (2, 2)$	$2a + 2b$
$C = (0, 4)$	$4b$

(A) z_{min} at only A:

$6a < 2a + 2b$ $6a < 4b$

$4a < 2b$ **and** $a < \frac{2}{3}b$ $\Rightarrow$ $a < \frac{b}{2}$

$2a < b$ $\Rightarrow$ $a < \frac{b}{2}$

(B) z_{min} at only B:

$2a + 2b < 6a$ $2a + 2b < 4b$

$2b < 4a$ $2a < 2b$

$b < 2a$ **and** $a < b$ $\Rightarrow$ $\frac{1}{2}b < a < b$

$\frac{1}{2}b < a$

(C) z_{min} at only C:

$4b < 6a$ $4b < 2a + 2b$

$b < 1.5a$ $2b < 2a$

or $a > \frac{2}{3}b$ **and** $b < a$ or $a > b \Rightarrow a > b$

(D) z_{min} at both A and B:

$6a = 2a + 2b$ $6a < 4b$

$4a = 2b$ **and** $6a < 8a$ $\checkmark$ $\Rightarrow$ $b = 2a$

$a = \frac{1}{2}b$ or $b = 2a$

(E) z_{min} at both B and C:

$2a + 2b = 4b$ $2a + 2b < 6a$

$2a = 2b$ $2a + 2a < 6a$

$a = b$ **and** $4a < 6a$ $\checkmark$ $\Rightarrow$ $a = b$

26. Let x = # of mice, y = # of rats.

$10x + 20y \leq 800$ $\Rightarrow$ $y \leq -\frac{1}{2}x + 40$

$20x + 10y \leq 640$ $\Rightarrow$ $y \leq -2x + 64$

$x, y \geq 0$

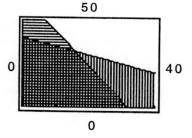

Corner points (x, y)	Objective function $z = x + y$
$(0, 0)$	0
$(0, 40)$	40
$(16, 32)$	48
$(32, 0)$	32

$z_{max} = 48$ at $(16, 32)$

48 maximum mice and rats can be used, with 16 mice and 32 rats.

28.

	students	chaperones	cost
x: bus	40	3	1200
y: van	8	1	100
	≥ 400	≤ 36	

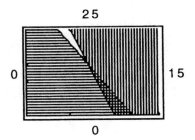

$$40x + 8y \geq 400 \implies y \geq -5x + 50$$
$$3x + y \leq 36 \implies y \leq -3x + 36$$
$$x,\ y \geq 0$$

Corner points $(x,\ y)$	Objective function $z = 1200x + 100y$
(10, 0)	12,000
(7, 15)	9,900
(12, 0)	14,400

$z_{min} = 9,900$ at (7, 15)

Rent 7 buses and 15 vans at a minimum cost of $9,900.

30.

	capital	labor	profit
x: desktop	400	40	320
y: portable	250	30	220
	$\leq 20,000$	≤ 2160	

$$400x + 250y \leq 20,000 \implies y \leq -1.6x + 80$$
$$40x + 30y \leq 2,160 \implies y \leq \frac{4}{3}x + 72$$
$$x,\ y \geq 0$$

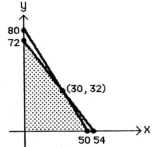

Corner points $(x,\ y)$	Objective function $z = 320x + 220y$
(0, 0)	0
(0, 72)	15,840
(30, 32)	16,640
(50, 0)	16,000

$z_{max} = 16,640$ at (30, 32)

(A) A company can produce a maximum of 72 computers, all portable (72 is the largest value for $(x,\ y)$, a corner point, and it is a y-value).

(B) By producing 72 portable computers, the profit will be $15,840. They could have a maximum profit of $16,640 by producing 30 desktop and 32 portable computers.

32. Let x = # of sociologists, y = # of research assistants.

$$10x + 30y \geq 280$$
$$30x + 10y \geq 360$$
$$x + y \leq 40$$
$$x, y \geq 0$$

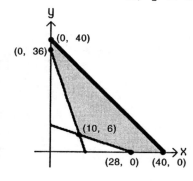

Corner points (x, y)	Objective function $C = 500x + 300y$
(0, 36)	10,800
(10, 6)	6,800
(28, 0)	14,000
(40, 0)	12,000
(0, 40)	20,000

(A) z_{min} = 6800 at (10, 6). Hire 10 sociologists and 6 research assistants for a minimum cost of $6,800.

(B) Add $y \geq x$ to the graph and delete $30x + 10y \geq 360$

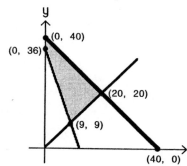

Corner points (x, y)	Objective function $C = 500x + 300y$
(0, 36)	10,800
(9, 9)	7,200
(0, 40)	12,000
(20, 20)	16,000

z_{min} = 7200 at (9, 9). Hire 9 sociologists and 9 research assistants for a minimum cost of $7,200.

34.

	calcium	iron	cholesterol	vitamin A
M	16	5	6	8
N	4	25	4	4
	≥ 320	≥ 575	≤ 300	

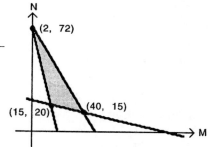

$$16M + 4N \geq 320$$
$$5M + 25N \geq 575$$
$$6M + 4N \leq 300$$
$$M, N \geq 0$$

Corner points (x, y)	Objective function $z = 8M + 4N$
(15, 20)	200
(2, 72)	304
(40, 15)	380

The amount of vitamin A will range from a minimum of 200 units when 15 ounces of food M and 20 ounces of food N are used to a maximum of 380 units when 40 ounces of food M and 15 ounces of food N are used.

CHAPTER   10

Exercise   10-1

2. $\begin{bmatrix} 0 & 8 \\ 2 & -1 \end{bmatrix} + \begin{bmatrix} 9 & -4 \\ 7 & 5 \end{bmatrix} = \begin{bmatrix} 0 + 9 & 8 - 4 \\ 2 + 7 & -1 + 5 \end{bmatrix} = \begin{bmatrix} 9 & 4 \\ 9 & 4 \end{bmatrix}$

4. $\begin{bmatrix} 6 & -2 & 3 \\ 4 & -8 & -7 \end{bmatrix} + \begin{bmatrix} 3 & 9 & -1 \\ 6 & -2 & 4 \end{bmatrix} = \begin{bmatrix} 6 + 3 & -2 + 9 & 3 - 1 \\ 4 + 6 & -8 - 2 & -7 + 4 \end{bmatrix} = \begin{bmatrix} 9 & 7 & 2 \\ 10 & -10 & -3 \end{bmatrix}$

6. $\begin{bmatrix} 6 & -2 & 3 \\ 4 & -8 & -7 \end{bmatrix} + \begin{bmatrix} 3 & 6 \\ 9 & -2 \\ -1 & 4 \end{bmatrix}$ is not defined.

8. $\begin{bmatrix} 6 & 2 \\ -4 & 1 \\ 3 & 0 \end{bmatrix} - \begin{bmatrix} 0 & 5 \\ -7 & 2 \\ -1 & 0 \end{bmatrix} = \begin{bmatrix} 6 - 0 & 2 - 5 \\ -4 + 7 & 1 - 2 \\ 3 + 1 & 0 \end{bmatrix} = \begin{bmatrix} 6 & -3 \\ 3 & -1 \\ 4 & 0 \end{bmatrix}$

10. $5 \begin{bmatrix} -7 & 3 & 0 & 9 \\ 4 & -5 & 6 & 2 \end{bmatrix} = \begin{bmatrix} -35 & 15 & 0 & 45 \\ 20 & -25 & 30 & 10 \end{bmatrix}$

12. $\underset{1 \times 2}{[-2 \quad 4]} \underset{2 \times 1}{\begin{bmatrix} 3 \\ -8 \end{bmatrix}} = [-2(3) + 4(-8)] = \underset{1 \times 1}{[-38]}$

14. $\underset{2 \times 2}{\begin{bmatrix} 3 & 7 \\ -1 & -9 \end{bmatrix}} \underset{2 \times 1}{\begin{bmatrix} 4 \\ -1 \end{bmatrix}} = \begin{bmatrix} 3(4) + 7(-1) \\ -1(4) - 9(-1) \end{bmatrix} = \underset{2 \times 1}{\begin{bmatrix} 5 \\ 5 \end{bmatrix}}$

16. $\begin{bmatrix} -2 & 7 \\ 3 & -1 \end{bmatrix} \begin{bmatrix} 4 & -1 \\ 0 & 5 \end{bmatrix} = \begin{bmatrix} -8 & 37 \\ 12 & -8 \end{bmatrix}$ **18.** $\begin{bmatrix} 7 & 0 \\ 0 & 3 \end{bmatrix} \begin{bmatrix} 9 & -2 \\ -4 & -1 \end{bmatrix} = \begin{bmatrix} 63 & -14 \\ -12 & -3 \end{bmatrix}$

20. $\underset{1 \times 2}{[-4 \quad 2]} \underset{2 \times 1}{\begin{bmatrix} -8 \\ -1 \end{bmatrix}} = [-4(-8) + 2(-1)] = \underset{1 \times 1}{[30]}$

22. $\underset{2 \times 1}{\begin{bmatrix} -8 \\ -1 \end{bmatrix}} \underset{1 \times 2}{[-4 \quad 2]} = \underset{2 \times 2}{\begin{bmatrix} 32 & -16 \\ 4 & -2 \end{bmatrix}}$

24. $\underset{1 \times 3}{[6 \quad -1 \quad 2]} \underset{3 \times 1}{\begin{bmatrix} 4 \\ 0 \\ -4 \end{bmatrix}} = [6(4) - 1(0) + 2(-4)] = \underset{1 \times 1}{[16]}$

26. $\underset{3 \times 1}{\begin{bmatrix} 4 \\ 0 \\ -4 \end{bmatrix}} \underset{1 \times 3}{[6 \quad -1 \quad 2]} = \underset{3 \times 3}{\begin{bmatrix} 24 & -4 & 8 \\ 0 & 0 & 0 \\ -24 & 4 & -8 \end{bmatrix}}$

28. $BA = \begin{bmatrix} 5 & -2 \\ 1 & 3 \end{bmatrix} \begin{bmatrix} 3 & 2 & 0 \\ -1 & 4 & -6 \end{bmatrix} = \begin{bmatrix} 17 & 2 & 12 \\ 0 & 14 & -18 \end{bmatrix}$

30. $CA = \begin{bmatrix} 1 & 2 & -4 \\ 0 & -2 & 3 \\ 5 & 0 & 4 \end{bmatrix} \begin{bmatrix} 3 & 2 & 0 \\ -1 & 4 & -6 \end{bmatrix}$ is not defined.

32. $B^2 = \begin{bmatrix} 5 & -2 \\ 1 & 3 \end{bmatrix} \begin{bmatrix} 5 & -2 \\ 1 & 3 \end{bmatrix} = \begin{bmatrix} 23 & -16 \\ 8 & 7 \end{bmatrix}$

34. $AD = \begin{bmatrix} 3 & 2 & 0 \\ -1 & 4 & -6 \end{bmatrix} \begin{bmatrix} 2 & 0 \\ -1 & 6 \\ -3 & 7 \end{bmatrix} = \begin{bmatrix} 4 & 12 \\ 12 & -18 \end{bmatrix}$

36. $-5DB = -5 \begin{bmatrix} 2 & 0 \\ -1 & 6 \\ -3 & 7 \end{bmatrix} \begin{bmatrix} 5 & -2 \\ 1 & 3 \end{bmatrix} = \begin{bmatrix} -50 & 20 \\ -5 & -100 \\ 40 & -135 \end{bmatrix}$

38. $2BA + CD = 2 \begin{bmatrix} 5 & -2 \\ 1 & 3 \end{bmatrix} \begin{bmatrix} 3 & 2 & 0 \\ -1 & 4 & -6 \end{bmatrix} + \begin{bmatrix} 1 & 2 & -4 \\ 0 & -2 & 3 \\ 5 & 0 & 4 \end{bmatrix} \begin{bmatrix} 2 & 0 \\ -1 & 6 \\ 3 & 7 \end{bmatrix}$ is not defined.

40. $3B - 2AD = 3 \begin{bmatrix} 5 & -2 \\ 1 & 3 \end{bmatrix} - 2 \begin{bmatrix} 3 & 2 & 0 \\ -1 & 4 & -6 \end{bmatrix} \begin{bmatrix} 2 & 0 \\ -1 & 6 \\ -3 & 7 \end{bmatrix} = \begin{bmatrix} 7 & -30 \\ -21 & 45 \end{bmatrix}$

42. $CDB = \begin{bmatrix} 1 & 2 & -4 \\ 0 & -2 & 3 \\ 5 & 0 & 4 \end{bmatrix} \begin{bmatrix} 2 & 0 \\ -1 & 6 \\ -3 & 7 \end{bmatrix} \begin{bmatrix} 5 & -2 \\ 1 & 3 \end{bmatrix} = \begin{bmatrix} 44 & -72 \\ -26 & 41 \\ 18 & 88 \end{bmatrix}$

44. $BAB = \begin{bmatrix} 5 & -2 \\ 1 & 3 \end{bmatrix} \begin{bmatrix} 3 & 2 & 0 \\ -1 & 4 & -6 \end{bmatrix} \begin{bmatrix} 5 & -2 \\ 1 & 3 \end{bmatrix}$ is not defined.

46. $\begin{bmatrix} w & x \\ y & z \end{bmatrix} + \begin{bmatrix} -3 & 6 \\ -2 & 1 \end{bmatrix} = \begin{bmatrix} -4 & 7 \\ 2 & -5 \end{bmatrix}$

$w - 3 = -4 \Rightarrow w = -1$
$x + 6 = 7 \Rightarrow x = 1$
$y - 2 = 2 \Rightarrow y = 4$
$z + 1 = -5 \Rightarrow z = -6$

48. $\begin{bmatrix} x & 5 \\ 8 & x \end{bmatrix} + \begin{bmatrix} 2y & 2 \\ 1 & -y \end{bmatrix} = \begin{bmatrix} 4 & 7 \\ 9 & 7 \end{bmatrix}$

$x + 2y = 4$
$x - y = 7$ which has solution $x = 6$, $y = -1$

50. $\begin{bmatrix} w & x \\ y & z \end{bmatrix} \begin{bmatrix} 1 & 5 \\ 0 & -1 \end{bmatrix} = \begin{bmatrix} 1 & 0 \\ 0 & 1 \end{bmatrix}$

$w(1) + x(0) = 1 \Rightarrow w = 1$
$w(5) + x(-1) = 0 \Rightarrow 5 - x = 0 \Rightarrow x = 5$
$y(1) + z(0) = 0 \Rightarrow y = 0$
$y(5) + z(-1) = 1 \Rightarrow 0 - z = 1 \Rightarrow z = -1$

52. $\begin{bmatrix} w & x \\ y & z \end{bmatrix} \begin{bmatrix} 4 & -3 \\ -3 & 2 \end{bmatrix} = \begin{bmatrix} 8 & 7 \\ 4 & -4 \end{bmatrix}$

$4w - 3x = 8$
$-3w + 2x = 7$ which has solution $w = -37$, $x = -52$

$4y - 3z = 4$
$-3y + 2z = -4$ which has solution $y = 4$, $z = 4$

54. True; $\begin{bmatrix} a & 0 \\ 0 & d \end{bmatrix}\begin{bmatrix} b & 0 \\ 0 & c \end{bmatrix} = \begin{bmatrix} ab & 0 \\ 0 & dc \end{bmatrix}$ is a 2 × 2 diagonal matrix.

56. False; $\begin{bmatrix} 1 & 3 \\ 2 & 4 \end{bmatrix}\begin{bmatrix} 2 & 3 \\ 4 & 1 \end{bmatrix} = \begin{bmatrix} 14 & 6 \\ 20 & 10 \end{bmatrix}$

$\begin{bmatrix} 2 & 3 \\ 4 & 1 \end{bmatrix}\begin{bmatrix} 1 & 3 \\ 2 & 4 \end{bmatrix} = \begin{bmatrix} 8 & 18 \\ 6 & 16 \end{bmatrix}$

58. True; $\begin{bmatrix} a & b \\ c & d \end{bmatrix} + \begin{bmatrix} e & f \\ g & h \end{bmatrix} = \begin{bmatrix} a+e & b+f \\ c+g & d+h \end{bmatrix} = \begin{bmatrix} e+a & f+b \\ g+c & h+d \end{bmatrix} = \begin{bmatrix} e & f \\ g & h \end{bmatrix} + \begin{bmatrix} a & b \\ c & d \end{bmatrix}$

60. False; $\begin{bmatrix} 1 & 0 \\ 0 & 0 \end{bmatrix}\begin{bmatrix} 0 & 0 \\ 0 & 1 \end{bmatrix} = \begin{bmatrix} 0 & 0 \\ 0 & 0 \end{bmatrix}$

62. False; Let $A = B = \begin{bmatrix} 1 & 0 \\ 0 & 0 \end{bmatrix}$; $AB = \begin{bmatrix} 1 & 0 \\ 0 & 0 \end{bmatrix} = B$. A is not the identity matrix.

64. True; $\begin{bmatrix} a & 0 \\ 0 & b \end{bmatrix}\begin{bmatrix} a & 0 \\ 0 & b \end{bmatrix} = \begin{bmatrix} a^2 & 0 \\ 0 & b^2 \end{bmatrix} = \begin{bmatrix} 0 & 0 \\ 0 & 0 \end{bmatrix} \Rightarrow a = 0,\ b = 0$

66. $\frac{1}{2}(1.2A + B) = \frac{1}{2}\left(1.2\begin{bmatrix} 30 & 25 \\ 60 & 80 \end{bmatrix} + \begin{bmatrix} 36 & 27 \\ 54 & 74 \end{bmatrix}\right) = \begin{matrix} \text{Guitar} & \text{Banjo} \\ \begin{bmatrix} \$36 & \$28.5 \\ \$63 & \$85 \end{bmatrix} & \begin{matrix} \text{Materials} \\ \text{Labor} \end{matrix} \end{matrix}$

68.

	Basic Car	Air	Markup AM/FM radio	Cruise control
Model A	$3,505	$82	$44	$29
Model B	$2,250	$99	$100	$53
Model C	$1,365	$120	$127	$55

$1.15N - 1.20M = $ (the matrix above)

70. (A) retail value of inventory at store 2 =
   $2(840) + 3(1800) + 5(2400) + 0(3300) + 6(4900) = \$48,480$

   (B) wholesale value of inventory at store 3 =
   $10(700) + 4(1400) + 3(1800) + 4(2700) + 3(3500) = \$39,300$

   (C) MN gives the total wholesale and retail values of each store.

   (D)

$$MN = \begin{matrix} W & R \\ \begin{bmatrix} \$33,400 & \$42,160 \\ \$35,600 & \$48,480 \\ \$39,300 & \$50,700 \end{bmatrix} & \begin{matrix} S1 \\ S2 \\ S3 \end{matrix} \end{matrix}$$

Total wholesale and retail values of each store.

   (E) $[1 \quad 1 \quad 1]M = [16 \quad 9 \quad 11 \quad 11 \quad 10]$

   (F) $M\begin{bmatrix} 1 \\ 1 \\ 1 \\ 1 \\ 1 \end{bmatrix} = \begin{bmatrix} 17 \\ 16 \\ 24 \end{bmatrix}$

72. $A = \begin{bmatrix} 0 & 0 & 0 & 1 & 1 \\ 1 & 0 & 0 & 1 & 0 \\ 0 & 1 & 0 & 0 & 0 \\ 1 & 0 & 0 & 0 & 1 \\ 0 & 1 & 1 & 0 & 0 \end{bmatrix}$; $A + A^2 + A^3 = \begin{bmatrix} 2 & 3 & 2 & 3 & 3 \\ 3 & 2 & 2 & 3 & 4 \\ 2 & 1 & 0 & 2 & 2 \\ 3 & 3 & 2 & 2 & 3 \\ 3 & 2 & 1 & 3 & 2 \end{bmatrix}$

It is possible to travel from any origin to any destination with at most 2 intermediate connections.

74. (A) $[4 \quad 2] \cdot \begin{bmatrix} 15 \\ 5 \end{bmatrix} = 70$ g of protein in mix X

(B) $[3 \quad 1] \cdot \begin{bmatrix} 5 \\ 15 \end{bmatrix} = 30$ g of fat in mix Z

(C) MN gives the total amounts in grams of protein, carbohydrates, and fat in 20 oz. of each mix.

(D) $\begin{bmatrix} 4 & 2 \\ 20 & 16 \\ 3 & 1 \end{bmatrix} \begin{bmatrix} 15 & 10 & 5 \\ 5 & 10 & 15 \end{bmatrix} = \begin{matrix} & X & Y & Z \\ \begin{bmatrix} 70g & 60g & 50g \\ 380g & 360g & 340g \\ 50g & 40g & 30g \end{bmatrix} & \end{matrix} \begin{matrix} \text{protein} \\ \text{carbohydrates} \\ \text{fat} \end{matrix}$

in 20 oz of each mix

Exercise 10-2

2. $\begin{bmatrix} 1 & 0 \\ 0 & 1 \end{bmatrix} \begin{bmatrix} -4 & 9 \\ 7 & -2 \end{bmatrix} = \begin{bmatrix} -4 & 9 \\ 7 & -2 \end{bmatrix}$

4. $\begin{bmatrix} 2 & 0 \\ -7 & -6 \end{bmatrix} \begin{bmatrix} 1 & 0 \\ 0 & 1 \end{bmatrix} = \begin{bmatrix} 2 & 0 \\ -7 & -6 \end{bmatrix}$

6. $\begin{bmatrix} 1 & 0 & 0 \\ 0 & 1 & 0 \\ 0 & 0 & 1 \end{bmatrix} \begin{bmatrix} 8 & 0 & 3 \\ -2 & -1 & -3 \\ 4 & -6 & 1 \end{bmatrix} = \begin{bmatrix} 8 & 0 & 3 \\ -2 & -1 & -3 \\ 4 & -6 & 1 \end{bmatrix}$

8. $\begin{bmatrix} 5 & 1 & 0 \\ 1 & -4 & 1 \\ 0 & 1 & 9 \end{bmatrix} \begin{bmatrix} 1 & 0 & 0 \\ 0 & 1 & 0 \\ 0 & 0 & 1 \end{bmatrix} = \begin{bmatrix} 5 & 1 & 0 \\ 1 & -4 & 1 \\ 0 & 1 & 9 \end{bmatrix}$

10. $\begin{bmatrix} 1 & 0 \\ -3 & 1 \end{bmatrix} \begin{bmatrix} 1 & 0 \\ 3 & 1 \end{bmatrix} = \begin{bmatrix} 1(1) + 0(3) & 1(0) + 0(1) \\ -3(1) + 1(3) & -3(0) + 1(1) \end{bmatrix} = \begin{bmatrix} 1 & 0 \\ 0 & 1 \end{bmatrix}$

12. $\begin{bmatrix} -6 & 5 \\ -5 & 4 \end{bmatrix} \begin{bmatrix} 4 & -5 \\ 5 & -6 \end{bmatrix} = \begin{bmatrix} 1 & 0 \\ 0 & 1 \end{bmatrix}$

14. $\begin{bmatrix} 1 & 0 & 0 \\ 2 & 1 & 0 \\ -6 & -3 & 1 \end{bmatrix} \begin{bmatrix} 1 & 0 & 0 \\ -2 & 1 & 0 \\ 0 & 3 & 1 \end{bmatrix} = \begin{bmatrix} 1 & 0 & 0 \\ 0 & 1 & 0 \\ 0 & 0 & 1 \end{bmatrix}$

16. $M = \begin{bmatrix} 0 & -1 \\ -1 & 3 \end{bmatrix}$, $M^{-1} = \begin{bmatrix} -3 & -1 \\ -1 & 0 \end{bmatrix}$; $M^{-1}M = \begin{bmatrix} -3 & -1 \\ -1 & 0 \end{bmatrix} \begin{bmatrix} 0 & -1 \\ -1 & 3 \end{bmatrix} = \begin{bmatrix} 1 & 0 \\ 0 & 1 \end{bmatrix}$

18. $M = \begin{bmatrix} 3 & -4 \\ -2 & 3 \end{bmatrix}$, $M^{-1} = \begin{bmatrix} 3 & 4 \\ 2 & 3 \end{bmatrix}$; $M^{-1}M = \begin{bmatrix} 3 & 4 \\ 2 & 3 \end{bmatrix}\begin{bmatrix} 3 & -4 \\ -2 & 3 \end{bmatrix} = \begin{bmatrix} 1 & 0 \\ 0 & 1 \end{bmatrix}$

20. $M = \begin{bmatrix} 11 & 4 \\ 3 & 1 \end{bmatrix}$, $M^{-1} = \begin{bmatrix} -1 & 4 \\ 3 & -11 \end{bmatrix}$; $M^{-1}M = \begin{bmatrix} -1 & 4 \\ 3 & -11 \end{bmatrix}\begin{bmatrix} 11 & 4 \\ 3 & 1 \end{bmatrix} = \begin{bmatrix} 1 & 0 \\ 0 & 1 \end{bmatrix}$

22. $M = \begin{bmatrix} 2 & -1 & 0 \\ 0 & 1 & 1 \\ 1 & 0 & 1 \end{bmatrix}$, $M^{-1} = \begin{bmatrix} 1 & 1 & -1 \\ 1 & 2 & -2 \\ -1 & -1 & 2 \end{bmatrix}$

$M^{-1}M = \begin{bmatrix} 1 & 1 & -1 \\ 1 & 2 & -2 \\ -1 & -1 & 2 \end{bmatrix}\begin{bmatrix} 2 & -1 & 0 \\ 0 & 1 & 1 \\ 1 & 0 & 1 \end{bmatrix} = \begin{bmatrix} 1 & 0 & 0 \\ 0 & 1 & 0 \\ 0 & 0 & 1 \end{bmatrix}$

24. $M = \begin{bmatrix} 1 & -1 & 1 \\ -2 & 3 & 2 \\ 3 & -3 & 2 \end{bmatrix}$, $M^{-1} = \begin{bmatrix} -12 & 1 & 5 \\ -10 & 1 & 4 \\ 3 & 0 & -1 \end{bmatrix}$

$M^{-1}M = \begin{bmatrix} -12 & 1 & 5 \\ -10 & 1 & 4 \\ 3 & 0 & -1 \end{bmatrix}\begin{bmatrix} 1 & -1 & 1 \\ -2 & 3 & 2 \\ 3 & -3 & 2 \end{bmatrix} = \begin{bmatrix} 1 & 0 & 0 \\ 0 & 1 & 0 \\ 0 & 0 & 1 \end{bmatrix}$

26. $\begin{bmatrix} 2 & -4 & | & 1 & 0 \\ -3 & 6 & | & 0 & 1 \end{bmatrix} \rightarrow \begin{bmatrix} 1 & -2 & | & -1 & -1 \\ 0 & 0 & | & -3 & -2 \end{bmatrix} \Rightarrow$ inverse does not exist

28. $\begin{bmatrix} -5 & 4 & | & 1 & 0 \\ 4 & -3 & | & 0 & 1 \end{bmatrix} \rightarrow \begin{bmatrix} 1 & 0 & | & 3 & 4 \\ 0 & 1 & | & 4 & 5 \end{bmatrix}$

30. $\begin{bmatrix} 4 & 2 & -1 & | & 1 & 0 & 0 \\ 1 & 1 & -1 & | & 0 & 1 & 0 \\ -3 & -1 & 1 & | & 0 & 0 & 1 \end{bmatrix} \rightarrow \begin{bmatrix} 1 & 0 & 0 & | & 0 & -\frac{1}{2} & -\frac{1}{2} \\ 0 & 1 & 0 & | & 1 & \frac{1}{2} & \frac{3}{2} \\ 0 & 0 & 1 & | & 1 & -1 & 1 \end{bmatrix}$

32. $\begin{bmatrix} 1 & -1 & 0 & | & 1 & 0 & 0 \\ 2 & -1 & 1 & | & 0 & 1 & 0 \\ 0 & 1 & 1 & | & 0 & 0 & 1 \end{bmatrix} \rightarrow \begin{bmatrix} 1 & 0 & 1 & | & -1 & 1 & 0 \\ 0 & 1 & 1 & | & -2 & 1 & 0 \\ 0 & 0 & 0 & | & 2 & -1 & 1 \end{bmatrix} \Rightarrow$ inverse does not exist

34. $\begin{bmatrix} 1 & -5 & -10 & | & 1 & 0 & 0 \\ 0 & 1 & 6 & | & 0 & 1 & 0 \\ 1 & -4 & -3 & | & 0 & 0 & 1 \end{bmatrix} \rightarrow \begin{bmatrix} 1 & 0 & 0 & | & 21 & 25 & -20 \\ 0 & 1 & 0 & | & 6 & 7 & -6 \\ 0 & 0 & 1 & | & -1 & -1 & 1 \end{bmatrix}$

36. $A = \begin{bmatrix} 3 & 4 \\ 2 & 3 \end{bmatrix}$, $A^{-1} = \begin{bmatrix} 3 & -4 \\ -2 & 3 \end{bmatrix}$, $B = \begin{bmatrix} 3 & 7 \\ 2 & 5 \end{bmatrix}$, $B^{-1} = \begin{bmatrix} 5 & -7 \\ -2 & 3 \end{bmatrix}$

$AB = \begin{bmatrix} 3 & 4 \\ 2 & 3 \end{bmatrix}\begin{bmatrix} 3 & 7 \\ 2 & 5 \end{bmatrix} = \begin{bmatrix} 17 & 41 \\ 12 & 29 \end{bmatrix}$, $(AB)^{-1} = \begin{bmatrix} 17 & 41 \\ 12 & 29 \end{bmatrix}^{-1} = \begin{bmatrix} 29 & -41 \\ -12 & 17 \end{bmatrix}$

$B^{-1}A^{-1} = \begin{bmatrix} 5 & -7 \\ -2 & 3 \end{bmatrix}\begin{bmatrix} 3 & -4 \\ -2 & 3 \end{bmatrix} = \begin{bmatrix} 29 & -41 \\ -12 & 17 \end{bmatrix}$

38. M^{-1} exists if and only if a and d are both nonzero.

40. $\begin{bmatrix} 1 & -2 & -1 & 0 \\ 2 & 1 & 3 & 5 \\ 1 & 0 & -3 & 2 \\ 0 & 4 & 2 & 6 \end{bmatrix}^{-1} = \begin{bmatrix} -1.55 & 0.9 & 0.75 & -1 \\ -1.3 & 0.4 & 0.5 & -0.5 \\ 0.05 & 0.1 & -0.25 & 0 \\ 0.85 & -0.3 & -0.25 & 0.5 \end{bmatrix}$

42. $\begin{bmatrix} 1 & -1 & -6 & -1 & 3 \\ -2 & 2 & 0 & 2 & 1 \\ 4 & -2 & 0 & -3 & 1 \\ 1 & 3 & 1 & 4 & 2 \\ -1 & 3 & 1 & 1 & 4 \end{bmatrix}^{-1} = \begin{bmatrix} -1 & 16.375 & 7.875 & -1.375 & -4.625 \\ -4 & 65.125 & 30.625 & -6.125 & -17.875 \\ 1 & -18.75 & -8.75 & 1.75 & 5.25 \\ 2 & -32.25 & -15.25 & 3.25 & 8.75 \\ 2 & -32 & -15 & 3 & 9 \end{bmatrix}$

44. F O X   I N   S O C K S
6 15 24 27 9 14 27 19 15 3 11 19

$\begin{bmatrix} 3 & 5 \\ 1 & 2 \end{bmatrix}\begin{bmatrix} 6 & 24 & 9 & 27 & 15 & 11 \\ 15 & 27 & 14 & 19 & 3 & 19 \end{bmatrix} \Rightarrow$ 93, 36, 207, 78, 97, 37, 176, 65, 60, 21, 128, 49

46. $\begin{bmatrix} 3 & 5 \\ 1 & 2 \end{bmatrix}^{-1}\begin{bmatrix} 99 & 154 & 115 & 121 & 20 & 149 & 86 & 196 & 99 \\ 38 & 58 & 43 & 43 & 7 & 56 & 29 & 73 & 38 \end{bmatrix} \Rightarrow$
8 15 18 20 15 14 27 8 5 1 18 19 27 1 27 23 8 15
H O R T O N   H E A R S   A   W H O

48. J O H N   F I T Z G E R A L D   K E N N E D Y
10 15 8 14 27 6 9 20 26 7 5 18 1 12 4 27 11 5 14 14 5 4 25

$\begin{bmatrix} 1 & 0 & 1 & 0 & 1 \\ 0 & 1 & 1 & 0 & 3 \\ 2 & 1 & 1 & 1 & 1 \\ 0 & 0 & 1 & 0 & 2 \\ 1 & 1 & 1 & 2 & 1 \end{bmatrix}\begin{bmatrix} 10 & 6 & 5 & 27 & 5 \\ 15 & 9 & 18 & 11 & 4 \\ 8 & 20 & 1 & 5 & 25 \\ 14 & 26 & 12 & 14 & 27 \\ 27 & 7 & 4 & 14 & 27 \end{bmatrix} \Rightarrow$

45, 104, 84, 62, 88, 33, 50, 74, 34, 94, 10, 31, 45, 9, 52, 46, 58, 98, 33, 85, 57, 110, 93, 79, 115

50. $\begin{bmatrix} 1 & 0 & 1 & 0 & 1 \\ 0 & 1 & 1 & 0 & 3 \\ 2 & 1 & 1 & 1 & 1 \\ 0 & 0 & 1 & 0 & 2 \\ 1 & 1 & 1 & 2 & 1 \end{bmatrix}^{-1}\begin{bmatrix} 22 & 54 & 46 & 51 & 68 \\ 15 & 58 & 80 & 68 & 135 \\ 57 & 89 & 87 & 116 & 136 \\ 5 & 45 & 53 & 39 & 81 \\ 47 & 84 & 96 & 113 & 149 \end{bmatrix} \Rightarrow$

18 9 3 8 1 18 4   27 13 9 12 8 15 21 19 27 14 9 24 15 14 27 27 27 27
R I C H A R D   M I L H O U S   N I X O N

Exercise 10-3

2. $\begin{bmatrix} -3 & 1 \\ -1 & 2 \end{bmatrix}\begin{bmatrix} x_1 \\ x_2 \end{bmatrix} = \begin{bmatrix} -2 \\ 5 \end{bmatrix} \Rightarrow \begin{array}{rcl} -3x_1 + x_2 &=& -2 \\ -x_1 + 2x_2 &=& 5 \end{array}$

4. $\begin{bmatrix} 1 & -2 & 0 \\ -3 & 1 & -1 \\ 2 & 0 & 4 \end{bmatrix}\begin{bmatrix} x_1 \\ x_2 \\ x_3 \end{bmatrix} = \begin{bmatrix} 3 \\ -2 \\ 5 \end{bmatrix} \Rightarrow \begin{array}{rcl} x_1 - 2x_2 + 0x_3 &=& 3 \\ -3x_1 + x_2 - x_3 &=& -2 \\ 2x_1 + 0x_2 + 4x_3 &=& 5 \end{array}$

6. $\begin{array}{rcl} x_1 - 2x_2 &=& 7 \\ -3x_1 + x_2 &=& -3 \end{array} \Rightarrow \begin{bmatrix} 1 & -2 \\ -3 & 1 \end{bmatrix}\begin{bmatrix} x_1 \\ x_2 \end{bmatrix} = \begin{bmatrix} 7 \\ -3 \end{bmatrix}$

8. $\begin{array}{rcl} 2x_1 \quad\quad + 3x_3 &=& 5 \\ x_1 - 2x_2 + x_3 &=& -4 \\ -x_1 + 3x_2 \quad\quad &=& 2 \end{array} \Rightarrow \begin{bmatrix} 2 & 0 & 3 \\ 1 & -2 & 1 \\ -1 & 3 & 0 \end{bmatrix}\begin{bmatrix} x_1 \\ x_2 \\ x_3 \end{bmatrix} = \begin{bmatrix} 5 \\ -4 \\ 2 \end{bmatrix}$

10. $\begin{bmatrix} x_1 \\ x_2 \end{bmatrix} = \begin{bmatrix} -2 & 1 \\ -1 & 2 \end{bmatrix}\begin{bmatrix} 3 \\ -2 \end{bmatrix} = \begin{bmatrix} -8 \\ -7 \end{bmatrix} \Rightarrow x_1 = -8, \ x_2 = -7$

12. $\begin{bmatrix} x_1 \\ x_2 \end{bmatrix} = \begin{bmatrix} 3 & -1 \\ 0 & 2 \end{bmatrix}\begin{bmatrix} -2 \\ 1 \end{bmatrix} = \begin{bmatrix} -7 \\ 2 \end{bmatrix} \Rightarrow x_1 = -7, \ x_2 = 2$

14. (A) $3x_1 - 4x_2 = 3$
$-2x_1 + 3x_2 = -1$

$\begin{bmatrix} 3 & -4 \\ -2 & 3 \end{bmatrix}\begin{bmatrix} x_1 \\ x_2 \end{bmatrix} = \begin{bmatrix} 3 \\ -1 \end{bmatrix}$

$\begin{bmatrix} x_1 \\ x_2 \end{bmatrix} = \begin{bmatrix} 3 & -4 \\ -2 & 3 \end{bmatrix}^{-1}\begin{bmatrix} 3 \\ -1 \end{bmatrix}$

$\begin{bmatrix} x_1 \\ x_2 \end{bmatrix} = \begin{bmatrix} 3 & 4 \\ 2 & 3 \end{bmatrix}\begin{bmatrix} 3 \\ -1 \end{bmatrix}$

$\begin{bmatrix} x_1 \\ x_2 \end{bmatrix} = \begin{bmatrix} 5 \\ 3 \end{bmatrix}$

(B) $3x_1 - 4x_2 = 6$
$-2x_1 + 3x_2 = 5$

$\begin{bmatrix} x_1 \\ x_2 \end{bmatrix} = \begin{bmatrix} 3 & 4 \\ 2 & 3 \end{bmatrix}\begin{bmatrix} 6 \\ 5 \end{bmatrix} = \begin{bmatrix} 38 \\ 27 \end{bmatrix}$

(C) $3x_1 - 4x_2 = 0$
$-2x_1 + 3x_2 = -4$

$\begin{bmatrix} x_1 \\ x_2 \end{bmatrix} = \begin{bmatrix} 3 & 4 \\ 2 & 3 \end{bmatrix}\begin{bmatrix} 0 \\ -4 \end{bmatrix} = \begin{bmatrix} -16 \\ -12 \end{bmatrix}$

16. (A) $11x_1 + 4x_2 = -2$
$3x_1 + x_2 = -3$

$\begin{bmatrix} 11 & 4 \\ 3 & 1 \end{bmatrix}\begin{bmatrix} x_1 \\ x_2 \end{bmatrix} = \begin{bmatrix} -2 \\ -3 \end{bmatrix}$

$\begin{bmatrix} x_1 \\ x_2 \end{bmatrix} = \begin{bmatrix} 11 & 4 \\ 3 & 1 \end{bmatrix}^{-1}\begin{bmatrix} -2 \\ -3 \end{bmatrix}$

$\begin{bmatrix} x_1 \\ x_2 \end{bmatrix} = \begin{bmatrix} -1 & 4 \\ 3 & -11 \end{bmatrix}\begin{bmatrix} -2 \\ -3 \end{bmatrix}$

$\begin{bmatrix} x_1 \\ x_2 \end{bmatrix} = \begin{bmatrix} -10 \\ 27 \end{bmatrix}$

(B) $11x_1 + 4x_2 = -1$
$3x_1 + x_2 = 9$

$\begin{bmatrix} x_1 \\ x_2 \end{bmatrix} = \begin{bmatrix} -1 & 4 \\ 3 & -11 \end{bmatrix}\begin{bmatrix} -1 \\ 9 \end{bmatrix} = \begin{bmatrix} 37 \\ -102 \end{bmatrix}$

(C) $11x_1 + 4x_2 = 4$
$3x_1 + x_2 = 5$

$\begin{bmatrix} x_1 \\ x_2 \end{bmatrix} = \begin{bmatrix} -1 & 4 \\ 3 & -11 \end{bmatrix}\begin{bmatrix} 4 \\ 5 \end{bmatrix} = \begin{bmatrix} 16 \\ -43 \end{bmatrix}$

18. (A) $2x_1 - x_2 \quad\quad = -2$
$x_2 + x_3 = 4$
$x_1 \quad\quad + x_3 = -1$

$\begin{bmatrix} 2 & -1 & 0 \\ 0 & 1 & 1 \\ 1 & 0 & 1 \end{bmatrix}\begin{bmatrix} x_1 \\ x_2 \\ x_3 \end{bmatrix} = \begin{bmatrix} -2 \\ 4 \\ -1 \end{bmatrix}$

$\begin{bmatrix} x_1 \\ x_2 \\ x_3 \end{bmatrix} = \begin{bmatrix} 2 & -1 & 0 \\ 0 & 1 & 1 \\ 1 & 0 & 1 \end{bmatrix}^{-1}\begin{bmatrix} -2 \\ 4 \\ -1 \end{bmatrix}$

$\begin{bmatrix} x_1 \\ x_2 \\ x_3 \end{bmatrix} = \begin{bmatrix} 1 & 1 & -1 \\ 1 & 2 & -2 \\ -1 & -1 & 2 \end{bmatrix}\begin{bmatrix} -2 \\ 4 \\ -1 \end{bmatrix}$

$\begin{bmatrix} x_1 \\ x_2 \\ x_3 \end{bmatrix} = \begin{bmatrix} 3 \\ 8 \\ -4 \end{bmatrix}$

(B) $2x_1 - x_2 \quad\quad = 2$
$x_2 + x_3 = -3$
$x_1 \quad\quad + x_3 = 1$

$\begin{bmatrix} x_1 \\ x_2 \\ x_3 \end{bmatrix} = \begin{bmatrix} 1 & 1 & -1 \\ 1 & 2 & -2 \\ -1 & -1 & 2 \end{bmatrix}\begin{bmatrix} 2 \\ -3 \\ 1 \end{bmatrix} = \begin{bmatrix} -2 \\ -6 \\ 3 \end{bmatrix}$

(C) $2x_1 - x_2 \quad\quad = -1$
$x_2 + x_3 = 2$
$x_1 \quad\quad + x_3 = -5$

$\begin{bmatrix} x_1 \\ x_2 \\ x_3 \end{bmatrix} = \begin{bmatrix} 1 & 1 & -1 \\ 1 & 2 & -2 \\ -1 & -1 & 2 \end{bmatrix}\begin{bmatrix} -1 \\ 2 \\ -5 \end{bmatrix} = \begin{bmatrix} 6 \\ 13 \\ -11 \end{bmatrix}$

20. (A) $\begin{aligned} x_1 - x_2 + x_3 &= 3 \\ -2x_1 + 3x_2 + 2x_3 &= -1 \\ 3x_1 - 3x_2 + 2x_3 &= 0 \end{aligned}$

$$\begin{bmatrix} 1 & -1 & 1 \\ -2 & 3 & 2 \\ 3 & -3 & 2 \end{bmatrix}\begin{bmatrix} x_1 \\ x_2 \\ x_3 \end{bmatrix} = \begin{bmatrix} 3 \\ -1 \\ 0 \end{bmatrix}$$

$$\begin{bmatrix} x_1 \\ x_2 \\ x_3 \end{bmatrix} = \begin{bmatrix} 1 & -1 & 1 \\ -2 & 3 & 2 \\ 3 & -3 & 2 \end{bmatrix}^{-1}\begin{bmatrix} 3 \\ -1 \\ 0 \end{bmatrix}$$

$$\begin{bmatrix} x_1 \\ x_2 \\ x_3 \end{bmatrix} = \begin{bmatrix} -12 & 1 & 5 \\ -10 & 1 & 4 \\ 3 & 0 & -1 \end{bmatrix}\begin{bmatrix} 3 \\ -1 \\ 0 \end{bmatrix}$$

$$\begin{bmatrix} x_1 \\ x_2 \\ x_3 \end{bmatrix} = \begin{bmatrix} -37 \\ -31 \\ 9 \end{bmatrix}$$

(B) $\begin{aligned} x_1 - x_2 + x_3 &= 0 \\ -2x_1 + 3x_2 + 2x_3 &= 4 \\ 3x_1 - 3x_2 + 2x_3 &= 5 \end{aligned}$

$$\begin{bmatrix} x_1 \\ x_2 \\ x_3 \end{bmatrix} = \begin{bmatrix} -12 & 1 & 5 \\ -10 & 1 & 4 \\ 3 & 0 & -1 \end{bmatrix}\begin{bmatrix} 0 \\ 4 \\ 5 \end{bmatrix} = \begin{bmatrix} 29 \\ 24 \\ -5 \end{bmatrix}$$

(C) $\begin{aligned} x_1 - x_2 + x_3 &= -2 \\ -2x_1 + 3x_2 + 2x_3 &= 0 \\ 3x_1 - 3x_2 + 2x_3 &= 1 \end{aligned}$

$$\begin{bmatrix} x_1 \\ x_2 \\ x_3 \end{bmatrix} = \begin{bmatrix} -12 & 1 & 5 \\ -10 & 1 & 4 \\ 3 & 0 & -1 \end{bmatrix}\begin{bmatrix} -2 \\ 0 \\ 1 \end{bmatrix} = \begin{bmatrix} 29 \\ 24 \\ -7 \end{bmatrix}$$

22. $\begin{aligned} AX + BX &= C + D \\ X(A + B) &= C + D \\ X &= (A + B)^{-1}(C + D) \end{aligned}$

24. $\begin{aligned} X + C &= AX - BX \\ C &= AX - BX - IX \\ C &= X(A - B - I) \\ X &= (A - B - I)^{-1}C \end{aligned}$

26. $\begin{aligned} AX + C &= BX - 7X + D \\ AX - BX + 7X &= D - C \\ X(A - B + 7I) &= D - C \\ X &= (A - B + 7I)^{-1}(D - C) \end{aligned}$

28. (A) $\begin{aligned} x_1 - 4.001x_2 &= 1 \\ x_1 - 4x_2 &= 1 \end{aligned}$

$$\begin{bmatrix} 1 & -4.001 \\ 1 & -4 \end{bmatrix}\begin{bmatrix} x_1 \\ x_2 \end{bmatrix} = \begin{bmatrix} 1 \\ 1 \end{bmatrix}$$

$$\begin{bmatrix} x_1 \\ x_2 \end{bmatrix} = \begin{bmatrix} 1 & -4.001 \\ 1 & -4 \end{bmatrix}^{-1}\begin{bmatrix} 1 \\ 1 \end{bmatrix}$$

$$\begin{bmatrix} x_1 \\ x_2 \end{bmatrix} = \begin{bmatrix} -4000 & 4001 \\ -1000 & 1000 \end{bmatrix}\begin{bmatrix} 1 \\ 1 \end{bmatrix}$$

$$\begin{bmatrix} x_1 \\ x_2 \end{bmatrix} = \begin{bmatrix} 1 \\ 0 \end{bmatrix}$$

(B) $\begin{aligned} x_1 - 4.001x_2 &= 1 \\ x_1 - 4x_2 &= 0 \end{aligned}$

$$\begin{bmatrix} x_1 \\ x_2 \end{bmatrix} = \begin{bmatrix} -4000 & 4001 \\ -1000 & 1000 \end{bmatrix}\begin{bmatrix} 1 \\ 0 \end{bmatrix} = \begin{bmatrix} -4000 \\ -1000 \end{bmatrix}$$

(C) $\begin{aligned} x_1 - 4.001x_2 &= 0 \\ x_1 - 4x_2 &= 1 \end{aligned}$

$$\begin{bmatrix} x_1 \\ x_2 \end{bmatrix} = \begin{bmatrix} -4000 & 4001 \\ -1000 & 1000 \end{bmatrix}\begin{bmatrix} 0 \\ 1 \end{bmatrix} = \begin{bmatrix} 4001 \\ 1000 \end{bmatrix}$$

Small changes in the constant terms can have large impact on the solution set.

30. $\begin{bmatrix} x_1 \\ x_2 \\ x_3 \end{bmatrix} = \begin{bmatrix} 1 & 5 & 4 \\ 6 & -1 & 7 \\ 4 & 6 & 1 \end{bmatrix}^{-1}\begin{bmatrix} 99 \\ 75 \\ 125 \end{bmatrix} = \begin{bmatrix} 9 \\ 14 \\ 5 \end{bmatrix}$

32. $\begin{bmatrix} x_1 \\ x_2 \\ x_3 \\ x_4 \end{bmatrix} = \begin{bmatrix} 1 & 9 & 1 & 2 \\ 4 & 8 & -5 & 1 \\ 2 & 5 & -6 & 3 \\ 6 & 4 & 1 & 8 \end{bmatrix}^{-1}\begin{bmatrix} 71 \\ 99 \\ 113 \\ 81 \end{bmatrix} = \begin{bmatrix} -3 \\ 7 \\ -9 \\ 10 \end{bmatrix}$

34. $\begin{bmatrix} 30 & 40 \\ 20 & 30 \end{bmatrix} \begin{bmatrix} A \\ B \end{bmatrix} = \begin{bmatrix} 1800 \\ 1200 \end{bmatrix}$

Allocation 1: $\begin{bmatrix} A \\ B \end{bmatrix} = \begin{bmatrix} 30 & 40 \\ 20 & 30 \end{bmatrix}^{-1} \cdot \begin{bmatrix} 1800 \\ 1200 \end{bmatrix} = \begin{bmatrix} 0.3 & -0.4 \\ -0.2 & 0.3 \end{bmatrix} \begin{bmatrix} 1800 \\ 1200 \end{bmatrix} = \begin{bmatrix} 60 \\ 0 \end{bmatrix}$

Allocation 2: $\begin{bmatrix} A \\ B \end{bmatrix} = \begin{bmatrix} 0.3 & -0.4 \\ -0.2 & 0.3 \end{bmatrix} \begin{bmatrix} 1750 \\ 1250 \end{bmatrix} = \begin{bmatrix} 25 \\ 25 \end{bmatrix}$

Allocation 3: $\begin{bmatrix} A \\ B \end{bmatrix} = \begin{bmatrix} 0.3 & -0.4 \\ -0.2 & 0.3 \end{bmatrix} \begin{bmatrix} 1720 \\ 1280 \end{bmatrix} = \begin{bmatrix} 4 \\ 40 \end{bmatrix}$

36. (A) $\begin{bmatrix} 1 & -1 & 1 \\ 1 & 2 & 0 \\ 0 & 2 & 2 \end{bmatrix} \begin{bmatrix} I_1 \\ I_2 \\ I_3 \end{bmatrix} = \begin{bmatrix} 0 \\ 10 \\ 10 \end{bmatrix}$

$\begin{bmatrix} I_1 \\ I_2 \\ I_3 \end{bmatrix} = \begin{bmatrix} 1 & -1 & 1 \\ 1 & 2 & 0 \\ 0 & 2 & 2 \end{bmatrix}^{-1} \begin{bmatrix} 0 \\ 10 \\ 10 \end{bmatrix} = \begin{bmatrix} \frac{1}{2} & \frac{1}{2} & -\frac{1}{4} \\ -\frac{1}{4} & \frac{1}{4} & \frac{1}{8} \\ \frac{1}{4} & -\frac{1}{4} & \frac{3}{8} \end{bmatrix} \begin{bmatrix} 0 \\ 10 \\ 10 \end{bmatrix} = \begin{bmatrix} \frac{5}{2} \\ \frac{15}{4} \\ \frac{5}{4} \end{bmatrix}$

(B) $\begin{bmatrix} I_1 \\ I_2 \\ I_3 \end{bmatrix} = \begin{bmatrix} \frac{1}{2} & \frac{1}{2} & -\frac{1}{4} \\ -\frac{1}{4} & \frac{1}{4} & \frac{1}{8} \\ \frac{1}{4} & -\frac{1}{4} & \frac{3}{8} \end{bmatrix} \begin{bmatrix} 0 \\ 10 \\ 15 \end{bmatrix} = \begin{bmatrix} \frac{5}{4} \\ \frac{35}{8} \\ \frac{25}{8} \end{bmatrix}$

(C) $\begin{bmatrix} I_1 \\ I_2 \\ I_3 \end{bmatrix} = \begin{bmatrix} \frac{1}{2} & \frac{1}{2} & -\frac{1}{4} \\ -\frac{1}{4} & \frac{1}{4} & \frac{1}{8} \\ \frac{1}{4} & -\frac{1}{4} & \frac{3}{8} \end{bmatrix} \begin{bmatrix} 0 \\ 15 \\ 10 \end{bmatrix} = \begin{bmatrix} 5 \\ 5 \\ 0 \end{bmatrix}$

38. $a(-1)^2 + b(-1) + c = k_1$
$a(0)^2 + b(0) + c = k_2$
$a(1)^2 + b(1) + c = k_3$

(A) $\begin{bmatrix} 1 & -1 & 1 \\ 0 & 0 & 1 \\ 1 & 1 & 1 \end{bmatrix} \begin{bmatrix} a \\ b \\ c \end{bmatrix} = \begin{bmatrix} k_1 \\ k_2 \\ k_3 \end{bmatrix} = \begin{bmatrix} -2 \\ 1 \\ 6 \end{bmatrix}$

$\begin{bmatrix} a \\ b \\ c \end{bmatrix} = \begin{bmatrix} 1 & -1 & 1 \\ 0 & 0 & 1 \\ 1 & 1 & 1 \end{bmatrix}^{-1} \begin{bmatrix} -2 \\ 1 \\ 6 \end{bmatrix} = \begin{bmatrix} \frac{1}{2} & -1 & \frac{1}{2} \\ -\frac{1}{2} & 0 & \frac{1}{2} \\ 0 & 1 & 0 \end{bmatrix} \begin{bmatrix} -2 \\ 1 \\ 6 \end{bmatrix} = \begin{bmatrix} 1 \\ 4 \\ 1 \end{bmatrix}$

(B) $\begin{bmatrix} a \\ b \\ c \end{bmatrix} = \begin{bmatrix} \frac{1}{2} & -1 & \frac{1}{2} \\ -\frac{1}{2} & 0 & \frac{1}{2} \\ 0 & 1 & 0 \end{bmatrix} \begin{bmatrix} 4 \\ 3 \\ -2 \end{bmatrix} = \begin{bmatrix} -2 \\ -3 \\ 3 \end{bmatrix}$

(C) $\begin{bmatrix} a \\ b \\ c \end{bmatrix} = \begin{bmatrix} \frac{1}{2} & -1 & \frac{1}{2} \\ -\frac{1}{2} & 0 & \frac{1}{2} \\ 0 & 1 & 0 \end{bmatrix} \begin{bmatrix} 8 \\ -5 \\ 4 \end{bmatrix} = \begin{bmatrix} 11 \\ -2 \\ -5 \end{bmatrix}$

Exercise 10-4

2. $\begin{vmatrix} 8 & -3 \\ 4 & 1 \end{vmatrix} = 8(1) - (-3)(4) = 8 + 12 = 20$

4. $\begin{vmatrix} 9 & -2 \\ 4 & 0 \end{vmatrix} = 9(0) - (-2)(4) = 0 + 8 = 8$

6. $\begin{vmatrix} -0.7 & -2.3 \\ 1.9 & -4.8 \end{vmatrix} = (-0.7)(-4.8) - (-2.3)(1.9) = 3.36 + 4.37 = 7.73$

8. minor of $a_{33} = \begin{vmatrix} 5 & -1 \\ 3 & 4 \end{vmatrix}$ **10.** minor of $a_{12} = \begin{vmatrix} 3 & 6 \\ 0 & 8 \end{vmatrix}$

12. cofactor of $a_{33} = (-1)^{3+3} \begin{vmatrix} 5 & -1 \\ 3 & 4 \end{vmatrix} = 23$

14. cofactor of $a_{12} = (-1)^{1+2} \begin{vmatrix} 3 & 6 \\ 0 & 8 \end{vmatrix} = (-1)(24) = -24$

16. $\begin{vmatrix} 2 & -3 & 5 \\ 0 & -3 & 1 \\ 0 & 6 & 2 \end{vmatrix} = (2)(-1)^{1+1} \begin{vmatrix} -3 & 1 \\ 6 & 2 \end{vmatrix} + 0(-1)^{2+1} \begin{vmatrix} -3 & 5 \\ 6 & 2 \end{vmatrix} + 0(-1)^{3+1} \begin{vmatrix} -3 & 5 \\ -3 & 1 \end{vmatrix}$

$= 2[(-3)(2) - (6)(1)] = -24$

18. $\begin{vmatrix} 4 & -2 & 0 \\ 9 & 5 & 4 \\ 1 & 2 & 0 \end{vmatrix} = (0)(-1)^{1+3} \begin{vmatrix} 9 & 5 \\ 1 & 2 \end{vmatrix} + 4(-1)^{2+3} \begin{vmatrix} 4 & -2 \\ 1 & 2 \end{vmatrix} + 0(-1)^{3+3} \begin{vmatrix} 4 & -2 \\ 9 & 5 \end{vmatrix}$

$= -4[(4)(2) - (1)(-2)]$

$= -40$

20. $\begin{vmatrix} 0 & 2 & -1 \\ -6 & 3 & 1 \\ 7 & -9 & -2 \end{vmatrix} = (0)(-1)^{1+1} \begin{vmatrix} 3 & 1 \\ -9 & -2 \end{vmatrix} + 2(-1)^{1+2} \begin{vmatrix} -6 & 1 \\ 7 & -2 \end{vmatrix} + (-1)(-1)^{1+3} \begin{vmatrix} -6 & 3 \\ 7 & -9 \end{vmatrix}$

$= -2[(-6)(-2) - (7)(1)] + (-1)[(-6)(-9) - (7)(3)]$

$= -43$

22. cofactor of $a_{44} = (-1)^{4+4} \begin{vmatrix} a_{11} & a_{12} & a_{13} \\ a_{21} & a_{22} & a_{23} \\ a_{31} & a_{32} & a_{33} \end{vmatrix}$ **24.** cofactor of $a_{23} = (-1)^{2+3} \begin{vmatrix} a_{11} & a_{12} & a_{14} \\ a_{31} & a_{32} & a_{34} \\ a_{41} & a_{42} & a_{44} \end{vmatrix}$

26. expansion by cofactors about third row gives

$\begin{vmatrix} 4 & -4 & 6 \\ 2 & 8 & -3 \\ 0 & -5 & 0 \end{vmatrix} = (-5)(-1)^{3+2} \begin{vmatrix} 4 & 6 \\ 2 & -3 \end{vmatrix} = 5[4(-3) - 2(6)] = -120$

28. expanding by cofactors about first row

$\begin{vmatrix} 3 & 2 & 1 \\ -1 & 5 & 1 \\ 2 & 3 & 1 \end{vmatrix} = 3[5(1) - 3(1)] - 2[-1(1) - 2(1)] + [(-1)(3) - 2(5)]$

$= -1$

30. expanding about first row

$\begin{vmatrix} 4 & -6 & 3 \\ -1 & 4 & 1 \\ 5 & -6 & 3 \end{vmatrix} = 4[(4)(3) - (-6)(1)] - (-6)[-1(3) - 5(1)] + 3[(-1)(-6) - (5)(4)]$

$= -18$

32. expanding about first column

$$\begin{vmatrix} 0 & 1 & 0 & 1 \\ 2 & 4 & 7 & 6 \\ 0 & 3 & 0 & 1 \\ 0 & 6 & 2 & 5 \end{vmatrix} = 2(-1)^{2+1} \begin{vmatrix} 1 & 0 & 1 \\ 3 & 0 & 1 \\ 6 & 2 & 5 \end{vmatrix} \quad \text{and expanding the 3×3 matrix} \\ \text{about the second column}$$

$$= -2(2)(-1)^{3+2} \begin{vmatrix} 1 & 1 \\ 3 & 1 \end{vmatrix}$$

$$= 4[1(1) - 3(1)] = -8$$

34. In a diagonal from the upper left to the lower right of a determinant, if all the off-diagonal elements are zero, then the value of the determinant may be found by multiplying the diagonal elements together; thus,

$$\begin{vmatrix} 2 & 0 & 0 & 0 & 0 \\ 0 & 3 & 0 & 0 & 0 \\ 0 & 0 & 2 & 0 & 0 \\ 0 & 0 & 0 & 1 & 0 \\ 0 & 0 & 0 & 0 & 4 \end{vmatrix} = 2(3)(2)(1)(4) = 48$$

36.

$$\begin{vmatrix} 4 & 1 & -5 \\ 1 & 2 & -6 \\ -3 & -1 & 7 \end{vmatrix} = \begin{matrix} 4(2)(7) + (1)(-6)(-3) + (-5)(1)(-1) \\ - (-5)(2)(-3) - 4(-6)(-1) - (1)(1)(7) = 18 \end{matrix}$$

38. False. $A = \begin{vmatrix} 1 & 2 & 3 \\ 0 & 4 & 5 \\ 0 & 0 & 6 \end{vmatrix}$, $B = \begin{vmatrix} 7 & 8 & 9 \\ 0 & 10 & 11 \\ 0 & 0 & 12 \end{vmatrix}$

$\det(A + B) = 2016$; $\det A + \det B = 24 + 840 = 864$

40. True. The product of two upper triangular matrices is an upper triangular matrix, whose determinant is the product of the elements of the principal diagonal. This is the same as the product of the first determinant and the second determinant. For example:

$$A = \begin{vmatrix} a_{11} & a_{12} & a_{13} \\ a_{21} & a_{22} & a_{23} \\ a_{31} & a_{32} & a_{33} \end{vmatrix}, \quad B = \begin{vmatrix} b_{11} & b_{12} & b_{13} \\ b_{21} & b_{22} & b_{23} \\ b_{31} & b_{32} & b_{33} \end{vmatrix}$$

$\det A = a_{11}a_{22}a_{33}$, $\det B = b_{11}b_{22}b_{33}$ $\Rightarrow$ $\det(AB) = a_{11}a_{22}a_{33}b_{11}b_{22}b_{33}$

$\det A \cdot \det B = a_{11}a_{22}a_{33}b_{11}b_{22}b_{33}$

42. $\begin{vmatrix} a & b \\ c & d \end{vmatrix} = ad - cb = -(bc - ad) = -\begin{vmatrix} b & a \\ d & c \end{vmatrix}$

Interchanging two columns changes the sign of the determinant.

44. $\begin{vmatrix} a & b \\ kc & kd \end{vmatrix} = akd - kcb = k(ad - cb) = k\begin{vmatrix} a & b \\ c & d \end{vmatrix}$

Multiplying a row by a constant multiplies the value of the determinant by the constant.

46. $\begin{vmatrix} a & ka + b \\ c & kc + d \end{vmatrix} = a(kc + d) - c(ka + b)$

$$= akc + ad - cka - cb$$
$$= ad - cb$$
$$= \begin{vmatrix} a & b \\ c & d \end{vmatrix}$$

Adding a multiple of one column to another column does not change the value of the determinant.

48. expanding about second row

$\begin{vmatrix} a_{11} & a_{12} & a_{13} \\ a_{21} & a_{22} & a_{23} \\ a_{31} & a_{32} & a_{33} \end{vmatrix} = a_{21}(-1)^{2+1}\begin{vmatrix} a_{12} & a_{13} \\ a_{32} & a_{33} \end{vmatrix} + a_{22}(-1)^{2+2}\begin{vmatrix} a_{11} & a_{13} \\ a_{31} & a_{33} \end{vmatrix} + a_{23}(-1)^{2+3}\begin{vmatrix} a_{11} & a_{12} \\ a_{31} & a_{32} \end{vmatrix}$

$$= -a_{21}[a_{12}a_{33} - a_{32}a_{13}] + a_{22}[a_{11}a_{33} - a_{31}a_{13}] - a_{23}[a_{11}a_{32} - a_{31}a_{12}]$$
$$= -a_{21}a_{12}a_{33} + a_{21}a_{32}a_{13} + a_{22}a_{11}a_{33} - a_{22}a_{31}a_{13} - a_{23}a_{11}a_{32} + a_{23}a_{31}a_{12}$$
$$= a_{13}a_{21}a_{32} - a_{13}a_{31}a_{22} - a_{23}a_{11}a_{32} + a_{23}a_{31}a_{12} + a_{33}a_{11}a_{22} - a_{33}a_{21}a_{12}$$

expanding about third column

$\begin{vmatrix} a_{11} & a_{12} & a_{13} \\ a_{21} & a_{22} & a_{23} \\ a_{31} & a_{32} & a_{33} \end{vmatrix} = a_{13}(-1)^{1+3}\begin{vmatrix} a_{21} & a_{22} \\ a_{31} & a_{32} \end{vmatrix} + a_{23}(-1)^{2+3}\begin{vmatrix} a_{11} & a_{12} \\ a_{31} & a_{32} \end{vmatrix} + a_{33}(-1)^{3+3}\begin{vmatrix} a_{11} & a_{12} \\ a_{21} & a_{22} \end{vmatrix}$

$$= a_{13}(a_{21}a_{32} - a_{31}a_{22}) - a_{23}(a_{11}a_{32} - a_{31}a_{12}) + a_{33}(a_{11}a_{22} - a_{21}a_{12})$$
$$= a_{13}a_{21}a_{32} - a_{13}a_{31}a_{22} - a_{23}a_{11}a_{32} + a_{23}a_{31}a_{12} + a_{33}a_{11}a_{22} - a_{33}a_{21}a_{12}$$

50. $AB = \begin{bmatrix} a & b \\ c & d \end{bmatrix}\begin{bmatrix} w & x \\ y & z \end{bmatrix} = \begin{bmatrix} aw + by & ax + bz \\ cw + dy & cx + dz \end{bmatrix}$

$\det(AB) = (aw + by)(cx + dz) - (cw + dy)(ax + bz)$
$$= awcx + awdz + bycx + bydz - cwax - dybz - cwbz - dyax$$
$$= awdz + bycx - cwbz - dyax$$
$$= adwz - adyx - bcwz + bcyx$$

$\det(A) = ad - bc; \det(B) = wz - yx$

$\det(A)\det(B) = (ad - bc)(wz - yx)$
$$= adwz - adyx - bcwz + bcyx$$

52. $f(x) = \left| x\begin{bmatrix} 1 & 0 \\ 0 & 1 \end{bmatrix} - \begin{bmatrix} 8 & -6 \\ 3 & -1 \end{bmatrix} \right|$

$$= \left| \begin{bmatrix} x & 0 \\ 0 & x \end{bmatrix} - \begin{bmatrix} 8 & -6 \\ 3 & -1 \end{bmatrix} \right|$$

$$= \begin{vmatrix} x - 8 & 6 \\ -3 & x + 1 \end{vmatrix} = (x - 8)(x + 1) - (-3)(6)$$

$$= x^2 - 7x + 10, \text{ characteristic polynomial}$$

$x^2 - 7x + 10 = (x - 5)(x - 2) = 0 \Rightarrow x = 5, x = 2, \text{ eigenvalues}$

54. $f(x) = \left| x \begin{bmatrix} 1 & 0 & 0 \\ 0 & 1 & 0 \\ 0 & 0 & 1 \end{bmatrix} - \begin{bmatrix} -2 & 2 & 0 \\ -1 & 1 & 0 \\ -2 & 4 & 2 \end{bmatrix} \right|$

$\qquad = \left| \begin{bmatrix} x & 0 & 0 \\ 0 & x & 0 \\ 0 & 0 & x \end{bmatrix} - \begin{bmatrix} -2 & 2 & 0 \\ -1 & 1 & 0 \\ -2 & 4 & 2 \end{bmatrix} \right|$

$\qquad = \begin{vmatrix} x+2 & -2 & 0 \\ 1 & x-1 & 0 \\ 2 & -4 & x-2 \end{vmatrix} = (x-2)(-1)^{3+3} \begin{vmatrix} x+2 & -2 \\ 1 & x-1 \end{vmatrix}$

$\qquad = (x-2)[(x+2)(x-1) - (1)(-2)]$

$\qquad = x^3 - x^2 - 2x$, characteristic polynomial

$x^3 - x^2 - 2x = x(x^2 - x - 2) = x(x-2)(x+1) \Rightarrow x = 0, 2, -1;$ eigenvalues

Exercise 10-5

2. $\begin{vmatrix} 1 & -9 \\ 0 & -6 \end{vmatrix} = -3 \begin{vmatrix} 1 & 3 \\ 0 & 2 \end{vmatrix}$ Theorem 1

4. $4 \begin{vmatrix} -1 & 3 \\ 2 & 1 \end{vmatrix} = \begin{vmatrix} -4 & 12 \\ 2 & 1 \end{vmatrix}$ Theorem 1

6. $\begin{vmatrix} 5 & -7 \\ 0 & 0 \end{vmatrix} = 0$ Theorem 2

8. $\begin{vmatrix} 6 & 9 \\ 0 & 1 \end{vmatrix} = - \begin{vmatrix} 0 & 1 \\ 6 & 9 \end{vmatrix}$ Theorem 3

10. $\begin{vmatrix} 3 & 2 \\ 5 & 1 \end{vmatrix} = \begin{vmatrix} 3+4 & 2 \\ 5+2 & 1 \end{vmatrix}$ Theorem 5

12. $\begin{vmatrix} -1 & 3 \\ 5 & -2 \end{vmatrix} = \begin{vmatrix} -1 & 3 \\ x & 13 \end{vmatrix} \Rightarrow$ $\begin{aligned} k(3) + (-2) &= 13; \quad k(-1) + 5 = x \\ 3k &= 15 \quad \ \ 5(-1) + 5 = x \\ k &= 5 \qquad \qquad 0 = x \end{aligned}$

$x = 0$

14. $\begin{vmatrix} -1 & 2 & 3 \\ 2 & 1 & 4 \\ 1 & 3 & 2 \end{vmatrix} = \begin{vmatrix} -1 & 0 & 3 \\ 2 & x & 4 \\ 1 & 5 & 2 \end{vmatrix}$ $\begin{aligned} k(-1) + 2 &= 0 \Rightarrow k = 2 \\ k(2) + 1 &= x \Rightarrow x = 5 \end{aligned}$

16. $\begin{vmatrix} 2a & 2b \\ c & d \end{vmatrix} = 2 \begin{vmatrix} a & b \\ c & d \end{vmatrix} = 2 \cdot 10 = 20$

18. $\begin{vmatrix} a+b & b \\ c+d & d \end{vmatrix} = \begin{vmatrix} a & b \\ c & d \end{vmatrix} = 10$

20. $\begin{vmatrix} a+c & b+d \\ -a & -b \end{vmatrix} = - \begin{vmatrix} a+c & b+d \\ a & b \end{vmatrix} = \begin{vmatrix} a & b \\ a+c & b+d \end{vmatrix} = \begin{vmatrix} a & b \\ c & d \end{vmatrix} = 10$

22. $\begin{vmatrix} -1 & 2 & 0 \\ 2 & 1 & 10 \\ 1 & 3 & 5 \end{vmatrix} \xrightarrow{-2R_3 + R_2 \to R_2} \begin{vmatrix} -1 & 2 & 0 \\ 0 & -5 & 0 \\ 1 & 3 & 5 \end{vmatrix} = 5(-1)^{3+3}[(-1)(-5) - 0(2)]$

$\qquad = 25$

24. $\begin{vmatrix} 2 & 0 & 1 \\ -1 & -3 & 4 \\ 1 & 2 & 3 \end{vmatrix} \xrightarrow{\ -2C_3 + C_1 \to C_1\ } \begin{vmatrix} 0 & 0 & 1 \\ -9 & -3 & 4 \\ -5 & 2 & 3 \end{vmatrix} = (1)(-1)^{1+3}[(-9)(2) - (-5)(-3)]$

$$= -33$$

26. $\begin{vmatrix} 8 & 0 & 1 \\ 12 & -1 & 0 \\ 4 & 3 & 2 \end{vmatrix} = 4 \begin{vmatrix} 2 & 0 & 1 \\ 3 & -1 & 0 \\ 1 & 3 & 2 \end{vmatrix}$ Theorem 1

28. $\begin{vmatrix} -2 & 5 & 13 \\ 1 & 7 & 12 \\ 0 & 8 & 15 \end{vmatrix} = - \begin{vmatrix} 5 & -2 & 13 \\ 7 & 1 & 12 \\ 8 & 0 & 15 \end{vmatrix}$ Theorem 3

30. $\begin{vmatrix} 7 & 7 & 1 \\ -3 & -3 & 11 \\ 2 & 2 & 0 \end{vmatrix} = 0$ Theorem 4

32. $\begin{vmatrix} 3 & -1 & 1 \\ -2 & 4 & 3 \\ 1 & 5 & 2 \end{vmatrix} = \begin{vmatrix} 0 & -1 & 0 \\ 10 & 4 & 7 \\ x & 5 & y \end{vmatrix}$ $\left.\begin{array}{l} k(-1) + 3 = 0 \\ k(4) - 2 = 10 \end{array}\right\} \Rightarrow k = 3$

$\qquad\qquad\qquad\qquad\qquad\qquad\qquad\qquad k(5) + 1 = x \Rightarrow x = 16$

$\left.\begin{array}{l} k(-1) + 1 = 0 \\ k(4) + 3 = 7 \end{array}\right\} \Rightarrow k = 1$

$k(5) + 2 = y \Rightarrow y = 7$

34. $\begin{vmatrix} 5 & 2 & 3 \\ 3 & 1 & 2 \\ -4 & -3 & 5 \end{vmatrix} = \begin{vmatrix} x & 0 & -1 \\ 3 & 1 & 2 \\ 5 & 0 & y \end{vmatrix}$ $\left.\begin{array}{l} k(1) + 2 = 0 \\ k(2) + 3 = -1 \end{array}\right\} \Rightarrow k = -2$

$\qquad\qquad\qquad\qquad\qquad\qquad\qquad\qquad k(3) + 5 = x \Rightarrow x = -1$

$\left.\begin{array}{l} k(3) - 4 = 5 \\ k(1) - 3 = 0 \end{array}\right\} \Rightarrow k = 3$

$k(2) + 5 = y \Rightarrow y = 11$

36. $\begin{vmatrix} -1 & 5 & 1 \\ 2 & 3 & 1 \\ 3 & 2 & 1 \end{vmatrix} \xrightarrow[\ -1R_3 + R_1 \to R_1\ ]{-1R_3 + R_2 \to R_2} \begin{vmatrix} -4 & 3 & 0 \\ -1 & 1 & 0 \\ 3 & 2 & 1 \end{vmatrix} = (1)(-1)^{3+3}[(-4)(1) - (-1)(3)]$

$$= -1$$

38. $\begin{vmatrix} 5 & 3 & -6 \\ -1 & 1 & 4 \\ 4 & 3 & -6 \end{vmatrix} \xrightarrow[\ -3R_2 + R_3 \to R_3\ ]{-3R_2 + R_1 \to R_1} \begin{vmatrix} 8 & 0 & -18 \\ -1 & 1 & 4 \\ 7 & 0 & -18 \end{vmatrix} = (1)(-1)^{2+2}[8(-18) - 7(-18)]$

$$= -18$$

40. $\begin{vmatrix} 2 & 3 & -1 \\ 5 & 4 & 7 \\ -4 & -6 & 2 \end{vmatrix} \xrightarrow[\ 2R_1 + R_3 \to R_3\ ]{7R_1 + R_2 \to R_2} \begin{vmatrix} 2 & 3 & -1 \\ 19 & 25 & 0 \\ 0 & 0 & 0 \end{vmatrix} = 0$

42. $\begin{vmatrix} 2 & 3 & 1 & -1 \\ 3 & 1 & 2 & 1 \\ 0 & 5 & 4 & 0 \\ -1 & 2 & 3 & 0 \end{vmatrix} \xrightarrow{\ 1R_2 + R_1 \to R_1\ } \begin{vmatrix} 5 & 4 & 3 & 0 \\ 3 & 1 & 2 & 1 \\ 0 & 5 & 4 & 0 \\ -1 & 2 & 3 & 0 \end{vmatrix} = (1)(-1)^{2+4} \begin{vmatrix} 5 & 4 & 3 \\ 0 & 5 & 4 \\ -1 & 2 & 3 \end{vmatrix}$

$$= 5(-1)^{1+1}[5(3) - 2(4)] + (-1)(-1)^{3+1}[(4)(4) - (5)(3)] = 34$$

44. $\begin{vmatrix} -1 & 4 & 2 & 1 \\ 5 & -1 & -3 & -1 \\ 2 & -1 & -2 & 3 \\ -3 & 3 & 3 & 3 \end{vmatrix}$ $\begin{matrix} 1R_1 + R_2 \to R_2 \\ -3R_1 + R_3 \to R_3 \\ -3R_1 + R_4 \to R_4 \end{matrix}$ $\begin{vmatrix} -1 & 4 & 2 & 1 \\ 4 & 3 & -1 & 0 \\ 5 & -13 & -8 & 0 \\ 0 & -9 & -3 & 0 \end{vmatrix}$

$\begin{vmatrix} -1 & 4 & 2 & 1 \\ 4 & 3 & -1 & 0 \\ 5 & -13 & -8 & 0 \\ 0 & -9 & -3 & 0 \end{vmatrix} = (1)(-1)^{1+4} \begin{vmatrix} 4 & 3 & -1 \\ 5 & -13 & -8 \\ 0 & -9 & -3 \end{vmatrix}$

$\qquad = -4(-1)^{1+1}[-13(-3) - (-9)(-8)]$
$\qquad\quad -3(-1)^{1+2}[5(-3) - 0(-8)]$
$\qquad\qquad + 1(-1)^{1+3}[5(-9) - 0(-13)]$

$\qquad = 42$

46. $\begin{vmatrix} a & b & c \\ kd & ke & kf \\ g & h & i \end{vmatrix}$ $= a(-1)^{1+1}[ke(i) - h(kf)]$
$\qquad\qquad\qquad\quad + b(-1)^{1+2}[kd(i) - g(kf)]$
$\qquad\qquad\qquad\quad + c(-1)^{1+3}[kd(h) - g(ke)]$
$\qquad\quad = akei - ahkf - bkdi + bgkf + ckdh - cgke$
$\qquad\quad = k[aei - ahf - bdi + bgf + cdh - cge]$
$\qquad\quad = k[a(ei - hf) - b(di - gf) + c(dh - ge)]$
$\qquad\quad = k \begin{vmatrix} a & b & c \\ d & e & f \\ g & h & i \end{vmatrix}$

48. $\begin{vmatrix} a_1 + kc_1 & b_1 & c_1 \\ a_2 + kc_2 & b_2 & c_2 \\ a_3 + kc_3 & b_3 & c_3 \end{vmatrix}$ $= (a_1 + kc_1)(b_2 c_3 - b_3 c_2)$
$\qquad\qquad\qquad\qquad\qquad\quad -b_1((a_2 + kc_2)c_3 - (a_3 + kc_3)c_2)$
$\qquad\qquad\qquad\qquad\qquad\quad + c_1((a_2 + kc_2)b_3 - (a_3 + kc_3)b_2)$

$\qquad = a_1 b_2 c_3 - a_1 b_3 c_2 + kc_1 b_2 c_3 - kc_1 b_3 c_2$
$\qquad\quad - b_1(a_2 c_3 + kc_2 c_3 - a_3 c_2 - kc_3 c_2)$
$\qquad\quad + c_1(a_2 b_3 + kc_2 b_3 - a_3 b_2 - kc_3 b_2)$

$\qquad = a_1 b_2 c_3 - a_1 b_3 c_2 + kc_1 b_2 c_3 - kc_1 b_3 c_2$
$\qquad\quad - b_1 a_2 c_3 - b_1 kc_2 c_3 + b_1 a_3 c_2 + b_1 kc_3 c_2$
$\qquad\quad + c_1 a_2 b_3 + c_1 kc_2 b_3 - c_1 a_3 b_2 - c_1 kc_3 b_2$

$\qquad = a_1 b_2 c_3 - a_1 b_3 c_2 - b_1 a_2 c_3 + b_1 a_3 c_2 + c_1 a_2 b_3 - c_1 a_3 b_2$

$\qquad = a_1(b_2 c_3 - b_3 c_2) - b_1(a_2 c_3 - a_3 c_2) + c_1(a_2 b_3 - a_3 b_2)$

$\qquad = \begin{vmatrix} a_1 & b_1 & c_1 \\ a_2 & b_2 & c_2 \\ a_3 & b_3 & c_3 \end{vmatrix}$

50. Equation of line through (2, 3) and (-1, 2)

$\qquad \dfrac{y - 3}{x - 2} = \dfrac{3 - 2}{2 - (-1)} \Rightarrow x - 3y + 7 = 0$

$\begin{vmatrix} x & y & 1 \\ 2 & 3 & 1 \\ -1 & 2 & 1 \end{vmatrix} = 0 \Rightarrow x(3(1) - 2(1)) - y(2(1) - (-1)(1)) + 1(2(2) - (-1)(3)) = 0$

$\qquad\qquad\qquad\qquad x - 3y + 7 = 0$

52. area $= \left| \frac{1}{2} \begin{vmatrix} -1 & 4 & 1 \\ 4 & 8 & 1 \\ 1 & 1 & 1 \end{vmatrix} \right|$

$= \left| \frac{1}{2} \{ -1[8(1) - (1)(1)] - 4[4(1) - (1)(1)] + 1[4(1) - 1(8)] \} \right|$

$= \left| \frac{1}{2} \{-23\} \right| = |-11.5| = 11.5$

54.

$\det = \begin{vmatrix} x_1 & y_1 & 1 \\ x_2 & y_2 & 1 \\ x_3 & y_3 & 1 \end{vmatrix} = x_1(y_2 - y_3) - y_1(x_2 - x_3) + (x_2y_3 - x_3y_2)$

$\det = x_1y_2 - x_1y_3 - y_1x_2 + y_1x_3 + x_2y_3 - x_3y_2$

from slopes

$\dfrac{y_2 - y_1}{x_2 - x_1} = \dfrac{y_3 - y_2}{x_3 - x_2}$

$(y_2 - y_1)(x_3 - x_2) - (x_2 - x_1)(y_3 - y_2) = 0$

$y_2x_3 - y_2x_2 - y_1x_3 + y_1x_2 - x_2y_3 + x_2y_2 + x_1y_3 - x_1y_2 = 0$

$x_1y_2 - x_1y_3 - y_1x_2 + y_1x_3 + x_2y_3 - x_3y_2 = 0 = \det$

Exercise 10-6

2. $x + 2y = 3$
$x + 3y = 5$

$x = \dfrac{\begin{vmatrix} 3 & 2 \\ 5 & 3 \end{vmatrix}}{\begin{vmatrix} 1 & 2 \\ 1 & 3 \end{vmatrix}} = \dfrac{9 - 10}{3 - 2} = \dfrac{-1}{1} = -1$

$y = \dfrac{\begin{vmatrix} 1 & 3 \\ 1 & 5 \end{vmatrix}}{1} = \dfrac{5 - 3}{1} = \dfrac{2}{1} = 2$

4. $x + 3y = 1$
$2x + 8y = 0$

$x = \dfrac{\begin{vmatrix} 1 & 3 \\ 0 & 8 \end{vmatrix}}{\begin{vmatrix} 1 & 3 \\ 2 & 8 \end{vmatrix}} = \dfrac{8}{2} = 4$

$y = \dfrac{\begin{vmatrix} 1 & 1 \\ 2 & 0 \end{vmatrix}}{2} = \dfrac{-2}{2} = -1$

6. $-3x + 2y = 1$
$2x - 3y = -3$

$x = \dfrac{\begin{vmatrix} 1 & 2 \\ -3 & -3 \end{vmatrix}}{\begin{vmatrix} -3 & 2 \\ 2 & -3 \end{vmatrix}} = \dfrac{3}{5}$

$y = \dfrac{\begin{vmatrix} -3 & 1 \\ 2 & -3 \end{vmatrix}}{5} = \dfrac{7}{5}$

8. $5x + 2y = -1$
$2x - 3y = 2$

$x = \dfrac{\begin{vmatrix} -1 & 2 \\ 2 & -3 \end{vmatrix}}{\begin{vmatrix} 5 & 2 \\ 2 & -3 \end{vmatrix}} = \dfrac{-1}{-19} = \dfrac{1}{19}$

$y = \dfrac{\begin{vmatrix} 5 & -1 \\ 2 & 2 \end{vmatrix}}{-19} = \dfrac{12}{-19} = -\dfrac{12}{19}$

10. $0.9877x - 0.9744y = 0$
$0.1564x + 0.2250y = 1900$

$$x = \frac{\begin{vmatrix} 0 & -0.9744 \\ 1900 & 0.2250 \end{vmatrix}}{\begin{vmatrix} 0.9877 & -0.9744 \\ 0.1564 & 0.2250 \end{vmatrix}} = \frac{1851.36}{0.37462866} \qquad y = \frac{\begin{vmatrix} 0.9877 & 0 \\ 0.1564 & 1900 \end{vmatrix}}{0.37462866} = \frac{1876.63}{0.37462866}$$

$x = 4941.853621$ $\qquad\qquad\qquad\qquad y = 5009.307083$
$x = 4900$, 2 significant digits $\qquad\quad y = 5000$, 2 significant digits

12. $x = \dfrac{\begin{vmatrix} 0 & -0.9957 \\ 112 & 0.0924 \end{vmatrix}}{\begin{vmatrix} 0.9973 & -0.9957 \\ 0.0732 & 0.0924 \end{vmatrix}} = \dfrac{111.5184}{0.16503576} = 675.7226434 = 680$, 2 significant digits

$y = \dfrac{\begin{vmatrix} 0.9973 & 0 \\ 0.0732 & 112 \end{vmatrix}}{0.16503576} = \dfrac{111.6976}{0.16503576} = 676.8084687 = 680$, 2 significant digits

14. $x = \dfrac{\begin{vmatrix} -4 & 1 & 0 \\ 0 & 2 & 1 \\ 5 & 0 & 1 \end{vmatrix}}{\begin{vmatrix} 1 & 1 & 0 \\ 0 & 2 & 1 \\ -1 & 0 & 1 \end{vmatrix}} = \dfrac{-3}{1} = -3$ $\qquad y = \dfrac{\begin{vmatrix} 1 & -4 & 0 \\ 0 & 0 & 1 \\ -1 & 5 & 1 \end{vmatrix}}{1} = \dfrac{-1}{1} = -1$

$\qquad\qquad\qquad\qquad\qquad\qquad\qquad z = \dfrac{\begin{vmatrix} 1 & 1 & -4 \\ 0 & 2 & 0 \\ -1 & 0 & 5 \end{vmatrix}}{1} = \dfrac{2}{1} = 2$

16. $x = \dfrac{\begin{vmatrix} -3 & 3 & 0 \\ 3 & 2 & 1 \\ 7 & 0 & 3 \end{vmatrix}}{\begin{vmatrix} 1 & 3 & 0 \\ 0 & 2 & 1 \\ -1 & 0 & 3 \end{vmatrix}} = \dfrac{-24}{3} = -8$ $\qquad$ **18.** $x = \dfrac{\begin{vmatrix} 3 & 0 & -1 \\ -3 & -1 & 0 \\ 1 & 1 & 1 \end{vmatrix}}{\begin{vmatrix} 1 & 0 & -1 \\ 2 & -1 & 0 \\ 1 & 1 & 1 \end{vmatrix}} = \dfrac{-1}{-4} = \dfrac{1}{4}$

$y = \dfrac{\begin{vmatrix} 1 & -3 & 0 \\ 0 & 3 & 1 \\ -1 & 7 & 3 \end{vmatrix}}{3} = \dfrac{5}{3}$ $\qquad\qquad\qquad y = \dfrac{\begin{vmatrix} 1 & 3 & -1 \\ 2 & -3 & 0 \\ 1 & 1 & 1 \end{vmatrix}}{-4} = \dfrac{-14}{-4} = \dfrac{7}{2}$

$z = \dfrac{\begin{vmatrix} 1 & 3 & -3 \\ 0 & 2 & 3 \\ -1 & 0 & 7 \end{vmatrix}}{3} = \dfrac{-1}{3} = -\dfrac{1}{3}$ $\qquad\qquad z = \dfrac{\begin{vmatrix} 1 & 0 & 3 \\ 2 & -1 & -3 \\ 1 & 1 & 1 \end{vmatrix}}{-4} = \dfrac{11}{-4} = -\dfrac{11}{4}$

20. $x = \dfrac{\begin{vmatrix} 2 & 1 & 0 \\ -1 & -1 & 0 \\ 2 & 1 & 1 \end{vmatrix}}{\begin{vmatrix} 2 & 1 & 0 \\ 1 & -1 & 1 \\ 1 & 1 & 1 \end{vmatrix}} = \dfrac{-1}{-4} = \dfrac{1}{4}$

$y = \dfrac{\begin{vmatrix} 2 & 2 & 0 \\ 1 & -1 & 1 \\ 1 & 2 & 1 \end{vmatrix}}{-4} = \dfrac{-6}{-4} = \dfrac{3}{2}$

$z = \dfrac{\begin{vmatrix} 2 & 1 & 2 \\ 1 & -1 & -1 \\ 1 & 1 & 2 \end{vmatrix}}{-4} = \dfrac{-1}{-4} = \dfrac{1}{4}$

22. $x = \dfrac{\begin{vmatrix} 25 & 4 & -3 \\ 2 & 1 & -1 \\ 1 & 1 & 2 \end{vmatrix}}{\begin{vmatrix} 1 & 4 & -3 \\ 3 & 1 & -1 \\ -4 & 1 & 2 \end{vmatrix}} = \dfrac{52}{-26} = -2$

24. $y = \dfrac{\begin{vmatrix} 2 & 15 & 4 \\ -1 & 5 & 2 \\ 3 & 4 & -2 \end{vmatrix}}{\begin{vmatrix} 2 & -1 & 4 \\ -1 & 1 & 2 \\ 3 & 4 & -2 \end{vmatrix}} = \dfrac{-52}{-52} = 1$

26. $z = \dfrac{\begin{vmatrix} 13 & 11 & 2 \\ 10 & 8 & 1 \\ 8 & 5 & 4 \end{vmatrix}}{\begin{vmatrix} 13 & 11 & 10 \\ 10 & 8 & 7 \\ 8 & 5 & 4 \end{vmatrix}} = \dfrac{-29}{-3} = \dfrac{29}{3}$

28. $D = \begin{vmatrix} 3 & -1 & 3 \\ 5 & 5 & -9 \\ -2 & 1 & -3 \end{vmatrix} = -6 \neq 0; \ x = 0, \ y = 0, \ z = 0$ is the only solution.

30. $\cos \alpha = \dfrac{\begin{vmatrix} c & a & 0 \\ b & 0 & a \\ a & c & b \end{vmatrix}}{\begin{vmatrix} b & a & 0 \\ c & 0 & a \\ 0 & c & b \end{vmatrix}} = \dfrac{c(-ac) - a(b^2 - a^2)}{b(-ac) - a(bc)}$

$= \dfrac{-ac^2 - ab^2 + a^3}{-abc - abc} = \dfrac{a(-c^2 - b^2 + a^2)}{-2abc}$

$= \dfrac{b^2 + c^2 - a^2}{2bc}$

32. (A) $R = xp + yq$

$= x(230 - 10x + 5y) + y(130 + 4x - 4y)$

$= 230x - 10x^2 + 5xy + 130y + 4xy - 4y^2$

$= 230x + 130y - 10x^2 + 9xy - 4y^2$

(B) $10x - 5y = 230 - p$

$4x - 4y = q - 130$

$$x = \frac{\begin{vmatrix} 230 - p & -5 \\ q - 130 & -4 \end{vmatrix}}{\begin{vmatrix} 10 & -5 \\ 4 & -4 \end{vmatrix}} = \frac{(230 - p)(-4) - (q - 130)(-5)}{10(-4) - 4(-5)} = \frac{-920 + 4p + 5q - 650}{-40 + 20}$$

$$= \frac{4p + 5q - 1570}{-20}$$

$x = -0.2p - 0.25q + 78.5$

$$y = \frac{\begin{vmatrix} 10 & 230 - p \\ 4 & q - 130 \end{vmatrix}}{-20} = \frac{10(q - 130) - 4(230 - p)}{-20} = \frac{10q + 4p - 2220}{-20}$$

$y = -0.2p - 0.5q + 111$

$R = xp + yq$

$= (-0.2p - 0.25q + 78.5)p + (-0.2p - 0.5q + 111)q$

$= -0.2p^2 - 0.25pq + 78.5p - 0.2pq - 0.5q^2 + 111q$

$= 78.5p + 111q - 0.2p^2 - 0.45pq - 0.5q^2$

CHAPTER 11

Exercise 11-1

2. $a_n = n^2 + 1$
$a_1 = 1^2 + 1 = 2$
$a_2 = 2^2 + 1 = 5$
$a_3 = 3^2 + 1 = 10$
$a_4 = 4^2 + 1 = 17$

4. $a_n = (n + 1)^n$
$a_1 = (1 + 1)^1 = 2^1 = 2$
$a_2 = (2 + 1)^2 = 3^2 = 9$
$a_3 = (3 + 1)^3 = 4^3 = 64$
$a_4 = (4 + 1)^4 = 5^4 = 625$

6. $a_n = \dfrac{(-1)^n}{n^3}$
$a_1 = \dfrac{(-1)^1}{1^3} = -1$
$a_2 = \dfrac{(-1)^2}{2^3} = \dfrac{1}{8}$
$a_3 = \dfrac{(-1)^3}{3^3} = -\dfrac{1}{27}$
$a_4 = \dfrac{(-1)^4}{4^3} = \dfrac{1}{64}$

8. $a_n = n^2 + 1$
$a_{50} = 50^2 + 1 = 2501$

10. $a_n = (n + 1)^n$
$a_{99} = (99 + 1)^{99} = 100^{99} = (10^2)^{99} = 10^{198}$

12. $\displaystyle\sum_{k=1}^{4} k^2 = 1^2 + 2^2 + 3^2 + 4^2$
$= 1 + 4 + 9 + 16$

14. $\displaystyle\sum_{k=1}^{5} \left(\dfrac{1}{3}\right)^k = \left(\dfrac{1}{3}\right)^1 + \left(\dfrac{1}{3}\right)^2 + \left(\dfrac{1}{3}\right)^3 + \left(\dfrac{1}{3}\right)^4 + \left(\dfrac{1}{3}\right)^5$
$= \dfrac{1}{3} + \dfrac{1}{9} + \dfrac{1}{27} + \dfrac{1}{81} + \dfrac{1}{243}$

16. $\displaystyle\sum_{k=1}^{6} (-1)^{k+1} k = (-1)^{1+1}(1) + (-1)^{2+1}(2) + (-1)^{3+1}(3) + (-1)^{4+1}(4)$
$+ (-1)^{5+1}(5) + (-1)^{6+1}(6)$
$= 1 - 2 + 3 - 4 + 5 - 6$

18. $a_n = (-1)^{n+1}\left(\dfrac{1}{2^n}\right)$
$a_1 = (-1)^{1+1}\dfrac{1}{2^1} = \dfrac{1}{2}$
$a_2 = (-1)^{2+1}\dfrac{1}{2^2} = -\dfrac{1}{4}$
$a_3 = (-1)^{3+1}\dfrac{1}{2^3} = \dfrac{1}{8}$
$a_4 = (-1)^{4+1}\dfrac{1}{2^4} = -\dfrac{1}{16}$
$a_5 = (-1)^{5+1}\dfrac{1}{2^5} = \dfrac{1}{32}$

20. $a_n = n[1 - (-1)^n]$
$a_1 = 1[1 - (-1)^1] = 2$
$a_2 = 2[1 - (-1)^2] = 0$
$a_3 = 3[1 - (-1)^3] = 6$
$a_4 = 4[1 - (-1)^4] = 0$
$a_5 = 5[1 - (-1)^5] = 10$

22. $a_n = \left(-\dfrac{3}{2}\right)^{n-1}$
$a_1 = \left(-\dfrac{3}{2}\right)^{1-1} = 1$
$a_2 = \left(-\dfrac{3}{2}\right)^{2-1} = -\dfrac{3}{2}$
$a_3 = \left(-\dfrac{3}{2}\right)^{3-1} = \dfrac{9}{4}$
$a_4 = \left(-\dfrac{3}{2}\right)^{4-1} = -\dfrac{27}{8}$
$a_5 = \left(-\dfrac{3}{2}\right)^{5-1} = \dfrac{81}{16}$

24. $a_n = a_{n-1} + a_{n-2}$, $n \geq 3$; $a_1 = a_2 = 1$
$a_1 = 1$
$a_2 = 1$
$a_3 = a_2 + a_1 = 1 + 1 = 2$
$a_4 = a_3 + a_2 = 2 + 1 = 3$
$a_5 = a_4 + a_3 = 3 + 2 = 5$

26. $a_n = 2a_{n-1}$, $n \geq 2$; $a_1 = 2$
$a_1 = 2$
$a_2 = 2a_1 = 2(2) = 4$
$a_3 = 2a_2 = 2(4) = 8$
$a_4 = 2a_3 = 2(8) = 16$
$a_5 = 2a_4 = 2(16) = 32$

28. $-2, -1, -4, -7, \ldots$
$a_n = 5 - 3n$

30. $24, 35, 48, 63, \ldots$
$a_n = (n + 3)(n + 5)$

32. $1, 4, 27, 256, \ldots$
$a_n = n^n$

34. $\dfrac{1}{2}, \dfrac{3}{4}, \dfrac{7}{8}, \dfrac{15}{16}, \ldots$
$a_n = \dfrac{2^n - 1}{2^n}$

36. $1, -\dfrac{1}{5}, \dfrac{1}{25}, -\dfrac{1}{125}, \ldots$
$a_n = \dfrac{1}{(-5)^{n-1}}$ or $\dfrac{(-1)^{n-1}}{5^{n-1}}$

38. $-x, -x^4, -x^7, x^{10}, \ldots$
$a_n = (-1)^n x^{3n-2}$

40.
```
WINDOW
 nMin=1
 nMax=20
 PlotStart=1
 PlotStep=1
 Xmin=0
 Xmax=21
↓Xscl=1■
```
```
WINDOW
↑PlotStep=1
 Xmin=0
 Xmax=21
 Xscl=1
 Ymin=-20
 Ymax=80
 Yscl=10■
```
```
Plot1 Plot2 Plot3
 nMin=1
\u(n)⊟2+πn
 u(nMin)⊟
\v(n)=
 v(nMin)=
\w(n)=
 w(nMin)=
```
```
u=2+πn              ×
                 ××
               ××
            ××
          ××
       ××
    ××
 ×
n=20
X=20      Y=64.831853
```

42.
```
WINDOW
 nMin=1
 nMax=20
 PlotStart=1
 PlotStep=1
 Xmin=0
 Xmax=21
↓Xscl=1■
```
```
WINDOW
↑PlotStep=1
 Xmin=0
 Xmax=21
 Xscl=1
 Ymin=-2
 Ymax=2
 Yscl=1■
```
```
Plot1 Plot2 Plot3
 nMin=1
∖u(n)⊟(2/3)u(n-1
)+1/2
 u(nMin)⊟(-1)
∖v(n)=
 v(nMin)=
∖w(n)=
```
```
u=(2/3)u(n-1)+1/2
          ········×
       ···
     ··
    ·
   ·
  ·
 ·
·
n=20
X=20      Y=1.4988723
```

44. $\displaystyle\sum_{k=1}^{5} (-1)^{k+1}(2k - 1)^2 = (-1)^{1+1}(2(1) - 1)^2 + (-1)^{2+1}(2(2) - 1)^2 + (-1)^{3+1}(2(3) - 1)^2$

$+ (-1)^{4+1}(2(4) - 1)^2 + (-1)^{5+1}(2(5) - 1)^2$

$= 1^2 - 3^2 + 5^2 - 7^2 + 9^2$

46. $\displaystyle\sum_{k=1}^{5} x^{k-1} = x^{1-1} + x^{2-1} + x^{3-1} + x^{4-1} + x^{5-1}$

$= 1 + x + x^2 + x^3 + x^4$

48. $\displaystyle\sum_{k=0}^{4} \dfrac{(-1)^k x^{2k+1}}{2k + 1} = \dfrac{(-1)^0 x^{2(0)+1}}{2(0) + 1} + \dfrac{(-1)^1 x^{2(1)+1}}{2(1) + 1} + \dfrac{(-1)^2 x^{2(2)+1}}{2(2) + 1} + \dfrac{(-1)^3 x^{2(3)+1}}{2(3)+1} + \dfrac{(-1)^4 x^{2(4)+1}}{2(4) +1}$

$= x - \dfrac{x^3}{3} + \dfrac{x^5}{5} - \dfrac{x^7}{7} + \dfrac{x^9}{9}$

50. $2 + 3 + 4 + 5 + 6 = \displaystyle\sum_{k=1}^{5} (k + 1)$

52. $1 - \dfrac{1}{2} + \dfrac{1}{3} - \dfrac{1}{4} = \displaystyle\sum_{k=1}^{4} \dfrac{(-1)^{k+1}}{k}$

54. $2 + \dfrac{3}{2} + \dfrac{4}{3} + \ldots + \dfrac{n + 1}{n} = \displaystyle\sum_{k=1}^{n} \dfrac{k + 1}{k}$

56. $\dfrac{1}{2} - \dfrac{1}{4} + \dfrac{1}{8} - \ldots + \dfrac{(-1)^{n+1}}{2^n} = \displaystyle\sum_{k=1}^{n} \dfrac{(-1)^{k+1}}{2^k}$

58. (A) $a_n = \dfrac{a_{n-1}^2 + 5}{2a_{n-1}}$, $n \geq 2$; $a_1 = 2$

$a_1 = 2$

$a_2 = \dfrac{2^2 + 5}{2(2)} = \dfrac{9}{4} = 2.25$

$a_3 = \dfrac{2.25^2 + 5}{2(2.25)} = 2.236\overline{1}$

$a_4 = \dfrac{2.236\overline{1}^2 + 5}{2(2.236\overline{1})} = 2.236067978$

(B) $\sqrt{5} = 2.236067978$ which, to nine decimal places,

$= a_4$ from (A)

(C) for

$a_1 = 3$

$a_2 = \dfrac{3^2 + 5}{2(3)} = 2.\overline{3}$

$a_3 = \dfrac{2.\overline{3}^2 + 5}{2(2.\overline{3})} = 2.238095238$

$a_4 = \dfrac{2.238095238^2 + 5}{2(2.238095238)} = 2.236068896$

$a_5 = \dfrac{2.236068896^2 + 5}{2(2.236068896)} = 2.236067978$

$\sqrt{5} = 2.236067978 = a_5$, to nine decimal places

60. $\{u_n\}$: $u_1 = 1$, $u_n = u_{n-1} + v_{n-1}$
$\{v_n\}$: $v_1 = 0$, $v_n = u_{n-1}$, $n \geq 2$

$u_1 = 1$	$v_1 = 0$
$u_2 = 1$	$v_2 = 1$
$u_3 = 2$	$v_3 = 1$
$u_4 = 3$	$v_4 = 2$
$u_5 = 5$	$v_5 = 3$
$u_6 = 8$	$v_6 = 5$
$u_7 = 13$	$v_7 = 8$
$u_8 = 21$	$v_8 = 13$
$u_9 = 34$	$v_9 = 21$
$u_{10} = 55$	$v_{10} = 34$

$\{u_n\}$ is the Fibonacci sequence
$\{v_n\}$ is the Fibonacci sequence preceded by 0.

62. $e^x = \displaystyle\sum_{k=0}^{\infty} \dfrac{x^k}{k!} \approx 1 + \dfrac{x}{1!} + \dfrac{x^2}{2!} + \ldots + \dfrac{x^n}{n!}$

$e^{-0.5} \approx 1 + \dfrac{-0.5}{1} + \dfrac{(-0.5)^2}{2!} + \dfrac{(-0.5)^3}{3!} + \dfrac{(-0.5)^4}{4!} = 0.6067708333$

$e^{-0.5} = 0.6065306597$, calculator

64. $\displaystyle\sum_{k=1}^{n} (a_k + b_k) = a_1 + b_1 + a_2 + b_2 + a_3 + b_3 + \ldots + a_n + b_n$

$= a_1 + a_2 + a_3 + \ldots + a_n + b_1 + b_2 + b_3 + \ldots + b_n$

$= \displaystyle\sum_{k=1}^{n} a_k + \sum_{k=1}^{n} b_k$

Exercise 11-2

2. $n^2 - 3n < 100$:

n	$n^2 - 3n$
1	-2
2	-2
3	0
4	4
5	10
6	18
7	28
8	40
9	54
10	70
11	88
12	108

$\Rightarrow$ 12 is first positive integer which fails

4. $n^2 = 5n - 6$:

n	n^2	$5n - 6$
1	1	-1

$\Rightarrow$ 1 is first positive integer which fails

6.

n	$4 + 8 + 12 + \cdots + 4n$	$2n(n + 1)$
1	4	$2(1)(1 + 1) = 4$
2	$4 + 8 = 12$	$2(2)(2 + 1) = 12$
3	$4 + 8 + 12 = 24$	$2(3)(3 + 1) = 24$

8.

n	$(a^5)^n$	a^{5n}
1	$(a^5)^1 = a^{5 \cdot 1} = a^5$	$a^{5 \cdot 1} = a^5$
2	$(a^5)^2 = a^{5 \cdot 2} = a^{10}$	$a^{5 \cdot 2} = a^{10}$
3	$(a^5)^3 = a^{5 \cdot 3} = a^{15}$	$a^{5 \cdot 3} = a^{15}$

10. P_1: $4^1 - 1 = 3$ which is divisible by 3
P_2: $4^2 - 1 = 15$ which is divisible by 3
P_3: $4^3 - 1 = 63$ which is divisible by 3

12. P_n: $4 + 8 + 12 + \cdots + 4n = 2n(n + 1)$
P_k: $4 + 8 + 12 + \cdots + 4k = 2k(k + 1)$
P_{k+1}: $4 + 8 + 12 + \cdots + 4k + 4(k + 1) = 2(k + 1)((k + 1) + 1) = 2(k + 1)(k + 2)$

14. P_n: $(a^5)^n = a^{5n}$
P_k: $(a^5)^k = a^{5k}$
P_{k+1}: $(a^5)^{k+1} = a^{5(k+1)}$

16. P_n: $4^n - 1$
P_k: $4^k - 1 = 3r, \ r \in N$
P_{k+1}: $4^{(k+1)} - 1 = 3s, \ s \in N$

18. P_n: $4 + 8 + 12 + \cdots + 4n = 2n(n + 1)$
Show P_1 is true.
P_1: $4(1) = 2(1)(1 + 1)$
$4 = 4$ Thus P_1 is true.

Show if P_k is true, then P_{k+1} is true.
P_k: $4 + 8 + 12 + \cdots + 4k = 2k(k + 1)$
P_{k+1}: $4 + 8 + 12 + \cdots + 4(k + 1) = 2(k + 1)(k + 2)$

Start with P_k: $4 + 8 + 12 + \cdots + 4k = 2k(k + 1)$
P_{k+1}: $4 + 8 + 12 + \cdots + 4k + 4(k + 1) = 2k(k + 1) + 4(k + 1)$
$= (2k + 4)(k + 1)$
$= 2(k + 2)(k + 1)$
$= 2(k + 1)(k + 2) \Rightarrow P_{k+1}$ is true

20. P_n: $(a^5)^n = a^{5n}$

Show P_1 is true.

P_1: $(a^5)^1 = a^{5 \cdot 1}$

$a^5 = a^5$ Thus P_1 is true.

Show if P_k is true, then P_{k+1} is true.

P_k: $(a^5)k = a^{5k}$

P_{k+1}: $(a^5)^{k+1} = a^{5(k+1)}$

Start with P_k: $(a^5)^k = a^{5k}$

$(a^5)^k \cdot a^5 = a^{5k} \cdot a^5$

$(a^{5k}) \cdot a^5 = a^{5k+5}$

$a^{5k+5} = a^{5(k+1)}$

$(a^5)^{k+1} = a^{5(k+1)} \Rightarrow P_{k+1}$ is true

22. P_n: $4^n - 1 = 3r$ for some integer r

Show P_1 is true.

P_1: $4^1 - 1 = 4 - 1 = 3 = 3 \cdot 1$ Thus P_1 is true.

Show if P_k is true, then P_{k+1} is true.

P_k: $4^k - 1 = 3s$ for some integer s

P_{k+1}: $4^{k+1} - 1 = 3t$ for some integer t

Start with P_k:

$4^k - 1 = 3s$ for some integer s

$4(4^k - 1) = 4(3s)$

$4^{k+1} - 4 = 4(3s)$

$4^{k+1} - 1 = 4(3s) + 3$

$4^{k+1} - 1 = 3(4s + 1)$; let $t = 4s + 1$

$4^{k+1} - 1 = 3t$ for some integer $t \Rightarrow P_{k+1}$ is true.

24.

n	n as sum of 3 or fewer positive integers		
8	$2^2 + 2^2 = 4 + 4 = 8$		
9	$3^2 = 9$		$1^2 = 1$
10	$1^2 + 3^2 = 1 + 9 = 10$		$2^2 = 4$
11	$1^2 + 1^2 + 3^2 = 1 + 1 + 9 = 11$		$3^2 = 9$
12	$2^2 + 2^2 + 2^2 = 4 + 4 + 4 = 12$		$4^2 = 16$
13	$2^2 + 3^2 = 4 + 9 = 13$		$5^2 = 25$
14	$1^2 + 2^2 + 3^2 = 1 + 4 + 9 = 14$		
15	fails		

26. Let $a = 1$, $b = 7$, $c = 5$, $d = 5$, then

$a^2 + b^2 = c^2 + d^2$ becomes

$1^2 + 7^2 = 5^2 + 5^2$

$1 + 49 = 25 + 25$

$50 = 50$ which is true but

$a = c$ or $a = d$ becomes

$1 = 5$ or $1 = 5$ which is false.

28. $P_n: \dfrac{1}{2} + \dfrac{1}{4} + \dfrac{1}{8} + \cdots + \dfrac{1}{2^n} = 1 - \left(\dfrac{1}{2}\right)^n$

Show P_1 is true.

$P_1: \dfrac{1}{2^1} = 1 - \left(\dfrac{1}{2}\right)^1$

$\dfrac{1}{2} = \dfrac{1}{2}$ Thus P_1 is true.

Show if P_k is true, then P_{k+1} is true.

$P_k: \dfrac{1}{2} + \dfrac{1}{4} + \dfrac{1}{8} + \cdots + \dfrac{1}{2^k} = 1 - \left(\dfrac{1}{2}\right)^k$

$P_{k+1}: \dfrac{1}{2} + \dfrac{1}{4} + \dfrac{1}{8} + \cdots + \dfrac{1}{2^k} + \dfrac{1}{2^{k+1}} = 1 - \left(\dfrac{1}{2}\right)^{k+1}$

Start with P_k:

$\dfrac{1}{2} + \dfrac{1}{4} + \dfrac{1}{8} + \cdots + \dfrac{1}{2^k} = 1 - \left(\dfrac{1}{2}\right)^k$

$\dfrac{1}{2} + \dfrac{1}{4} + \dfrac{1}{8} + \cdots + \dfrac{1}{2^k} + \dfrac{1}{2^{k+1}} = 1 - \left(\dfrac{1}{2}\right)^k + \dfrac{1}{2^{k+1}}$

$= 1 - \left(\dfrac{1}{2}\right)^k + \left(\dfrac{1}{2}\right)^{k+1}$

$= 1 - \left(\dfrac{1}{2}\right)^k + \left(\dfrac{1}{2}\right)^k\left(\dfrac{1}{2}\right)$

$= 1 - \left(\dfrac{1}{2}\right)^k\left(1 - \dfrac{1}{2}\right)$

$= 1 - \left(\dfrac{1}{2}\right)^k\left(\dfrac{1}{2}\right)$

$= 1 - \left(\dfrac{1}{2}\right)^{k+1} \Rightarrow P_{k+1}$ is true

30. $P_n: 1 + 8 + 16 + \cdots + 8(n - 1) = (2n - 1)^2; \ n > 1$

Show P_2 is true.

$1 + 8(2 - 1) = (2(2) - 1)^2$

$9 = 9$ Thus P_2 is true.

Show if P_k is true, then P_{k+1} is true.

$P_k: 1 + 8 + 16 + \cdots + 8(k - 1) = (2k - 1)^2; \ k > 2$

$P_{k+1}: 1 + 8 + 16 + \cdots + 8(k - 1) + 8((k + 1) - 1) = (2(k + 1) - 1)^2; \ k > 2$

Start with P_k:

$1 + 8 + 16 + \cdots + 8(k - 1) = (2k - 1)^2; \ k > 2$

$1 + 8 + 16 + \cdots + 8(k - 1) + 8((k + 1) - 1) = (2k - 1)^2 + 8((k + 1) - 1)$

$= 4k^2 - 4k + 1 + 8k$

$= 4k^2 + 4k + 1$

$= (2k + 1)^2$

$= (2(k + 1) - 1)^2 \Rightarrow P_{k+1}$ is true

32. P_n: $1 \cdot 2 + 2 \cdot 3 + 3 \cdot 4 + \cdots + n(n + 1) = \dfrac{n(n + 1)(n + 2)}{3}$

Show P_1 is true.

$$1 \cdot 2 = \frac{1(2)(3)}{3}$$

$2 = 2$ Thus P_1 is true.

Show if P_k is true, then P_{k+1} is true.

P_k: $1 \cdot 2 + 2 \cdot 3 + 3 \cdot 4 + \cdots + k(k + 1) = \dfrac{k(k + 1)(k + 2)}{3}$

P_{k+1}: $1 \cdot 2 + 2 \cdot 3 + 3 \cdot 4 + \cdots + (k + 1)(k + 1 + 1) = \dfrac{(k + 1)(k + 1 + 1)(k + 1 + 2)}{3}$

Start with P_k:

$$1 \cdot 2 + 2 \cdot 3 + 3 \cdot 4 + \ldots + k(k + 1) = \frac{k(k + 1)(k + 2)}{3}$$

$$1 \cdot 2 + 2 \cdot 3 + 3 \cdot 4 + \cdots + k(k + 1) + (k + 1)(k + 2)$$

$$= \frac{k(k + 1)(k + 2)}{3} + (k + 1)(k + 2)$$

$$= \frac{k(k + 1)(k + 2)}{3} + \frac{3(k + 1)(k + 2)}{3}$$

$$= \frac{(k + 1)(k + 2)(k + 3)}{3}$$

$$= \frac{(k + 1)(k + 1 + 1)(k + 1 + 2)}{3}$$

Thus P_{k+1} is true.

34. P_n: $\dfrac{a^5}{a^n} = \dfrac{1}{a^{n-5}}$; $n > 5$

Show true for $n = 6$.

$$\frac{a^5}{a^6} = \frac{1}{a^{6-5}}$$

$$\frac{1}{a} = \frac{1}{a}$$ Thus P_6 is true.

Show if P_k is true, then P_{k+1} is true; $n > 6$.

$$P_k: \frac{a^5}{a^k} = \frac{1}{a^{k-5}}$$

$$P_{k+1}: \frac{a^5}{a^{k+1}} = \frac{1}{a^{(k+1)-5}}$$

Start with P_k: $\dfrac{a^5}{a^k} = \dfrac{1}{a^{k-5}}$

$$\frac{a^5}{a^k} \cdot \frac{1}{a} = \frac{1}{a^{k-5}} \cdot \frac{1}{a}$$

$$\frac{a^5}{a^{k+1}} = \frac{1}{a^{k-4}}$$

$$\frac{a^5}{a^{k+1}} = \frac{1}{a^{(k+1)-5}} \Rightarrow P_{k+1} \text{ is true.}$$

36. P_n: $(a^n)^m = a^{mn}$; $m, n \in N$

Show true for P_1: $(a^1)^m = a^{m \cdot 1}$

$$a^m = a^m \quad \text{Thus } P_1 \text{ is true.}$$

Show if P_k is true, then P_{k+1} is true.

$$P_k: (a^k)^m = a^{mk}$$
$$P_{k+1}: (a^{k+1})^m = a^{m(k+1)}$$

Start with P_k:

$$(a^k)^m = a^{mk}$$
$$(a^k)^m \cdot a^m = a^{mk} \cdot a^m$$
$$a^{km} \cdot a^m = a^{mk+m}$$
$$a^{km+m} = a^{m(k+1)}$$
$$a^{(k+1)m} = a^{m(k+1)}$$
$$(a^{k+1})^m = a^{m(k+1)} \implies P_{k+1} \text{ is true.}$$

38. P_n: $x^n - y^n$ is divisible by $x - y$; $x \neq y$

Show true for P_1: $\dfrac{x' - y'}{x - y} = 1$ Thus P_1 is true.

Show if P_k is true, then P_{k+1} is true.

$$P_k: x^k - y^k = (x - y)[Q_1(x, y)]$$
$$P_{k+1}: x^{k+1} - y^{k+1} = (x - y)[Q_2(x, y)]$$

Start with P_k:
$$
\begin{aligned}
x^k - y^k &= (x - y)[Q_1(x, y)] \\
&= (x - y)[x^k + yQ_2(x, y)] \\
&= x^k(x - y) + y(x - y)[Q_2(x, y)] \\
&= x^k(x - y) + y(x^k - y^k) \\
&= x^{k+1} - x^k y + x^k y - y^{k+1} \\
&= x^{k+1} - y^{k+1} \quad \text{Thus } P_{k+1} \text{ is true.}
\end{aligned}
$$

40. P_n: $x^{2n} - 1$ is divisible by $x + 1$, $x \neq -1$

Show true for P_1: $x^2 - 1 = (x - 1)(x + 1) = (x + 1)[Q(x)]$

Thus P_1 is true.

Show if P_k is true, then P_{k+1} is true.

$$P_k: x^{2k} - 1 = (x + 1)[Q_1(x)]$$
$$P_{k+1}: x^{2(k+1)} - 1 = (x + 1)[Q_2(x)]$$

Consider
$$
\begin{aligned}
x^{2(k+1)} - 1 &= x^{2(k+1)} - x^2 + x^2 - 1 \\
&= x^{2k+2} - x^2 + x^2 - 1 \\
&= x^2(x^{2k} - 1) + (x - 1)(x + 1), \text{ using } P_k \\
&= x^2[(x + 1)[Q_1(x)]] + (x + 1)(x - 1) \\
&= (x + 1)[x^2 Q_1(x) + x - 1] \\
&= (x + 1)Q_2(x) \implies P_{k+1} \text{ is true.}
\end{aligned}
$$

42. P_n: $\dfrac{1}{1\cdot2\cdot3} + \dfrac{1}{2\cdot3\cdot4} + \dfrac{1}{3\cdot4\cdot5} + \cdots + \dfrac{1}{n(n+1)(n+2)} = \dfrac{n(n+3)}{4(n+1)(n+2)}$

Show P_1 is true.

$$\frac{1(1+3)}{4(1+1)(1+2)} = \frac{1(4)}{4(2)(3)} = \frac{1}{1\cdot2\cdot3} \Rightarrow P_n \text{ is true for } n = 1$$

Show if P_k is true, then P_{k+1} is true.

P_k: $\dfrac{1}{1\cdot2\cdot3} + \dfrac{1}{2\cdot3\cdot4} + \dfrac{1}{3\cdot4\cdot5} + \cdots + \dfrac{1}{k(k+1)(k+2)} = \dfrac{k(k+3)}{4(k+1)(k+2)}$

P_{k+1}: $\dfrac{1}{1\cdot2\cdot3} + \dfrac{1}{2\cdot3\cdot4} + \cdots + \dfrac{1}{k(k+1)(k+2)} + \dfrac{1}{(k+1)(k+2)(k+3)}$

$$= \frac{(k+1)(k+4)}{4(k+2)(k+3)}$$

$\dfrac{1}{1\cdot2\cdot3} + \dfrac{1}{2\cdot3\cdot4} + \dfrac{1}{3\cdot4\cdot5} + \cdots + \dfrac{1}{k(k+1)(k+2)} + \dfrac{1}{(k+1)(k+2)(k+3)}$

$$= \frac{k(k+3)}{4(k+1)(k+2)} + \frac{1}{(k+1)(k+2)(k+3)}$$

$$= \frac{1}{(k+1)(k+2)} \cdot \left[\frac{k(k+3)}{4} + \frac{1}{k+3}\right]$$

$$= \frac{1}{(k+1)(k+2)} \cdot \left[\frac{k(k+3)^2 + 4}{4(k+3)}\right]$$

$$= \frac{1}{(k+1)(k+2)} \cdot \left[\frac{k(k^2+6k+9) + 4}{4(k+3)}\right]$$

$$= \frac{1}{(k+1)(k+2)} \cdot \left[\frac{k^3 + 6k^2 + 9k + 4}{4(k+3)}\right]$$

$$= \frac{1}{(k+1)(k+2)} \cdot \frac{(k+1)^2(k+4)}{4(k+3)}$$

$$= \frac{(k+1)(k+4)}{4(k+2)(k+3)} \Rightarrow P_{k+1} \text{ is true}$$

44. P_n: $\dfrac{1}{1\cdot2} + \dfrac{1}{2\cdot3} + \dfrac{1}{3\cdot4} + \cdots + \dfrac{1}{n(n+1)} = \dfrac{n}{n+1}$

Show P_1 is true.

$$\frac{1}{1+1} = \frac{1}{2} = \frac{1}{1\cdot2} \Rightarrow P_n \text{ is true for } n = 1$$

Show if P_k is true, then P_{k+1} is true.

P_k: $\dfrac{1}{1\cdot2} + \dfrac{1}{2\cdot3} + \dfrac{1}{3\cdot4} + \cdots + \dfrac{1}{k(k+1)} = \dfrac{k}{k+1}$

$$P_{k+1}: \frac{1}{1\cdot 2} + \frac{1}{2\cdot 3} + \cdots + \frac{1}{(k+1)(k+2)} = \frac{k+1}{k+2}$$

$$\frac{1}{1\cdot 2} + \frac{1}{2\cdot 3} + \frac{1}{3\cdot 4} + \cdots + \frac{1}{k(k+1)} + \frac{1}{(k+1)(k+2)} = \frac{k}{k+1} + \frac{1}{(k+1)(k+2)}$$

$$= \frac{1}{(k+1)} \cdot \left[k + \frac{1}{k+2} \right]$$

$$= \frac{1}{(k+1)} \cdot \left[\frac{k(k+2)+1}{k+2} \right]$$

$$= \frac{1}{(k+1)} \cdot \frac{k^2+2k+1}{k+2}$$

$$= \frac{1}{k+1} \cdot \frac{(k+1)^2}{k+2}$$

$$= \frac{k+1}{k+2} \Rightarrow P_{k+1} \text{ is true}$$

46. The number of diagonals in a polygon with n sides.

$$P_n: 2 + 3 + 4 + \cdots + (n-2) = \frac{n(n-3)}{2}, \ n > 3$$

Show P_4 is true.

$$\frac{4(4-3)}{2} = 2 \Rightarrow \text{true for } n = 4$$

Show if P_k is true, then P_{k+1} is true.

$$P_k: 2 + 3 + 4 + \cdots + (k-2) = \frac{k(k-3)}{2}, \ k > 3$$

$$P_{k+1}: 2 + 3 + 4 + \cdots + (k-2) + (k-1) = \frac{(k+1)(k-2)}{2}, \ k > 3$$

$$2 + 3 + 4 + \cdots + (k-2) + (k-1) = \frac{k(k-3)}{2} + k - 1$$

$$= \frac{k(k-3) + 2(k-1)}{2}$$

$$= \frac{k^2 - 3k + 2k - 2}{2}$$

$$= \frac{k^2 - k - 2}{2}$$

$$= \frac{(k+1)(k-2)}{2} \Rightarrow P_{k+1} \text{ is true}$$

48. Prove: $0 < a < 1 \Rightarrow 0 < a^n < 1: P_n \quad (n \in N)$

Show P_1 is true.

$0 < a < 1 \Rightarrow 0 < a^1 < 1$, P_n is true for $n = 1$

Show if P_k is true, then P_{k+1} is true.

$$P_k: 0 < a^k < 1$$

$$P_{k+1}: 0 < a^{k+1} < a < 1$$

Start with P_k: $0 < a^k < 1$

$$0 < a^k \cdot a < 1 \cdot a$$

$$0 < a^{k+1} < a < 1 \Rightarrow P_{k+1} \text{ is true}$$

50. P_n: $2^n > n^2$, $n \geq 5$

Show P_5 is true.

$$2^5 > 5^2$$
$$32 > 25 \Rightarrow P_5 \text{ is true}$$

Show if P_k is true, then P_{k+1} is true, $k \geq 5$.
$$P_k: 2^k > k^2, \quad k \geq 5$$
$$P_{k+1}: 2^{k+1} > (k+1)^2, \quad k \geq 5$$

Start with P_k:

$$2^k > k^2 \qquad\qquad\qquad * \quad k \geq 5$$
$$2 \cdot 2^k > 2k^2 \qquad\qquad\qquad k^2 \geq 25 \quad \text{and} \quad 2k \geq 10$$
$$2^{k+1} > k^2 + k^2 \qquad\qquad\qquad k^2 - 2k \geq 15$$
$$2^{k+1} > k^2 + 2k + 1 \; * \qquad\qquad k^2 \geq 2k + 15 > 2k + 1$$
$$2^{k+1} > (k+1)^2 \quad \Rightarrow P_{k+1} \text{ is true.}$$

52. $n^2 + 21n + 1$, $n \in N$, is prime. Prove or disprove: $n = 18$ gives $18^2 + 21(18) + 1 = 703 = 19(37)$, a counterexample.

54. $a_1 = 2$, $a_n = a_{n-1} + 2$; $b_n = 2n$

Show P_1 is true:
$$a_1 = 2 = 2 \cdot 1 = b_1: \{a_n\} = \{b_n\} \text{ is true for } n = 1$$

Assume $a_k = b_k$ and show $a_{k+1} = b_{k+1}$.
$$a_{k+1} = a_k + 2 = b_k + 2 = 2k + 2 = 2(k+1) = b_{k+1} \Rightarrow \{a_n\} = \{b_n\} \text{ for all } n$$

56. $a_1 = 2$, $a_n = 3a_{n-1}$; $b_n = 2 \cdot 3^{n-1}$

Show P_1 is true:
$$a_1 = 2 = 2 \cdot 1 = 2 \cdot 3^0 = 2 \cdot 3^{1-1} = b_1 \Rightarrow \{a_n\} = \{b_n\} \text{ is true for } n = 1.$$

Assume $a_k = b_k$ and show $a_{k+1} = b_{k+1}$.
$$a_{k+1} = 3a_k = 3b_k = 3 \cdot (2 \cdot 3^{k-1}) = 2 \cdot 3^k = b_{k+1} \Rightarrow \{a_n\} = \{b_n\} \text{ for all } n.$$

Exercise 11-3

2. (A) 5, 20, 100, …

Since $\dfrac{20 - 5 = 15}{100 - 20 = 80}$ and $\dfrac{\frac{20}{5} = 4}{\frac{100}{20} = 5}$ the sequence 5, 20, 100, … is neither arithmetic nor geometric.

(B) -5, -5, -5, …

Since $-5 - (-5) = 0$ and $\dfrac{-5}{-5} = 1$ the sequence -5, -5, -5, … is arithmetic with $d = 0$, and geometric with $r = 1$. The next two terms are -5, -5 in both cases.

(C) 7, 6.5, 6, …

Since $6.5 - 7 = -0.5$ and $6 - 6.5 = -0.5$, the sequence is arithmetic with $d = -0.5$. The next two terms are 5.5, 5. Since $\dfrac{6.5}{7} = 0.92857\ldots$ and $\dfrac{6}{6.5} = 0.92307\ldots$ the sequence is not geometric.

(D) 512, 256, 128, …

Since $256 - 512 = -256$ and $128 - 256 = -128$, the sequence is not arithmetic.
Since $\dfrac{256}{512} = \dfrac{1}{2}$ and $\dfrac{128}{256} = \dfrac{1}{2}$, the sequence is geometric with $r = \dfrac{1}{2}$. The next two terms are 64, 32.

4. $a_1 = -11, \ d = 4$
$a_2 = -11 + 4 = -7$
$a_3 = -7 + 4 = -3$
$a_4 = -3 + 4 = 1$

6. $a_1 = 20, \ d = -6$
$a_n = a_1 + d(n - 1)$
$a_{12} = 20 + (-6)(12 - 1)$
$\quad = 20 - 66$
$\quad = -46$
$S_n = \frac{n}{2}(a_1 + a_n)$
$S_{12} = \frac{12}{2}(20 + (-46))$
$\quad = 6(-26)$
$\quad = -156$

8. $a_1 = 2, \ a_2 = 9 \Rightarrow d = 7$
$a_n = a_1 + d(n - 1)$
$a_{30} = 2 + 7(29) = 205$

10. $a_1 = -8, \ a_2 = 2$
$d = 2 - (-8) = 10$
$a_n = a_1 + d(n - 1)$
$a_{29} = -8 + 10(28) = 272$

12. $a_1 = 12, \ r = \frac{2}{3}$
$a_n = a_{n-1}r$
$a_2 = 12\left(\frac{2}{3}\right) = 8$
$a_3 = 8\left(\frac{2}{3}\right) = \frac{16}{3}$
$a_4 = \frac{16}{3} \cdot \frac{2}{3} = \frac{32}{9}$

14. $a_1 = 64, \ r = \frac{1}{2}$
$a_n = a_1 r^{n-1}$
$a_{13} = 64\left(\frac{1}{2}\right)^{12} = \frac{1}{64}$

16. $a_1 = 1, \ a_7 = 729, \ r = -3$
$S_n = \frac{a_1 - a_1 r^n}{1 - r}$
$S_7 = \frac{1 - (1)(-3)^7}{1 - (-3)} = 547$

18. $a_1 = -7, \ a_8 = 7$
$a_n = a_1 + (n - 1)d$
$7 = -7 + 7d \Rightarrow d = 2$
$S_n = \frac{n}{2}[2a_1 + (n - 1)d]$
$S_{100} = \frac{100}{2}[2(-7) + 99(2)]$
$\quad = 50[-14 + 198]$
$\quad = 9200$

20. $a_1 = -9, \ a_{12} = -31$
$a_n = a_1 + (n - 1)d$
$-31 = -9 + 11d \Rightarrow d = -2$
$a_{45} = -9 + 44(-2)$
$\quad = -97$

22. $a_6 = 26, \ a_{10} = 50$
$a_n = a_1 + (n - 1)d$
(1) $a_6 = a_1 + (5)d$
$\quad 26 = a_1 + 5d \Rightarrow a_1 = 26 - 5d$
(2) $a_{10} = a_1 + 9d$
$\quad 50 = a_1 + 9d$
(1) $\rightarrow$ (2): $50 = 26 - 5d + 9d$
$\qquad 50 = 26 + 4d$
$\qquad 24 = 4d$
$\qquad d = 6$
(1): $a_1 = 26 - 30 = -4$
$S_n = \frac{n}{2}[2a_1 + (n - 1)d]$
$S_{10} = \frac{10}{2}[2(-4) + 9(6)]$
$\quad = 5[-8 + 54]$
$\quad = 230$

24. $a_1 = -3, \; S_{12} = 60$

$$S_n = \frac{n}{2}[2a_1 + (n-1)d]$$

$$60 = \frac{12}{2}[2(-3) + 11d]$$

$$10 = -6 + 11d$$

$$16 = 11d$$

$$d = \frac{16}{11}$$

$$a_n = a_1 + (n-1)d$$

$$a_{12} = -3 + 11\left(\frac{16}{11}\right)$$

$$= -3 + 16$$

$$= 13$$

26. $a_1 = 324, \; a_9 = 4$

$$a_n = a_1 r^{n-1}$$

$$a_9 = 324r^8$$

$$4 = 324r^8$$

$$\frac{1}{81} = r^8$$

$$\frac{1}{3^4} = r^8$$

$$\frac{1}{\pm\sqrt{3}} = r$$

$$r = \pm\frac{1}{\sqrt{3}}$$

28. $a_1 = 20, \; r = 2$

$$S_n = \frac{a_1 - a_1 r^n}{1 - r}$$

$$S_{12} = \frac{20 - 20(2^{12})}{1 - 2}$$

$$= 81,900$$

30. $a_1 = 625, \; a_6 = -\dfrac{32}{5}$

$$a_n = a_1 r^{n-1} \qquad\qquad a_n = ra_{n-1}$$

$$a_6 = a_1 r^5 \qquad\qquad a_2 = -\frac{2}{5}(625) = -250$$

$$-\frac{32}{5} = 625r^5 \qquad a_3 = -\frac{2}{5}(-250) = 100$$

$$\frac{-32}{3125} = r^5 \qquad\qquad a_4 = -\frac{2}{5}(100) = -40$$

$$r^5 = -\frac{2^5}{5^5} \qquad\qquad a_5 = -\frac{2}{5}(-40) = 16$$

$$r = -\frac{2}{5}$$

32. $S_{40} = \displaystyle\sum_{k=1}^{40}(2k - 3) \Rightarrow$ arithmetic seq: $a_1 = -1, \; d = 2$

$$S_n = \frac{n}{2}[2a_1 + (n-1)d]$$

$$S_{40} = \frac{40}{2}[2(-1) + 39(2)] = 1520$$

34. $S_7 = \displaystyle\sum_{k=1}^{7}3k \Rightarrow$ geometric seq: $a_1 = 3, \; r = 3$

$$S_n = \frac{a_1 - a_1 r^n}{1 - r}$$

$$S_7 = \frac{3 - 3(3)^7}{1 - 3} = 3279$$

36. $f(x) = 2x - 5$: arithmetic seq: $a_1 = -3, \; d = 2$

$$S_n = \frac{n}{2}[2a_1 + (n-1)d]$$

$$f(1) + f(2) + f(3) + \cdots + f(20) = S_{20} = \frac{20}{2}[2(-3) + 19(2)] = 320$$

38. $f(x) = 2^x$; geometric seq: $a_1 = 2, \; r = 2$

$$S_n = \frac{a_1 - a_1 r^n}{1 - r}$$

$$f(1) + f(2) + \cdots + f(10) = S_{10} = \frac{2 - 2 \cdot 2^{10}}{1 - 2} = 2046$$

40. $S = 101 + 103 + 105 + \cdots + 499 \Rightarrow$ arithmetic seq: $a_1 = 101$, $d = 2$

$$a_n = a_1 + (n - 1)d$$
$$499 = 101 + (n - 1)2$$
$$398 = 2n - 2$$
$$400 = 2n \Rightarrow n = 200$$
$$S_n = \frac{n}{2}[a_1 + a_n]$$
$$S_{200} = \frac{200}{2}[101 + 499] = 60,000$$

42. $2 + 4 + 6 + \cdots + 2n = n + n^2$; arithmetic seq: $a_1 = 2$, $d = 2$

$$S_n = \frac{n}{2}[2a_1 + (n - 1)d]$$
$$= \frac{n}{2}[2(2) + (n - 1)2]$$
$$= \frac{n}{2}[2n + 2]$$
$$= n^2 + n = n + n^2$$

44. $6 + x + 8$; geometric series: $a_1 = 6$, $a_3 = 8$

$$a_n = a_1 r^{n-1}$$
$$a_3 = a_1 r^2$$
$$8 = 6r^2 \qquad\qquad a_2 = a_1 r$$
$$r^2 = \frac{4}{3} \qquad\qquad = 6 \cdot \frac{2\sqrt{3}}{3}$$
$$r = \frac{2}{\sqrt{3}} = \frac{2\sqrt{3}}{3} \qquad\qquad = 4\sqrt{3}$$

46. No. For $S_\infty = \dfrac{a_1}{1 - r}$, if $|r| < 1$, then $0 < 1 - r < 2$ and $\dfrac{2}{1 - r} > 1$. So the sum of an infinite geometric series with $a_1 = 2$ is never less than or equal to 1.

48.

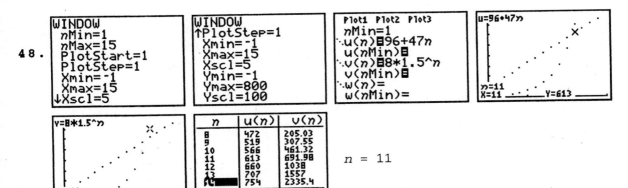

$n = 11$

50.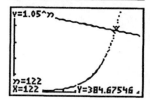

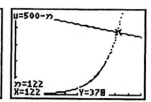

n	$u(n)$	$v(n)$
120	380	348.91
121	379	366.36
122	378	384.68
123	377	403.91
124	376	424.1
125	375	445.31
126	374	467.58

$n = 120$

$n = 122$

52. $16 + 4 + 1 + \cdots$

$a_1 = 16 \qquad S_\infty = \dfrac{a_1}{1 - r}$

$r = \dfrac{1}{4} \qquad\qquad = \dfrac{16}{1 - \frac{1}{4}} = \dfrac{64}{3}$

54. $4 + 6 + 9 + \cdots$

$a_1 = 4$

$r = \dfrac{3}{2} > 1 \Rightarrow$ no sum

56. $21 - 3 + \dfrac{3}{7} - \cdots$

$a_1 = 21 \qquad S_\infty = \dfrac{a_1}{1 - r}$

$r = -\dfrac{1}{7} \qquad\qquad = \dfrac{21}{1 - (-\frac{1}{7})} = \dfrac{147}{8}$

58. $0.\overline{5} = 0.5 + 0.05 + 0.005 + \cdots$

$a_1 = 0.5 \qquad S_\infty = \dfrac{a_1}{1 - r}$

$r = 0.1 \qquad\qquad = \dfrac{0.5}{1 - 0.1} = \dfrac{5}{9}$

60. $0.\overline{27} = 0.27 + 0.0027 + 0.000027 + \cdots$

$a_1 = 0.27 \qquad S_\infty = \dfrac{a_1}{1 - r}$

$r = 0.01 \qquad\qquad = \dfrac{0.27}{1 - 0.01} = \dfrac{3}{11}$

62. $5.\overline{63} = 5 + 0.63 + 0.0063 + \cdots$

$a_1 = 0.63 \qquad\qquad\quad 5 + S_\infty = 5 + \dfrac{a_1}{1 - r}$

$r = 0.01 \qquad\qquad\qquad\qquad\quad = 5 + \dfrac{0.63}{1 - 0.01} = 5 + \dfrac{7}{11} = \dfrac{62}{11}$

64. $S_n = a_1 + (a_1 + d) + (a_1 + 2d) + \cdots + (a_1 + (n - 1)d)$

$S_n = \dfrac{n}{2}[2a_1 + (n - 1)d]$

Show S_1 is true.

$S_1 = \dfrac{1}{2}[2a_1 + (1 - 1)d] = a_1 \Rightarrow$ true for $n = 1$

Assume $S_k = \dfrac{k}{2}[2a_1 + (k - 1)d]$ is true.

$$S_{k+1} = S_k + a_{k+1} = S_k + a_1 + kd$$

$$= \frac{k}{2}[2a_1 + (k-1)d] + a_1 + kd$$

$$= ka_1 + \frac{k}{2}(k-1)d + a_1 + kd$$

$$= ka_1 + a_1 + \left(\frac{k}{2}(k-1) + k\right)d$$

$$= (k+1)a_1 + \left(\frac{k(k-1) + 2k}{2}\right)d$$

$$= (k+1)a_1 + \left(\frac{k^2 - k + 2k}{2}\right)d$$

$$= (k+1)a_1 + \left(\frac{k^2 + k}{2}\right)d$$

$$= (k+1)a_1 + \frac{k(k+1)}{2}d$$

$$= \frac{k+1}{2}[2a_1 + kd] \Rightarrow \text{true for } k+1 \Rightarrow \text{true for all } n.$$

66. $a_1 = -2$, $a_n = -3a_{n-1}$, $n > 1 \Rightarrow a_1 = -2$, $r = -3$

$$S_n = \sum_{k=1}^{n} a_k = \frac{a_1 - a_1 r^n}{1 - r} = \frac{-2 - (-2)(-3)^n}{1 - (-3)} = \frac{(-3)^n - 1}{2}$$

68.

$a_n = 2 + (n-1)5$	$b_n = 2 + (n-1)3$
$a_1 = 2$	$b_1 = 2$
$a_2 = 7$	$b_2 = 5$
$\vdots$	$\vdots$
$a_{121} = 602$	$b_{121} = 362$

Observe that $b_{121} = 362 = a_{73}$. Note also that $b_{116} = 347 = a_{70}$ which implies that every reduction of n by five from 121 in b_n is equal to the corresponding a_n reduced by 3. Thus every time b_n is reduced by 5 an a_n is produced. b_n can be reduced 24 times $\left(\frac{121}{5} = 24.2\right)$ in this manner. Hence, there are $25 = 24 + 1$, ($a_1 = b_1 = 2$ is common) numbers in common.

70. S_n: $a_1 + a_1 r + a_1 r^2 + \cdots + a_1 r^{n-1} = \dfrac{a_1 - a_1 r^n}{1 - r}$

Show true for S_1.

$$S_1 = a_1 = a_1 \cdot \frac{1 - r}{1 - r} = \frac{a_1 - a_1 r^1}{1 - r} \Rightarrow \text{true for } n = 1$$

Assume $S_k = a_1 + a_1 r + a_1 r^2 + \cdots + a_1 r^{k-1} = \dfrac{a_1 - a_1 r^k}{1 - r}$ is true.

$$S_{k+1} = a_1 + a_1 r + a_1 r^2 + \cdots + a_1 r^{k-1} + a_1 r^k$$

$$= \frac{a_1 - a_1 r^k}{1 - r} + a_1 r^k$$

$$= \frac{a_1 - a_1 r^k}{1 - r} + \frac{a_1 r^k \cdot (1 - r)}{1 - r}$$

$$= \frac{a_1 - a_1 r^k + a_1 r^k - a_1 r^{k+1}}{1 - r}$$

$$= \frac{a_1 - a_1 r^{k+1}}{1 - r} \Rightarrow S_{k+1} \text{ is true}$$

72. $a_1 + a_4 = 2 \Rightarrow a_1 = 2 - a_4$
$(a_1)^2 + (a_4)^2 = 20 \Rightarrow (2 - (a_4)^2) + (a_4)^2 = 20$
$(a_4)^2 - 2a_4 - 8 = 0$
$(a_4 - 4)(a_4 + 2) = 0$

I. $a_4 = 4$
$a_1 = 2 - a_4 = -2$
$a_4 = a_1 + 3d$
$4 = -2 + 3d$
$d = 2$
$S_8 = \dfrac{8}{2}[2(-2) + 7(2)]$
$= 40$

II. $a_4 = -2$
$a_1 = 2 - a_4 = 4$
$a_4 = a_1 + 3d$
$-2 = 4 + 3d$
$d = -2$
$S_8 = \dfrac{8}{2}[2(4) + 7(-2)]$
$= -24$

74. <u>Firm A</u>
$a_1 = 25,000$
$d = 1200$
$a_{10} = 25,000 + 9(1200)$
$a_{10} = \$35,800$

<u>Firm B</u>
$a_1 = 28,000$
$d = 800$
$a_{10} = 28,000 + 9(800)$
$a_{10} = \$35,200$

76. $S_\infty = \dfrac{a_1}{1 - r}$

$600(0.7) + 600(0.7)^2 + \cdots = \dfrac{600(0.7)}{1 - 0.7} = \$1400$

78.

time	population
1	$A_0 + rA_0 = A_0(1 + r)$
2	$A_0(1 + r) + A_0(1 + r)r = A_0(1 + r)(1 + r) = A_0(1 + r)^2$
$\vdots$	
t	$A_0(1 + r)^t$

If $r = 2\%$:
$A_0(1 + r)^t = 2A_0$
$(1 + 0.02)^t = 2$
$t = \dfrac{\ln 2}{\ln 1.02} \approx 35$ years

80. (A) arithmetic sequence   (B) $T_n = 80 + (n)(-5)$

82. $10 + 10(0.9) + 10(0.9)^2 + \cdots$

$S_\infty = \dfrac{a_1}{1 - r}$

$= \dfrac{10}{1 - 0.9} = 100$ in

84. $\dfrac{600}{30} = 20$ generations
direct ancestors $= 2^{20} = 1,048,576$

86.

n	s	
1	$16 = 16 \cdot 1$	$1, 3, 5, \cdots, a_n, \cdots$
2	$48 = 16 \cdot 3$	$a_n = 1 + (n - 1)2$
3	$80 = 16 \cdot 5$	
$\vdots$		
20	(A) $d = 16 \cdot a_{20} = 16(1 + 19(2)) = 624$ feet	
$\vdots$		
t	(B) $d = 16 \cdot a_t = 16(1 + (t - 1)2) = 16(2t + 1 - 2) = 32t - 16$	

88.

$$\text{cells after } t \text{ days} = 2^{2t} = 1,000,000,000$$
$$\ln 2^{2t} = \ln 1,000,000,000$$
$$2t \ln 2 = \ln 1,000,000,000$$
$$t = \frac{\ln 1,000,000,000}{2 \ln 2}$$
$$t \approx 14.95 \text{ days}$$

The mouse dies on the 15th day (discrete model; round up).

90. (A) $a_1 = 400$, $a_{13} = 800$ (B) Find a_4: $a_4 = a_1 r^3$
$$a_n = a_1 r^{n-1}$$ $$= 400(1.059)^3$$
$$800 = 400r^{12}$$ $$\approx 475 \text{ cps}$$
$$2 = r^{12}$$
$$r \approx 1.059$$

92. If $a_1 = 0.001$, $r = 2$, find a_{33}:
$$a_n = a_1 r^{n-1}$$
$$a_{33} = 0.001(2)^{32} \text{ in} \times \frac{1 \text{ ft}}{12 \text{ in}} \times \frac{1 \text{ mi}}{5280 \text{ ft}}$$
$$\approx 68 \text{ miles}$$

If $a_1 = 0.002$, $r = 2$, find a_{32}:
$$a_n = a_1 r^{n-1}$$
$$a_{32} = 0.002(2)^{31} \text{ in} \times \frac{1 \text{ ft}}{12 \text{ in}} \times \frac{1 \text{ mi}}{5280 \text{ ft}}$$
$$\approx 68 \text{ miles}$$

94. $a_1 = \dfrac{220}{440}$, $a_2 = \dfrac{110}{440}$, $a_3 = \dfrac{55}{440}$, $\cdots$ $r = \dfrac{1}{2}$

$$S_\infty = \frac{a_1}{1-r}$$

$$= \frac{\frac{220}{440}}{1-\frac{1}{2}} = \frac{\frac{1}{2}}{1-\frac{1}{2}} \cdot \frac{2}{2} = \frac{1}{1} = 1 \text{ min}$$

96. shutter speeds: $1, \dfrac{1}{2}, \dfrac{1}{4}, \dfrac{1}{8}, \cdots$ $r = \dfrac{1}{2}$

  f-stops: $1.4, 2, 2.8, 4, \cdots$ $r = 1.42857\ldots \approx 1.4$

Exercise 11-4

2. $5! = 5 \cdot 4 \cdot 3 \cdot 2 \cdot 1 = 120$ **4.** $\dfrac{20!}{17!} = \dfrac{20 \cdot 19 \cdot 18 \cdot 17!}{17!} = 6840$

6. $(4 + 5)! = 9! = 9 \cdot 8 \cdot 7 \cdot 6 \cdot 5 \cdot 4 \cdot 3 \cdot 2 \cdot 1 = 362,880$

8. $\dfrac{10!}{2!8!} = \dfrac{10 \cdot 9 \cdot 8!}{2 \cdot 1 \cdot 8!} = \dfrac{10 \cdot 9}{2} = 45$ **10.** $\dfrac{12!}{12!(12-12)!} = \dfrac{1}{0!} = \dfrac{1}{1} = 1$

12. $\dfrac{10!}{3!} = \dfrac{10 \cdot 9 \cdot 8 \cdot 7 \cdot 6 \cdot 5 \cdot 4 \cdot 3!}{3!} = 604,800$ **14.** $12 = \dfrac{12 \cdot 11!}{11!} = \dfrac{12!}{11!}$

16. $9 \cdot 10 \cdot 11 \cdot 12 = \dfrac{12 \cdot 11 \cdot 10 \cdot 9 \cdot 8!}{8!} = \dfrac{12!}{8!}$ **18.** $\dbinom{12}{5} = \dfrac{12!}{5!7!} = 792$

20. $\dbinom{16}{8} = \dfrac{16!}{8!8!} = 12,870$

22. $\dbinom{100}{3} = \dfrac{100!}{3!97!} = 161,700$

24.

n	$\dbinom{2n}{n}$
165	9.599589238E97
166	3.828269925E98
167	1.526723216E99
168	6.088717586E99
169	overflow

26. $(3u + 2v)^3 = (3u)^3 + \dfrac{3!}{2!1!}(3u)^2(2v) + \dfrac{3!}{1!2!}(3u)(2v)^2 + (2v)^3$

$\qquad = 27u^3 + 54u^2v + 36uv^2 + 8v^3$

28. $(3p - q)^4 = (3p)^4 + \dfrac{4!}{3!1!}(3p)^3(-q) + \dfrac{4!}{2!2!}(3p)^2(-q)^2 + \dfrac{4!}{1!3!}(3p)(-q)^3 + (-q)^4$

$\qquad = 81p^4 - 108p^3q + 54p^2q^2 - 12pq^3 + q^4$

30. $(2x - y)^6 = (2x)^6 + \dfrac{6!}{5!1!}(2x)^5(-y) + \dfrac{6!}{4!2!}(2x)^4(-y)^2 + \dfrac{6!}{3!3!}(2x)^3(-y)^3$

$\qquad + \dfrac{6!}{2!4!}(2x)^2(-y)^4 + \dfrac{6!}{1!5!}(2x)^1(-y)^5 + (-y)^6$

$\qquad = 64x^6 - 192x^5y + 240x^4y^2 - 160x^3y^3 + 60x^2y^4 - 12xy^5 + y^6$

32. $(a + b)^{12}$: fifth term $= \dfrac{12!}{8!4!}a^8b^4 = 495a^8b^4$

34. $(x + 3y)^{13}$; third term $= \dfrac{13!}{11!2!}x^{11}(3y)^2 = 702x^{11}y^2$

36. $(2x - 5y)^8$; sixth term $= \dfrac{8!}{3!5!}(2x)^3(-5y)^5$

$\qquad\qquad = 56(8x^3)(-3125y^5)$

$\qquad\qquad = -1,400,000x^3y^5$

38. $(2p - 3q)^7$: fourth term $= \dfrac{7!}{4!3!}(2p)^4(-3q)^3 = -15,120p^4q^3$

40.

```
WINDOW
nMin=1
nMax=40
PlotStart=1
PlotStep=1
Xmin=-1
Xmax=40
↓Xscl=0▪
```

```
WINDOW
↑PlotStep=1
Xmin=-1
Xmax=40
Xscl=0
Ymin=-1
Ymax=(1E12)/6
Yscl=0
```

```
Plot1 Plot2 Plot3
nMin=0
··u(n)⊟(40 nCr n)
 u(nMin)⊟
··v(n)=▪
 v(nMin)=
··w(n)=
```

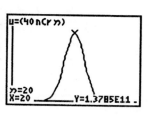

```
 n  │ u(n)
17  │ 8.9E10
18  │ 1.1E11
19  │ 1.3E11
20  │ 1.4E11
21  │ 1.3E11
22  │ 1.1E11
23  │ 8.9E10
n=17
```

```
40 nCr 20
      1.378465288E11
Ans/2
      6.892326441E10
▪
```

As both the graph and table show, $\dbinom{40}{20} = 1.378465288 \times 10^{11}$ is the largest term and one half of this largest term is $6.892326441 \times 10^{10}$. An examination of the table shows $\dbinom{40}{17}$ through $\dbinom{40}{23}$, a total of 7 terms, have values larger than one half the largest term.

42. (A)

k	$\dbinom{10}{k}(0.3)^{10-k}(0.7)^k$
0	5.9049×10^{-6}
1	1.37781×10^{-4}
2	0.0014467005
3	0.009001692
4	0.036756909
5	0.1029193452
6	0.200120949
7	0.266827932 ← largest
8	0.2334744405
9	0.121060821
10	0.0282475249
	1.000000000

(B) According to the binomial formula, the sum of $a_0 + a_1 + a_2 + \dots + a_{10} = 1$.

44. $(0.99)^6 = (1 - 0.01)^6$

$$= 1^6 + \frac{6!}{5!1!}(1)^5(-0.01) + \frac{6!}{4!2!}(1)^4(-0.01)^2 + \frac{6!}{3!3!}(1)^3(-0.01)^3$$

$$+ \frac{6!}{2!4!}(1)^2(-0.01)^4 + \frac{6!}{1!5!}(1)(-0.01)^5 + (-0.01)^6$$

$$= 1 - 0.06 + 0.0015 - 0.00002 + 0.00000015 - 0.0000000006$$
$$+ 0.000000000001$$

$$= 0.9414801494$$

$$= 0.9415 \text{ to four decimal places}$$

46. False. If $n = 6$, $p = 3$, $r = 3$ then 6 is divisible by 3, but $\dbinom{6}{3} = 20$ is not divisible by 3.

48. $\dbinom{2p}{p} = \dfrac{(2p)!}{p!p!} = \dfrac{(2p)(2p-1)(2p-2)\dots 1}{[(p)(p-1)(p-2)\dots 1][p(p-1)(p-2)\dots 1]}$ will have the factor containing p in the numerator reduced by a factor of p in the denominator, so it will not be divisible by p since no other factors in the numerator are divisible by p (prime).

50. $\dbinom{k}{0} = \dfrac{k!}{0!(k-0)!} = \dfrac{k!}{k!} = 1$

$\dbinom{k+1}{0} = \dfrac{(k+1)!}{0!(k+1-0)!} = \dfrac{(k+1)!}{(k+1)!} = 1$

52. $\dfrac{n-r+1}{r}\dbinom{n}{r-1} = \dfrac{n-r+1}{r} \cdot \dfrac{n!}{(r-1)!(n-(r-1))!}$

$$= \dfrac{n-r+1}{r(r-1)!} \cdot \dfrac{n!}{(n-r+1)!}$$

$$= \dfrac{n-r+1}{r!} \cdot \dfrac{n!}{(n-r+1)(n-r)!}$$

$$= \dfrac{n!}{r!(n-r)!}$$

$$= \dbinom{n}{r}$$

54.

Exercise 11-5

2. $\dfrac{20!}{18!} = \dfrac{20 \cdot 19 \cdot 18!}{18!} = 380$

4. $\dfrac{25!}{24!1!} = \dfrac{25 \cdot 24!}{24! \cdot 1} = 25$

6. $\dfrac{7!}{5!2!} = \dfrac{7 \cdot 6 \cdot 5!}{5! \cdot 2} = 21$

8. $\dfrac{18!}{3!(18-3)!} = \dfrac{18 \cdot 17 \cdot 16 \cdot 15!}{3 \cdot 2 \cdot 15!} = 816$

10. $C_{8,5} = \dfrac{8!}{5!3!} = 56$

12. $P_{13,5} = \dfrac{13!}{(13-5)!} = \dfrac{13!}{8!} = 154{,}440$

14. $C_{13,4} = \dfrac{13!}{4!9!} = 715$

16. $P_{20,4} = \dfrac{20!}{(20-4)!} = \dfrac{20!}{16!} = 116{,}280$

18. $3 \cdot 5 \cdot 2 = 30$

20. $P_{50,5} = \dfrac{50!}{(50-5)!} = 254{,}251{,}200$

22. (A) $P_{9,3} = \dfrac{9!}{6!} = 504$ (B) $C_{9,3} = \dfrac{9!}{3!6!} = 84$ **24.** $C_{7,2} = \dfrac{7!}{2!5!} = 21$

26. $P_{10,3} = \dfrac{10!}{7!} = 720$ with no digit repeated

$10 \cdot 10 \cdot 10 = 10^3 = 1000$ with repeated digits

28. $C_{12,5} = \dfrac{12!}{5!7!} = 792$ with all face cards

$C_{8,5} = \dfrac{8!}{5!3!} = 56$ with only jacks and queens

30. $10 \cdot 10 \cdot 10 \cdot 10 \cdot 10 = 10^5 = 100{,}000$ possible 5 digit zip codes

$P_{10,5} = \dfrac{10!}{5!} = 30{,}240$ contain no repeated digits

32. $C_{13,2} \cdot C_{13,3} = \dfrac{13!}{2!11!} \cdot \dfrac{13!}{3!10!} = 22{,}308$

34. $P_{12,2} \cdot P_{15,2} \cdot P_{18,2} = \dfrac{12!}{10!} \cdot \dfrac{15!}{13!} \cdot \dfrac{18!}{16!} = 8{,}482{,}320$

36. (A) As the tables show, they are equal.

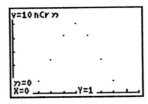

n	$u(n)$	$v(n)$
0	1	1
1	10	10
2	45	45
3	120	120
4	210	210
5	252	252
6	210	210

$n=0$

n	$u(n)$	$v(n)$
4	210	210
5	252	252
6	210	210
7	120	120
8	45	45
9	10	10
10	1	1

$n=10$

(B) As the graphs show, they are equal.

```
u=(10 nPr n)/n!




n=0
X=0          Y=1
```

```
v=10 nCr n




n=0
X=0          Y=1
```

38. $6 \cdot 5 = 30$

40. (A) $C_{5,2} = \dfrac{5!}{2!3!} = 10$ (B) $C_{5,3} = \dfrac{5!}{3!2!} = 10$ **42.** $2 \cdot 5!5! = 28,800$

44. (A) $C_{9,4} = \dfrac{9!}{5!4!} = 126$ (B) $C_{7,2} = \dfrac{7!}{5!2!} = 21$ (C) $2C_{7,3} = \dfrac{2 \cdot 7!}{4!3!} = 70$

46. There are $C_{26,10} = 5,311,735$ hands whose cards are all red and $C_{48,6} = 12,271,512$ hands containing all four aces, so the hand with four aces is more likely.

48. First give each student 1 doughnut. The number of distributions is then the number of ways of distributing the 3 remaining doughnuts among 9 students. There are 9 ways of choosing one student to get all 3 remaining doughnuts, 9×8 ways of choosing one student to get 2 doughnuts and another to get 1, and $C(9, 3)$ ways of choosing 3 students to get one more doughnut each: $9 + 72 + C(9, 3) = 165$.

CHAPTER 12

Exercise 12-1

2. $y^2 = 8x = 4(2)x$
opens right
Vertex $(0, 0)$; $a = 2$

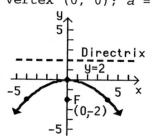

4. $x^2 = 4y = 4(1)y$
opens up
Vertex $(0, 0)$; $a = 1$

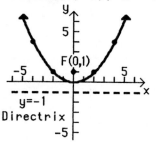

6. $y^2 = -4x = 4(-1)x$
opens left
Vertex $(0, 0)$; $a = -1$

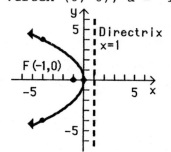

8. $x^2 = -8y = 4(-2)y$
opens down
Vertex $(0, 0)$; $a = -2$

10. $x^2 = -24y = 4(-6)y$
opens down
Vertex $(0, 0)$; $a = -6$

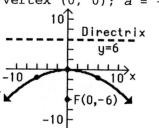

12. $y^2 = 6x = 4(1.5)x$
opens right
Vertex $(0, 0)$; $a = 1.5$

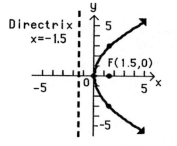

14. $x^2 = 58y$
$4a = 58$
$a = 14.5$; opens up
$F(0, 14.5)$

16. $y^2 = -93x$
$4a = -93$
$a = -23.25$; opens left
$F(-23.25, 0)$

18. $x^2 = -205y$
$4a = -205$
$a = -51.25$; opens down
$F(0, -51.25)$

20. Directrix: $y = 8 \Rightarrow a = -8$
$x^2 = 4ay$
$x^2 = -32y$

22. Focus $(3, 0) \Rightarrow a = 3$
$y^2 = 4ax$
$y^2 = 12x$

24. Directrix: $y = -\frac{1}{2} \Rightarrow a = \frac{1}{2}$
$x^2 = 4ay$
$x^2 = 2y$

26. y axis; $(30, -15)$
$x^2 = 4ay$
$30^2 = 4a(-15)$
$900 = -60a$
$a = -15 \Rightarrow x^2 = -60y$

28. x axis; $(121, 11)$
$y^2 = 4ax$
$(11)^2 = 4a(121)$
$121 = 484a$
$a = \frac{1}{4} \Rightarrow y^2 = x$

30. y axis; $(-\sqrt{2}, 3)$
$x^2 = 4ay$
$(-\sqrt{2})^2 = 4a(3)$
$2 = 12a$
$a = \frac{1}{6} \Rightarrow x^2 = \frac{2}{3}y$

32. (A) $y^2 = 3x \Rightarrow x = \dfrac{y^2}{3}$ (B)

$$x^2 = 3y$$

$$\left(\dfrac{y^2}{3}\right)^2 = 3y$$

$$y^4 = 27y$$

$$y^4 - 27y = 0$$

$$y(y^3 - 27) = 0$$

$y = 0 \qquad y = 3$

$x = 0 \qquad x = 3$

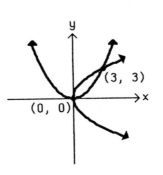

34. (A) $\qquad x^2 = 7y \Rightarrow y = \dfrac{x^2}{7}$ (B)

$$y^2 = 2x$$

$$\left(\dfrac{x^2}{7}\right)^2 = 2x$$

$$x^4 = 98x$$

$$x(x^3 - 98) = 0$$

$x = 0, \qquad x = \sqrt[3]{98} \approx 4.610$

$y = 0, \qquad y \approx 3.037$

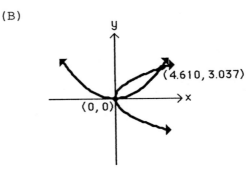

36. $\begin{array}{ll} x^2 = 4ay \\ y^2 = 4bx \end{array}$ $\begin{array}{l} x^4 = 16a^2y^2 \\ x^4 = 16a^2 \cdot 4bx \end{array}$

$$x^4 - 16a^2 \cdot 4bx = 0$$

$$x(x^3 - 64a^2b) = 0$$

$x = 0 \qquad\qquad x^3 = 64a^2b$

$$x = 4\sqrt[3]{a^2b}$$

$x = 0 \Rightarrow y = 0 \qquad\qquad x^2 = 16(a^{2/3})^2(b^{1/3})^2$

$$x^2 = 16a^{4/3}b^{2/3}$$

$$\dfrac{x^2}{4a} = y = \dfrac{16a^{4/3}b^{2/3}}{4a}$$

$$y = 4a^{1/3}b^{2/3} = 4\sqrt[3]{ab^2}$$

Intersections at:

$(0, 0), \left(4\sqrt[3]{a^2b}, \ 4\sqrt[3]{ab^2}\right)$

38. $x^2 = 4ay$ is a parabola opening upwards with focus at $(0, a)$. The two endpoints of the focal chord have coordinates (x, a) and $(-x, a)$.

For (x, a): $x^2 = 4a^2$

$\qquad\qquad x = \pm 2a$

The distance from $(-2a, a)$ to $(2a, a)$ will be the length of the focal chord,

and $d = \sqrt{(-2a - 2a)^2 + (a - a)^2}$

$\qquad = \sqrt{16a^2}$

$\qquad = |4a|$

40. True; the graph of $y^2 = 4ax$ is a parabola opening right if $a > 0$ and is a parabola opening left if $a < 0$.

42. False; for example the line $y = \dfrac{1}{2}x - 4$ does not intersect the graph of $x^2 = 4y$.

44. Directrix $y = 2$; focus $(-3, 6)$
$$(x_2 - x_1)^2 + (y_2 - y_1)^2 = d^2$$
$$(x - (-3))^2 + (y - 6)^2 = (y - 2)^2$$
$$x^2 + 6x + 9 + y^2 - 12y + 36 = y^2 - 4y + 4$$
$$x^2 + 6x - 8y + 41 = 0$$

46. Directrix $x = -3$; focus $(1, 4)$
$$(x_2 - x_1)^2 + (y_2 - y_1)^2 = d^2$$
$$(x - 1)^2 + (y - 4)^2 = (x - (-3))^2$$
$$x^2 - 2x + 1 + y^2 - 8y + 16 = x^2 + 6x + 9$$
$$y^2 - 8y - 8x + 8 = 0$$

48.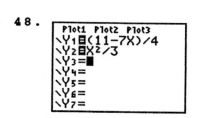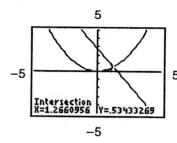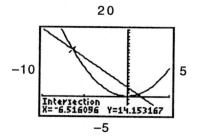

Intersection: $(1.27, 0.53)$, $(-6.52, 14.15)$

50.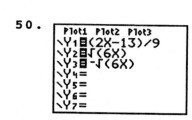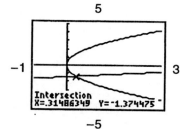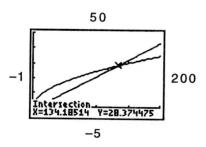

Intersection: $(0.31, -1.37)$, $(134.19, 28.37)$

52. (A) $x^2 = 4ay$
$3^2 = 4a(0.15)$
$4a = 60$
$x^2 = 60y$

(B) $4a = 60$
$a = 15$ inches

54. (A) $y^2 = 4ax$
$y^2 = 4(1.5)x$
$y^2 = 6x$, $0 \le x \le 6$

(B) $(x, 6) \Rightarrow 6^2 = 6x \Rightarrow x = 6$
$(6, 6)$
depth = 6 inches

Exercise 12-2

2. $\dfrac{x^2}{9} + \dfrac{y^2}{4} = 1$ $a^2 = b^2 + c^2$
$$9 = 4 + c^2$$
$$c = \pm\sqrt{5}$$
$F(\sqrt{5}, 0)$; $F'(-\sqrt{5}, 0)$
major axis length = 6
minor axis length = 4

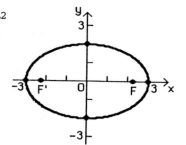

To check this graph:
$$4x^2 + 9y^2 = 36$$
$$9y^2 = 36 - 4x^2$$
$$y^2 = 4 - \frac{4}{9}x^2$$
$$y = \pm\sqrt{4 - \frac{4}{9}x^2}$$

4. $\dfrac{x^2}{4} + \dfrac{y^2}{9} = 1$ $c^2 + 4 = 9$

$c = \pm\sqrt{5}$

$F(0, \sqrt{5})$; $F'(0, -\sqrt{5})$
major axis length = 6
minor axis length = 4

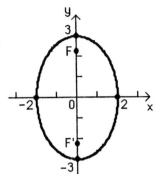

To check this graph:

$9x^2 + 4y^2 = 36$

$4y^2 = 36 - 9x^2$

$y^2 = 9 - \dfrac{9}{4}x^2$

$y = \pm\sqrt{9 - \dfrac{9}{4}x^2}$

6. $4x^2 + y^2 = 4$ $c^2 + 1 = 4$

$\dfrac{x^2}{1} + \dfrac{y^2}{4} = 1$ $c = \pm\sqrt{3}$

$F(0, \sqrt{3})$; $F'(0, -\sqrt{3})$
major axis length = 4
minor axis length = 2

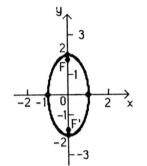

To check this graph:

$y^2 = 4 - 4x^2$

$y = \pm\sqrt{4 - 4x^2}$

8. $16x^2 + 25y^2 = 400$ $c^2 + 16 = 25$

$\dfrac{x^2}{25} + \dfrac{y^2}{16} = 1$ $c = \pm 3$

$F(3, 0)$; $F'(-3, 0)$
major axis length = 10
minor axis length = 8

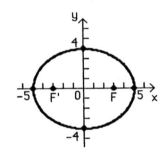

To check this graph:

$25y^2 = 400 - 16x^2$

$y^2 = 16 - \dfrac{16}{25}x^2$

$y = \pm\sqrt{16 - \dfrac{16}{25}x^2}$

10. $4x^2 + 3y^2 = 24$ $c^2 + 6 = 8$

$\dfrac{x^2}{6} + \dfrac{y^2}{8} = 1$ $c = \pm\sqrt{2}$

$F(0, \sqrt{2})$; $F'(0, -\sqrt{2})$
major axis length = $2\sqrt{8} \approx 5.66$
minor axis length = $2\sqrt{6} \approx 4.90$

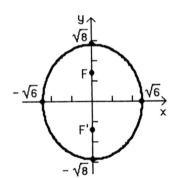
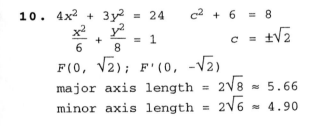

To check this graph:

$3y^2 = 24 - 4x^2$

$y^2 = 8 - \dfrac{4}{3}x^2$

$y = \pm\sqrt{8 - \dfrac{4}{3}x^2}$

12. $3x^2 + 2y^2 = 24$ $c^2 + 8 = 12$

$\dfrac{x^2}{8} + \dfrac{y^2}{12} = 1$ $c = \pm 2$

$F(0, 2)$; $F'(0, -2)$
major axis length = $2\sqrt{12} \approx 6.93$
minor axis length = $2\sqrt{8} \approx 5.66$

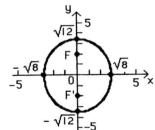
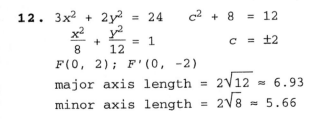

To check this graph:

$2y^2 = 24 - 3x^2$

$y^2 = 12 - 1.5x^2$

$y = \pm\sqrt{12 - 1.5x^2}$

14. Major axis on x axis, length $2a = 32 \Rightarrow a = 16$
minor axis length $2b = 30 \Rightarrow b = 15$

$$\frac{x^2}{16^2} + \frac{y^2}{15^2} = 1$$

$$\frac{x^2}{256} + \frac{y^2}{225} = 1$$

16. Major axis on y axis, length $2a = 16 \Rightarrow a = 8$
distance of foci from center $= 7 \Rightarrow c = 7$

$$
\begin{aligned}
c^2 &= a^2 - b^2 \\
49 &= 64 - b^2 \\
b^2 &= 15 \\
b &= \sqrt{15}
\end{aligned}
$$

$$\frac{x^2}{(\sqrt{15})^2} + \frac{y^2}{8^2} = 1$$

$$\frac{x^2}{15} + \frac{y^2}{64} = 1$$

18. Major axis on x axis
minor axis length $2b = 4 \Rightarrow b = 2$
distance between foci $= 50 = 2c \Rightarrow c = 25$

$$
\begin{aligned}
c^2 &= a^2 - b^2 \\
25^2 &= a^2 - 2^2 \\
a^2 &= 629 \\
a &= \sqrt{629}
\end{aligned}
$$

$$\frac{x^2}{(\sqrt{629})^2} + \frac{y^2}{2^2} = 1$$

$$\frac{x^2}{629} + \frac{y^2}{4} = 1$$

20. An ellipse having $(0, \pm 1)$ as the ends of the minor axis is almost circular when the foci are close to the origin and becomes more elongated as the distance of the foci from the origin increases.

22. $5x + 8y = 20 \rightarrow y = \dfrac{20 - 5x}{8}$

$$25x^2 + 16y^2 = 400$$

$$25x^2 + 16\left(\frac{20 - 5x}{8}\right)^2 = 400$$

$$25x^2 + 16\left(\frac{400 - 200x + 25x^2}{64}\right) = 400$$

$$100x^2 + 400 - 200x + 25x^2 = 1600$$

$$125x^2 - 200x - 1200 = 0$$

Using the quadratic formula:

$x = 4$ $x = -2.4$
$y = 0$ $y = 4$

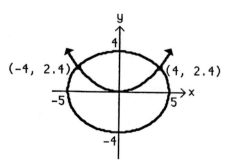

24. $3x^2 - 20y = 0 \rightarrow y = \dfrac{3x^2}{20}$

$$16x^2 + 25y^2 = 400$$

$$16x^2 + 25\left(\frac{3x^2}{20}\right)^2 = 400$$

$$256x^2 + 9x^4 = 6400$$

$$9x^4 + 256x^2 - 6400 = 0$$

$$x^2 = 16, \quad x^2 = -\frac{400}{9} \text{ (discard)}$$

Solving for x:

$x = 4,$ $x = -4$
$y = 2.4$ $y = 2.4$

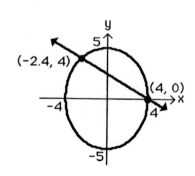

26. $x - 2y = 0 \rightarrow x = 2y$ $y = \dfrac{\sqrt{57}}{4}, \ x = \dfrac{\sqrt{57}}{2}$

$$3x^2 + 4y^2 = 57$$ $y = -\dfrac{\sqrt{57}}{4}, \ x = -\dfrac{\sqrt{57}}{2}$

$$3(2y)^2 + 4y^2 = 57$$
$$12y^2 + 4y^2 = 57$$ $(3.775, \ 1.887)$
$$16y^2 = 57$$
$$y = \pm\dfrac{\sqrt{57}}{4}$$

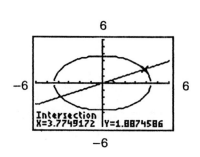

28. $x^2 - 12y = 0 \rightarrow x^2 = 12y$ $y \approx 1.124, \ x \approx 3.673$
$$3x^2 + 2y^2 = 43$$ $x \approx -3.673$
$$3(12y) + 2y^2 = 43$$
$$2y^2 + 36y - 43 = 0$$
$$y = \dfrac{-36 \pm \sqrt{1640}}{4}$$ $(3.673, \ 1.124)$
$$y \approx 1.124, \ -19.124 \ \text{(discard)}$$

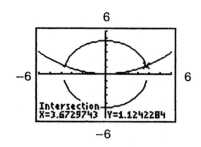

30. False. Both ellipses, $\dfrac{x^2}{26} + \dfrac{y^2}{25} = 1$ and $\dfrac{x^2}{16} + \dfrac{y^2}{15} = 1$ have center $(0, 0)$
and foci $(\pm1, 0)$.

32. True. The only line tangent to the ellipse at either $(-4, 0)$ or $(4, 0)$ is
vertical. All other lines through either point will intersect the ellipse
twice.

34. $\sqrt{(x - 0)^2 + (y - 9)^2} = \dfrac{3}{4}\sqrt{(x - x)^2 + (y - 16)^2}$

$$x^2 + y^2 - 18y + 81 = \dfrac{9}{16}(y^2 - 32y + 256)$$
$$16x^2 + 16y^2 - 288y + 1296 = 9y^2 - 288y + 2304$$
$$16x^2 + 7y^2 = 1008$$
$$\dfrac{x^2}{63} + \dfrac{y^2}{144} = 1: \text{ellipse}$$

36. $8x^2 + 35y^2 = 3600$ $x^2 = -25y$
$$35y^2 = 3600 - 8x^2$$ $x \approx \pm13.86$
$$y^2 = \dfrac{3600 - 8x^2}{35}$$

$$y = \pm\sqrt{\dfrac{3600 - 8x^2}{35}} \approx -7.68, \ 7.68 \ \text{(discard)}$$

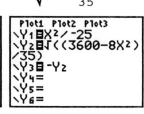
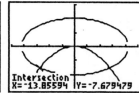
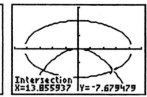

$(-13.86, -7.68)$
$(13.86, -7.68)$

38.
$$2x^2 + 7y^2 = 95 \qquad\qquad 13x^2 + 6y^2 = 63$$
$$7y^2 = 95 - 2x^2 \qquad\qquad 6y^2 = 63 - 13x^2$$
$$y^2 = \frac{95 - 2x^2}{7} \qquad\qquad y^2 = \frac{63 - 13x^2}{6}$$
$$y = \pm\sqrt{\frac{95 - 2x^2}{7}} \qquad\qquad y = \pm\sqrt{\frac{63 - 13x^2}{6}}$$

There are no points of intersection.

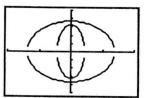

```
WINDOW
 Xmin=-10
 Xmax=10
 Xscl=5
 Ymin=-5
 Ymax=5
 Yscl=1
 Xres=1■
```

```
Plot1 Plot2 Plot3
\Y1◪√((95-2X²)/7
)
\Y2◪-Y1
\Y3◪√((63-13X²)/
6)
\Y4◪-Y3
\Y5=
```

40. Let the center of the table be (0, 0) on the coordinate system. For
$$\frac{x^2}{a^2} + \frac{y^2}{b^2} = 1, \quad a = 4, \quad b = 2.$$
$$c^2 + 2^2 = 4^2$$
$$c = \sqrt{12}, \text{ distance from center to focus}$$
$4 - \sqrt{12} \approx 0.54$ ft, distance from edge to focus
length of string = length of major axis = 8 ft

42. (A)
$$\frac{x^2}{a^2} + \frac{y^2}{b^2} = 1$$
$$\frac{x^2}{6^2} + \frac{y^2}{b^2} = 1$$
$$\frac{5.5^2}{6^2} + \frac{1^2}{b^2} = 1$$
$$30.25b^2 + 36 = 36b^2$$
$$5.75b^2 = -36$$
$$b^2 \approx 6.26$$
$$\frac{x^2}{36} + \frac{y^2}{6.26} = 1$$

(B)
$$\frac{5^2}{36} + \frac{y^2}{6.26} = 1$$
$$156.5 + 36y^2 = 225.36$$
$$36y^2 = 68.86$$
$$y^2 \approx 1.91278$$
$$y \approx 1.38$$

width = 1.38 + 1 = 2.38 feet to 2 decimal places

Exercise 12-3

2. $\frac{x^2}{9} - \frac{y^2}{25} = 1$; opens left/right
$b^2 = 25 \Rightarrow b = 5 \Rightarrow$ conjugate axis length $2b = 10$
$a^2 = 9 \Rightarrow a = 3 \Rightarrow$ transverse axis length $2a = 6$
$c^2 = a^2 + b^2 = 9 + 25 \Rightarrow c = \sqrt{34}$
foci: $F'(-\sqrt{34}, 0), F(\sqrt{34}, 0)$

To check: $25x^2 - 9y^2 = 225$
$$y^2 = \frac{25x^2 - 225}{9}$$
$$y = \pm\sqrt{\frac{25x^2 - 225}{9}}$$

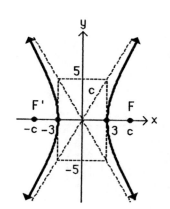

4. $\dfrac{y^2}{25} - \dfrac{x^2}{9} = 1$; opens up/down

$a^2 = 25 \Rightarrow a = 5 \Rightarrow$ transverse axis length $2a = 10$
$b^2 = 9 \Rightarrow b = 3 \Rightarrow$ conjugate axis length $2b = 6$
$c^2 = a^2 + b^2 = 25 + 9 = 34 \Rightarrow c = \sqrt{34}$

foci: $F'(0, -\sqrt{34})$, $F(0, \sqrt{34})$

To check: $9y^2 - 25x^2 = 225$
$$y^2 = \dfrac{25x^2 + 225}{9}$$
$$y = \pm\sqrt{\dfrac{25x^2 + 225}{9}}$$

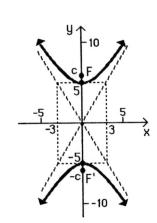

6. $x^2 - 9y^2 = 9$

$\dfrac{x^2}{9} - \dfrac{y^2}{1} = 1$; opens left/right

$a^2 = 9 \Rightarrow a = 3 \Rightarrow$ transverse axis length $2a = 6$
$b^2 = 1 \Rightarrow b = 1 \Rightarrow$ conjugate axis length $2b = 2$
$c^2 = a^2 + b^2 = 9 + 1 = 10 \Rightarrow c = \sqrt{10}$
foci: $F'(-\sqrt{10}, 0)$, $F(\sqrt{10}, 0)$

To check: $-9y^2 = 9 - x^2$
$$y^2 = \dfrac{x^2 - 9}{9}$$
$$y = \pm\sqrt{\dfrac{x^2 - 9}{9}}$$

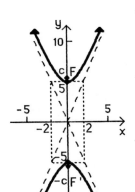

8. $4y^2 - 25x^2 = 100$

$\dfrac{y^2}{25} - \dfrac{x^2}{4} = 1$; opens up/down

$a^2 = 25 \Rightarrow a = 5 \Rightarrow$ transverse axis length $2a = 10$
$b^2 = 4 \Rightarrow b = 2 \Rightarrow$ conjugate axis length $2b = 4$
$c^2 = a^2 + b^2 = 25 + 4 = 29 \Rightarrow c = \sqrt{29}$
foci: $F'(0, -\sqrt{29})$, $F(0, \sqrt{29})$

To check: $4y^2 = 25x^2 + 100$
$$y = \pm\sqrt{\dfrac{25x^2 + 100}{4}}$$

10. $3x^2 - 4y^2 = 24$

$\dfrac{x^2}{8} - \dfrac{y^2}{6} = 1$; opens right/left

$a^2 = 8 \Rightarrow a = \sqrt{8} \Rightarrow$ transverse axis length $2a = 2\sqrt{8} \approx 5.66$
$b^2 = 6 \Rightarrow b = \sqrt{6} \Rightarrow$ conjugate axis length $2b = 2\sqrt{6} \approx 4.90$
$c^2 = a^2 + b^2 = 8 + 6 \Rightarrow c = \sqrt{14}$
foci: $F'(-\sqrt{14}, 0)$, $F(\sqrt{14}, 0)$
To check: $-4y^2 = -3x^2 + 24$
$$y^2 = \dfrac{3x^2 - 24}{4}$$
$$y = \pm\sqrt{\dfrac{3x^2 - 24}{4}}$$

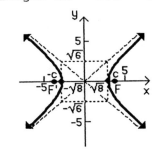

12. $3y^2 - 2x^2 = 24$

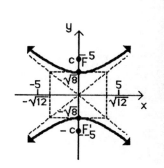

$\dfrac{y^2}{8} - \dfrac{x^2}{12} = 1$; opens up/down

$a^2 = 8 \Rightarrow a = \sqrt{8} \Rightarrow$ transverse axis length $2a = 2\sqrt{8} \approx 5.66$

$b^2 = 12 \Rightarrow b = \sqrt{12} \Rightarrow$ conjugate axis length $2b = 2\sqrt{12} \approx 6.93$

$c^2 = a^2 + b^2 = 8 + 12 = 20 \Rightarrow c = \sqrt{20}$

foci: $F'(0, -\sqrt{20})$, $F(0, \sqrt{20})$

To check: $3y^2 = 2x^2 + 24$

$$y = \pm\sqrt{\dfrac{2x^2 + 24}{3}}$$

14. Transverse axis on x axis
Transverse axis length $2a = 22 \Rightarrow a = 11$
Conjugate axis length $2b = 2 \Rightarrow b = 1$

$$\dfrac{x^2}{11^2} - \dfrac{y^2}{1^2} = 1$$

$$\dfrac{x^2}{121} - \dfrac{y^2}{1} = 1 \quad \text{or} \quad \dfrac{x^2}{121} - y^2 = 1$$

16. Transverse axis on y axis
Conjugate axis length $2b = 30 \Rightarrow b = 15$
Distance of foci from center $= 25$

$$c^2 = a^2 + b^2$$
$$25^2 = a^2 + 15^2$$
$$a^2 = 400$$
$$a = 20$$
$$\dfrac{y^2}{20^2} - \dfrac{x^2}{15^2} = 1$$
$$\dfrac{y^2}{400} - \dfrac{x^2}{225} = 1$$

18. Conjugate axis on y axis
Transverse axis length $2a = 2 \Rightarrow a = 1$
Distance between foci $2c = 48 \Rightarrow c = 24$

$$c^2 = a^2 + b^2$$
$$24^2 = 1^2 + b^2$$
$$b^2 = 575$$
$$b = \sqrt{575}$$
$$\dfrac{x^2}{1^2} - \dfrac{y^2}{575} = 1$$
$$x^2 - \dfrac{y^2}{575} = 1$$

20. Infinitely many; $\dfrac{x^2}{a^2} - \dfrac{y^2}{4a^2} = 1$, $\dfrac{y^2}{a^2} - \dfrac{4x^2}{a^2} = 1$ $(a > 0)$ are two examples.

22.

$\begin{aligned} y^2 - x^2 &= 3 \\ \underline{y^2 + x^2} &= 5 \\ 2y^2 &= 8 \\ y^2 &= 4, \end{aligned}$

$\begin{aligned} x^2 &= 5 - y^2 \\ x^2 &= 5 - (\pm 2)^2 \\ x &= \pm 1 \end{aligned}$

$\begin{aligned} y &= 2, & y &= -2 \\ x &= \pm 1 & x &= \pm 1 \\ (1, \ 2) & & (1, \ -2) \\ (-1, \ 2) & & (-1, \ -2) \end{aligned}$

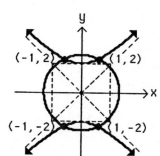

24.
$$2x^2 + y^2 = 17$$
$$\underline{x^2 - y^2 = -5}$$
$$3x^2 \quad\quad = 12$$
$$x^2 = 4$$
$$x = 2, \quad\quad x = -2$$
$$y = \pm3 \quad\quad y = \pm3$$
$$(2, 3) \quad\quad (-2, 3)$$
$$(2, -3) \quad\quad (-2, -3)$$

$$y^2 = 17 - 2x^2$$
$$y^2 = 17 - 2(\pm2)^2$$
$$y^2 = 9$$
$$y = \pm3$$

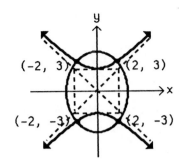

$(-2, 3)$ $(2, 3)$
$(-2, -3)$ $(2, -3)$

26.
$$y^2 - x^2 = 4$$
$$y - x = 6 \Rightarrow x = y - 6$$

$$y^2 - (y - 6)^2 = 4$$
$$y^2 - y^2 + 12y - 36 = 4$$
$$12y = 40$$
$$y = 3\tfrac{1}{3}$$
$$x = 3\tfrac{1}{3} - 6 = -2\tfrac{2}{3}$$

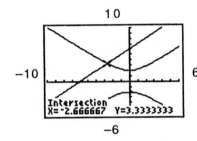

$(-2.667, 3.333)$

28.
$$y^2 - x^2 = 1$$
$$\underline{2y^2 + x^2 = 16}$$
$$3y^2 \quad\quad = 17$$
$$y = \pm\sqrt{\frac{17}{3}}$$
$$y \approx \pm2.380$$

$$x^2 = y^2 - 1$$
$$x^2 = \frac{17}{3} - 1$$
$$x \approx \pm2.160$$

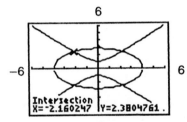

$(2.160, 2.380),\quad (2.160, -2.380),$
$(-2.160, 2.380),\quad (-2.160, -2.380)$

30. True. Since $c^2 = a^2 + b^2$, then $c > a$ and $2c > 2a$.

32. True. Since a vertical line through the vertex of $4x^2 - y^2 = 16$, $(-2, 0)$ or $(2, 0)$ is tangent to the graph, thus intersecting it 1 time, any non-vertical line through the vertex will intersect the graph twice.

34.
$$\sqrt{(x - 0)^2 + (y - 4)^2} = \frac{4}{3}\sqrt{(x - x)^2 + \left(y - \frac{9}{4}\right)^2}$$
$$x^2 + y^2 - 8y + 16 = \frac{16}{9}\left(y^2 - \frac{9}{2}y + \frac{81}{16}\right)$$
$$9x^2 + 9y^2 - 72y + 144 = 16y^2 - 72y + 81$$
$$7y^2 - 9x^2 = 63$$
$$\frac{y^2}{9} - \frac{x^2}{7} = 1: \text{hyperbola}$$

36. $y^2 - 3x^2 = 8$ $\qquad\qquad$ $x^2 = -\dfrac{y}{3}$

$\qquad$ $y^2 = 3x^2 + 8$ $\qquad\qquad$ $y = -3x^2$ $\qquad$ (−1.06, −3.37), (1.06, −3.37)

$\qquad\qquad$ $y = \pm\sqrt{3x^2 + 8}$

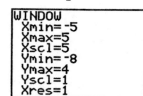 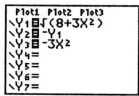 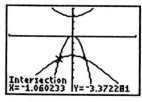 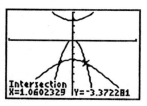

38. $8x^2 - 7y^2 = 58$ $\qquad\qquad\qquad$ $4y^2 - 11x^2 = 45$

$\qquad\qquad$ $y^2 = \dfrac{8x^2 - 58}{7}$ $\qquad\qquad$ $y^2 = \dfrac{11x^2 + 45}{4}$

$\qquad\qquad$ $y = \pm\sqrt{\dfrac{8x^2 - 58}{7}}$ $\qquad\qquad$ $y = \pm\sqrt{\dfrac{11x^2 + 45}{4}}$ $\qquad$ There are no points of intersection.

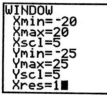 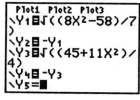 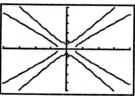

40. $\dfrac{x^2}{100^2} - \dfrac{y^2}{150^2} = 1$ $\qquad\qquad\qquad\qquad\qquad$ $\dfrac{x^2}{100^2} - \dfrac{y^2}{150^2} = 1$

$\quad$ $\dfrac{x^2}{100^2} - \dfrac{150^2}{150^2} = 1$ $\qquad\qquad\qquad\qquad$ $\dfrac{x^2}{100^2} - \dfrac{(-350)^2}{150^2} = 1$

$\qquad\qquad$ $x^2 = 2(100)^2$ $\qquad\qquad\qquad\qquad$ $\dfrac{x^2}{10000} - \dfrac{49}{9} = 1$

$\qquad\qquad$ $x \approx 141$ ft, top radius $\qquad\qquad$ $9x^2 - 490000 = 90000$

$\qquad\qquad\qquad\qquad\qquad\qquad\qquad\qquad\qquad$ $9x^2 = 580000$

$\qquad\qquad\qquad\qquad\qquad\qquad\qquad\qquad\qquad$ $x^2 = 64444.\overline{4}$

$\qquad\qquad\qquad\qquad\qquad\qquad\qquad\qquad$ $x \approx 254$ ft, base radius

$\quad$ $a^2 = 100^2$

$\quad$ $a = 100$ ft, radius of smallest circular cross section

Exercise 12-4

2. (A) $(x - 3)^2 = 8(y + 2)$ $\qquad\qquad$ (B) $x'^2 = 8y'$ $\qquad\qquad$ (C) parabola

$\qquad\quad$ $x' = x - 3$

$\qquad\quad$ $y' = y + 2$

4. (A) $(x + 2)^2 + (y + 6)^2 = 36$ $\qquad$ (B) $x'^2 + y'^2 = 36$ $\qquad$ (C) circle

$\qquad\qquad\quad$ $x' = x + 2$

$\qquad\qquad\quad$ $y' = y + 6$

6. (A) $\dfrac{(y - 9)^2}{10} - \dfrac{(x + 5)^2}{6} = 1$ $\qquad$ (B) $\dfrac{y'^2}{10} - \dfrac{x'^2}{6} = 1$ $\qquad$ (C) hyperbola

$\qquad\qquad\qquad$ $x' = x + 5$

$\qquad\qquad\qquad$ $y' = y - 9$

8. (A) $\dfrac{(x + 7)^2}{25} - \dfrac{(y - 8)^2}{50} = 1$ $\qquad$ (B) $\dfrac{x'^2}{25} - \dfrac{y'^2}{50} = 1$ $\qquad$ (C) hyperbola

$\qquad\qquad\qquad$ $x' = x + 7$

$\qquad\qquad\qquad$ $y' = y - 8$

10. (A) $(y + 2)^2 - 12(x - 3) = 0$ $\qquad\qquad\qquad\qquad\qquad$ (B) parabola

$\qquad\qquad$ $(y + 2)^2 = 12(x - 3)$

12. (A) $12(y - 5)^2 - 8(x - 3)^2 = 24$

$$\frac{(y - 5)^2}{2} - \frac{(x - 3)^2}{3} = 1$$

(B) hyperbola

14. (A) $4(x - 7)^2 + 7(y - 3)^2 = 28$

$$\frac{(x - 7)^2}{7} + \frac{(y - 3)^2}{4} = 1$$

(B) ellipse

16. $16x^2 + 9y^2 + 64x + 54y + 1 = 0$

$16x^2 + 64x + 9y^2 + 54y + 1 = 0$

$16(x^2 + 4x + 4) + 9(y^2 + 6y + 9) = -1 + 64 + 81$

$16(x + 2)^2 + 9(y + 3) = 144$

$$\frac{(x + 2)^2}{9} + \frac{(y + 3)^2}{16} = 1: \text{ellipse}$$

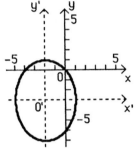

18. $y^2 + 12x + 4y - 32 = 0$

$y^2 + 4y + 4 = -12x + 32 + 4$

$(y + 2)^2 = -12(x - 3):$

parabola

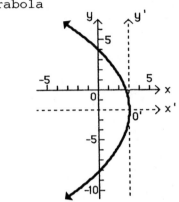

20. $x^2 + y^2 - 8x - 6y = 0$

$x^2 - 8x + 16 + y^2 - 6y + 9 = 16 + 9$

$(x - 4)^2 + (y - 3)^2 = 25: \text{circle}$

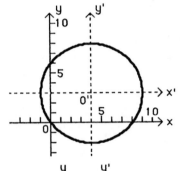

22. $16x^2 - 25y^2 - 160x = 0$

$16(x^2 - 10x + 25) - 25y^2 = 400$

$$\frac{(x - 5)^2}{25} - \frac{y^2}{16} = 1: \text{hyperbola}$$

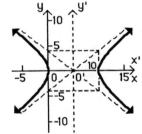

24. $Cy^2 + Ey + Dx = -F$

$$C\left(y^2 + \frac{E}{C}y + \frac{E^2}{4C^2}\right) = -Dx - F + \frac{E^2}{4C}$$

$$\left(y + \frac{E}{2C}\right)^2 = \frac{-D}{C}x - \frac{F}{C} + \frac{E^2}{4C^2}$$

$$\left(y + \frac{E}{2C}\right)^2 = \frac{-D}{C}\left(x + \frac{F}{D} - \frac{E^2}{4CD}\right)$$

$$y - k = y + \frac{E}{2C} \qquad x - h = x + \frac{F}{D} - \frac{E^2}{4CD}$$

$$k = \frac{-E}{2C} \qquad\qquad h = \frac{E^2}{4CD} - \frac{F}{D} \cdot \frac{4C}{4C}$$

$$h = \frac{E^2 - 4CF}{4CD}$$

26. Parabola, focus at $(2, 3)$, directrix the y axis

$y^2 = 4ax$; The x-coordinate of the vertex will be half-way between
$x = 2$ and $x = 0$ at $x = 1 \Rightarrow a = 1$
Focus $(h + a, k) = (1 + 1, 3) \Rightarrow h = 1$, $k = 3$

$(y - k)^2 = 4a(x - h)$
$(y - 3)^2 = 4(1)(x - 1)$
$y^2 - 6y + 9 = 4x - 4$
$y^2 - 4x - 6y + 13 = 0$

28. Hyperbola, vertices $(-2, -8)$ and $(4, -8)$ $\Rightarrow$ center is at $(1, -8)$, transverse axis length $2a = 6$; conjugate axis length $2b = 24$.

$a = 3$, $b = 12$, $h = 1$, $k = -8$

$$\frac{(x - h)^2}{a^2} - \frac{(y - k)^2}{b^2} = 1$$

$$\frac{(x - 1)^2}{9} - \frac{(y + 8)^2}{144} = 1$$

$16(x - 1)^2 - (y + 8)^2 = 144$
$16(x^2 - 2x + 1) - (y^2 + 16y + 64) - 144 = 0$
$16x^2 - 32x + 16 - y^2 - 16y - 64 - 144 = 0$
$16x^2 - y^2 - 32x - 16y - 192 = 0$

30. Ellipse, foci $(-3, 0)$ and $(-3, 6)$ $\Rightarrow 2c = 6$, $c = 3$
$\Rightarrow$ center is at $(-3, 3)$: $h = -3$, $k = 3$
vertices $(-3, -2)$ and $(-3, 8)$ $\Rightarrow 2a = 10$, $a = 5$

$c^2 = a^2 - b^2$ $\qquad$ $\dfrac{(x - h)^2}{b^2} + \dfrac{(y - k)^2}{a^2} = 1$
$9 = 25 - b^2$
$b^2 = 16$ $\qquad$ $\dfrac{(x + 3)^2}{16} + \dfrac{(y - 3)^2}{25} = 1$

$25(x + 3)^2 + 16(y - 3)^2 = 400$
$25(x^2 + 6x + 9) + 16(y^2 - 6y + 9) = 400$
$25x^2 + 150x + 225 + 16y^2 - 96y + 144 - 400 = 0$
$25x^2 + 16y^2 + 150x - 96y - 31 = 0$

32. Parabola, vertex at $(-6, 2)$, axis the line $y = 2$, passing through $(0, 7)$.

$(y - k)^2 = 4a(x - h)$ $\qquad\qquad$ $(y - 2)^2 = \dfrac{25}{6}(x + 6)$
$(y - 2)^2 = 4a(x + 6)$
$(0, 7)$: $(7 - 2)^2 = 4a(0 + 6)$ $\qquad$ $y^2 - 4y + 4 = \dfrac{25}{6}x + 25$
$25 = 24a$
$\qquad\qquad$ $a = \dfrac{25}{24}$ $\qquad\qquad$ $6y^2 - 24y + 24 = 25x + 150$
$\qquad\qquad\qquad\qquad$ $6y^2 - 25x - 24y - 126 = 0$

34. Hyperbola, vertices at $(2, 3)$ and $(2, 5)$ $\Rightarrow$ center at $(2, 4)$
$\Rightarrow 2a = 2$, $a = 1$

$$\frac{(y - k)^2}{a^2} - \frac{(x - h)^2}{b^2} = 1$$

$$\frac{(y - 4)^2}{1} - \frac{(x - 2)^2}{b^2} = 1$$

$(4, 0)$: $\dfrac{(-4)^2}{1} - \dfrac{(4 - 2)^2}{b^2} = 1$

$16b^2 - 4 = b^2$
$15b^2 = 4$
$b^2 = \dfrac{4}{15}$

$$\frac{(y - 4)^2}{1} - \frac{(x - 2)^2}{4/15} = 1$$

$4(y - 4)^2 - 15(x - 2)^2 = 4$
$4(y^2 - 8y + 16) - 15(x^2 - 4x + 4) = 4$
$4y^2 - 32y + 64 - 15x^2 + 60x - 60 - 4 = 0$
$-15x^2 + 4y^2 + 60x - 32y = 0$
$15x^2 - 4y^2 - 60x + 32y = 0$

36. $\dfrac{(x+2)^2}{9} + \dfrac{(y+3)^2}{16} = 1 \Rightarrow \dfrac{x'^2}{9} + \dfrac{y'^2}{16} = 1$

$c = \pm\sqrt{16 - 9} = \pm\sqrt{7}$

$x' = x + 2, \ y' = y + 3$ foci: $(0, \sqrt{7})'$, $(0, -\sqrt{7})'$

$\qquad\qquad\qquad\qquad\qquad$: $(-2, \sqrt{7} - 3)$, $(-2, -\sqrt{7} - 3)$

38 $(y + 2)^2 = -12(x - 3)$

$\qquad\quad y'^2 = -12x' \Rightarrow 4p = -12 \Rightarrow p = -3$

$y' = y + 2, \ x' = x - 3$

$\qquad\qquad\qquad\qquad$ focus: $(-3, 0)'$

$\qquad\qquad\qquad\qquad$: $(0, -2)$

40. $\dfrac{(x-5)^2}{25} - \dfrac{y^2}{16} = 1$

$x' = x - 5, \ y' = y$ foci: $(\sqrt{41}, 0)'$, $(-\sqrt{41}, 0)'$

$c^2 = 25 + 16 = 41$: $(\sqrt{41} + 5, 0)$, $(-\sqrt{41} + 5, 0)$

$\quad c = \pm\sqrt{41}$

42. (1) $8x^2 + 3y^2 - 14x + 17y - 39 = 0$

(2) $5x - 11y = 23$

Write (1) as $3y^2 + 17y + (8x^2 - 14x - 39) = 0$ and solve for y:

$$y = \frac{-17 \pm \sqrt{17^2 - 4\cdot 3(8x^2 - 14x - 39)}}{2\cdot 3} = \frac{-17}{6} \pm \frac{\sqrt{-96x^2 + 168x + 757}}{6} \ .$$

Solving (2) for y gives $y = \dfrac{5x - 23}{11}$.

Graph these three equations to obtain $(-2.06, -3.03)$ and $(3.45, -0.52)$.

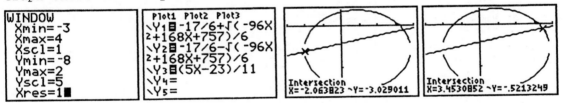

44. (1) $4x^2 - y^2 - 24x - 2y + 35 = 0$

$\qquad y^2 + 2y + (-4x^2 + 24x - 35) = 0$; solving for y

$$y = \frac{-2 \pm \sqrt{2^2 - 4(-4x^2 + 24x - 35)}}{2}$$

$$= \frac{-2 \pm \sqrt{16x^2 - 96x + 144}}{2}$$

$$= -1 \pm \sqrt{4x^2 - 24x + 36}$$

(2) $2x^2 + 6y^2 - 3x - 34 = 0$

$\qquad 6y^2 = -2x^2 + 3x + 34$

$\qquad\ y^2 = \dfrac{-2x^2 + 3x + 34}{6}$

$\qquad\ y = \dfrac{\pm\sqrt{-2x^2 + 3x + 34}}{\sqrt{6}}$

Graph these four equations to obtain (1.30, 2.40), (2.39, -2.23), (3.43, -1.86), (4.19, 1.38).

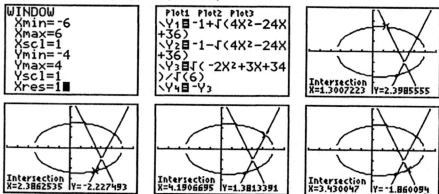

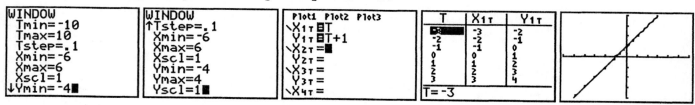

Exercise 12-5

2. Eliminating the parameter gives $y = x + 1$.

The graph is a straight line.

4. Eliminating the parameter gives $y = x + 1$, $x \geq 0$.

The graph is a ray (part of a straight line).

6. Eliminating the parameter gives $y = \dfrac{x}{2}$.

The graph is a straight line.

8. Eliminating the parameter gives $y = \dfrac{x^2}{4}$ ($x^2 = 4y$).

The graph is a parabola.

10. Eliminating the parameter gives $y = \dfrac{x^2}{4}$ $(x^2 = 4y)$, $x \geq 0$.

The graph is a parabola; the right half of the parabola in problem 8.

12. $x = 3 \sin \theta$, $y = 3 \cos \theta$, $0 \leq \theta \leq 2\pi$

$\sin \theta = \dfrac{x}{3}$ $\cos \theta = \dfrac{y}{3}$

$\cos^2\theta + \sin^2\theta = 1$

$\dfrac{y^2}{9} + \dfrac{x^2}{9} = 1$

$x^2 + y^2 = 9$; circle

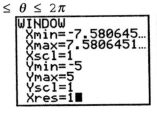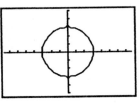

14. $x = 3 + 4 \sin \theta$, $y = 2 + 2 \cos \theta$, $0 \leq \theta \leq 2\pi$

$\sin \theta = \dfrac{x - 3}{4}$ $\cos \theta = \dfrac{y - 2}{2}$

$\cos^2\theta + \sin^2\theta = 1$

$\dfrac{(y - 2)^2}{4} + \dfrac{(x - 3)^2}{16} = 1$

$\dfrac{(x - 3)^2}{16} + \dfrac{(y - 2)^2}{4} = 1$; ellipse

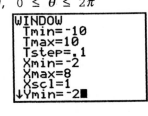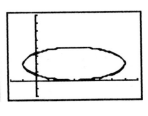

16. $x = t - 1$ $y = \dfrac{2}{t - 1}$, $t \neq 1$

$t = x + 1$ $y = \dfrac{2}{x + 1 - 1}$

$y = \dfrac{2}{x}$, $x \neq 0$; a rotated hyperbola

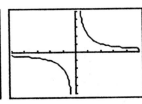

18. $x = t^3$ $y = t^2 + 1$
$t = x^{1/3}$ $y = x^{2/3} + 1$

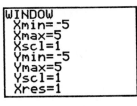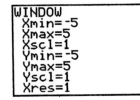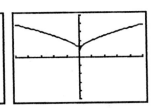

20. $Cy^2 + Dx + Ey + F = 0$; Answers may vary.

Let $y = t$. Then $Dx = -Ct^2 - Et - F$

$x = \dfrac{-(Ct^2 + Et + F)}{D}$, $y = t$; parabola; $t \in (-\infty, \infty)$.

22. $x = e^t$ $y = e^{-t}$
$t = \ln x$ $y = e^{-\ln x}$
        $y = e^{\ln x^{-1}}$

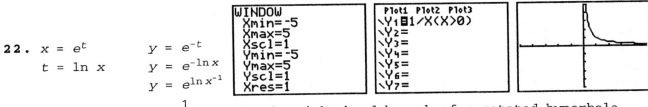

$y = \dfrac{1}{x}$, $x > 0$; the right hand branch of a rotated hyperbola

24. $x = 3 \sec^2 \theta \Rightarrow \sec^2 \theta = \dfrac{x}{3}$, $x \geq 3$ $\tan^2 \theta + 1 = \sec^2 \theta$

$y = 2 \tan^2 \theta \Rightarrow \tan^2 \theta = \dfrac{y}{2}$ $\dfrac{y}{2} + 1 = \dfrac{x}{3}$

$3y + 6 = 2x$

$3y = 2x - 6$

$y = \dfrac{2}{3}x - 2$, $x \geq 3$; a ray

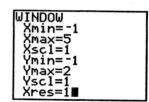
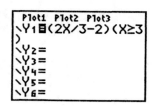
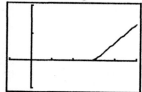

26. $x = \dfrac{4t}{t^2 + 1}$ (1), $y = \dfrac{4t^2}{t^2 + 1}$ (2)

Solve (2) for t^2: $yt^2 + y = 4t^2$

$y = 4t^2 - yt^2$

$\dfrac{y}{4 - y} = t^2$, $y \neq 4$

Substitute (2) → (1): $x = \dfrac{4\sqrt{\frac{y}{4-y}}}{\frac{y}{4-y} + 1}$

$\dfrac{xy}{4 - y} + x = 4\sqrt{\dfrac{y}{4 - y}}$

$\dfrac{xy + 4x - xy}{4 - y} = 4\sqrt{\dfrac{y}{4 - y}}$

$\dfrac{x}{4 - y} = \sqrt{\dfrac{y}{4 - y}}$

$\dfrac{x^2}{(4 - y)^2} = \dfrac{y}{4 - y}$

$\dfrac{x^2}{4 - y} = y$

$x^2 = 4y - y^2$

$x^2 + y^2 - 4y = 0$

$x^2 + (y - 2)^2 = 4$; circle with hole at (0, 4).

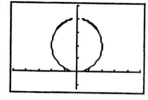

28. $x = 2\theta - 2 \sin \theta$, $y = 1 \cos \theta$, $0 \leq \theta \leq 2\pi$

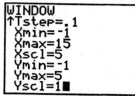

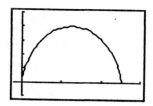

30. $x = 1 + 3 \sec t$, $y = -2 + 2 \tan 2$, $0 \leq t \leq 2\pi$, $t \neq \dfrac{\pi}{2}$, $\dfrac{3\pi}{2}$

$\sec t = \dfrac{x - 1}{3}$ $\tan t = \dfrac{y + 2}{2}$

$\sec^2 t - \tan^2 t = 1$

$\dfrac{(x - 1)^2}{9} - \dfrac{(y + 2)^2}{4} = 1$;

hyperbola with center $(1, -2)$.

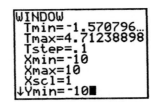
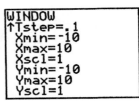

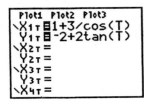
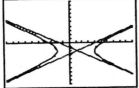
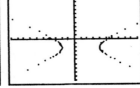

32. $x = -4 + 5 \cos t$, $y = 1 + 8 \sin t$, $0 \leq t \leq 2\pi$

$\cos t = \dfrac{x + 4}{5}$ $\sin t = \dfrac{y - 1}{8}$

$\cos^2 t + \sin^2 t = 1$

$\dfrac{(x + 4)^2}{25} + \dfrac{(y - 1)^2}{64} = 1$; ellipse with center $(-4, 1)$.

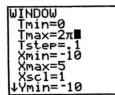
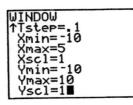

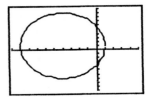

34. $x = \cot t$, $y = \dfrac{3t \cot t}{|t|}$, $-\pi < t < \pi$, $t \neq 0$

$x^2 = \cot^2 t$ $y^2 = \dfrac{9t^2 \cot^2 t}{t^2}$

$y^2 = 9 \cot^2 t$

$y^2 = 9x^2$

$9x^2 - y^2 = 0$

36. $36x^2 + 360x + 4y^2 - 8y + 760 = 0$

$36(x^2 + 10x + 25) + 4(y^2 - 2y + 1) = -760 + 900 + 4$

$36(x + 5)^2 + 4(y - 1)^2 = 144$

$\dfrac{(x + 5)^2}{4} + \dfrac{(y - 1)^2}{36} = 1$; Ellipse, center at $(-5, 1)$

Let $\cos^2 t = \dfrac{(x + 5)^2}{4}$ and $\sin^2 t = \dfrac{(y - 1)^2}{36}$

$\cos t = \dfrac{x + 5}{2}$ $\sin t = \dfrac{y - 1}{6}$

$2 \cos t = x + 5$ $6 \sin t = y - 1$

$x = 2 \cos t - 5$ $y = 6 \sin t + 1$, $0 \leq t \leq 2\pi$

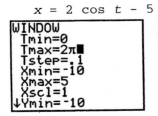
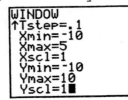

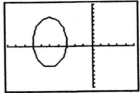

38. $16x^2 + 32x - 9y^2 - 36y - 164 = 0$

$16(x^2 + 2x + 1) - 9(y^2 + 4y + 4) = 164 + 16 - 36$

$16(x + 1)^2 - 9(y + 2)^2 = 144$

$$\frac{(x + 1)^2}{9} - \frac{(y + 2)^2}{16} = 1 \text{ ; Hyperbola, center at } (-1, -2)$$

Let $\sec^2 t = \dfrac{(x + 1)^2}{9}$ and $\tan^2 t = \dfrac{(y + 2)^2}{16}$

$\sec t = \dfrac{x + 1}{3}$ $\qquad\qquad \tan t = \dfrac{y + 2}{4}$

$3 \sec t = x + 1$ $\qquad\qquad 4 \tan t = y + 2$

$x = 3 \sec t - 1$ $\qquad\qquad y = 4 \tan t - 2, \ -\dfrac{\pi}{2} \le t \le \dfrac{3\pi}{2}, \ t \ne \dfrac{\pi}{2}$

 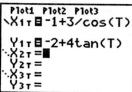

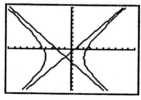 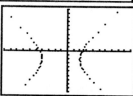

40. $x = 4 \sin \pi t, \ y = 2 \cos \pi t, \ t \ge 0$

(A)

T	X₁ₜ	Y₁ₜ
.1	1.2361	1.9021
1.1	-1.236	-1.902
2.1	1.2361	1.9021
3.1	-1.236	-1.902
4.1	1.2361	1.9021
5.1	-1.236	-1.902
6.1	1.2361	1.9021
T=.1		

$(1.2, \ 1.9)$

(B) $\sin^2 \pi t + \cos^2 \pi t = 1$

$$\left(\frac{x}{4}\right)^2 + \left(\frac{y}{2}\right)^2 = 1$$

$$\frac{x^2}{16} + \frac{y^2}{4} = 1; \text{ an ellipse}$$

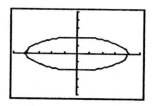

42. $\alpha = 40°, \ v_0 = 300, \ a_0 = 0$:

The equations of motion are $x = 300 \cos 40° \cdot t$ and $y = -4.9t^2 + 300 \sin 40° \cdot t$.

(A) At impact $y = 0 = -4.9t^2 + 300 \sin 40° \cdot t$
from which $t \approx 39.354343 \approx 39.354$ sec.

(B) Range $\approx 300 \cos 40° \cdot 39.354 \approx 9044.153$ m ≈ 9.044 km

(C) Maximum height occurs at one half of the impact time.

Maximum height $= -4.9\left(\dfrac{39.354}{2}\right)^2 + 300 \sin 40° \cdot \left(\dfrac{39.354}{2}\right) \approx 1897.236$ m

PART II
ANSWERS

CHAPTER 1

Exercise 1-1

1. True **2.** True **3.** False **4.** True **5.** False **6.** True

7. True **8.** True **9.** $7 + x$ **10.** vu **11.** $(xy)z$ **12.** $(3 + 7) + y$

13. $9m$ **14.** $u + v$ **15.** Commutative$(\cdot)$ **16.** Associative$(\cdot)$

17. Distributive **18.** Negatives **19.** Inverse$(\cdot)$ **20.** Subtraction

21. Inverse $(+)$ **22.** Division **23.** Identity $(+)$ **24.** Distributive **25.** Negatives **26.** Zero **27.** $\{-2, 0, 2, 4\}$

28. $\{-3, -1, 1, 3, 5\}$ **29.** $\{a, s, t, u\}$ **30.** $\{c, o, n, s, e, u\}$

31. $\varnothing$ **32.** $\varnothing$ **33.** (A) 4 (B) 8 (C) 16

34. 2^n **35.** Negatives **36.** Commutative $(\cdot)$ **37.** Associative $(\cdot)$

38. Associative $(+)$ **39.** Distributive **40.** Distributive

41. Zero **42.** Negatives **43.** Yes **44.** No

45. (A) T (B) F (C) T **46.** (A) F (B) T (C) T

47. $\frac{3}{5}$ and -1.43 are two examples of infinitely many

48. $\sqrt{2}$ and π are two examples of infinitely many

49. (A) $S = \{1, 12\}$ (B) $S = \{-3, 0, 1, 12\}$ (C) $S = \left\{-3, -\frac{2}{3}, 0, 1, \frac{9}{5}, 12\right\}$

50. (A) $S = \{2, 6\}$ (B) $S = \{-1, 2, 6\}$ (C) $S = \left\{-1, -\frac{1}{2}, 2, 6, \frac{25}{3}\right\}$

51. (A) $0.888\ 888\ldots$; repeating; repeated digit: 8
(B) $0.272\ 727\ldots$; repeating; repeated digits: 27
(C) $2.236\ 067\ 977\ldots$; nonrepeating and nonterminating
(D) 1.375; terminating

52. (A) $2.166\ 666\ldots$; repeating; repeated digit: 6
(B) $4.582\ 575\ 695\ldots$; nonrepeating and nonterminating
(C) 0.4375; terminating
(D) $0.261\ 261\ 261\ldots$; repeating; repeated digits: 261

53. (A) True (B) False; for example $3 - 5 \neq 5 - 3$.
(C) True (D) False; for example $9 \div 3 \neq 3 \div 9$.

54. (A) True (B) False, since, for example, $(8 - 4) - 2 \neq 8 - (4 - 2)$
(C) True (D) False, since, for example, $(8 \div 4) \div 2 \neq 8 \div (4 \div 2)$

55. (A) $\{1, 2, 3, 4, 6\}$ (B) $\{2, 4\}$ **56.** (A) $\{-2, -1, 0, 1, 2\}$ (B) $\{0, 2\}$

57. $\frac{1}{11}$ **58.** $\frac{2}{11}$ **59.**

$$
\begin{array}{r}
23 \\
12 \\
\hline
46 \\
230 \\
\hline
276
\end{array}
$$

$23 \cdot 2$
$23 \cdot 10$

$23 \cdot 12 = 23(2 + 10)$
$\quad = 23 \cdot 2 + 23 \cdot 10$
$\quad = 46 + 230$
$\quad = 276$

60. (1) Commutative (2) Associative (3) Inverse (4) Identity

Exercise 1-2

1. 3 **2.** 2 **3.** $2x^3 - x^2 + 2x + 4$ **4.** $2x^2 + 4x - 3$

5. $2x^3 - 5x^2 + 6$ **6.** $2x^2 - 2x + 1$ **7.** $6x^4 - 13x^3 + 9x^2 + 13x - 10$

8. $6x^3 - x^2 - 5x + 2$ **9.** $4x - 6$ **10.** $-5u + 2$ **11.** $6y^2 - 16y$

12. $6a^2 + 6a$ **13.** $m^2 - n^2$ **14.** $a^2 - b^2$ **15.** $4t^2 - 11t + 6$

16. $6x^2 - 7x - 5$ **17.** $3x^2 - 7xy - 6y^2$ **18.** $2x^2 + xy - 6y^2$ **19.** $4m^2 - 49$

20. $9y^2 - 4$ **21.** $30x^2 - 2xy - 12y^2$ **22.** $6m^2 - mn - 35n^2$ **23.** $9x^2 - 4y^2$

24. $16m^2 - 9n^2$ **25.** $16x^2 - 8xy + y^2$ **26.** $9u^2 + 24uv + 16v^2$

27. $a^3 + b^3$ **28.** $a^3 - b^3$ **29.** $-x + 27$ **30.** 1

31. $32a - 34$ **32.** $-b + 6$ **33.** $2x^4 - x^3 - 6x^2 + 7x - 2$

34. $x^4 - 7x^2y^2 + y^4$ **35.** $x^4 - 8x^2y^2 + 16y^4$ **36.** $m^4 - 14n^2m^2 + n^4$

37. $5u^2 - 12uv + 13v^2$ **38.** $3a^2 - 8ab - 3b^2$ **39.** $z^3 - 1$ **40.** $y^3 + 2$

41. $8m^3 - 12m^2n + 6mn^2 - n^3$ **42.** $27a^3 + 54a^2b + 36ab^2 + 8b^3$

43. $3h$ **44.** $2xh + h^2$ **45.** $4hx - 3h + 2h^2$ **46.** $-8xh + 6h - 4h^2$

47. $4hx - 4h + 2h^2$ **48.** $6hx + 5h + 3h^2$ **49.** $3hx^2 - 4hx + 3h^2x - 2h^2 + h^3$

50. $3hx^2 + 3h^2x + 3h + h^3$ **51.** $m^3 - 3m^2 - 5$ **52.** $2x^2 - 2xy + 3y^2$

53. $2x^3 - 13x^2 + 25x - 18$ **54.** $8x^3 - 20x^2 + 20x + 1$

55. $9x^3 - 9x^2 - 18x$ **56.** $4x^3 - 14x^2 + 8x - 6$

57. $(1 + 1)^2 \neq 1^2 + 1^2$; either a or b must be zero

58. $(2 - 1)^2 \neq 2^2 - 1^2$; b must be zero **59.** m **60.** $m + n$

61. Now the degree is less than or equal to m. **62.** It doesn't change.

63. Perimeter = $4x - 10$ **64.** Area = $x^2 + 8x$

65. Value = $40x - 125$ **66.** Value = $35x + 40$

67. Volume = $1.2\pi x^2 + 0.36\pi x + 0.036\pi$ **68.** Volume = $12x^2 + 48x + 64$

Exercise 1-3

1. $2x^2(3x^2 - 4x - 1)$ **2.** $3m^2(2m^2 - 3m - 1)$ **3.** $5xy(2x^2 + 4xy - 3y^2)$

4. $2uv(4u^2 - 3uv + 2v^2)$ **5.** $(x + 1)(5x - 3)$ **6.** $(2m - 3)(7m + 5)$

7. $(y - 2z)(2w - x)$ **8.** $(3c + d)(a - 4b)$ **9.** $(x - 2)(x + 3)$

10. $(y - 3)(2y + 5)$ **11.** $(3m + 5)(2m - 1)$ **12.** $(x - 8)(5x - 1)$

13. $(x - 2y)(2x - 3y)$ **14.** $(a - 4b)(3a - 2b)$ **15.** $(2c - d)(4a - 3b)$

16. $(r + 2s)(3p - q)$ **17.** $(2x + 3)(x - 1)$ **18.** $(3y + 1)(y - 3)$

19. Prime **20.** $(u - 2v)(u + 6v)$ **21.** $(m - 2)(m + 3)$

22. $(x + 5y)(x - 2y)$ **23.** $(2a + 3b)(2a - 3b)$ **24.** Prime

25. $(2x - 5)^2$ **26.** $(ab + c)(ab - c)$ **27.** Prime

28. $(3x - 2)(3x + 2)$ **29.** $6(x + 2)(x + 6)$ **30.** Prime

31. $2y(y - 3)(y - 8)$ **32.** $2x^2(x - 10)(x - 2)$ **33.** $y(4x - 1)^2$

34. $x(2y - 3)^2$ **35.** Prime **36.** $(2m - 3n)(3m + 4n)$

37. $xy(x - 3y)(x + 3y)$ **38.** $uv(2u - v)(2u + v)$

39. $3m(m^2 - 2m + 5)$ **40.** $2x(x^2 - x + 4)$ **41.** $(m + n)(m^2 - mn + n^2)$

42. $(r - t)(r^2 + rt + t^2)$　　　**43.** $2x(3x + 1)(x + 1)^3$

44. $(x - 1)^2(4x - 1)$　　　**45.** $2(3x - 5)(2x - 3)(12x - 19)$

46. $2(x - 3)(4x + 7)(8x - 5)$　　　**47.** $9x^4(9 - x)^3(5 - x)$

48. $7x^3(x - 7)^2(x - 4)$　　　**49.** $2(x + 1)(x^2 - 5)(3x + 5)(x - 1)$

50. $2(x - 3)^3(x^2 + 2)^2(5x - 4)(x - 1)$

51. $[(a - b) - 2(c - d)][(a - b) + 2(c - d)]$

52. Prime　　　**53.** $(2m - 3n)(a + b)$　　　**54.** $(5a + b)(3c - 4d)$

55. Prime　　　**56.** $(u + v)(5u - v)$　　　**57.** $(x - 3)^2(x + 3)$　　　**58.** $(x + 1)(x - 1)^2$

59. $(a - 2)(a + 1)(a - 1)$　　　**60.** $(t^2 + 1)(t - 2)$　　**61.** Prime

62. $(x - y + 4)(6x - 6y - 1)$　　　**63.** $(m - n)(m + n)(m^2 + n^2)$

64. $(y - 2)(y + 2)(y^2 + 1)$　　　**65.** Prime

66. $a^2(3 + ab)(9 - 3ab + a^2b^2)$　　　**67.** $(m + n)(m + n - 1)$

68. $(y - x)(y - x - 1)$　　　**69.** $2a[3a - 2(x + 4)][3a + 2(x + 4)]$

70. $[10x - 15y + 3ab][10x - 15y - 3ab]$

71. $(x^2 - x + 1)(x^2 + x + 1)$　　　**72.** $(a^2 + b^2 - ab)(a^2 + b^2 + ab)$

73. (A) $4(10 - x)(10 + x) = 400 - 4x^2$　(B) $4x(10 - x)^2 = 400x - 80x^2 + 4x^3$

74. (A) $4(6 - x)(6 + x) = 144 - 4x^2$　　(B) $2x(8 - x)(9 - 2x) = 144x - 50x^2 + 4x^3$

Exercise 1-4

1. $\dfrac{a^2}{2}$　　**2.** $8d^6$　　**3.** $\dfrac{22y + 9}{252}$　　**4.** $\dfrac{15x^2 + 10x - 6}{180}$　　**5.** $\dfrac{x^2 + 8}{8x^3}$

6. $\dfrac{15m^2 + 14m - 6}{36m^3}$　　**7.** $\dfrac{1}{x + 2}$　　**8.** $\dfrac{1}{x(3x + 2)}$　　**9.** $\dfrac{1}{2m + n}$

10. $\dfrac{2y - 1}{y - 2}$　　**11.** $\dfrac{2b^2}{(a + b)^2(a - b)}$　　**12.** $\dfrac{2x}{(x + 1)(x - 1)^2}$　　**13.** $\dfrac{m^2}{m - 1}$

14. $\dfrac{x^2 + 1}{x - 1}$　　**15.** $\dfrac{5}{x - 2}$　　**16.** $\dfrac{3}{a - 3}$　　**17.** $\dfrac{1}{y + 2}$

18. $\dfrac{5}{x + y}$　　**19.** $\dfrac{x - y}{y}$　　**20.** $x + 2$

21. $\dfrac{4(x^2 + 2)^2(x + 1)(x - 1)}{x^3}$　　**22.** $\dfrac{(x + 3)(x - 3)(x^2 + 3)}{x^4}$

23. $\dfrac{x(2 + 3x)}{(1 - 3x)^4}$　　**24.** $\dfrac{2x(3 - 2x)}{(2x + 3)^5}$　　**25.** $\dfrac{(x + 1)(x - 9)}{(x + 4)^4}$

26. $\dfrac{3(x + 2)(x - 2)}{(x + 1)^4}$　　**27.** $\dfrac{1}{y - 1}$　　**28.** $\dfrac{2x}{x - 3}$　　**29.** -1　　**30.** $-\dfrac{1}{x}$

31. $\dfrac{7y - 9x}{xy(a - b)}$　　**32.** $\dfrac{-17c + 16}{15(c - 1)}$　　**33.** $\dfrac{x^2 - x + 1}{2(x - 9)}$

34. 1　　**35.** $\dfrac{(x - y)^2}{y^2(x + y)}$　　**36.** $\dfrac{x^2(x + y)}{(x - y)^2}$　　**37.** $\dfrac{1}{x - 4}$

38. $\dfrac{2x + 5}{(x + 1)(x + 4)}$　　**39.** $\dfrac{x - 3}{x - 1}$　　**40.** $\dfrac{x - y}{x + y}$　　**41.** $\dfrac{-1}{x(x + h)}$

42. $\dfrac{-2x - h}{x^2(x + h)^2}$　　**43.** $\dfrac{x^2 + hx + 4x + 2h}{(x + h + 2)(x + 2)}$　　**44.** $\dfrac{-3}{x(x + h)}$

45. (A) Incorrect (B) $x + 1$ **46.** (A) Incorrect (B) $x + 1$

47. (A) Incorrect (B) $2x + h$ **48.** (A) Incorrect (B) $3x^2 + 3xh + h^2$

49. (A) Incorrect (B) $\dfrac{x^2 - 2}{x + 1}$ **50.** (A) Correct **51.** (A) Correct

52. (A) Incorrect (B) $\dfrac{x^2 - x + 1}{x - 1}$ **53.** $\dfrac{-x(x + y)}{y}$ **54.** 1 **55.** $\dfrac{a - 2}{a}$ **56.** x

Exercise 1-5

1. 1 **2.** 1 **3.** $60x^{11}$ **4.** $42a^{16}$ **5.** $\dfrac{4x^8}{z^6}$ **6.** $\dfrac{u^4}{9v^6}$ **7.** $\dfrac{r^{10}s^{15}}{p^5 q^{20}}$

8. $\dfrac{a^6 b^4}{4c^{10}}$ **9.** 10^7 **10.** $\dfrac{1}{10^9}$ **11.** $\dfrac{3a^4}{b^3}$ **12.** $\dfrac{5v^8}{u^8}$ **13.** $\dfrac{1}{y}$ **14.** $\dfrac{1}{w^4}$

15. 4×10^{11} **16.** $\dfrac{3}{10^3}$ **17.** 4.532×10^7 **18.** 3.67×10^3

19. 6.6×10^{-2} **20.** 2.9×10^{-2} **21.** 8.4×10^{-8} **22.** 4.97×10^{-4}

23. 0.000 09 **24.** 0.003 **25.** 3,480,000 **26.** 863,000,000

27. 0.000 000 004 2 **28.** 0.000 000 16

29. $\dfrac{3y^4}{2}$ **30.** $\dfrac{4}{3n^3}$ **31.** $\dfrac{x^{12}}{y^8}$ **32.** $\dfrac{n^8}{m^{12}}$ **33.** $\dfrac{4x^8}{y^6}$

34. $\dfrac{n^{12}}{8m^6}$ **35.** $\dfrac{w^{12}}{u^{20}v^4}$ **36.** $\dfrac{t^2}{x^2 y^{10}}$ **37.** $\dfrac{1}{(x + y)^2}$ **38.** $\dfrac{1}{a^2 - b^2}$ **39.** $\dfrac{x}{x - 1}$

40. x **41.** $\dfrac{-1}{xy}$ **42.** uv **43.** $\dfrac{-9x^2}{(x^3 + 3)^4}$ **44.** $\dfrac{-2(2x + 3)}{(x^2 + 3x)^3}$ **45.** 64

46. $2^{(3^2)} = 2^9 = 512$ while $(2^3)^2 = 8^2 = 64$ which is the calculator result.

49. $2x - 6x^{-1}$ **50.** $2 + 3x^{-2}$ **51.** $\dfrac{5}{3}x - \dfrac{2}{3}x^{-2}$ **52.** $\dfrac{7}{4} - \dfrac{1}{4}x^{-3}$

53. $x - \dfrac{3}{2} + \dfrac{1}{2}x^{-1}$ **54.** $\dfrac{3}{4}x - x^{-1} - \dfrac{1}{4}x^{-3}$ **55.** 6.65×10^{-17} **56.** 5.74×10^{-21}

57. 1.54×10^{12} **58.** 1.77×10^{-18} **59.** 1.0295×10^{11} **60.** -2.2911×10^{17}

61. -4.3647×10^{-18} **62.** 9.7137×10^{-12} **63.** 9.4697×10^{29} **64.** 1.8527×10^{37}

65. $2(a + 2b)^5$ **66.** $\dfrac{1}{2(x - 3)^2}$ **67.** $\dfrac{x^2 + xy + y^2}{xy}$ **68.** $\dfrac{bc(c + b)}{c^2 + bc + b^2}$

69. $\dfrac{y - x}{y}$ **70.** $\dfrac{v - u}{v + u}$ **71.** 1.3×10^{25} lb **72.** 3.3×10^{18} lb

73. 10^{10} or 10 billion, 6×10^{11} or 600 billion

74. 1.86×10^{-5} mi, 9.82×10^{-2} ft, 1.18 in

75. 2.07×10^4 dollars per person; \$20,700 per person

76. 3.24×10^4 dollars per person; \$32,400 per person

Exercise 1-6

1. 5   **2.** 3   **3.** 27   **4.** 4   **5.** -4 **6.** 16

7. Not a real number   **8.** 16   **9.** $\dfrac{9}{25}$ **10.** $\dfrac{125}{216}$ **11.** $\dfrac{1}{32}$ **12.** $\dfrac{1}{243}$

13. $a^{5/3}$ **14.** $b^{6/5}$ **15.** $c^{2/5}$ **16.** $\dfrac{1}{d^{2/5}}$ **17.** $\dfrac{1}{u^{1/2}}$ **18.** $\dfrac{1}{v^6}$ **19.** $\dfrac{2x^2}{y}$

20. $\dfrac{3y^3}{x^2}$ **21.** $\dfrac{1}{a^{1/4}b^{1/3}}$ **22.** $\dfrac{m^4}{n^3}$ **23.** $\dfrac{xy^2}{2}$ **24.** $\dfrac{3}{xw^2}$

25. $\dfrac{2b^2}{3a^2}$ **26.** $\dfrac{5}{4}x^4y^2$ **27.** $\dfrac{2}{3x^{7/12}}$ **28.** $\dfrac{2}{5}a^{13/12}$ **29.** $\dfrac{a^{1/3}}{b^2}$ **30.** $\dfrac{y}{x^{1/2}}$

31. $6m - 2m^{19/3}$ **32.** $12x - 6x^{35/4}$ **33.** $a - a^{1/2}b^{1/2} - 6b$

34. $3u - 13u^{1/2}v^{1/2} + 4v$ **35.** $4x - 9y$ **36.** $25m - n$

37. $x + 4x^{1/2}y^{1/2} + 4y$ **38.** $9x - 6x^{1/2}y^{1/2} + y$ **39.** 29.52   **40.** 103.2

41. 0.03093   **42.** 0.08053   **43.** 5.421   **44.** 4588   **45.** 107.6

46. 2.883×10^{20} **47.** $x = y = 1$ is one of many choices

48. $x = y = 1$ is one of many choices.   **49.** $x = y = 1$ is one of many choices.

50. $x = y = 1$ is one of many choices.   **51.** $3 - \dfrac{3}{4}x^{-1/2}$ **52.** $\dfrac{1}{2}x^{1/3} + x^{-1/3}$

53. $\dfrac{3}{5}x^{-1/3} + \dfrac{1}{5}x^{-1/2}$ **54.** $\dfrac{2}{3}x^{-1/4} + x^{-2/3}$ **55.** $\dfrac{1}{2}x^{5/3} - 2x^{1/6}$ **56.** $\dfrac{1}{2}x^{-1/6} - \dfrac{1}{4}$

57. $a^{1/n}b^{1/m}$ **58.** $a^{1/2}b^{1/3}$ **59.** $\dfrac{1}{x^{3m}y^{4n}}$ **60.** $\dfrac{1}{a^{2m}b^{3n}}$

61. (A) $x = -2$, for example (B) $x = 2$, for example (C) Not possible

62. (A) $x = 1$, for example (B) $x = -1$, for example (C) $x = 0$ is the only choice

63. No   **64.** No   **65.** $\dfrac{x - 3}{(2x - 1)^{3/2}}$ **66.** $\dfrac{x - 2}{2(x - 1)^{3/2}}$

67. $\dfrac{4x - 3}{(3x - 1)^{4/3}}$ **68.** $\dfrac{x + 6}{3(x + 2)^{5/3}}$ **69.** 1,920 units   **70.** 9600 units

71. 428 feet   **72.** 195 feet

Exercise 1-7

1. $\sqrt[3]{m^2}$ or $(\sqrt[3]{m})^2$ (first preferred)   **2.** $\sqrt[5]{n^4}$ **3.** $6\sqrt[5]{x^3}$ **4.** $7\sqrt[5]{y^2}$

5. $\sqrt[5]{(4xy^3)^2}$ **6.** $\sqrt[7]{(7x^2y)^5}$ **7.** $\sqrt{x + y}$ **8.** $\sqrt{x} + \sqrt{y}$

9. $b^{1/5}$ **10.** $c^{1/2}$ **11.** $5x^{3/4}$ **12.** $7mn^{2/5}$ **13.** $(2x^2y)^{3/5}$ **14.** $(3m^4n)^{2/9}$

15. $x^{1/3} + y^{1/3}$ **16.** $(x + y)^{1/3}$ **17.** -2 **18.** -3 **19.** $3x^4y^2$

20. $4m^2y^4$ **21.** $2mn^2$ **22.** $2a^3b^2$ **23.** $2ab^2\sqrt{2ab}$ **24.** $3mn^3\sqrt{3n}$

25. $2xy^2\sqrt[3]{2xy}$ **26.** $2xy^2\sqrt[4]{x}$ **27.** $\sqrt{m}$ **28.** $\sqrt[5]{n^3}$ **29.** $\sqrt[15]{xy}$

30. $\sqrt[8]{5x}$ **31.** $3x\sqrt[3]{3}$ **32.** $4x\sqrt{y}$ **33.** $\dfrac{\sqrt{5}}{5}$ **34.** $\dfrac{\sqrt{7}}{7}$

35. $2\sqrt{3x}$

36. $2y\sqrt{6y}$

37. $2\sqrt{2} + 2$

38. $2\sqrt{6} + 4$

39. $\sqrt{3} - \sqrt{2}$

40. $\dfrac{\sqrt{5} + \sqrt{2}}{3}$

41. $3x^2y^2\sqrt[5]{3x^2y}$

42. $4a^3b^4\sqrt[3]{a^2b}$

43. $n\sqrt[4]{2m^3n}$

44. $2u\sqrt[5]{u^2v^3}$

45. $\sqrt[3]{a^2(b - a)}$

46. $\sqrt[4]{3^3(u + v)^3}$

47. $\sqrt[4]{a^3b}$

48. $\sqrt[6]{x^4y^3}$

49. $x^2y\sqrt[3]{6xy^2}$

50. $m^2n\sqrt[4]{24n}$

51. In simplified form

52. In simplified form

53. $\dfrac{\sqrt{2}}{2}$ or $\dfrac{1}{2}\sqrt{2}$

54. $\dfrac{2\sqrt{6}}{3}$

55. $2a^2b\sqrt[3]{4a^2b}$

56. $4x^2y^4\sqrt[3]{2xy^2}$

57. $\dfrac{\sqrt[4]{12xy^3}}{2x}$ or $\dfrac{1}{2x}\sqrt[4]{12xy^3}$

58. $\dfrac{\sqrt[5]{8x^2y^2}}{2y}$

59. $\dfrac{6y + 9\sqrt{y}}{4y - 9}$

60. $\dfrac{15\sqrt{x} + 10x}{9 - 4x}$

61. $\dfrac{38 + 11\sqrt{10}}{117}$

62. $\dfrac{5\sqrt{6} - 6}{19}$

63. $\sqrt{x^2 + 9} + 3$

64. $2 + \sqrt{y^2 + 4}$

65. $\dfrac{1}{\sqrt{t} + \sqrt{x}}$

66. $\dfrac{x - y}{x + 2\sqrt{xy} + y}$

67. $\dfrac{1}{\sqrt{x + h} + \sqrt{x}}$

68. $\dfrac{1}{\sqrt{2 + h} - \sqrt{2}}$

69. 0.1816

70. 20.49

71. 3.557

72. 0.5603

73. 0.092 75

74. 242.2

75. 1.602

76. 1.483

77. Both are 1.259

78. Both are 1.344

79. Both are 0.4807

80. Both are 0.7937

81. $x \le 0$

82. $x \ge 0$

83. All real numbers

84. $x = 0$

85. A and E, B and F, C and D

86. A and F, B and D, C and E

87. $\dfrac{\sqrt[3]{a^2} + \sqrt[3]{ab} + \sqrt[3]{b^2}}{a - b}$

88. $\dfrac{\sqrt[3]{m^2} - \sqrt[3]{mn} + \sqrt[3]{n^2}}{m + n}$

89. $\dfrac{(\sqrt{x} - \sqrt{y} - \sqrt{z})[(x + y - z) + 2\sqrt{xy}]}{(x + y - z)^2 - 4xy}$

90. $\dfrac{(\sqrt{x} + \sqrt{y} + \sqrt{z})(x + y - z - 2\sqrt{x}\sqrt{y})}{(x + y - z)^2 - 4xy}$

91. $\dfrac{1}{\sqrt[3]{(x + h)^2} + \sqrt[3]{x(x + h)} + \sqrt[3]{x^2}}$

92. $\dfrac{1}{\sqrt[3]{t^2} + \sqrt[3]{t}\sqrt[3]{x} + \sqrt[3]{x^2}}$

93. $\sqrt[kn]{x^{km}} = (x^{km})^{1/kn} = x^{km/kn} = x^{m/n} = \sqrt[n]{x^m}$

CHAPTER 1 REVIEW

1. (A) True (B) True (C) False (D) True (E) False (F) False (*1-1*)

2. (A) $(y + z)x$ (B) $(2 + x) + y$ (C) $2x + 3x$ (*1-1*)

3. $x^3 + 3x^2 + 5x - 2$ (*1-2*)   **4.** $x^3 - 3x^2 - 3x + 22$ (*1-2*)

5. $3x^5 + x^4 - 8x^3 + 24x^2 + 8x - 64$ (*1-2*)   **6.** 3 (*1-2*)   **7.** 1 (*1-2*)

8. $14x^2 - 30x$ (*1-2*)   **9.** $9m^2 - 25n^2$ (*1-2*) **10.** $6x^2 - 5xy - 4y^2$ (*1-2*)

11. $4a^2 - 12ab + 9b^2$ (*1-2*)   **12.** $(3x - 2)^2$ (*1-3*) **13.** Prime (*1-3*)

14. $3n(2n - 5)(n + 1)$ *(1-3)*   **15.** $\dfrac{12a^3b - 40b^2 - 5a}{30a^3b^2}$ *(1-4)*

16. $\dfrac{7x - 4}{6x(x - 4)}$ *(1-4)*   **17.** $\dfrac{y + 2}{y(y - 2)}$ *(1-4)*   **18.** u *(1-4)*   **19.** $6x^5y^{15}$ *(1-5)*

20. $\dfrac{3u^4}{v^2}$ *(1-5)*   **21.** 6×10^2 *(1-5)*   **22.** $\dfrac{x^6}{y^4}$ *(1-5)*   **23.** $u^{7/3}$ *(1-6)*

24. $\dfrac{3a^2}{b}$ *(1-6)*   **25.** $3\sqrt[5]{x^2}$ *(1-7)*   **26.** $-3(xy)^{2/3}$ *(1-7)*

27. $3x^2y\sqrt[3]{x^2y}$ *(1-7)*   **28.** $6x^2y^3\sqrt{xy}$ *(1-7)*   **29.** $2b\sqrt{3a}$ *(1-7)*   **30.** $\dfrac{3\sqrt{5} + 5}{4}$ *(1-7)*

31. $\sqrt[4]{y^3}$ *(1-7)*   **32.** $\{-3, -1, 1\}$ *(1-1)*   **33.** Subtraction *(1-1)*

34. Commutative (+) *(1-1)*   **35.** Distributive *(1-1)*

36. Associative ($\cdot$) *(1-1)*   **37.** Negatives *(1-1)*

38. Identity (+) *(1-1)*   **39.** (A) T   (B) F *(1-1)*

40. 0 and -3 are two examples of infinitely many *(1-1)*

41. (A) a and d   (B) None *(1-2)*   **42.** $4xy - 2y^2$ *(1-2)*   **43.** $m^4 - 6m^2n^2 + n^4$ *(1-2)*

44. $10xh + 5h^2 - 7h$ *(1-2)*   **45.** $2x^3 - 4x^2 + 12x$ *(1-2)*

46. $x^3 - 6x^2y + 12xy^2 - 8y^3$ *(1-2)*   **47.** $(x - y)(7x - y)$ *(1-3)*   **48.** Prime *(1-3)*

49. $3xy(2x^2 + 4xy - 5y^2)$ *(1-3)*   **50.** $(y - b)(y - b - 1)$ *(1-3)*

51. $3(x + 2y)(x^2 - 2xy + 4y^2)$ *(1-3)*   **52.** $(y - 2)(y + 2)^2$ *(1-3)*

53. $x(x - 4)^2(5x - 8)$ *(1-3)*   **54.** $\dfrac{(x + 2)^2(x - 4)}{x^3}$ *(1-4)*

55. $\dfrac{2m}{(m - 2)^2(m + 2)}$ *(1-4)*   **56.** $\dfrac{y^2}{x}$ *(1-4)*   **57.** $\dfrac{x - y}{x + y}$ *(1-4)*

58. $\dfrac{-ab}{a^2 + ab + b^2}$ *(1-4, 1-5)*

59. Incorrect; correct final form is $\dfrac{x^2 + 2x - 2}{x - 1}$ *(1-4)*   **60.** $\dfrac{1}{4}$ *(1-5)*

61. $\dfrac{5}{9}$ *(1-5)*   **62.** $\dfrac{3x^2}{2y^2}$ *(1-6)*   **63.** $\dfrac{27a^{1/6}}{b^{1/2}}$ *(1-6)*

64. $x + 2x^{1/2}y^{1/2} + y$ *(1-6)*   **65.** $6x + 7x^{1/2}y^{1/2} - 3y$ *(1-6)*

66. 2×10^{-7} *(1-5)*   **67.** 3.213×10^6 *(1-5)*   **68.** 4.434×10^{-5} *(1-5)*

69. -4.541×10^{-6} *(1-5)*   **70.** $128,800$ *(1-6)*   **71.** 0.01507 *(1-6)*

72. 0.3664 *(1-7)*   **73.** 1.640 *(1-7)*   **74.** 0.08726 *(1-6)*

75. $-6x^2y^2\sqrt[5]{3x^2y}$ *(1-7)*   **76.** $x\sqrt[3]{2x^2}$ *(1-7)*   **77.** $\dfrac{\sqrt[5]{12x^3y^2}}{2x}$ *(1-7)*

78. $y\sqrt[3]{2x^2y}$ *(1-7)*   **79.** $\sqrt[3]{2x^2}$ *(1-7)*   **80.** $2x - 3\sqrt{xy} - 5y$ *(1-7)*

81. $\dfrac{6x + 3\sqrt{xy}}{4x - y}$ *(1-7)*   **82.** $\dfrac{4u - 12\sqrt{uv} + 9v}{4u - 9v}$ *(1-7)*   **83.** $\sqrt{y^2 + 4} + 2$ *(1-7)*

84. $\dfrac{1}{\sqrt{t} + \sqrt{5}}$ *(1-7)*   **85.** $2 - \dfrac{3}{2}x^{-1/2}$ *(1-7)*   **86.** $\dfrac{6}{11}$; rational *(1-1)*

87. (A) $\{-4, -3, 0, 2\}$ (B) $\{-3, 2\}$ *(1-1)*   **88.** 0 *(1-7)*

89. $x^3 + 8x^2 - 6x + 1$ *(1-2)*   **90.** $x(2a + 3x - 4)(2a - 3x - 4)$ *(1-3)*

91. All three have the same value. *(1-7)*

92. $\dfrac{2}{3}(x - 2)(x + 3)^4$ *(1-5)*   **93.** $\dfrac{a^2b^2}{a^3 + b^3}$ *(1-5)*

94. $x - y$ *(1-6)*   **95.** x^{m-1} *(1-6)*   **96.** $\dfrac{1 + \sqrt[3]{x} + \sqrt[3]{x^2}}{1 - x}$ *(1-7)*

97. $\dfrac{1}{\sqrt[3]{t^2} + \sqrt[3]{5t} + \sqrt[3]{25}}$ *(1-7)*   **98.** x^{n+1} *(1-7)*

99. Volume $= 12\pi x + 12\pi$ ft^3 *(1-2)*

100. 2.84×10^4 dollars per person; $28,400 per person *(1-5)*

101. (A) $24,000$ units   (B) Production doubles to $48,000$ units

  (C) At any production level, doubling the units of capital and labor doubles production. *(1-6)*

102. $R = \dfrac{R_1 R_2 R_3}{R_2 R_3 + R_1 R_3 + R_1 R_2}$ *(1-4)*

103. (A) $A = 480 - 6x^2 = 6(80 - x^2)$

  (B) $V = x(16 - 2x)(15 - 1.5x) = 240x - 54x^2 + 3x^3$ *(1-3)*

CHAPTER 2

Exercise 2-1

1. $x = 16$ **2.** $y = 6$ **3.** No solution   **4.** No solution

5. $a = -\dfrac{23}{4}$ or -5.75 **6.** $b = -\dfrac{21}{20}$ or -1.05 **7.** $x = \dfrac{16}{5}$ or 3.2

8. $x = \dfrac{35}{4}$ or 8.75 **9.** No solution   **10.** $w = -1.3$ **11.** $s = -5.93$

12. No solution   **13.** $y = \dfrac{16}{9}$ or $1.\overline{7}$ **14.** No solution   **15.** No solution

16. $t = 0$ **17.** $m = \dfrac{5}{2}$ or 2.5 **18.** $x = \dfrac{23}{4}$ or 5.75 **19.** No solution

20. $x = 2$ **21.** $x = -\dfrac{15}{2}$ or -7.5 **22.** No solution

23. $a = -\dfrac{9}{8}$ or -1.125 **24.** $b = 10$ **25.** 1.83

26. -0.456 **27.** -8.55 **28.** -0.933 **29.** $d = \dfrac{a_n - a_1}{n - 1}$

30. $C = \dfrac{5}{9}(F - 32)$ **31.** $f = \dfrac{d_1 d_2}{d_2 + d_1}$ **32.** $R_1 = \dfrac{RR_2}{R_2 - R}$ **33.** $a = \dfrac{A - 2bc}{2b + 2c}$

34. $c = \dfrac{A - 2ab}{2a + 2b}$ **35.** $x = \dfrac{5y + 3}{2 - 3y}$ **36.** $y = \dfrac{3x + 2}{x - 3}$

37. Wrong. There is no solution.   **38.** Wrong. There is no solution.

39. 4   **40.** solution set $= \varnothing$ **41.** All real numbers except 0 and 1.

42. $y = \dfrac{x^3}{3x^2 - 3x + 1}$ **43.** $x = \dfrac{cy + by - ac}{a - y}$

44. $m - n - p = 0$, and division by zero is not permitted

45. 24   **46.** 36   **47.** 8, 10, 12, 14   **48.** 4, 6, and 8 are the integers.

49. 17 meters $\times$ 10 meters   **50.** The rectangle is 24m long and 6m wide.

51. 42 feet   **52.** 20 cm   **53.** $90   **54.** $90   **55.** $19,750

56. (A) $39,900

    (B) They are never the same. Employees should always choose the first method.

57. (A) $T = 30 + 25(x - 3)$ (B) $330°C$ (C) 13 km

58. (A) $V = V_S(1 + 0.03A)$ (B) 143 mph   (C) 99.6 mph   (D) 4,940 ft.

59. 90 miles   **60.** 55,000 ft.   **61.** 5,000 trout   **62.** 9000 trout in lake

63. 10 gallons   **64.** 2 gallons   **65.** 11.25 liters   **66.** 24,000 gallons

67. 1.5 hours   **68.** $t = \dfrac{24}{5}$ hours   **69.** (A) 216 mi   (B) 225 mi

70. 10 AM; 24 miles   **71.** 330 hertz; 396 hertz   **72.** 264 hertz; 330 hertz

73. 150 centimeters   **74.** 141.2 cm   **75.** 150 feet   **76.** 20 miles

77. $5\frac{5}{11}$ minutes after 1 PM

Exercise 2-2

1. $x = -2$, $y = -1$ **2.** $x = 4$, $y = 12$ **3.** $x = 3$, $y = -4$

4. $x = -5$, $y = 2$ **5.** $x = -1$, $y = 2$ **6.** $x = -3$, $y = 5$

7. $s = -\dfrac{5}{2}$ or -2.5, $t = \dfrac{9}{2}$ or 4.5 **8.** $s = \dfrac{19}{5}$ or 3.8, $t = -\dfrac{8}{5}$ or -1.6

9. $m = 0$, $n = \dfrac{10}{3}$ or $3.\overline{3}$ **10.** $m = \dfrac{1}{6}$ or $0.1\overline{6}$, $n = 0$ **11.** $x = 10{,}500$, $y = 57{,}330$

12. $x = 4{,}200$, $y = 30{,}030$ **13.** $u = 0.8$, $v = 0.3$ **14.** $u = 0.2$, $v = -0.7$

15. $a = -\dfrac{7}{4}$ or -1.75, $b = -\dfrac{19}{15}$ or $-1.2\overline{6}$ **16.** $a = \dfrac{14}{3}$ or $4.\overline{6}$, $b = -0.5$

17. The system has no solution

18. The system has an infinite number of solutions.

19. $q = x + y - 5$, $p = 3x + 2y - 12$ **20.** $p = x + y - 3$, $q = x + 2y - 7$

21. $x = \dfrac{dh - bk}{ad - bc}$, $y = \dfrac{ak - ch}{ad - bc}$, $ad - bc \neq 0$

22. If $ad - bc = 0$, there may be no solutions or an infinite number of solutions.

23. airspeed = 330 mph; wind rate = 90 mph   **24.** 1,440 miles

25. 2.475 km   **26.** 5/3 mph

27. 40 milliliters of 50% solution and 60 milliliters of 80% solution

28. $6\frac{2}{3}$ grams of 12-carat gold; $3\frac{1}{3}$ grams of 18-carat gold

29. $x = 5{,}200$ records   **30.** $x = 600$ units to break even

31. $7,200 invested at 10% and $4,800 invested at 15%

32. $5,000 at 8% and $15,000 at 12%

33. Mexico plant: 75 hours; Taiwan plant: 50 hours

34. Green Bay plant: 60 hrs; Sheboygan plant: 28.5 hrs

35. Mix A: 80g; Mix B: 60g

36. 55 bags of Brand A and 40 bags of Brand B

37. (A) $p = 0.001q + 0.15$ (B) $p = -0.002q + 1.89$
    (C) Equilibrium price = $0.73; equilibrium quantity = 580 bushels

38. (A) $p = 0.0004x + 0.97$ (B) $p = -0.0005x + 1.69$
    (C) Equilibrium price = $1.29; equilibrium quantity = 800 bushels

39. (A) $a = 196$, $b = -16$ (B) 196 feet   (C) 3.5 seconds

40. (A) $a = 256$, $b = -16$ (B) 256 ft   (C) 4 sec, fall time of object

41. 40 seconds, 24 seconds, 120 mi

42. $t = 1\frac{9}{13}$ sec, $t + 6 = 7\frac{9}{13}$ sec; $d = 8{,}462$ ft

Exercise 2-3

1. $-8 \leq x \leq 7$; x

2. $-4 < x < 8$; x

3. $-6 \leq x < 6$; x

4. $-3 < x \leq 3$; x

5. $x \geq -6$; ![number line with closed bracket at -6 shaded right, marks -10 -5 0 5 10] x

6. $x < 7$; ![number line shaded left with open paren at 7] x

7. $(-2, 6]$; ![number line open paren at -2 to bracket at 6, marks -10 -5 0 5 10] x

8. $[-5, 5]$; ![number line bracket -5 to bracket 5 shaded] x

9. $(-7, 8)$; ![number line open paren -7 to open paren 8, marks -10 -5 0 5 10] x

10. $[-4, 5)$; ![number line bracket -4 to paren 5 shaded] x

11. $(-\infty, -2]$; ![number line shaded left with bracket at -2, marks -10 -5 0 5 10] x

12. $(3, \infty)$; ![number line open paren at 3 shaded right] x

13. $[-7, 2)$; $-7 \leq x < 2$

14. $[-5, 6]$; $-5 \leq x \leq 6$

15. $(-\infty, 0]$; $x \leq 0$

16. $(1, \infty)$; $x > 1$

17. $x < 5$ or $(-\infty, 5)$; ![number line shaded left with open paren at 5] x

18. $x \geq -3$; $[-3, \infty)$; ![number line bracket at -3 shaded right] x

19. $x \geq 3$ or $[3, \infty)$; ![number line bracket at 3 shaded right] x

20. $x < 2$; $(-\infty, 2)$; ![number line shaded left with open paren at 2] x

21. $N < -8$ or $(-\infty, -8)$; ![number line shaded left with open paren at -8] N

22. $M \geq 6$; $[6, \infty)$; ![number line bracket at 6 shaded right] M

23. $t > 2$ or $(2, \infty)$; ![number line open paren at 2 shaded right] t

24. $n \leq -3$; $(-\infty, -3]$; ![number line shaded left with bracket at -3] n

25. $m > 3$ or $(3, \infty)$; ![number line open paren at 3 shaded right] m

26. $u \leq \frac{2}{7}$; $\left(-\infty, \frac{2}{7}\right]$; ![number line shaded left with bracket at 2/7] u

27. $B \geq -4$ or $[-4, \infty)$; ![number line bracket at -4 shaded right] B

28. $y < -7$; $(-\infty, -7)$; ![number line shaded left with open paren at -7] y

29. $-2 < t \leq 3$ or $(-2, 3]$; ![number line open paren -2 to bracket 3] t

30. $3 \leq m < 7$; $[3, 7)$; ![number line bracket 3 to paren 7] m

31. $-5 < x \leq 7$; $(-5, 7]$![number line open paren -5 to bracket 7] x

32. $4 \leq x < 5$; $[4, 5)$![number line bracket 4 to paren 5] x

33. $2 < x < 4$; $(2, 4)$![number line open paren 2 to paren 4] x

34. $-1 \leq x \leq 6$; $[-1, 6]$![number line bracket -1 to bracket 6] x

35. $-\infty < x < \infty$; $(-\infty, \infty)$![number line fully shaded both directions] x

36. $\varnothing$, the empty set ![number line unshaded] x

37. $x < -1$ or $3 \leq x < 7$; $(-\infty, -1) \cup [3, 7)$![number line shaded left to paren -1, bracket 3 to paren 7]

38. $1 < x \leq 6$ or $x \geq 9$; $(1, 6] \cup [9, \infty)$![number line paren 1 to bracket 6, bracket 9 shaded right] x

39. $1 < x < 5$; $(1, 5)$![number line paren 1 to paren 5] x

40. $2 \leq x \leq 3$; $[2, 3]$![number line bracket 2 to bracket 3] x

41. $x \leq 6$; $(-\infty, 6]$![number line shaded left with bracket at 6] x

42. $x > -3$; $(-3, \infty)$![number line open paren at -3 shaded right] x

43. $q < -14$ or $(-\infty, -14)$; 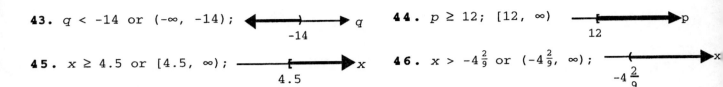   **44.** $p \geq 12$; $[12, \infty)$

45. $x \geq 4.5$ or $[4.5, \infty)$;   **46.** $x > -4\frac{2}{9}$ or $(-4\frac{2}{9}, \infty)$;

47. $-20 \leq x \leq 20$ or $[-20, 20]$;

48. $-9 \leq A \leq 9$ or $[-9, 9]$

49. $-30 \leq x < 18$ or $[-30, 18)$;

50. $41 \leq x < 59$ or $[41, 59)$

51. $-8 \leq x < -3$ or $[-8, -3)$;

52. $2 < x \leq 5$ or $(2, 5]$

53. $-14 < x \leq 11$ or $(-14, 11]$;

54. $-35 \leq x \leq -20$ or $[-35, -20]$

55. $x \geq -0.60$ **56.** $x < 2.11$ **57.** $-0.255 < x < 0.362$

58. $-0.29 < x < 1.34$ **59.** $x \leq 1$ **60.** $x + 5 \geq 0$ or $x \geq -5$

61. $x \geq -\frac{5}{3}$ **62.** $x \leq \frac{7}{2}$ **63.** $x > -\frac{3}{2}$ **64.** $x < \frac{5}{6}$

65. (A) and (C) $a > 0$ and $b > 0$, or $a < 0$ and $b < 0$
(B) and (D) $a > 0$ and $b < 0$, or $a < 0$ and $b > 0$

66. (A) two of three numbers must be negative and one positive or all three must be positive

(B) two of three numbers must be positive and one negative or all three must be negative

(C) two of three numbers must be negative and one positive or all three must be positive

(D) $a \neq 0$ and b and c must have opposite signs

67. (A) > (B) <   **68.** $q < 0$ which is true for all real p and negative q

69. positive   **70.** negative   **71.** (A) False (B) True (C) True

72. When both sides are divided by $n - m$ the order of the inequality should be changed, because $n - m$ is negative.

77. $9.8 \leq x \leq 13.8$ (from 9.8 km to 13.8 km)

78. $8000 \leq h \leq 20,000$ or (8, 000 ft to 20,000 ft)

79. (A) $x > 40,625$ (B) $x = 40,625$ **80.** (A) $x > 27,500$ (B) 27,500

81. (B) $x > 52,000$ (C) Raise wholesale price \$3.50 to \$66.50

82. (B) $x > 33,000$ (C) Raise wholesale price \$4 to \$144

83. $2 \leq I \leq 25$ or $[2, 25]$ **84.** $9.6 \leq MA \leq 16.8$ or $[9.6, 16.8]$

85. \$2,060 $\leq$ Benefit reduction $\leq$ \$3,560

86. \$1,373.33 $\leq$ Benefit reduction $\leq$ \$2,373.33

Exercise 2-4

1. $\sqrt{5}$ **2.** $\frac{3}{4}$ **3.** 4   **4.** 4   **5.** $5 - \sqrt{5}$

6. $\sqrt{7} - 2$ since $\sqrt{7} > 2$ or $\sqrt{7} - 2 > 0$ **7.** $5 - \sqrt{5}$ **8.** $\sqrt{7} - 2$

9. 12   **10.** 9   **11.** 12   **12.** 8   **13.** 4   **14.** 5   **15.** 4

16. 5   **17.** 9   **18.** 3   **19.** $|x - 3| = 4$ **20.** $|y - 1| = 3$

21. $|m + 2| = 5$ **22.** $|n + 5| = 7$ **23.** $|x - 3| < 5$ **24.** $|z + 2| < 8$

25. $|p + 2| > 6$ **26.** $|c + 3| \leq 7$ **27.** $|q - 1| \geq 2$ **28.** $|d - 5| \leq 4$

29. x is no more than 7 units from the origin. $-7 \leq x \leq 7$ or $[-7,7]$;

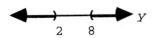

30. t is no more than 5 units from the origin. $-5 \leq t \leq 5$ or $[-5, 5]$;

31. x is at least 7 units from the origin. $x \leq -7$ or $x \geq 7$ or $(-\infty, -7] \cup [7, \infty)$;

32. x is at least 5 units from the origin. $x \leq -5$ or $x \geq 5$ or $(-\infty, -5] \cup [5, \infty)$;

33. y is 3 units from 5. $y = 2, 8$;

34. t is 4 units from 3. $t = 7$ or -1;

35. y is less than 3 units from 5. $2 < y < 8$ or $(2, 8)$;

36. t is less than 4 units from 3. $-1 < t < 7$ or $(-1, 7)$;

37. y is more than 3 units from 5. $y < 2$ or $y > 8$ or $(-\infty, 2) \cup (8, \infty)$;

38. t is more than 4 units from 3. $t < -1$ or $t > 7$ or $(-\infty, -1) \cup (7, \infty)$;

39. u is 3 units from -8. $u = -11$ or -5;

40. x is 5 units from -1. $x = -6$ or 4;

41. u is no more than 3 units from -8. $-11 \leq u \leq -5$ or $[-11, -5]$;

42. x is no more than 5 units from -1. $-6 \leq x \leq 4$ or $[-6, 4]$;

43. u is at least 3 units from -8. $u \leq -11$ or $u \geq -5$ or $(-\infty, -11] \cup [-5, \infty)$;

44. x is at least 5 units from -1. $x \leq -6$ or $x \geq 4$ or $(-\infty, -6] \cup [4, \infty)$;

45. $1 \leq x \leq \dfrac{11}{3}$; $\left[1, \dfrac{11}{3}\right]$ **46.** $y \leq -2$ or $y \geq 1.2$; $(-\infty, -2] \cup [1.2, \infty)$

47. $t < -1$ or $t > 5$; $(-\infty, -1) \cup (5, \infty)$ **48.** $-4 < s < -1$; $(-4, -1)$

49. $m = -2, \ -\dfrac{8}{7}$ **50.** $-0.8 \leq n \leq 2.4$; $[-0.8, 2.4]$

51. $-2.5 < w < 5.5$; $(-2.5, 5.5)$ **52.** $z = -5.5, \ 0.5$

53. $u \leq -11$ or $u \geq -6$; $(-\infty, -11] \cup [-6, \infty)$

54. $v < 1.8$ or $v > 8.2$; $(-\infty, 1.8) \cup (8.2, \infty)$

55. $-35 < C < -\dfrac{5}{9}$ or $\left(-35, \ -\dfrac{5}{9}\right)$

56. $-40 < F < 104$ or $(-40, 104)$ **57.** $-2 < x < 2$ or $(-2, 2)$

58. $m < -3$ or $m > 3$ or $(-\infty, -3) \cup (3, \infty)$ **59.** $-\dfrac{1}{3} \leq t \leq 1$ or $\left[-\dfrac{1}{3}, \ 1\right]$

60. $-1 < x < 4$ or $(-1, 4)$ **61.** $t < 0$ or $t > 3$ or $(-\infty, 0) \cup (3, \infty)$

62. $m \leq -3$ or $m \geq -\dfrac{1}{3}$ or $(-\infty, -3] \cup \left[-\dfrac{1}{3}, \ \infty\right)$

63. $(2.9, 3) \cup (3, 3.1)$;

64. $(4.99, 5) \cup (5, 5.01)$;

65. $(c - d, c) \cup (c, c + d)$;

66. $(4 - d, 4) \cup (4, 4 + d)$;

$$\begin{array}{ccc} 4 - d & 4 & 4 + d \end{array}$$

67. $x \geq 2$ **68.** $x \leq -4$ **69.** $x \leq 1.5$ **70.** $x \geq 3$

71. $x = -2.2, 1$ **72.** $x = 2, 4$ **73.** $-3 \leq x \leq 0$ **74.** $x \geq 5$

75. $x = 1.4, 5$ **76.** $x = -1.8, 2.6$ **77.** ± 1 **78.** ± 1

91. $42.2 < x < 48.6$ **92.** $15.6 < x < 41.6$ **93.** $|P - 500| \leq 20$

94. $|T - 200| \leq 10$ **95.** $|A - 12.436| < 0.001$, $(12.435, 12.437)$

96. $|V - 6.94| < 0.02$, $(6.92, 6.96)$ **97.** $|N - 2.37| \leq 0.005$

98. $|N - 3.65 \times 10^{-3}| \leq 5 \times 10^{-6}$

Exercise 2-5

1. $5 + 9i$ **2.** $9 + 4i$ **3.** $3 + 3i$ **4.** $3 - 5i$

5. $3 + 3i$ **6.** $1 + 2i$ **7.** $8 - 10i$ **8.** $-5 - 3i$

9. $7 + 3i$ **10.** $7 - 2i$ **11.** -8 **12.** -15

13. $-12 - 8i$ **14.** $-12 - 8i$ **15.** $11 + 2i$ **16.** $-4 + 17i$

17. $13 - i$ **18.** $26 - 7i$ **19.** 85 **20.** 73

21. $0.1 - 0.2i$ **22.** $0.1 + 0.3i$ **23.** $2 - i$ **24.** $2.2 - 1.4i$

25. $3 - i$ **26.** $1 + 2i$

27. $7 - 5i$ **28.** $-5 + 3i$ **29.** $-3 + 2i$ **30.** $-6 - 13i$

31. $8 + 25i$ **32.** $13 + i$ **33.** $\frac{5}{7} - \frac{2}{7}i$ **34.** $3 - 4i$

35. $\frac{2}{13} + \frac{3}{13}i$ **36.** $\frac{3}{25} + \frac{4}{25}i$ **37.** $-\frac{2}{5}i$ or $0 - \frac{2}{5}i$

38. $-\frac{1}{3}i$ or $0 - \frac{1}{3}i$ **39.** $\frac{3}{2} - \frac{1}{2}i$ **40.** $-\frac{1}{3} - \frac{2}{3}i$ **41.** $-6i$ or $0 - 6i$

42. $4 - 7i$ **43.** 0 or $0 + 0i$ **44.** 0 or $0 + 0i$

45. $i^{18} = -1$, $i^{32} = 1$, $i^{67} = -i$ **46.** $i, -i, 1$ **47.** $x = 3, y = -2$

48. $x = 1, y = 3$ **49.** $x > 3$ **50.** $x < -5$ **51.** $x > \frac{2}{3}$

52. $x < -\frac{3}{2}$ **53.** $33.89 - 20.38i$ **54.** $35.98 - 21.95i$ **55.** $0.85 - 0.89i$

56. $0.92 + 1.23i$ **57.** $(a + c) + (b + d)i$ **58.** $(a - c) + (b - d)i$

59. $a^2 + b^2$ or $(a^2 + b^2) + 0i$ **60.** $u^2 + v^2$ or $(u^2 + v^2) + 0i$

61. $(ac - bd) + (ad + bc)i$ **62.** $\frac{ac + bd}{c^2 + d^2} + \frac{(bc - ad)}{c^2 + d^2}i$

63. $i^{4k} = (i^4)^k = (i^2 \cdot i^2)^k = [(-1)(-1)]^k = 1^k = 1$

65. (1) Definition of addition; (2) Commutative (+) property for R;
(3) Definition of addition

66. (1) Definition of multiplication; (2) Commutative (·);
(3) Definition of multiplication

Exercise 2-6

1. $x = 0, 4$

2. $y = -3, \dfrac{1}{2}$

3. $t = \dfrac{3}{2}$ (double root)

4. $s = -2, 0$

5. $w = -5, \dfrac{2}{3}$

6. $x = \dfrac{3}{4}$ (double root)

7. $m = \pm 5$

8. $n = \pm 4i$

9. $c = \pm 3i$

10. $d = \pm 6$

11. $y = \pm\dfrac{3}{2}i$

12. $x = \pm\dfrac{5}{3}$

13. $z = \pm\dfrac{4\sqrt{2}}{5}$

14. $w = \pm\dfrac{3\sqrt{3}}{4}i$

15. $s = -1 \pm \sqrt{5}$

16. $t = 2 \pm\sqrt{3}i$

17. $n = 3 \pm 2i$

18. $m = -5, -3$

19. $x = 1 \pm \sqrt{2}$

20. $y = 2 \pm i\sqrt{3}$

21. $x = 1 \pm i\sqrt{2}$

22. $y = 2 \pm \sqrt{3}$

23. $t = \dfrac{3 \pm i\sqrt{7}}{2}$

24. $s = \dfrac{2 \pm \sqrt{2}}{3}$

25. $t = \dfrac{3 \pm\sqrt{7}}{2}$

26. $s = \dfrac{2 \pm i\sqrt{3}}{3}$

27. $x = 2 \pm \sqrt{5}$

28. $y = -2 \pm \sqrt{7}$

29. $r = \dfrac{-5 \pm \sqrt{3}}{2}$

30. $s = \dfrac{3 \pm i\sqrt{5}}{2}$

31. $u = \dfrac{-2 \pm i\sqrt{11}}{2}$

32. $v = \dfrac{-4 \pm i\sqrt{7}}{2}$

33. $w = \dfrac{-2 \pm i\sqrt{5}}{3}$

34. $z = \dfrac{4 \pm \sqrt{13}}{3}$

35. $x = -\dfrac{5}{4}, \dfrac{2}{3}$

36. $x = -\dfrac{4}{3}, \dfrac{1}{3}$

37. $y = \dfrac{3 \pm \sqrt{5}}{2}$

38. $m = -\dfrac{2}{3} \pm \dfrac{2}{3}i$

39. $x = \dfrac{3 \pm \sqrt{13}}{2}$

40. $x = -1 \pm \sqrt{3}$

41. $n = -\dfrac{4}{7}, 0$

42. $u = 0, -\dfrac{3}{8}$

43. $x = 2 \pm 2i$

44. $u = 1 \pm i\sqrt{2}$

45. $m = -50, 2$

46. $y = 3, \dfrac{2}{5}$

47. $x = \dfrac{-5 \pm \sqrt{57}}{2}$

48. $x = \dfrac{1}{6} \pm \dfrac{\sqrt{119}}{6}i$

49. $x = \dfrac{-3 \pm \sqrt{57}}{4}$

50. $x = \dfrac{1}{3} \pm \dfrac{\sqrt{2}}{3}i$

51. $u = 1, 2, \dfrac{-3 \pm \sqrt{17}}{2}$

52. $-4, -3, \dfrac{7 \pm \sqrt{97}}{2}$

53. $t = \sqrt{\dfrac{2s}{g}}$

54. $a = \sqrt{c^2 - b^2}$

55. $I = \dfrac{E + \sqrt{E^2 - 4RP}}{2R}$

56. $r = \sqrt{\dfrac{A}{P}} - 1$

57. $x = 1.35, 0.48$

58. $x = 6.25, 0.77$

59. $x = -1.05, 0.63$

60. $x = -1.87, 0.45$

61. If $c < 4$ there are two distinct real roots, if $c = 4$ there is one real double root, and if $c > 4$ there are two distinct imaginary roots.

62. If $c < 1$ there are two distinct real roots, if $c = 1$ there is one real double root, and if $c > 1$ there are two distinct imaginary roots.

63. Since the discriminant is positive, the equation has real solutions.

64. $0.02634736 > 0$, real solutions

65. Since $b^2 - 4ac$, the discriminant, is negative, the equation has no real solutions.

66. $-0.0346424 < 0$, no real solutions **67.** $x = \dfrac{4\sqrt{6} \pm 2\sqrt{15}}{3}$ or $\dfrac{4}{3}\sqrt{6} \pm \dfrac{2}{3}\sqrt{15}$

68. $x = \dfrac{\sqrt{6} \pm \sqrt{15}}{3}$ **69.** $x = \sqrt{2} - i$, $-\sqrt{2} - i$ **70.** $x = 3i$ and $x = -i$

71. $x = 1$, $-\dfrac{1}{2} \pm \dfrac{1}{2}i\sqrt{3}$ **72.** $x = 1$, $x = -1$, $x = i$, $x = -i$

74. No **75.** $\dfrac{c}{a}$ **76.** $-\dfrac{b}{a}$

77. The $\pm$ in front still yields the same two numbers even if a is negative.

78. $(a - b)^2 = (b - a)^2$ does not imply $a - b = b - a$

79. 8, 13 **80.** $x = 0, 2$ **81.** 12, 14 **82.** $x = 3, \dfrac{1}{3}$

83. 5.12 by 3.12 inches **84.** base = 4 ft.; $b - 3 = 1$ ft. = height

85. 20% **86.** $p = \$15$ **87.** 100 mph, 240 mph **88.** $r = 2$ mph

89. 13.09 h and 8.09 h **90.** larger gear: 3 rpm; smaller gear: 4 rpm

91. $v = 50$ mph

92. (A) $t = 0$ when projectile leaves the ground; $t = 11$ sec. when projectile returns to ground

(B) $t = 10.91$ sec and 0.09 sec

93. 50 ft wide and 300 ft long or 150 ft wide and 100 ft long.

94. 14 ft wide and 14 ft high or 10.5 ft wide and 18.67 ft high

95. 52 mi **96.** straightaways: 348 ft; diameters: 198 ft

Exercise 2-7

1. T **2.** F **3.** F **4.** T **5.** F **6.** F **7.** $x = 14$

8. $x = 8$ **9.** $y = 6$ **10.** $y = 2$ **11.** $w = -1, 2$ **12.** No solution **13.** No solution

14. $t = 1, 9$ **15.** $m = \pm\sqrt{3}, \pm i\sqrt{5}$ **16.** $m = \pm\sqrt{2}, \pm i\sqrt{6}$ **17.** $x = \dfrac{1}{2}i$

18. $x = \dfrac{3}{2}i$ **19.** $y = -64, \dfrac{27}{8}$ **20.** $y = -8, \dfrac{64}{27}$ **21.** $m = -1, 3, 1 \pm 2i$

22. $m = -4, 2, -1 \pm i$ **23.** No solution **24.** $x = 5, 41$ **25.** $w = -2, 1$

26. $w = 2$ **27.** $z = -1$ **28.** No solution **29.** $x = -\dfrac{3}{2} + \dfrac{1}{2}i$

30. $x = \dfrac{5}{2} + \dfrac{1}{2}i$ **31.** $y = \dfrac{1}{3} \pm \dfrac{i\sqrt{2}}{3}$ **32.** $y = \dfrac{3}{8} \pm \dfrac{i\sqrt{7}}{8}$ **33.** $t = \pm\dfrac{\sqrt{2}}{2}, \pm\sqrt{2}$

34. $t = \pm\dfrac{\sqrt{3}}{2}, \pm\sqrt{5}$ **35.** $z = \dfrac{3}{2} \pm \dfrac{3i\sqrt{3}}{2}$ **36.** $z = \dfrac{1}{8} \pm \dfrac{3i\sqrt{7}}{8}$ **37.** $m = 0.25$

38. $m = 2.25$ **39.** $w = 4$ **40.** $w = \dfrac{16}{9}$ **41.** $x = -1$

42. $x = \dfrac{1}{2}, \; -2$ **43.** $x = \pm\sqrt{\dfrac{5 \pm \sqrt{13}}{6}}$ (four roots)

44. $x = \pm\sqrt{\dfrac{7 \pm \sqrt{17}}{4}}$ (four roots)

45. $x = -4, \; 39{,}596$ **46.** $x = 2, \; 3{,}482$ **47.** $x = \left(\dfrac{4}{5 \pm \sqrt{17}}\right)^5 \approx 0.016203, \; 1974.98$

48. $x = \left(\dfrac{2}{3 \pm \sqrt{5}}\right)^5 \approx 0.008131, \; 122.991869$

49. 13.1 in. by 9.1 in.   **50.** 5.3 in. by 2.8 in.

51. 1.65 ft or 3.65 ft   **52.** $r = 3.73$ cm   **53.** $30; 1,600 telephones

Exercise 2-8

1. $(-5, 2)$. $-5 < x < 2$. ———(———)——→ x
$\qquad\qquad\qquad$ −5 2

2. $(-4, 3)$. $-4 < x < 3$. ———(———)——→ x
$\qquad\qquad\qquad$ −4 3

3. $(-\infty, 3) \cup (7, \infty)$. $x < 3$ or $x > 7$. ←———)——(———→ x
$\qquad\qquad\qquad$ 3 7

4. $(-\infty, -5) \cup (-2, \infty)$. $x < -5$ or $x > -2$. ←———)——(———→ x
$\qquad\qquad\qquad$ −5 −2

5. $[0,8]$. $0 \le x \le 8$. ———[———]——→ x
$\qquad\qquad\qquad$ 0 8

6. $(-\infty, -6] \cup [0, \infty)$. $x \le -6$ or $x \ge 0$. ←———]——[———→ x
$\qquad\qquad\qquad$ −6 0

7. $[-5,0]$. $-5 \le x \le 0$. ———[———]——→ x
$\qquad\qquad\qquad$ −5 0

8. $[0, 4]$. $0 \le x \le 4$. ———[———]——→ x
$\qquad\qquad\qquad$ 0 4

9. $(-\infty, -2) \cup (2, \infty)$. $x < -2$ or $x > 2$. ←———)——(———→ x
$\qquad\qquad\qquad$ −2 2

10. $[-3, 3]$. $-3 \le x \le 3$. ———[———]——→ x
$\qquad\qquad\qquad$ −3 3

11. $(-4, 2]$. $-4 < x \le 2$. ———(———]——→ x
$\qquad\qquad\qquad$ −4 2

12. $(-\infty, -3] \cup (1, \infty)$. $x \le -3$ or $x > 1$. ←———]——(———→ x
$\qquad\qquad\qquad$ −3 1

13. $(-\infty, -4] \cup (1, \infty)$. $x \le -4$ or $x > 1$. ←———]——(———→ x
$\qquad\qquad\qquad$ −4 1

14. $(-\infty, -5) \cup [3, \infty)$. $x < -5$ or $x \geq 3$.

15. $[-5, 0] \cup (3, \infty)$. $-5 \leq x \leq 0$ or $3 < x$.

16. $(-\infty, -2) \cup (0, 4]$. $x < -2$ or $0 < x \leq 4$.

17. $-3 < x < 1$. $(-3, 1)$.

18. $[-3, 4]$. $-3 \leq x \leq 4$.

19. $(-\infty, 0) \cup \left(\frac{1}{4}, \infty\right)$. $x < 0$ or $\frac{1}{4} < x$

20. $\left(0, \frac{5}{3}\right)$. $0 < x < \frac{5}{3}$.

21. $\left(-4, \frac{3}{2}\right]$. $-4 < x \leq \frac{3}{2}$

22. $\left(-\infty, -\frac{2}{3}\right] \cup (5, \infty)$. $x \leq -\frac{2}{3}$ or $x > 5$.

23. $(-1, 2) \cup [5, \infty)$. $-1 < x < 2$ or $5 \leq x$

24. $(-\infty, -12] \cup (-2, 3)$. $x \leq -12$ or $-2 < x < 3$.

25. $(-\infty, -4] \cup [0, 2]$. $x \leq -4$ or $0 \leq x \leq 2$

26. $(-2, 0) \cup \left(\frac{3}{2}, \infty\right)$. $-2 < x < 0$ or $x > \frac{3}{2}$.

27. $(-\infty, -3] \cup [3, \infty)$. $x \leq -3$ or $x \geq 3$ **28.** $-2 \leq x \leq 2$. $[-2, 2]$

29. $(-\infty, -2] \cup \left[\frac{3}{2}, \infty\right)$. $x \leq -2$ or $x \geq \frac{3}{2}$ **30.** $x \leq -\frac{2}{3}$ or $x \geq 3$

31. $-7 \leq x < 3$ **32.** $x < -3$ or $x \geq 1$

33. If $a > 0$, the solution set is $(-\infty, r_1) \cup (r_2, \infty)$. If $a < 0$, the solution set is (r_1, r_2).

34. If $a > 0$, the solution set is $[r_1, r_2]$. If $a < 0$, the solution set is $(-\infty, r_1] \cup [r_2, \infty)$.

35. If $a > 0$, the solution set is R, the set of real numbers. If $a < 0$, the solution set is $\{r\}$.

36. If $a > 0$, the solution set is $\emptyset$, the empty set. If $a < 0$, the solution set is $(-\infty, r) \cup (r, \infty)$.

37. $x^2 \geq 0$ **38.** $x^2 < 0$ **39.** $\emptyset$ is the solution set.

40. $\emptyset$ is the solution set.   **41.** $\emptyset$ is the solution set.

42. all x, $(-\infty, \infty)$

43. $(-\infty, 2 - \sqrt{5}] \cup [2 + \sqrt{5}, \infty)$. $x \leq 2 - \sqrt{5}$ or $x \geq 2 + \sqrt{5}$

44. $(1 - \sqrt{3}, 1 + \sqrt{3})$. $1 - \sqrt{3} < x < 1 + \sqrt{3}$.

45. $(1 - \sqrt{2}, 0) \cup (1 + \sqrt{2}, \infty)$. $1 - \sqrt{2} < x < 0$ or $x > 1 + \sqrt{2}$

46. $(-\infty, 2 - \sqrt{7}] \cup [0, 2 + \sqrt{7}]$. $x \leq 2 - \sqrt{7}$ or $0 \leq x \leq 2 + \sqrt{7}$.

47. $\left[-2, -\frac{1}{2}\right] \cup \left[\frac{1}{2}, 2\right]$. $-2 \leq x \leq -\frac{1}{2}$ or $\frac{1}{2} \leq x \leq 2$.

48. $(-\infty, -3] \cup [-2, 2] \cup [3, \infty)$. $x \leq -3$ or $-2 \leq x \leq 2$ or $x \geq 3$.

49. $-2 \leq x \leq 2$. $[-2, 2]$

50. $\left(-\frac{1}{3}, 0\right) \cup (0, 1)$. $-\frac{1}{3} < x < 0$ or $0 < x < 1$.

51. (A) profit: $\$4 < p < \$7$ or $(\$4, \$7)$;
(B) loss: $\$0 \leq p < \$4$ or $p > \$7$. $[\$0, \$4) \cup (\$7, \infty)$

52. (A) profit: $\$3 < p < \$9$. $(\$3, \$9)$
(B) loss: $\$0 \leq p < \$3$ or $p > \$9$. $[\$0, \$3) \cup (\$9, \infty)$

53. $2 \leq t \leq 5$. $[2, 5]$ **54.** $0 < t < 7$ **55.** $v > 75$ mph

56. $0 \leq v < 59.3$ mph   **57.** $5 \leq t \leq 20$ **58.** $1 \leq t \leq 2$ sec

CHAPTER 2 REVIEW

1. $x = 21$ (2-1)   **2.** $x = \frac{30}{11}$ (2-1)   **3.** $x = 3$, $y = 3$ (2-2)

4. $x \geq 1$; $[1, \infty)$ (2-3)

5. $-14 < y < -4$; $(-14, -4)$ (2-4)

6. $-1 \le x \le 4$; $[-1, 4]$ x (2-4)

7. $(-5, 4)$; $-5 < x < 4$. x (2-8)

8. $(-\infty, -3] \cup [7, \infty)$; $x \le -3$ or $x \ge 7$ x (2-8)

9. (A) $3 - 6i$ (B) $15 + 3i$ (C) $2 + i$ (2-5)   **10.** $x = \pm \dfrac{\sqrt{14}}{2}$ (2-6)

11. $x = 0, 2$ (2-6)   **12.** $x = \dfrac{1}{2}, 3$ (2-6)   **13.** $m = -\dfrac{1}{2} \pm \dfrac{\sqrt{3}}{2} i$ (2-6)

14. $y = \dfrac{3 \pm \sqrt{33}}{4}$ (2-6)   **15.** $x = 2, 3$ (2-7)   **16.** $x = 3$, $y = -2$ (2-2)

17. $x \le \dfrac{3}{5}$ (2-3)   **18.** $x = -15$ (2-1)   **19.** No solution   (2-1)

20. $m = 2$, $n = -\dfrac{4}{3}$ (2-2)   **21.** $x \ge -19$; $[-19, \infty)$ x (2-3)

22. $x < 2$ or $x > \dfrac{10}{3}$; $(-\infty, 2) \cup \left(\dfrac{10}{3}, \infty\right)$ x (2-4)

23. $(-\infty, 0) \cup \left(\dfrac{1}{2}, \infty\right)$; $x < 0$ or $x > \dfrac{1}{2}$ x (2-8)

24. $(-\infty, 1] \cup (3, 4)$; $x \le 1$ or $3 < x < 4$ x (2-8)

25. $-1 \le m \le 2$; $[-1, 2]$ m (2-4)

26. $[-4, 2)$; $-4 \le x < 2$ (2-8)   **27.** (A) $d(A,B) = 6$ (B) $d(B,A) = 6$ (2-4)

28. (A) $5 + 4i$ (B) $-i$ (2-5)

29. (A) $-1 + i$ (B) $\dfrac{4}{13} - \dfrac{7}{13} i$ (C) $\dfrac{5}{2} - 2i$ (2-5)   **30.** $u = \dfrac{-5 \pm \sqrt{5}}{2}$ (2-6)

31. $u = 1 \pm i\sqrt{2}$ (2-6)   **32.** $x = \dfrac{1 \pm \sqrt{43}}{3}$ (2-6)

33. $x = -\dfrac{27}{8}, 64$ (2-7)   **34.** $m = \pm 3i, \pm 2$ (2-7)

35. $y = \dfrac{9}{4}, 3$ (2-7)   **36.** $x = 0.45$ (2-1)

37. $-2.24 \le x \le 1.12$ or $[-2.24, 1.12]$ (2-3)   **38.** $0.89 - 0.32i$ (2-5)

39. $x = -1.64, 0.89$ (2-6)   **40.** $x = 0.94$, $y = 1.02$ (2-2)

41. $M = \dfrac{P}{1 - dt}$ (2-1)   **42.** $I = \dfrac{E \pm \sqrt{E^2 - 4PR}}{2R}$ (2-6)

43. $y = \dfrac{5 - x}{2x - 4}$ (2-1)   **44.** The correct answer is $x = -1$.   (2-1)

45. If $c < 9$ there are two distinct real roots, if $c = 9$ there is one real double root, and if $c > 9$ there are two distinct imaginary roots.   *(2-6)*

46. True for all real b and all negative a.   *(2-3)*

47. $\dfrac{a}{b}$ is less than 1.   *(2-3)*   **48.** $x = \dfrac{1}{1 - y}$ *(2-1)*

49. $6 - d < x < 6 + d$, $x \neq 6$. $(6 - d, 6) \cup (6, 6 + d)$

(2-4)

50. $x = \dfrac{\sqrt{3}}{4} \pm \dfrac{1}{4} i$ *(2-6)*

51. $x = \pm\sqrt{\dfrac{2 \pm \sqrt{3}}{2}}$ (four real roots)   *(2-7)*

52. 1   *(2-5)*   **53.** no solution   *(2-8)*

54. Set of all real numbers   *(2-8)*

55. $x \leq -4$ or $-2 \leq x < 0$ or $0 < x \leq 2$ or $x \geq 4$
$(-\infty, -4] \cup [-2, 0) \cup (0, 2] \cup [4, \infty)$ *(2-8)*

56. $u = -31 + 5x - 7y$, $v = 13 - 2x + 3y$ *(2-2)*

57. (A) Infinite number of solutions   (B) No solution   *(2-2)*

58. $x = -\dfrac{3}{5}, \dfrac{5}{3}$ *(2-6)*

59. (A) $H = 0.7(220 - A)$ (B) $H = 140$ beats per minute   (C) $A = 40$ years old   *(2-2)*

60. 30 mL of 80% solution and 20 mL of 30% solution   *(2-2)*

61. rate = 3 mph   *(2-6)*

62. (A) 3 km   (B) 16.2 km/hr   (C) 20.6 min   *(2-1, 2-6)*

63. 85 bags of Brand A and 45 bags of Brand B *(2-2)*

64. (A) 2000 and 8000 (B) 5000   *(2-6)*

65. $x = \dfrac{13 \pm \sqrt{45}}{2}$ thousand or approximately 3,146 and 9,854 units   *(2-6)*

66. $3.146 < x < 9.854$, x in thousands   *(2-8)*

67. $|T - 110| \leq 5$ *(2-4)*   **68.** 20 cm by 24 cm   *(2-6)*

69. $B = 14.58$ ft or 6.58 ft   *(2-7)*

CUMULATIVE REVIEW EXERCISE (Chapters 1 and 2)

1. $x = \dfrac{5}{2}$ *(2-1)*   **2.** (A) $ca + cb$ (B) $a + (b + c)$ (C) $c(a + b)$ *(1-1)*

3. $x = 1$, $y = -2$ *(2-2)*   **4.** $4x^2 - 6x + 10$ *(1-2)* **5.** $3x^2 - 26x + 9$ *(1-2)*

6. $6x^2 - 7xy - 20y^2$ *(1-2)* **7.** $4a^2 - 9b^2$ *(1-2)*   **8.** $25m^2 + 20mn + 4n^2$ *(1-2)*

9. $y \geq 5$; $[5, \infty)$ **10.** $-5 < x < 9$; $(-5, 9)$

(2-3) x *(2-4)*

11. $x \leq -5$ or $x \geq 2$; $(-\infty, -5] \cup [2, \infty)$ x *(2-8)*

12. Prime *(1-3)*   **13.** $(3t + 5)(2t - 1)$ *(1-3)* **14.** $\dfrac{2}{(x - 2)(x - 3)}$ *(1-4)*

15. $2y$ *(1-4)*   **16.** (A) $7 - 10i$ (B) $23 + 7i$ (C) $1 - i$ *(2-5)*

17. $3x^7y^{10}$ *(1-5)*   **18.** $\dfrac{2y^2}{x}$ *(1-5)*   **19.** $\dfrac{a^6}{b^9}$ *(1-6)*

20. $x = 0, -4$ *(2-6)*   **21.** $x = \pm\sqrt{5}$ *(2-6)*   **22.** $x = 3 \pm \sqrt{7}$ *(2-6)*

23. $x = 3$ *(2-7)*   **24.** $5\sqrt[4]{a^3}$ *(1-7)*   **25.** $2x^{2/5}y^{3/5}$ *(1-7)*

26. $x^2y^4\sqrt[3]{xy^2}$ *(1-7)*   **27.** $2xy^2\sqrt{3x}$ *(1-7)*   **28.** $\dfrac{\sqrt{2}}{2}$ or $\dfrac{1}{2}\sqrt{2}$ *(1-7)*

29. $x \geq -\dfrac{2}{3}$ or $\left[-\dfrac{2}{3}, \infty\right)$ *(2-3)*   **30.** $\{2, 3, 5\}$ *(1-1, 1-2)*

31. (A) False (B) True (C) False *(1-1)*   **32.** No solution: -1 is excluded *(2-1)*

33. $x = \dfrac{1}{2}, 3$ *(2-6)*   **34.** $x = \dfrac{5}{2}, 1$ *(2-7)*   **35.** $x = \dfrac{87}{16}$, $y = \dfrac{5}{8}$ *(2-2)*

36. (a) is a second degree polynomial. (c) is a fourth degree polynomial.   *(1-2)*

37. $10ab$ *(1-2)*   **38.** $6xh + 3h^2 - 4h$ *(1-2)*

39. $64m^3 + 144m^2n + 108mn^2 + 27n^3$ *(1-2)*   **40.** $(y + 4)(3y + 4)$ *(1-3)*

41. $(a + 3)(a + 2)(a - 2)$ *(1-3)*   **42.** $x^3(x + 1)^2(7x + 4)$ *(1-3)*

43. $\dfrac{x^3(x + 4)}{(x + 1)^4}$ *(1-4)*   **44.** $\dfrac{5}{a - 2b}$ *(1-4)*   **45.** $\dfrac{x + 2y}{x - 2y}$ *(1-4)*

46. Correct answer is $x + 1$ *(1-4)*   **47.** Correct answer is $x = 2$ *(2-1)*

48. $x < \dfrac{3}{2}$ or $x > 3$; $\left(-\infty, \dfrac{3}{2}\right) \cup (3, \infty)$ **49.** $\dfrac{2}{3} \leq m \leq 2$; $\left[\dfrac{2}{3}, 2\right]$

x *(2-4)* m *(2-4)*

50. $(-1, 2) \cup [5, \infty)$; $-1 < x < 2$ or   **51.** $x \geq 2$, $x \neq 4$, or $[2, 4) \cup (4, \infty)$.
$5 \leq x$.

x *(2-8)* x *(2-3)*

52. (A) $0 + 0i$ or 0 (B) $\dfrac{6}{5}$ (C) $i^{35} = i^{32}i^3 = (i^4)^8(-i) = 1^8(-i) = -i$ *(2-5)*

53. (A) $3 + 18i$ (B) $-2.9 + 10.7i$ (C) $-4 - 6i$ *(2-5)*

54. (A) 0.1767 (B) 1.434 (C) 1.435 (D) 5.724×10^{14} *(1-5, 1-7)*

55. $6x^2y^4\sqrt[3]{2x^2y}$ *(1-7)*   **56.** $\dfrac{\sqrt[5]{14a^3b}}{2b}$ *(1-7)*   **57.** $y\sqrt{2y}$ *(1-7)*

58. $\sqrt{t+9} + 3$ *(1-7)*   **59.** All three have the same value.   *(1-7)*

60. (A) $\dfrac{2}{5}x + 2x^{-2}$ (B) $\dfrac{1}{2} - \dfrac{5}{4}x^{-1/2}$ or $\dfrac{1}{2}x^0 - \dfrac{5}{4}x^{-1/2}$ *(1-5, 1-7)*

61. $y = 3 \pm \sqrt{-5}$, $y = 3 \pm i\sqrt{5}$ *(2-6)*   **62.** $x = \dfrac{27}{8}$, $-\dfrac{1}{8}$ *(2-7)*

63. $u = \pm 2i$, $\pm\sqrt{3}$ *(2-7)*   **64.** $t = \dfrac{9}{4}$ *(2-7)*

65. $-18.36 \le x < 16.09$ or $[-18.36, 16.09)$ *(2-3)*

66. $-5.68, 1.23$ *(2-6)*   **67.** $x = 1.49$, $y = 0.55$ *(2-2)*

68. $y = \dfrac{3 - 3x}{x + 4}$ *(2-1)*   **69.** $s = 5 + x - 2y$, $t = -12 - 2x + 5y$ *(2-2)*

70. 0 *(1-7)*   **71.** 0 *(2-5)*   **72.** $6x^2 + 2$ *(1-2)*

73. All a and b such that $a < b$.   *(2-3)*

74. $b^2(3b - 4a + 4)(3b + 4a - 4)$ *(1-3)*   **75.** $\dfrac{2 - m}{4m}$ *(1-4)*

76. $y = \dfrac{x^2 + x}{x - 1}$ *(2-1)*   **77.** $x = \dfrac{\sqrt{2} \pm i}{3}$ *(2-6)*

78. If $b < -2$ or $b > 2$ there are two distinct real roots; if $b = -2$ or $b = 2$, there is one real double root; and if $-2 < b < 2$ there are two distinct imaginary roots.   *(2-6, 2-8)*

79. $x = -3$ *(2-7)*   **80.** (A) $a - b$ (B) $\dfrac{x^2 - y^2}{x^2 + y^2}$ *(1-5, 1-7)*

81. $\dfrac{1}{(8 + h)^{2/3} + 2(8 + h)^{1/3} + 4}$ *(1-7)*   **82.** $\dfrac{a^2 - b^2}{a^2 + b^2} + \dfrac{2ab}{a^2 + b^2}i$ *(2-5)*

83. $x < -1$ or $x > 2$; $(-\infty, -1) \cup (2, \infty)$ *(2-8)*   **84.** x^2 *(1-7)*

85. $x = -\dfrac{1}{2}$, 2 *(2-6)*   **86.** $t = 10.5$ min   *(2-2)*

87. $x = 2.5$ mph   *(2-6)*   **88.** $x = 12$ gal   *(2-2)*

89. $x = 8{,}800$ books   *(2-2)*   **90.** $|p - 200| \le 10$ *(2-4)*

91. \$16.50, 5,500 cheese heads   *(2-2)*   **92.** $V = 2x - 1$ cubic feet   *(1-2)*

93. (A) Profit: $\$5.5 < p < \$8$ or $(\$5.5, \$8)$
(B) Loss: $\$0 \le p < \$5.5$ or $p > \$8$. $[\$0, \$5.5) \cup (\$8, \infty)$ *(2-8)*

94. 40 mi from A to B and 75 mi from B to C *or* 75 mi from A to B and 40 mi from B to C *(2-6)*

95. (A) $a = 2{,}500$, $b = -16$ (B) 2,500 ft   (C) 12.5 sec   *(2-1, 2-6)*

CHAPTER 3

Exercise 3-1

1. The y axis   **2.** Quadrant I   **3.** Quadrant III   **4.** The x axis

5. Quadrant IV   **6.** Quadrant III and quadrant IV

7. Quadrant II and quadrant IV   **8.** Quadrant II

9. Quadrant I and quadrant IV   **10.** Quadrant I and quadrant III

11.

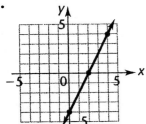

12.

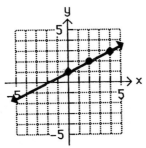

13. Symmetric with respect to the origin

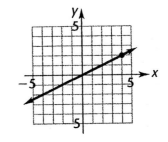

14. Symmetric with respect to the origin

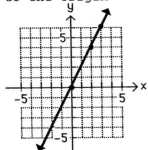

15. Symmetric with respect to the x axis

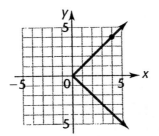

16. Symmetric with respect to the x axis

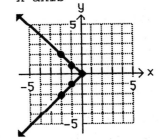

17. Symmetric with respect to the x axis, y axis, and origin

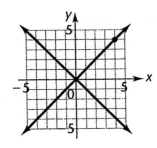

18. Symmetric with respect to the origin

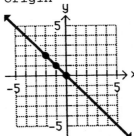

19. $\sqrt{106}$ **20.** $\sqrt{89}$ **21.** $\sqrt{82}$ **22.** $\sqrt{61}$ **23.** $x^2 + y^2 = 16$ **24.** $x^2 + y^2 = 36$

25. $(x - 3)^2 + (y + 2)^2 = 1$ **26.** $(x + 4)^2 + (y - 2)^2 = 25$

27. $(x - 2)^2 + (y - 6)^2 = 3$ **28.** $(x + 1)^2 + (y + 3)^2 = 5$

29. (A) 3   (B) -2   (C) -3, -1, 4   (D) -4, 1, 3

30. (A) -4   (B) 5   (C) -3, 1   (D) -2, 0

31. (A) 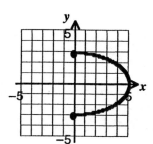   (B) 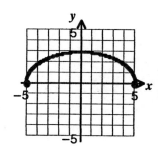   (C) 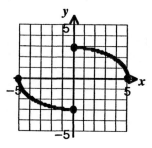   (D)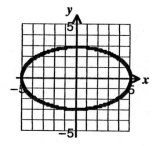

32. (A) 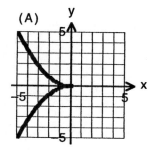   (B) (C) 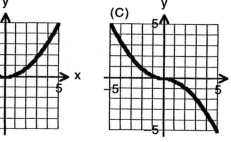   (D)

33. Symmetric with respect to the *x* axis

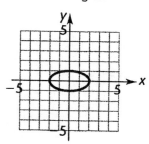

34. Symmetric with respect to the *x* axis

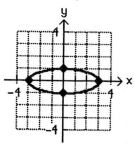

35. Symmetric with respect to the *y* axis

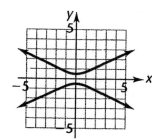

36. Symmetric with respect to the *y* axis

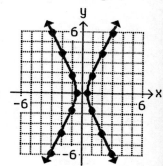

37. Symmetric with respect to the *x* axis, *y* axis, and origin

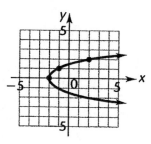

38. Symmetric with respect to the *x* axis, *y* axis, and origin.

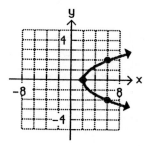

39. Symmetric with respect to the *x* axis, *y* axis, and origin

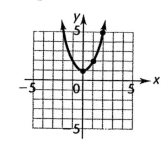

40. Symmetric with respect to the *x* axis, *y* axis and origin

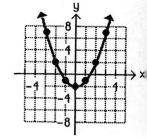

41. Symmetric with respect to the origin

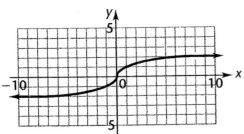

42. Symmetric with respect to the *y* axis

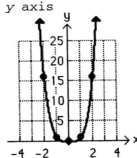

43. Symmetric with respect to the *y* axis

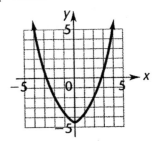

44. Symmetric with respect to the *x* axis

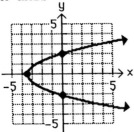

45. Symmetric with respect to the *y* axis

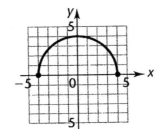

46. Symmetric with respect to the *y* axis

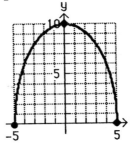

47. Symmetric with respect to the *y* axis

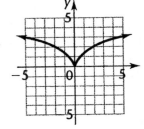

48. Symmetric with respect to the *x* axis

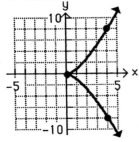

49. Area = 28, perimeter = 26.96

50. Area = 50, perimeter = 34.44   **51.** $x = -12, 4$ **52.** No solution

53. $y = 4$ **54.** $y = -3, 7$

55. Center $(-4, 2)$; **56.** $(h, k) = (5, -7)$; **57.** Center $(3, 2)$; **58.** Center = $(1, 5$
    Radius = $\sqrt{7}$ $r = \sqrt{15}$ Radius = 7   radius = 9

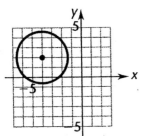

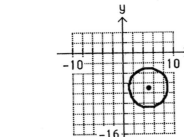

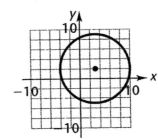

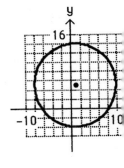

59. Center $(-4, 3)$; Radius $= \sqrt{17}$

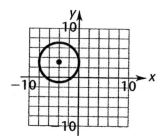

60. Center $= (-2, -5)$; radius $= \sqrt{14}$

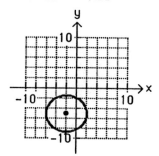

61.

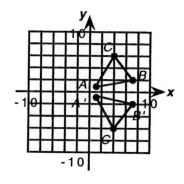

62.

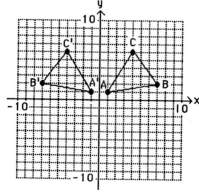

63.

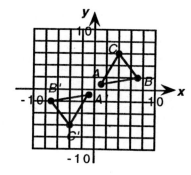

64.

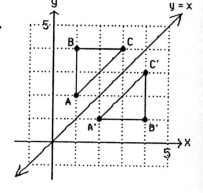

65. $y = \pm\sqrt{3 - x^2}$

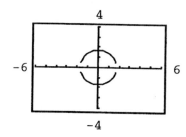

66. $y = \pm\sqrt{5 - x^2}$

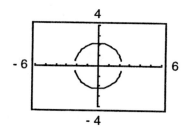

67. $y = -1 \pm \sqrt{2 - (x + 3)^2}$

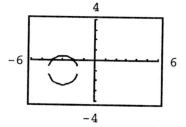

68. $y = 1 \pm\sqrt{3 - (x - 2)^2}$

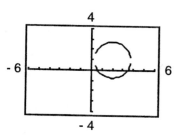

69. Center: $(1, 0)$; radius: 1; $(x - 1)^2 + y^2 = 1$

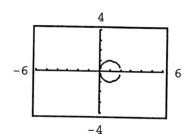

70. $x^2 + (y - 1)^2 = 1$; center $= (0, 1)$; radius $= 1$

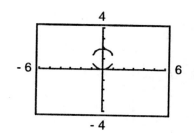

71. Center: (2, 1);
   radius: 3;
   $(x - 2)^2 + (y - 1)^2 = 9$

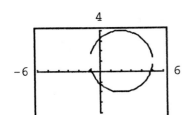

72. $(x - 2)^2 + (y + 1)^2 = 2^2$
   center = (2, -1);
   radius = 2

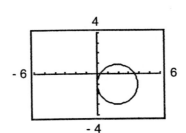

73. Symmetric with respect
   to the y axis

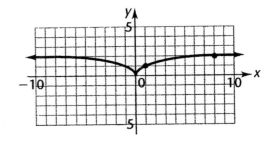

74. Symmetric with respect
   to the x axis

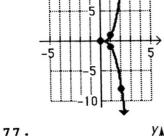

75. Symmetric with respect
   to the origin

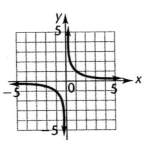

76. Symmetric with respect
   to the origin

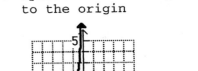

77.

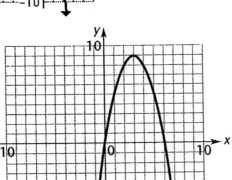

78.

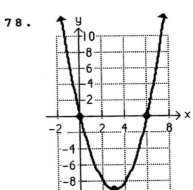

79. $5x + 3y = -2$

81. $(x - 4)^2 + (y - 2)^2 = 34$

82. $(x - 2)^2 + (y + 1)^2 = 34$

83. $(x - 2)^2 + (y - 2)^2 = 50$

84. $(x + 5)^2 + (y - 4)^2 = 98$

85. Yes

86. Yes

87. (A) 3,000 cases   (B) Demand decreases by 400 cases
   (C) Demand increases by 600 cases

88. (A) 3,000 cases   (B) Supply increases by 300 cases
   (C) Supply decreases by 400 cases

89. (A) 53°   (B) 68° at 3 PM   (C) 1 AM, 7 AM, and 11 PM

90. (A) 60°   (B) 44° at 5 AM   (C) 9 AM, 10 PM

91.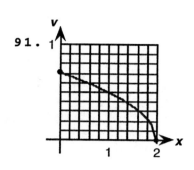

92.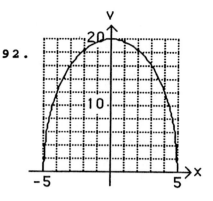

93. $r = \dfrac{5}{2}$ or 2.5 ft

94. $r = 6.5$ mm

95. (A) $676 = (x + 12)^2 + (y + 5)^2$; center: $(-12, -5)$; radius: 26
(B) 13.5 mi

96. (A) Center = $(48, 20)$; radius = 26   (B) $x = 64.6$ mi or $x = 31.4$ mi

Exercise 3-2

1. x intercept = -2; y intercept = 2; slope = 1; equation: $y = x + 2$

2. x intercept = 1; y intercept = 1; slope = -1; equation: $y = -x + 1$

3. x intercept = -2; y intercept = -4; slope = -2; equation: $y = -2x - 4$

4. x intercept = -1; y intercept = -3; slope = -3; equation: $y = -3x - 3$

5. x intercept = 3; y intercept = -1; slope = $\dfrac{1}{3}$; equation: $y = \dfrac{1}{3}x - 1$

6. x intercept = 4; y intercept = -2; slope = $\dfrac{1}{2}$; equation: $y = \dfrac{1}{2}x - 2$

7. slope = $-\dfrac{3}{5}$

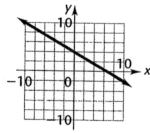

8. slope = $-\dfrac{3}{2}$

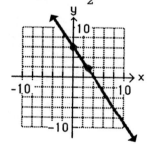

9. slope = $-\dfrac{3}{4}$

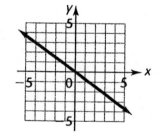

10. slope = $\dfrac{2}{3}$

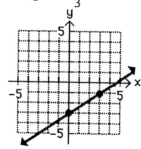

11. slope = $\dfrac{2}{3}$

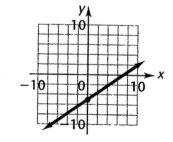

12. slope = $-\dfrac{4}{3}$

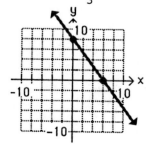

13. slope = $\frac{4}{5}$

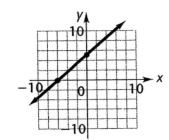

14. slope = $\frac{6}{7}$

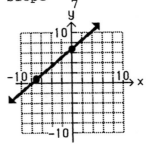

15. slope = 2

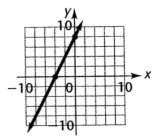

16. slope = $\frac{6}{5}$

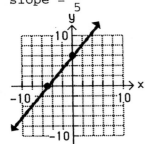

17. slope not defined

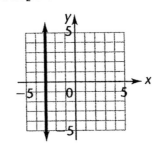

18. slope = 0

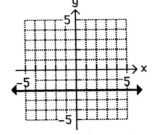

19. slope = 0

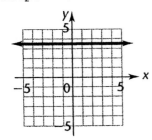

20. slope not defined

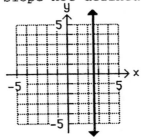

21. $x - y = 0$

22. $x + y = 7$

23. $2x + 3y = -12$

24. $5x - 3y = -18$

25. $y = -2x + 3$

26. $y = 3x - 12$

27. $y = \frac{3}{2}x + \frac{23}{2}$

28. $y = -\frac{4}{5}x - \frac{7}{5}$

29. $y = -4x + 13$

30. $y = -\frac{1}{2}x + \frac{7}{2}$

31. $x = -3$

32. $y = 5$

33. $y = 2$

34. $x = 5$

35. $3x + y = 5$

36. $4x - y = -14$

37. $2x + 3y = -12$

38. $3x - 4y = -6$

39. $y = 3$

40. $x = -2$

41. $2x + 3y = 23$

42. $5x - 3y = -14$

43. $2x + 5y = 10$

44. $x - 2y = -6$

45. $x = -2$

46. $y = -7$

47. Trapezoid

48. Parallelogram

49. Rectangle

50. None of these

51. $y = -\frac{6}{7}x - \frac{5}{14}$

52. $12x + 14y = -5$, which is equivalent to $y = -\frac{6}{7}x - \frac{5}{14}$

53. $3x + 4y = 25$

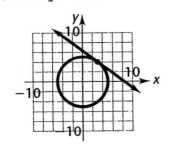

54. $4x - 3y = -50$

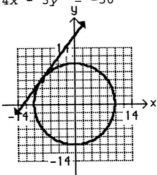

55. $x - y = 10$

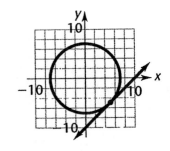

56. $x + 2y = -20$

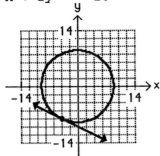

57. $232 = 5x - 12y$

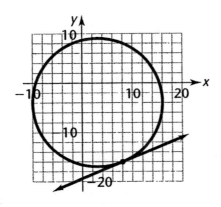

58. $8x + 15y = -194$

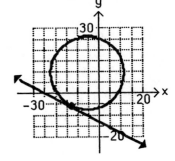

59. (A)

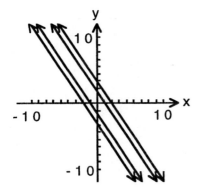

60. (A)

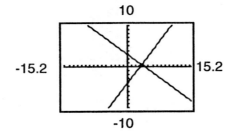

(B)

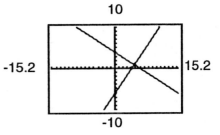

61.

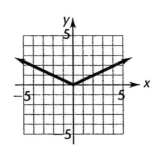

62.

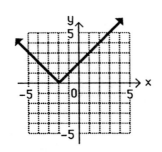

63.

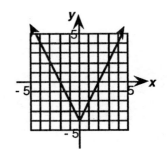

64.

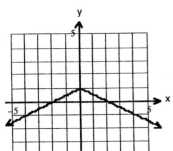

65.

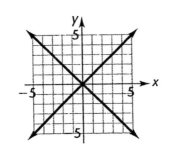

66.

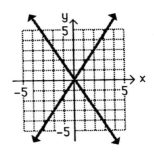

70. $5x + 3y = 15$

71. $7x - 2y = -14$

73. (A)

x	0	5,000	10,000	15,000	20,000	25,000	30,000
$212 - 0.0018x = B$	212	203	194	185	176	167	158

(B) The boiling point drops 9°F for each 5,000 foot increase in altitude.

74. (A)

x	0	1	2	3	4	5
A	25	16	7	-2	-11	-20

(B) For every kilometer increase in altitude the air temperature decreases 9°C.

75. The rental charges are $25 per day plus $0.25 per mile driven.

76. The installation charges are $15 for travel to the installation site plus $0.70 per minute spent at the site.

77. (A)

x	0	1	2	3	4
Sales	5.9	6.5	7.7	8.6	9.7
$5.74 + 0.97x = y$	5.7	6.7	7.7	8.6	9.6

(B) (C) $10.6 billion, $17.4 billion

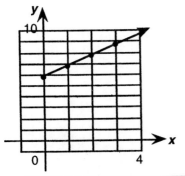

78. (A)

x	0	1	2	3	4
net income	1.2	1.5	1.8	2.1	2.4
y	1.2	1.5	1.8	2.1	2.4

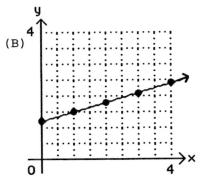

(C) $2.7 billion, $4.8 billion

79. (A) $F = \dfrac{9}{5}C + 32$ (B) 68°F, 30°C   (C) $\dfrac{9}{5}$

80. (A) $s = 0.4w$ (B) 9 lbs.   (C) slope = 0.4

81. (A) $V = -1,600t + 8,000, \; 0 \le t \le 5$ (B) $V = \$3,200$ (C) $-1,600$

82. (A) $R = 1.5C + 3 \; (C > 10)$ (B) $158   (C) slope = 1.5

83. (A) $T = -5A + 70, \; A \ge 0$ (B) $A = 14$ thousand feet
(C) slope = -5; the temperature changes $-5°F$ for each 1,000 foot rise in altitude.

84. (A) $T = 4A + 200 \; (A \ge 0)$ (B) $T = 226$ mph
(C) slope = 4 which indicates that true air speed increases 4 mph for each one thousand foot increase in altitude.

85. (A) $h = 1.13t + 12.8$ (B) $t = 32.9$ hours

86. (A) $p = \dfrac{5}{11}d + 15$ (B) $d = 55$ ft

87. (A) $R = 0.00152C - 0.159, \; C \ge 210$ (B) $R = 0.236$
(C) slope = 0.00152; coronary risk increases 0.00152 per unit increase in cholesterol above the 210 cholesterol level.

88. (A) $N = -0.0251t + 4.76 \; (t \ge 0)$ (B) $N = 2.25$ people per household

Exercise 3-3

1. A function   **2.** A function   **3.** Not a function

4. Not a function   **5.** A function   **6.** A function

7. A function; Domain = {2, 3, 4, 5}; Range = {4, 6, 8, 10}

8. A function; Domain = {-1, 0, 1, 2}; Range = {4, 3, 2, 1}

9. Not a function

10. A function; Domain = {-10, -5, 0, 5, 10}; Range = {0, 5, 10}

11. A function; Domain = {0, 1, 2, 3, 4, 5}; Range = {1, 2}

12. Not a function   **13.** A function   **14.** A function

15. Not a function   **16.** A function   **17.** Not a function

18. Not a function   **19.** 4   **20.** -9   **21.** 0   **22.** 8   **23.** 10

24. -5   **25.** 4   **26.** -4   **27.** 5.25   **28.** Not defined   **29.** 7

30. -5   **31.** -1, -5, 6   **32.** -6, 1, 5

33. A function with domain all real numbers

34. Not a function; for example, when $x = 0$, $y = \pm 1$

35. Not a function; for example, when $x = 0$, $y = \pm 2$

36. A function with domain all real numbers

37. A function with domain all real numbers

38. Not a function; for example, when $x = 0$, $y = \pm 6$

39. Not a function; for example, when $x = 0$, y can be any real number

40. A function with domain all real numbers except 0

41. A function with domain all real numbers except 0

42. Not a function; for example, when $x = 0$, y can be any real number

43. Domain: $x \geq 2$ **44.** Domain: all real numbers

45. Domain: all real numbers   **46.** Domain: $s \leq -1$

47. Domain: all real numbers except 4   **48.** Domain: all real numbers

49. Domain: all real numbers except −2 and 1

50. Domain: all real numbers except −2 and 3

51. Domain: $y \leq -1$ or $y \geq 3$ **52.** Domain: all real numbers

53. Domain: all real numbers   **54.** Domain: $1 \leq t < 5$

55. Domain: $y < -2$ or $y \geq 3$ **56.** Domain: $z < -3$ or $z > -1$

57. $g(x) = 2x^3 - 5$ **58.** $f(x) = -3x + 4$

59. $G(x) = 2\sqrt{x} - x^2$ **60.** $F(x) = -8x^3 + 3\sqrt{3}$

61. Function f multiplies the domain element by 2 and subtracts 3 from the result.

62. Function g multiplies the domain element by −2 and adds 7 to the result.

63. Function F multiplies the cube of the domain element by 3 and subtracts twice the square root of the domain element from the result.

64. Function G multiplies the square root of the domain element by 4 and subtracts the square of the domain element from the result.

65. 3   **66.** −4   **67.** $-6 - h$ **68.** $8 + 2h$

69. $11 - 2h$ **70.** $-3h + 2$ **71.** $f(x) = 3x^2 - 5x + 9$

72. $g(w) = -4w^3 + 7w - 5$ **73.** $m(t) = -2t^2 - 5\sqrt{t} - 2$

74. $s(z) = 3z + 9\sqrt{z} + 1$ **75.** (A) 4   (B) 4

76. (A) −5   (B) −5   **77.** (A) $4x + 2h$ (B) $2x + 2a$

78. (A) $-6x - 3h$ (B) $-3x - 3a$ **79.** (A) $-8x + 3 - 4h$ (B) $-4x - 4a + 3$

80. (A) $6x - 5 + 3h$ (B) $3x + 3a - 5$

81. (A) $3x^2 - 2 + 3xh + h^2$ (B) $x^2 + ax + a^2 - 2$

82. (A) $2x - 3x^2 - 3xh - h^2 + h$ (B) $x - x^2 - ax + a - a^2$

83. $P(w) = 2w + \dfrac{128}{w}$, $w > 0$ **84.** $A(w) = -w^2 + 25w$, $0 < w < 25$

85. $h(b) = \sqrt{b^2 + 25}$, $b > 0$ **86.** $b(h) = \sqrt{h^2 - 16}$, $h > 4$

87. $C(x) = 300 + 1.75x$ **88.** $C(x) = 68x + 3750$

89. (A) $s(0) = 0$, $s(1) = 16$, $s(2) = 64$, $s(3) = 144$ (B) $64 + 16h$
(C) Value of expression tends to 64; this number appears to be the speed of the object at the end of 2 s.

90. (A) $S(8) = 640$, $S(9) = 810$, $S(10) = 1000$, $S(11) = 1210$ (B) $220 + h$

(C) $220 + h \to 220$ as h tends to 0. This is the speed of the automobile at the instant $t = 11$ sec.

91. $V(x) = (12 - 2x)(8 - 2x)x$; Domain: $0 < x < 4$

92. $A(x) = x(20 - 2x)$ where $0 < x < 10$

93. $F(x) = 8x + \dfrac{250}{x} - 12$; $F(4) = 82.5$; $F(5) = 78$; $F(6) = 77.7$; $F(7) = 79.7$

94. $P(x) = x\left(1 + \dfrac{\pi}{4}\right) + \dfrac{48}{x}$

x	$P(x) = x\left(1 + \dfrac{\pi}{4}\right) + \dfrac{48}{x}$
4	19.1
5	18.5
6	18.7
7	19.4

95. $C(x) = 10{,}000(20 - x) + 15{,}000\sqrt{64 + x^2}$; Domain: $0 \le x \le 20$

96. $d(h) = \sqrt{h^2 + 100}$ **97.** $C(v) = 100v + \dfrac{200{,}000}{v}$ **98.** $C(t) = \dfrac{50{,}000}{t} + 400t$

Exercise 3-4

1. (A) $[-4, 4)$ (B) $[-3, 3)$ (C) 0   (D) 0   (E) $[-4, 4)$ (F) None
   (G) None   (H) None

2. (A) $(-5, 5]$ (B) $[-4, 4)$ (C) 0   (D) 0   (E) None   (F) $(-5, 5]$
   (G) None   (H) None

3. (A) $(-\infty, \infty)$ (B) $(-4, \infty)$ (C) $-3, 1$ (D) -3 (E) $[-1, \infty)$ (F) $(-\infty, -1]$
   (G) None   (H) None

4. (A) $(-\infty, \infty)$ (B) $(-\infty, 3]$ (C) 0, 4   (D) 0   (E) $(-\infty, 2]$
   (F) $[2, \infty)$ (G) none   (H) none

5. (A) $(-\infty, 2) \cup (2, \infty)$ (The function is not defined at $x = 2$.)
   (B) $(-\infty, -1) \cup [1, \infty)$ (C) None   (D) 1   (E) None   (F) $(-\infty, -2] \cup (2, \infty)$
   (G) $[-2, 2)$ (H) $x = 2$

6. (A) $(-\infty, -3) \cup (-3, \infty)$ (B) $(-\infty, -2) \cup [2, \infty)$ (C) none   (D) 2
   (E) $(-\infty, -3) \cup [3, \infty)$ (F) none   (G) $(-3, 3]$ (H) $x = -3$

7. One possible answer:

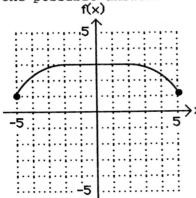

8. One possible answer:

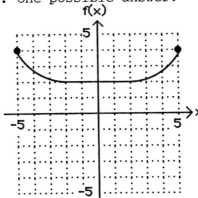

9. One possible answer:

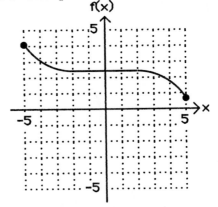

10. One possible answer:

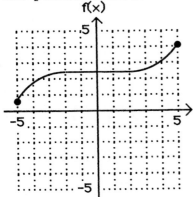

11. One possible answer:

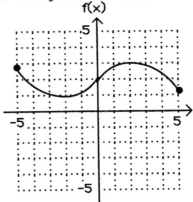

12. One possible answer:

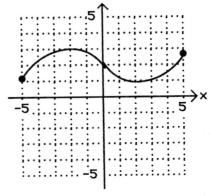

13. y intercept is
$f(0) = 4$;
slope is 2;
x intercept = -2

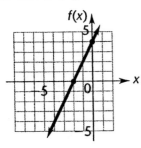

14. $x = 1$ x int
$f(0) = -3$ y int
slope = 3

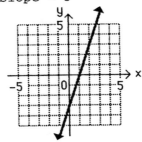

15. y intercept is
$f(0) = -\frac{5}{3}$;
slope is $-\frac{1}{2}$;
x intercept = $\frac{-10}{3}$

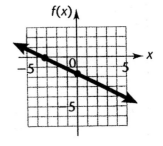

16. $x = \frac{8}{5}$ x int

$f(0) = \frac{6}{5}$ y int

slope = $-\frac{3}{4}$

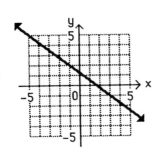

17. $f(x) = -\frac{3}{2}x + 4$

18. $f(x) = \frac{3}{4}x + \frac{1}{4}$

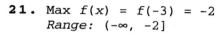

19. Min $f(x) = f(3) = 2$
Range: $[2, \infty)$

20. min $f(x) = f(-2) = -4$
range $= [-4, \infty]$

21. Max $f(x) = f(-3) = -2$
Range: $(-\infty, -2]$

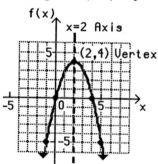

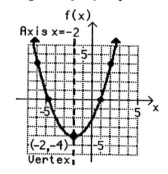

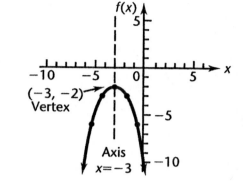

22. max $f(x) = f(2) = 4$
range $= (-\infty, 4]$

23. y intercept: $f(0) = -5$
x intercepts: $5, -1$

24. $(0, 5)$ y int
$(1, 0)$, $(5, 0)$ x int

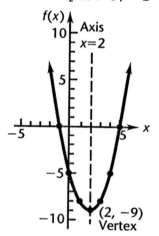

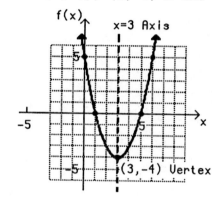

25. y intercept: $f(0) = 0$
x intercepts: $0, 6$

26. $(0, 8)$ y int
$(4, 0)$, $(-2, 0)$ x int

27. f is decreasing on
$(-\infty, -3]$ and
increasing on $[-3, \infty)$

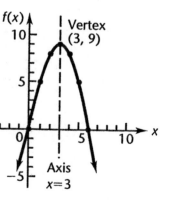

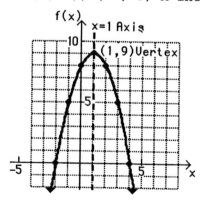

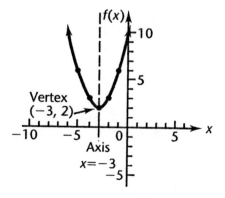

28. *f* is increasing on [4, ∞); *f* is decreasing on (–∞, 4]

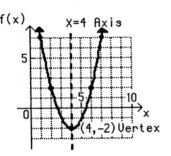

29. *f* is increasing on (–∞, 3] and decreasing on [3, ∞)

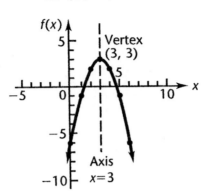

30. *f* is increasing on (–∞, –5]; *f* is decreasing on [–5, ∞)

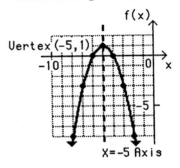

31. Domain: [–1, 1]; Range: [0, 1]

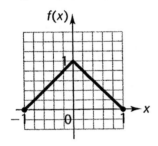

32. Domain: [–2, 2]; Range: [–2, 1]

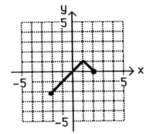

33. Domain: [–3, –1) ∪ (–1, 2] Range: {–2, 4} (a set, not an interval) Discontinuous: at *x* = –1

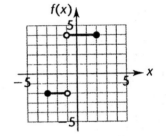

34. Domain: [–2, 2) ∪ (2, 5]; Range: {–3, 1} Discontinuous at *x* = 2

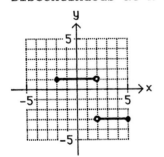

35. Domain: All real numbers Range: All real numbers Discontinuous at *x* = –1

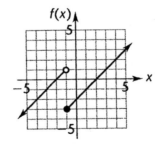

36. Domain: all real numbers Range: all real numbers Discontinuous at *x* = 2

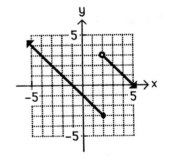

37. Domain: $(-\infty, 0) \cup (0, \infty)$
Discontinuous at $x = 0$
Range: $(-\infty, -1) \cup$
$(1, \infty)$

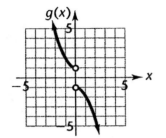

38. Domain: $x \neq 0 \Leftrightarrow$
$(-\infty, 0) \cup (0, \infty)$
Range: $(-\infty, -2) \cup$
$(2, \infty)$
Discontinuous at $x = 0$

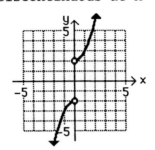

39. Min $f(x) = f(-2) = 1$
Range: $[1, \infty)$
Increasing on $[-2, \infty)$
Decreasing on $(-\infty, -2]$
y intercept: $f(0) = 3$
no x intercepts

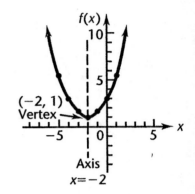

40. min $f(x) = -4$; range: $[-4, \infty)$
$f(0) = 14$, y-int
$x = 3 + \sqrt{2}$ and
$x = 3 - \sqrt{2}$ for x intercepts
f is increasing on $[3, \infty)$
f is decreasing on $(-\infty, 3]$

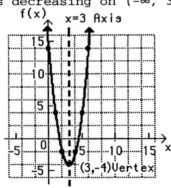

41. Min $f(x) = = f\left(\dfrac{3}{2}\right) = 0$; Range: $[0, \infty)$

Increasing on $\left[\dfrac{3}{2}, \infty\right)$

Decreasing on $\left(-\infty, \dfrac{3}{2}\right]$

y intercept: $f(0) = 9$

x intercept: $x = \dfrac{3}{2}$

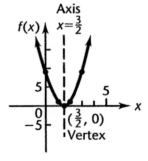

42. max $f(x) = -2$; range: $(-\infty, -2]$
$f(0) = -10$, y int
no x intercepts
f is increasing on $(-\infty, 4]$
f is decreasing on $[4, \infty)$

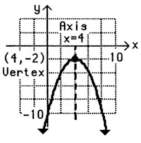

43. Max $f(x) = f(-2) = 6$; Range: $(-\infty, 6]$
Decreasing on $[-2, \infty)$
Increasing on $(-\infty, -2]$
y intercept: $f(0) = -2$
x intercepts: $x = -2 \pm \sqrt{3}$

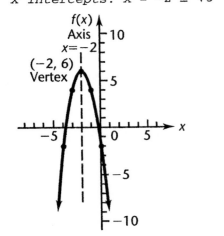

44. max $f(x) = f\left(-\frac{1}{2}\right) = 0$

range: $(-\infty, 0]$
$f(0) = -1$, y int
$x = -\frac{1}{2}$, x int

f is increasing on $\left(-\infty, -\frac{1}{2}\right]$

f is decreasing on $\left[-\frac{1}{2}, \infty\right)$

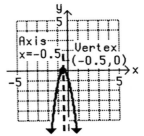

45. $f(x) = \begin{cases} -1 & \text{if } x < 0 \\ 1 & \text{if } x > 0 \end{cases}$

Domain: $(-\infty, 0) \cup (0, \infty)$, that is,
$x \neq 0$
Range: $\{-1, 1\}$ (a set, not an
interval)
Discontinuous at $x = 0$

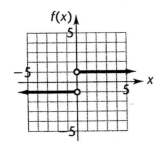

46. $f(x) = \begin{cases} -x^2 & \text{if } x < 0 \\ x^2 & \text{if } x \geq 0 \end{cases}$

Domain: all real numbers
Range: all real numbers

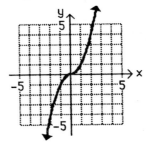

47. $f(x) = \begin{cases} x - 1 & \text{if } x < 1 \\ x + 1 & \text{if } x > 1 \end{cases}$

Domain: $(-\infty, 1) \cup (1, \infty)$
Range: $(-\infty, 0) \cup (2, \infty)$
Discontinuous at $x = 1$

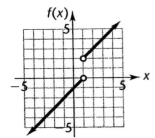

48. $f(x) = \begin{cases} x - 2 & \text{if } x < -1 \\ x + 2 & \text{if } x > -1 \end{cases}$

Domain: $x \neq -1$ or
$(-\infty, -1) \cup (-1, \infty)$
Range: $(-\infty, -3) \cup (1, \infty)$
Discontinuous at $x = -1$

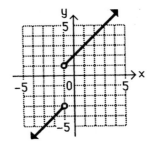

49. $f(x) = \begin{cases} 2 - 2x & x < 0 \\ 2 & 0 \le x < 2 \\ 2x - 2 & x \ge 2 \end{cases}$

Domain: All real numbers
Range: $[2, \infty)$
No discontinuities

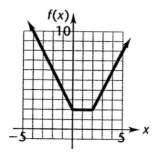

50. $f(x) = \begin{cases} -3 & x < 0 \\ 2x - 3 & 0 \le x < 3 \\ 3 & x \ge 3 \end{cases}$

Domain: all real numbers
Range: $[-3, 3]$
no discontinuity

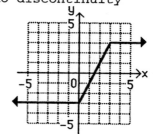

51. Domain: All real numbers
Range: All integers
Discontinuous at the even integers

$f(x) = \begin{cases} \vdots & & & \vdots \\ -2 & \text{if} & -4 \le x < -2 \\ -1 & \text{if} & -2 \le x < 0 \\ 0 & \text{if} & 0 \le x < 2 \\ 1 & \text{if} & 2 \le x < 4 \\ 2 & \text{if} & 4 \le x < 6 \\ \vdots & & & \vdots \end{cases}$

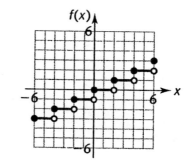

52. $f(x) = \begin{cases} -2 & \text{if} & -6 \le x < -3 \\ -1 & \text{if} & -3 \le x < 0 \\ 0 & \text{if} & 0 \le x < 3 \\ 1 & \text{if} & 3 \le x < 6 \\ 2 & \text{if} & 6 \le x < 9 \end{cases}$

Domain: all real numbers
Range: all integers
Discontinuous at all integers
divisible by 3

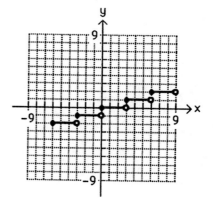

53. Domain: All real numbers
Range: All integers
Discontinuous at rational numbers of the form $\frac{k}{3}$ where k is an integer

$f(x) = \begin{cases} \vdots & & & \vdots \\ -2 & \text{if} & -\frac{2}{3} \le x < -\frac{1}{3} \\ -1 & \text{if} & -\frac{1}{3} \le x < 0 \\ 0 & \text{if} & 0 \le x < \frac{1}{3} \\ 1 & \text{if} & \frac{1}{3} \le x < \frac{2}{3} \\ 2 & \text{if} & \frac{2}{3} \le x < 1 \\ \vdots & & & \vdots \end{cases}$

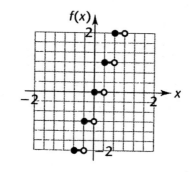

54. $f(x) = \begin{cases} \vdots \\ -2 & \text{if } -1 \le x < -\frac{1}{2} \\ -1 & \text{if } -\frac{1}{2} \le x < 0 \\ 0 & \text{if } 0 \le x < \frac{1}{2} \\ 1 & \text{if } \frac{1}{2} \le x < 1 \\ 2 & \text{if } 1 \le x < \frac{3}{2} \\ \vdots \end{cases}$

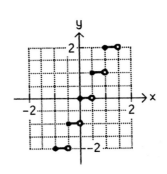

Domain: all real numbers
Range: all integers
Discontinuous at all rational numbers of the form $\frac{k}{2}$ where k is an integer.

55. Domain: all real numbers
Range: [0, 1)
Discontinuous at all integers.

$f(x) = \begin{cases} \vdots & \vdots \\ x + 2 & \text{if } -2 \le x < -1 \\ x + 1 & \text{if } -1 \le x < 0 \\ x & \text{if } 0 \le x < 1 \\ x - 1 & \text{if } 1 \le x < 2 \\ x - 2 & \text{if } 2 \le x < 3 \\ \vdots & \vdots \end{cases}$

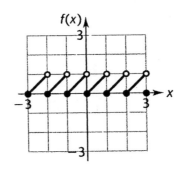

56. $f(x) = \begin{cases} \vdots \\ -2 - x & \text{if } -2 \le x < -1 \\ -1 - x & \text{if } -1 \le x < 0 \\ 0 - x & \text{if } 0 \le x < 1 \\ 1 - x & \text{if } 1 \le x < 2 \\ 2 - x & \text{if } 2 \le x < 3 \\ \vdots \end{cases}$

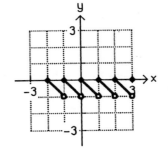

Domain: all real numbers
Range: (-1, 0]
Discontinuous at all integers.

57. vertex = (2, 4); axis is $x = 2$; range is [4, ∞); no x intercepts

58. vertex = (-3, -5), axis: $x = -3$; range: (-∞, -5]; no x intercepts

59. (A) One possible answer:

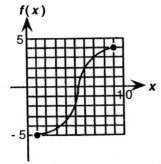

(B) The graph must cross the x axis exactly once.

60. (A) One possible answer:

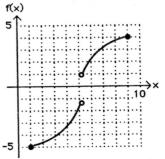

(B) The graph can cross the x axis at most one time.

61. (A) One possible answer:

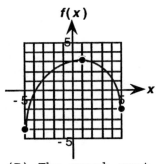

(B) The graph must cross the *x* axis at least twice. There is no upper limit on the number of times it can cross the *x* axis.

62. (A) One possible answer:

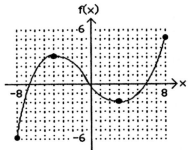

(B) The graph must cross the *x* axis three times. There is no upper limit on the number of times it can cross the *x* axis.

63. $y = 2x - 1$

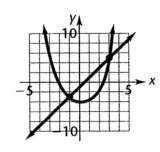

64. $y = -2x + 1$

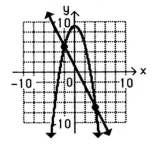

65. (A) $1 + h$ (B)

h	$slope = 1 + h$
1	2
0.1	1.1
0.01	1.01
0.001	1.001

; The slope seems to be approaching 1.

66. $f(x) = x^2 + 2x - 6$
(A) $6 + h$

(B)

h	1	0.1	0.01	0.001
m_{SL}	7	6.1	6.01	6.001

Slope seems to be approaching 6.

67. Graphs of *f* and *g*   Graph of *m*   Graph of *n*

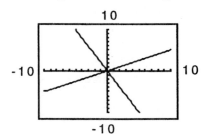
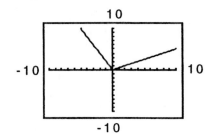
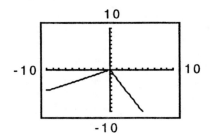

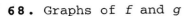

68. Graphs of f and g Graph of m Graph of n

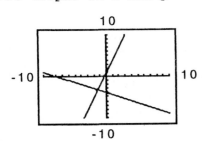 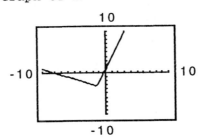 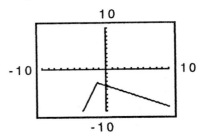

69. Graphs of f and g Graph of m Graph of n

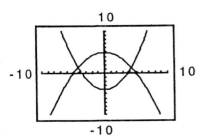 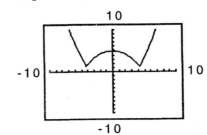 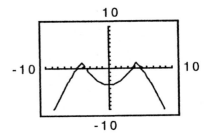

70. Graphs of f and g Graph of m Graph of n

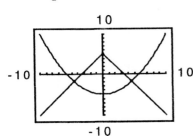 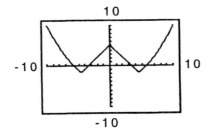 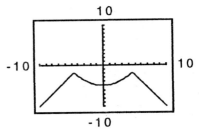

71. Graphs of f and g Graph of m Graph of n

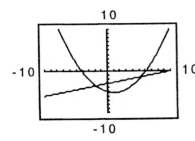 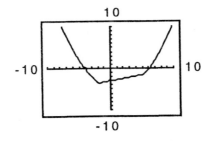 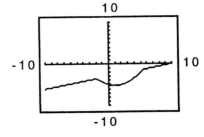

72. Graphs of f and g Graph of m Graph of n

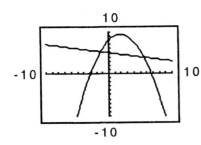 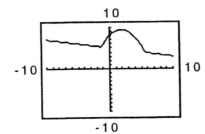 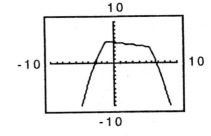

73. $\max[f(x), g(x)] = m(x)$ **74.** $n(x) = \min[f(x), g(x)]$

75. (A)

x	28	30	32	34	36
Mileage	45	52	55	51	47
$-0.518x^2 + 33.3x - 481 = f(x)$	45.3	51.8	54.2	52.4	46.5

(C) $f(31) \approx 53.50$ thousand miles
$f(35) \approx 49.95$ thousand miles

(B)

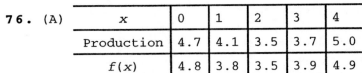

76. (A)

x	0	1	2	3	4
Production	4.7	4.1	3.5	3.7	5.0
$f(x)$	4.8	3.8	3.5	3.9	4.9

(B)

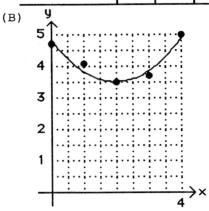

(C) 1994: $f(5) \approx 6.55$ million vehicles;
1995: $f(6) \approx 8.88$ million vehicles

77. (A) $s = f(w) = \dfrac{w}{10}$; (B) $f(15) = 1.5$
inches and $f(30) = 3$ inches

(C) slope $= \dfrac{1}{10}$

(D)

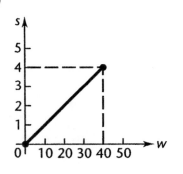

78. (A) $V = f(t) = -1800t + 20,000$
(B) $f(4) = \$12,800$; $f(8) = \$5600$
(C) slope $= -1,800$
(D)

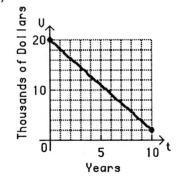

79. $E(x) = \begin{cases} 200 & \text{if} & 0 \le x \le 3{,}000 \\ 80 + 0.04x & \text{if } 3{,}000 < x < 8{,}000 \\ 180 + 0.04x & \text{if } 8{,}000 \le x \end{cases}$

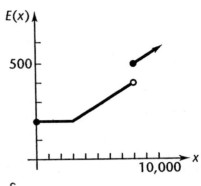

$E(5{,}750) = \$310; \; E(9{,}200) = \$548$
discontinous at $x = 8{,}000$

80. $S(x) = \begin{cases} 2x \text{ if } 0 \le x \le 30 \\ 2(30) + 1(x - 30) = x + 30 \text{ if } x > 30 \end{cases}$

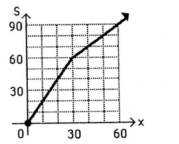

No points of discontinuity.
$S(25) = 50; \; S(45) = 75$

81. (A) $A(x) = x(50 - x) = 50x - x^2$ (B) $0 < x < 50$ or $(0, 50)$ is the domain

(C)   (D) 25 feet by 25 feet

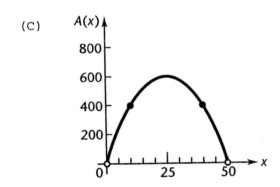

82. (A) $A(x) = x(100 - 2x)$ (B) $0 < x < 50$

(C)   (D) 25 ft by 50 ft

83.

$$\begin{array}{rcllr}
f(4) & = & 10[\![0.5 + 0.4]\!] & = 10(0) & = 0 \\
f(-4) & = & 10[\![0.5 - 0.4]\!] & = 10(0) & = 0 \\
f(6) & = & 10[\![0.5 + 0.6]\!] & = 10(1) & = 10 \\
f(-6) & = & 10[\![0.5 - 0.6]\!] & = 10(-1) & = -10 \\
f(24) & = & 10[\![0.5 + 2.4]\!] & = 10(2) & = 20 \\
f(25) & = & 10[\![0.5 + 2.5]\!] & = 10(3) & = 30 \\
f(247) & = & 10[\![0.5 + 24.7]\!] & = 10(25) & = 250 \\
f(-243) & = & 10[\![0.5 - 24.3]\!] & = 10(-24) & = -240 \\
f(-245) & = & 10[\![0.5 - 24.5]\!] & = 10(-24) & = -240 \\
f(-246) & = & 10[\![0.5 - 24.6]\!] & = 10(-25) & = -250 \\
\end{array}$$
$\Big\}$ f rounds numbers to the tens place

84.

x	40	−40	60	−60	740	750	7,551	−601	−649	−651
$f(x)$	0	0	100	−100	700	800	7,600	−600	−600	−700

$f(x)$ rounds to the nearest hundred.

85. $f(x) = [\![100x + 0.5]\!]/100$ **86.** $f(x) = \dfrac{1}{1000}[\![0.5 + 1000x]\!]$

87. (A) $C(x) = \begin{cases} 15 & 0 < x \le 1 \\ 18 & 1 < x \le 2 \\ 21 & 2 < x \le 3 \\ 24 & 3 < x \le 4 \\ 27 & 4 < x \le 5 \\ 30 & 5 < x \le 6 \end{cases}$

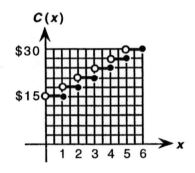

(B) No, since $f(x) \ne C(x)$ at $x = 1, 2, 3, 4, 5,$ or 6

88. (A) $C(x) = \begin{cases} 4 & 0 < x \le 1 \\ 6 & 1 < x \le 2 \\ 8 & 2 < x \le 3 \\ 10 & 3 < x \le 4 \\ 12 & 4 < x \le 5 \\ 14 & 5 < x \le 6 \end{cases}$

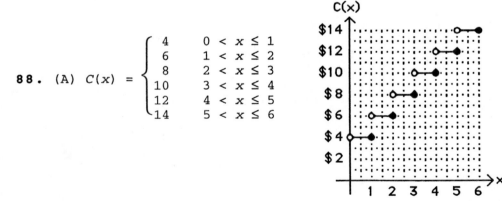

(B) No, since $f(x) \ne C(x)$ at $x = 1, 2, 3, 4, 5,$ or 6

89. \$50 a day; maximum income = \$12,500

90. \$90 per room will maximize profit; P_{max} = \$25,600

91. (A) $v = 32\sqrt{5} \approx 71.55$ ft/sec (B) 15 ft   **92.** (A) $x = 100$ at landing (B) 35 ft

Exercise 3-5

1. Domain: $[0, \infty)$; Range: $(-\infty, 0]$ **2.** Domain: R; Range: R

3. Domain: R; Range: $(-\infty, 0]$ **4.** Domain: R; Range: $(-\infty, 0]$

5. Domain: R; Range R

6. Domain: R; Range: R

7. $(f + g)(x) = 5x + 1$; $(f - g)(x) = 3x - 1$; $(fg)(x) = 4x^2 + 4x$

$\left(\dfrac{f}{g}\right)(x) = \dfrac{4x}{x + 1}$; Domain $f + g$, $f - g$, $fg = (-\infty, \infty)$;

Domain of $f/g = (-\infty, -1) \cup (-1, \infty)$

8. $(f + g)(x) = 4x - 2$; $(f - g)(x) = 2x + 2$; $(fg)(x) = f(x)g(x) = 3x^2 - 6x$;

$\left(\dfrac{f}{g}\right)(x) = \dfrac{3x}{x - 2}$; Domain $f + g$, $f - g$, fg: $(-\infty, \infty)$

Domain $\dfrac{f}{g}$: $(-\infty, 2) \cup (2, \infty)$

9. $(f + g)(x) = 3x^2 + 1$; $(f - g)(x) = x^2 - 1$; $(fg)(x) = 2x^4 + 2x^2$;

$\left(\dfrac{f}{g}\right)(x) = \dfrac{2x^2}{x^2 + 1}$; Domain of each function: $(-\infty, \infty)$

10. $(f + g)(x) = x^2 + 3x + 4$; $(f - g)(x) = f(x) - g(x) = -x^2 + 3x - 4$;

$(fg)(x) = 3x^3 + 12x$; $\left(\dfrac{f}{g}\right)(x) = \dfrac{3x}{x^2 + 4}$; Domain $f + g$, $f - g$, fg, $\dfrac{f}{g}$: $(-\infty, \infty)$

11. $(f \circ g)(x) = x^4 - 8x^3 + 16x^2 + 3$, $(g \circ f)(x) = x^4 + 2x^2 - 3$;

Domain of $f \circ g$ = Domain of $g \circ f$ = $(-\infty, \infty)$

12. $(f \circ g)(x) = x^4 - 3x^2 - 4$, $(g \circ f)(x) = x^4 - 10x^3 + 25x^2 + 1$;

Domain of $f \circ g$ = Domain of $g \circ f$ = $(-\infty, \infty)$

13. $(f \circ g)(x) = 2(x^3 - 1)^{2/3}$, $(g \circ f)(x) = 8x^2 - 1$;

Domain of $f \circ g$ = Domain of $g \circ f$ = $(-\infty, \infty)$

14. $(f \circ g)(x) = 4 - 27x$, $(g \circ f)(x) = 3(4 - x^3)^{1/3}$;

Domain of $f \circ g$ = Domain of $g \circ f$ = $(-\infty, \infty)$

15.

16.

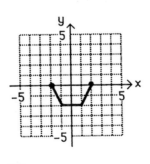

17.

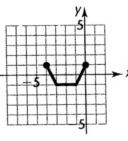

18.

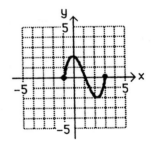

19.

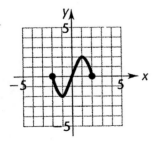

20.

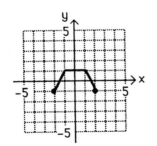

21.

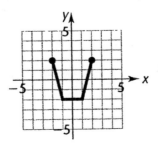

22.

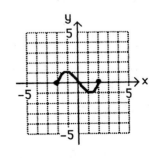

23. The graph of $y = |x|$ is shifted two units to the left and refelected in the x axis.

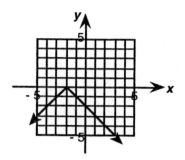

24. The graph of $|x|$ is shifted 4 units to the right and reflected in the x axis.

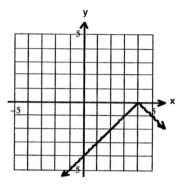

25. The graph of $y = x^2$ is shifted 2 units to the right and 4 units down.

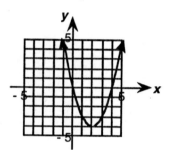

26. The graph of x^2 is shifted 1 unit to the left and 3 units up.

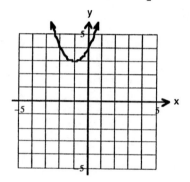

27. The graph of $y = \sqrt{x}$ is vertically expanded by a factor of 2, reflected in the x axis, and shifted 4 units up.

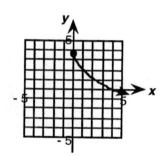

28. The graph of $\sqrt[3]{x}$ is vertically expanded by a factor of 3 and shifted down two units.

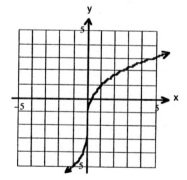

29. $(f + g)(x) = \sqrt{x + 2} + \sqrt{4 - x}$,
$(f - g)(x) = \sqrt{x + 2} - \sqrt{4 - x}$,
$(fg)(x) = \sqrt{8 + 2x - x^2}$,
$(f/g)(x) = \sqrt{(x + 2)/(4 - x)}$;
Domain of $f + g =$ Domain of $f - g =$
Domain of $fg = [-2, 4]$,
Domain of $f/g = [-2, 4)$

30. $(f + g)(x) = \sqrt{5 - x} + \sqrt{x + 1}$,
$(f - g)(x) = \sqrt{5 - x} - \sqrt{x + 1}$,
$(fg)(x) = \sqrt{5 + 4x - x^2}$,
$(f/g)(x) = \sqrt{(5 - x)/(x + 1)}$;
Domain of $f + g =$ Domain of $f - g =$
Domain of $fg = [-1, 5]$,
Domain of $f/g = (-1, 5]$

31. $(f + g)(x) = 8 - 3\sqrt{x}$,
$(f - g)(x) = 2 - \sqrt{x}$,
$(fg)(x) = 15 - 11\sqrt{x} + 2x$,
$(f/g)(x) = (5 - 2\sqrt{x})/(3 - \sqrt{x})$;
Domain of $f + g$ = Domain of $f - g$ =
Domain of $fg = [0, \infty)$,
Domain of $f/g = [0, 9) \cup (9, \infty)$

32. $(f + g)(x) = 4\sqrt{x} + 5$,
$(f - g)(x) = 2\sqrt{x} + 7$,
$(fg)(x) = 3x + 3\sqrt{x} - 6$,
$(f/g)(x) = (3\sqrt{x} + 6)/(\sqrt{x} - 1)$;
Domain of $f + g$ = Domain of $f - g$ =
Domain of $fg = [0, \infty)$,
Domain of $f/g = [0, 1) \cup (1, \infty)$

33. $(f + g)(x) = \sqrt{x^2 + x - 2} + \sqrt{24 + 2x - x^2}$,
$(f - g)(x) = \sqrt{x^2 + x - 2} - \sqrt{24 + 2x - x^2}$,
$(fg)(x) = \sqrt{-x^4 + x^3 + 28x^2 + 20x - 48}$,
$(f/g)(x) = \sqrt{(x^2 + x - 2)/(24 + 2x - x^2)}$;
Domain of $f + g$ = Domain of $f - g$ = Domain of $fg = [-4, -2] \cup [1, 6]$,
Domain of $f/g = (-4, -2] \cup [1, 6)$

34. $(f + g)(x) = \sqrt{x^2 + 3x - 10} + \sqrt{x^2 - x - 12}$,
$(f - g)(x) = \sqrt{x^2 + 3x - 10} - \sqrt{x^2 - x - 12}$,
$(fg)(x) = \sqrt{x^4 + 2x^3 - 25x^2 - 26x + 120}$,
$(f/g)(x) = \sqrt{(x^2 + 3x - 10)/(x^2 - x - 12)}$;
Domain of $f + g$ = Domain of $f - g$ = Domain of $fg = (-\infty, -5] \cup [4, \infty)$,
Domain of $f/g = (-\infty, -5] \cup (4, \infty)$

35. $(f \circ g)(x) = \sqrt{4 - x} + 2$,
$(g \circ f)(x) = \sqrt{2 - x}$;
Domain of $f \circ g = (-\infty, 4]$,
Domain of $g \circ f = (-\infty, 2]$

36. $(f \circ g)(x) = \sqrt{x - 1}$,
$(g \circ f)(x) = \sqrt{x + 1} - 2$;
Domain of $f \circ g = [1, \infty)$,
Domain of $g \circ f = [-1, \infty)$

37. $(f \circ g)(x) = (3x - 5)/(x - 2)$,
$(g \circ f)(x) = 1/(x + 1)$;
Domain of $f \circ g = (-\infty, 2) \cup (2, \infty)$,
Domain of $g \circ f = (-\infty, -1) \cup (-1, \infty)$

38. $(f \circ g)(x) = (2 - x)/(6 - x)$,
$(g \circ f)(x) = (x + 8)/(x + 4)$;
Domain of $f \circ g = (-\infty, 6) \cup (6, \infty)$,
Domain of $g \circ f = (-\infty, -4) \cup (-4, \infty)$

39. $(f \circ g)(x) = 3|(x - 2)/(x - 3)|$,
$(g \circ f)(x) = |x + 2|/(|x + 2| - 3)$;
Domain of $f \circ g = (-\infty, 3) \cup (3, \infty)$,
Domain of $g \circ f = (-\infty, -5) \cup (-5, 1) \cup (1, \infty)$

40. $(f \circ g)(x) = |x + 3|/(|x + 3| - 4)$,
$(g \circ f)(x) = 4|(x - 3)/(x - 4)|$;
Domain of $f \circ g = (-\infty, -7) \cup (-7, 1) \cup (1, \infty)$,
Domain of $g \circ f = (-\infty, 4) \cup (4, \infty)$

41. $y = |x + 1| - 2$ **42.** $y = 4 - (x - 2)^2$ **43.** $y = 3 - \sqrt[3]{x}$

44. $y = -2 - \sqrt{x}$ **45.** $y = 1 - (x + 2)^3$ **46.** $y = (x - 3)^3 - 1$

47. $y = \sqrt{x + 2} + 3$

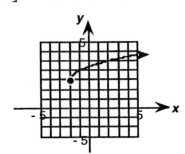

48. $y = \sqrt[3]{x - 3} - 2$

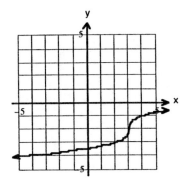

49. $y = -|x - 3|$

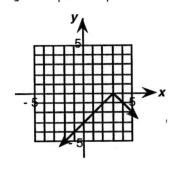

50. $y = -|x + 1|$

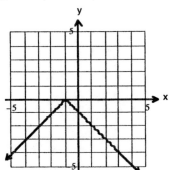

51. $y = -(x + 2)^3 + 1$

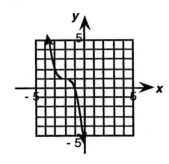

52. $y = -(x - 2)^2 - 4$

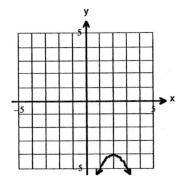

53. Reversing the order does not change the result.

54. Reversing the order does not change the result.

55. Reversing the order can change the result.

56. Reversing the order can change the result.

57. Reversing the order does not change the result.

58. Reversing the order does not change the result.

59. $g(x) = 2x - 7$; $f(x) = x^4$; $h(x) = (f \circ g)(x)$

60. $f(x) = x^7$; $g(x) = 3 - 5x$; $h(x) = (f \circ g)(x)$

61. $g(x) = 4 + 2x$; $f(x) = x^{1/2}$; $h(x) = (f \circ g)(x)$

62. $f(x) = x^{1/2}$; $g(x) = 3x - 11$; $h(x) = (f \circ g)(x)$

63. $f(x) = x^7$; $g(x) = 3x - 5$; $h(x) = (g \circ f)(x)$

64. $g(x) = 5x + 3$; $f(x) = x^6$; $h(x) = (g \circ f)(x)$

65. $f(x) = x^{-1/2}$; $g(x) = 4x + 3$; $h(x) = (g \circ f)(x)$

66. $g(x) = -2x + 1$; $f(x) = x^{-1/2}$; $h(x) = (g \circ f)(x)$

67. The graph of $y = |x|$ is reflected in the x axis and vertically expanded by a factor of 3. Equation: $y = -3|x|$

68. The graph of $y = x^2$ is vertically contracted by a factor of 0.25. Equation: $y = 0.25x^2$.

69. The graph of $y = x^3$ is reflected in the x axis and vertically contracted by a factor of 0.5. Equation: $y = -0.5x^3$.

70. The graph of $y = \sqrt[3]{x}$ is reflected in the axis and vertically expanded by a factor of 2. Equation: $y = -2\sqrt[3]{x}$.

75. $(f + g)(x) = 2x$; $(f - g)(x) = \dfrac{2}{x}$; $(fg)(x) = x^2 - \dfrac{1}{x^2}$; $\left(\dfrac{f}{g}\right)(x) = \dfrac{x^2 + 1}{x^2 - 1}$

The domain of $f + g$, $f - g$, and $fg = (-\infty, 0) \cup (0, \infty)$.

The domain of $\dfrac{f}{g}$ is $(-\infty, -1) \cup (-1, 0) \cup (0, 1) \cup (1, \infty)$.

76. $(f + g)(x) = 2x - 1 - \dfrac{6}{x - 1}$; $(f - g)(x) = -1 + \dfrac{6}{x - 1}$; $(fg)(x) = x^2 - x - 6$

$\left(\dfrac{f}{g}\right)(x) = \dfrac{(x - 1)^2}{(x - 3)(x + 2)}$

Domain $f + g$, $f - g$, fg: $(-\infty, 1) \cup (1, \infty)$

Domain $\dfrac{f}{g}$: $(-\infty, -2) \cup (-2, 1) \cup (1, 3) \cup (3, \infty)$

77. $(f + g)(x) = 2$; $(f - g)(x) = \dfrac{-2x}{|x|}$; $(fg)(x) = 0$; $\left(\dfrac{f}{g}\right)(x) = 0$

The domain of $f + g$, $f - g$, and fg is $(-\infty, 0) \cup (0, \infty)$. Domain of $\dfrac{f}{g}$ is $(0, \infty)$.

78. $(f + g)(x) = 2x$; $(f - g)(x) = 2|x|$; $(fg)(x) = 0$; $\left(\dfrac{f}{g}\right)(x) = 0$

Domain $f + g$, $f - g$, fg: $(-\infty, \infty)$; Domain $\dfrac{f}{g}$: $(-\infty, 0)$

79. $(f \circ g)(x) = 9 - x$,
$(g \circ f)(x) = \sqrt{9 - x^2}$;
Domain of $f \circ g = (-\infty, 9]$, Domain of $g \circ f = [-3, 3]$

80. $(f \circ g)(x) = \sqrt{x^2 - 16}$,
$(g \circ f)(x) = x - 16$;
Domain of $f \circ g = (-\infty, -4] \cup [4, \infty)$, Domain of $g \circ f = [16, \infty)$

81. $(f \circ g)(x) = (3x + 1)/(8 - x)$,
$(g \circ f)(x) = (4x - 3)/(7 - x)$;
Domain of $f \circ g = (-\infty, 3) \cup (3, 8) \cup (8, \infty)$,
Domain of $g \circ f = (-\infty, 2) \cup (2, 7) \cup (7, \infty)$

82. $(f \circ g)(x) = (1 - x)/(x + 3)$,
$(g \circ f)(x) = (11 - 2x)/(x - 1)$;
Domain of $f \circ g = (-\infty, -3) \cup (-3, -1) \cup (-1, \infty)$,
Domain of $g \circ f = (-\infty, 1) \cup (1, 4) \cup (4, \infty)$

83. $(f \circ g)(x) = \sqrt{x^2 + 1}$,
$(g \circ f)(x) = \sqrt{x^2 + 1}$;
Domain of $f \circ g = (-\infty, -2] \cup [2, \infty)$,
Domain of $g \circ f = (-\infty, \infty)$

84. $(f \circ g)(x) = \sqrt{x^2 - 1}$,
$(g \circ f)(x) = \sqrt{x^2 - 1}$;
Domain of $f \circ g = (-\infty, -3] \cup [3, \infty)$,
Domain of $g \circ f = (-\infty, -1] \cup [1, \infty)$

85. $P(p) = -70,000 + 6,000p - 200p^2$

86. $P(p) = -100p^2 + 7000p - 140,000$

87.

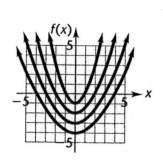

88.

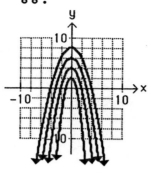

89.

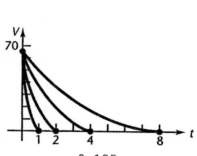

90.

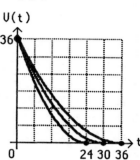

91. (A) $r(h) = \frac{1}{2}h$ (B) $V(h) = \frac{1}{12}\pi h^3$ (C) $V(t) = \frac{0.125}{12}\pi t^{3/2}$

92. (A) $w(h) = 2h$ (B) $V = 6h^2$ (C) $V(t) = 6(2 - 0.2\sqrt{t})^2$

Exercise 3-6

1. one-to-one **2.** not one-to-one **3.** not one-to-one **4.** one-to-one

5. one-to-one **6.** not one-to-one **7.** not one-to-one **8.** one-to-one

9. one-to-one **10.** not one-to-one **11.** not one-to-one **12.** one-to-one

13. one-to-one **14.** not one-to-one **15.** one-to-one **16.** one-to-one

17. one-to-one **18.** one-to-one **19.** not one-to-one **20.** one-to-one

21. one-to-one **22.** not one-to-one

23. one-to-one **24.** not one-to-one **25.** not one-to-one

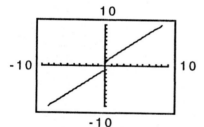

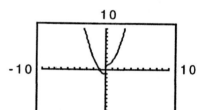

26. one-to-one **27.** not one-to-one **28.** not one-to-one

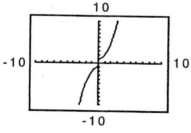

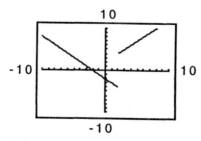

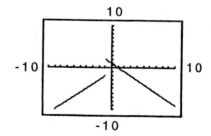

29. one-to-one **30.** one-to-one

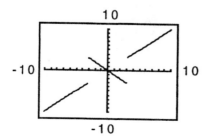

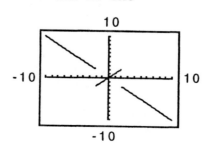

31. Range of f^{-1} = [-4, 4];
Domain of f^{-1} = [1, 5]

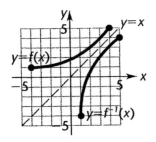

32. $D_{f^{-1}}$: $-4 \leq x \leq 3$; $R_{f^{-1}}$: $-2 \leq y \leq 5$

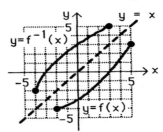

33. Range of f^{-1} = [-5, 3];
Domain of f^{-1} = [-3, 5]

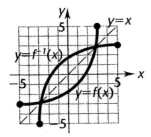

34. $D_{f^{-1}}$: $-5 \leq x \leq 5$;
$R_{f^{-1}}$: $0 \leq y \leq 5$

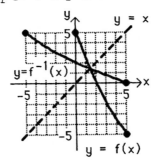

35.

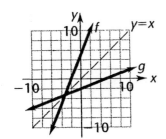

36.

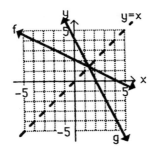

37.

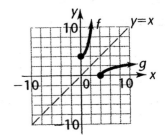

38.

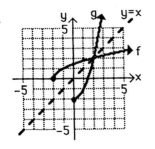

39.

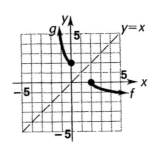

40.

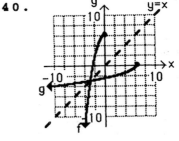

41. $f^{-1}(x) = 5x$

42. $f^{-1}(x) = \dfrac{1}{4}x$

43. $f^{-1}(x) = \dfrac{1}{2}x - \dfrac{7}{2}$

44. $f^{-1}(x) = 4x - 9$

45. $f^{-1}(x) = 5x - 2$

46. $f^{-1}(x) = -\dfrac{1}{8}x + \dfrac{7}{8}$

47. $f^{-1}(x) = \dfrac{2}{3 - x}$

48. $f^{-1}(x) = \dfrac{4}{x - 5}$

49. $f^{-1}(x) = \dfrac{x}{2 - x}$

50. $f^{-1}(x) = \dfrac{2x}{x + 4}$

51. $f^{-1}(x) = \dfrac{5x + 4}{2 - x}$

52. $f^{-1}(x) = \dfrac{0.5x + 0.2}{1 - x}$

53. $f^{-1}(x) = 0.5\sqrt[3]{x + 5}$

54. $f^{-1}(x) = \sqrt[5]{\dfrac{x - 9}{2}}$

55. $f^{-1}(x) = \frac{1}{3}(x - 2)^5 + \frac{7}{3}$ **56.** $f^{-1}(x) = \frac{4}{5} - \frac{1}{5}(x + 1)^3$

57. $f^{-1}(x) = 9 - \frac{1}{4}x^2, \ x \geq 0$ **58.** $f^{-1}(x) = 4 + \frac{1}{9}x^2, \ x \geq 0$

59. $f^{-1}(x) = -x^2 + 4x - 1, \ x \geq 2$ **60.** $f^{-1}(x) = x^2 - 8x + 11, \ x \leq 4$

61. The x intercept of f is the y intercept of f^{-1} and the y intercept of f is the x intercept of f^{-1}.

62. A constant function cannot have an inverse because it is not 1-1.

63. $f^{-1}(x) = 1 + \sqrt{x - 2}$ **64.** $f^{-1}(x) = 5 - \sqrt{3 - x}$

65. $f^{-1}(x) = -1 - \sqrt{x + 3}$ **66.** $f^{-1}(x) = -4 + \sqrt{9 + x}$

67. $f^{-1}(x) = \sqrt{9 - x^2}$;
Domain of
$\quad f^{-1} = [-3, 0]$;
Range of $f^{-1} = [0, 3]$

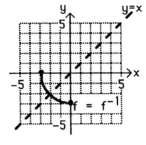

68. $f^{-1}(x) = \sqrt{9 - x^2}$;
Domain of
$\quad f^{-1}: 0 \leq x \leq 3$;
Range of $f^{-1}: 0 \leq y \leq 3$

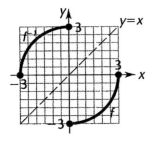

69. $f^{-1}(x) = -\sqrt{9 - x^2}$;
Domain: $f^{-1} = [0, 3]$;
Range of $f^{-1} = [-3, 0]$

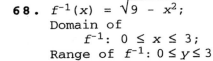
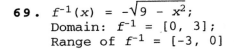

70. $f^{-1}(x) = -\sqrt{9 - x^2}$;
Domain of f^{-1}:
$\quad -3 \leq x \leq 0$;
Range of $f^{-1}: -3 \leq y \leq 0$

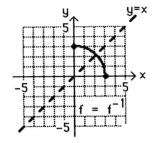
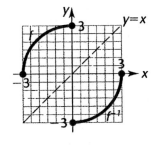

71. $f^{-1}(x) = \sqrt{2x - x^2}$;
Domain of
$\quad f^{-1} = [1, 2]$;
Range of $f^{-1} = [0, 1]$

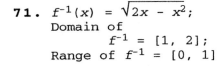
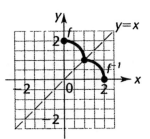

72. $f^{-1}(x) = \sqrt{2x - x^2}$;
Domain of $f^{-1}: 0 \leq x \leq 1$;
Range of $f^{-1}: 0 \leq y \leq 1$

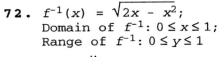
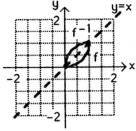

73. $f^{-1}(x) = -\sqrt{2x - x^2}$;
Domain of $f^{-1} = [0, 1]$;
Range of $f^{-1} = [-1, 0]$

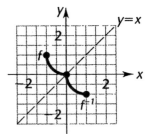

74. $f^{-1}(x) = -\sqrt{2x - x^2}$;
Domain of $f^{-1}: 1 \leq x \leq 2$;
Range of $f^{-1}: -1 \leq y \leq 0$

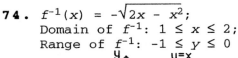
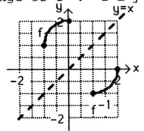

75. $f^{-1}(x) = \dfrac{x - b}{a}$

76. $f^{-1}(x) = \sqrt{a^2 - x^2}$, $0 \leq x \leq a$

77. $a = 1$ and $b = 0$ or $a = -1$ and b arbitrary.

78. The graph must be symmetric with respect to the line $y = x$.

81. (A) $f^{-1}(x) = 2 - \sqrt{x}$ (B) $f^{-1}(x) = 2 + \sqrt{x}$

82. (A) $f^{-1}(x) = -1 - \sqrt{x}$ (B) $f^{-1}(x) = -1 + \sqrt{x}$

83. (A) $f^{-1}(x) = 2 - \sqrt{4 - x^2}$, $0 \leq x \leq 2$ (B) $f^{-1}(x) = 2 + \sqrt{4 - x^2}$, $0 \leq x \leq 2$

84. (A) $f^{-1}(x) = 3 - \sqrt{9 - x^2}$, $0 \leq x \leq 3$ (B) $f^{-1}(x) = 3 + \sqrt{9 - x^2}$, $0 \leq x \leq 3$

CHAPTER 3 REVIEW

1. (A) $\sqrt{45}$ (B) $m = -\dfrac{1}{2}$ (C) $m_1 = 2$ *(3-1, 3-2)*

2. (A) $x^2 + y^2 = 7$ (B) $(x - 3)^2 + (y + 2)^2 = 7$ *(3-1)*

3. Center: $C(h, k) = C(-3, 2)$; Radius: $r = \sqrt{5}$ *(3-1)*

4. slope: $-\dfrac{3}{2}$ **5.** $2x + 3y = 12$ *(3-2)* **6.** $y = -\dfrac{2}{3}x + 2$ *(3-2)*

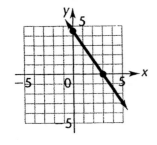

(3-2)

7. *vertical:* $x = -3$, slope not defined; *horizontal:* $y = 4$, slope $= 0$ *(3-2)*

8. (A) Function; domain $= \{ 1, 2, 3\}$, range $= \{1, 4, 9\}$
   (B) Not a function
   (C) Function; domain $= \{-2, -1, 0, 1, 2\}$, range $= \{2\}$ *(3-3)*

9. (A) Not a function   (B) A function
   (C) A function   (D) Not a function   *(3-3)*

10. (A) Function   (B) Not a function   (C) Function   (D) Not a function   *(3-3)*

11. 16   *(3-3)*   **12.** 1   *(3-3)*   **13.** 3   *(3-3)*

14. $-2a - h$ *(3-3)*   **15.** $9 + 3x - x^2$ *(3-5)* **16.** $x^2 + 3x + 1$ *(3-5)*

17. $20 + 12x - 5x^2 - 3x^3$ *(3-5)*   **18.** $\dfrac{3x + 5}{4 - x^2}$; Domain: $\{x \mid x \neq \pm 2\}$ *(3-5)*

19. $7 - 3x^2$ *(3-5)*   **20.** $-21 - 30x - 9x^2$ *(3-5)*

21. (A)   (B)   (C)   (D)

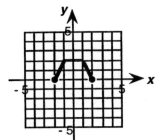 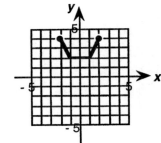 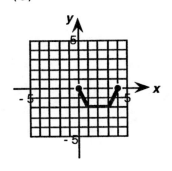 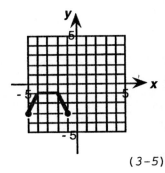

(3–5)

22. (A) *g*   (B) *m*   (C) *n*   (D) *f*   *(3–4, 3–5)*

23. (A) *x* intercepts: −4, 0; *y* intercept: 0
    (B) Vertex: (−2, −4)   (C) Minimum: −4
    (D) Range: $y \geq -4$ or $[-4, \infty)$
    (E) Increasing on $[-2, \infty)$ (F) Decreasing on $(-\infty, -2]$ *(3–4)*

24. *Min* $f(x) = f(3) = 2.$; *Vertex:* (3, 2)   *(3–4)*

25. (A) Reflected across *x*-axis   (B) Shifted down 3 units
    (C) Shifted left 3 units   *(3–5)*

26. (A) 0   (B) 1   (C) 2   (D) 0   *(3–4)*

27. (A) −2, 0   (B) 1   (C) No solution   (D) $x = 3$ and $x < -2$ *(3–4)*

28. Domain = $(-\infty, \infty)$ **29.** $[-2, -1]$, $[1, \infty)$ *(3–4)*   **30.** $[-1, 1)$ *(3–4)*
Range = $(-3, \infty)$ *(3–4)*

31. $(-\infty, -2)$ *(3–4)*   **32.** $x = -2$, $x = 1$ *(3–4)*   **33.** $f(x) = 4x^3 - \sqrt{x}$ *(3–3)*

34. The function *f* multiplies the square of the domain element by 3, adds 4 times
the domain element, and then subtracts 6.   *(3–3)*

35. (A) $3x + 2y = -6$ (B) $\sqrt{52}$ *(3–1, 3–2)*

36. (A) $y = -2x - 3$ (B) $y = \frac{1}{2}x + 2$ *(3–2)*

37. It is symmetric with respect to all three.   *(3–1)*

38. $(-\infty, 3)$ *(3–3)*

39. Min $f(x) = f(3) = -4$
    Range: $[-4, \infty)$
    y intercept: $f(0) = 5$
    x intercepts: $x = 1$,
    $x = 5$

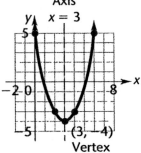

40. $[0, 16) \cup (16, \infty)$ *(3–3)*

(3–4)

41. (A) $(f \circ g)(x) = \sqrt{|x|} - 8$; $(g \circ f)(x) = |\sqrt{x} - 8|$

(B) Domain of $f \circ g$ is the set of all real numbers. The domain of $(g \circ f)$ is $[0, \infty)$ *(3-5)*

42. (A) one-to-one (B) not one-to-one (C) one-to-one (D) one-to-one   *(3-6)*

43. (A) $f^{-1}(x) = \dfrac{x + 7}{3}$ (B) $f^{-1}(5) = 4$ (C) $f^{-1}[f(x)] = x$ (D) increasing   *(3-6)*

44. Domain: $[-1, 1]$
Range: $[0, 1] \cup (2, 3]$
Discontinuous at $x = 0$

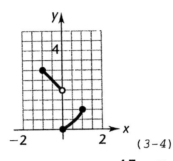

(3-4)

45. The graph of $y = x^2$ is vertically expanded by a factor of 2, reflected in the x axis, and shifted to the left 3 units.
Equation: $y = -2(x + 3)^2$.
     (3-5)

46. $g(x) = 5 - 3|x - 2|$

47. $y = -(x - 4)^2 + 3$ *(3-4, 3-5)*

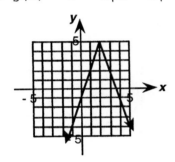

(3-5)

48. (A)

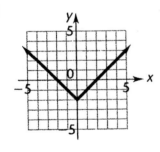

B)

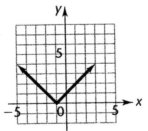

(C)

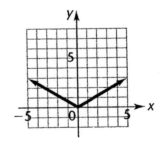

(3-5)

49. (A) $f^{-1}(x) = 1 + x^2$
(B) Domain of $f = [1, \infty)$ = Range of f^{-1}; Range of $f = [0, \infty)$ = Domain of f^{-1}

(C)

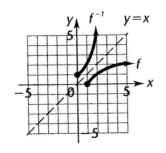

(3-6)

50. $(x - 3)^2 + y^2 = 32$ *(3-1)*

51. Center: $C(h, k) = C(-2, 3)$; Radius $r = \sqrt{16} = 4$ *(3-1)*

52.

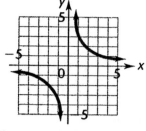

The graph has symmetry with respect to the origin. *(3-1)*

53. decreasing *(3-2, 3-3)*

54. (A) Domain of $f = [0, \infty)$ = Range of f^{-1}; Range of $f = [-1, \infty)$ = Domain of f^{-1}
(B) $f^{-1}(x) = \sqrt{x + 1}$ (C) $f^{-1}(3) = 2$ (D) $f^{-1}[f(4)] = 4$
(E) $f^{-1}[f(x)] = x$
(3-6)

55. The graph of $y = \sqrt[3]{x}$ is vertically expanded by a factor of 2, reflected in the x axis, shifted 1 unit left and 1 unit down. Equation $y = -2\sqrt[3]{x + 1} - 1$. *(3-4)*

56. It is the same as the graph of g shifted to the right 2 units, reflected in the x axis, and shifted down 1 unit.
(3-5)

57. This is the same as the graph of $y = |x|$, reflected across the x-axis, and shifted to the left 1 unit and down 1 unit.

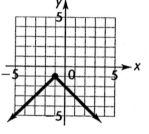

(3-5)

58. $[-5, 5]$ *(2-8, 3-3)*

59. (A) $(fg)(x) = x^2\sqrt{1 - x}$; domain is $(-\infty, 1]$

(B) $\left(\dfrac{f}{g}\right)(x) = \dfrac{x^2}{\sqrt{1 - x}}$; domain of $\dfrac{f}{g}$ is $(-\infty, 1)$

(C) $(f \circ g)(x) = 1 - x$; domain of $f \circ g$ is $(-\infty, 1]$

(D) $(g \circ f)(x) = \sqrt{1 - x^2}$; domain of $g \circ f$ is $[-1, 1]$
(3-5)

60. (A) $f^{-1}(x) = \dfrac{3x + 2}{x - 1}$ (B) $f^{-1}(3) = \dfrac{11}{2}$ (C) $f^{-1}[f(x)] = x$
(3-6)

61. Piecewise definition for f: $f(x) = \begin{cases} -2 & \text{if } x < -1 \\ 2x & \text{if } -1 \leq x < 1 \\ 2 & \text{if } x \geq 1 \end{cases}$

Domain: $(-\infty, \infty)$; Range: $[-2, 2]$
(3-4)

62. $x - y = 3$; This is the equation of a line.
(3-1, 3-2)

65. (A) 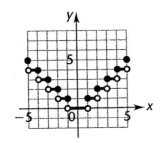 (B)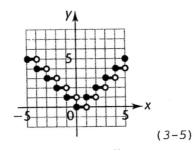

(3-5)

66. Domain: All real numbers except $x = 2$, range: $y > -3$ or $(-3, \infty)$
Discontinuous at $x = 2$

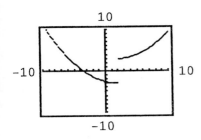

(3-4)

67. (A) 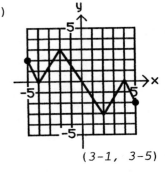 (B)

(3-1, 3-5)

68. (A) The graph must cross the x axis exactly once.
(B) The graph can cross the x axis either once or not at all.   *(3-4)*

69. (A) $V = -1,250t + 12,000$ (B) $V = \$5,750$ *(3-2)*

70. (A) $R = 1.6C$ (B) $R = \$168$ *(3-2)*

71. $E(x) = \begin{cases} 200 & \text{if } 0 \le x \le 3,000 \\ 0.1x - 100 & \text{if } x > 3,000 \end{cases}$; $E(2,000) = 200$, $E(5,000) = 400$ *(3-4)*

72. (A)

x	0	5	10	15	20
Consumption	309	276	271	255	233
$303.4 - 3.46x = f(x)$	303	286	269	252	234

(B)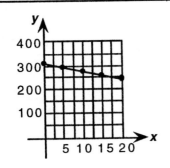

(C) 217 in 1995, 200 in 2000

(D) Per capita egg consumption is dropping about 17 eggs every five years.

(3-4)

73. (A) $\begin{cases} 0.49x & \text{for } 0 \le x < 36 \\ 0.44x & \text{for } 36 \le x < 72 \\ 0.39x & \text{for } 72 \le x \end{cases}$ (B) Discontinuous at $x = 36$ and $x = 72$

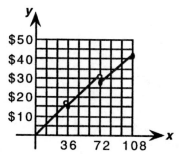

$(3-4)$

74. (A) $C = 84,000 + 15x;\ R = 50x$

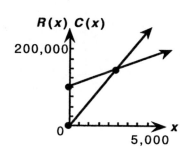

(B) $R = C$ at $x = 2,400$ units; $R < C$ for $0 \le x < 2,400$; $R > C$ for $x > 2,400$ $(3-2)$

75. $P(p) = -14,000 + 700p - 10p^2$ $(3-5)$

76. $r = 5$ feet $(3-1)$

77. (A) $A(x) = 60x - \dfrac{3}{2}x^2$ (B) $0 < x < 40$ (C) $x = 20,\ y = 15$ $(3-4)$

78. (A) $f(1) = 0$ (B) $f(2) = 1$ (C) $f(3) = 2$ (D) $f(4) = 0$
(E) $f(5) = 1$ (F) $f(n^2) = 0$ $(3-4)$

CHAPTER 4

Exercise 4-1

1. c **2.** a **3.** d **4.** b **5.** h **6.** f **7.** h, k

8. g **9.** $a - 2$; $R = 0$ **10.** $a - 2$; $R = 8$ **11.** $b - 3$; $R = -18$

12. $b - 3$; $R = 0$ **13.** $x^2 + 3$; $R = 5$ **14.** $-x^2 + 4$; $R = 0$

15. $4y^2 - 4y + 1$; $R = 0$ **16.** $4y^2 + 3y + 1$; $R = 6$ **17.** $x + 7 + \dfrac{6}{x - 3}$

18. $x + 2 + \dfrac{7}{x - 4}$ **19.** $3x - 7 + \dfrac{7}{x + 2}$ **20.** $4x - 2 + \dfrac{14}{x + 5}$

21. $2x^2 - 3x + 1 - \dfrac{2}{x + 3}$ **22.** $3x^2 + 2x - 3 + \dfrac{3}{x - 2}$ **23.** 4 **24.** 6

25. -7 **26.** -8 **27.** -2 **28.** 5 **29.** $2x^4 + 2x^3 + 2x^2 - 3x - 3$; $R = 0$

30. $3x^3 - 3x^2 + 3x - 5$; $R = 0$ **31.** $x^3 - 4x^2 + 16x - 64$; $R = 240$

32. $x^4 + 2x^3 + 4x^2 + 8x + 16$; $R = 0$ **33.** $4x^3 + 3x^2 + x + 1$; $R = -4$

34. $2x^3 - 4x + 7$; $R = -14$ **35.** $x^5 + 2x^4 - x$; $R = 0$

36. $x^5 + 2x^3 - 3$; $R = 0$ **37.** $2x^3 + 6x^2 - 4x + 2$; $R = 0$

38. $2x^3 + 4x^2 - 2x + 6$; $R = 5$ **39.** $3x^3 + 6x^2 - 3x + 9$; $R = 2$

40. $4x^3 - 8x^2 + 12x + 4$; $R = 7$ **41.** $5x^3 - 3x^2 - 0.6x + 1.88$; $R = -4.624$

42. $3x^3 - 2.4x^2 - 2.08x + 6.664$; $R = 2.6688$

43. $5x^4 - x^3 + 4.6x^2 + 3.24x - 1.944$; $R = -4.8336$

44. $10x^4 + 2x + 4.8$; $R = 0.92$

45. The graph has three x intercepts and two turning points; $P(x) \to \infty$ as $x \to \infty$ and $P(x) \to -\infty$ as $x \to -\infty$

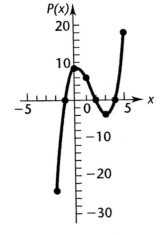

46. The graph has three x intercepts and two turning points; $P(x) \to \infty$ as $x \to \infty$ and $P(x) \to -\infty$ as $x \to -\infty$

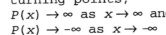
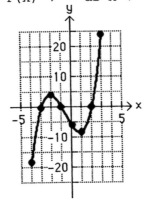

47. The graph has three x intercepts and two turning points; $P(x) \to \infty$ as $x \to \infty$ and $P(x) \to -\infty$ as $x \to -\infty$

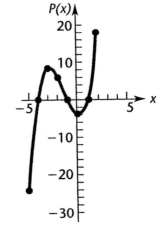

48. The graph has three x intercepts and two turning points; $P(x) \rightarrow \infty$ as $x \rightarrow \infty$ and $P(x) \rightarrow -\infty$ as $x \rightarrow -\infty$

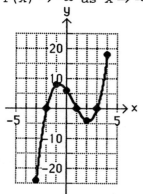

49. The graph has one x intercept and two turning points; $P(x) \rightarrow -\infty$ as $x \rightarrow \infty$ and $P(x) \rightarrow \infty$ as $x \rightarrow -\infty$

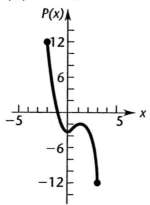

50. The graph has no turning points and one x intercept; $P(x) \rightarrow \infty$ as $x \rightarrow -\infty$ and $P(x) \rightarrow -\infty$ as $x \rightarrow \infty$

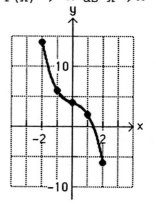

51. The graph has one x intercept and no turning points; $P(x) \rightarrow -\infty$ as $x \rightarrow \infty$ and $P(x) \rightarrow \infty$ as $x \rightarrow -\infty$

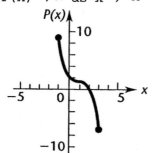

52. The graph has one x intercept and two turning points; $P(x) \rightarrow \infty$ as $x \rightarrow -\infty$ and $P(x) \rightarrow -\infty$ as $x \rightarrow \infty$

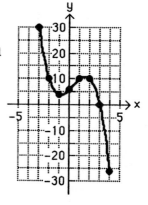

53. $P(x) = x^3$

54. $P(x) = x^4 + 1$

55. No such polynomial exists

56. No such polynomial exists

57. $x^2 + x + 2$; R = 0

58. $x^2 + 2x + 1$; R = 0

59. $x^2 - 2x + 1$; R = $x + 3$

60. $x^2 - 3x + 2$; R = $2x - 1$

61. $x^3 + (2 + i)x^2 + (-3 + 2i)x - 3i$; R = 0

62. $x^3 + (2 - i)x^2 + (-3 - 2i)x + 3i$; R = 0

63. (A) -5 (B) $-40i$ (C) 0   (D) 0

64. (A) $40i$ (B) -8 (C) 0   (D) 0

65. The graph has two x intercepts and one turning point; $P(x) \to \infty$ as $x \to \infty$ and as $x \to -\infty$

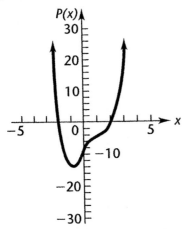

66. The graph has two x intercepts and one turning point; $P(x) \to \infty$ as $x \to \infty$ and as $x \to -\infty$

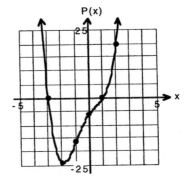

67. The graph has two x intercepts and three turning points; $P(x) \to \infty$ as $x \to \infty$ and as $x \to -\infty$

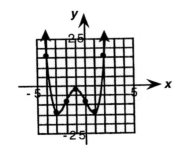

68. The graph has two x intercepts and three turning points; $P(x) \to \infty$ as $x \to \infty$ and as $x \to -\infty$

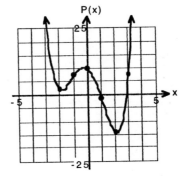

69. The graph has four x intercepts and three turning points; $P(x) \to -\infty$ as $x \to \infty$ and as $x \to -\infty$

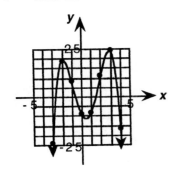

70. The graph has four x intercepts and three turning points; $P(x) \to -\infty$ as $x \to \infty$ and as $x \to -\infty$

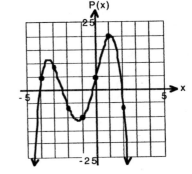

71. The graph has five x intercepts and four turning points; $P(x) \to \infty$ as $x \to \infty$ and $P(x) \to -\infty$ as $x \to -\infty$

72. The graph has five x intercepts and four turning points; $P(x) \to \infty$ as $x \to \infty$ and $P(x) \to -\infty$ as $x \to -\infty$

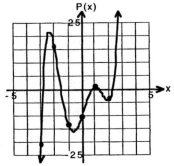

73. (A) In both cases the coefficient of x is a_2, the constant term $a_2 r + a_1$, and the remainder is $(a_2 r + a_1)r + a_0$.
(B) The remainder expanded is $a_2 r^2 + a_1 r + a_0 = P(r)$.

74. (A) In both cases: the coefficient of x^2 is a_3, of x is $a_3 r + a_2$, and the constant term is $(a_3 r + a_2)r + a_1$. The remainder is $[(a_3 r + a_2)r + a_1]r + a_0$.
(B) $P(r) = a_3 r^3 + a_2 r^2 + a_1 r + a_0 = $ remainder

75. $P(-2) = 81$; $P(1.7) = 6.2452$ or 6.2 **76.** $P(-2) = -12$; $P(1.3) = -1.6347$

Exercise 4-2

1. -2 (multiplicity 5), 3 (multiplicity 4); degree of $P(x)$ is 9

2. -6 (multiplicity 2), 5 (multiplicity 3); degree of $P(x)$ is 5

3. -1, 1 (multiplicity 4), 7 (multiplicity 3); degree of $P(x)$ is 8

4. -4 (multiplicity 3), 3 (multiplicity 2), 4; degree of $P(x)$ is 6

5. $P(x) = (x - 2)^3 (x + 1)$; degree 4

6. $P(x) = (x + 4)^2 x(x - 2)^3$; degree 6

7. $P(x) = x(x - 2)(x + 1 - \sqrt{3})(x + 1 + \sqrt{3})$; degree 4

8. $P(x) = (x - 1)^3 (x + 3 - \sqrt{2})(x + 3 + \sqrt{2})$; degree 5

9. $P(x) = (x + 2)^2 (x - 2)^2 (x - 3 + i)(x - 3 - i)$; degree 6

10. $P(x) = (x - 2i)^2 (x + 2i)^2 (x - 2)^3$; degree 7

11. $(x + 2)(x - 1)(x - 3)$, degree 3   **12.** $(x + 2)(x + 1)(x - 1)(x - 3)$, degree 4

13. $(x + 2)^2 (x - 1)^2$, degree 4   **14.** $(x - 1)^2 (x + 3)$, degree 3

15. $(x + 3)(x + 2) x(x - 1)(x - 2)$, degree 5   **16.** $(x + 2)^2 x(x - 2)^2$, degree 5

17. Yes   **18.** No   **19.** No   **20.** Yes   **21.** $\pm 1, \pm 2, \pm 5, \pm 10$

22. $\pm 1, \pm 2, \pm 7, \pm 14$ **23.** $\pm 1, \pm 5, \pm \frac{1}{2}, \pm \frac{5}{2}$ **24.** $\pm 1, \pm 2, \pm \frac{1}{3}, \pm \frac{2}{3}$

25. $\pm 1, \pm 5, \pm 25, \pm \frac{1}{2}, \pm \frac{5}{2}, \pm \frac{25}{2}, \pm \frac{1}{3}, \pm \frac{5}{3}, \pm \frac{25}{3}, \pm \frac{1}{6}, \pm \frac{5}{6}, \pm \frac{25}{6}$

26. $\pm 1, \pm 3, \pm 9, \pm \frac{1}{2}, \pm \frac{3}{2}, \pm \frac{9}{2}, \pm \frac{1}{5}, \pm \frac{3}{5}, \pm \frac{9}{5}, \pm \frac{1}{10}, \pm \frac{3}{10}, \pm \frac{9}{10}$

27. $P(x) = (x + 4)^2 (x + 1)$ **28.** $P(x) = (x - 3)(x - 3)(x + 2)$

29. $P(x) = (x - 1)(x + 1)(x - i)(x + i)$

30. $P(x) = (x + i)(x + i)(x - i)(x - i)$

31. $P(x) = (2x - 1)[x - (4 + 5i)][x - (4 - 5i)]$

32. $P(x) = (3x + 2)[x - (2 + 3i)][x - (2 - 3i)]$ **33.** $\frac{3}{2}$, $1 \pm \sqrt{3}$

34. $-\frac{1}{2}$, $2 \pm \sqrt{5}$ **35.** -1 (double root), $\pm\sqrt{3}$

36. 2 (double root), $-2 \pm \sqrt{3}$ **37.** ± 3, $-1 \pm \sqrt{2}$

38. ± 1, $1 \pm 3i$ **39.** -2, $-\frac{1}{2}$, 1, $1 \pm i$

40. -1, $\frac{2}{3}$, 1, $-2 \pm i$ **41.** -4, -3, 2

42. -3, 3, 4 **43.** -0.2, 0, 1.5, 2

44. -0.5, 0, 0.6, 4 **45.** 3 (double zero), $-2 \pm \sqrt{3}$

46. -4 (double zero), $-\frac{1}{2} \pm \frac{\sqrt{5}}{2}$ **47.** -1 (double zero), $\frac{2}{3}$, $1 \pm 2i$

48. 2 (double zero), $-\frac{1}{2}$, $\frac{1}{2} \pm \frac{i}{2}$ **49.** $P(x) = (2x + 3)(3x - 1)(x + 2)$

50. $P(x) = (3x + 2)(2x - 1)(x - 2)$ **51.** $P(x) = (x + 3)[x - (2 + \sqrt{5})][x - (2 - \sqrt{5})]$

52. $P(x) = [x - (1 + \sqrt{3})][x - (1 - \sqrt{3})](x - 2)$

53. $P(x) = (x + 2)(2x + 1)(2x - 3)(x - 2)$

54. $P(x) = (x + 3)(2x + 3)(2x + 1)(x - 1)$

55. Interval notation: $[2 - \sqrt{3}, 2 + \sqrt{3}]$; Inequality notation: $2 - \sqrt{3} \le x \le 2 + \sqrt{3}$

56. Inequality notation: $x < 1 - \sqrt{2}$ or $x > 1 + \sqrt{2}$
Interval notation: $(-\infty, 1 - \sqrt{2}) \cup (1 + \sqrt{2}, \infty)$

57. Interval notation: $(-\infty, -1]$ or $[1, 3]$; Inequality notation: $x \le -1$ or $1 \le x \le 3$

58. Inequality notation: $-3 \le x \le -1$ or $x \ge 3$; Interval notation: $[-3, -1] \cup [3, \infty)$

59. Interval notation: $\left[-3, \frac{1}{2}\right] \cup [2, \infty)$; Inequality notation: $-3 \le x \le \frac{1}{2}$ or $x \ge 2$

60. Inequality notation: $x < -\sqrt{2}$ or $\frac{3}{5} < x < \sqrt{2}$; Interval notation: $(-\infty, -\sqrt{2}) \cup \left(\frac{3}{5}, \sqrt{2}\right)$

61. $x^2 - 8x + 41$ **62.** $x^2 - 10x + 29$ **63.** $x^2 - 2ax + a^2 + b^2$

64. $x^2 + b^2$ **65.** $1 - 2i$, -2 **66.** zeros: $-2 - i$, 2

67. $3i$, -4 **68.** $-2i$, $2i$, 5 **69.** $3 + 2i$, $1 \pm \sqrt{2}$

70. $1 - 3i$, $1 + 3i$, $2 \pm \sqrt{3}$

71. Interval notation: $\left(-\frac{5}{2}, -1\right) \cup (1, \infty)$; Inequality notation: $-\frac{5}{2} < x < -1$ or $x > 1$

72. Inequality notation: $x < -2$ or $\frac{1}{2} < x < 2$; Interval notation: $(-\infty, -2) \cup \left(\frac{1}{2}, 2\right)$

73. Interval notation: $(-\infty, -2] \cup (-1, 2) \cup (3, 5]$
Inequality notation: $x \le -2$ or $-1 < x < 2$ or $3 < x \le 5$

74. Inequality notation: $-7 \le x < -5$ or $-3 < x < 1$ or $x \ge 3$
Interval notation: $[-7, -5) \cup (-3, 1) \cup [3, \infty)$

75. $\frac{1}{3}$, $6 \pm 2\sqrt{3}$ **76.** $\frac{5}{2}$, $1 \pm \sqrt{7}$ **77.** $\frac{3}{2}$, $-\frac{5}{2}$, $\pm 4i$

78. $\frac{8}{3}$, $-\frac{9}{2}$, $-2 \pm i$ **79.** $\frac{3}{2}$ (double), $4 \pm \sqrt{6}$ **80.** 2 (triple zero), $\pm\sqrt{6}$.

81. (A) 3   (B) $-\frac{1}{2} + \frac{\sqrt{3}}{2}i$ and $-\frac{1}{2} - \frac{\sqrt{3}}{2}i$

82. (A) 3   (B) $-1 \pm i\sqrt{3}$ **83.** maximum of n; minimum of 1   **84.** n, 0

85. No, since $P(x)$ is not a polynomial with real coefficients (the coefficient of x is the imaginary number $2i$).

86. They must be identities; hence, are equal for <u>all</u> values of x (real or complex).

87. 2 feet   **88.** 1 foot   **89.** 0.5 × 0.5 inches or 1.59 × 1.59 inches

90. 1 ft by 1 ft or 2 ft by 2 ft

Exercise 4-3

1. There is at least one x intercept in each of the intervals $(-5, -1)$, $(-1, 3)$, and $(5, 8)$

2. There is at least one x intercept in each of the intervals $(-8, -2)$, $(2, 4)$, and $(4, 9)$.

3. There is at least one x intercept in each of the intervals $(-6, -4)$, $(-4, 0)$, $(2, 4)$, and $(4, 7)$

4. There is at least one x intercept in each of the intervals $(-1, 0)$, $(0, 2)$, and $(2, 5)$.

5. Zeros in $(0, 1)$, $(3, 4)$, and $(4, 5)$ **6.** Zeros in $(2, 3)$, $(3, 4)$, and $(6, 7)$

7. Zeros in $(-3, -2)$, $(-2, -1)$, and $(1, 2)$

8. Zeros in $(-3, -2)$, $(-1, 0)$, and $(1, 2)$

9. Upper bound: 2; lower bound: -2 **10.** Upper bound: 4; lower bound: -1

11. Upper bound: 3; lower bound: -2 **12.** Upper bound: 4; lower bound: -1

13. Upper bound: 2; lower bound: -3 **14.** Upper bound: 3; lower bound: -1

15. (A) Upper bound: 4; lower bound: -2; real zeros in $(-2, -1)$, $(0, 1)$, and $(3, 4)$
(B) 3.2

16. (A) Upper bound: 2; lower bound: -3; real zeros in $(-3, -2)$, $(-1, 0)$, and $(1, 2)$
(B) 1.7

17. (A) Upper bound: 3; lower bound: -2; real zero in $(-2, -1)$ (B) -1.4

18. (A) Upper bound: 4; lower bound: -1; real zero in $(3, 4)$ (B) 3.5

19. (A) Upper bound: 4; lower bound: -3; real zeros in $(-3, -2)$, $(-1, 0)$, $(1, 2)$, and $(3, 4)$ (B) 3.1

20. (A) Upper bound: 4; lower bound: -3; real zeros in $(-3, -2)$, $(-1, 0)$, $(1, 2)$, and $(2, 3)$ (B) 2.9

21. (A) Upper bound: 3; lower bound: -2; real zeros in $(-2, -1)$ and $(-1, 0)$
(B) -0.5

22. (A) Upper bound: 4; lower bound: -1; real zeros in $(1, 2)$ and $(2, 3)$ (B) 2.9

23. (A) Upper bound: 3; lower bound: -1 (B) 2.25

24. (A) Upper bound: 1; lower bound: -3 (B) -2.21

25. (A) Upper bound: 3; lower bound: -4   (B) -3.51, 2.12

26. (A) Upper bound: 5; lower bound: -3   (B) -2.29, 4.07

27. (A) Upper bound: 2; lower bound: -3   (B) -2.09, 0.75, 1.88

28. (A) Upper bound: 3; lower bound: -1   (B) 2.12

29. (A) Upper bound: 1; lower bound: -1   (B) 0.83

30. (A) Upper bound: 3; lower bound: -2   (B) -1.35 0.72, 2.92

31. (A) Upper bound: 5; lower bound: -2; real zeros in (-2, -1), (1, 2), and (3, 4)
(B) 3.22

32. (A) Upper bound: 4; lower bound: -3; real zeros in (-2, -1), (0, 1), (1, 2),
and (3, 4)   (B) 3.07

33. (A) Upper bound: 4; lower bound: -4; real zeros in (-4, -3), (1, 2), and (2, 3)
(B) 2.92

34. (A) Upper bound: 3; lower bound: -4; real zeros in (-3, -2), (-2, -1) and (2, 3)
(B) 2.55

35. (A) Upper bound: 30; lower bound: -10   (B) -1.29, 0.31, 24.98

36. (A) Upper bound: 40; lower bound: -10   (B) 0.35, 1.63, 35.02

37. (A) Upper bound: 30; lower bound: -40   (B) -36.53, -2.33, 2.40, 24.46

38. (A) Upper bound: 30; lower bound: -20   (B) -14.70, -4.46, 3.92, 27.25

39. (A) Upper bound: 20; lower bound: -10   (B) -7.47, 14.03

40. (A) Upper bound: 20; lower bound: -10   (B) No real zeros

41. (A) Upper bound: 30; lower bound: -20   (B) -17.66, 2.5 (double zero), 22.66

42. (A) Upper bound: 20; lower bound: -30   (B) -23.22, -3.67 (double zero), 17.22

43. (A) Upper bound: 40; lower bound: -40   (B) -30.45, 9.06, 39.80

44. (A) Upper bound: 20; lower bound: -20   (B) -3.5 (double zero), 17.69

45. $x^4 - 3x^2 - 2x + 4 = 0$; (1, 1) and (1.7, 2.9)

46. $x^4 - x^2 - 4x + 4 = 0$; (1, 1) and (1.3, 1.7)

47. $4x^3 - 84x^2 + 432x - 600 = 0$; 2.3 in or 4.6 in

48. $3x^3 - 70x^2 + 400x - 500 = 0$; 1.7 in or 6.2 in   **49.** $x^3 - 15x^2 + 30 = 0$; 1.5 ft

50. $8x^3 - 20x^2 + 8 = 0$; 0.8 × 0.8 × 3.5 ft or 2.3 × 2.3 × 0.4 ft

Exercise 4-4

1. $g(x)$ **2.** $k(x)$ **3.** $h(x)$ **4.** $f(x)$

5. Domain: $(-\infty, -1) \cup (-1, \infty)$; x intercept: 2

6. Domain: all x except 1 or $(-\infty, 1) \cup (1, \infty)$; $x = -2$, x intercept

7. Domain: $(-\infty, -4) \cup (-4, 4) \cup (4, \infty)$; x intercepts: -1, 1

8. Domain: all x except ± 5 or $(-\infty, -5) \cup (-5, 5) \cup (5, \infty)$; $x = \pm 6$, x intercepts

9. Domain: $(-\infty, -3) \cup (-3, 4) \cup (4, \infty)$; x intercepts: -2, 3

10. Domain: all x except -3 and 2 or $(-\infty, -3) \cup (-3, 2) \cup (2, \infty)$;
-4, 3: x intercepts

11. Domain: all real numbers; x intercept: 0

12. Domain: all real numbers; x intercepts: 0

13. Vertical asymptote: $x = 4$; horizontal asymptote: $y = 2$

14. Vertical asymptote: $x = -5$; horizontal asymptote: $y = 3$

15. Vertical asymptote: $x = -4$, $x = 4$; horizontal asymptote: $y = \frac{2}{3}$

16. Vertical asymptote: $x = \pm 5$; horizontal asymptote: $y = \frac{5}{2}$

17. No vertical asymptotes; horizontal asymptote: $y = 0$

18. Vertical asymptote: $x = \frac{1}{2}$ and $x = -2$; no horizontal asymptote

19. Vertical asymptotes: $x = 1$, $x = \frac{5}{3}$; no horizontal asymptote

20. No vertical asymptote; horizontal asymptote: $y = 0$

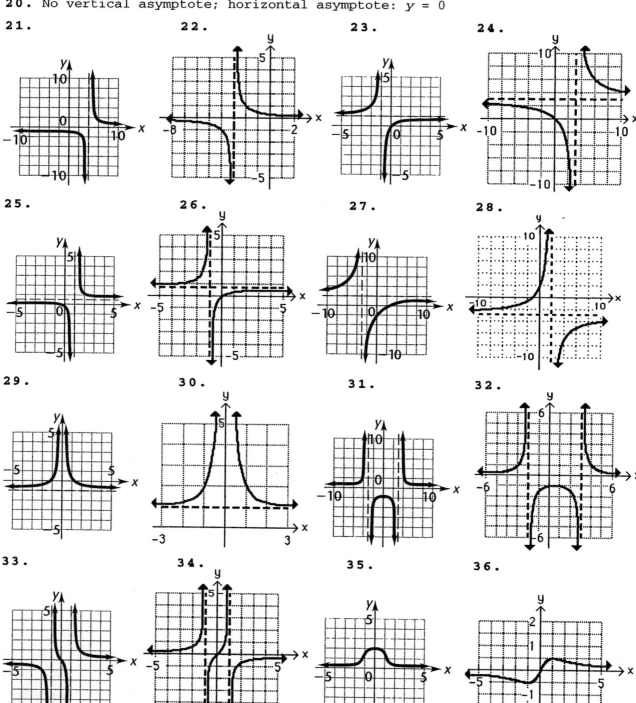

37.   **38.**   **39.**   **40.**

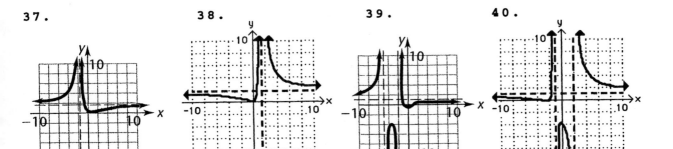

41. The maximum number of x intercepts is 2 and the minimum number is 0. For example, $\dfrac{x^2 - 1}{x^2}$ has two x intercepts and $\dfrac{x^2 + 1}{x^2}$ has none.

42. The maximum number of vertical asymptotes is 2 as in $\dfrac{x^2}{x^2 - 1}$ and the minimum number is 0 as in $\dfrac{x^2}{x^2 + 1}$.

43. Vertical asymptote: $x = 1$; oblique asymptote: $y = 2x + 2$

44. $x = -2$ vertical asymptote; $y = 3x - 6$ is an oblique asymptote

45. Oblique asymptote: $y = x$

46. $x = 2$ vertical asymptote

47. Vertical asymptote: $x = 0$; oblique asymptote: $y = 2x - 3$

48. Vertical asymptote: $x = 0$; oblique asymptote: $y = -3x + 5$

49. $f(x) \to 5$ as $x \to \infty$ and $f(x) \to -5$ as $x \to -\infty$; the lines $y = 5$ and $y = -5$ are horizontal asymptotes

50. $f(x) \to 2$ as $x \to \infty$ and $f(x) \to -2$ as $x \to -\infty$; the lines $y = \pm 2$ are horizontal asymptotes

51. $f(x) \to 4$ as $x \to \infty$ and $f(x) \to -4$ as $x \to -\infty$; the lines $y = 4$ and $y = -4$ are horizontal asymptotes

52. $f(x) \to 3$ as $x \to \infty$ and $f(x) \to -3$ as $x \to -\infty$; the lines $y = \pm 3$ are horizontal asymptotes

53.   **54.**   **55.**   **56.**

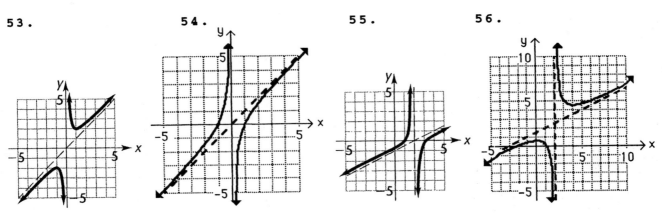

57.

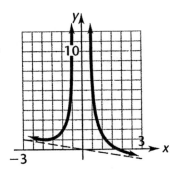

58.

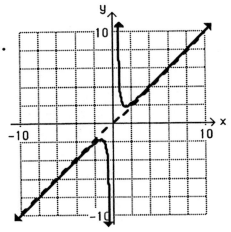

59. Let $p(x) = x^2 - 1$; $[f(x) - p(x)] \to 0$ as $x \to \infty$ and as $x \to -\infty$

60. $p(x) = x^3 - x$, $[f(x) - p(x)] \to 0$ as $x \to \pm\infty$

61. $p(x) = x^3 + x$; $[f(x) - p(x)] \to 0$ as $x \to \infty$ and as $x \to -\infty$

62. $p(x) = x^2$, $[f(x) - p(x)] \to 0$ as $x \to \pm\infty$

63. Domain: $x \neq 2$, or $(-\infty, 2) \cup (2, \infty)$;
  $f(x) = x + 2$

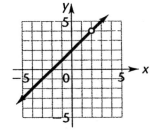

64. $g(x) = x - 1$ for $x \neq -1$;
  Domain: $x \neq -1$ or $(-\infty, -1) \cup (-1, \infty)$

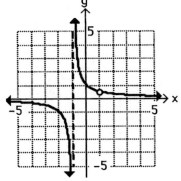

65. Domain: $x \neq 2$, -2 or
  $(-\infty, -2) \cup (-2, 2) \cup (2, \infty)$;
  $r(x) = \dfrac{1}{x - 2}$

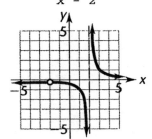

66. $S(x) = \dfrac{1}{x + 1}$, $x \neq \pm 1$;
  Domain: $x \neq \pm 1$ or
  $(-\infty, -1) \cup (-1, 1) \cup (1, \infty)$

67. As $t \to \infty$, $N \to 50$

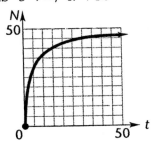

68.

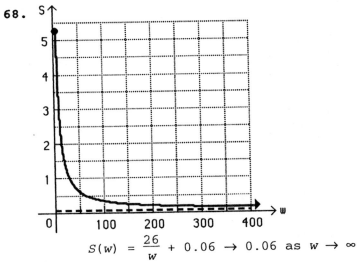

$$S(w) = \frac{26}{w} + 0.06 \to 0.06 \text{ as } w \to \infty$$

69. As $t \to \infty$, $N \to 5$

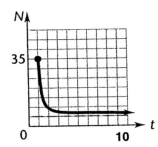

70. $f(x) \to 50$ as $x \to \infty$

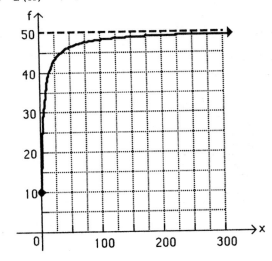

71. (A) $\overline{C}(n) = 25n + 175 + \dfrac{2,500}{n}$

(B) 10 yr

(C)

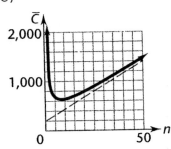

72. (A) $\overline{C}(x) = \dfrac{1}{5}x + 2 + \dfrac{2000}{x}$

(B) 100 units

(C)

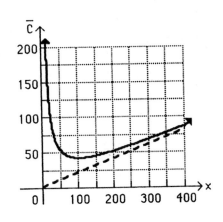

73. (A) $L(x) = 2x + \dfrac{450}{x} = \dfrac{2x^2 + 450}{x}$

(B) $(0, \infty)$

(C) 15 ft by 15 ft

(D)

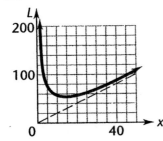

74. (A) $L(x) = 3x + \dfrac{450}{x}$ (B) $(0, \infty)$

(C) $x = 5\sqrt{6}$ ft by $\ell = \dfrac{15\sqrt{6}}{2}$ ft will require the least amount of fencing, $30\sqrt{6}$ ft

(D)

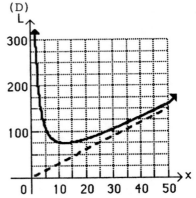

Exercise 4-5

1. $A = 2$, $B = 3$ **2.** $A = -4$, $B = 7$ **3.** $A = 3$, $B = -5$

4. $A = -5$, $B = -6$ **5.** $A = 2$, $B = 3$, $C = -4$ **6.** $A = -1$, $B = 2$, $C = 3$

7. $A = 3$, $B = -2$, $C = 5$ **8.** $A = -4$, $B = 7$, $C = -2$

9. $A = 2$, $B = -1$, $C = -3$, $D = 0$ **10.** $A = 0$, $B = 4$, $C = 2$, $D = -3$

11. $\dfrac{-4}{x - 4} + \dfrac{7}{x + 3}$ **12.** $\dfrac{9}{x + 5} - \dfrac{5}{x - 2}$ **13.** $\dfrac{4}{2x + 7} - \dfrac{2}{3x - 2}$

14. $\dfrac{8}{5x + 1} - \dfrac{3}{2x - 3}$ **15.** $\dfrac{4}{x} - \dfrac{5}{2x - 1} - \dfrac{3}{(2x - 1)^2}$

16. $\dfrac{-2}{x} + \dfrac{6}{3x - 2} - \dfrac{5}{(3x - 2)^2}$ **17.** $\dfrac{3}{x} + \dfrac{4x + 1}{2x^2 + x + 1}$ **18.** $\dfrac{7}{x} + \dfrac{2x - 7}{x^2 + x + 2}$

19. $\dfrac{4x - 5}{x^2 + 1} + \dfrac{2x}{(x^2 + 1)^2}$ **20.** $\dfrac{2x - 1}{x^2 + 4} + \dfrac{3x + 4}{(x^2 + 4)^2}$ **21.** $\dfrac{3}{x + 1} + \dfrac{x - 3}{x^2 - x + 2}$

22. $\dfrac{2}{x - 2} + \dfrac{3x - 4}{x^2 + x + 2}$ **23.** $x + 2 + \dfrac{3}{x - 2} + \dfrac{2}{(x - 2)^2} + \dfrac{x + 6}{x^2 + 2x + 4}$

24. $2x + 2 - \dfrac{2}{x + 1} + \dfrac{1}{(x + 1)^2} - \dfrac{4x + 3}{x^2 - 2x + 3}$

25. $2x + \dfrac{7}{x - 3} + \dfrac{1}{x + 1} - \dfrac{3}{x^2 + 2x + 3}$ **26.** $x + 2 + \dfrac{2}{x - 2} - \dfrac{3}{x + 1} + \dfrac{2x + 4}{x^2 + x + 2}$

27. $\dfrac{1}{x + a} - \dfrac{a}{(x + a)^2}$ **28.** $\dfrac{1}{a^2 x} - \dfrac{1}{a^2 (x + a)} - \dfrac{1}{a(x + a)^2}$

29. $\dfrac{1}{(a - b)(x - a)} - \dfrac{1}{(a - b)(x - b)}$ **30.** $\dfrac{a}{(a - b)(x - a)} - \dfrac{b}{(a - b)(x - b)}$

CHAPTER 4 REVIEW

1. $2x^3 + 3x^2 - 1 = (x + 2)(2x^2 - x + 2) - 5$ *(4-1)*

2. $P(3) = -8$ *(4-1, 4-2)*   **3.** $2, -4, -1$ *(4-2)*   **4.** $1 - i$ is a zero *(4-3)*

5. (A) $P(x) = (x + 2)x(x - 2) = x^3 - 4x$

(B) $P(x) \to \infty$ as $x \to \infty$ and $P(x) \to -\infty$ as $x \to -\infty$ *(4-1)*

6. Lower bound: -2; upper bound: 4   *(4-3)*

7. $P(1) = -5$ and $P(2) = 1$ are of opposite sign.   *(4-3)*

8. $\pm 1, \pm 2, \pm 3, \pm 6$ *(4-2)*   **9.** $-1, 2, 3$ *(4-2)*

10. (A) Domain is $(-\infty, -4) \cup (-4, \infty)$; x intercept is $\frac{3}{2}$

  (B) Domain is $(-\infty, -2) \cup (-2, 3) \cup (3, \infty)$; x intercept is 0   *(4-4)*

11. (A) Horizontal asymptote: $y = 2$; Vertical asymptote: $x = -4$
  (B) Horizontal asymptote: $y = 0$; Vertical asymptotes: $x = -2$, $x = 3$ *(4-4)*

12. $\dfrac{2}{x - 3} + \dfrac{5}{x + 2}$ *(4-5)*

13. (A) The graph of $P(x)$ has three x intercepts and two turning points; $P(x) \to \infty$ as $x \to \infty$ and $P(x) \to -\infty$ as $x \to -\infty$

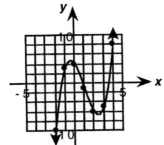

  (B) 3.5   *(4-1)*

14. $Q(x) = 8x^3 - 12x^2 - 16x - 8$, R = 5; $P\left(\frac{1}{4}\right) = 5$ *(4-1)*

15. -4 *(4-1)*   **16.** $P(x) = [x - (1 + \sqrt{2})][x - (1 - \sqrt{2})]$ *(4-2)*

17. Yes, since $P(-1) = 0$, $x - (-1) = x + 1$ must be a factor.   *(4-2)*

18. $4, -\frac{1}{2}, -2$ *(4-2)*   **19.** $(x - 4)(2x + 1)(x + 2)$ *(4-2)*

20. no rational zeros   *(4-2)*   **21.** $-1, \frac{1}{2}$, and $\dfrac{1 \pm i\sqrt{3}}{2}$ *(4-2)*

22. $(x + 1)(2x - 1)\left(x - \dfrac{1 + i\sqrt{3}}{2}\right)\left(x - \dfrac{1 - i\sqrt{3}}{2}\right)$ *(4-2)*

23. Interval notation: $(-\infty, -3]$, and $\left[-\dfrac{1}{2}, 2\right]$

  Inequality notation: $x \leq -3$ or $-\dfrac{1}{2} \leq x \leq 2$ *(4-2, 2-8)*

24. (A) Upper bound: 7; lower bound: -5   (B) 6.62   (C) -4.67, 6.62   *(4-3)*

25. (A) Domain is $(-\infty, -1) \cup (-1, \infty)$;

  x intercept: $x = 1$; y intercept: $y = -\dfrac{1}{2}$

  (B) Vertical asymptote: $x = -1$.

  Horizontal asymptote: $y = \dfrac{1}{2}$

(C)

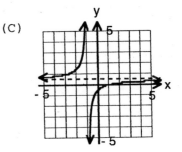

(4-4)

26. $\dfrac{1}{x} - \dfrac{2}{x - 2} + \dfrac{3}{(x - 2)^2}$ *(4-5)*   **27.** $\dfrac{3}{x} + \dfrac{2x - 1}{2x^2 - 3x + 3}$ *(4-5)*

28. $P(x) = [x^2 + (1 + i)x + (3 + 2i)][x - (1 + i)] + 3 + 5i$ (*4-1*)

29. $P(x) = \left(x + \dfrac{1}{2}\right)^2 (x + 3)(x - 1)^3$. The degree is 6.   (*4-2*)

30. $P(x) = (x + 5)[x - (2 - 3i)][x - (2 + 3i)]$. The degree is 3.   (*4-2*)

31. $\dfrac{1}{2}$, ±2, $1 \pm \sqrt{2}$ (*4-2*)

32. $(x - 2)(x + 2)(2x - 1)[x - (1 - \sqrt{2})][x - (1 + \sqrt{2})]$ (*4-2*)

33. Interval notation: $\left(-3, -\dfrac{3}{2}\right] \cup \left(-\dfrac{1}{2}, \dfrac{1}{2}\right] \cup (2, \infty)$

Inequality notation: $-3 < x \le -\dfrac{3}{2}$ or $-\dfrac{1}{2} < x \le \dfrac{1}{2}$ or $x > 2$ (*4-2, 2-8*)

34. Since $P(x)$ changes sign three times, the minimal degree is 3.   (*4-3*)

35. $P(x) = a(x - r)(x^2 - 2x + 5)$ and since the constant term, $-5ar$, must be an integer, r must be a rational number.   (*4-2*)

36. (A) 3   (B) $-\dfrac{3}{2} \pm \dfrac{3i\sqrt{3}}{2}$ (*4-2*)

37. (A) Upper bound: 30; lower bound: -30 (B) -23.54, 21.57 (*4-3*)

38.

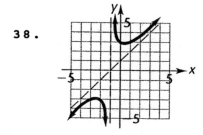

(*4-4*)

39. $y = 2$ and $y = -2$ (*4-4*)

40. $\dfrac{2}{x - 3} - \dfrac{3}{x} + \dfrac{x - 1}{x^2 + 1}$ (*4-5*)

41. $2x^3 - 32x + 48 = 0$, 4×12 ft or 5.2×9.2 ft   (*4-2*)

42. $x^3 + 27x^2 - 729 = 0$, 4.8 ft   (*4-3*)

43. $4x^3 - 70x^2 + 300x - 300$, 1.4 in or 4.5 in   (*4-3*)

CHAPTER 5
Exercise 5-1

1.

x	y
-3	0.04
-2	0.11
-1	0.33
0	1.00
1	3.00
2	9.00
3	27.00

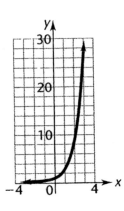

2.

x	y
-2	0.04
-1	0.2
0	1
1	5
2	25

3.

x	y
-3	27.00
-2	9.00
-1	3.00
0	1.00
1	0.33
2	0.11
3	0.04

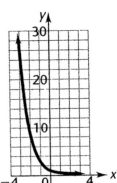

4.

x	y
-2	25
-1	5
0	1
1	0.2
2	0.04

5.

x	y = g(x)
-3	-27.00
-2	-9.00
-1	-3.00
0	-1.00
1	-0.33
2	-0.11
3	-0.04

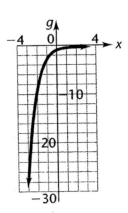

6.

x	f(x)
-2	-0.04
-1	-0.2
0	-1
1	-5
2	-25

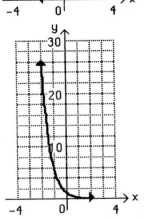

7.

x	y = h(x)
-3	0.19
-2	0.56
-1	1.67
0	5.00
1	15.00
2	45.00
3	135.00

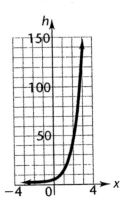

8.

x	f(x)
-2	0.16
-1	0.8
0	4
1	20
2	100

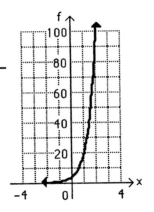

9.

x	y
-6	-4.96
-5	-4.89
-4	-4.67
-3	-4.00
-2	-2.00
-1	4.00
0	22.00

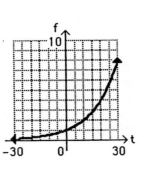

10.

x	y
-4	4.04
-3	4.2
-2	5
-1	9
0	29

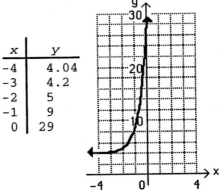

11. 2^{3x+4}

12. 5^{3-2x}

13. 3^{-4x+7y}

14. 7^{3x+3y}

15. 4^{3x}

16. x^{12}

17. 10^{4x}

18. $2^{x^3+x^2}$

19. $\dfrac{5^{3x}}{4^{3y}}$

20. $\dfrac{3^{4x}}{7^{6y}}$

21. $a^2b^2c^4$

22. $a^6b^3c^9$

23. $x = -3.5$

24. $x = -1.5$

25. $x = 0,\ 2$

26. $x = -2,\ 5$

27. $x = 0.5$

28. $x = -0.5$

29. $x = 6$

30. $x = -3$

31. $x = 2$

32. $x = 4$

33. $x = 1,\ 1.5$

34. $x = -2,\ 4$

35. $a = 1$ or $a = -1$

36. $a = 2,\ b = -2$, for example

37.

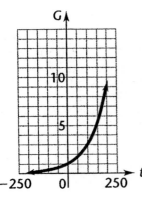

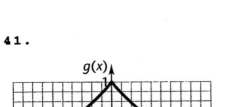

38.

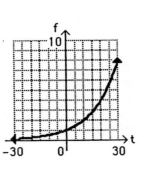

39.

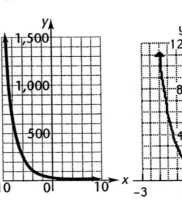

40.

41.

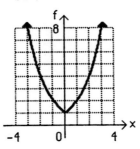

42.

43.

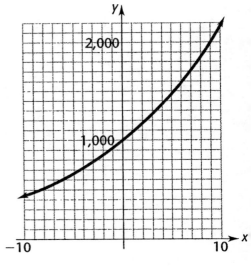

44.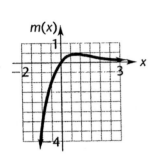

45.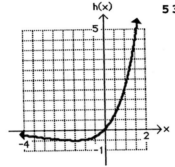

46.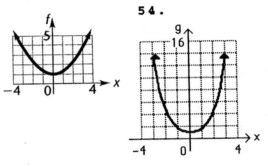

47. $6^{2x} - 6^{-2x}$

48. $3^{2x} - 3^{-2x}$

49. 4

50. $2(3^{2x}) + 2(3^{-2x})$

51.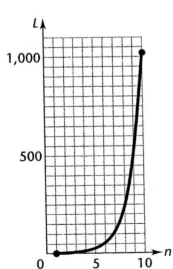

52.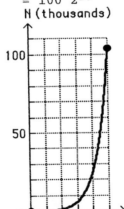

53.

54.

55. (A) 1.46
(B) As $x \to \infty$, $f(x) \to \infty$. As $x \to -\infty$, $f(x) \to -5$. The line $y = -5$ is a horizontal asymptote.

56. (A) No real zeros.
(B) $f(x) \to 4$ as $x \to \infty$, $f(x) \to \infty$ as $x \to -\infty$. $y = 4$ is an horizontal asymptote.

57. (A) -1.08
(B) As $x \to \infty$, $f(x) \to \infty$. As $x \to -\infty$, $f(x) \to -\infty$; none

58. (A) 2.85
(B) $f(x) \to \infty$ as $x \to -\infty$, $f(x) \to -\infty$ as $x \to \infty$. No horizontal asymptotes.

59.

60. $P = P_0 2^{t/d} = 100 \; 2^{t/(1/2)}$
         $= 100 \; 2^{2t}$

61. (A) 76 flies   (B) 570 flies
62. (A) 43,000,000   (B) 90,000,000
63. (A) 19 pounds   (B) 7.9 pounds
64. (A) 8.49 mg   (B) 0.750 mg
65. (A) \$4,225.92   (B) \$12,002.75
66. (A) \$2633.56   (B) \$7079.54

67. $9,841

68. $9,217

69. No

70. $r \geq 0.125973313$, about 12.6%

Exercise 5-2

1.

x	y
-3	-0.05
-2	-0.14
-1	-0.37
0	-1.00
1	-2.72
2	-7.39
3	-20.09

2.

x	y
-3	-20.09
-2	-7.39
-1	-2.72
0	-1.00
1	-0.37
2	-0.14
3	-0.05

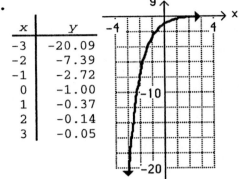

3.

x	y
-5	3.68
-4	4.49
-3	5.49
-2	6.7
-1	8.19
0	10
1	12.21
2	14.92
3	18.22
4	22.26
5	27.18

4.

x	y
-5	60.65
-4	67.03
-3	74.08
-2	81.87
-1	90.48
0	100
1	110.52
2	122.14
3	134.99
4	149.18
5	164.87

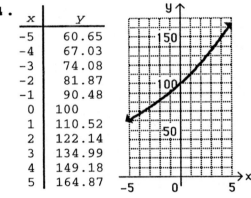

5.

t	f(t)
-5	164.87
-4	149.18
-3	134.99
-2	122.14
-1	110.52
0	100
1	90.48
2	81.87
3	74.08
4	67.03
5	60.65

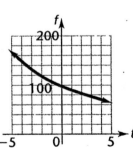

6.

t	g(t)
-5	27.18
-4	22.26
-3	18.22
-2	14.92
-1	12.21
0	10
1	8.19
2	6.70
3	5.49
4	4.49
5	3.68

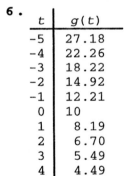
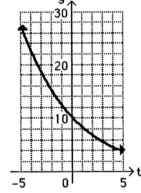

7. e^{-x}

8. e^{-4x}

9. e^{3x} **10.** e^{2x}

11. e^{3x-1}

12. e^{2x+2}

13. (A) $1 + \dfrac{1}{m}$ is not equal to 1   (B) e

14. (A) $\left(1 + \dfrac{1}{m}\right)$ is not constant and b is.   (B) e

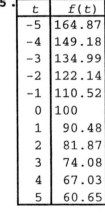

15.

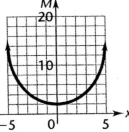

16.

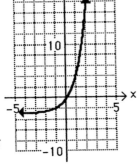

17.

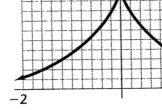

18.

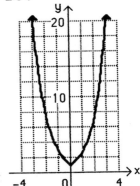

19.

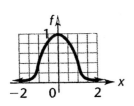

20.

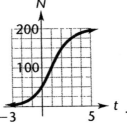

21.

22.

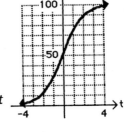

23. $\dfrac{e^{-2x}(-2x - 3)}{x^4}$

24. $\dfrac{e^{5x}(5x - 4)}{x^5}$

25. $2e^{2x} + 2e^{-2x}$

26. $e^x - e^{-x}$

27. $2e^{2x}$

28. $\dfrac{2}{e^{2x}}$

29. $x = 0$

30. $(x - 3)e^x = 0 \Rightarrow x - 3 = 0$, $e^x = 0$, no solution, $e^x > 0$
        $x = 3$

31. $x = 0,\ 5$

32. $x = 0,\ -3$

33.

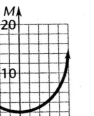

34.

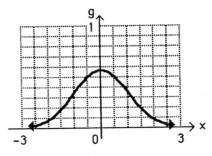

35. (A)

s	f(s)	s	f(s)
-0.5	4.0000	0.5	2.2500
-0.2	3.0518	0.2	2.4883
-0.1	2.8680	0.1	2.5937
-0.01	2.7320	0.01	2.7048
-0.001	2.7196	0.001	2.7169
-0.0001	2.7184	0.0001	2.7181

(B) Both tables are "closing in" on 2.7182… or e.

36.

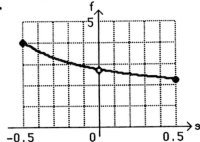

37.

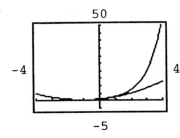

38.

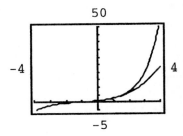

39.

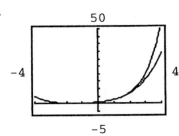

40.

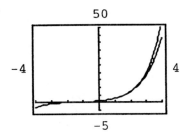

41. As $x \to \infty$, $f_n(x) \to 0$; The line $y = 0$ is a horizontal asymptote.
As $x \to -\infty$, $f_1(x) \to -\infty$ and $f_3(x) \to -\infty$, while $f_2(x) \to \infty$. As $x \to -\infty$, $f_n(x) \to \infty$ if n is even and $f_n(x) \to -\infty$ if n is odd.

42. as $x \to \infty$, $g(x) \to \infty$, as $x \to -\infty$, $g(x) \to 0$. $y = 0$ is an horizontal asymptote.

43. 7.1 billion **44.** 120 million **45.** 2006 **46.** 2009

47.

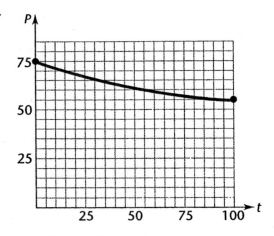

48.

49. (A) 62% (B) 39% **50.** (A) 10% (B) 1%

51. (A) $10,691.81 (B) $36,336.69 **52.** (A) $11,871.65 (B) $20,427.93

53. Gill Savings: $1,230.60; Richardson S & L: $1,231.00; U.S.A. Savings: $1,229.03

54. Alamo: $10,850.88; Lamar: $10,838.29 **55.** $12,197.09

56. $P = P_0 e^{rt} \Rightarrow 50,000 = P_0 e^{0.1(5.5)} \Rightarrow P_0 = \$28,847.49$

57. (A) 15 million (B) 30 million

58. (A) 59.87... million (B) 128.02... million

59. 40 boards

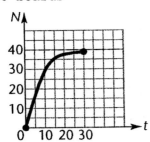

60. N tends to 2 as t increases without bound

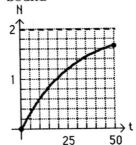

61. $T = 50°F$

62. $T = 44°F$

63. 0.0009 coulomb

64. 0.000 008 coulombs

65. 100 deer

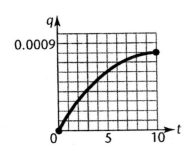

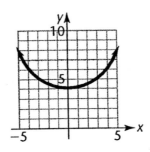

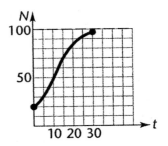

66. $N_{max} = 50$ computers

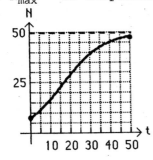

67.

68. $y = \dfrac{e^{0.4x} + e^{-0.4x}}{2(0.4)}$

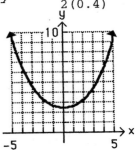

Exercise 5-3

1. $2^6 = 64$ **2.** $6^3 = 216$ **3.** $10^5 = 100,000$ **4.** $10^{-6} = 0.000001$

5. $9^{1/2} = 3$ **6.** $16^{1/4} = 2$ **7.** $(1/4)^{-3} = 64$ **8.** $(1/5)^{-2} = 25$

9. $\log_{10} 0.001 = -3$ **10.** $\log_{10} 10,000,000 = 7$ **11.** $\log_8 4 = 2/3$

12. $\log_{16} 64 = 3/2$ **13.** $\log_{81} (1/3) = -1/4$ **14.** $\log_{32} (1/4) = -2/5$

15. $\log_{125} 5 = 1/3$ **16.** $\log_{121} 11 = 1/2$ **17.** 1

18. 0   **19.** 0   **20.** 1   **21.** 3

22. 6   **23.** 1/2   **24.** 1/3   **25.** -3

26. -4   **27.** x^2 **28.** $\sqrt{x}$ **29.** $(x - 1)^3$

30. $1/(x + 1)^2$ **31.** 8   **32.** 9   **33.** 1/25

34. 1/64   **35.** 4   **36.** 3   **37.** 64

38. 4   **39.** -3   **40.** -4   **41.** 4

42. 64 **43.** 100 **44.** 0.1

45. $6 \log_b x + 9 \log_b y$

46. $(2/3)\log_b x + (4/3)\log_b y$

47. $(3/2)\log_b u - (5/3)\log_b v$

48. $7 \log_b v - 8 \log_b u$

49. $\log_b m + \log_b n - \log_b p - \log_b q$

50. $\log_b m + \log_b n + \log_b p - \log_b q$

51. $-4 \log_b a$ **52.** $-3 \log_b a$ **53.** $(1/2)\log_b (c^2 + d^2)$

54. $(1/4)\log_b (c^4 + d^4)$ **55.** $(1/2)\log_b u - \log_b v - 2 \log_b w$

56. $3 \log_b u + 4 \log_b v - (1/2)\log_b w$ **57.** $(2/3)\log_b x + (1/6)\log_b y - \log_b z$

58. $(3/8)\log_b x - (3/2)\log_b y - (9/4)\log_b z$

59. $\log_b \dfrac{x^2}{y}$ **60.** $\log_b \dfrac{m}{\sqrt{n}}$ **61.** $\log_b \dfrac{w}{xy}$ **62.** $\log_b \dfrac{wx}{y}$

63. $\log_b \dfrac{x^3 y^2}{z^{1/4}}$ **64.** $\log_b \dfrac{\sqrt[3]{w}}{x^3 y^5}$ **65.** $\log_b \left(\dfrac{u^{1/2}}{v^2}\right)^5$ **66.** $\log_b (m^4 \sqrt[3]{n})^7$

67. $\log_b \sqrt[5]{x^2 y^3}$ **68.** $\log_b \sqrt[3]{\dfrac{x^4}{y^2}}$ **69.** $5 \log_b(x + 3) + 2 \log_b(2x - 7)$

70. $3 \log_b(5x - 4) + 4 \log_b(3x + 2)$ **71.** $7 \log_b(x + 10) - 2 \log_b(1 + 10x)$

72. $5 \log_b(x - 3) - 3 \log_b(5 + x)$ **73.** $2 \log_b x - \dfrac{1}{2} \log_b(x + 1)$

74. $\dfrac{1}{2} \log_b(x - 1) - 3 \log_b x$ **75.** $2 \log_b x + \log_b(x + 5) + \log_b(x - 4)$

76. $3 \log_b x + \log_b(x + 7) + \log_b(x - 2)$ **77.** $x = 4$

78. $x = -3$ **79.** $x = \dfrac{1}{3}$ **80.** $x = 3$ **81.** $x = \dfrac{8}{7}$

82. $x = 1$ **83.** $x = 2$ **84.** $x = 1$ **85.** $x = 2$

86. $x = 8$ **87.** 3.40 **88.** 2.48 **89.** -0.92

90. 0.51 **91.** 3.30 **92.** 2.76 **93.** 0.23

94. 0.55 **95.** -0.05 **96.** 0.137

97.
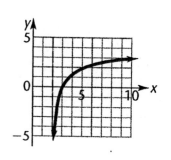

98.
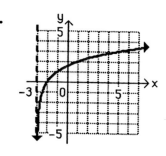

99.
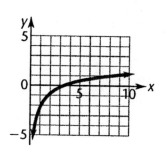

100.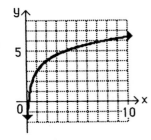

101. (A)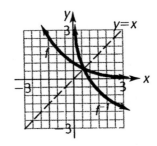

(B) Domain $f = (-\infty, \infty)$ = Range f^{-1}
Range $f = (0, \infty)$ = Domain f^{-1}

(C) $f^{-1}(x) = \log_{1/2} x = -\log_2 x$

103. $f^{-1}(x) = \frac{1}{3}[1 + \log_5(x - 4)]$

102. (A)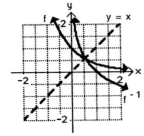

(B) domain of $f(x) = (-\infty, \infty)$ = range of $f^{-1}(x)$,
range of $f(x) = (0, \infty)$ = domain of $f^{-1}(x)$

(C) $f^{-1}(x) = -\log_3 x = \log_{1/3} x$

104. $g^{-1}(x) = \frac{1}{2}[\log_3(x + 2) + 3]$

105. $g^{-1}(x) = \frac{1}{5}(e^{x/3} + 2)$

106. $f^{-1}(x) = \frac{1}{5}(e^{x-2} + 3)$

107. The reflection is not a function since $y = 3^{x^2}$ is not one-to-one.

108. The reflection is not a function since $y = 2^{|x|}$ is not one-to-one.

109. $x = 100e^{-0.08t}$

110. $x = Ce^{-kt}$

Exercise 5-4

1. 4.4408
2. -3.2684
3. -2.3644
4. 5.0812
5. -7.3324
6. -3.7637
7. 6.1242
8. 4.8861
9. 32.45
10. 0.7419
11. 0.1039
12. 919.3
13. 0.055 68
14. 0.002 442
15. 3,407
16. 317.4
17. 1.238
18. 0.097
19. 2.320
20. 0.203
21. -51.083
22. -30.980
23. 5.192
24. 5.192
25. 35.779
26. -23.848
27. -12.169
28. 14.709
29. 4.6505×10^{21}
30. 2.1077×10^6
31. 1.4925×10^{-5}
32. 2.5122×10^{-16}

33.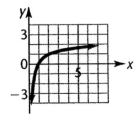

34.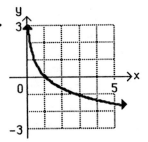

35.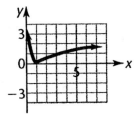

36.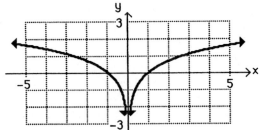

37.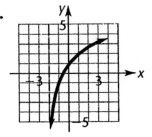

38.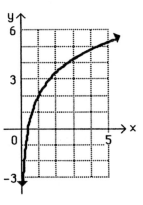

39.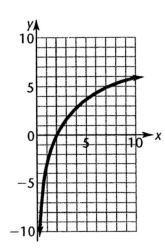

40.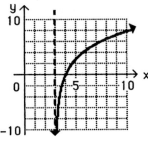

41. The inequality sign in the last step reverses because $\log \frac{1}{3}$ is negative.

42. $\log \frac{1}{2} = -0.3010 < 0$, thus when $3 > 2$ is multiplied on both sides by $\log \frac{1}{2}$ (a negative number) the order of the inequality should be reversed: $3 \log \frac{1}{2} < 2 \log \frac{1}{2}$ rather than $3 \log \frac{1}{2} > 2 \log \frac{1}{2}$ as shown.

43. (B) Domain $= (1, \infty)$; Range $= (-\infty, \infty)$

44. (B) Domain $= (1, \infty)$; Range $= (-\infty, \infty)$

45. $(0.90, -0.11)$, $(38.51, 3.65)$

46. $(1.93, 0.28)$

47. $(6.41, 1.86)$, $(93.35, 4.54)$

48. $(3.06, 0.19)$

49.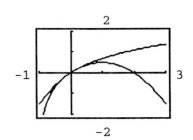

50.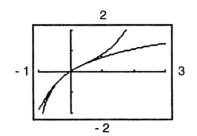

51.

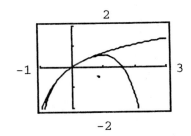

52.

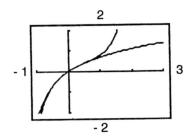

53. (A) 0 decibels   (B) 120 decibels
55. 30 decibels   **56.** 40 decibels
59. 1000 times as powerful

61. 7.67 km/s

63. (A) 8.3, basic   (B) 3.0, acidic
65. 6.3×10^{-6} moles per liter

54. (A) 65 decibels   (B) 150 decibels
57. 8.6   **58.** 8.3
60. $E_1 \approx 32,000$ times as powerful

62. $9.49 \dfrac{\text{km}}{\text{sec}}$

64. (A) 6.5 acidic   (B) 5.4 acidic
66. 2.0×10^{-6} moles per liter

Exercise 5-5

1. 1.44   **2.** 2.26   **3.** 5.88   **4.** −0.0969
5. −1.68   **6.** −0.421   **7.** 0.0967   **8.** 1.17
9. 3.24   **10.** −4.25   **11.** −3.43   **12.** 6.64
13. 5/2   **14.** $e/4$ **15.** $8/e^2$ **16.** 2/25
17. $x = 10$ **18.** $x = 35$ **19.** 86.7   **20.** 91.6
21. −921   **22.** 0.008 93   **23.** 5.18   **24.** −7.70
25. ±4.01   **26.** ±1.86   **27.** $x = 5$ **28.** $x = \dfrac{2}{3}$

29. $2 + \sqrt{3}$ **30.** $x = 1 + \sqrt{2}$ **31.** $\dfrac{1 + \sqrt{89}}{4}$ **32.** $x = 3$

33. $1, e^2, e^{-2}$ **34.** $x = 1, x = 10^{\pm 2}$ **35.** $x = e^e$ **36.** $x = 10^{10}$
37. $x = 100, 0.1$
                        38. $x = 10^{(\log 3)/(\log 3 - 1)}$
39. (B) 2   **40.** (B) 1   **41.** (B) −1.252, 1.707   **42.** (B) 1.248, 10.738
43. 3.6776   **44.** 2.2618   **45.** −1.6094   **46.** −7.5224

47. −1.7372   **48.** 2.4455   **49.** $r = \dfrac{1}{t} \ln \dfrac{A}{P}$

50. $t = \dfrac{\ln \frac{A}{P}}{n \ln(1 + \frac{r}{n})}$ **51.** $I = I_0(10^{D/10})$ **52.** $A = A_0 e^{-kt}$

53. $I = I_0[10^{(6-M)/2.5}]$ **54.** $D = 10^{(L-8.8)/5.1}$

55. $t = -\dfrac{L}{R} \ln \left(1 - \dfrac{RI}{E}\right)$ **56.** $n = \dfrac{\ln(\frac{Si}{R} + 1)}{\ln(1 + i)}$

57. $x = \ln(y \pm \sqrt{y^2 - 1})$ **58.** $x = \ln[y + \sqrt{y^2 + 1}]$

59. $x = \dfrac{1}{2} \ln \dfrac{1 + y}{1 - y}$

60. $x = \dfrac{1}{2} \ln \dfrac{y + 1}{y - 1}$

61.

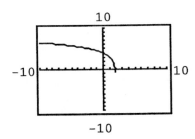

62.

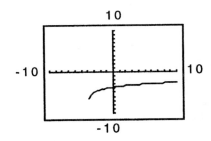

63.

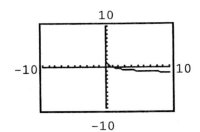

64.

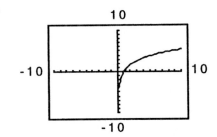

65. 0.38   **66.** 0.25   **67.** 0.55   **68.** 0.64

69. 0.57   **70.** 0.43   **71.** 0.85   **72.** 0.35

73. 0.43   **74.** 0.65   **75.** 0.27   **76.** 0.57

77. $n = 5$ years to the nearest year   **78.** 8 yrs. to nearest year

79. $r = 0.0916$ or 9.16%   **80.** 5.22 years

81. (A) $m = 6$ (B) 100 times brighter   **82.** (A) 12.8   (B) 206 in.

83. $t = 35$ years to the nearest year   **84.** 533 years

85. $t = 18,600$ years old   **86.** 5590 years

87. $t = 7.52$ seconds   **88.** 43 days

89. $k = 0.40$, $t = 2.9$ hours   **90.** $k = 0.0485$, $d = 95.0$ ft.

91. $t = 10$ years   **92.** 30 days

CHAPTER 5 REVIEW

1. $\log m = n$ *(5-3)*   **2.** $\ln x = y$ *(5-3)*

3. $x = 10^y$ *(5-3)*   **4.** $y = e^x$ *(5-3)*

5. 7^{2x} *(5-1)*   **6.** e^{2x^2} *(5-1)*

7. $x = 8$ *(5-3)*   **8.** $x = 5$ *(5-3)*

9. $3 = x$ *(5-3)*   **10.** $x = 1.24$ *(5-3)*

11. $x = 11.9$ *(5-3)*   **12.** $x = 0.984$ *(5-3)*

13. $x = 103$ *(5-3)*   **14.** $x = 4$ *(5-3)*

15. $x = 2$ *(5-3)*   **16.** $x = 3, -1$ *(5-2)*

17. $x = 1$ *(5-1)*

18. $x = 3, -3$ *(5-2)*

19. $-2 = x$ *(5-3)*

20. $x = \dfrac{1}{3}$ *(5-3)*

21. $x = 64$ *(5-3)*

22. $x = e$ *(5-3)*

23. $x = 33$ *(5-3)*

24. $x = 1$ *(5-3)*

25. 1.145 *(5-3)*

26. Not defined   *(5-3)*

27. 2.211 *(5-3)*

28. 11.59 *(5-3)*

29. $x = 41.8$ *(5-1)*

30. $x = 1.95$ *(5-3)*

31. $x = 0.0400$ *(5-3)*

32. $x = -6.67$ *(5-3)*

33. $x = 1.66$ *(5-3)*

34. $x = 2.32$ *(5-5)*

35. $x = 3.92$ *(5-5)*

36. $x = 92.1$ *(5-5)*

37. $x = 2.11$ *(5-5)*

38. $x = 0.881$ *(5-5)*

39. $x = 300$ *(5-5)*

40. $x = 2$ *(5-5)*

41. $x = 1$ *(5-5)*

42. $x = \dfrac{3 + \sqrt{13}}{2}$ *(5-5)*

43. $x = 1, 10^3, 10^{-3}$ *(5-5)*

44. $x = 10^e$ *(5-5)*

45. $e^{-x} - 1$ *(5-2)*

46. $2 - 2e^{-2x}$ *(5-2)*

47.
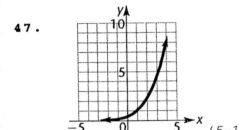
(5-1)

48.
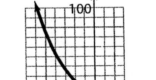
(5-2)

49.
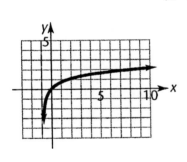
(5-3)

50.
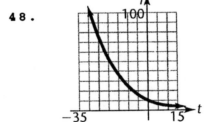
(5-2)

51. $y = e^{-x}$ or $y = \dfrac{1}{e^x}$ or $y = \left(\dfrac{1}{e}\right)^x$ *(5-3)*

52. (A) $y = e^{-x/3}$ is decreasing while $y = 4 \ln(x + 1)$ is increasing without bound.
     (B) 0.258 *(5-5)*

53. $0.018, 2.187$ *(5-3)*

54. $(1.003, 0.010), (3.653, 4.502)$ *(5-4)*

55. $I = I_0(10^{D/10})$ *(5-5)*

56. $x = \pm\sqrt{-2 \ln(\sqrt{2\pi}y)}$ *(5-5)*

57. $I = I_0(e^{-kx})$ *(5-5)*

58. $n = -\dfrac{\ln\left(1 - \dfrac{Pi}{r}\right)}{\ln(1 + i)}$ *(5-5)*

59. $f^{-1}(x) = e^{x/2} + 1$ *(5-5, 3-6)*

60. $f^{-1}(x) = \ln(x + \sqrt{x^2 + 1})$ *(5-5, 3-6)*

61. $y = ce^{-5t}$ *(5-3, 5-5)*

62. Domain $f = (0, \infty) = $ Range f^{-1}
Range $f = (-\infty, \infty) = $ Domain f^{-1}

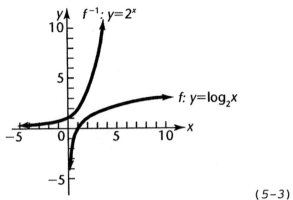

                               (5-3)

63. If $\log_1 x = y$, then we would have to have $1^y = x$; that is, $1 = x$ for arbitrary positive x, which is impossible.   *(5-3)*

64. Let $u = \log_b M$ and $v = \log_b N$; then $M = b^u$ and $N = b^v$. Thus, $\log(M/N) = \log_b(b^u/b^v) = \log_b b^{u-v} = u - v = \log_b M - \log_b N$.   *(5-3)*

65. $t = 23.4$ years *(5-5)*

66. $t = 23.1$ years   *(5-5)*

67. $t = 37,100$ years   *(5-5)*

68. (A) $N = 2^{2t}$ (or $N = 4^t$)   (B) $t = 15$ days   *(5-5)*

69. $A = 1.1 \times 10^{26}$ dollars   *(5-2)*

70. (A)

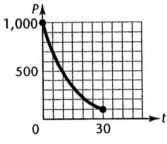

                              (B) 0

                               (5-2)

71. $M = 6.6$ *(5-4)*

72. $I = 10^{16.85}$ or 7.08×10^{16} joules   *(5-4)*

73. The level of the louder sound is 50 decibels more.   *(5-4)*

74. $k = 0.00942$, $d = 489$ feet   *(5-2)*

75. $t = 3$ years   *(5-5)*

CUMULATIVE REVIEW EXERCISE (Chapters 3, 4 and 5)

1. (A) $2\sqrt{5}$ (B) $m = 2$ (C) $m_1 = -\dfrac{1}{2}$ *(3-1, 3-2)*

2. (A) $x^2 + y^2 = 2$ (B) $(x + 3)^2 + (y - 1)^2 = 2$ *(3-1)*

3. slope: $\dfrac{2}{3}$ y intercept: -2

x intercept: 3

4. (A) Function; domain: {1, 2, 3};
range: {1}
(B) Not a function
(C) Function; domain: {-2, -1, 0, 1, 2};
range: {-1, 0, 2} *(3-3)*

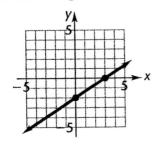

(3-2)

5. (A) 20 (B) $x^2 + x + 3$ (C) $9x^2 - 18x + 13$ (D) $2a + h - 2$ *(3-2, 3-5)*

6. (A) $P(x) = (x + 1)^2(x - 1)(x - 2)$
(B) $P(x) \to \infty$ as $x \to \infty$ and as $x \to -\infty$ *(4-1)*

7. (A) Expanded by a factor of 2 (B) Shifted right 2 units
(C) Shifted down 2 units *(3-5)*

8. (A) (B)

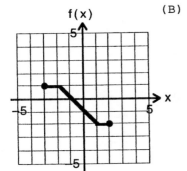 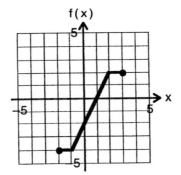

(3-5)

9. $3x^3 + 5x^2 - 18x - 3 = (x + 3)(3x^2 - 4x - 6) + 15$ *(4-1)*

10. $-2, 3, 5$ *(4-2)*

11. $P(1) = -5$ and $P(2) = 5$ are of opposite sign. *(4-3)*

12. $1, 2, -4$ *(4-2)*

13. $\dfrac{2}{x - 2} + \dfrac{3}{x + 1}$ *(4-5)*

14. (A) $x = \log y$ (B) $x = e^y$ *(5-4)*

15. (A) $8e^{3x}$ (B) e^{5x} *(5-2)*

16. (A) 9 (B) 4 (C) $\dfrac{1}{2}$ *(5-3)*

17. (A) 0.371 (B) 11.4 (C) 0.0562 (D) 15.6 *(5-4)*

18. (A) All real numbers $(-\infty, \infty)$ (B) $\{-2\} \cup [1, \infty)$ (C) 1
(D) $[-3, -2]$ and $[2, \infty)$ (E) $-2, 2$. *(3-3, 3-4)*

19. (A) $y = -\dfrac{3}{2}x - 8$ (B) $y = \dfrac{2}{3}x + 5$ *(3-2)*

20. $[-4, \infty)$ *(3-3)*

21. Range: $[-9, \infty)$

Min $f(x) = f\left(-\dfrac{b}{2a}\right) = -9$

y intercept: $f(0) = -8$
x intercepts: $x = 4$ and $x = -2$

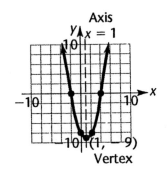

(3-4)

22. $(f \circ g)(x) = \dfrac{x}{3 - x}$; Domain: $(-\infty, 0) \cup (0, 3) \cup (3, \infty)$ (3-5)

23. $f^{-1}(x) = \dfrac{x - 5}{2}$ or $\dfrac{1}{2}x - \dfrac{5}{2}$ (3-8)

24. $f(x) = 3 \ln x - \sqrt{x}$ (3-3, 5-3)

25. The function f multiplies the base e raised to power of one-half the domain element by 100 and then subtracts 50. (3-3, 5-2)

26. Domain: all real numbers
Range: $(-\infty, -1) \cup [1, \infty)$
Discontinuous at: $x = 0$

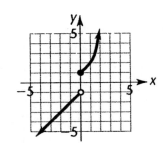

(3-4)

27. (A)   (B)

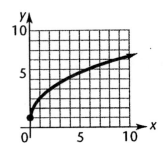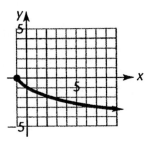

(3-5)

28. The graph of $y = |x|$ is contracted by $\dfrac{1}{2}$, reflected in the x axis, shifted two units to the right and three units up; $y = -\dfrac{1}{2}|x - 2| + 3$. (3-5)

29. (A) Domain: $x \neq -2$;
x intercept: $x = -4$;
y intercept: $y = 4$

(B) *Vertical asymptote:* $x = -2$
Horizontal asymptote: $y = 2$

(C)

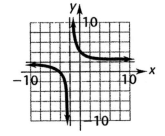

(4-4)

30. (A) $f^{-1}(x) = x^2 - 4$, Domain: $x \geq 0$

(B) Domain of $f = [-4, \infty) = $ Range of f^{-1}
Range of $f = [0, \infty) = $ Domain of f^{-1}

(C)

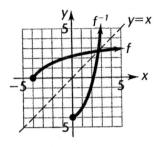

(3-6)

31. Center: $(3, -1)$;
Radius: $\sqrt{10}$

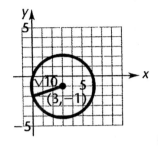

(3-1)

32. symmetry with respect to the origin   *(3-1)*

33. $y = (x + 2)^2 - 3$ *(3-4)*   **34.** $P\left(\dfrac{1}{2}\right) = \dfrac{5}{2}$ *(4-2)*   **35.** (B)   *(4-2)*

36. (A) The graph of $P(x)$ has four x
intercepts and three turning points;
$P(x) \to \infty$ as $x \to \infty$ and as $x \to -\infty$

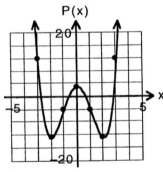

(B) 2.8   *(4-1, 4-3)*

37. (A) Upper bound: 4; lower bound: -6
(B) 3.80
(C) -5.68, 3.80   *(4-3)*

38. $3,\ 1 \pm \dfrac{1}{2}i$ *(4-2)*

39. $P(x) = (x + 1)(x + 4)(x^2 - 3) = (x + 1)(x + 4)(x - \sqrt{3})(x + \sqrt{3})$.
The four zeros are -1, -4, $\pm\sqrt{3}$.   *(4-2)*

40. Interval notation: $(-\infty, -2] \cup [3, 6]$;
Inequality notation: $x \leq -2$ or $3 \leq x \leq 6$ *(4-2)*

41. $\dfrac{1}{x} + \dfrac{2}{x + 1} - \dfrac{5}{(x + 1)^2}$ *(4-5)*   **42.** $\dfrac{-2}{x} + \dfrac{3x - 1}{x^2 - x + 1}$ *(4-5)*

43. $x = 4, -2$ *(5-1)*   **44.** $\dfrac{1}{2}, -1$ *(5-2)*

45. $x = 2.5$ *(5-3)*   **46.** $x = 10$ *(5-3)*

47. $x = \dfrac{1}{27}$ *(5-3)*   **48.** $x = 5$ *(5-5)*

49. $x = 7$ *(5-5)*   **50.** $x = 5$ *(5-5)*

51. $x = e^{0.1}$ *(5-4)*   **52.** $x = 1,\ e^{0.5}$ *(5-5)*

53. $x = 3.38$ *(5-5)*   **54.** $x = 4.26$ *(5-4)*

55. $x = 2.32$ *(5-4)*   **56.** $x = 3.67$ *(5-5)*

57. $x = 0.549$ *(5-5)*

58.

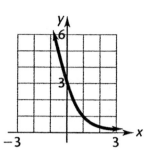

(5-1)

59.

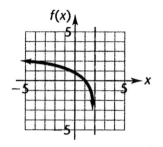

(5-4)

60.

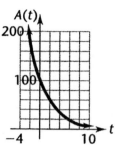

(5-2)

61.

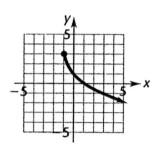

(3-5)

62.

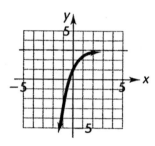

(5-2)

63. A reflection in the x axis transforms the graph of $y = \ln x$ into the graph of $y = -\ln x$. A reflection in the y axis transforms the graph of $y = \ln x$ into the graph of $y = \ln(-x)$.   *(3-5, 5-3)*

64. (A) For $x > 0$, $y = e^{-x}$ decreases from 1 to 0 while ln x increases from $-\infty$ to ∞. Consequently, the graphs can intersect at exactly one point.

(B) 1.31   *(5-3)*

65. $f(x) = \begin{cases} -2x & \text{if } x < -2 \\ 4 & \text{if } -2 \le x \le 2 \\ 2x & \text{if } x > 2 \end{cases}$

Domain: all real numbers; Range $[4, \infty)$

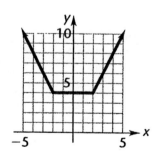

(3-4)

66. (A) Domain g: $[-2, 2]$

(B) $\left(\dfrac{f}{g}\right)(x) = \dfrac{x^2}{\sqrt{4 - x^2}}$; domain of f/g is $(-2, 2)$

(C) $(f \circ g)(x) = 4 - x^2$; domain of $f \circ g$ is $[-2, 2]$ *(3-5)*

67. (A) $f^{-1}(x) = 1 + \sqrt{x + 4}$

(B) Domain of f^{-1} is $[-4, \infty)$
Range of f^{-1} = Domain of f
is $[1, \infty)$

(C)

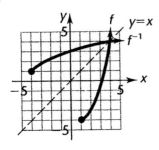

$(3-6)$

68. *Vertical asymptote: $x = -2$*
Oblique asymptote: $y = x + 2$

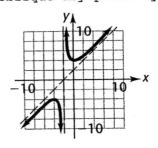

$(4-4)$

69. $f(x) = \begin{cases} \vdots & \vdots \\ 2x + 2 & \text{if} \quad -1 \le x < -\frac{1}{2} \\ 2x + 1 & \text{if} \quad -\frac{1}{2} \le x < 0 \\ 2x & \text{if} \quad 0 \le x < \frac{1}{2} \\ 2x - 1 & \text{if} \quad \frac{1}{2} \le x < 1 \\ 2x - 2 & \text{if} \quad 1 \le x < \frac{3}{2} \\ 2x - 3 & \text{if} \quad \frac{3}{2} \le x < 2 \\ \vdots & \vdots \end{cases}$

Domain: All real numbers
Range: $[0, 1)$
Discontinous at $x = k/2$, k an integer

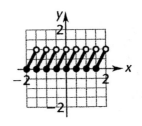

$(3-4)$

70. $P(x) = (x + 1)^2 x^3 (x - 3 - 5i)(x - 3 + 5i)$; degree 7 $(4-2)$

71. Yes, for example:
$P(x) = (x + i)(x - i)(x + \sqrt{2})(x - \sqrt{2}) = x^4 - x^2 - 2$ $(4-2)$

72. (A) Upper bound: 20; lower bound: -30   (B) -26.68, -6.22, 7.23, 16.67 $(4-3)$

73. 2, -1 (double), and $2 \pm i\sqrt{2}$;
$P(x) = (x - 2)(x + 1)^2 (x - 2 - i\sqrt{2})(x - 2 + i\sqrt{2})$ $(4-2)$

74. -2(double), -1.88, 0.35, 1.53 $(4-3)$

75. $\dfrac{-2}{x - 1} + \dfrac{2}{(x - 1)^2} + \dfrac{2x + 3}{x^2 + x + 2}$ $(4-5)$

76. (A) $f^{-1}(x) = e^{x/3} + 2$

(B) Domain of $f = (2, \infty)$ = Range of f^{-1}
Range of $f = (-\infty, \infty)$ = Domain of f^{-1}

(C)

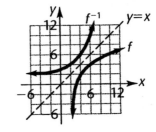

$(3-6, 5-5)$

77. $n = \dfrac{\ln(1 + \frac{Ai}{P})}{\ln(1 + i)}$ $(5-5)$ **78.** $y = Ae^{5x}$ $(5-5)$

79. $x = \ln(y + \sqrt{y^2 + 2})$ $(5-5)$

80. $x = -900(3.29) + 4{,}571$; 1,610 bottles $(3-2)$

81. $C(x) = \begin{cases} 0.06x & \text{if} & 0 \le x \le 60 \\ 0.05x + 0.6 & \text{if} & 60 < x \le 150 \\ 0.04x + 2.1 & \text{if} & 150 < x \le 300 \\ 0.03x + 5.1 & \text{if} & 300 < x \end{cases}$

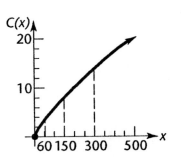

(3-4)

82. (A) $A(x) = 80x - 2x^2$

(B) $0 < x < 40$

(C) 20 feet by 40 feet

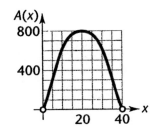

(3-4)

83. (A) $f(1) = 1$; $f(2) = 0$; $f(3) = 1$; $f(4) = 0$

(B) $f(n) = \begin{cases} 1 \text{ if } n \text{ is an odd integer} \\ 0 \text{ if } n \text{ is an even integer} \end{cases}$

(3-4)

84. $x = 2$ feet and $y = 2$ feet, or $x = 1.3$ feet and $y = 4.8$ feet   (4-2)

85. 1.8 feet by 3.3 feet   (4-3)

86. (A) 46.8 million (B) 103 million   (5-1)

87. $t = 10.2$ years   (5-5)   **88.** $t = 9.90$ years   (5-5)

89. 63.1 times as powerful   (5-4)   **90.** $I = 6.31 \times 10^{-4}$ W/m^2 (5-4)

CHAPTER 6

Exercise 6-1

1. $40°$

2. $72°$

3. $270°$

4. $420°$

5. 6

6. $\theta = 2$

7. 2.5

8. $\theta = 1.5$

9. $\dfrac{\pi}{4}$

10. $\dfrac{\pi}{3}$

11. $\dfrac{3\pi}{2}$

12. $\dfrac{11\pi}{4}$

13. $\dfrac{\pi}{6}, \dfrac{\pi}{3}, \dfrac{\pi}{2}, \dfrac{2\pi}{3}, \dfrac{5\pi}{6}, \pi$

14. $\dfrac{\pi}{3}, \dfrac{2\pi}{3}, \pi, \dfrac{4\pi}{3}, \dfrac{5\pi}{3}, 2\pi$

15. $-\dfrac{\pi}{4}, -\dfrac{\pi}{2}, -\dfrac{3\pi}{4}, -\pi$

16. $-\dfrac{\pi}{2}, -\pi, -\dfrac{3\pi}{2}, -2\pi$

17. $60°, 120°, 180°, 240°, 300°, 360°$

18. $30°, 60°, 90°, 120°, 150°, 180°$

19. $-90°, -180°, -270°, -360°$

20. $-45°, -90°, -135°, -180°$

21. False

22. True

23. False

24. True

25. False

26. False

27. $5.859°$

28. $14.310°$

29. $354.141°$

30. $184.519°$

31. $3°2'31"$

32. $49°42'54"$

33. $403°13'23"$

34. $156°48'29"$

35. 0.314

36. 1.379

37. 0.415

38. 0.854

39. $87.09°$

40. $36.67°$

41. $-47.56°$

42. $-151.83°$

43. Quadrant II

44. Quadrant II

45. Quadrant IV

46. Quadrant I

47. Quadrant IV

48. Quadrant II

49. Quadrantal angle

50. Quadrant I

51. Quadrant III

52. Quadrantal angle

53. Quadrant III

54. Quadrant IV

55. Coterminal

56. Not coterminal

57. Not coterminal

58. Coterminal

59. Coterminal

60. Not coterminal

61. Not coterminal

62. Coterminal

63. Coterminal

64. Coterminal

65. Coterminal

66. Not coterminal

67. $24,000$ mi

68. $25,000$ mi

69. The $7.5°$ angle and θ have a common side. (An extended vertical pole in Alexandria will pass through the center of the earth.) The sun's rays are essentially parallel when they arrive at the earth. Thus, the other two sides of the angles are parallel, since a sun ray to the bottom of the well, when extended, will pass through the center of the earth. From geometry we know that the alternate interior angles made by a line intersecting two parallel lines are equal. Therefore, $\theta = 7.5°$.

70. Since the circumference of the earth is given by $C = 2\pi r$, if C is known, then r can be found by using $r = C/2\pi$. Once the radius is known, the surface area and volume can be found using the formulas $S = 4\pi r^2$ and $V = 4\pi r^3/3$, respectively.

71. $\dfrac{7\pi}{4}$ radians

72. $\dfrac{3\pi}{4}$

73. 200 radians

74. 16 rad

75. $\dfrac{\pi}{26} \approx 0.12$ rad

76. $\dfrac{3\pi}{4}$ rad ≈ 2.36 rad

77. 12

78. $\theta = 10$ rad

79. $865,000$ mi

80. $3,500$ km

81. 33 ft

82. 70 ft

Exercise 6-2

1. $a/b = \cot\theta$, $a/c = \cos\theta$, $b/a = \tan\theta$, $b/c = \sin\theta$, $c/a = \sec\theta$, $c/b = \csc\theta$

2. $\sin(90° - \theta) = a/c$, $\cos(90° - \theta) = b/c$, $\tan(90° - \theta) = a/b$, $\csc(90° - \theta) = c/a$, $\sec(90° - \theta) = c/b$, $\cot(90° - \theta) = b/a$

3. 0.9666   **4.** 0.6924   **5.** 1.203   **6.** 47.10

7. 21.36   **8.** 1.040   **9.** 1.079   **10.** 0.4554

11. 67.56°   **12.** 58.15°   **13.** 84.01°   **14.** 1.82°

15. 42.06°   **16.** 76.90°   **17.** 3°30'   **18.** 53°40'

19. 21°40'   **20.** 89°20'   **21.** 72°20'   **22.** 29°10'

23. $\alpha = 72.2°$, $a = 3.28$, $b = 1.05$ **24.** $\alpha = 56.3°$, $a = 33.6$, $c = 40.4$

25. $\alpha = 46°40'$, $b = 116$, $c = 169$ **26.** $\alpha = 27°30'$, $a = 19.6$, $b = 37.7$

27. $\beta = 67°0'$, $b = 127$, $c = 138$ **28.** $\beta = 36°$, $a = 3.5$, $b = 2.5$

29. $\beta = 36.79°$, $a = 31.85$, $c = 39.77$ **30.** $\beta = 54.27°$, $a = 4.663$, $c = 7.985$

31. $\beta = 54.6°$ or $54°40'$, $\alpha = 35°20'$, $c = 10.4$

32. $a = 157$, $\alpha = 72°20'$, $\beta = 17°40'$ **33.** True   **34.** False

35. True   **36.** False   **37.** True   **38.** False

39. (A) $\cos \theta = OA/1 = OA$ (B) Angle $OED = \theta$; $\cot \theta = DE/1 = DE$
(C) $\sec \theta = OC/1 = OC$

40. (A) $\sin \theta = AD/1 = AD$ (B) $\tan \theta = CD/1 = CD$
(C) Angle $OED = \theta$; $\csc \theta = OE/1 = OE$

41. (A) As θ approaches 90°, $OA = \cos \theta$ approaches 0.
(B) As θ approaches 90°, $DE = \cot \theta$ approaches 0.
(C) As θ approaches 90°, $OC = \sec \theta$ increases without bound.

42. (A) As θ approaches 90°, $AD = \sin \theta$ approaches 1.
(B) As θ approaches 90°, $CD = \tan \theta$ increases without bound.
(C) As θ approaches 90°, $OE = \csc \theta$ approaches 1.

43. (A) As θ approaches 0°, $AD = \sin \theta$ approaches 0.
(B) As θ approaches 0°, $CD = \tan \theta$ approaches 0.
(C) As θ approaches 0°, $OE = \csc \theta$ increases without bound.

44. (A) As θ approaches 0°, $OA = \cos \theta$ approaches 1.
(B) As θ approaches 0°, $DE = \cot \theta$ increases without bound.
(C) As θ approaches 0°, $OC = \sec \theta$ approaches 1.

47. 228 ft   **48.** $h = 315$ meters   **49.** 127.5 ft   **50.** 6 min.

51. 2,225 mi   **52.** $D = 870,000$ miles   **53.** 44°

54. 2.78 in.   **55.** $g = 9.8$ meters/second^2 **56.** $g = 32.3 \dfrac{\text{ft.}}{\text{sec}^2}$

57. (B)

θ	$C(\theta)$
10°	$368,222
20°	$363,435
30°	$360,622
40°	$360,146
50°	$363,050

58. (B)

θ	$C(\theta) = 120{,}000\ \sec\theta - 80{,}000\ \tan\theta + 400{,}000$
10°	$507,745
20°	$498,584
30°	$492,376
40°	$489,521
50°	$491,347

59. $r = 0.77$ m   **60.** 1.2 inches

Exercise 6-3

1. $\sin\theta = \dfrac{4}{5}$, $\csc\theta = \dfrac{5}{4}$, $\cos\theta = \dfrac{3}{5}$, $\sec\theta = \dfrac{5}{3}$, $\tan\theta = \dfrac{4}{3}$, $\cot\theta = \dfrac{3}{4}$

2. $\sin\theta = \dfrac{3}{5}$, $\cos\theta = \dfrac{4}{5}$, $\tan\theta = \dfrac{3}{4}$, $\sec\theta = \dfrac{5}{4}$, $\csc\theta = \dfrac{5}{3}$, $\cot\theta = \dfrac{4}{3}$

3. $\sin\theta = \dfrac{4}{5}$, $\csc\theta = \dfrac{5}{4}$, $\cos\theta = -\dfrac{3}{5}$, $\sec\theta = -\dfrac{5}{3}$, $\tan\theta = -\dfrac{4}{3}$, $\cot\theta = -\dfrac{3}{4}$

4. $\sin\theta = \dfrac{-3}{5}$, $\cos\theta = \dfrac{-4}{5}$, $\tan\theta = \dfrac{3}{4}$, $\sec\theta = -\dfrac{5}{4}$, $\csc\theta = -\dfrac{5}{3}$, $\cot\theta = \dfrac{4}{3}$

5. $\sin\theta = -\dfrac{1}{\sqrt{5}}$, $\csc\theta = -\sqrt{5}$, $\cos\theta = -\dfrac{2}{\sqrt{5}}$, $\sec\theta = -\dfrac{\sqrt{5}}{2}$, $\tan\theta = \dfrac{1}{2}$, $\cot\theta = 2$

6. $\sin\theta = \dfrac{-2}{\sqrt{5}}$, $\cos\theta = \dfrac{1}{\sqrt{5}}$, $\tan\theta = -2$, $\sec\theta = \sqrt{5}$, $\csc\theta = -\dfrac{\sqrt{5}}{2}$, $\cot\theta = -\dfrac{1}{2}$

7. $\cos\theta = \dfrac{4}{5}$, $\csc\theta = \dfrac{5}{3}$, $\tan\theta = \dfrac{3}{4}$, $\sec\theta = \dfrac{5}{4}$, $\cot\theta = \dfrac{4}{3}$

8. $\cos\theta = \dfrac{3}{5}$, $\sin\theta = \dfrac{4}{5}$, $\tan\theta = \dfrac{4}{3}$, $\sec\theta = \dfrac{5}{3}$, $\csc\theta = \dfrac{5}{4}$, $\cot\theta = \dfrac{3}{4}$

9. $\cos\theta = -\dfrac{4}{5}$, $\csc\theta = \dfrac{5}{3}$, $\tan\theta = -\dfrac{3}{4}$, $\sec\theta = -\dfrac{5}{4}$, $\cot\theta = -\dfrac{4}{3}$

10. $\sin\theta = \dfrac{-4}{5}$, $\tan\theta = \dfrac{-4}{3}$, $\sec\theta = \dfrac{5}{3}$, $\csc\theta = -\dfrac{5}{4}$, $\cot\theta = -\dfrac{3}{4}$

11. $\sin\theta = \dfrac{4}{5}$, $\csc\theta = \dfrac{5}{4}$, $\cos\theta = -\dfrac{3}{5}$, $\sec\theta = -\dfrac{5}{3}$, $\cot\theta = -\dfrac{3}{4}$

12. $\sin\theta = \dfrac{-4}{5}$, $\cos\theta = \dfrac{-3}{5}$, $\tan\theta = \dfrac{4}{3}$, $\sec\theta = -\dfrac{5}{3}$, $\cot\theta = \dfrac{3}{4}$

13. $\sin\theta = -\dfrac{4}{5}$, $\csc\theta = -\dfrac{5}{4}$, $\cos\theta = \dfrac{3}{5}$, $\sec\theta = \dfrac{5}{3}$, $\cot\theta = -\dfrac{3}{4}$

14. $\sin\theta = \dfrac{-4}{5}$, $\cos\theta = \dfrac{3}{5}$, $\tan\theta = \dfrac{-4}{3}$, $\sec\theta = \dfrac{5}{3}$, $\cot\theta = -\dfrac{3}{4}$

15. 0.9272   **16.** 0.3839   **17.** −0.2958   **18.** 1.000

19. 0.9806   **20.** 0.2495   **21.** −1.030   **22.** −14.77

23. 108.6   **24.** −30.53   **25.** 3.303   **26.** −0.1022

27. $\sin \theta = \dfrac{1}{2}$, $\csc \theta = 2$, $\cos \theta = \dfrac{\sqrt{3}}{2}$, $\sec \theta = \dfrac{2}{\sqrt{3}}$, $\tan \theta = \dfrac{1}{\sqrt{3}}$, $\cot \theta = \sqrt{3}$

28. $\sin \theta = \dfrac{1}{\sqrt{2}}$, $\cos \theta = \dfrac{1}{\sqrt{2}}$, $\tan \theta = 1$, $\csc \theta = \sqrt{2}$, $\sec \theta = \sqrt{2}$, $\cot \theta = 1$

29. $\sin \theta = \dfrac{\sqrt{3}}{2}$, $\csc \theta = \dfrac{2}{\sqrt{3}}$, $\cos \theta = -\dfrac{1}{2}$, $\sec \theta = -2$, $\tan \theta = -\sqrt{3}$, $\cot \theta = \dfrac{-1}{\sqrt{3}}$

30. $\sin \theta = \dfrac{-\sqrt{3}}{2}$, $\cos \theta = \dfrac{1}{2}$, $\tan \theta = -\sqrt{3}$, $\csc \theta = -\dfrac{2}{\sqrt{3}}$, $\sec \theta = 2$, $\cot \theta = -\dfrac{1}{\sqrt{3}}$

31. $\sin \theta = -\dfrac{1}{\sqrt{2}}$, $\csc \theta = -\sqrt{2}$, $\cos \theta = -\dfrac{1}{\sqrt{2}}$, $\sec \theta = -\sqrt{2}$, $\tan \theta = 1$, $\cot \theta = 1$

32. $\sin \theta = \dfrac{-\sqrt{2}}{2}$, $\cos \theta = \dfrac{\sqrt{2}}{2}$, $\tan \theta = -1$, $\csc \theta = -\dfrac{2}{\sqrt{2}}$, $\sec \theta = \dfrac{2}{\sqrt{2}}$, $\cot \theta = -1$

33. III and IV quadrants, since $\sin \theta = b/r$ and b is negative only in these quadrants (r is always positive).

34. I and III quadrants, since $\tan \theta = b/a$ and a and b are either both positive or both negative in these quadrants.

35. I and IV quadrants, since $\cos \theta = a/r$ and a is positive only in these quadrants (r is always positive).

36. I and II quadrants, since $\sin \theta = b/r$ and b is positive only in these quadrants (r is always positive).

37. II and IV quadrants, since $\tan \theta = b/a$ and b and a have opposite signs only in these quadrants.

38. II and III quadrants, since $\cos \theta = a/r$ and a is negative only in these quadrants (r is always positive).

39. II and IV quadrants, since $\cot \theta = a/b$ and a and b have opposite signs only in these quadrants.

40. II and III quadrants, since $\sec \theta = r/a$ and a is negative only in these quadrants (r is always positive).

41. I and II quadrants, since $\csc \theta = r/b$ and b is positive only in these quadrants.

42. I and III quadrants, since $\cot \theta = a/b$ and a and b are either both positive or both negative in these quadrants.

43. III and IV quadrants, since $\csc \theta = r/b$ and b is negative only in these quadrants (r is always positive)

44. I and IV quadrants, since $\sec \theta = r/a$ and a is positive only in these quadrants (r is always positive).

45. $\sin \theta = \dfrac{2}{3}$, $\csc \theta = \dfrac{3}{2}$, $\tan \theta = -\dfrac{2}{\sqrt{5}}$, $\sec \theta = -\dfrac{3}{\sqrt{5}}$, $\cot \theta = -\dfrac{\sqrt{5}}{2}$

46. $\cos \theta = \dfrac{-\sqrt{5}}{3}$, $\tan \theta = \dfrac{2}{\sqrt{5}}$, $\csc \theta = -\dfrac{3}{2}$, $\sec \theta = -\dfrac{3}{\sqrt{5}}$, $\cot \theta = \dfrac{\sqrt{5}}{2}$

47. $\sin \theta = -\dfrac{2}{3}$, $\csc \theta = -\dfrac{3}{2}$, $\tan \theta = \dfrac{2}{\sqrt{5}}$, $\sec \theta = -\dfrac{3}{\sqrt{5}}$, $\cot \theta = \dfrac{\sqrt{5}}{2}$

48. $\cos \theta = \dfrac{\sqrt{5}}{3}$, $\tan \theta = \dfrac{-2}{\sqrt{5}}$, $\csc \theta = -\dfrac{3}{2}$, $\sec \theta = \dfrac{3}{\sqrt{5}}$, $\cot \theta = -\dfrac{\sqrt{5}}{2}$

49. $\sin \theta = \dfrac{\sqrt{2}}{\sqrt{3}}$, $\csc \theta = \dfrac{\sqrt{3}}{\sqrt{2}}$, $\cos \theta = -\dfrac{1}{\sqrt{3}}$, $\sec \theta = -\sqrt{3}$, $\cot \theta = -\dfrac{1}{\sqrt{2}}$

50. $\sin \theta = \dfrac{-\sqrt{2}}{\sqrt{3}}$, $\cos \theta = \dfrac{1}{\sqrt{3}}$, $\tan \theta = -\sqrt{2}$, $\csc \theta = -\dfrac{\sqrt{3}}{\sqrt{2}}$, $\cot \theta = -\dfrac{1}{\sqrt{2}}$

53. tangent and secant, since $\tan \theta = b/a$ and $\sec \theta = r/a$ and $a = 0$ if $P(a, b)$ is on the vertical axis (division by zero is not defined).

54. cotangent and cosecant, since $\cot = a/b$ and $\csc \theta = r/b$ and b is 0 if $P(a, b)$ is on the horizontal axis (division by zero is not defined).

55. (A) 1.75 radians (B) (-0.713, 3.936) **56.** (A) 4 radians (B) (-1.307, -1.514)

57. 9.27 units **58.** $s = 5.13$ units

59. (A) k, $0.866k$, $0.5k$ (B) $\theta = 75.5°$ **60.** (A) $0.940k$, $0.643k$, 0 (B) $36.9°$

62. $y = 3.33$ inches

63. (A) 3.31371, 3.14263, 3.14160, 3.14159 (B) $\pi = 3.1415926...$

64. (A) 2.82843, 3.13953, 3.14157, 3.14159 (B) $\pi = 3.1415926...$

65. (A) 44.07; -0.32 (B) $y = -0.93x + 1.28$

66. (A) 0.09; -23.86 (B) $y = -3.49x + 16.92$

Exercise 6-4

1. 60° **2.** $\alpha = 45°$ **3.** $\dfrac{\pi}{6}$ **4.** $\alpha = \dfrac{\pi}{4}$

5. $\dfrac{\pi}{3}$ **6.** $\alpha = \dfrac{\pi}{4}$ **7.** 0 **8.** 1

9. $\dfrac{\sqrt{3}}{2}$ **10.** $\dfrac{\sqrt{2}}{2}$ **11.** $\dfrac{1}{2}$ **12.** $\dfrac{1}{2}$

13. 0 **14.** 1 **15.** $\dfrac{1}{\sqrt{3}}$ **16.** $\sqrt{3}$

17. 1 **18.** $\dfrac{\sqrt{2}}{2}$ **19.** not defined **20.** 0

21. $\dfrac{2}{\sqrt{3}}$ **22.** 1 **23.** $\dfrac{2}{\sqrt{3}}$ **24.** not defined

25. $\dfrac{-1}{\sqrt{3}}$ or $\dfrac{-\sqrt{3}}{3}$ **26.** -1 **27.** 0 **28.** $-\dfrac{1}{2}$

29. $\dfrac{-2}{\sqrt{3}}$ or $\dfrac{-2\sqrt{3}}{3}$ **30.** $\sqrt{2}$ **31.** -1 **32.** $-\dfrac{1}{2}$

33. $\dfrac{1}{2}$ **34.** 1 **35.** $\dfrac{\sqrt{3}}{2}$ **36.** $\dfrac{1}{2}$

37. $\sqrt{2}$ **38.** $\dfrac{-2}{\sqrt{3}}$ or $\dfrac{-2\sqrt{3}}{3}$ **39.** 0 **40.** $\dfrac{1}{\sqrt{3}}$ or $\dfrac{\sqrt{3}}{3}$

41. $\dfrac{2}{\sqrt{3}}$ or $\dfrac{2\sqrt{3}}{3}$ **42.** Not defined **43.** $\dfrac{1}{2}$ **44.** $\dfrac{1}{\sqrt{3}}$ or $\dfrac{\sqrt{3}}{3}$

45. -1 **46.** $\dfrac{1}{2}$ **47.** $\dfrac{2}{\sqrt{3}}$ or $\dfrac{2\sqrt{3}}{3}$ **48.** $-\dfrac{1}{2}$

49. Defined for all θ, since $\cos \theta = a/r$ and r is never zero.
50. $90°$ and $270°$, since $\sec \theta = r/a$ and $a = 0$ at $\theta = 90°$ and $270°$.
51. $90°$ and $270°$, since $\tan \theta = b/a$ and $a = 0$ at $\theta = 90°$, $270°$.
52. $0°$ and $180°$, since $\cot \theta = a/b$ and $b = 0$ at $\theta = 0°$ and $180°$.
53. $0°$ and $180°$, since $\csc \theta = r/b$ and $b = 0$ at $\theta = 0°$ and $180°$.
54. Defined for all θ, since $\sin \theta = b/r$ and r is never zero.
55. Defined for all x, since $\sin x = \sin(x \text{ rad}) = b/r$ and r is never zero.
56. $\pi/2$ and $3\pi/2$, since $\tan x = \tan(x \text{ rad}) = b/a$ and $a = 0$ at $x = \pi/2$ and $3\pi/2$.
57. 0 and π, since $\cot x = \cot(x \text{ rad}) = a/b$ and $b = 0$ at $x = 0$ and π.
58. 0 and π, since $\csc x = \csc(x \text{ rad}) = r/b$ and $b = 0$ at $x = 0$ and π.
59. $\pi/2$ and $3\pi/2$, since $\sec x = \sec(x \text{ rad}) = r/a$ and $a = 0$ at $x = \pi/2$ and $3\pi/2$.
60. Defined for all x, since $\cos x = \cos(x \text{ rad}) = a/r$ and r is never zero.

61. $225°$ **62.** $150°$ **63.** $120°$ **64.** $210°$

65. $45°$ **66.** $135°$ **67.** $\theta = \dfrac{4\pi}{3}$ **68.** $x = \pi$

69. $\theta = \dfrac{5\pi}{6}$ **70.** $x = \dfrac{3\pi}{4}$ **71.** $\theta = \dfrac{5\pi}{6}$ **72.** $x = \dfrac{5\pi}{4}$

73. $\theta = 150°, 210°$ **74.** $120°, 300°$ **75.** $\theta = \dfrac{\pi}{4}$ or $\dfrac{5\pi}{4}$ **76.** $\theta = \dfrac{3\pi}{4}, \dfrac{5\pi}{4}$

79. 18 in^2; 36 in^2 **80.** $24\sqrt{3} \approx 41.57$ in^2; $32\sqrt{3} \approx 55.43$ in^2
81. 282.8 cm^2; 331.4 cm^2 **82.** 75 m^2; 80.38 m^2

83. (A) $x = \dfrac{1}{2}$; $y = \dfrac{\sqrt{3}}{2}$ (B) $x = \dfrac{\sqrt{2}}{2}$ or $\dfrac{1}{\sqrt{2}}$; $y = \dfrac{\sqrt{2}}{2}$ or $\dfrac{1}{\sqrt{2}}$

84. (A) $y = \dfrac{1}{2}$; $x = \dfrac{\sqrt{3}}{2}$ (B) $y = \dfrac{\sqrt{2}}{2}$; $x = \dfrac{\sqrt{2}}{2}$

85. (A) $x = 2\sqrt{3}$; $y = \sqrt{3}$ (B) $x = \sqrt{2}$; $y = \sqrt{2}$ (C) $x = 12$; $y = 6\sqrt{3}$

86. (A) $x = 3\sqrt{3}$; $y = 3$ (B) $x = 8\sqrt{2}$; $y = 8$ (C) $y = \dfrac{5}{2}$; $x = \dfrac{5\sqrt{3}}{2}$

Exercise 6-5

1. (A) $\frac{\pi}{2}$ (B) $\frac{\pi}{3}$ (C) $\frac{\pi}{4}$ **2.** (A) π (B) $\frac{\pi}{6}$ (C) $\frac{3\pi}{2}$

3. (A) $(-1, 0)$ (B) $(0, -1)$ (C) $(0, -1)$ (D) $(0, -1)$ (E) $(-1, 0)$ (F) $(1, 0)$

4. (A) $(0, 1)$ (B) $(0, 1)$ (C) $(0, 1)$ (D) $(1, 0)$ (E) $(-1, 0)$ (F) $(-1, 0)$

5. (A) y decreases from 1 to 0   (B) y decreases from 0 to -1
    (C) y increases from -1 to 0   (D) y increases from 0 to 1
    (E) y decreases from 1 to 0

6. (A) y increases from 0 to 1   (B) y decreases from 1 to 0
    (C) y decreases from 0 to -1 (D) y increases from -1 to 0
    (E) y increases from 0 to 1

7. (A) y decreases from 0 to -1 (B) y increases from -1 to 0
    (C) y increases from 0 to 1   (D) y decreases from 1 to 0
    (E) y decreases from 0 to -1

8. (A) y decreases from 1 to 0   (B) y decreases from 0 to -1
    (C) y increases from -1 to 0   (D) y increases from 0 to 1
    (E) y decreases from 1 to 0

9. $\pi/2,\ 5\pi/2$ **10.** $0,\ 2\pi,\ 4\pi$ **11.** $\pi/4,\ 5\pi/4,\ 9\pi/4,\ 13\pi/4$

12. $3\pi/4,\ 7\pi/4,\ 11\pi/4,\ 15\pi/4$ **13.** $0,\ 2\pi,\ 4\pi$ **14.** $3\pi/2,\ 7\pi/2$

15. $-7\pi/4,\ -5\pi/4,\ \pi/4,\ 3\pi/4$ **16.** $-5\pi/4,\ -3\pi/4,\ 3\pi/4,\ 5\pi/4$

17. $-2\pi,\ -\pi,\ 0,\ \pi,\ 2\pi$ **18.** $-3\pi/2,\ -\pi/2,\ \pi/2,\ 3\pi/2$

19. $-2\pi,\ -\pi,\ 0,\ \pi,\ 2\pi$ **20.** $-\frac{3\pi}{2},\ -\frac{\pi}{2},\ \frac{\pi}{2},\ \frac{3\pi}{2}$

21. $-\frac{3\pi}{2},\ -\frac{\pi}{2},\ \frac{\pi}{2},\ \frac{3\pi}{2}$ **22.** $-2\pi,\ -\pi,\ 0,\ \pi,\ 2\pi$

23. -1.493 **24.** 1.904 **25.** -12.20 **26.** 0.9654

27. -0.4872 **28.** -196.1 **29.** $P(-0.342, -0.940)$; quadrant III

30. $P(0.529, -0.849)$; quadrant IV   **31.** $P(0.345, -0.939)$; quadrant IV

32. $P(-0.163, 0.987)$; quadrant II   **33.** $\frac{1}{2}$ **34.** $\frac{\sqrt{2}}{2}$

35. 1 **36.** -1 **37.** -2 **38.** -2

39. All are 0.7015

40. $\sin(x + 2\pi) = \sin(x - 2\pi) = \sin(x + 50\pi) = \sin(x - 66\pi) = -0.1377$

41. (A) Both are 0.540 (B) Both are 0.965 (C) Both are 0.292 (D) Both are -0.955

42. (A) Both -0.841 (B) Both -0.789 (C) Both -0.602 (D) Both 0.954

43. (A) Both are 0.827 (B) Both are 0.572 (C) Both are 0.0506 (D) Both are 0.540

44. (A) Both 0.080 (B) Both 0.034 (C) Both 0.165 (D) Both 0.090

45. (A) (5);   (B) (9);   (C) (1)   **46.** (A) (4);   (B) (9);   (C) (2)

47. $\sec x$ **48.** $\csc x$ **49.** 1 **50.** 1

51. $\cot^2 x$ **52.** $\cot^2 x$ **53.** $-\sin x$ **54.** $-\tan x$

55. 2π **56.** 2π **59.** True   **60.** True

61. True   **62.** False   **63.** origin   **64.** origin

65. origin   **66.** y axis

67.

x	0.05	0.15	0.25	0.35	0.45
$x - (x^3/6)$	0.04998	0.1494	0.2474	0.3429	0.4348
$\sin x$	0.04998	0.1494	0.2474	0.3429	0.4350

68.

x	0.05	0.15	0.25	0.35	0.45
$1 - x^2/2$	0.9988	0.9888	0.9688	0.9388	0.8988
$\cos x$	0.9988	0.9888	0.9689	0.9394	0.9004

69. $a_1 = 0.5$, $a_2 = 1.377583$, $a_3 = 1.569596$, $a_4 = 1.570796$, $a_5 = 1.570796$;
$\dfrac{\pi}{2} = 1.570796$
The sequence appears to approach $\pi/2$ as n increases.

70. $a_1 = 1$, $a_2 = 1.540302$, $a_3 = 1.570792$, $a_4 = 1.570796$, $a_5 = 1.570796$; $\dfrac{\pi}{2} = 1.570796$
The sequence appears to approach $\pi/2$ as n increases.

Exercise 6-6

1. 2π, π, 2π **2.** 2π, π, 2π

3. (A) 1 unit   (B) Indefinitely far   (C) Indefinitely far

4. (A) 1 unit   (B) Indefinitely far   (C) Indefinitely far

5. (A) -2π, $-\pi$, 0, π, 2π (B) $-3\pi/2$, $-\pi/2$, $\pi/2$, $3\pi/2$ (C) No x intercepts

6. (A) $-3\pi/2$, $-\pi/2$, $\pi/2$, $3\pi/2$ (B) -2π, $-\pi$, 0, π, 2π (C) No x intercepts

7. $y = \cot x$, $y = \csc x$ **8.** $y = \tan x$, $y = \sec x$

9. (A) No vertical asymptotes   (B) $-3\pi/2$, $-\pi/2$, $\pi/2$, $3\pi/2$ (C) -2π, $-\pi$, 0, π, 2π

10. (A) No vertical asymptotes   (B) -2π, $-\pi$, 0, π, 2π (C) $-3\pi/2$, $-\pi/2$, $\pi/2$, $3\pi/2$

11. (A) $y = \cos x$ (B) $y = \tan x$ (C) $y = \csc x$

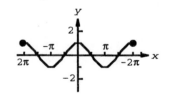
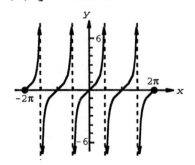
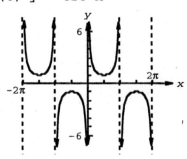

12. (A) $y = \sin x$ (B) $y = \cot x$ (C) $y = \sec x$

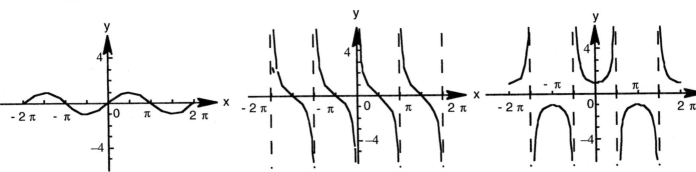

13. (A) A shift of $\pi/2$ to the left will transform the cosecant graph into the secant graph. [The answer is not unique—see part (B).]   (B) The graph of $y = -\csc(x - \pi/2)$ is a $\pi/2$ shift to the right and a reflection in the x axis of the graph of $y = \csc x$. The result is the graph of $y = \sec x$.

14. (A) A shift of $\pi/2$ to the right will transform the secant graph into the cosecant graph. [The answer is not unique—see part (B).]

(B) The graph of $y = -\sec(x + \pi/2)$ is a $\pi/2$ shift to the left and a reflection in the x axis of the graph of $y = \sec x$. The result is the graph of $y = \csc x$.

15. (A)

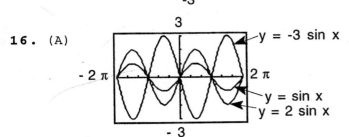

(B) No

(C) 1 unit; 2 units; 3 units

(D) The deviation of the graph from the x axis is changed by changing A. The deviation appears to be $|A|$.

16. (A)

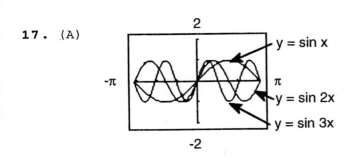

(B) No

(C) 1 unit; 2 units; 3 units

(D) The deviation of the graph from the x axis is changed by changing A. The deviation appears to be $|A|$.

17. (A)

(B) 1; 2; 3

(C) n

18. (A)

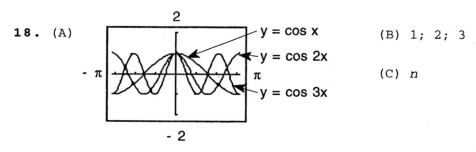

(B) 1; 2; 3

(C) n

19. (A)

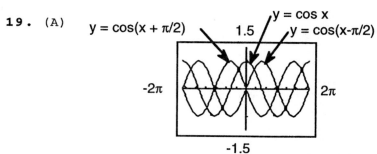

(B) The graph of $y = \cos x$ is shifted $|C|$ units to the right if $C < 0$ and $|C|$ units to the left if $C > 0$.

20. (A)

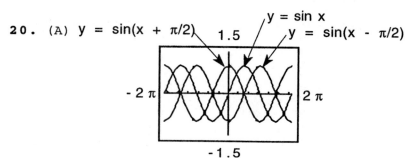

(B) The graph of $y = \sin x$ is shifted $|C|$ units to the right if $C < 0$ and $|C|$ units to the left if $C > 0$.

21. True   **22.** True   **23.** False   **24.** True

25. For each case, the number is not in the domain of the function and an error message of some type will appear.

26. For each case, the number is not in the domain of the function and an error message of some type will appear.

27. (A) Both graphs are almost indistinguishable the closer x is to the origin.

(B)

x	-0.3	-0.2	-0.1	0.0	0.1	0.2	0.3
$\sin x$	-0.296	-0.199	-0.100	0.000	0.100	0.199	0.296

28. (A) Both graphs are almost indistinguishable the closer x is to the origin.

(B)

x	-0.3	-0.2	-0.1	0.0	0.1	0.2	0.3
$\tan x$	-0.309	-0.203	-0.100	0.000	0.100	0.203	0.309

Exercise 6-7

1. $A = 3$, $P = 2\pi$

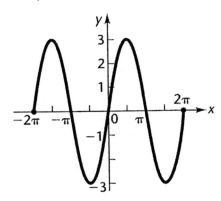

2. $A = \dfrac{1}{4}$, $P = 2\pi$

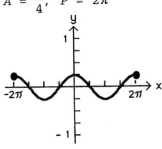

3. $|A| = \dfrac{1}{2}$ $P = 2\pi$

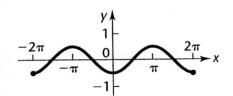

4. $A = 2$, $P = 2\pi$

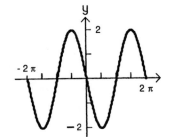

5. $A = 1$, $P = \dfrac{2\pi}{3}$

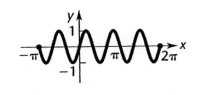

6. $y = \cos 2x$, $-\pi \le x \le \pi$
Amplitude = 1
$$\text{Period} = \frac{2\pi}{2} = \pi$$

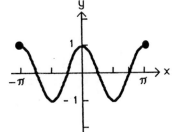

7. $A = 1$ $P = 2\pi \div \left(\dfrac{1}{2}\right) = 4\pi$

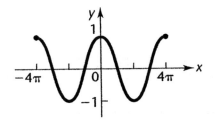

8. $y = \sin\left(\dfrac{x}{3}\right)$, $-6\pi \le x \le 6\pi$
Amplitude = 1
$$\text{Period} = \frac{2\pi}{\frac{1}{3}} = 6\pi$$

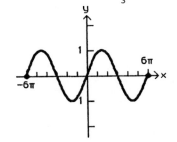

9. $A = 1$ $P = \dfrac{2\pi}{\pi} = 2$

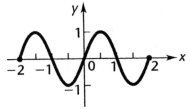

10. $y = \cos(\pi x)$, $-2 \leq x \leq 2$

Amplitude = 1

Period = $\dfrac{2\pi}{\pi} = 2$

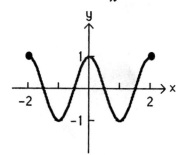

11. $A = 3$ $\quad P = \dfrac{2\pi}{2} = \pi$

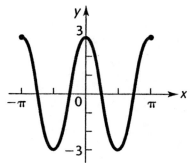

12. $y = 2\sin 4x$, $-\pi \leq x \leq \pi$

Amplitude = 2

Period = $\dfrac{2\pi}{4} = \dfrac{\pi}{2}$

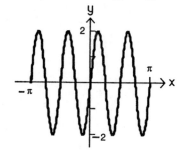

13. $A = \dfrac{1}{2}$ $\quad P = \dfrac{2\pi}{2\pi} = 1$

The graph of $-\dfrac{1}{2}\sin 2\pi x$ is the graph of $\dfrac{1}{2}\sin 2\pi x$ turned upside down.

14. $y = -\dfrac{1}{3}\cos 2\pi x$, $-2 \leq x \leq 2$

Amplitude = $\dfrac{1}{3}$

Period = $\dfrac{2\pi}{2\pi} = 1$

15. $A = 3$ $\quad P = 2\pi \div \left(\dfrac{1}{2}\right) = 4\pi$

The graph of $-3\cos \dfrac{x}{2}$ is the graph of $3\cos \dfrac{x}{2}$ turned upside down.

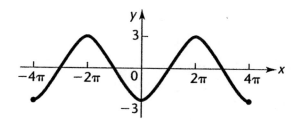

16. $y = -\dfrac{1}{4} \sin\left(\dfrac{x}{2}\right), \quad -4\pi \le x \le 4\pi$

Amplitude $= \dfrac{1}{4}$

Period $= \dfrac{2\pi}{\frac{1}{2}} = 4\pi$

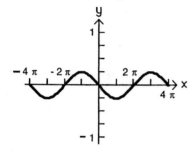

17. The graph is the same as the graph of $y = 2 \sin \dfrac{\pi x}{2}$ shifted 2 units up.

$A = 2, \quad P = 4$

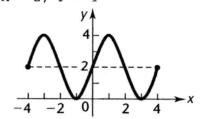

18. $y = 3 + 3 \cos\left(\dfrac{\pi x}{2}\right), \quad -4 \le x \le 4$

Amplitude $= 3$

Period $= \dfrac{2\pi}{\frac{\pi}{2}} = 4$

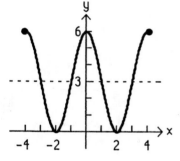

19. The graph is the same as the graph of $y = 2 \cos \dfrac{x}{2}$, turned upside down and shifted up 4 units.

$A = 2 \qquad P = 2\pi \div \dfrac{1}{2} = 4\pi$

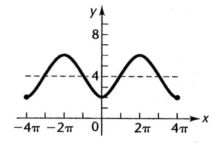

20. $y = 3 - 2 \sin\left(\dfrac{x}{2}\right), \quad -4\pi \le x \le 4\pi$

Amplitude $= 2$

Period $= \dfrac{2\pi}{\frac{1}{2}} = 4\pi$

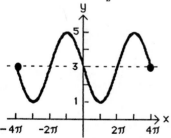

21. $A = 3 \quad P = \dfrac{\pi}{2} = \dfrac{2\pi}{4}; \quad B = 4, \quad y = 3 \sin 4x, \quad -\dfrac{\pi}{4} \le x \le \dfrac{\pi}{2}$

22. Amplitude $= \dfrac{1}{4}$ and period $= 8\pi \Rightarrow y = \dfrac{1}{4} \sin\left(\dfrac{x}{4}\right), \quad -4\pi \le x \le 8\pi$

23. $|A| = 10$ $P = 2 = \dfrac{2\pi}{\pi}$; $B = \pi$, $A = -10$, $y = -10 \sin \pi x$ $-1 \leq x \leq 2$

24. Amplitude $= \dfrac{1}{2}$ and period $= 4 \Rightarrow y = -\dfrac{1}{2} \sin \left(\dfrac{\pi x}{2}\right)$, $-2 \leq x \leq 4$

25. $A = 5$ $P = 8\pi = 2\pi \cdot 4 = 2\pi \div \dfrac{1}{4}$; $B = \dfrac{1}{4}$, $y = 5 \cos \dfrac{1}{4}x$ $-4\pi \leq x \leq 8\pi$

26. Amplitude $= 0.1$ and period $= \dfrac{\pi}{4} \Rightarrow y = 0.1 \cos 8x$, $-\dfrac{\pi}{8} \leq x \leq \dfrac{\pi}{4}$

27. $|A| = 0.5$, $P = 8 = 2\pi \cdot \dfrac{4}{\pi} = 2\pi \div \dfrac{\pi}{4}$; $B = \dfrac{\pi}{4}$, $A = -0.5$, $y = -0.5 \cos \dfrac{\pi x}{4}$, $-4 \leq x \leq 8$

28. Amplitude $= 1$ and period $= \dfrac{1}{2} \Rightarrow y = -\cos(4\pi x)$, $-0.25 \leq x \leq 0.5$

29. $y = \cos 2x$ **30.** $y = \dfrac{1}{2} \sin 2x$ **31.** $y = 1 - \cos 2x$ **32.** $y = 1 + \cos 2x$

33. $A = 1$, $P = 2\pi$, Phase shift $= -\pi$ **34.** $A = 1$, $P = 2\pi$, Phase shift $= \pi$

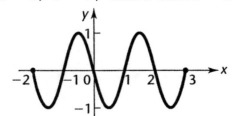

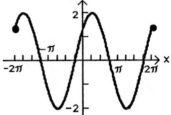

35. $A = \dfrac{1}{2}$, $P = 2\pi$, Phase shift $= \dfrac{\pi}{4}$ **36.** $A = 2$, $P = 2\pi$, Phase Shift $= -\dfrac{\pi}{4}$

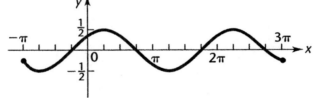

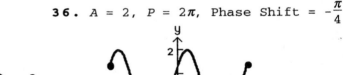

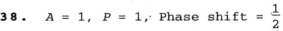

37. $A = 1$, $P = 2$, Phase shift $= 1$ **38.** $A = 1$, $P = 1$, Phase shift $= \dfrac{1}{2}$

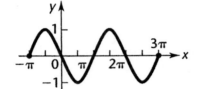

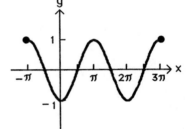

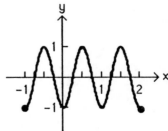

39. $A = 3$, $P = 2$, Phase shift $= -\dfrac{1}{2}$

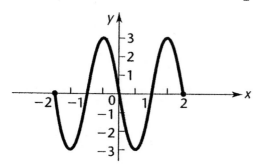

40. $A = 2$, $P = 2$, Phase shift $= \dfrac{1}{4}$

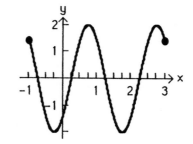

41.

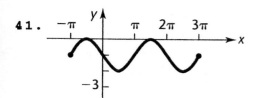

42.

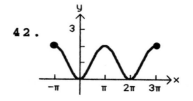

43.

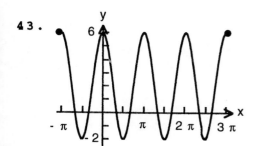

44.

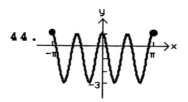

45. $y = -4 \sin\left(\dfrac{\pi}{2}x - \dfrac{\pi}{2}\right)$

46. $y = 4 \sin\left(\dfrac{\pi}{2}x + \dfrac{\pi}{2}\right)$

47. $y = \dfrac{1}{2}\cos\left(\dfrac{1}{4}x - \dfrac{3\pi}{4}\right)$

48. $y = -\dfrac{1}{2}\cos\left(\dfrac{x}{4} + \dfrac{\pi}{4}\right)$

49. 2; $y = 4\sin\left(2x + \dfrac{2\pi}{3}\right)$, $y = -4\sin\left(2x + \dfrac{2\pi}{3}\right)$

50. 2; $y = 8\cos\left(\dfrac{2\pi x}{5} - \dfrac{4\pi}{5}\right)$, $y = -8\cos\left(\dfrac{2\pi x}{5} - \dfrac{4\pi}{5}\right)$

51. $A = 3.5$, $P = 4$, Phase shift $= -0.5$

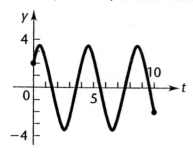

52. $A = 5.4$, $P = 5$, Phase shift $= 1$

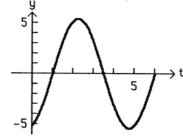

53. $A = 50$, $P = 1$, Phase shift = 0.25

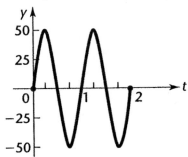

54. $A = 25$, $P = \frac{2}{5}$, Phase shift = 0.1

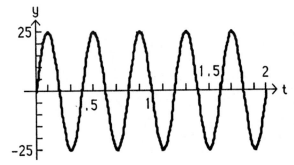

55. $y = 2 \sin(x + 0.785)$

56. $y = 2 \sin(x - 0.785)$

57. $y = 2 \sin(x - 0.524)$

58. $y = 2 \sin(x + 1.047)$

59. $y = 5 \sin(2x - 0.284)$

60. $y = 5 \sin(2x + 1.288)$

61. True   **62.** True

63. True   **64.** False

65.

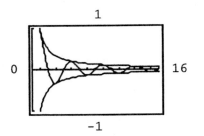

The amplitude is decreasing with time. This is often referred to as a *damped sine wave*. Examples are the vertical motion of a car after going over a bump (which is damped by the suspension system) and the slowing down of a pendulum that is released away from the vertical line of suspension (air resistance and friction).

66.

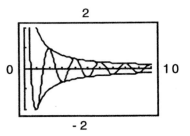

The amplitude is decreasing with time. This is often referred to as a **damped sine wave**. Examples are a car's vertical motion, which is damped by the suspension system after the car goes over a bump, and the slowing down of a pendulum that is released away from the vertical line of suspension (air resistance and friction).

67.

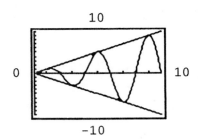

The amplitude is increasing with time. In physical and electrical systems this is referred to as *resonance*. Some examples are the swinging of a bridge during high winds and the movement of tall buildings during an earthquake. Some bridges and buildings are destroyed when the resonance reaches the elastic limits of the structure.

68.

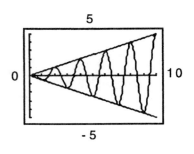

The amplitude is increasing with time. In physical and electrical systems this is referred to as **resonance**. Some examples are the swinging of a bridge during high winds and the movement of tall buildings during an earthquake. Some bridges and buildings are destroyed when the resonance reaches the elastic limits of the structure.

69.

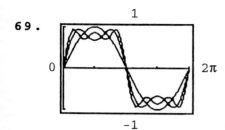

70.

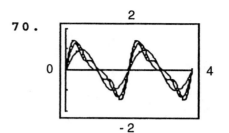

71. $A = \dfrac{1}{3}$

$P = \dfrac{2\pi}{8} = \dfrac{\pi}{4}$

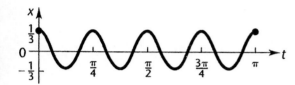

72. $I = 30 \sin 120t$

$A = 30, \quad P = \dfrac{2\pi}{120} = \dfrac{\pi}{60}, \quad f = \dfrac{60}{\pi} \text{ Hz}$

73. $y = -8 \cos 4\pi t$

74. $A = 110, \quad P = \dfrac{1}{60} = \dfrac{2\pi}{B} \Rightarrow B = 120\pi$

$E = 110 \cos(120\pi t)$

75. The graph shows the seasonal changes of sulfur dioxide pollutant in the atmosphere; more is produced during winter months because of increased heating.

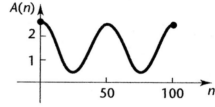

76. The graph shows the volume of air in the lungs t seconds after exhaling.

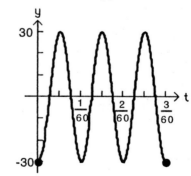

77. $A = 15, \quad P = \dfrac{1}{60},$ Phase shift $= -\dfrac{1}{240}$

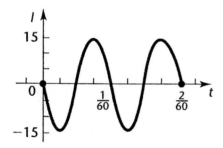

78. $A = 30, \quad P = \dfrac{1}{60},$ Phase shift $= \dfrac{1}{120}$

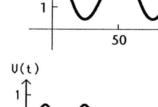

79.

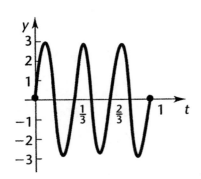

80.

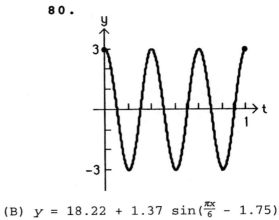

81. (A)

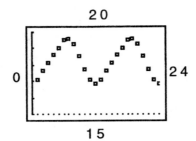

(B) $y = 18.22 + 1.37 \sin(\frac{\pi x}{6} - 1.75)$

(C)

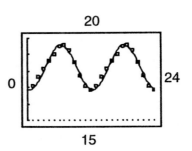

82. (A)

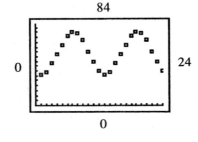

(B) $y = 53.5 + 22.5 \sin(\pi x/6 - 2.1)$

(C)

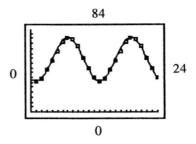

Exercise 6-8

1. Period = $\frac{\pi}{4}$

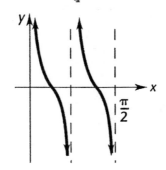

2. Period = $\frac{\pi}{2}$

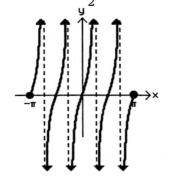

3. Period = $\frac{1}{8}$

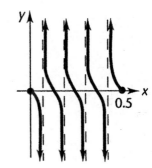

4. Period = $\frac{1}{2}$

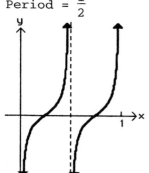

5. Period = 4π

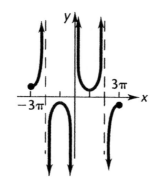

6. Period = 2

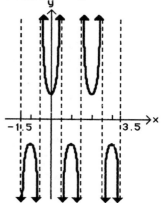

7. Period = 2

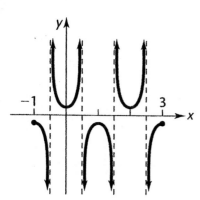

8. Period = 4π

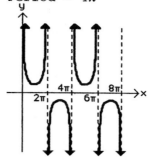

9. Period = π,
Phase shift = $-\frac{\pi}{2}$

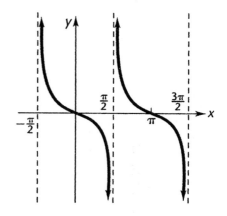

10. Period = π,
Phase shift = $\frac{\pi}{2}$

11. Period = $\frac{\pi}{2}$,
Phase shift = $-\frac{\pi}{2}$

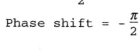

12. Period = $\frac{\pi}{2}$,
Phase shift = $\frac{\pi}{2}$

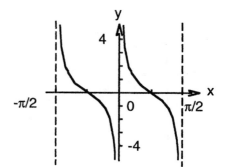

13. Period = 2, Phase shift = $-\dfrac{1}{2}$

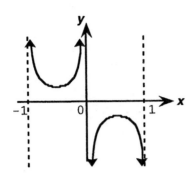

14. Period = 2, Phase shift = $\dfrac{1}{2}$

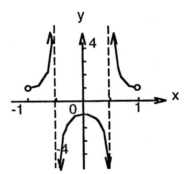

15. False

16. True

17. False

18. False

19. $y = 2 \cot 2x$

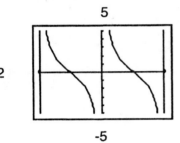

20. $y = 2 \csc 2x$

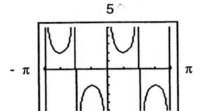

21. $y = \cot(x/2)$

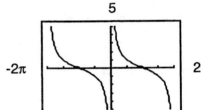

22. $y = \tan(x/2)$

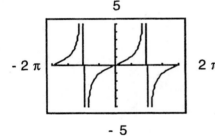

23. Period = 4, Phase shift = 1

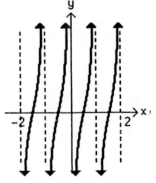

24. Period = 1, Phase shift = 1

25. Period = 4,
Phase shift = -1

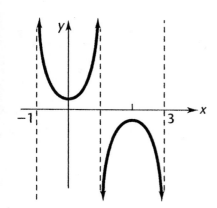

26. Period = 2,
Phase shift = $\frac{1}{2}$

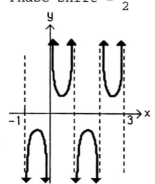

27. $y = \csc 3x$

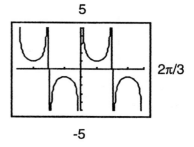

-2π/3 ... 2π/3

28. $y = \sec 2x$

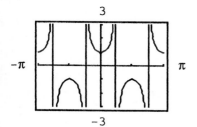

29. $y = \tan 2x$

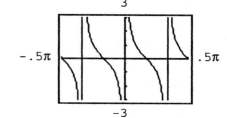

30. $y = \cot 3x$

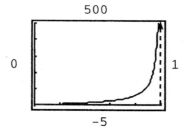

31. (A) $c = 20\sec(\pi t/2)$, [0, 1]
(B)

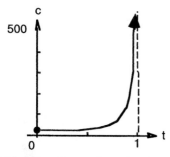

(C) The length of the light beam starts at 20 ft and increases slowly at first, then increases rapidly without end.

32. (A) $a = 20\tan(\pi t/2)$, [0, 1]
(B)

(C) The distance a starts at 0 and increases slowly at first, then increases rapidly without end.

Exercise 6-9

1. $\frac{\pi}{2}$ **2.** 0 **3.** $\frac{\pi}{3}$ **4.** $\frac{\pi}{6}$ **5.** $\frac{\pi}{3}$ **6.** $\frac{\pi}{4}$ **7.** $\frac{\pi}{4}$

8. $\frac{\pi}{3}$ **9.** 0 **10.** $\frac{\pi}{6}$ **11.** $\frac{\pi}{6}$ **12.** 0 **13.** 0.6064 **14.** 0.5974

15. 1.563 **16.** 1.558 **17.** Not defined **18.** 1.454 **19.** $\frac{5\pi}{6}$ **20.** Not defined

21. $\frac{-\pi}{4}$ **22.** $\frac{3\pi}{4}$ **23.** $\frac{-\pi}{6}$ **24.** $\frac{-\pi}{6}$ **25.** 25 **26.** -0.6 **27.** $\frac{1}{2}$

28. $\sqrt{3}$ **29.** -0.9810   **30.** 1.001 **31.** 2.645 **32.** 2.456   **33.** -45°

34. 120° **35.** -60° **36.** -45° **37.** 180° **38.** -90° **39.** 43.51°   **40.** 85.40°

41. -21.48°   **42.** 157.01°

43. $\sin^{-1}(\sin 2) = 1.1416 \neq 2$. For the identity $\sin^{-1}(\sin x) = x$ to hold, x must be in the restricted domain of the sine function; that is, $-\dfrac{\pi}{2} \leq x \leq \dfrac{\pi}{2}$. The number 2 is not in the restricted domain.

44. $\cos^{-1}[\cos(-0.5)] = 0.5$. For the identity $\cos^{-1}(\cos x) = x$ to hold, x must be in the restricted domain of the cosine function; that is, $0 \leq x \leq \pi$. The number -0.5 is not in the restricted domain.

45.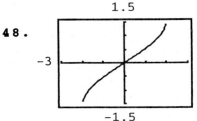

46.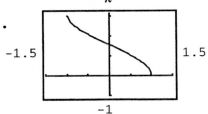

47.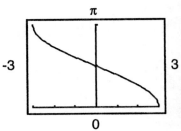

48.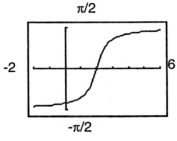

49.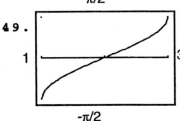

50.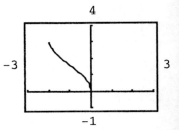

51.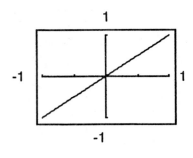

52.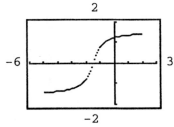

53. (A)

(B) The domain of $\cos^{-1}$ is restricted to $-1 \leq x \leq 1$; hence no graph will appear for other x.

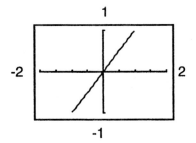

54. (A)

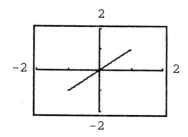

(B) The graph is the same. The domain of the inverse sine is the interval [-1, 1].

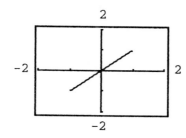

55. $\dfrac{\sqrt{2}}{2}$

56. 0

57. $\dfrac{1}{2}$

58. -1, 1

59. $\sqrt{1 - x^2}$

60. $\sqrt{1 - x^2}$

61. $\dfrac{1}{\sqrt{1 + x^2}}$

62. $\dfrac{x}{\sqrt{1 - x^2}}$

63. $f^{-1}(x) = 3 + \cos^{-1}\dfrac{x - 4}{2}$; $2 \le x \le 6$

64. $f^{-1}(x) = 1 + \sin^{-1}\dfrac{x - 3}{5}$; $2 \le x \le 8$

65. (A)

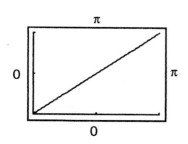

(B) The domain for cos x is $(-\infty, \infty)$ and the range is [-1, 1], which is the domain for $\cos^{-1} x$. Thus, $y = \cos^{-1}(\cos x)$ has a graph over the interval $(-\infty, \infty)$, but $\cos^{-1}(\cos x) = x$ only on the restricted domain of cos x, [0, π].

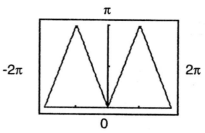

66. (A)

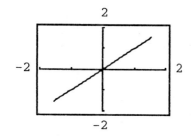

(B) The domain for sin x is $(-\infty, \infty)$ and the range is [-1, 1], which is the domain for $\sin^{-1} x$. Thus, $y = \sin^{-1}(\sin x)$ has a graph over the interval $(-\infty, \infty)$, but $\sin^{-1}(\sin x) = x$ only on the restricted domain of sin x, $[-\pi/2, \pi/2]$.

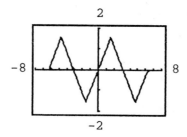

67. 75.38°; 24.41°

68. 103.68°; 34.35°

69. (A)

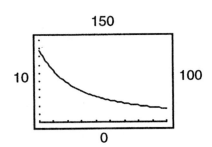

(B) 59.44 mm

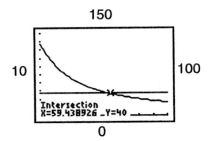

70. (A)

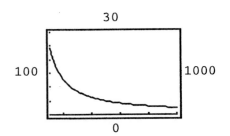

(B)

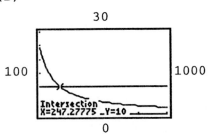

71. 21.59 inches   **72.** 35.81 inches

73. (A)

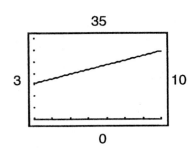

(B) 7.22 inches

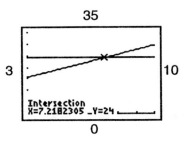

74. (A)

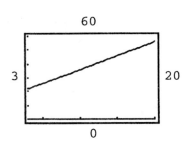

(B) 10.10 inches

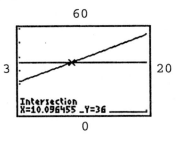

75. (B) 76.10 feet   **76.** 46.36 feet

CHAPTER 6 REVIEW

1. 2.5 radians (*6-1*)

2. 7.5 centimeters (*6-1*)

3. α = 54.8°, a = 16.5 ft, b = 11.6 ft (*6-2*)

4. (A) $\frac{\pi}{3}$ (B) 60° (C) $\frac{\pi}{6}$ (D) 30° (*6-2, 6-4*)

5. (A) III, IV (B) II, III (C) II, IV (*6-3*)

6. (A) $-\dfrac{3}{5}$ (B) $\dfrac{5}{4}$ (C) $-\dfrac{4}{3}$ (*6-3*)

7.

$\theta°$	θ rad	$\sin\theta$	$\cos\theta$	$\tan\theta$	$\csc\theta$	$\sec\theta$	$\cot\theta$
0°	0	0	1	0	ND*	1	ND
30°	$\pi/6$	1/2	$\sqrt{3}/2$	$1/\sqrt{3}$	2	$2/\sqrt{3}$	$\sqrt{3}$
45°	$\pi/4$	$1/\sqrt{2}$	$1/\sqrt{2}$	1	$\sqrt{2}$	$\sqrt{2}$	1
60°	$\pi/3$	$\sqrt{3}/2$	1/2	$\sqrt{3}$	$2/\sqrt{3}$	2	$1/\sqrt{3}$
90°	$\pi/2$	1	0	ND	1	ND	0
180°	π	0	-1	0	ND	-1	ND
270°	$3\pi/2$	-1	0	ND	-1	ND	0
360°	2π	0	1	0	ND	1	ND

*ND = not defined (*6-4*)

8. (A) 2π (B) 2π (C) π (*6-6*)

9. (A) Domain = $(-\infty, \infty)$, range = $[-1, 1]$

(B) Domain is set of all real numbers except $x = \dfrac{2k+1}{2}\pi$, k an integer, Range = all real numbers (*6-6*)

10.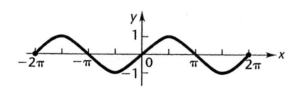

(*6-6*)

11.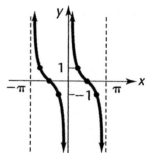

(*6-6*)

12. The central angle in a circle subtended by an arc of half the length of the radius. (*6-1*)

13. If the graph of $y = \sin x$ is shifted $\dfrac{\pi}{2}$ units to the left, the result will be the graph of $y = \cos x$. (*6-6, 6-7*)

14. 78.50° (*6-1*)

15. $\alpha = 49.7°$; $\beta = 40.3°$; $c = 20.6$ cm (*6-2*)

16. (A) II (B) Quadrantal (C) III (*6-1*)

17. (A) and (C) (*6-1*)   **18.** (B) and (C) (*6-3, 6-5*)

19. (A) $\dfrac{\pi}{2}, \dfrac{3\pi}{2}$ (B) $0, \pi$ (C) $0, \pi$ (*6-3, 6-5*)

20. Since the coordinates of a point on a unit circle are given by $P(a, b) = P(\cos x, \sin x)$, we evaluate $P(\cos(-8.305), \sin(-8.305))$--using a calculator set in radian mode--to obtain $P(-0.436, -0.900)$. Note that $x = -8.305$, since P is moving clockwise. The quadrant in which $P(a, b)$ lies can be determined by the signs of a and b. In this case P is in the third quadrant, since a is negative and b is negative. (*6-5*)

21. $-\dfrac{1}{2}$ (*6-4*)   **22.** $\dfrac{1}{\sqrt{2}}$ or $\dfrac{\sqrt{2}}{2}$ (*6-4*)

23. -1 $(6-4)$

24. $\dfrac{1}{\sqrt{3}}$ or $\dfrac{\sqrt{3}}{3}$ $(6-4)$

25. $\dfrac{\pi}{2}$ $(6-4,\ 6-9)$

26. $\dfrac{-\pi}{2}$ $(6-4,\ 6-9)$

27. $\dfrac{\pi}{4}$ $(6-4,\ 6-9)$

28. $\dfrac{-\pi}{3}$ $(6-4,\ 6-9)$

29. Not defined $(6-4,\ 6-9)$

30. $\dfrac{2\pi}{3}$ $(6-4,\ 6-9)$

31. $\dfrac{\pi}{3}$ $(6-4,\ 6-9)$

32. Not defined $(6-4,\ 6-9)$

33. $\dfrac{2}{3}$ $(6-4,\ 6-9)$

34. $\dfrac{5\pi}{6}$ $(6-4,\ 6-9)$

35. $\sqrt{5}$ $(6-4,\ 6-9)$

36. $\dfrac{\sqrt{7}}{4}$ $(6-4,\ 6-9)$

37. 0.4431 $(6-3)$ **38.** -15.17 $(6-3)$

39. -2.077 $(6-3,\ 6-5)$ **40.** -0.9750 $(6-2,\ 6-9)$ **41.** Not defined $(6-2,\ 6-9)$

42. 1.557 $(6-2,\ 6-9)$ **43.** 1.095 $(6-9)$ **44.** Not defined $(6-9)$

45. (A) $\theta = -30°$ (B) $\theta = 120°$ $(6-9)$

46. (A) $\Theta = 151.20°$ (B) $\Theta = 82.28°$ $(6-9)$

47. $\cos^{-1}[\cos(-2)] = 2$ For the identity $\cos^{-1}(\cos x) = x$ to hold, x must be in the restricted domain of the cosine function; that is, $0 \le x \le \pi$. The number -2 is not in the restricted domain. $(6-9)$

48. $A = 2$, $P = 2$

49.

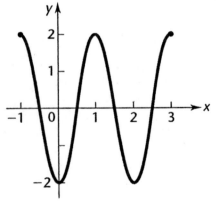

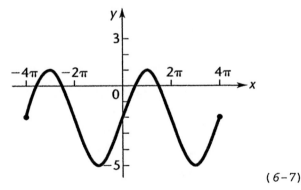

$(6-7)$

$(6-7)$

50. $y = 6 \cos 2x$; $-\dfrac{\pi}{2} \le x \le \pi$ $(6-7)$

51. $y = -0.5 \sin \pi x$; $-1 \le x \le 2$ $(6-7)$

52. If the graph of $y = \tan x$ is shifted $\dfrac{\pi}{2}$ units to the right and reflected in the x axis, the result will be the graph of $y = \cot x$. $(6-6,\ 6-7)$

53. (A) $\cos x$ (B) $\tan^2 x$ $(6-5)$

54.

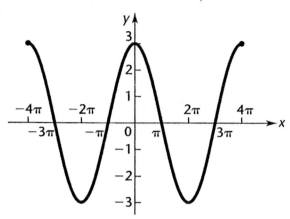

$(6-7)$

55. $A = 2$, $P = 4$,
Phase shift $= \frac{1}{2}$ $(6-7)$

56. Domain $= [-1, 1]$
Range $= [0, \pi]$

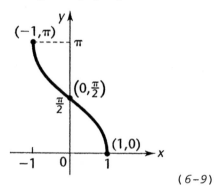

$(6-9)$

57. $y = \frac{1}{2} \cos 2x + \frac{1}{2}$

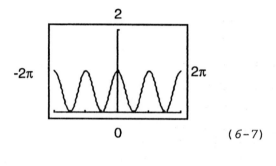

$(6-7)$

58. (A) $y = \tan x$

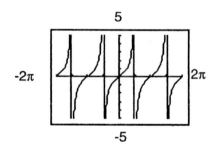

(B) $y = \cot x$

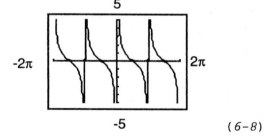

$(6-8)$

59. (A) 2.5 rad (B) $(-6.41, 4.79)$ $(6-1, 6-3)$ **60.** (A) $\frac{2\pi}{3}$ (B) $\frac{5\pi}{4}$ $(6-5)$

61.

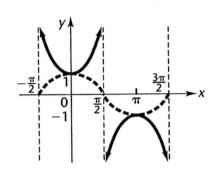

(6-6)

62.

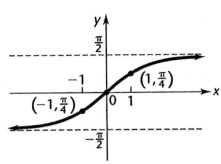

Domain = all real numbers

Range = $\left(-\dfrac{\pi}{2},\ \dfrac{\pi}{2}\right)$

(6-6)

63. Phase Shift = $-\dfrac{1}{2}$; Period $P = 1$ *(6-8)*

64. Phase shift = $\dfrac{\pi}{2}$; Period = 4π *(6-8)*

65. (A) sine has origin symmetry   (B) cosine has y axis symmetry
(C) tangent has origin symmetry   *(6-6)*

66. $\dfrac{1}{\sqrt{1 - x^2}}$ *(6-9)*

67. For each case, the number is not in the domain of the function and an error
message of some type will appear.   *(6-5, 6-9)*

68. $y = 2\,\sin\left(\pi x + \dfrac{\pi}{4}\right)$ *(6-7)*   **69.** True   *(6-1)*   **70.** True   *(6-2)*

71. False   *(6-3)*   **72.** False   *(6-5)*   **73.** True   *(6-5)*

74. False   *(6-9)*   **75.** False   *(6-7)*   **76.** True   *(6-7)*

77. $y = 2\,\sin(2x + 0.928)$

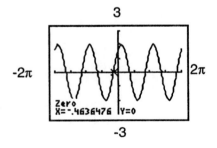

(6-7)

78. (A)

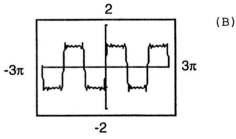

(B)

(6-7)

79. $\frac{2\pi}{5}$ radians   *(6-1)*   **80.** 28.3 cm   *(6-2)*   **81.** $I = 30 \cos 120\pi t$ *(6-7)*

82. (A) $L = 10 \csc \theta + 15 \sec \theta;\ 0 < \theta < \frac{\pi}{2}$

(B) θ radians	0.4	0.5	0.6	0.7	0.8	0.9	1.0
L feet	42.0	38.0	35.9	35.1	35.5	36.9	39.6

35 feet is the length of the longest log that can make the corner.

(C) Length of longest log that can make the corner is 35.1 feet.

(D) Length L increases without bound.

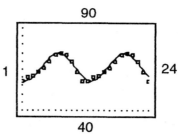

     (6-2, 6-5)

83. (A) $R(t) = 4 - 3 \cos \frac{\pi}{6} t$.

(B) The graph shows the seasonal changes in soft drink consumption. Most is consumed in August and the least in February.   *(6-7)*

84. (A)

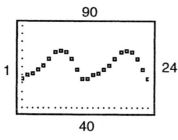

(C)

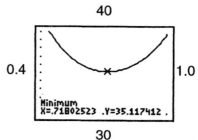

(B) $y = 66.5 + 8.5 \sin\left(\frac{\pi}{6} x - 2.4\right)$

     (6-7)

CHAPTER 7

Exercise 7-1

25.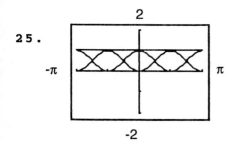

26.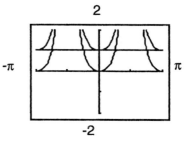

27.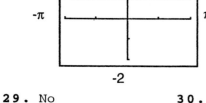

28.

29. No   **30.** Yes   **31.** Yes   **32.** No

33. No   **34.** No   **35.** No   **36.** No

65. Not an identity   **66.** Not an identity   **67.** An identity

68. An identity   **69.** Not an identity   **70.** Not an identity

71. An identity   **72.** An identity   **73.** An identity

74. An identity   **75.** Not an identity   **76.** Not an identity

83. $g(x) = \cot x$ **84.** $g(x) = \tan x$ **85.** $g(x) = -1 + \csc x$

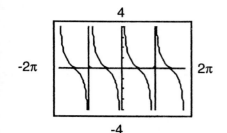 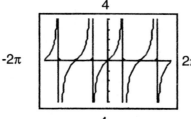

86. $g(x) = 1 + \sec x$ **87.** $g(x) = 3 \cos x$ **88.** $g(x) = 2 \sin x$

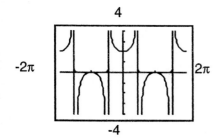 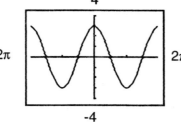

89. III, IV   **90.** QI or QIV   **91.** I, II

92. QII or QIII   **93.** All quadrants   **94.** QI, II, III, IV

95. I, IV   **96.** QII, III   **97.** $a \cos x$

98. $a \sin x$ **99.** $a \sec x$ **100.** $a \csc x$

Exercise 7-2

1. Yes   **2.** Yes   **3.** No   **4.** Yes

5. Yes   **6.** No   **7.** No   **8.** Yes

9. Yes   **10.** Yes   **15.** $\dfrac{\sqrt{2}}{2}(\cos x - \sin x)$

16. $\dfrac{1}{2}(\sqrt{3}\sin x + \cos x)$ **17.** $\dfrac{\sqrt{3} + \tan x}{1 - \sqrt{3}\tan x}$ **18.** $-\cos x$ **19.** $-\cos x$

20. $\dfrac{\tan x - 1}{1 + \tan x}$ **21.** $\dfrac{\sqrt{2}}{2}$ **22.** $\dfrac{\sqrt{3}}{2}$ **23.** $\dfrac{\sqrt{3}}{3}$

24. $\sqrt{3}$ **25.** $\dfrac{\sqrt{2}}{4}(\sqrt{3} - 1)$ **26.** $\dfrac{\sqrt{2}}{4}(\sqrt{3} + 1)$ **27.** $-\dfrac{\sqrt{2}}{4}(1 + \sqrt{3})$

28. $\dfrac{\sqrt{2}}{4}(1 - \sqrt{3})$ **29.** $\sin(x - y) = \dfrac{-3 - 4\sqrt{8}}{15}$; $\tan(x + y) = \dfrac{4\sqrt{8} - 3}{4 + 3\sqrt{8}}$

30. $\sin(x - y) = \dfrac{-2 - 5\sqrt{3}}{12}$; $\tan(x + y) = \dfrac{-2 + 5\sqrt{3}}{\sqrt{5} + 2\sqrt{15}}$

31. $\sin(x - y) = \dfrac{-2}{\sqrt{5}}$; $\tan(x + y) = \dfrac{2}{11}$

32. $\sin(x - y) = \dfrac{-4\sqrt{2} - 1}{3\sqrt{5}}$; $\tan(x + y) = \dfrac{1 - 4\sqrt{2}}{2 + 2\sqrt{2}}$

46. $\dfrac{\sin(x + h) - \sin x}{h} = \sin x\left(\dfrac{\cos h - 1}{h}\right) + \cos x\left(\dfrac{\sin h}{h}\right)$

47. -0.3685, -0.3685; 0.9771, 0.9771   **48.** 0.6115, -1.155

49. -0.4429, -0.4429; -2.682, -2.682   **50.** 0.9756, -0.4895

51. Evaluate each side for a particular set of values of x and y for which each side is defined. If the left side is not equal to the right side, then the equation is not an identity. For example, for $x = 2$ and $y = 1$, both sides are defined, but are not equal.

52. Evaluate each side for a particular set of values of x and y for which each side is defined. If the left side is not equal to the right side, then the equation is not an identity. For example, for $x = 2$ and $y = 1$, both sides are defined, but are not equal.

53. $y_1 = \sin(x + \pi/6)$

$y_2 = \dfrac{\sqrt{3}}{2}\sin x + \dfrac{1}{2}\cos x$

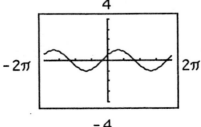

54. $y_1 = \sin(x - \pi/3)$

$y_2 = \dfrac{1}{2}\sin x - \dfrac{\sqrt{3}}{2}\cos x$

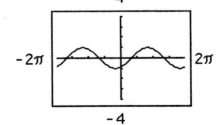

55. $y_1 = \cos(x - 3\pi/4)$

$y_2 = -\dfrac{\sqrt{2}}{2}\cos x + \dfrac{\sqrt{2}}{2}\sin x$

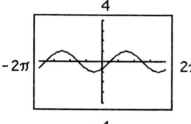

56. $y_1 = \cos(x + 5\pi/6)$

$y_2 = -\dfrac{\sqrt{3}}{2}\cos x - \dfrac{1}{2}\sin x$

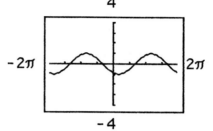

57. $y_1 = \tan(x + 2\pi/3)$

$y_2 = \dfrac{\tan x - \sqrt{3}}{1 + \sqrt{3}\,\tan x}$

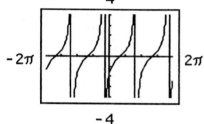

58. $y_1 = \tan(x - \pi/4)$

$y_2 = \dfrac{\tan x - 1}{1 + \tan x}$

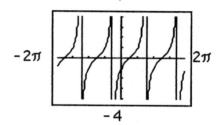

59. $\dfrac{24}{25}$ **60.** 1

61. $-\dfrac{1}{2}$ **62.** -1

63. $xy + \sqrt{1 - x^2}\,\sqrt{1 - y^2}$

64. $y\sqrt{1 - x^2} + x\sqrt{1 - y^2}$

67. $y_1 = \cos 1.2x \cos 0.8x -$
              $\sin 1.2x \sin 0.8x$

$y_2 = \cos 2x$

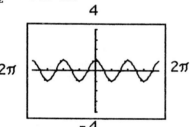

68. $y_1 = \sin 0.8x \cos 0.3x -$
              $\cos 0.8x \sin 0.3x$

$y_2 = \sin 0.5x$

70. $45°$ **72.** $18°$

73. (C) 3,510 ft

Exercise   7-3

1. $\dfrac{1}{2} = \dfrac{1}{2}$ **2.** $1 = 1$ **3.** $-\sqrt{3} = -\sqrt{3}$ **4.** $\sqrt{3} = \sqrt{3}$

5. $1 = 1$ **6.** $\dfrac{\sqrt{2}}{2} = \dfrac{\sqrt{2}}{2}$ **7.** $2 - \sqrt{3}$ **8.** $\dfrac{\sqrt{2} - \sqrt{3}}{2}$

9. $-\dfrac{\sqrt{2} - \sqrt{2}}{2}$ **10.** $1 - \sqrt{2}$

11.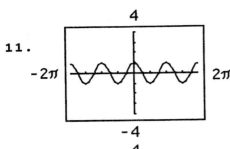

12.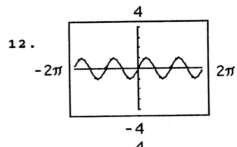

13.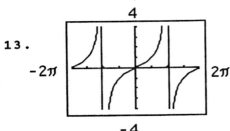

14.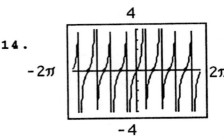

29. No   **30.** No   **31.** Yes   **32.** No   **33.** No   **34.** Yes

35. $\sin 2x = -\dfrac{24}{25}$, $\cos 2x = \dfrac{7}{25}$, $\tan 2x = -\dfrac{24}{7}$

36. $\sin 2x = -\dfrac{24}{25}$, $\cos 2x = \dfrac{7}{25}$, $\tan 2x = -\dfrac{24}{7}$

37. $\sin 2x = -\dfrac{120}{169}$, $\cos 2x = \dfrac{119}{169}$, $\tan 2x = -\dfrac{120}{119}$

38. $\sin 2x = -\dfrac{120}{169}$, $\cos 2x = -\dfrac{119}{169}$, $\tan 2x = \dfrac{120}{119}$

39. $\sin \dfrac{1}{2}x = \sqrt{\dfrac{3 + 2\sqrt{2}}{6}}$, $\cos \dfrac{1}{2}x = -\sqrt{\dfrac{3 - 2\sqrt{2}}{6}}$, $\tan \dfrac{1}{2}x = -3 - 2\sqrt{2}$

40. $\sin \dfrac{x}{2} = \dfrac{\sqrt{10}}{4}$, $\cos \dfrac{x}{2} = \dfrac{-\sqrt{6}}{4}$, $\tan \dfrac{x}{2} = -\dfrac{\sqrt{15}}{3}$

41. $\sin \dfrac{1}{2}x = -\dfrac{2\sqrt{5}}{5}$, $\cos \dfrac{1}{2}x = \dfrac{\sqrt{5}}{5}$, $\tan \dfrac{1}{2}x = -2$

42. $\sin \dfrac{x}{2} = \dfrac{-3\sqrt{10}}{10}$, $\cos \dfrac{x}{2} = \dfrac{\sqrt{10}}{10}$, $\tan \dfrac{x}{2} = -3$

43. (A) 2θ is a second quadrant angle, since θ is a first quadrant angle and $\tan 2\theta$ is negative for 2θ in the second quadrant and not for 2θ in the first.

(B) Construct a reference triangle for 2θ in the second quadrant with $(a, b) = (-3, 4)$. Use the pythagorean theorem to find $r = 5$. Thus, $\sin 2\theta = 4/5$ and $\cos 2\theta = -3/5$.

(C) The double angle identities $\cos 2\theta = 1 - 2 \sin^2 \theta$ and $\cos 2\theta = 2 \cos^2 \theta - 1$.

(D) Use the identities in part (C) in the form
$$\sin \theta = \sqrt{\dfrac{1 - \cos 2\theta}{2}} \quad \text{and} \quad \cos \theta = \sqrt{\dfrac{1 + \cos 2\theta}{2}}$$
The positive radicals are used because θ is in quadrant one.

(E) $\sin \theta = 2\sqrt{5}/5$; $\cos \theta = \sqrt{5}/5$

44. (A) 2θ is a second quadrant angle, since θ is a first quadrant angle and sec 2θ is negative for 2θ in the second quadrant and not for 2θ in the first.

(B) Construct a reference triangle for 2θ in the second quadrant with $a = -4$ and $r = 5$. Use the pythagorean theorem to find $b = 3$. Thus, sin $2\theta = 3/5$ and cos $2\theta = -4/5$.

(C) The double angle identities $\cos 2\theta = 1 - 2 \sin^2 \theta$ and $\cos 2\theta = 2 \cos^2 \theta - 1$.

(D) Use the identities in part (C) in the form

$$\sin \theta = \sqrt{\frac{1 - \cos 2\theta}{2}} \quad \text{and} \quad \cos \theta = \sqrt{\frac{1 + \cos 2\theta}{2}}$$

The positive radicals are used because θ is in quadrant one.

(E) $\sin \theta = 3\sqrt{10}/10$; $\cos \theta = \sqrt{10}/10$

45. (A) $-0.72335 = -0.72335$ (B) $-0.58821 = -0.58821$

46. (A) $-0.70762 = -0.70762$ (B) $0.80718 = 0.80718$

47. (A) $-3.2518 = -3.2518$ (B) $0.89279 = 0.89279$

48. (A) $-6.7997 = -6.7997$ (B) $-0.41615 = -0.41615$

49. $y_1 = y_2$ for $[-\pi, \pi]$

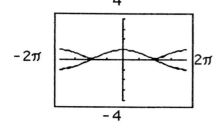

50. $y_1 = y_2$ for $[-2\pi, -\pi]$ and $[\pi, 2\pi]$

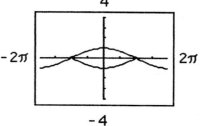

51. $y_1 = y_2$ for $[-2\pi, 0]$

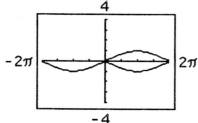

52. $y_1 = y_2$ for $[0, 2\pi]$

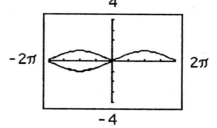

57. $-\dfrac{7}{25}$ **58.** $\dfrac{24}{25}$ **59.** $-\dfrac{24}{7}$ **60.** $-\dfrac{24}{7}$ **61.** $\dfrac{\sqrt{5}}{5}$ **62.** $-\dfrac{\sqrt{5}}{5}$

63. $\tan \dfrac{x}{2}$

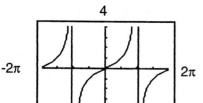

64. $\cot \dfrac{x}{2}$

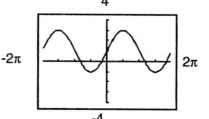

65. $1 + 2 \sin x$

66. $-1 + 2 \cos x$ **67.** $\sec 2x$ **68.** $\csc 2x$

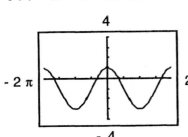 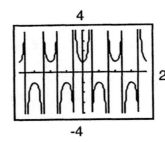 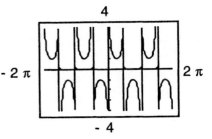

69. $x = \dfrac{224}{17} \approx 13.176$ m; $\theta = 28.955°$ **70.** $x = 2\sqrt{3} \approx 3.464$ ft, $\theta = 30.000°$

71. (A) $d = \dfrac{v_0^2 \sin 2\theta}{32 \text{ ft/sec}^2}$ (B) $\theta = 45°$ **72.** $\dfrac{4}{5}$

73. (B) TABLE 1

n	10	100	1,000	10,000
A_n	2.93893	3.13953	3.14157	3.14159

(C) A_n appears to approach π, the area of the circle with radius 1.

(D) A_n will not exactly equal the area of the circumscribing circle for any n no matter how large n is chosen; however, A_n can be made as close to the area of the circumscribing circle as we like by making n sufficiently large.

Exercise 7-4

1. $\dfrac{1}{2} \sin 4m + \dfrac{1}{2} \sin 2m$ **2.** $\dfrac{1}{2} \cos 12A + \dfrac{1}{2} \cos 2A$ **3.** $\dfrac{1}{2} \cos 2u - \dfrac{1}{2} \cos 4u$

4. $\dfrac{1}{2} \sin 5\theta + \dfrac{1}{2} \sin \theta$ **5.** $2 \sin 2t \cos t$ **6.** $2 \cos 6\theta \cos \theta$

7. $2 \sin 7w \sin 2w$ **8.** $-2 \cos 3u \sin 2u$

9. $\dfrac{1}{4}$ **10.** $\dfrac{\sqrt{3} - 2}{4}$ **11.** $\dfrac{1 + \sqrt{2}}{4}$ **12.** $\dfrac{\sqrt{3} + \sqrt{2}}{4}$

13. $-\dfrac{\sqrt{6}}{2}$ **14.** $\dfrac{\sqrt{6}}{2}$ **15.** $-\dfrac{\sqrt{2}}{2}$ **16.** $-\dfrac{\sqrt{6}}{2}$

19. Let $x = u + v$ and $y = u - v$ and solve the resulting system for u and v in terms of x and y, then substitute the results into the first identity. The second identity will result after a small amount of algebraic manipulation.

20. Let $x = u - v$ and $y = u + v$ and solve the resulting system for u and v in terms of x and y, then substitute the results into the first identity. The second identity will result after a small amount of algebraic manipulation.

25. Yes   **26.** No   **27.** No   **28.** Yes

29. No   **30.** Yes

31. (A) $-0.34207 = -0.34207$ (B) $-0.05311 = -0.05311$

32. (A) $0.19853 = 0.19853$ (B) $1.5918 = 1.5918$

33. (A) $-0.19115 = -0.19115$ (B) $-0.46541 = -0.46541$

34. (A) $0.57285 = 0.57285$ (B) $1.8186 = 1.8186$

35. $y_2 = 2 \sin \frac{3x}{2} \cos \frac{x}{2}$

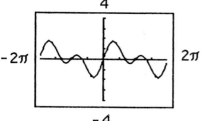

36. $y_2 = 2 \cos 2x \cos x$

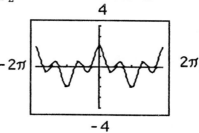

37. $y_2 = -2 \sin x \sin 0.7x$

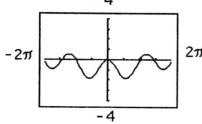

38. $y_2 = 2 \cos 1.3x \sin 0.8x$

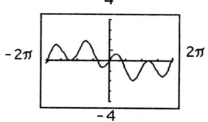

39. $y_2 = \frac{1}{2} (\sin 4x + \sin 2x)$

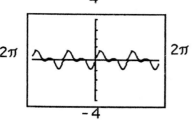

40. $y_2 = \frac{1}{2} (\cos 8x + \cos 2x)$

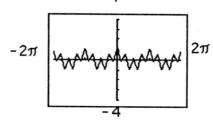

41. $y_2 = \frac{1}{2} (\cos 1.6x - \cos 3x)$

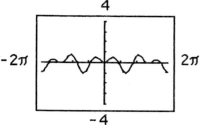

42. $y_2 = \frac{1}{2} (\sin 2.4x - \sin 1.4x)$

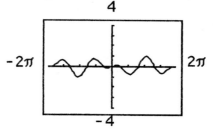

45. (A)

(B) $y_1 = \cos(30\pi x) + \cos(26\pi x)$
Graph same as part (A)

46. (A)

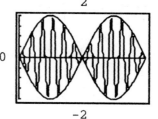

(B) $y_1 = \cos(22\pi x) - \cos(26\pi x)$
Graph same as part (A)

47. (A)

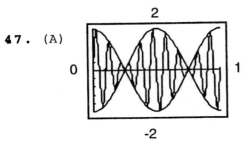

(B) $y_1 = \sin(22\pi x) + \sin(18\pi x)$
Graph same as part (A)

48. (A)

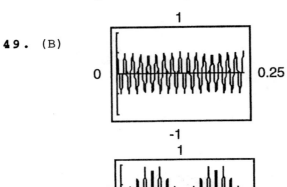

(B) $y_1 = \sin(18\pi x) - \sin(14\pi x)$
Graph same as part (A)

49. (B)

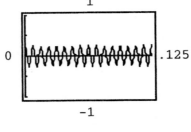

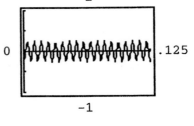

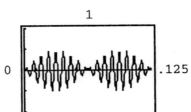

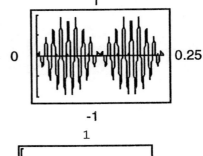

50. (B)

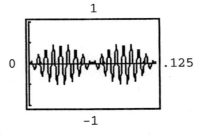

Exercise 7-5

1. $7\pi/6$, $11\pi/6$ **2.** $2\pi/3$, $4\pi/3$

3. $7\pi/6 + 2k\pi$, $11\pi/6 + 2k\pi$, k any integer

4. $2\pi/3 + 2k\pi$, $4\pi/3 + 2k\pi$, k any integer   **5.** $2\pi/3$ **6.** $5\pi/6$

7. $2\pi/3 + k\pi$, k any integer

8. $5\pi/6 + k\pi$, k any integer

9. $30°$, $330°$ **10.** $45°$, $135°$ **11.** 1.1279, 5.1553

12. 1.1593, 5.1239   **13.** 74.0546°   **14.** 104.9314°

15. 3.5075 + $2k\pi$, 5.9172 + $2k\pi$, k any integer

16. 0.6696 + $2k\pi$, 2.4720 + $2k\pi$, k any integer

17. 0.3376   **18.** 0.4502   **19.** 2.7642   **20.** 0.6167

21. $k(180°)$, 135° + $k(180°)$, k any integer

22. 90° + $k180°$, 45° + $k180°$, k any integer

23. 0, $2\pi/3$, π, $4\pi/3$ **24.** $\dfrac{\pi}{2}$, $\dfrac{3\pi}{2}$ **25.** 210°, 330°   **26.** 180°

27. 60°, 180°, 300°   **28.** 90°, 270°   **29.** $\pi/3$, π, $5\pi/3$

30. $\dfrac{\pi}{6}$, $\dfrac{7\pi}{6}$, $\dfrac{5\pi}{6}$, $\dfrac{11\pi}{6}$ **31.** 41.81°   **32.** 104.5°   **33.** 1.911

34. 0.2527   **35.** 0.3747, 2.767   **36.** 0.9987, 5.284

37. Infinitely many **38.** None   **39.** One   **40.** Three

41. Infinitely many **42.** Infinitely many

43. 0.3747, 2.7669   **44.** 0.9987, 5.2845

45. 0.3747 + $2k\pi$, 2.7669 + $2k\pi$, k any integer

46. 0.9987 + $2k\pi$, 5.2845 + $2k\pi$, k any integer

47. (–1.1530, 1.1530)   **48.** (–1.5099, 1.8281)

49. [3.5424, 5.3778], [5.9227, ∞)   **50.** [0.4204, 1.2346], [2.9752, ∞)

51. 1.8183   **52.** 2.4652

53. $\tan^{-1}(-5.377)$ has exactly one value, –1.387; the equation $\tan x = -5.377$ has infinitely many solutions, which are found by adding $k\pi$, k any integer, to each solution in one period of $\tan x$.

54. $\cos^{-1}(-0.7334)$ has exactly one value, 2.3941; the equation $\cos x = -0.7334$ has infinitely many solutions, which are found by adding $2\pi k$, k any integer, to each solution in one period of $\cos x$.

55. 0, $3\pi/2$ **56.** 0, $\dfrac{\pi}{2}$ **57.** π **58.** 0

59. 0.1204, 0.1384   **60.** 0.006104, 0.006137

61. (A) The largest zero for f is 0.3183. As x increases without bound, $1/x$ tends to 0 through positive numbers, and $\sin(1/x)$ tends to 0 through positive numbers. $y = 0$ is a horizontal asymptote for the graph of f.

(B) Infinitely many zeros exist between 0 and b, for any b, however small. The exploration graphs suggest this conclusion, which is reinforced by the following reasoning: Note that for each interval $(0, b]$, however small, as x tends to zero through positive numbers, $1/x$ increases without bound, and as $1/x$ increases without bound, $\sin(1/x)$ will cross the x axis an unlimited number of times. The function f does not have a smallest zero, because, between 0 and b, no matter how small b is, there is always an unlimited number of zeros.

62. (A) The largest zero for g is 0.6366. As x increases without bound, $1/x$ tends to 0 through positive numbers, and $\cos(1/x)$ tends to 1. $y = 1$ is a horizontal asymptote for the graph of g.

(B) Infinitely many zeros exist between 0 and b, for any b, however small. The exploration graphs suggest this conclusion, which is reinforced by the following reasoning: Note that for each interval $(0, b]$, however small, as x tends to zero through positive numbers, $1/x$ increases without bound, and as $1/x$ increases without bound, $\cos(1/x)$ will cross the x axis an unlimited number of times. The function g does not have a smallest zero, because, between 0 and b, no matter how small b is, there is always an unlimited number of zeros.

63. 0.009235 sec   **64.** 0.002613 sec   **65.** 50.77°   **66.** 33.21°

67. 123°   **68.** 64.1°   **69.** 2.267 rad   **70.** 1.779 rad

71. (A) 12.4575 mm   (B) 2.6496 mm   **72.** (A) 12.1703 mm   (B) 2.2318 mm

73. $(r, \theta) = (0, 0)$, $(0, 180°)$, $(0, 360°)$ **74.** $(r, \theta) = (1, 30°)$, $(1, 150°)$

75. $\theta = 45°$ **76.** $\theta = 45°$

CHAPTER 7 REVIEW

5. $\frac{1}{2}(\cos 5\alpha + \cos \alpha)$ $(7\text{-}4)$ **6.** $2\cos 7x \sin 2x$ $(7\text{-}4)$

7. $\cos x$ $(7\text{-}2)$ **8.** $135° + k360°$, $225° + k360°$, k any integer $(7\text{-}5)$

9. $k\pi$ or $\frac{\pi}{4} + k\pi$, k any integer $(7\text{-}5)$

10. $\pm34.7648° + k(360°)$, k any integer $(7\text{-}5)$ **11.** -0.0065 $(7\text{-}5)$

12. $0.5943 + 2k\pi$, $2.5473 + 2k\pi$, k any integer $(7\text{-}5)$

13. 3.1855 $(7\text{-}5)$ **14.** (A) Not an identity (B) An identity $(7\text{-}1)$

24. $\frac{-2 - \sqrt{3}}{4}$ $(7\text{-}4, 6\text{-}4)$ **25.** $-\frac{\sqrt{6}}{2}$ $(7\text{-}4, 6\text{-}4)$ **26.** No $(7\text{-}1)$ **27.** Yes $(7\text{-}3)$

28. Yes $(7\text{-}2)$ **29.** No $(7\text{-}2)$ **30.** $\frac{\pi}{3}, \frac{2\pi}{3}, \frac{4\pi}{3}, \frac{5\pi}{3}$ $(7\text{-}5)$

31. 0°, 120° $(7\text{-}5)$

32. $x = 0 + 2k\pi$, $x = \pi + 2k\pi$, $x = \frac{\pi}{6} + 2k\pi$, $x = \frac{5\pi}{6} + 2k\pi$, k any integer. The first two can also be written together as $x = k\pi$, k any integer. $(7\text{-}5)$

33. $x = 0 + 2k\pi$, $x = \pi + 2k\pi$, $x = \frac{\pi}{6} + 2k\pi$, $x = \frac{11\pi}{6} + 2k\pi$, k any integer. The first two can also be written together as $x = k\pi$, k any integer. $(7\text{-}5)$

34. $120° + k360°$, $240° + k360°$, k any integer $(7\text{-}5)$

35. $14.34° + k180°$ $(7\text{-}5)$ **36.** $x = \begin{cases} 0.6259 + 2k\pi \\ 2.516 + 2k\pi \end{cases}$ k any integer $(7\text{-}5)$

37. 1.178, 2.749   (7-5)   **38.** Two   (7-5)   **39.** Infinitely many   (7-5)

40. None   (7-5)   **41.** Infinitely many   (7-5)   **42.** 1.4903   (7-5)

43. $(-\infty, 1.4903)$ (7-5)   **44.** -0.6716, 0.6716   (7-5)

45. [-0.6716, 0.6716]   (7-5)

46. (A) Yes
(B) Conditional equation, since the equation is false for $x = 1$ and $y = 1$, for example, and both sides are defined at $x = 1$ and $y = 1$.   (7-1)

47. $\sin^{-1} 0.3351$ has exactly one value, while the equation $\sin x = 0.3351$ has infinitely many solutions.   (6-9, 7-5)

48. (A) Not an identity   (B) An identity   (7-1)

49. $y2 = \dfrac{1}{2} \cos x + \dfrac{\sqrt{3}}{2} \sin x$

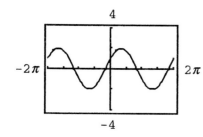

   (7-2)

50.   (A) $0, \dfrac{2\pi}{3}, \dfrac{4\pi}{3}$
   (B) 2.0944 and 4.1888   (7-5)

51.   0.149 and -2.233   (7-5)

52.   (A) $\dfrac{3}{\sqrt{10}}$ or $\dfrac{3\sqrt{10}}{10}$
   (B) $\dfrac{7}{25}$ (7-3)

53. $-\dfrac{24}{25}$ (7-3)   **54.** $\dfrac{24}{25}$ (7-2)   **55.** (A) $0, \dfrac{\pi}{3}, \dfrac{2\pi}{3}$ (B) 0, 1.0472, 2.0944   (7-5)

56.   (A) 0.6817, 1.3183

(B) As x increases without bound, $\dfrac{1}{x - 1}$ tends to 0 through positive numbers and $\sin \dfrac{1}{x - 1}$ tends to 0 through positive numbers. $y = 0$ is a horizontal asymptote for the graph of f.

(C) The exploratory graphs are left to the student. There are infinitely many zeros in any interval containing $x = 1$. The number $x = 1$ is not a zero because $\sin \dfrac{1}{x - 1}$ is not defined at $x = 1$.   (7-5)

57. $x = \sqrt{27}$; $x = 5.196$ cm, $\theta = 30.000°$ (7-3)   **58.** 0.00346 sec   (7-5)

59. $y = 0.6 \cos 184\pi t$

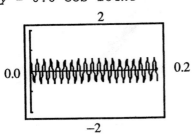

$y = -0.6 \cos 208\pi t$

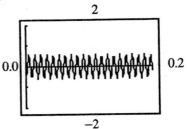

$y = 0.6 \cos 184\pi t - 0.6 \cos 208\pi t$

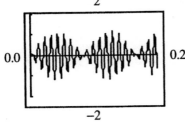

$y = 1.2 \sin 12\pi t \sin 196\pi t$

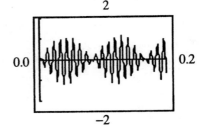

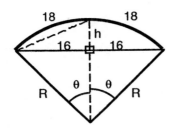

(7-4)

60. Height = 7.057 ft, raduis = 21.668 ft

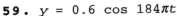

From the figure, $R\theta = 18$ and $\sin \theta = \dfrac{16}{R}$. From these two equations, solving each for R in terms of θ and setting the results equal to each other, we obtain the desired trigonometric equation.   (7-5)

CHAPTER 8

Exercise 8-1

1. $\gamma = 79°$, $a = 41$ ft, $b = 20$ ft

2. $\gamma = 106°$, $a = 14$ cm, $b = 12$ cm

3. $\beta = 40°$, $a = 16$ km, $c = 5.8$ km

4. $\alpha = 101°$, $b = 64$ mm, $c = 55$ mm

5. $\alpha = 49°$, $a = 53$ yd, $b = 66$ yd

6. $\beta = 23°$, $a = 38$ m, $b = 19$ m

7. $\beta = 81°$, $b = 16$ cm, $c = 12$ cm

8. $\alpha = 20°$, $b = 25$ mi, $a = 8.8$ mi

9. Two triangles; case (c)

10. One triangle; case (d)

11. One triangle; case (b)

12. Zero triangles; case (a)

13. Zero triangles; case (a)

14. Two triangles; case (c)

15. Zero triangles; case (e)

16. One triangle; case (f)

17. One triangle; case (d)

18. Two triangles; case (c)

19. One triangle; none of the cases

20. Zero triangles; none of the cases

21. $\beta = 49.5°$, $a = 20.0$ ft, $c = 4.81$ ft

22. $\alpha = 98.0°$, $b = 4.32$ in, $c = 7.62$ in

23. $\gamma = 58.1°$, $a = 140$ m, $c = 129$ m

24. $\gamma = 22.9°$, $a = 27.3$ km, $c = 12.6$ km

25. no solution

26. no solution

27. Triangle 1: $\beta = 63.4°$, $\gamma = 77.7°$, $c = 46.7$ in.; Triangle 2: $\beta = 116.6°$, $\gamma = 24.5°$, $c = 19.8$ in.

28. Triangle 1: $\beta = 56.0°$, $\gamma = 96.7°$, $c = 292$ cm; Triangle 2: $\beta = 124.0°$, $\gamma = 28.7°$, $c = 141$ cm

29. no solution   30. no solution

31. $\alpha = 22°10'$, $\gamma = 128°20'$, $c = 89.9$ mm

32. $\alpha = 17°40'$, $c = 1740$ m, $\gamma = 128°30'$

33. $k = 25.2 \sin 42.3° = 16.9599$

34. $k = 42.8 \sin 37.3° = 25.9$

35. Left side: 16.204; right side: 16.073

36. (B) Right side: 0.3415; Left side: 0.3443

37. 4.06 mi, 2.47 mi

38. 8.08 mi, 4.82 mi

39. 353 ft   40. 14,490 ft.

41. 5.8 in, 3.1 in   42. 7.4", 5.0"

43. 4.42×10^7 km, 2.39×10^8 km

44. 46.5°

45. 159 ft   46. 109 ft

47. $R = 7.76$ mm, $s = 13.4$ mm

48. $R = 9.73$ mm, $s = 10.7$ mm

Exercise 8-2

1. Angle γ is acute. A triangle can have at most one obtuse angle. Since α is acute, then, if the triangle has an obtuse angle it must be the angle opposite the longer of the two sides, b and c. Thus, γ, the angle opposite the shorter of the two sides, c, must be acute.

2. A triangle can have at most one obtuse angle. Since α is obtuse, both β and γ must be acute.

3. $a = 6.03$ yd, $\beta = 56.6°$, $\gamma = 52.2°$

4. $b = 5.48$ cm, $\alpha = 69.0°$, $\gamma = 53.7°$

5. $c = 14.0$ mm, $\alpha = 20°40'$, $\beta = 39°0'$

6. $a = 27.0$ in, $\beta = 12°30'$, $\gamma = 31°40'$

7. If the triangle has an obtuse angle, then it must be the angle opposite the longest side; in this case, β.

8. Sides a and c are not long enough to construct a triangle ($a + c < b$).

9. $\alpha = 23.0°$, $\beta = 94.9°$, $\gamma = 62.1°$ **10.** $\alpha = 22.4°$, $\beta = 131.4°$, $\gamma = 26.2°$

11. $\alpha = 67.3°$, $\beta = 54.6°$, $\gamma = 58.1°$ **12.** $\alpha = 59.4°$, $\beta = 53.5°$, $\gamma = 67.1°$

13. No solution   **14.** No solution

15. $b = 23.5$ inches, $\alpha = 28.3°$, $\gamma = 25.5°$

16. $c = 13.8$ yards, $\alpha = 22.9°$, $\beta = 138.0°$

17. No solution   **18.** No solution

19. $\alpha = 30.7°$, $\gamma = 110.9°$, $c = 21.0$ in   **20.** $\beta = 66.4°$, $\alpha = 47.2°$, $a = 20.4$ m

21. $\alpha = 49.1°$, $\beta = 102.9°$, $\gamma = 28.0°$ **22.** $\alpha = 95°$, $\beta = 29.7°$, $\gamma = 55.3°$

23. Triangle I: $\beta = 109.7°$, $\alpha = 11.9°$, $a = 1.58$ m
Triangle II: $\beta = 70.3°$, $\alpha = 51.3°$, $a = 5.99$ m

24. $\beta = 65.3° \Rightarrow \gamma = 68.0° \Rightarrow c = 23.1$ m
$\beta = 114.7° \Rightarrow \gamma = 18.6° \Rightarrow c = 7.93$ m

25. no solution   **26.** no solution

33. 120 yd   **34.** 130 m

35. 5.81 ft   **36.** 10.6 ft

37. 121 mi   **38.** 713 mi   **39.** 74.1 m   **40.** 43.6 cm

41. 0.284 radian   **42.** 0.446 radian   **43.** $\alpha = 31°50'$, $\beta = 50°10'$, $\gamma = 98°0'$

44. $\alpha = 32°10'$, $\beta = 49°40'$, $\gamma = 98°10'$ **45.** $\angle CAB = 33°$ **46.** $\angle ACB = 80°$

47. 24,800 mi   **48.** 638 mi

Exercise 8-3

1. $|u + v| = 78$ mph, $\theta = 67°$ **2.** $|u + v| = 225$ mph, $\theta = 16°$

3. $|u + v| = 41$ kg, $\theta = 45°$ **4.** $|u + v| = 90$ kg, $\theta = 30°$

5. $|u| = 12$ lb, $|v| = 21$ lb   **6.** $|u| = 34$ lb, $|v| = 34$ lb

7. $|u| = 388$ mph, $|v| = 41$ mph   **8.** $|u| = 12$ mph, $|v| = 74$ mph

9. $|u + v| = 77$g, $\alpha = 15°$ **10.** $|u + v| = 190$ gm, $\alpha = 18°$

11. $|u + v| = 23$ knots, $\alpha = 6°$ **12.** $|u + v| = 9.1$ knots, $\alpha = 11°$

13. $|u| = 12$ kg, $|v| = 6.0$ kg   **14.** $|v| = 14$ kg, $|u| = 21$ kg

15. $|u| = 109$ mi/hr, $|v| = 160$ mi/hr   **16.** $|v| = 173$ mph and $|u| = 306$ mph

17. True   **18.** True   **19.** False   **20.** True

21. True   **22.** False   **23.** False   **24.** False

25. 260 mph at 282°   **26.** 14 mph at 40°

27. 288°, 7.6 knots   **28.** 251 mph at 349.6°

29. 3,900 lbs @ 72°   **30.** 6300 kg @ 178°

31. (A) 388 lb (B) 4,030 lb   **32.** (A) 650 lb (B) 2400 lb

33. to the right   **34.** slide left

Exercise 8-4

1. $\langle 7, 2 \rangle$ **2.** $\langle -5, -3 \rangle$ **3.** $\langle -4, 8 \rangle$ **4.** $\langle 6, 5 \rangle$

5. $\langle -2, 9 \rangle$ **6.** $\langle 15, 4 \rangle$ **7.** 15   **8.** 32

9. 75   **10.** 52   **11.** 493   **12.** 845

13. (A) $\langle 1, 4 \rangle$ (B) $\langle 3, -2 \rangle$ (C) $\langle 14, -1 \rangle$ **14.** (A) $\langle 2, 0 \rangle$ (B) $\langle -4, 4 \rangle$ (C) $\langle -5, 0 \rangle$

15. (A) $\langle -2, 1 \rangle$ (B) $\langle -6, -3 \rangle$ (C) $\langle -10, -1 \rangle$ **16.** (A) $\langle -5, 4 \rangle$ (B) $\langle -1, 0 \rangle$ (C) $\langle -13, 2 \rangle$

17. $v = -8i$ **18.** $v = 14j$ **19.** $v = 6i - 12j$ **20.** $v = -5i - 18j$

21. $v = -5i - 2j$ **22.** $2i + 3j$ **23.** $5i + 2j$ **24.** $i - 6j$

25. $-16j$ **26.** $13i + 2j$ **27.** $-8j$ **28.** $i - 14j$

29. $u = \left\langle -\dfrac{1}{\sqrt{2}}, \dfrac{1}{\sqrt{2}} \right\rangle$ **30.** $u = \left\langle \dfrac{2}{\sqrt{5}}, \dfrac{1}{\sqrt{5}} \right\rangle$

31. $u = \left\langle -\dfrac{12}{13}, \dfrac{5}{13} \right\rangle$ **32.** $u = \left\langle -\dfrac{7}{25}, -\dfrac{24}{25} \right\rangle$

33. False   **34.** True   **35.** False   **36.** False

45. 760 lb to the left; 761 lb to the right

46. $T_L = 676$ lb, $T_R = 677$ lb

47. 897 lb to the left; 732 lb to the right

48. $T_L = 518$ lb, $T_R = 390$ lb

49. This corresponds to a tension force of 462 lb in member *CB*.
This corresponds to a compression force of 231 lb in member *AB*.

50. *BC* = 2000 kg, tension; *AB* = 1730 kg, compression

51. *AB* = a compression of 2,360 lb; *BC* = a tension of 2,000 lb

52. *AB* = 9050 kg, compression; *BC* = 7540 kg, tension

Exercise 8-5

1.

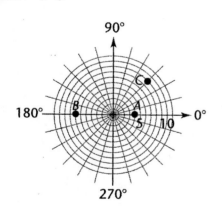

2.

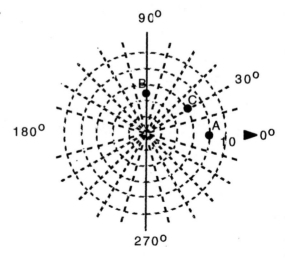

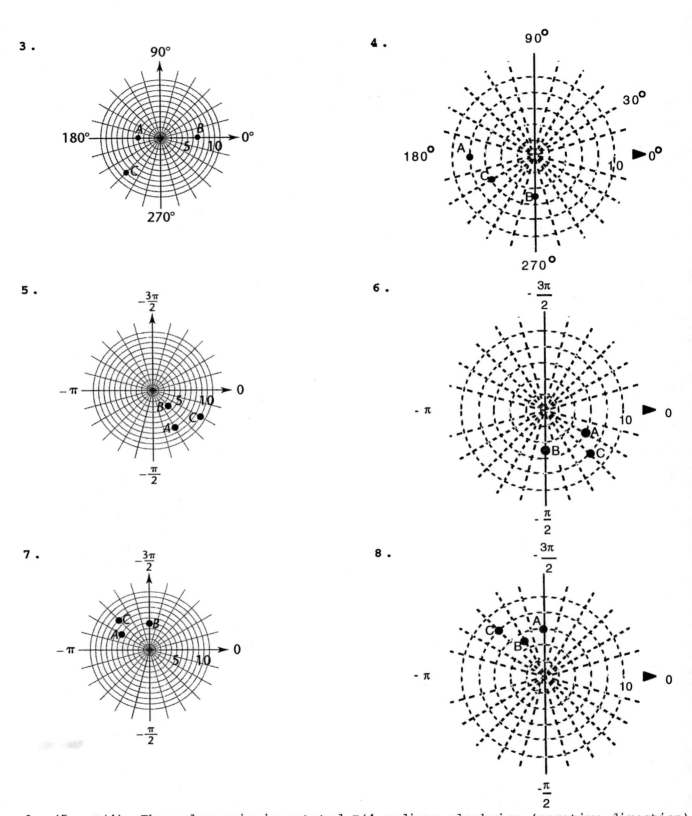

9. (5, −π/4): The polar axis is rotated π/4 radians clockwise (negative direction) and the point is located 5 units from the pole along the positive polar axis. (5, 7π/4): The polar axis is rotated 7π/4 radians counterclockwise (positive direction) and the point is located 5 units from the positive polar axis. (−5, −5π/4): The polar axis is rotated 5π/4 radians clockwise (negative direction) and the point is located 5 units from the pole along the negative polar axis.

10. $(-6, -210°)$: The polar axis is rotated 210° clockwise (negative direction) and the point is located 6 units from the pole along the negative polar axis. $(-6, 150°)$: The polar axis is rotated 150° counterclockwise (positive direction) and the point is located 6 units from the pole along the negative polar axis. $(6, 330°)$: The polar axis is rotated 330° counterclockwise (positive direction) and the point is located 6 units along the positive polar axis.

11.

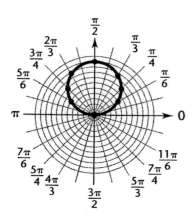

12.

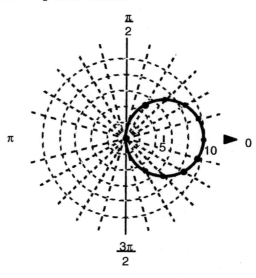

13.

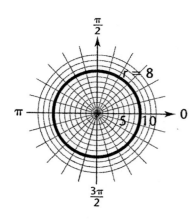

14.

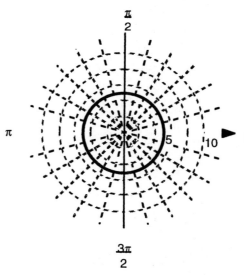

15.

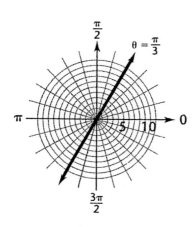

16.

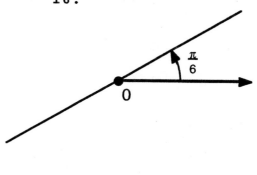

17. $(5.196, 3.000)$ **18.** $(-3.500, 6.062)$ **19.** $(1.848, -0.765)$

20. (0.668, -2.925)   **21.** (2.078, 3.688)   **22.** (-7.115, 5.557)

23. (8, 180°)   **24.** (5, -90°)   **25.** $(5\sqrt{2}, -135°)$

26. (2, -60°)   **27.** (11.05, 27.7°)   **28.** (31.4, 97.8°)

29.

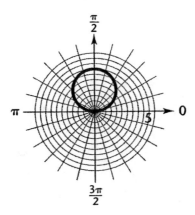

30.

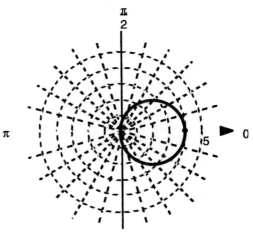

31.

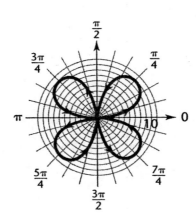

32.

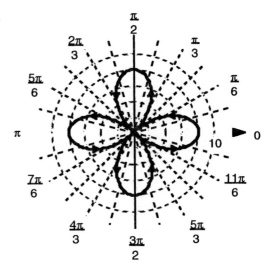

33.

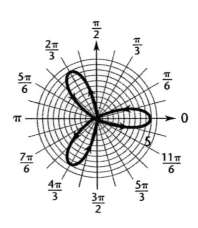

34.

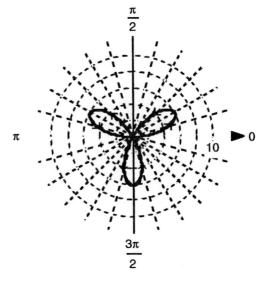

35.

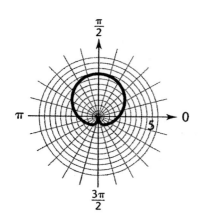

36.

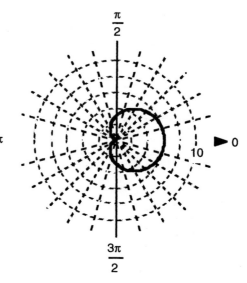

37.

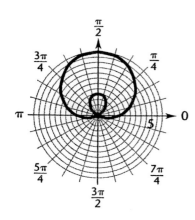

38.

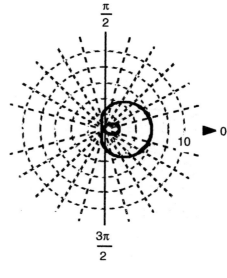

39.

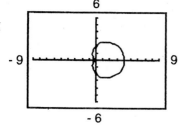
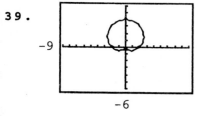
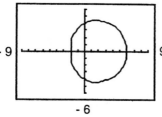

40.

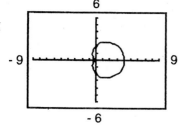
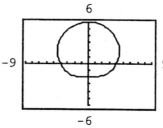
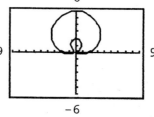

41. (A)

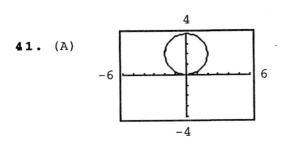 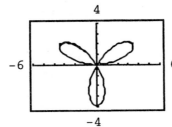 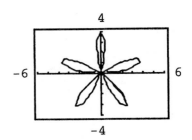

(B) 7   (C) n

42. (A)

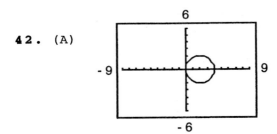 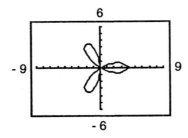 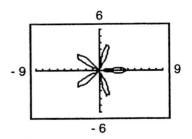

(B) 7   (C) n

43. (A)

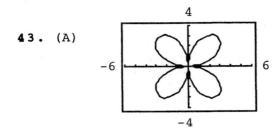 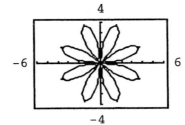 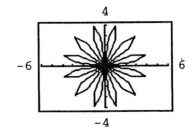

(B) 16   (C) $2n$

44. (A)

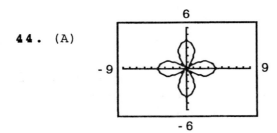 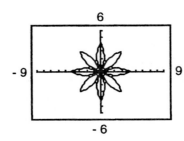 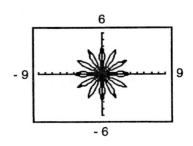

(B) 16   (C) $2n$

45. $r = 2$; circle

46. $\tan \theta = -1$ or $\theta = 3\pi/4$; line

47. $\tan \theta = 1/\sqrt{3}$ or $\theta = \pi/6$; line

48. $r = -8 \cos \theta$;   circle

49. $r = 5 \tan \theta \sec \theta$, parabola

50. $r^2 = \sec 2\theta$;   hyperbola

51. $x^2 + y^2 = 3x$;   circle

52. $y = -\sqrt{3}x$; line

53. $4y - x = 1$; line

54. $x^2 + y^2 = -5y$; circle

55. $3x^2 + 4y^2 = 1 - 2x$; ellipse

56. $y^2 = 1 - 2x$;   parabola

57. For each n, there are n large petals and n small petals. For n odd, the small petals are within the large petals; for n even, the small petals are between the large petals.

58. For each n, there are n large petals and n small petals. For n odd, the small petals are within the large petals; for n even, the small petals are between the large petals.

59.

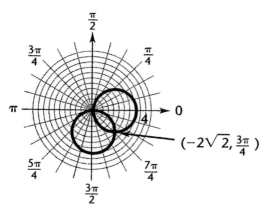

$(r, \theta) = \left(-2\sqrt{2}, \dfrac{3\pi}{4}\right)$ [Note: (0, 0) is not a solution of the system even though the graphs cross at the origin.]

60.

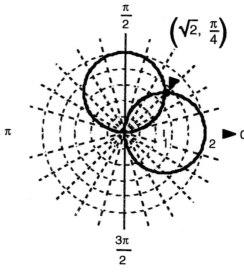

$(r, \theta) = \left(\sqrt{2}, \dfrac{\pi}{4}\right)$

[Note: (0, 0) is not a solution to the system even though the graphs cross at the origin.]

61.

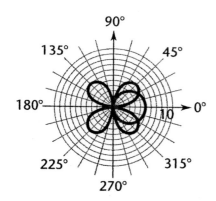

$(r, \theta) = (0, 90°)$, $(0, 270°)$, $(3\sqrt{3}, 30°)$, $(-3\sqrt{3}, 150°)$
[Note: (0, 0) is not a solution of the system even though the graphs cross at the origin.]

62.

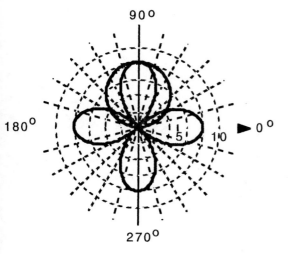

$(r, \theta) = (4, 30°)$, $(4, 150°)$, $(-8, 270°)$ [Note: (0, 0) is not a solution to the system even though the graphs cross at the origin.]

63. 3.368 units

64. 1.615

65. 6 k, 13 k, 12 k, 9 k

66. 9 k, 14 k, 13 k, 11 k

67. (A) Ellipse (B) Parabola (C) Hyperbola

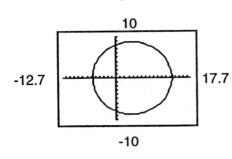

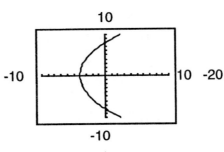

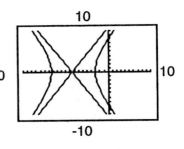

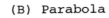

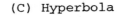

68. (A) Ellipse (B) Parabola (C) Hyperbola

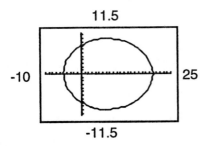

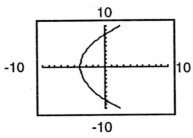

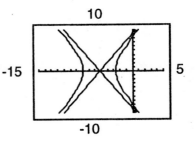

69. (A) Aphelion: 4.34×10^7 mi; Perihelion: 2.85×10^7 mi

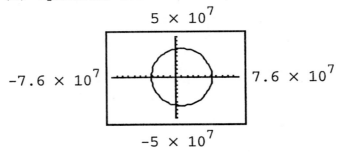

(B) Faster at perihelion. Since the distance from the sun to Mercury is less at perihelion than at aphelion, the planet must move faster near perihelion in order for the line joining Mercury to the sun to sweep out equal areas in equal intervals of time.

Exercise 8-6

1.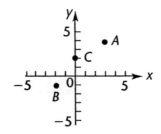

2.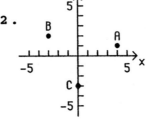

3.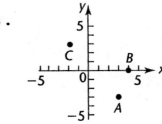

4.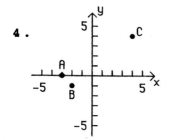

5.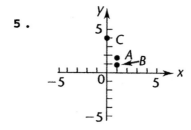

6.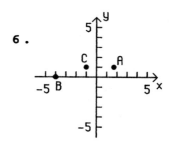

7.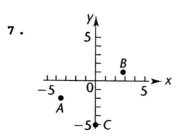

8.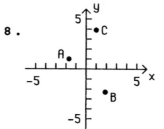

9. (A) $2e^{30°i}$ (B) $\sqrt{2}e^{(-135°)i}$ (C) $7.81e^{(-50.19°)i}$

10. (A) $2e^{120°i}$ (B) $3e^{(-90°)i}$ (C) $8.06e^{(-150.26°)i}$

11. (A) $\sqrt{3}e^{(-\pi/2)i}$ (B) $2e^{(-5\pi/6)i}$ (C) $9.43e^{2.58i}$

12. (A) $2e^{(-\pi/6)i}$ (B) $2\sqrt{2}e^{(3\pi/4)i}$ (C) $7.81e^{(-0.69)i}$

13. (A) $1 + i\sqrt{3}$ (B) $1 - i$ (C) $-2.35 + 1.99i$

14. (A) $\sqrt{3} + i$ (B) $-1 - i$ (C) $5.06 - 2.64i$

15. (A) $3\sqrt{3} + 3i$ (B) $-i\sqrt{7}$ (C) $-2.22 - 3.43i$

16. (A) $-i\sqrt{3}$ (B) $-1 + i$ (C) $-2.20 - 6.46i$

17. $14e^{113°i}$; $3.5e^{51°i}$ **18.** $18e^{225°i}$; $2e^{39°i}$ **19.** $10e^{135°i}$; $2.5e^{(-31°)i}$

20. $6e^{164°i}$; $1.5e^{(-30°)i}$ **21.** $36.42\,e^{4.35i}$; $0.26e^{(-0.83i)}$

22. $18.91e^{1.86i}$; $2.67e^{(-0.28)i}$ **23.** $4i$; $4e^{90°i}$

24. $2 + 2i\sqrt{3}$; $4e^{60°i}$ **25.** $2 + 2i$; $2\sqrt{2}e^{45°i}$

26. $\sqrt{3} - 3 + (3 + \sqrt{3})i$; $2\sqrt{6}e^{105°i}$ **27.** i; $e^{90°i}$

28. $-i$; $e^{-90°i}$ **29.** $re^{i(-\theta)} = re^{-i\theta}$

30. The product of z with its conjugate is the square of the modulus of z.

33. $z^n = r^n e^{n\theta i}$

35. (A) $(20 + 0i) + (5 + 5i\sqrt{3}) = 25 + 5i\sqrt{3}$ (B) $26.5\,e^{19.1°i}$

(C) 26.5 pounds at an angle of $19.1°$

36. (A) $(8 + 0i) + (3\sqrt{3} + 3i) = (8 + 3\sqrt{3}) + 3i$ (B) $13.5\,e^{12.8°i}$

(C) 13.5 lb at $12.8°$

Exercise 8-7

1. $81e^{160°i}$ **2.** $4\sqrt{2}e^{75°i}$ **3.** $8e^{90°i}$ **4.** $64e^{180°i}$

5. $e^{120°i}$ **6.** $256e^{-120°i}$ **7.** $-8 + 8\sqrt{3}i$ **8.** -4

9. 16 **10.** $16\sqrt{3} + 16i$ **11.** 1 **12.** 1

13. $w_1 = 2e^{10°i}$, $w_2 = 2e^{130°i}$, $w_3 = 2e^{250°i}$

14. $w_1 = 2e^{15°i}$, $w_2 = 2e^{135°i}$, $w_3 = 2e^{255°i}$

15. $w_1 = 3e^{15°i}$, $w_2 = 3e^{105°i}$, $w_3 = 3e^{195°i}$, $w_4 = 3e^{285°i}$

16. $w_1 = 2e^{22.5°i}$, $w_2 = 2e^{112.5°i}$, $w_3 = 2e^{202.5°i}$, $w_4 = 2e^{292.5°i}$

17. $w_1 = 2^{1/10}e^{(-9°)i}$, $w_2 = 2^{1/10}e^{63°i}$, $w_3 = 2^{1/10}e^{135°i}$, $w_4 = 2^{1/10}e^{207°i}$, $w_5 = 2^{1/10}e^{279°i}$

18. $w_1 = 2^{1/6}e^{45°i}$, $w_2 = 2^{1/6}e^{165°i}$, $w_3 = 2^{1/6}e^{285°i}$

19. $w_1 = 2e^{0°i}$, $w_2 = 2e^{120°i}$, $w_3 = 2e^{240°i}$

20. $w_1 = 1e^{0°i}$, $w_2 = 1e^{90°i}$, $w_3 = 1e^{180°i}$, $w_4 = 1e^{270°i}$

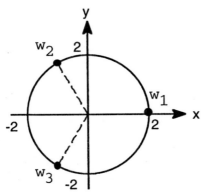

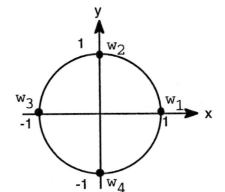

21. $w_1 = 2e^{45°i}$, $w_2 = 2e^{135°i}$, $w_3 = 2e^{225°i}$, $w_4 = 2e^{315°i}$

22. $w_1 = 2e^{60°i}$, $w_2 = 2e^{180°i}$, $w_3 = 2e^{300°i}$

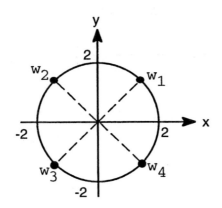

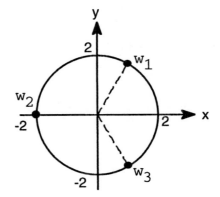

23. $w_1 = 1e^{15°i}$, $w_2 = 1e^{75°i}$,
$w_3 = 1e^{135°i}$, $w_4 = 1e^{195°i}$,
$w_5 = 1e^{255°i}$, $w_6 = 1e^{315°i}$

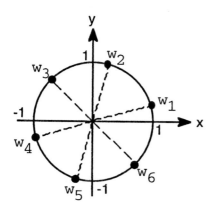

24. $w_1 = 1e^{(-18°)i}$, $w_2 = 1e^{54°i}$,
$w_3 = 1e^{126°i}$, $w_4 = 1e^{198°i}$,
$w_5 = 1e^{270°i}$

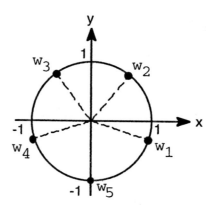

25. True   **26.** False

27. False   **28.** True

29. (A) $(1 + i)^4 + 4 = -4 + 4 = 0$
There are three other roots.

(B) The four roots are equally spaced around the circle. Since there are 4 roots, the angle between successive roots on the circle is $360°/4 = 90°$.

30. (A) $(-2)^3 + 8 = -8 + 8 = 0$; There are two other roots.

(B) The three roots are equally spaced around a circle of radius 2. The angle between successive roots on the circle is $360°/3 = 120°$.

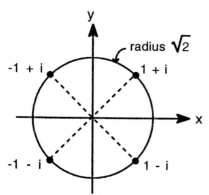

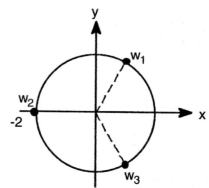

(C) $(-1 + i)^4 + 4 = -4 + 4 = 0$;
$(-1 - i)^4 + 4 = -4 + 4 = 0$;
$(1 - i)^4 + 4 = -4 + 4 = 0$

(C) $(1 + i\sqrt{3})^3 + 8 = -8 + 8 = 0$;
$(1 - i\sqrt{3})^3 + 8 = -8 + 8 = 0$

31. $x_1 = 4e^{60°i} = 2 + 2\sqrt{3}\,i$, $x_2 = 4e^{180°i} = -4$, $x_3 = 4e^{300°i} = 2 - 2\sqrt{3}\,i$

32. $x_1 = 4e^{0°i} = 4$, $x_2 = 4e^{120°i} = -2 + 2\sqrt{3}\,i$, $x_3 = 4e^{240°i} = -2 - 2\sqrt{3}\,i$

33. $x_1 = 3e^{0°i} = 3$, $x_2 = 3e^{120°i} = -\frac{3}{2} + \frac{3\sqrt{3}}{2}\,i$, $x_3 = 3e^{240°i} = -\frac{3}{2} - \frac{3\sqrt{3}}{2}\,i$

34. $x_1 = 3e^{60°i} = \frac{3}{2} + \frac{3\sqrt{3}}{2}\,i$, $x_2 = 3e^{180°i} = -3$, $x_3 = 3e^{300°i} = \frac{3}{2} - \frac{3\sqrt{3}}{2}\,i$

35. $w_1 = 2i$, $w_2 = -2i$ **36.** $w_1 = \frac{5\sqrt{2}}{2} + \frac{5\sqrt{2}}{2}\,i$, $w_2 = -\frac{5\sqrt{2}}{2} - \frac{5\sqrt{2}}{2}\,i$

37. $w_1 = \sqrt{3} + i$, $w_2 = -\sqrt{3} + i$, $w_3 = -2i$

38. $w_1 = 4i$, $w_2 = -2\sqrt{3} - 2i$, $w_3 = 2\sqrt{3} - 2i$

41. $x_1 = 2e^{0°i}$, $x_2 = 2e^{72°i}$, $x_3 = 2e^{144°i}$, $x_4 = 2e^{216°i}$, $x_5 = 2e^{288°i}$

42. $x_1 = 1e^{30°i}$, $x_2 = 1e^{90°i}$, $x_3 = 1e^{150°i}$, $x_4 = 1e^{210°i}$, $x_5 = 1e^{270°i}$, $x_6 = 1e^{330°i}$

43. $x_1 = e^{36°i}$, $x_2 = e^{108°i}$, $x_3 = e^{180°i}$, $x_4 = e^{252°i}$, $x_5 = e^{324°i}$

44. $x_1 = 1e^{30°i}$, $x_2 = 1e^{150°i}$, $x_3 = 1e^{270°i}$

45. $P(x) = (x - 2i)(x + 2i)[x - (-\sqrt{3} + i)][x - (-\sqrt{3} - i)]$
$$[x - (\sqrt{3} + i)][x - (\sqrt{3} - i)]$$

46. $(x - 1)(x + 1)\left[x - \left(\frac{1}{2} + \frac{\sqrt{3}}{2}i\right)\right]\left[x - \left(\frac{1}{2} - \frac{\sqrt{3}}{2}i\right)\right]\left[x - \left(-\frac{1}{2} + \frac{\sqrt{3}}{2}i\right)\right]\left[x - \left(-\frac{1}{2} - \frac{\sqrt{3}}{2}i\right)\right]$

CHAPTER 8 REVIEW

1. 1   *(8-1)*   **2.** 0   *(8-1)*   **3.** 2   *(8-1)*

4. Angle β is acute. A triangle can have at most one obtuse angle. Since α is acute, then, if the triangle has an obtuse angle it must be the angle opposite the longer of the two sides, b and c. Thus, β, the angle opposite the shorter of the two sides, b, must be acute.   *(8-2)*

5. $\gamma = 75°$, $a = 47$ m, $b = 31$ m   *(8-1)*

6. $a = 4.00$ ft, $\beta = 36°$, $\gamma = 129°$ *(8-1, 8-2)*

7. $\beta = 19°$, $\alpha = 40°$, $a = 8.2$ cm   *(8-1)*

8. $|\mathbf{u} + \mathbf{v}| = 170$ mi/hr, $\theta = 19°$ *(8-3)*   **9.** $\langle 3, -7 \rangle$ *(8-4)*   **10.** $\sqrt{34}$ *(8-4)*

11.   **12.**   **13.**

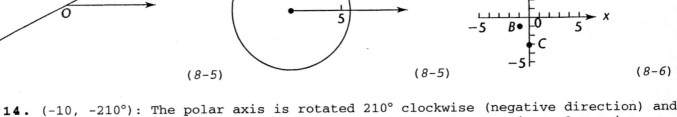

(8-5)   *(8-5)*   *(8-6)*

14. $(-10, -210°)$: The polar axis is rotated 210° clockwise (negative direction) and the point is located 10 units from the pole along the negative polar axis. $(-10, 150°)$: The polar axis is rotated 150° counterclockwise (positive direction) and the point is located 10 units from the pole along the negative polar axis. $(10, 330°)$: The polar axis is rotated 330° counterclockwise and the point is located 10 units from the pole along the positive polar axis.   *(8-5)*

15.

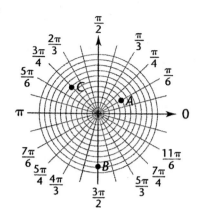

$(8-6)$

16. (A) $2e^{(-60°)i}$ (B) $2\sqrt{3} - 2i$ $(8-6)$

17. (A) 1   (B) 1 $(8-7)$ **18.** $8 + i\,8\sqrt{3}$ $(8-7)$

19. If the triangle has an obtuse angle, then it must be the angle opposite the longest side; in this case, α. $(8-2)$

20. $b = 10.5$ cm, $\alpha = 27.2°$, $\gamma = 37.4°$ $(8-2)$

21. No solution $(8-1)$

22. Two solutions. Obtuse case: $\beta = 133.9°$, $\gamma = 19.7°$, $c = 39.6$ km $(8-1)$

23. $\alpha = 41.1°$, $\beta = 74.2°$, $\gamma = 64.7°$ $(8-1, 8-2)$

24. The sum of all of the force vectors must be the zero vector for the object to remain at rest. $(8-4)$

25. $|\mathbf{u} + \mathbf{v}| = 98.0$ kg, $\alpha = 17.1°$ $(8-3)$

26. $\mathbf{u} = 11\mathbf{i} - 7\mathbf{j}$ $(8-4)$ **27.** $\langle 105, 45 \rangle$ $(8-4)$

28. $u = \left\langle -\dfrac{4}{5}, \dfrac{3}{5} \right\rangle$ $(8-4)$ **29.** $k = \dfrac{6 \pm \sqrt{6}}{10}$ $(8-4)$

30. $k_1 = \dfrac{1}{5}$, $k_2 = \dfrac{2}{5}$ $(8-4)$ **31.** $\left\langle \dfrac{15}{13}, -\dfrac{36}{13} \right\rangle$ $(8-4)$

32.

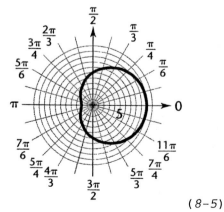

$(8-5)$

33.

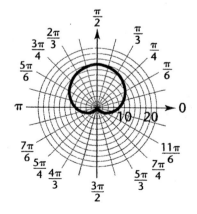

$(8-5)$

34.

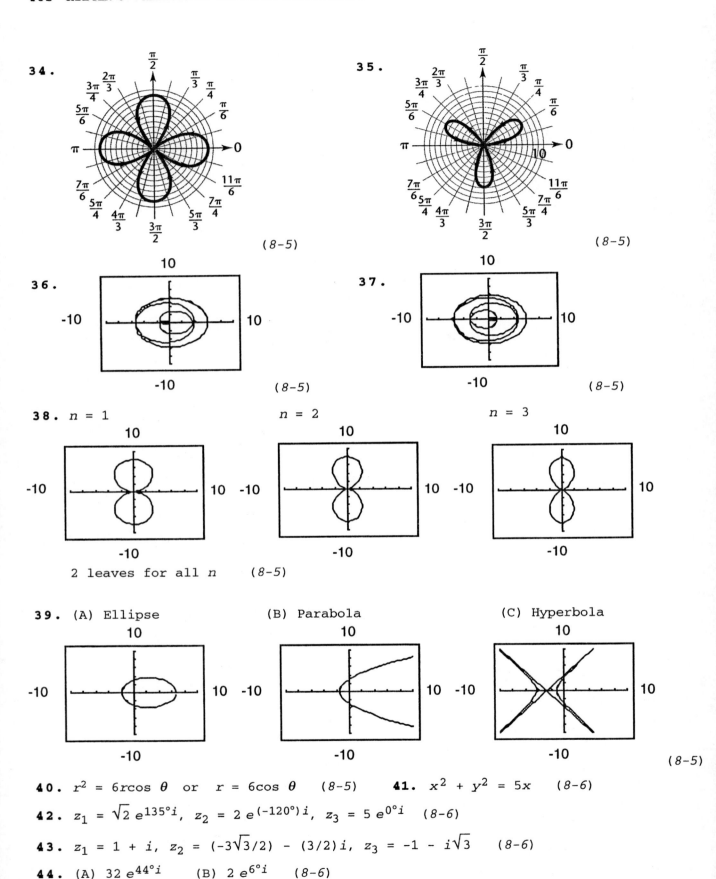

$(8-5)$

35.

$(8-5)$

36.

$(8-5)$

37.

$(8-5)$

38. $n = 1$

$n = 2$

$n = 3$

2 leaves for all n $(8-5)$

39. (A) Ellipse

(B) Parabola

(C) Hyperbola

$(8-5)$

40. $r^2 = 6r\cos\theta$ or $r = 6\cos\theta$ $(8-5)$ **41.** $x^2 + y^2 = 5x$ $(8-6)$

42. $z_1 = \sqrt{2}\,e^{135°i}$, $z_2 = 2\,e^{(-120°)i}$, $z_3 = 5\,e^{0°i}$ $(8-6)$

43. $z_1 = 1 + i$, $z_2 = (-3\sqrt{3}/2) - (3/2)i$, $z_3 = -1 - i\sqrt{3}$ $(8-6)$

44. (A) $32\,e^{44°i}$ (B) $2\,e^{6°i}$ $(8-6)$

45. (A) $-8 - 8\sqrt{3}\,i$ (B) $-8 - 13.86i$ $(8-7)$

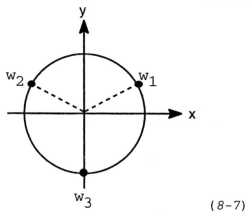

46. $w_1 = (\sqrt{3}/2) + (1/2)i$

$w_2 = (-\sqrt{3}/2) + (1/2)i$

$w_3 = -i$

47. $2 e^{50°i}$, $2 e^{170°i}$, $2 e^{290°i}$ (*8-7*)   **48.** $(4 e^{15°i})^2 = 16 e^{30°i} = 8\sqrt{3} + 8i$ (*8-7*)

49. $(5.76, -26.08°)$ (*8-5*)   **50.** $(-5.30, -2.38)$ (*8-5*)

51. $5.26e^{127.20°i}$ (*8-6*)   **52.** $-7.27 - 2.32i$ (*8-6*)

53. (A) There are a total of three cube roots and they are spaced equally around a circle of radius 2.

(B) $w_2 = -\sqrt{3} - i$, $w_3 = \sqrt{3} - i$

(C) The cube of each cube root is $-8i$.

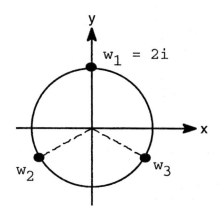

(*8-7*)

54. $k = 44.6 \sin 23.4°$ (*8-1*)

57. False   (*8-7*)   **58.** False   (*8-7*)   **59.** True   (*8-7*)   **60.** False   (*8-7*)

61. (A)

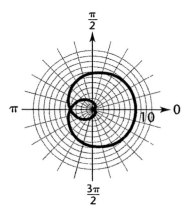

(B)

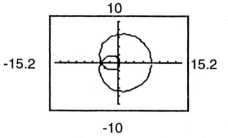

(*8-5*)

62. (A) The coordinates of P represent a simultaneous solution.

(B) $r = -4\sqrt{2}$, $\theta = 3\pi/4$

(C) The two graphs go through the pole at different values of θ.

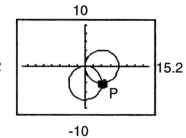

(*8-5*)

63. 1, -1, i, $-i$, $\dfrac{\sqrt{2}}{2} + i\dfrac{\sqrt{2}}{2}$, $\dfrac{\sqrt{2}}{2} - i\dfrac{\sqrt{2}}{2}$, $-\dfrac{\sqrt{2}}{2} + i\dfrac{\sqrt{2}}{2}$, $-\dfrac{\sqrt{2}}{2} - i\dfrac{\sqrt{2}}{2}$ *(8-7)*

64. $P(x) = (x + 2i)[x - (-\sqrt{3} + i)][x - (\sqrt{3} + i)]$ *(8-7)*

65. 438 miles   *(8-3)*   **66.** 438 miles per hour at 83°   *(8-3)*

67. 86°, 464 miles per hour   *(8-3)*   **68.** 0.6 miles   *(8-1)*

69. 177 pounds at 15.2° relative to **v**   *(8-3)*

70. 19 kg at 204° relative to **u**   *(8-4)*

71. (A) Distance at aphelion: 1.56×10^8 miles
         Distance at perihelion: 1.29×10^8 miles

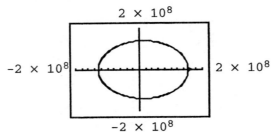

   (B) Distance at aphelion: 1.56×10^8 miles
         Distance at perihelion: 1.29×10^8 miles   *(8-5)*

72. 5,740 lb   *(8-4)*

CUMULATIVE REVIEW EXERCISE (Chapters 6, 7 and 8)

1. 1.86 meters   *(6-1)*   **2.** θ = 57.3°, 14.5 cm, 7.83 cm   *(6-2)*

3. (A) I, II (B) I, IV (C) I, III   *(6-3)*

4. (A) $-\dfrac{3}{5}$ (B) $\dfrac{5}{4}$ (C) $-\dfrac{4}{3}$ *(6-3)*   **5.** (A) $\dfrac{\pi}{4}$ (B) 65° (C) 30°   *(6-4)*

6. (A) Domain: all real numbers; Range: $-1 \le y \le 1$; Period: 2π

   (B) Domain: all real numbers; Range: $-1 \le y \le 1$; Period: 2π

   (C) Domain: all real numbers except $x = \dfrac{\pi}{2} + k\pi$, k an integer;
   Range: all real numbers; Period: π *(6-6)*

7.

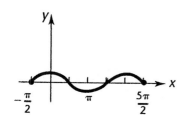

(6-6)

8.

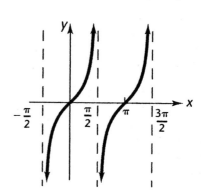

(6-6)

9. The central angle of a circle subtended by an arc of twice the length of the radius.   *(6-1)*

10. If the graph of $y = \cos x$ is shifted $\pi/2$ units to the right, the result will be the graph of $y = \sin x$.   *(6-6, 6-7)*

15. (A) Not an identity   (B) An identity   *(7-1)*

16. Angle α is acute. A triangle can have at most one obtuse angle. Since β is acute, then, if the triangle has an obtuse angle it must be the angle opposite the longer of the two sides, a and c. Thus, α, the angle opposite the shorter of the two sides, a, must be acute.   *(8-2)*

17. 0.3245, 2.8171   *(7-5)*   **18.** -76.2154°   *(7-5)*

19. b = 22 ft, α = 28°, γ = 31°   *(8-2, 8-1)*   **20.** ⟨6, -3⟩   *(8-4)*

21. (5, -30°): The polar axis is rotated 30° clockwise (negative direction) and the point is located 5 units from the pole along the positive polar axis.
(-5, -210°): The polar axis is rotated 210° clockwise (negative direction) and the point is located 5 units from the pole along the negative polar axis.
(5, 330°): The polar axis is rotated 330° counterclockwise (positive direction) and the point is located 5 units from the pole along the positive polar axis.
                                                                (8-5)

22.

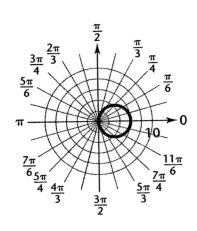

(8-5)

23.

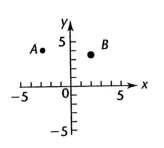

(8-6)

24. $4\sqrt{3} + 4i$ (8-7)

25. $-\dfrac{7\pi}{6}$, 870°   (6-1)

26. 75.06°   (6-1)

27. (A) and (C)   (6-3, 6-5)

28. $-\dfrac{\sqrt{3}}{2}$ (6-4)

29. $-\sqrt{2}$ (6-4)

30. Not defined   (6-3, 6-4, 6-5)

31. $-\dfrac{\sqrt{3}}{3}$ (6-4)

32. $\dfrac{\pi}{3}$ (6-9)

33. $-\dfrac{\pi}{3}$ (6-9)

34. Not defined   (6-9)

35. $-\dfrac{3\sqrt{10}}{10}$ (6-9, 6-3)

36. $\dfrac{\sqrt{2}}{3}$ (6-9)

37. $\dfrac{\pi}{4}$ (6-9)

38. (A) 9.871   (B) -3.748   (C) -1.559   (D) not defined   (6-3, 6-5, 6-9)

39.

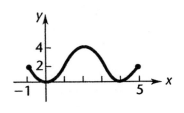

(6-7)

40. (A) 150°   (B) -19.755°   (6-9)

41. $\sin^{-1}(\sin 3) = 0.142$. For the identity $\sin^{-1}(\sin x) = x$ to hold, x must be in the restricted domain of the sine function; that is , $-\pi/2 \le x \le \pi/2$. The number 3 is not in the restricted domain.   (6-9)

42. Since the coordinates of a point on a unit circle are given by $P(a, b) = P(\cos x, \sin x)$, we evaluate $P(\cos(11.205), \sin(11.205))$--using a calculator set in radian mode--to obtain $P(0.208, -0.978)$. The quadrant in which $P(a, b)$ lies can be determined by the signs of a and b. In this case P is in the fourth quadrant, since a is positive and b is negative.   (6-5)

43. The equation has infinitely many solutions [$x = \tan^{-1}(-24.5) + k\pi$, k any integer]; $\tan^{-1}(-24.5)$ has a unique value (-1.530 to three decimal places). *(6-9, 7-5)*

44. $y = 3 + 2 \sin \pi x$ *(6-7)*

45. $A = 3$, $P = \pi$, P.S. $= \dfrac{\pi}{2}$

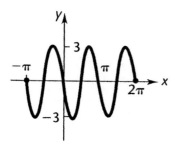

(6-7)

46. Phase shift = 1, Period = 2

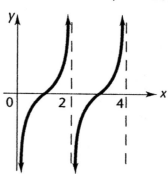

(6-8)

47.

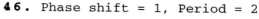

(6-6)

48. If the graph of $y = \cot x$ is shifted to the left $\pi/2$ units and reflected in the x axis, the result will be the graph of $y = \tan x$.   *(6-6, 6-7)*

49. $y = \dfrac{1}{2} - \dfrac{1}{2} \cos 2x$ *(6-7)*

50. $y = \cot x$ *(6-7, 6-8)*

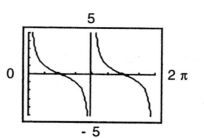

51. (A) Yes

(B) Conditional, since both sides are defined at $x = \pi/2$, for example, but $\pi/2$ is not a solution.   *(7-1)*

58. (A) Not an identity   (B) An identity   *(7-1)*   **59.** 0   *(7-2)*

60. $\sin 2x = \dfrac{-24}{25}$, $\cos \dfrac{x}{2} = \sqrt{\dfrac{1}{10}}$ or $\dfrac{\sqrt{10}}{10}$ *(6-4, 7-3)*

61. $30°$, $150°$, $270°$ *(7-5)*

62. $x = k\pi$, $\dfrac{\pi}{3} + 2k\pi$, $-\dfrac{\pi}{3} + 2k\pi$, k any integer   *(7-5)*

63. (A) $\pi/2$, $3\pi/2$, $7\pi/6$, $11\pi/6$ (B) 1.571, 3.665, 4.712, 5.760   *(7-5)*

64. $x = 0.926$ *(7-5)*   **65.** $\gamma = 107.2°$, $\alpha = 25.0°$, $\beta = 47.8°$ *(8-1, 8-2)*

66. No solution   *(8-1)*   **67.** $\beta = 120.7°$, $\gamma = 6.4°$ $c = 4.81$ in   *(8-1)*

68. β must be acute. A triangle can have at most one obtuse angle, and since γ is acute, the obtuse angle, if present, must be opposite the longer of the two sides a and b.   *(8-2)*

69. $|u + v| = 35.6$ lb, $\alpha = 16.3°$ *(8-1, 8-2, 8-3)*

70. (A) $\langle 1, 3 \rangle$ (B) $3i + j$ *(8-4)*   **71.** $r = 8 \sin \theta$ *(8-5)*

72. $x^2 + y^2 = -4x$ *(8-5)*

73.

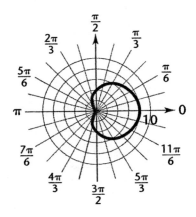

(8-5)

74.

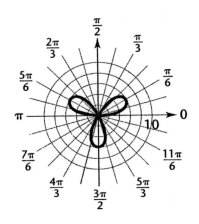

(8-5)

75. $n = 1$ $n = 2$ $n = 3$

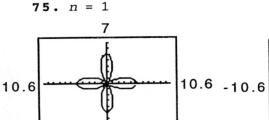 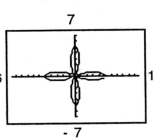 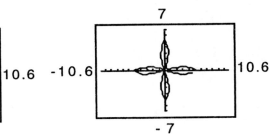

4 leaves for all n *(8-5)*

76.

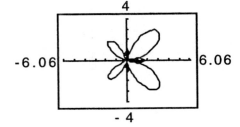

(8-5)

77. $(4.23, -131.07°)$ *(8-5)*   **78.** $(-3.68, 5.02)$ *(8-5)*

79. $\sqrt{3} - i$ *(8-6)*   **80.** $z = 2e^{120°i}$ *(8-6)*

81. $64 + 0i = 64$ *(8-7)*

82. $w_1 = \dfrac{\sqrt{3}}{2} - \dfrac{1}{2}i,$
$w_2 = i,$
$w_3 = -\dfrac{\sqrt{3}}{2} - \dfrac{1}{2}i$

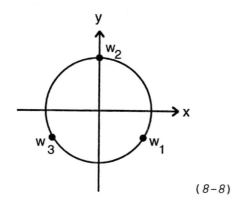

$(8\text{-}8)$

83. $5.82e^{(-146.99°)i}$ $(8\text{-}6)$

84. $-6.70 + 1.94i$ $(8\text{-}6)$

85. (A) There are a total of four fourth roots and they are spaced equally around a circle of radius $\sqrt{2}$.

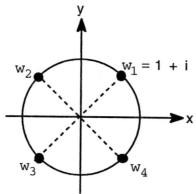

(B) $w_2 = -1 + i,$
$w_3 = -1 - i,$
$w_4 = 1 - i$

(C) The fourth power of each fourth root is -4.

$(8\text{-}7)$

86. $a = \cos 1.2 = 0.362$
$b = \sin 1.2 = 0.932$ $(6\text{-}5)$

87.

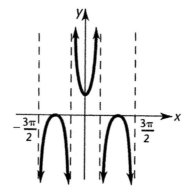

$(6\text{-}8)$

88. $y = 3\cos(2\pi x - \pi/4)$; Amplitude = 3, Period = 1, P.S. = 1/8 $(6\text{-}7)$

89. $y = 2\sin(2x - 0.644)$

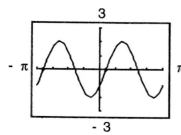

$(6\text{-}7)$

90. $\dfrac{1}{\sqrt{1 - x^2}}$ $(6\text{-}9)$

91. $\dfrac{24}{25}$ $(6\text{-}9,\ 7\text{-}3)$

92. (A) $\dfrac{2}{\sqrt{5}}$ or $\dfrac{2\sqrt{5}}{5}$ (B) $-\dfrac{7}{25}$ $(7\text{-}3)$

93. (A) $\pi/3,\ 5\pi/3$ (B) $1.0472,\ 5.2360$ $(7\text{-}5)$

94. (A)

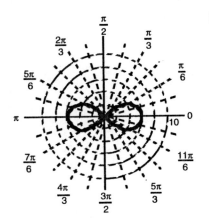

(B)

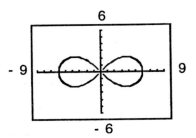

(8-5)

95. (A)

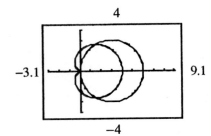

(B) 6

(C) $(3, \pi/3)$, $(3, 5\pi/3)$

(D) The points on $r2$ and $r1$ arrive at the intersection points for different values of θ, except for the two found in part (C).

(8-5)

96. $P(x) = (x - i)[x - (\sqrt{3}/2 - i/2)][x - (-\sqrt{3}/2 - i/2)]$ (8-7)

97. No   (8-1, 8-2)   **98.** False   (6-9)

99. True   (6-9)   **100.** True   (8-7)

101. False   (8-7)   **102.** False   (8-3, 8-4)

103. False   (8-4)   **104.** False   (6-5)

105. True   (6-5)   **106.** $\frac{2\pi}{73}$ radians   (6-1)

107. 1,088 m   (6-2)   **108.** 5.88 in   (6-2, 8-2)

109. 76°   (8-2)   **110.** $I = 50 \cos 220\pi t$ (6-7)

111. 274 miles per hour at 117°   (8-3)

112. Both have a tension of 234 lb   (8-4)

113. (A) Add the perpendicular bisector of the chord as shown in the figure. Then, $\sin \theta = 4/R$ and $\theta = 5/R$. Substituting the second into the first, we obtain $\sin 5/R = 4/R$.

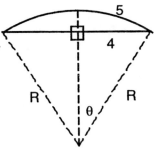

(B) R cannot be isolated on one side of the equation.

(C) Plot $y_1 = \sin 5/R$ and $y_2 = 4/R$ in the same viewing window and solve for R at the point of intersection using a built-in routine (see figure).
$R = 4.420$ cm.

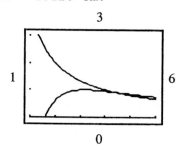

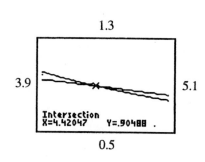

(7-5)

114. (A)

 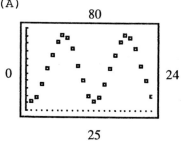

(C)

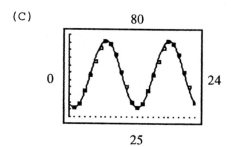

(B) $y = 53.5 + 22.5 \sin(\pi x/6 - 2.1)$ (6-7)

CHAPTER 9

Exercise 9-1

1. B, no solution   **2.** A, $(2, 1)$ **3.** D, $(1, -3)$

4. C, infinitely many solutions: for any real number s, $x = s$, $y = 2s - 5$

5. $(5, 2)$ **6.** $(3, 1)$ **7.** $(2, -3)$ **8.** $(2, 4)$

9. No solution (parallel lines)   **10.** parallel lines, no solution

11. $(2, -1)$ **12.** $(8, 6)$ **13.** $(3, -1)$ **14.** $(-1, 3)$

15. 2×3, 1×3 **16.** 3×3, 2×1 **17.** C   **18.** D

19. B   **20.** 1   **21.** $-2, -6$ **22.** $4, 0$

23. $-2, 6, 0$ **24.** $3, 1$ **25.** $\begin{bmatrix} 4 & -6 & | & -8 \\ 1 & -3 & | & 2 \end{bmatrix}$ **26.** $\begin{bmatrix} 1 & -3 & | & 2 \\ 2 & -3 & | & -4 \end{bmatrix}$

27. $\begin{bmatrix} -4 & 12 & | & -8 \\ 4 & -6 & | & -8 \end{bmatrix}$ **28.** $\begin{bmatrix} -2 & 6 & | & -4 \\ 4 & -6 & | & -8 \end{bmatrix}$ **29.** $\begin{bmatrix} 1 & -3 & | & 2 \\ 8 & -12 & | & -16 \end{bmatrix}$ **30.** $\begin{bmatrix} 1 & -3 & | & 2 \\ -4 & 6 & | & 8 \end{bmatrix}$

31. $\begin{bmatrix} 1 & -3 & | & 2 \\ 0 & 6 & | & -16 \end{bmatrix}$ **32.** $\begin{bmatrix} -1 & 0 & | & 6 \\ 4 & -6 & | & -8 \end{bmatrix}$ **33.** $\begin{bmatrix} 1 & -3 & | & 2 \\ 2 & 0 & | & -12 \end{bmatrix}$ **34.** $\begin{bmatrix} 1 & -3 & | & 2 \\ 1 & 3 & | & -14 \end{bmatrix}$

35. $\begin{bmatrix} 1 & -3 & | & 2 \\ 3 & -3 & | & -10 \end{bmatrix}$ **36.** $\begin{bmatrix} 1 & -3 & | & 2 \\ 5 & -9 & | & -6 \end{bmatrix}$

37. $x_1 = 4$, $x_2 = 3$; each pair of lines has the same intersection point.

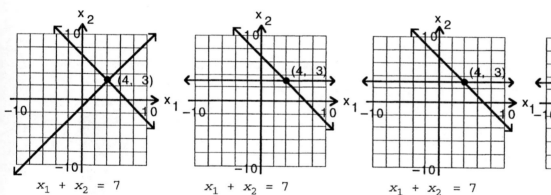 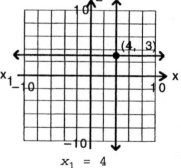

| $x_1 + x_2 = 7$ | $x_1 + x_2 = 7$ | $x_1 + x_2 = 7$ | $x_1 = 4$ |
| $x_1 - x_2 = 1$ | $-2x_2 = -6$ | $x_2 = 3$ | $x_2 = 3$ |

38. $x_1 = 1$, $x_2 = 4$; each pair of lines has the same intersection point.

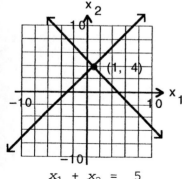 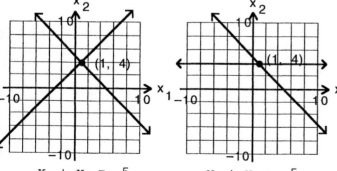

| $x_1 + x_2 = 5$ | $x_1 + x_2 = 5$ | $x_1 + x_2 = 5$ | $x_1 = 1$ |
| $x_1 - x_2 = -3$ | $-2x_2 = -8$ | $x_2 = 4$ | $x_2 = 4$ |

39. $x_1 = 2$ and $x_2 = 1$ **40.** $x_1 = -2$, $x_2 = 1$ **41.** $x_1 = 2$ and $x_2 = 4$

42. $x_1 = -1$, $x_2 = 2$ **43.** no solution   **44.** no solution

45. $x_1 = 1$ and $x_2 = 4$ **46.** $x_1 = -1$, $x_2 = 2$

47. Infinitely many solutions for any real number s, $x_2 = s$, $x_1 = 2s - 3$

48. Infinitely many solutions for $x_2 = s$, $x_1 = 2s - 1$ for any real number s

49. Infinitely many solutions for any real number s, $x_2 = s$, $x_1 = \frac{1}{2}s + \frac{1}{2}$

50. Infinitely many solutions for $x_2 = s$, $x_1 = \frac{1}{3}s - \frac{2}{3}$ for any real number s

51. $(1.12, 2.41)$ **52.** $(2.21, -1.52)$ **53.** $(-2.24, -3.31)$ **54.** $(-3.35, 1.23)$

55. (A) $(-24, 20)$ (B) $(6, -4)$ (C) No solution

56. (A) $(10, 10)$ (B) $(-2, 0)$ (C) Infinite number of solutions

57. $(-23.125, 7.8125)$ **58.** $(1.25, -1.5625)$ **59.** $(3.225, -6.9375)$

60. $(6.2625, 8.375)$ **61.** 25 32-cent stamps, 50 23-cent stamps

62. 57 nickels, 32 dimes   **63.** \$107,500 in bond A and \$92,500 in bond B

64. 25% in fund A and 75% in fund B

65. 30 liters of 20% solution and 70 liters of 80% solution

66. 56 liters of 40% solution and 24 liters of 70% solution

67. 200 grams of mix A and 80 grams of mix B

68. 50 bags of brand A and 40 bags of brand B

69. Base price = \$17.95, surcharge = \$2.45 per pound

70. (A) Base price = \$22.15, surcharge = \$1.95

(B) Ship packages weighing more than 9 pounds with Federated Shipping and all others with United Express.

71. 5,720 pounds of the robust blend and 6,160 pounds of the mild blend.

72. (A) The company can produce 8,448 pounds of the mild blend by blending 3,168 pounds of Columbian beans with 5,280 pounds of Brazilian beans. There will be 3,432 pounds of Columbian beans that are not used.

(B) The company can produce 8,800 pounds of the robust blend by blending 6,600 pounds of Columbian beans with 2,200 pounds of Brazilian beans. There will be 3,080 pounds of Brazilian beans that are not used.

Exercise 9-2

1. No   **2.** Yes   **3.** Yes   **4.** No   **5.** No   **6.** No   **7.** Yes

8. Yes   **9.** $x_1 = -2$, $x_2 = 3$, $x_3 = 0$ **10.** $x_1 = -2$, $x_2 = 0$, $x_3 = 1$, $x_4 = 3$

11. $x_1 = 2t + 3$, $x_2 = -t - 5$, $x_3 = t$ is the solution for t any real number

12. $x_1 = 2t - 3$, $x_2 = t$, $x_3 = 5$, t any real number

13. No solution   **14.** $x_1 = 5$, $x_2 = -3$

15. $x_1 = 2s + 3t - 5$, $x_2 = s$, $x_3 = -3t + 2$, $x_4 = t$ is the solution, for s and t any real numbers

16. $x_1 - 2x_3 + 3x_4 = 4$, $x_2 - x_3 + 2x_4 = -1$; $x_1 = 2s - 3t + 4$, $x_2 = s - 2t - 1$, $x_3 = s$, $x_4 = t$, s and $t = $ any real number

17. $\begin{bmatrix} 1 & 0 & | & -7 \\ 0 & 1 & | & 3 \end{bmatrix}$ **18.** $\begin{bmatrix} 1 & 0 & | & 7 \\ 0 & 1 & | & -2 \end{bmatrix}$ **19.** $\begin{bmatrix} 1 & 0 & 0 & | & -5 \\ 0 & 1 & 0 & | & 4 \\ 0 & 0 & 1 & | & -2 \end{bmatrix}$

20. $\begin{bmatrix} 1 & 0 & 0 & | & 4 \\ 0 & 1 & 0 & | & -4 \\ 0 & 0 & 1 & | & -1 \end{bmatrix}$ **21.** $\begin{bmatrix} 1 & 0 & 2 & | & -\frac{5}{3} \\ 0 & 1 & -2 & | & \frac{1}{3} \\ 0 & 0 & 0 & | & 0 \end{bmatrix}$ **22.** $\begin{bmatrix} 1 & 0 & -1 & | & -\frac{5}{2} \\ 0 & 1 & -4 & | & -\frac{1}{2} \\ 0 & 0 & 0 & | & 0 \end{bmatrix}$

23. $x_1 = -2$, $x_2 = 3$, and $x_3 = 1$ **24.** $x_1 = -2$, $x_2 = 0$, $x_3 = 1$

25. $x_1 = 0$, $x_2 = -2$, and $x_3 = 2$ **26.** $x_1 = 1$, $x_2 = -2$, $x_3 = 0$

27. $x_1 = 2t + 3$, $x_2 = t - 2$, $x_3 = t$, t any real number

28. $x_3 = t$, $x_1 = -t - 1$, $x_2 = 3 + 2t$, t any real number

29. $x_1 = 1$, $x_2 = 2$ **30.** No solution

31. No solution   **32.** No solution

33. $x_1 = 2t + 4$, $x_2 = t + 1$, $x_3 = t$, t any real number

34. $x_1 = 3t - 1$, $x_2 = -2t - 1$, $x_3 = t$, t any real number

35. $x_1 = s + 2t - 1$, $x_2 = s$, $x_3 = t$, s and t any real numbers

36. $x_2 = s$ and $x_3 = t$, $x_1 = -4s + 3t + 2$, s, t any real numbers

37. No solution   **38.** No solution

39. $x_1 = 2.5t - 4$, $x_2 = t$, $x_3 = -5$ for t any real number

40. $x_1 = 1.5t - 2.5$, $x_2 = -0.5t - 2$, $x_3 = t$ for t any real number

41. $x_1 = 1$, $x_2 = -2$, $x_3 = 1$

42. $x_1 = -1$, $x_2 = 1$, $x_3 = 3$

43. (A) Dependent with two parameters   (B) Dependent with one parameter
(C) Independent   (D) Impossible

44. (A) $\begin{bmatrix} 1 & 0 & m & | & a \\ 0 & 1 & n & | & b \\ 0 & 0 & 0 & | & 0 \end{bmatrix}$, $\begin{bmatrix} 1 & m & 0 & | & a \\ 0 & 0 & 1 & | & b \\ 0 & 0 & 0 & | & 0 \end{bmatrix}$, $\begin{bmatrix} 1 & m & n & | & a \\ 0 & 0 & 0 & | & 0 \\ 0 & 0 & 0 & | & 0 \end{bmatrix}$

(B) $\begin{bmatrix} 1 & 0 & m & | & 0 \\ 0 & 1 & n & | & 0 \\ 0 & 0 & 0 & | & 1 \end{bmatrix}$, $\begin{bmatrix} 1 & m & n & | & 0 \\ 0 & 0 & 0 & | & 1 \\ 0 & 0 & 0 & | & 0 \end{bmatrix}$

45. $x_1 = 2s - 3t + 3$, $x_2 = s + 2t + 2$, $x_3 = s$, $x_4 = t$, s and t any real numbers

46. $x_1 = 3t - 2s - 1$, $x_2 = s$ and $x_3 = -2t + 2$, $x_4 = t$; s, t any real numbers

47. $x_1 = -0.5$, $x_2 = 0.2$, $x_3 = 0.3$, $x_4 = -0.4$

48. $x_1 = -1.2$, $x_2 = 0.6$, $x_3 = 0.7$, $x_4 = -0.9$

49. $x_1 = 2s - 1.5t + 1$, $x_2 = s$, $x_3 = -t + 1.5$, $x_4 = 0.5t - 0.5$, $x_5 = t$ for s and t any real numbers

50. $x_1 = -5.5s + 3.5t + 10.5$, $x_2 = -1.5s + 1.5t + 2.5$, $x_3 = s$, $x_4 = -t - 1$, $x_5 = t$
for s and t any real numbers

51. $x_1 = (3t - 100)$ 15-cent stamps, $x_2 = (145 - 4t)$ 20-cent stamps,
$x_3 = t$ 35-cent stamps, where $t = 34$, 35, or 36

52. if $Q = t = 24$, 25, 26 then $N = 3t - 72$ and $D = 104 - 4t$

53. $x_1 = (6t - 24)$, 500-cc containers of 10% solution
$x_2 = (48 - 8t)$, 500-cc containers of 20% solution
$x_3 = t$, 1000-cc containers of 50% solution
where $t = 4$, 5, or 6

54. $x = 9t - 24$, 10% containers; $y = 48 - 12t$, 20% containers;
$z = t$, 50% containers, where $t = 3$, 4

55. $a = 3$, $b = 2$, $c = 1$ **56.** $a = 8$, $b = -7$, $c = 2$

57. $a = -2$, $b = -4$, and $c = -20$ **58.** $a = 2$, $b = 6$, $c = -15$

59. $x_1 = 20$ one-person boats, $x_2 = 220$ two-person boats, $x_3 = 100$ four-person boats

60. 150 one-person boats, 200 two-person boats, 50 four-person boats

61. $x_1 = (t - 80)$ one-person boats, $x_2 = (-2t + 420)$ two-person boats,
$x_3 = t$ four-person boats $80 \leq t \leq 210$, t an integer

62. $x = 100 + t$, one-person; $y = 300 - 2t$, two-person;
$z = t$, four-person, $0 \leq t \leq 150$, $t = $ integer

63. No solution; no production schedule will use all the work-hours in all
departments.

64. No production schedule will use all work hours in all departments.

65. $x_1 = 8$ ounces food A, $x_2 = 2$ ounces food B, $x_3 = 4$ ounces food C

66. 12 oz. food A, 4 oz. food B, 0 oz. food C

67. No solution

68. 12 oz. food A, 4 oz. food B

69. $x_1 = 8$ ounces food A, $x_2 = -2t + 10$ ounces food B, $x_3 = t$ ounces food C
$0 \leq t \leq 5$

70. 12 oz. food A, $4 - 2t$ oz. of food B, t oz. of food C where $0 \leq t \leq 2$

71. $x_1 = 10$ hours company A, $x_2 = 15$ hours company B

72. 15 hours company A, 10 hours company B

Exercise 9-3

1. $(-12, 5)$, $(-12, -5)$ **2.** $(3, -4)$, $(-3, -4)$ **3.** $(2, 4)$, $(-2, -4)$

4. $\left(\dfrac{1}{2}, 1\right)$ **5.** $(5, -5)$, $(-5, 5)$ **6.** $(-4, 2)$, $(4, -2)$

7. $(4 + 2\sqrt{3}, 1 + \sqrt{3})$, $(4 - 2\sqrt{3}, 1 - \sqrt{3})$ **8.** $(3 + \sqrt{5}, 7 + 3\sqrt{5})$, $(3 - \sqrt{5}, 7 - 3\sqrt{5})$

9. $(2, 4)$, $(2, -4)$, $(-2, 4)$, $(-2, -4)$ **10.** $(2, 1)$, $(2, -1)$, $(-2, -1)$, $(-2, 1)$

11. $(1, 3)$, $(1, -3)$, $(-1, 3)$, $(-1, -3)$ **12.** $(3, 2)$, $(3, -2)$, $(-3, 2)$, $(-3, -2)$

13. $(1 + \sqrt{5}, -1 + \sqrt{5})$, $(1 - \sqrt{5}, -1 - \sqrt{5})$

14. $(2 + \sqrt{10}, -2 + \sqrt{10})$, $(2 - \sqrt{10}, -2 - \sqrt{10})$

15. $(\sqrt{2}, \sqrt{2})$, $(-\sqrt{2}, -\sqrt{2})$, $(2, 1)$, $(-2, -1)$

16. $(1, 4)$, $(-1, -4)$, $(2\sqrt{2}, \sqrt{2})$, $(-2\sqrt{2}, -\sqrt{2})$

17. $(2, 2i)$, $(-2, 2i)$, $(2, -2i)$, $(-2, -2i)$

18. $(i, 2i)$, $(-i, 2i)$, $(i, -2i)$, $(-i, -2i)$

19. $(2, \sqrt{2})$, $(2, -\sqrt{2})$, $(-1, i)$, $(-1, -i)$

20. $(2, 4)$, $(-2, 4)$, $(\sqrt{5}i, -5)$, $(-\sqrt{5}i, -5)$

21. $(3, 0)$, $(-3, 0)$, $(\sqrt{5}, 2)$, $(-\sqrt{5}, 2)$

22. $(4, 0)$, $(-3, \sqrt{7})$, $(-3, -\sqrt{7})$

23. $(2, 1)$, $(-2, -1)$, $(i, -2i)$, $(-i, 2i)$

24. $(i, -2i)$, $(-i, 2i)$, $\left(\frac{2\sqrt{5}}{5}, \sqrt{5}\right)$, $\left(\frac{-2\sqrt{5}}{5}, -\sqrt{5}\right)$

25. $(3, -4)$, $(-1, 4)$ **26.** $(1, 4)$, $(3, 6)$ **27.** $(0, 0)$, $(3, 6)$

28. $(1, 3)$, $(0, 0)$ **29.** $(1, 4)$, $(4, 1)$ **30.** $(1, 6)$, $(-1, 2)$

31. $(4, 8)$, $(-1, 3)$ **32.** $(4, -10)$, $(-3, 11)$

33. (A) The lines are tangent to the circle.

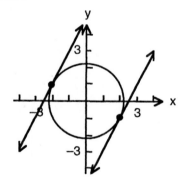

(B) $b = 5$, intersection point is $(2, -1)$; $b = -5$, intersection point is $(-2, 1)$

(C) The line $x + 2y = 0$ is perpendicular to all the lines in the family and intersects the circle at the intersection points found in part B. Solving the system $x^2 + y^2 = 5$, $x + 2y = 0$ would determine the intersection points.

34. (A) The lines are tangent to the circle.

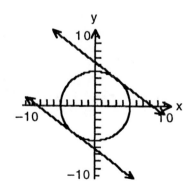

(B) $b = 25$, intersection point is $(3, 4)$; $b = -25$, intersection point is $(-3, -4)$

(C) The line $4x - 3y = 0$ is perpendicular to all the lines in the family and intersects the circle at the intersection points found in part B. Solving the system $x^2 + y^2 = 25$, $4x - 3y = 0$ would determine the intersection points.

35. $\left(-\frac{3}{2}, -2\right)$, $\left(-5, -\frac{3}{5}\right)$ **36.** $\left(3, \frac{5}{3}\right)$, $\left(\frac{5}{2}, 2\right)$ **37.** $(0, -1)$, $(-4, -3)$

38. (4, 7), (-1, 2)   **39.** (2, 2), (-2, -2), (-$\sqrt{2}$, $\sqrt{2}$), ($\sqrt{2}$, -$\sqrt{2}$)

40. (0, 6), (0, -6), (3, 3), (-3, -3)   **41.** (-*i*, *i*), (*i*, -*i*), (-3, 1), (3, -1)

42. (4, 4), (-4, -4), $\left(\dfrac{4\sqrt{5}}{5}, \dfrac{-4\sqrt{5}}{5}\right)$, $\left(\dfrac{-4\sqrt{5}}{5}, \dfrac{4\sqrt{5}}{5}\right)$

43. (-1.41, -0.82), (-0.13, 1.15), (0.13, -1.15), (1.41, 0.82)

44. (-1.12, -0.64), (-0.39, 2.43), (0.39, -2.43), (1.12, 0.64)

45. (-1.66, -0.84), (-0.91, 3.77), (0.91, -3.77), (1.66, 0.84)

46. (-1.48, 1.60), (-0.65, 3.19), (0.65, -3.19), (1.48, -1.60)

47. (-2.96, -3.47), (-0.89, -3.76), (1.39, 4.05), (2.46, 4.18)

48. (-2.09, -0.66), (0.18, -3.64), (0.58, 2.83), (1.73, 1.28)

49. $\frac{1}{2}$(3 - $\sqrt{5}$) and $\frac{1}{2}$(3 + $\sqrt{5}$)   **50.** $\left(\dfrac{1 + \sqrt{5}}{2}, \dfrac{-1 + \sqrt{5}}{2}\right)$, $\left(\dfrac{1 - \sqrt{5}}{2}, \dfrac{-1 - \sqrt{}}{2}\right)$

51. 5 inches and 12 inches   **52.** 2 meters by 16 meters

53. 6 inches by 4.5 inches   **54.** 2*x* = 6 in by 2*y* = 2.5 in

55. 22 feet by 26 feet   **56.** 24 in by 32 in

57. *x* = 25 mph = average speed of Boat *B*; *x* + 5 = 30 mph = average speed of Boat *A*

58. 3:30 PM

Exercise 9-4

1.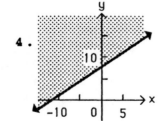

2.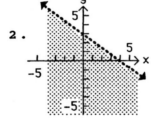

3.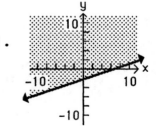

4.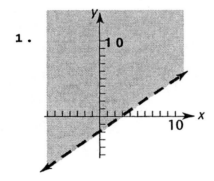

5.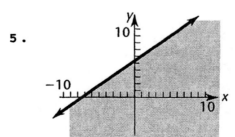

6.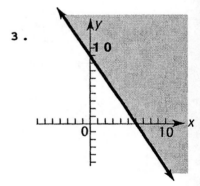

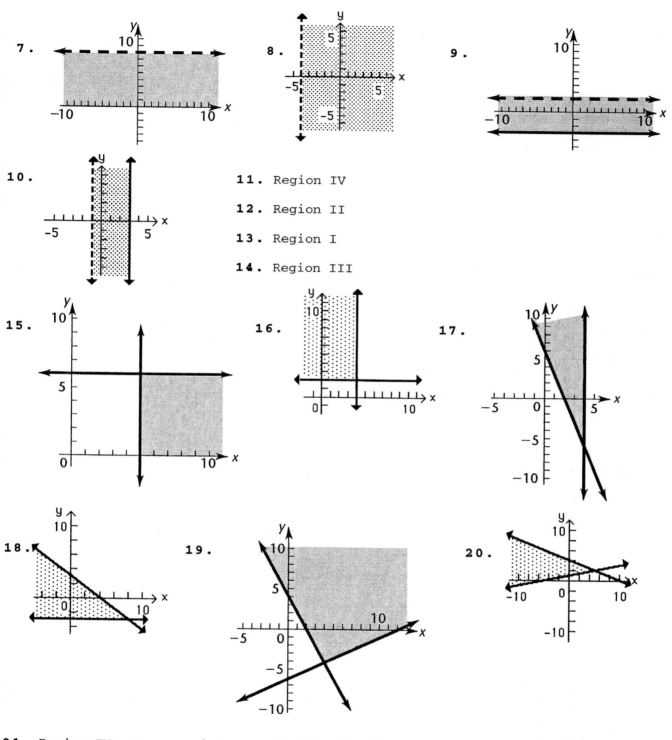

7.

8.

9.

10.

11. Region IV

12. Region II

13. Region I

14. Region III

15.

16.

17.

18.

19.

20.

21. Region IV; corner points are (6, 4), (8, 0), and (18, 0)

22. Region III; corner points: (0, 0), (0, 6), (6, 4), (8, 0)

23. Region I; corner points are (0, 16), (6, 4), and (18, 0)

24. Region II; corner points: (6, 4), (0, 6), (0, 16)

25.

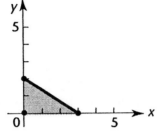

corner points: (0, 0), (0, 2), (3, 0); bounded

26.

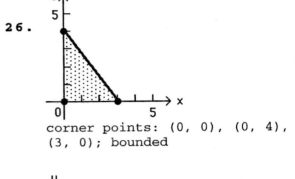

corner points: (0, 0), (0, 4), (3, 0); bounded

27.

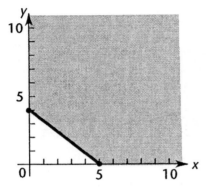

corner points: (0, 4) and (5, 0); unbounded

28.

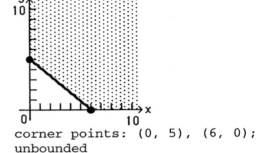

corner points: (0, 5), (6, 0); unbounded

29.

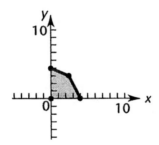

corner points: (0, 4), (0, 0), $\left(\dfrac{12}{5}, \dfrac{16}{5}\right)$, (4, 0); bounded

30.

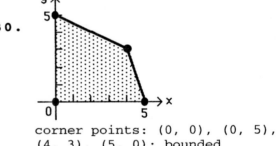

corner points: (0, 0), (0, 5), (4, 3), (5, 0); bounded

31.

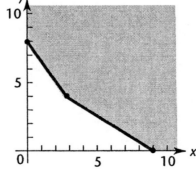

corner points: (9, 0), (0, 8), and (3, 4); unbounded

32.

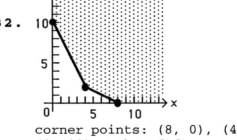

corner points: (8, 0), (4, 2), (0, 10); unbounded

33.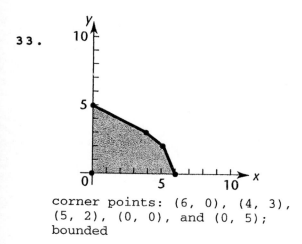

corner points: (6, 0), (4, 3), (5, 2), (0, 0), and (0, 5); bounded

34.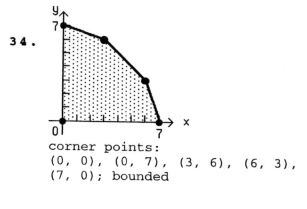

corner points: (0, 0), (0, 7), (3, 6), (6, 3), (7, 0); bounded

35.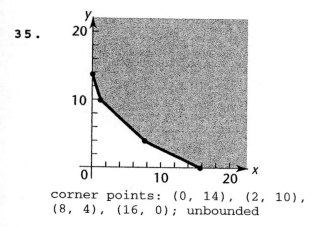

corner points: (0, 14), (2, 10), (8, 4), (16, 0); unbounded

36.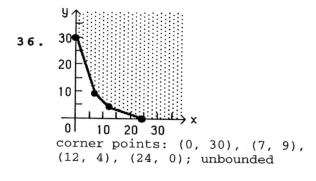

corner points: (0, 30), (7, 9), (12, 4), (24, 0); unbounded

37.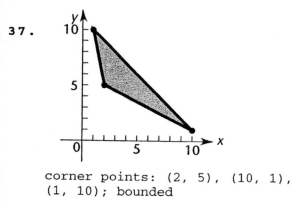

corner points: (2, 5), (10, 1), (1, 10); bounded

38.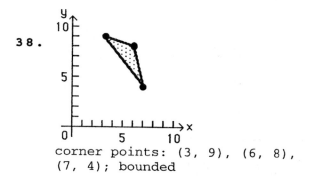

corner points: (3, 9), (6, 8), (7, 4); bounded

39. The feasible region is empty.

40. The feasible region is empty.

41.

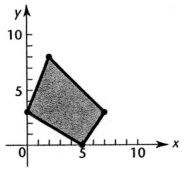

corner points: (0, 3), (5, 0), (7, 3), (2, 8); bounded

42.

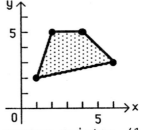

corner points: (1, 2), (2, 5), (4, 5), (6, 3); bounded

43.

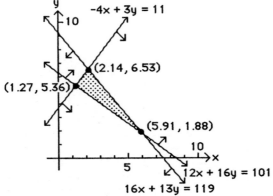

corner points: (1.27, 5.36), (2.14, 6.52), (5.91, 1.88); bounded

44.

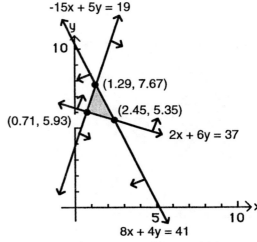

corner points: (0.71, 5.93), (1.29, 7.67), (2.45, 5.35); bounded

45. $6x + 4y \leq 108$
$x + y \leq 24$
$x \geq 0$
$y \geq 0$

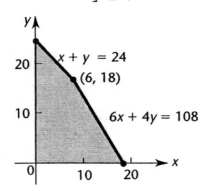

46. $8x + 2y \leq 400$
$2x + y \leq 120$
$x \geq 0$
$y \geq 0$

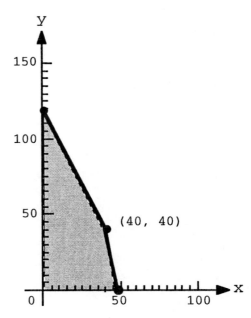

47. (A) All production schedules in the feasible region that are on the graph of $50x + 60y = 1{,}100$ will result in a profit of $1,100.

(B) There are many possible choices. For example, producing 5 trick and 15 slalom skies will produce a profit of $1,150. The graph of the line $50x + 60y = 1{,}150$ includes all the production schedules in the feasible region that result in a profit of $1,150.

48. (A) All production schedules in the feasible region that are on the graph of $50x + 15y = 1{,}300$ will result in a profit of $1,300.

(B) There are many possible choices. For example, producing 30 tables and 30 chairs will produce a profit of $1,950. The graph of the line $50x + 15y = 1{,}950$ includes all the production schedules in the feasible region that result in a profit of $1,950.

49.
$$20x + 10y \geq 460$$
$$30x + 30y \geq 960$$
$$5x + 10y \geq 220$$
$$x \geq 0$$
$$y \geq 0$$

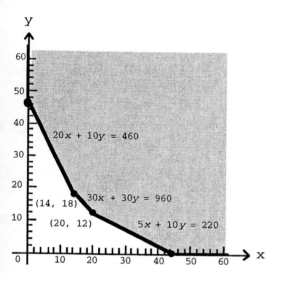

50.
$$30x + 10y \geq 360$$
$$10x + 10y \geq 160$$
$$10x + 30y \geq 240$$
$$x \geq 0$$
$$y \geq 0$$

51.
$$10x + 30y \geq 280$$
$$30x + 10y \geq 360$$
$$x \geq 0$$
$$y \geq 0$$

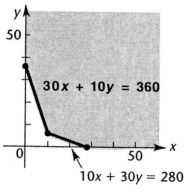

52.
$$10x + 20y \leq 800$$
$$20x + 10y \leq 640$$
$$x \geq 0$$
$$y \geq 0$$

Exercise 9-5

1. maximum value of z on S is 16 at $(7, 9)$ 2. $z_{max} = 40$ at $(10, 0)$

3. maximum value of z on S is 84 at both $(0, 12)$ and $(7, 9)$

4. $z_{max} = 90$ at $(7, 9)$ and $(10, 0)$ (multiple optimal solutions)

5. minimum value of z on S is 32 at $(0, 8)$ 6. $z_{min} = 55$ at $(4, 3)$

7. minimum value of z on S is 36 at both $(12, 0)$ and $(4, 3)$

8. $z_{min} = 32$ at $(0, 8)$ and $(4, 3)$ (multiple optimal solutions)

9. maximum value of z on S is 18 at $(4, 3)$ 10. $z_{max} = 42$ at $(3, 6)$

11. minimum value of z on S is 12 at $(4, 0)$ 12. $z_{min} = 8$ at $(0, 8)$

13. maximum value of z on S is 52 at $(4, 10)$ 14. $z_{max} = 44$ at $(7, 3)$

15. minimum value of z on S is 44 at $(4, 4)$ 16. $z_{min} = 15$ at $(15, 0)$

17. The minimum value of z on S is 1,500 at $(60, 0)$. The maximum value of z on S is 3,000 at $(60, 30)$ and $(120, 0)$ (multiple optimal solutions).

18. $z_{max} = 6000$ at $(0, 200)$; $z_{min} = 1500$ at $(0, 50)$ and $(20, 40)$ (multiple optimal solutions)

19. The minimum value of z on S is 300 at $(0, 20)$. The maximum value of z on S is 1,725 at $(60, 15)$.

20. $z_{min} = 1200$ at $(0, 40)$; $z_{max} = 4600$ at $(40, 120)$

21. Max $P = 5,507$ at $x = 6.62$ and $y = 4.25$

22. Max $P = 4,484$ at $x = 4.52$ and $y = 6.8$

23. (A) $a > 2b$ (B) $\frac{1}{3}b < a < 2b$ (C) $a < \frac{1}{3}b$ or $b > 3a$ (D) $a = 2b$ (E) $b = 3a$

24. (A) $2a < b$ (B) $\frac{1}{2}b < a < b$ (C) $a > b$ (D) $b = 2a$ (E) $b = a$

25. (A) 6 trick skis, 18 slalom skis; $780

(B) The maximum profit decreases to $720 when 18 trick and no slalom skis are produced.

(C) The maximum profit increases to $1,080 when no trick and 24 slalom skis are produced.

26. 48; 16 mice, 32 rats

27. 9 model A trucks and 6 model B trucks to realize the minimum cost of $279,000

28. 7 buses, 15 vans; $9,900

29. (A) 40 tables, 40 chairs; $4,600

(B) The maximum profit decreases to $3,800 when 20 tables and 80 chairs are produced.

30. (A) 72 (all portable)

(B) Profit on 72 portable computers is $15,840. Maximum profit is $16,640 when 30 desktop and 32 portable computers are manufactured.

31. (A) Max P = \$450 when 750 gallons are produced using the old process exclusively.

(B) The maximum profit decreases to \$380 when 400 gallons are produced using the old process and 700 gallons using the new process.

(C) The maximum profit decreases to \$288 when 1,440 gallons are produced using the new process exclusively.

32. (A) 10 sociologists, 6 research assistants; \$6,800

(B) The minimum cost will increase to \$7,200 when 9 sociologists and 9 research assistants are hired.

33. The nitrogen will range from a minimum of 940 pounds when 40 bags of brand A and 100 bags of brand B are used to a maximum of 1,190 pounds when 140 bags of brand A and 50 bags of brand B are used.

34. The amount of vitamin A will range from a minimum of 200 units when 15 ounces of food M and 20 ounces of food N are used to a maximum of 380 units when 40 ounces of food M and 15 ounces of food N are used.

CHAPTER 9 REVIEW

1. (2, 3)   *(9-1)*

2. No solution   *(9-1)*

3. Infinitely many solutions $\left(t, \dfrac{4t + 8}{3}\right)$ for any real number t *(9-1)*

4. (5, -3), (-1, 3)   *(9-3)*

5. (1, -1), $\left(\dfrac{7}{5}, -\dfrac{1}{5}\right)$ *(9-3)*

6. (1, 3), (1, -3), (-1, 3), (-1, -3)   *(9-3)*

7.

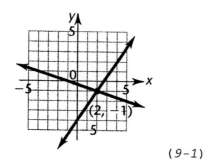

(9-1)

8.

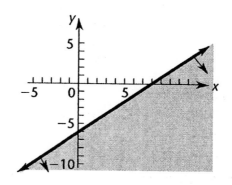

(9-4)

9.

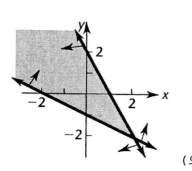

(9-4)

10. $\begin{bmatrix} 3 & -6 & | & 12 \\ 1 & -4 & | & 5 \end{bmatrix}$ *(9-1)*

11. $\begin{bmatrix} 1 & -4 & | & 5 \\ 1 & -2 & | & 4 \end{bmatrix}$ *(9-1)*

12. $\begin{bmatrix} 1 & -4 & | & 5 \\ 0 & 6 & | & -3 \end{bmatrix}$ *(9-1)*

13. $x_1 = 4$
$x_2 = -7$
The solution is $(4, -7)$ *(9-2)*

14. $x_1 - x_2 = 4$
$0 = 1$
No solution   *(9-2)*

15. $x_1 - x_2 = 4$
$x_1 = t + 4$, $x_2 = t$ is the solution, for t any real number   *(9-2)*

16. The maximum value of z on S is 42 at $(6, 4)$. The minimum value of z on S is 18 at $(0, 6)$.   *(9-5)*

17. $x_1 = 2$, $x_2 = -2$; each pair of lines has the same interesection point.

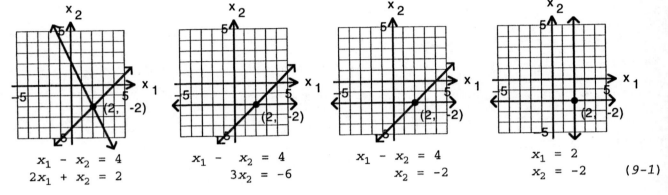

$x_1 - x_2 = 4$
$2x_1 + x_2 = 2$

$x_1 - x_2 = 4$
$3x_2 = -6$

$x_1 - x_2 = 4$
$x_2 = -2$

$x_1 = 2$
$x_2 = -2$ *(9-1)*

18. $(2.54, 2.15)$ *(9-1)*

19. $x_1 = -1$, $x_2 = 3$ *(9-2)*

20. $x_1 = -1$, $x_2 = 2$, $x_3 = 1$ *(9-2)*

21. $x_1 = 2$, $x_2 = 1$, $x_3 = -1$ *(9-2)*

22. $x_1 = -5t - 12$, $x_2 = 3t + 7$, $x_3 = t$ is a solution for every real number t. There are infinitely many solutions.   *(9-2)*

23. no solution   *(9-2)*

24. $x_1 = -\frac{3}{7}t - \frac{4}{7}$, $x_2 = \frac{5}{7}t + \frac{9}{7}$, $x_3 = t$ is a solution for every real number t. There are infinitely many solutions.   *(9-2)*

25. $(2, \sqrt{2})$, $(2, -\sqrt{2})$, $(-1, i)$, $(-1, -i)$ *(9-3)*

26. $(2, -1)$, $(-2, 1)$, $(1, -2)$, $(-1, 2)$ *(9-3)*

27. $(\sqrt{2}, \sqrt{2})$, $(-\sqrt{2}, -\sqrt{2})$, $(2, -2)$, $(-2, 2)$ *(9-3)*

28. corners: $(0, 4)$, $(0, 0)$, $(4, 0)$, and $(3, 2)$; bounded

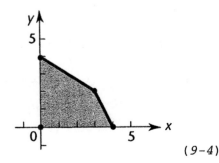

(9-4)

29. corners: $(0, 8)$, $(12, 0)$, and $\left(\dfrac{12}{5}, \dfrac{16}{5}\right)$; unbounded

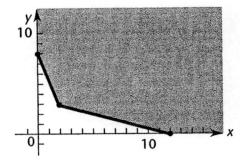

(9-4)

30. corners: (4, 4), (10, 10), (20, 0)
bounded

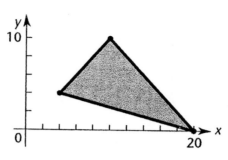

(9-4)

31. The maximum value of z on S is 46 at (4, 2).   (9-5)

32. The minimum value of z on S is 75 at (3, 6) and (15, 0) (multiple optimal solutions).
(9-5)

33. The minimum value of z on S is 44 at (4, 3). The maximum value of z on S is 82 at (2, 9).
(9-5)

34. $x_1 = 1000$, $x_2 = 4000$, $x_3 = 2000$ (9-2)

35. $\left(\dfrac{4\sqrt{7}}{7}, -\dfrac{2\sqrt{7}}{7}\right)$, $\left(-\dfrac{4\sqrt{7}}{7}, \dfrac{2\sqrt{7}}{7}\right)$, (2, 2), (-2, -2)   (9-3)

36. The maximum value of z on S is 26,000 at (600, 400).   (9-5)

37. (-2.16, -0.37), (-1.09, 5.59), (1.09, -5.59), (2.16, 0.37)   (9-3)

38. (A) A unique solution   (B) No solution   (C) An infinite number of solutions
(9-2)

39. 48 $\frac{1}{2}$-pound packages and 72 $\frac{1}{3}$-pound packages   (9-1, 9-2)

40. 6 meters by 8 meters   (9-3)

41. $x_1 = 40$ grams Mix A, $x_2 = 60$ grams Mix B, $x_3 = 30$ grams Mix C (9-2)

42. (A) $x_1 = 22$ nickels, $x_2 = 8$ dimes

(B) $x_1 = 3t + 22$ nickels, $x_2 = 8 - 4t$ dimes, $x_3 = t$ quarters, $t = 0, 1,$ or 2
(9-1, 9-2)

43. (A) Maximum profit is $P = \$7,800$ when 80 regular and 30 competition sails are produced.

(B) The maximum profit increases to $8,750 when 70 competition and no regular sails are produced.

(C) The maximum profit decreases to $7,200 when no competition and 120 regular sails are produced.   (9-5)

44. (A) The minimum cost is $C = \$13$ when 100 grams of mix A and 150 grams of mix B are used.

(B) The minimum cost decreases to $9 when 50 grams of mix A and 275 grams of mix B are used.

(C) The minimum cost increases to $28.75 when 250 grams of mix A and 75 grams of mix B are used.
(9-5)

CHAPTER 10

Exercise 10-1

1. $\begin{bmatrix} 2 & 5 \\ 4 & -6 \end{bmatrix}$ 　　**2.** $\begin{bmatrix} 9 & 4 \\ 9 & 4 \end{bmatrix}$ 　　**3.** $\begin{bmatrix} 3 & 2 \\ -2 & 8 \\ 12 & -5 \end{bmatrix}$ 　　**4.** $\begin{bmatrix} 9 & 7 & 2 \\ 10 & -10 & -3 \end{bmatrix}$

5. Not defined 　　**6.** Not defined 　　**7.** $\begin{bmatrix} 3 & -5 & 6 \\ 1 & 1 & 8 \end{bmatrix}$ 　　**8.** $\begin{bmatrix} 6 & -3 \\ 3 & -1 \\ 4 & 0 \end{bmatrix}$

9. $\begin{bmatrix} 12 & -16 & 28 \\ -8 & 36 & 20 \end{bmatrix}$ 　　**10.** $\begin{bmatrix} -35 & 15 & 0 & 45 \\ 20 & -25 & 30 & 10 \end{bmatrix}$ 　　**11.** $[41]$ 　　**12.** $[-38]$

13. $\begin{bmatrix} 3 \\ -13 \end{bmatrix}$ 　　**14.** $\begin{bmatrix} 5 \\ 5 \end{bmatrix}$ 　　**15.** $\begin{bmatrix} 13 & 8 \\ 26 & 48 \end{bmatrix}$ 　　**16.** $\begin{bmatrix} -8 & 37 \\ 12 & -8 \end{bmatrix}$

17. $\begin{bmatrix} 16 & -18 \\ -10 & 18 \end{bmatrix}$ 　　**18.** $\begin{bmatrix} 63 & -14 \\ -12 & -3 \end{bmatrix}$ 　　**19.** $[-36]$ 　　**20.** $[30]$

21. $\begin{bmatrix} -6 & 12 \\ 15 & -30 \end{bmatrix}$ 　　**22.** $\begin{bmatrix} 32 & -16 \\ 4 & -2 \end{bmatrix}$ 　　**23.** $[-13]$ 　　**24.** $[16]$

25. $\begin{bmatrix} 5 & 0 & -3 \\ -10 & 0 & 6 \\ 30 & 0 & -18 \end{bmatrix}$ 　　**26.** $\begin{bmatrix} 24 & -4 & 8 \\ 0 & 0 & 0 \\ -24 & 4 & -8 \end{bmatrix}$ 　　**27.** Not defined 　　**28.** $\begin{bmatrix} 17 & 2 & 12 \\ 0 & 14 & -18 \end{bmatrix}$

29. $\begin{bmatrix} 3 & 2 & -6 \\ -31 & -10 & -8 \end{bmatrix}$ 　　**30.** Not defined 　　**31.** Not defined 　　**32.** $\begin{bmatrix} 23 & -16 \\ 8 & 7 \end{bmatrix}$

33. $\begin{bmatrix} -19 & -2 & -14 \\ 15 & 4 & 6 \\ 25 & 10 & -4 \end{bmatrix}$ 　　**34.** $\begin{bmatrix} 4 & 12 \\ 12 & -18 \end{bmatrix}$ 　　**35.** $\begin{bmatrix} 24 & -32 \\ -14 & 18 \\ -4 & 56 \end{bmatrix}$ 　　**36.** $\begin{bmatrix} -50 & 20 \\ -5 & -100 \\ 40 & -135 \end{bmatrix}$

37. Not defined 　　**38.** Not defined 　　**39.** $\begin{bmatrix} 24 & 8 & 24 \\ -45 & 122 & -198 \\ -110 & 110 & -234 \end{bmatrix}$ **40.** $\begin{bmatrix} 7 & -30 \\ -21 & 45 \end{bmatrix}$

41. $\begin{bmatrix} 6 & 4 & -12 \\ -189 & -62 & -42 \\ -226 & -76 & -38 \end{bmatrix}$ **42.** $\begin{bmatrix} 44 & -72 \\ -26 & 41 \\ 18 & 88 \end{bmatrix}$ 　　**43.** $\begin{bmatrix} 32 & 28 \\ 42 & -78 \end{bmatrix}$ 　　**44.** Not defined

45. $a = 4$, $b = 5$, $c = -9$, $d = -4$ 　　**46.** $w = -1$, $x = 1$, $y = 4$, $z = -6$

47. $x = 5$, $y = 2$ 　　**48.** $x = 6$, $y = -1$ 　　**49.** $a = 1$, $b = -4$, $c = 0$, $d = 1$

50. $w = 1$, $x = 5$, $y = 0$, $z = -1$ 　　**51.** $a = -3$, $b = 6$, $c = 2$, $d = -1$

52. $w = -37$, $x = -52$, $y = 4$, $z = 4$ 　　**53.** True 　　**54.** True

55. True 　　**56.** False 　　**57.** True 　　**58.** True

59. True 　　**60.** False 　　**61.** True 　　**62.** False

63. False 　　**64.** True

65. $\begin{array}{cc} \text{Guitar} & \text{Banjo} \\ \begin{bmatrix} \$33 & \$26 \\ \$57 & \$77 \end{bmatrix} & \begin{array}{l} \text{Materials} \\ \text{Labor} \end{array} \end{array}$ 　　**66.** $\begin{array}{cc} \text{Guitar} & \text{Banjo} \\ \begin{bmatrix} \$36 & \$28.5 \\ \$63 & \$85 \end{bmatrix} & \begin{array}{l} \text{Materials} \\ \text{Labor} \end{array} \end{array}$

67.

	Basic Car	Markup Air	AM/FM radio	Cruise control
Model A	$3,330	$77	$42	$27
Model B	$2,125	$93	$95	$50
Model C	$1,270	$113	$121	$52

68.

	Basic Car	Markup Air	AM/FM radio	Cruise control
Model A	$3,505	$82	$44	$29
Model B	$2,250	$99	$100	$53
Model C	$1,365	$120	$127	$55

69. (A) $11.80 (B) $30.30   (C) *MN* gives the labor costs per boat at each plant.

(D)

$MN =$	Plant I	Plant II	
	$11.80	$13.80	One-person
	$18.50	$21.60	Two-person
	$26.00	$30.30	Four-person

70. (A) $48,480   (B) $39,300

(C) *MN* gives the total wholesale and retail values of each store.

(D)

	W	R	
	$33,400	$42,160	S1
	$35,600	$48,480	S2
	$39,300	$50,700	S3

(E) $[1 \quad 1 \quad 1]M = [16 \quad 9 \quad 11 \quad 11 \quad 10]$ (F) $M \begin{bmatrix} 1 \\ 1 \\ 1 \\ 1 \\ 1 \end{bmatrix} = \begin{bmatrix} 17 \\ 16 \\ 24 \end{bmatrix}$

71. (A) $A^2 = \begin{bmatrix} 0 & 0 & 2 & 0 & 0 \\ 1 & 0 & 0 & 0 & 1 \\ 0 & 1 & 0 & 2 & 0 \\ 1 & 0 & 0 & 0 & 1 \\ 0 & 0 & 1 & 0 & 0 \end{bmatrix}$;

There is one way to travel from Baltimore to Atlanta with one intermediate connection; there are two ways to travel from Atlanta to Chicago with one intermediate connection. In general, the elements in A^2 indicate the number of different ways to travel from the *i*th city to the *j*th city with one intermediate connection.

(B) $A^3 = \begin{bmatrix} 2 & 0 & 0 & 0 & 2 \\ 0 & 1 & 0 & 2 & 0 \\ 0 & 0 & 3 & 0 & 0 \\ 0 & 1 & 0 & 2 & 0 \\ 1 & 0 & 0 & 0 & 1 \end{bmatrix}$;

There is one way to travel from Denver to Baltimore with two intermediate connections; there are two ways to travel from Atlanta to El Paso with two intermediate connections. In general, the elements in A^3 indicate the number of different ways to travel from the ith city to the jth city with two intermediate connections.

(C) $A + A^2 + A^3 + A^4 = \begin{bmatrix} 2 & 3 & 2 & 5 & 2 \\ 1 & 1 & 4 & 2 & 1 \\ 4 & 1 & 3 & 2 & 4 \\ 1 & 1 & 4 & 2 & 1 \\ 1 & 1 & 1 & 3 & 1 \end{bmatrix}$;

It is possible to travel from any origin to any destination with at most 3 intermediate connections

72. $A = \begin{bmatrix} 0 & 0 & 0 & 1 & 1 \\ 1 & 0 & 0 & 1 & 0 \\ 0 & 1 & 0 & 0 & 0 \\ 1 & 0 & 0 & 0 & 1 \\ 0 & 1 & 1 & 0 & 0 \end{bmatrix}$; $A + A^2 + A^3 = \begin{bmatrix} 2 & 3 & 2 & 3 & 3 \\ 3 & 2 & 2 & 3 & 4 \\ 2 & 1 & 0 & 2 & 2 \\ 3 & 3 & 2 & 2 & 3 \\ 3 & 2 & 1 & 3 & 2 \end{bmatrix}$;

It is possible to travel from any origin to any destination with at most 2 intermediate connections.

73. (A) \$3,550   (B) \$6,000   (C) NM gives the total cost per town.

(D) $NM = \begin{bmatrix} \$3,550 \\ \$6,000 \end{bmatrix} \begin{matrix} \text{Berkeley} \\ \text{Oakland} \end{matrix}$

Cost/town appears above the matrix.

(E) $\begin{bmatrix} 1 & 1 \end{bmatrix} N = \begin{bmatrix} 3,000 & 1,300 & 13,000 \end{bmatrix}$

with headings Telephone call, House call, Letter.

(F) $N \begin{bmatrix} 1 \\ 1 \\ 1 \end{bmatrix} = \begin{bmatrix} 6,500 \\ 10,800 \end{bmatrix} \begin{matrix} \text{Berkeley} \\ \text{Oakland} \end{matrix}$

with heading Total contacts.

74. (A) 70 g   (B) 30 g

(C) MN gives total amounts in grams of protein, carbohydrates, and fat in 20 ounces of each mix.

(D)
$\begin{matrix} X & Y & Z \end{matrix}$

$\begin{bmatrix} 70g & 60g & 50g \\ 380g & 360g & 340g \\ 50g & 40g & 30g \end{bmatrix} \begin{matrix} \text{protein} \\ \text{carbohydrates} \\ \text{fat} \end{matrix}$

Exercise 10-2

1. $\begin{bmatrix} 6 & -3 \\ 5 & 8 \end{bmatrix}$

2. $\begin{bmatrix} -4 & 9 \\ 7 & -2 \end{bmatrix}$

3. $\begin{bmatrix} 2 & -5 \\ 8 & -4 \end{bmatrix}$

4. $\begin{bmatrix} 2 & 0 \\ -7 & -6 \end{bmatrix}$

5. $\begin{bmatrix} 4 & -2 & 5 \\ 6 & 0 & -3 \\ -1 & 2 & 7 \end{bmatrix}$

6. $\begin{bmatrix} 8 & 0 & 3 \\ -2 & -1 & -3 \\ 4 & -6 & 1 \end{bmatrix}$

7. $\begin{bmatrix} -3 & 2 & -5 \\ 4 & -1 & 6 \\ -3 & 4 & -2 \end{bmatrix}$

8. $\begin{bmatrix} 5 & 1 & 0 \\ 1 & -4 & 1 \\ 0 & 1 & 9 \end{bmatrix}$

15. $\begin{bmatrix} 1 & -9 \\ 0 & 1 \end{bmatrix}$

16. $\begin{bmatrix} -3 & -1 \\ -1 & 0 \end{bmatrix}$

17. $\begin{bmatrix} -5 & -2 \\ 2 & 1 \end{bmatrix}$

18. $\begin{bmatrix} 3 & 4 \\ 2 & 3 \end{bmatrix}$

19. $\begin{bmatrix} -3 & -7 \\ -2 & -5 \end{bmatrix}$

20. $\begin{bmatrix} -1 & 4 \\ 3 & -11 \end{bmatrix}$

21. $\begin{bmatrix} 0 & -1 & -1 \\ -1 & -1 & -1 \\ -1 & -1 & 0 \end{bmatrix}$

22. $\begin{bmatrix} 1 & 1 & -1 \\ 1 & 2 & -2 \\ -1 & -1 & 2 \end{bmatrix}$

23. $\begin{bmatrix} -19 & 9 & -7 \\ 15 & -7 & 6 \\ -2 & 1 & -1 \end{bmatrix}$

24. $\begin{bmatrix} -12 & 1 & 5 \\ -10 & 1 & 4 \\ 3 & 0 & -1 \end{bmatrix}$

25. does not exist

26. inverse does not exist

27. $\begin{bmatrix} 5 & -3 \\ -3 & 2 \end{bmatrix}$

28. $\begin{bmatrix} 3 & 4 \\ 4 & 5 \end{bmatrix}$

29. $\begin{bmatrix} 1 & 0 & 1 \\ \frac{1}{2} & \frac{1}{2} & 1 \\ 2 & 1 & 4 \end{bmatrix}$

30. $\begin{bmatrix} 0 & -\frac{1}{2} & -\frac{1}{2} \\ 1 & \frac{1}{2} & \frac{3}{2} \\ 1 & -1 & 1 \end{bmatrix}$

31. does not exist

32. inverse does not exist

33. $\begin{bmatrix} -9 & -15 & 10 \\ 4 & 5 & -4 \\ -1 & -1 & 1 \end{bmatrix}$

34. $\begin{bmatrix} 21 & 25 & -20 \\ 6 & 7 & -6 \\ -1 & -1 & 1 \end{bmatrix}$

37. M^{-1} exists if and only if all the elements on the main diagonal are nonzero.

38. M^{-1} exists if and only if all the elements on the main diagonal are nonzero.

39. $\begin{bmatrix} -0.4 & 0.8 & 1.8 & -1.4 \\ 0.1 & -0.2 & -0.7 & 0.6 \\ -0.85 & 1.7 & 3.95 & -3.6 \\ -0.1 & -0.8 & -1.3 & 1.4 \end{bmatrix}$

40. $\begin{bmatrix} -1.55 & 0.9 & 0.75 & -1 \\ -1.3 & 0.4 & 0.5 & -0.5 \\ 0.05 & 0.1 & -0.25 & 0 \\ 0.85 & -0.3 & -0.25 & 0.5 \end{bmatrix}$

41. $\begin{bmatrix} 0.75 & 3.75 & -4 & -0.75 & 3.5 \\ -0.5 & -0.5 & 1 & -0.5 & -1 \\ 2.5 & -10.5 & 11.5 & -1.5 & -9.5 \\ 0.125 & 1.375 & -1.75 & 0.375 & 1.5 \\ -0.75 & 0.75 & -0.5 & -0.25 & 0 \end{bmatrix}$

42. $\begin{bmatrix} -1 & 16.375 & 7.875 & -1.375 & -4.625 \\ -4 & 65.125 & 30.625 & -6.125 & -17.875 \\ 1 & -18.75 & -8.75 & 1.75 & 5.25 \\ 2 & -32.25 & -15.25 & 3.25 & 8.75 \\ 2 & -32 & -15 & 3 & 9 \end{bmatrix}$

43. 14 5 195 74 97 37 181 67 49 18 121 43 103 41

44. 93 36 207 78 97 37 176 65 60 21 128 49

45. GREEN EGGS AND HAM   **46.** HORTON HEARS A WHO

47. 21 56 55 25 58 46 97 94 48 75 45 58 63 45 59 48 64 80 44 69 68 104 123 72 127

48. 45 104 84 62 88 33 50 74 34 94 10 31 45 9 52 46 58 98 33 85 57 110 93 79 115

49. LYNDON BAINES JOHNSON   **50.** RICHARD MILHOUS NIXON

Exercise 10-3

1. $2x_1 - x_2 = 3$
$x_1 + 3x_2 = -2$

2. $-3x_1 + x_2 = -2$
$-x_1 + 2x_2 = 5$

3. $-2x_1 + x_3 = 3$
$x_1 + 2x_2 + x_3 = -4$
$x_2 - x_3 = 2$

4. $x_1 - 2x_2 + 0x_3 = 3$
$-3x_1 + x_2 - x_3 = -2$
$2x_1 + 0x_2 + 4x_3 = 5$

5. $\begin{bmatrix} 4 & -3 \\ 1 & 2 \end{bmatrix}\begin{bmatrix} x_1 \\ x_2 \end{bmatrix} = \begin{bmatrix} 2 \\ 1 \end{bmatrix}$

6. $\begin{bmatrix} 1 & 2 \\ -3 & 1 \end{bmatrix}\begin{bmatrix} x_1 \\ x_2 \end{bmatrix} = \begin{bmatrix} 7 \\ -3 \end{bmatrix}$

7. $\begin{bmatrix} 1 & -2 & 1 \\ -1 & 1 & 0 \\ 2 & 3 & 1 \end{bmatrix}\begin{bmatrix} x_1 \\ x_2 \\ x_3 \end{bmatrix} = \begin{bmatrix} -1 \\ 2 \\ -3 \end{bmatrix}$

8. $\begin{bmatrix} 2 & 0 & 3 \\ 1 & -2 & 1 \\ -1 & 3 & 0 \end{bmatrix}\begin{bmatrix} x_1 \\ x_2 \\ x_3 \end{bmatrix} = \begin{bmatrix} 5 \\ -4 \\ 2 \end{bmatrix}$

9. $x_1 = -8$ and $x_2 = 2$

10. $x_1 = -8$, $x_2 = -7$

11. $x_1 = 0$ and $x_2 = 4$

12. $x_1 = -7$, $x_2 = 2$

13. (A) $x_1 = -20$, $x_2 = 9$ (B) $x_1 = 18$, $x_2 = -7$ (C) $x_1 = 19$, $x_2 = -8$

14. (A) $x_1 = 5$, $x_2 = 3$ (B) $x_1 = 38$, $x_2 = 27$ (C) $x_1 = -16$, $x_2 = -12$

15. (A) $x_1 = 8$, $x_2 = 5$ (B) $x_1 = 4$, $x_2 = 4$ (C) $x_1 = -18$, $x_2 = -12$

16. (A) $x_1 = -10$, $x_2 = 27$ (B) $x_1 = 37$, $x_2 = -102$ (C) $x_1 = 16$, $x_2 = -43$

17. (A) $x_1 = -3$, $x_2 = -4$, $x_3 = -2$ (B) $x_1 = 4$, $x_2 = 5$, $x_3 = 1$
(C) $x_1 = 2$, $x_2 = -1$, $x_3 = -1$

18. (A) $x_1 = 3$, $x_2 = 8$, $x_3 = -4$ (B) $x_1 = -2$, $x_2 = -6$, $x_3 = 3$
(C) $x_1 = 6$, $x_2 = 13$, $x_3 = -11$

19. (A) $x_1 = -19$, $x_2 = 17$, $x_3 = -3$ (B) $x_1 = -104$, $x_2 = 82$, $x_3 = -11$
(C) $x_1 = 100$, $x_2 = -78$, $x_3 = 10$

20. (A) $x_1 = -37$, $x_2 = -31$, $x_3 = 9$ (B) $x_1 = 29$, $x_2 = 24$, $x_3 = -5$
(C) $x_1 = 29$, $x_2 = 24$, $x_3 = -7$

21. $X = (A - B)^{-1}C$ **22.** $X = (A + B)^{-1}(C + D)$ **23.** $X = (I - A)^{-1}C$

24. $X = (A - B - I)^{-1}C$ **25.** $X = (3I - A)^{-1}C$ **26.** $X = (A - B + 7I)^{-1}(D - C)$

27. (A) $x_1 = 1$, $x_2 = 0$ (B) $x_1 = -5,000$, $x_2 = 1,000$
(C) $x_1 = 5,001$, $x_2 = -1000$

28. (A) $x_1 = 1$, $x_2 = 0$ (B) $x_1 = -4,000$, $x_2 = -1,000$ (C) $x_1 = 4,001$, $x_2 = -1,000$

29. $x_1 = 13$, $x_2 = 21$, $x_3 = -12$ **30.** $x_1 = 9$, $x_2 = 14$, $x_3 = 5$

31. $x_1 = 35$, $x_2 = -5$, $x_3 = 15$, $x_4 = 20$ **32.** $x_1 = -3$, $x_2 = 7$, $x_3 = -9$, $x_4 = 10$

33. Concert 1: 6,000 \$4 tickets and 4,000 \$8 tickets; Concert 2: 5,000 \$4 tickets and 5,000 \$8 tickets; Concert 3: 3,000 \$4 tickets and 7,000 \$8 tickets

34. Allocation 1: $\begin{bmatrix} A \\ B \end{bmatrix} = \begin{bmatrix} 60 \\ 0 \end{bmatrix}$; Allocation 2: $\begin{bmatrix} A \\ B \end{bmatrix} = \begin{bmatrix} 25 \\ 25 \end{bmatrix}$; Allocation 3: $\begin{bmatrix} A \\ B \end{bmatrix} = \begin{bmatrix} 4 \\ 40 \end{bmatrix}$

35. (A) $I_1 = 4$, $I_2 = 6$, $I_3 = 2$ (B) $I_1 = 3$, $I_2 = 7$, $I_3 = 4$
(C) $I_1 = 7$, $I_2 = 8$, $I_3 = 1$

36. (A) $\begin{bmatrix} I_1 \\ I_2 \\ I_3 \end{bmatrix} = \begin{bmatrix} \frac{5}{2} \\ \frac{15}{4} \\ \frac{5}{4} \end{bmatrix}$ (B) $\begin{bmatrix} I_1 \\ I_2 \\ I_3 \end{bmatrix} = \begin{bmatrix} \frac{5}{4} \\ \frac{35}{8} \\ \frac{25}{8} \end{bmatrix}$ (C) $\begin{bmatrix} I_1 \\ I_2 \\ I_3 \end{bmatrix} = \begin{bmatrix} 5 \\ 5 \\ 0 \end{bmatrix}$

37. (A) $a = 1$, $b = 0$, $c = -3$ (B) $a = -2$, $b = 5$, $c = 1$
(C) $a = 11$, $b = -46$, $c = 43$

38. (A) $\begin{bmatrix} a \\ b \\ c \end{bmatrix} = \begin{bmatrix} 1 \\ 4 \\ 1 \end{bmatrix}$ (B) $\begin{bmatrix} a \\ b \\ c \end{bmatrix} = \begin{bmatrix} -2 \\ -3 \\ 3 \end{bmatrix}$ (C) $\begin{bmatrix} a \\ b \\ c \end{bmatrix} = \begin{bmatrix} 11 \\ -2 \\ -5 \end{bmatrix}$

39. Diet 1: 60 ounces Mix A and 80 ounces Mix B; Diet 2: 20 ounces Mix A and 60 ounces Mix B; Diet 3: 0 ounces Mix A and 100 ounces Mix B

Exercise 10-4

1. 7   **2.** 20   **3.** -17   **4.** 8

5. 9.79   **6.** 7.73   **7.** $\begin{vmatrix} 4 & 6 \\ -2 & 8 \end{vmatrix}$ **8.** $\begin{vmatrix} 5 & -1 \\ 3 & 4 \end{vmatrix}$

9. $\begin{vmatrix} 5 & -1 \\ 0 & -2 \end{vmatrix}$ **10.** $\begin{vmatrix} 3 & 6 \\ 0 & 8 \end{vmatrix}$ **11.** $(-1)^{1+1} \begin{vmatrix} 4 & 6 \\ -2 & 8 \end{vmatrix} = 44$

12. $(-1)^{3+3} \begin{vmatrix} 5 & -1 \\ 3 & 4 \end{vmatrix} = 23$ **13.** $(-1)^{2+3} \begin{vmatrix} 5 & -1 \\ 0 & -2 \end{vmatrix} = 10$ **14.** $(-1)^{1+2} \begin{vmatrix} 3 & 6 \\ 0 & 8 \end{vmatrix} = -24$

15. 10   **16.** -24   **17.** -21   **18.** -40   **19.** -40   **20.** -43

21. $(-1)^{1+1} \begin{vmatrix} a_{22} & a_{23} & a_{24} \\ a_{32} & a_{33} & a_{34} \\ a_{42} & a_{43} & a_{44} \end{vmatrix}$ **22.** $(-1)^{4+4} \begin{vmatrix} a_{11} & a_{12} & a_{13} \\ a_{21} & a_{22} & a_{23} \\ a_{31} & a_{32} & a_{33} \end{vmatrix}$

23. $(-1)^{4+3} \begin{vmatrix} a_{11} & a_{12} & a_{14} \\ a_{21} & a_{22} & a_{24} \\ a_{31} & a_{32} & a_{34} \end{vmatrix}$ **24.** $(-1)^{2+3} \begin{vmatrix} a_{11} & a_{12} & a_{14} \\ a_{31} & a_{32} & a_{34} \\ a_{41} & a_{42} & a_{44} \end{vmatrix}$

25. 22   **26.** -120   **27.** -12   **28.** -1   **29.** 0   **30.** -18

31. 6   **32.** -8   **33.** 60   **34.** 48   **35.** 114   **36.** 18

37. False   **38.** False   **39.** True   **40.** True

41. $\begin{vmatrix} a & b \\ c & d \end{vmatrix} = -\begin{vmatrix} c & d \\ a & b \end{vmatrix}$; interchanging the rows of this determinant changes the sign.

42. $\begin{vmatrix} a & b \\ c & d \end{vmatrix} = -\begin{vmatrix} b & a \\ d & c \end{vmatrix}$; interchanging the columns of this determinant changes the sign.

43. $\begin{vmatrix} ka & b \\ kc & d \end{vmatrix} = k\begin{vmatrix} a & b \\ c & d \end{vmatrix}$; multiplying a column of this determinant by a number k multiplies the value of the determinant by k.

44. $\begin{vmatrix} a & b \\ kc & kd \end{vmatrix} = k\begin{vmatrix} a & b \\ c & d \end{vmatrix}$; multiplying a row of this determinant by a number k multiplies the value of the determinant by k.

45. $\begin{vmatrix} kc + a & kd + b \\ c & d \end{vmatrix} = \begin{vmatrix} a & b \\ c & d \end{vmatrix}$; adding a multiple of one row to the other row does not change the value of the determinant.

46. $\begin{vmatrix} a & ka + b \\ c & kc + d \end{vmatrix} = \begin{vmatrix} a & b \\ c & d \end{vmatrix}$; adding a multiple of one column to the other column does not change the value of the determinant.

49. $49 = (-7)(-7)$

51. $f(x) = x^2 - 4x + 3$; $x = 1, 3$

52. $f(x) = x^2 - 7x + 10$; $x = 5, x = 2$

53. $f(x) = x^3 + 2x^2 - 8x$; $x = 0, -4, 2$

54. $f(x) = x^3 - x^2 - 2x$; $x = 0, 2, -1$

Exercise 10-5

1. Theorem 1

2. Theorem 1

3. Theorem 1

4. Theorem 1

5. Theorem 2

6. Theorem 2

7. Theorem 3

8. Theorem 3

9. Theorem 5

10. Theorem 5

11. $x = 0$

12. $x = 0$

13. $x = 5$

14. $x = 5$

15. -10

16. 20

17. 10

18. 10

19. -10

20. 10

21. 25

22. 25

23. -12

24. -33

25. Theorem 1

26. Theorem 1

27. Theorem 2

28. Theorem 3

29. Theorem 5

30. Theorem 4

31. $x = 5, y = 0$

32. $x = 16, y = 7$

33. $x = -3, y = 10$

34. $x = -1, y = 11$

35. -28

36. -1

37. 106

38. -18

39. 0

40. 0

41. 6

42. 34

43. 14

44. 42

45. Expand the left side of the equation using minors.

46. Expand both members of the equation and compare.

47. Expand both sides of the equation and compare.

48. Expand both members of the equation and compare.

49. This follows from Theorem 4.

50. Expand the determinant about the first row to obtain $x - 3y + 7 = 0$, then show that the two points satisfy this linear equation.

51. Expand the determinant about the first row to obtain
$(y_1 - y_2)x - (x_1 - x_2)y + (x_1 y_2 - x_2 y_1) = 0$.

52. 11.5

53. If the determinant is 0, then the area of the triangle formed by the three points is zero. The only way this can happen is if the three points are on the same line; that is, the points are colinear.

54. det = 0

Exercise 10-6

1. $x = 5$, $y = -2$ **2.** $x = -1$, $y = 2$ **3.** $x = 1$, $y = -1$ **4.** $x = 4$, $y = -1$

5. $x = -\frac{6}{5}$, $y = \frac{3}{5}$ **6.** $x = \frac{3}{5}$, $y = \frac{7}{5}$ **7.** $x = \frac{2}{17}$, $y = -\frac{20}{17}$

8. $x = \frac{1}{19}$, $y = -\frac{12}{19}$ **9.** $x = 6,400$, $y = 6,600$

10. $x = 4,900$, $y = 5,000$ **11.** $x = 760$, $y = 760$

12. $x = 680$, $y = 680$ **13.** $x = 2$, $y = -2$, $z = -1$

14. $x = -3$, $y = -1$, $z = 2$ **15.** $x = \frac{4}{3}$, $y = -\frac{1}{3}$, $z = \frac{2}{3}$

16. $x = -8$, $y = \frac{5}{3}$, $z = -\frac{1}{3}$ **17.** $x = -9$, $y = -\frac{7}{3}$, $z = 6$

18. $x = \frac{1}{4}$, $y = \frac{7}{2}$, $z = -\frac{11}{4}$ **19.** $x = \frac{3}{2}$, $y = -\frac{7}{6}$, $z = \frac{2}{3}$

20. $x = \frac{1}{4}$, $y = \frac{3}{2}$, $z = \frac{1}{4}$ **21.** $x = 4$ **22.** $x = -2$

23. $y = 2$ **24.** $y = 1$ **25.** $z = \frac{5}{2}$ **26.** $z = \frac{29}{3}$

27. Since $D = 0$, the system either has no solution or infinitely many. Since $x = 0$, $y = 0$, $z = 0$ is a solution, the second case must hold.

28. Since $D \neq 0$, by Cramer's Rule, $x = 0$, $y = 0$, $z = 0$ is the only solution.

31. (A) $R = 200p + 300q - 6p^2 + 6pq - 3q^2$

   (B) $p = -0.3x - 0.4y + 180$, $q = -0.2x - 0.6y + 220$,
       $R = 180x + 220y - 0.3x^2 - 0.6xy - 0.6y^2$

32. (A) $R = 230x + 130y - 10x^2 + 9xy - 4y^2$

   (B) $x = -0.2p - 0.25q + 78.5$, $y = -0.2p - 0.5q + 111$,
       $R = 78.5p + 111q - 0.2p^2 - 0.45pq - 0.5q^2$

CHAPTER 10 REVIEW

1. $\begin{bmatrix} 4 & 8 \\ -12 & 18 \end{bmatrix}$ *(10-1)*   **2.** [-11]   *(10-1)*   **3.** [-15 19]   *(10-1)*

4. $\begin{bmatrix} 16 \\ -6 \end{bmatrix}$ *(10-1)*   **5.** $\begin{bmatrix} 3 & 3 \\ -4 & 9 \end{bmatrix}$ *(10-1)*   **6.** Not defined   *(10-1)*

7. Not defined   *(10-1)*   **8.** $\begin{bmatrix} 13 & -29 \\ 20 & -24 \end{bmatrix}$ *(10-1)*   **9.** [-5 18]   *(10-1)*

10. $\begin{bmatrix} 2 & 7 \\ -1 & -4 \end{bmatrix}$ *(10-2)*

11. (A) $x_1 = -1$, $x_2 = 3$ (B) $x_1 = 1$, $x_2 = 2$ (C) $x_1 = 8$, $x_2 = -10$ *(10-3)*

12. -17 *(10-4)*   **13.** 0   *(10-4, 10-5)*   **14.** $x = 2$, $y = -1$ *(10-6)*

15. (A) -2   (B) 6   (C) 2   *(10-5)*   **16.** $\begin{bmatrix} 7 & 16 & -9 \\ 28 & 40 & -30 \\ -21 & -8 & 17 \end{bmatrix}$ *(10-1)*

17. $\begin{bmatrix} 22 & 19 \\ 38 & 42 \end{bmatrix}$ *(10-1)*   **18.** $\begin{bmatrix} 12 & 24 & -6 \\ 0 & 0 & 0 \\ -8 & -16 & 4 \end{bmatrix}$ *(10-1)*   **19.** [16]   *(10-1)*

20. Not defined   *(10-1)*   **21.** $\begin{bmatrix} 63 & -24 & -39 \\ -42 & 16 & 26 \end{bmatrix}$ *(10-1)*

22. $\begin{bmatrix} -1 & 1 & 1 \\ -2 & 3 & 2 \\ \frac{1}{2} & -\frac{1}{4} & -\frac{1}{4} \end{bmatrix}$ *(10-1)*

23. (A) $x_1 = 2$, $x_2 = 1$, $x_3 = -1$ (B) $x_1 = 1$, $x_2 = -2$, $x_3 = 1$
(C) $x_1 = -1$, $x_2 = 2$, $x_3 = -2$ *(10-3)*

24. $-\frac{11}{12}$ *(10-4)*   **25.** 35   *(10-4, 10-5)*   **26.** $y = \dfrac{10}{5} = 2$ *(10-6)*

27. (A) A unique solution
(B) Either no solution or an infinite number   *(10-3)*

28. No   *(10-3)*   **29.** $X = (A - C)^{-1}B$ *(10-3)*

30. $\begin{bmatrix} -\frac{11}{12} & -\frac{1}{12} & 5 \\ \frac{10}{12} & \frac{2}{12} & -4 \\ \frac{1}{12} & -\frac{1}{12} & 0 \end{bmatrix}$ or $\frac{1}{12}\begin{bmatrix} -11 & -1 & 60 \\ 10 & 2 & -48 \\ 1 & -1 & 0 \end{bmatrix}$ *(10-2)*

31. $x_1 = 1,000$, $x_2 = 4,000$, $x_3 = 2,000$ *(10-3)*   **32.** 42   *(10-5)*

33. $\begin{vmatrix} u + kv & v \\ w + kx & x \end{vmatrix} = (u + kv)x - (w + kx)v = ux + kvx - wv - kvx = ux - wv$

$$= \begin{vmatrix} u & v \\ w & x \end{vmatrix}$$ *(10-5)*

34. Theorem 4 in Section 10-5 implies that both points satisfy the equation. All other points on the line through the given points will also satisfy the equation. *(10-5)*

35. (A) 60 tons of ore must be produced at Big Bend, 20 tons of ore at Saw Pit.

(B) 30 tons of ore must be produced at Big Bend, 50 tons of ore at Saw Pit.

(C) 40 tons of ore must be produced at Big Bend, 40 tons of ore at Saw Pit. *(10-3)*

36. (A) $27

(B) Elements in LH give the total cost of manufacturing each product at each plant.

(C)
$$LH = \begin{matrix} & \text{N.C.} & \text{S.C.} \\ & \begin{bmatrix} \$46.35 & \$41.00 \\ \$30.45 & \$27.00 \end{bmatrix} & \begin{matrix} \text{Desk} \\ \text{Stands} \end{matrix} \end{matrix}$$
(10-1)

37. (A) $\begin{bmatrix} 1,600 & 1,730 \\ 890 & 720 \end{bmatrix}$ (B) $\begin{bmatrix} 200 & 160 \\ 80 & 40 \end{bmatrix}$

(C) $\begin{bmatrix} 3,150 \\ 1,550 \end{bmatrix} \begin{matrix} \text{Desks} \\ \text{Stands} \end{matrix}$

This matrix represents the total production of each item in January. *(10-1)*

38. GRAPHING UTILITY   *(10-2)*

CUMULATIVE REVIEW EXERCISE (Chapters 9 and 10)

1. $(2, -1)$ $(9-1)$ **2.** $(-1, 2)$ $(9-1)$

3. $\left(-\dfrac{1}{5}, -\dfrac{7}{5}\right)$, $(1, 1)$ $(9-3)$ **4.**

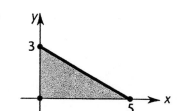

$(9-4)$

5. The minimum value of z on S is 10 at $(5, 0)$.
   The maximum value of z on S is 33 at $(6, 7)$. $(9-5)$

6. (A) $\begin{bmatrix} 0 & -3 \\ 3 & -9 \end{bmatrix}$ (B) not defined (C) $[3]$ (D) $\begin{bmatrix} 1 & 7 \\ 4 & -7 \end{bmatrix}$ (E) $[-1 \quad 8]$
   (F) not defined $(10-1)$

7. -10 $(10-4)$

8. (A) $x_1 = 3$, $x_2 = -4$
   (B) $x_1 = 2t + 3$, $x_2 = t$ is a solution for every real number t
   (C) No solution. $(9-1)$

9. (A) $\begin{bmatrix} 1 & 1 & | & 3 \\ -1 & 1 & | & 5 \end{bmatrix}$ (B) $\begin{bmatrix} 1 & 0 & | & -1 \\ 0 & 1 & | & 4 \end{bmatrix}$ (C) $x_1 = -1$, $x_2 = 4$ $(9-1, 9-2)$

10. (A) $\begin{bmatrix} 1 & -3 \\ 2 & -5 \end{bmatrix}\begin{bmatrix} x_1 \\ x_2 \end{bmatrix} = \begin{bmatrix} k_1 \\ k_2 \end{bmatrix}$ (B) $A^{-1} = \begin{bmatrix} -5 & 3 \\ -2 & 1 \end{bmatrix}$ (C) $x_1 = 13$, $x_2 = 5$

   (D) $x_1 = -11$, $x_2 = -4$ $(10-3)$

11. (A) 2 (B) $x = \dfrac{1}{2}$, $y = 0$ $(10-6)$

12. $x_1 = 1$, $x_2 = 3$; each pair of lines has the same intersection point.

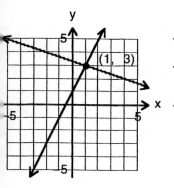
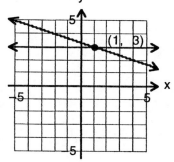
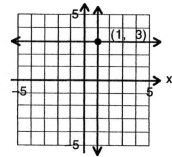

$x_1 + 3x_2 = 10$ $x_1 + 3x_2 = 10$ $x_1 + 3x_2 = 10$ $x_1 = 1$
$2x_1 - x_2 = -1$ $-7x_2 = -21$ $x_2 = 3$ $x_2 = 3$ $(9-1)$

13. (1.53, 3.35)   *(9-1)*

14. $x_1 = 1$, $x_2 = 0$, $x_3 = -2$ *(9-2)*   **15.** no solution   *(9-2)*

16. $x_1 = t - 3$, $x_2 = t - 2$, $x_3 = t$ is a solution for every real number t *(9-2)*

17. (1, 1), (-1, -1), $\left(\sqrt{3}, \dfrac{\sqrt{3}}{3}\right)$, $\left(-\sqrt{3}, -\dfrac{\sqrt{3}}{3}\right)$ *(9-3)*

18. (1, 1), (-1, -1), (0, i), (0, $-i$)   *(9-3)*

19. (A) [-3]   (B) $\begin{bmatrix} 1 & 2 & -1 \\ -1 & -2 & 1 \\ 2 & 4 & -2 \end{bmatrix}$ *(10-1)*

20. (A) $\begin{bmatrix} -1 & 2 \\ 2 & 3 \end{bmatrix}$ (B) not defined   *(10-1)*

21.

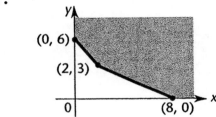

22. 63   *(9-5)*

(9-4)

23. (A) $\begin{bmatrix} 1 & 4 & 2 \\ 2 & 6 & 3 \\ 2 & 5 & 2 \end{bmatrix}\begin{bmatrix} x_1 \\ x_2 \\ x_3 \end{bmatrix} = \begin{bmatrix} k_1 \\ k_2 \\ k_3 \end{bmatrix}$ (B) $A^{-1} = \begin{bmatrix} -3 & 2 & 0 \\ 2 & -2 & 1 \\ -2 & 3 & -2 \end{bmatrix}$

(C) $x_1 = 7$, $x_2 = -5$, $x_3 = 6$ (D) $x_1 = -6$, $x_2 = 3$, $x_3 = -2$ *(10-3)*

24. (A) $D = 1$ (B) $z = 32$ *(10-5, 10-6)*

25. (-1.35, 0.28), (-0.87, -1.60), (0.87, 1.60), (1.35, -0.28)   *(9-3)*

26. (A) Infinite number of solutions   (B) No solution   (C) Unique solution   *(9-2)*

27. $A = I$, the $n \times n$ identity   *(10-3)*

28. L, M, and P *(9-2)*

32. True   *(10-1)*   **33.** True   *(10-1)*   **34.** False   *(10-1)*   **35.** False   *(10-1)*

36. True   *(10-2)*   **37.** True   *(10-2)*   **38.** True   *(10-4)*   **39.** True   *(10-4)*

40. $8,000 at 8% and $4,000 at 14%   *(9-1, 9-2)*

41. $x_1 = 60$g Mix A, $x_2 = 50$g Mix B, $x_3 = 40$g Mix C *(9-2)*

42. 1 model A truck, 6 model B trucks, and 5 model C trucks; or 3 model A trucks, 3 model B trucks, and 6 model C trucks; or 5 model A trucks and 7 model C trucks.

(9-2)

43. 8 meters by 4 meters

(9-3)

44. (A) Manufacturing 400 standard and 200 deluxe day packs produces a maxmimum weekly profit of $5,600.

(B) The maximum weekly profit incresaes to $6,000 when 0 standard and 400 deluxe day packs are manufactured.

(C) The maximum weekly profit incresaes to $6,600 when 600 standard and 0 deluxe day packs are manufactured.

(9-5)

45. (A) $M \begin{bmatrix} 0.25 \\ 0.25 \\ 0.25 \\ 0.25 \end{bmatrix} = \begin{bmatrix} 82.25 \\ 83 \\ 92 \\ 83.75 \\ 82 \end{bmatrix} \begin{matrix} \text{Ann} \\ \text{Bob} \\ \text{Carol} \\ \text{Dan} \\ \text{Eric} \end{matrix}$ (B) $M \begin{bmatrix} 0.2 \\ 0.2 \\ 0.2 \\ 0.4 \end{bmatrix} = \begin{bmatrix} 83 \\ 84.8 \\ 91.8 \\ 85.2 \\ 80.8 \end{bmatrix} \begin{matrix} \text{Ann} \\ \text{Bob} \\ \text{Carol} \\ \text{Dan} \\ \text{Eric} \end{matrix}$

Class averages

(C) $[0.2 \quad 0.2 \quad 0.2 \quad 0.2 \quad 0.2]M = [84.4 \quad 81.8 \quad 85 \quad 87.2]$

Test 1   Test 2   Test 3   Test 4

(10-1)

CHAPTER 11

Exercise 11-1

1. 7, 9, 11, 13, …

2. 2, 5, 10, 17, …

3. 2, $\dfrac{7}{3}$, $\dfrac{5}{2}$, $\dfrac{13}{5}$, …

4. 2, 9, 64, 625, …

5. 1, 13, 19, 97, …

6. -1, $\dfrac{1}{8}$, $-\dfrac{1}{27}$, $\dfrac{1}{64}$, …

7. 205

8. 2501

9. $\dfrac{601}{201}$

10. 10^{198}

11. $1 + 2 + 3 + 4 + 5$

12. $1 + 4 + 9 + 16$

13. $\dfrac{1}{10} + \dfrac{1}{100} + \dfrac{1}{1000}$

14. $\dfrac{1}{3} + \dfrac{1}{9} + \dfrac{1}{27} + \dfrac{1}{81} + \dfrac{1}{243}$

15. $-1 + 1 - 1 + 1$

16. $1 - 2 + 3 - 4 + 5 - 6$

17. 1, -4, 9, -16, 25

18. $\dfrac{1}{2}$, $-\dfrac{1}{4}$, $\dfrac{1}{8}$, $-\dfrac{1}{16}$, $\dfrac{1}{32}$

19. 0.3, 0.33, 0.333, 0.3333, 0.33333

20. 2, 0, 6, 0, 10

21. 1, $-\dfrac{1}{2}$, $\dfrac{1}{4}$, $-\dfrac{1}{8}$, $\dfrac{1}{16}$

22. 1, $-\dfrac{3}{2}$, $\dfrac{9}{4}$, $-\dfrac{27}{8}$, $\dfrac{81}{16}$

23. 7, 3, -1, -5, -9

24. 1, 1, 2, 3, 5

25. 4, 1, $\dfrac{1}{4}$, $\dfrac{1}{16}$, $\dfrac{1}{64}$

26. 2, 4, 8, 16, 32

27. $a_n = 1 + 2n$

28. $a_n = 5 - 3n$

29. $a_n = (n + 1)^2$

30. $a_n = (n + 3)(n + 5)$

31. $a_n = 2^{n+1}$

32. $a_n = n^n$

33. $a_n = \dfrac{2n - 1}{n}$

34. $a_n = \dfrac{2^n - 1}{2^n}$

35. $a_n = 7(-1)^{n+1}$

36. $a_n = \dfrac{1}{(-5)^{n-1}}$

37. $a_n = \dfrac{x^n}{2^{n-1}}$

38. $a_n = (-1)^n x^{3n-2}$

39.

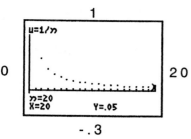

40.

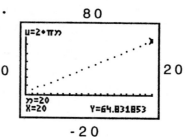

41.

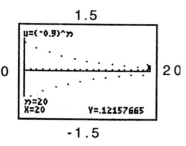

42.

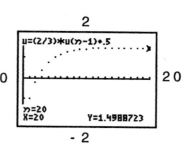

43. $\dfrac{4}{1} - \dfrac{8}{2} + \dfrac{16}{3} - \dfrac{32}{4}$

44. $1^2 - 3^2 + 5^2 - 7^2 + 9^2$

45. $x^2 + \dfrac{x^3}{2} + \dfrac{x^4}{3}$

46. $1 + x + x^2 + x^3 + x^4$

47. $x - \dfrac{x^2}{2} + \dfrac{x^3}{3} - \dfrac{x^4}{4} + \dfrac{x^5}{5}$

48. $x - \dfrac{x^3}{3} + \dfrac{x^5}{5} - \dfrac{x^7}{7} + \dfrac{x^9}{9}$ **49.** $\displaystyle\sum_{k=1}^{4} k^2$ **50.** $\displaystyle\sum_{k=1}^{5} (k+1)$

51. $\displaystyle\sum_{k=1}^{5} \dfrac{1}{2^k}$ **52.** $\displaystyle\sum_{k=1}^{4} \dfrac{(-1)^{k+1}}{k}$ **53.** $\displaystyle\sum_{k=1}^{n} \dfrac{1}{k^2}$

54. $\displaystyle\sum_{k=1}^{n} \dfrac{k+1}{k}$ **55.** $\displaystyle\sum_{k=1}^{n} (-1)^{k+1} k^2$ **56.** $\displaystyle\sum_{k=1}^{n} \dfrac{(-1)^{k+1}}{2^k}$

57. (A) 3, 1.83, 1.46, 1.415 (B) Calculator $\sqrt{2} = 1.4142135\ldots$
(C) $a_1 = 1$; 1, 1.5, 1.417, 1.414

58. (A) 2, 2.25, $2.236\overline{1}$, 2.236067978 (B) $\sqrt{5} = 2.236067978$
(C) 3, $2.\overline{3}$, 2.238095238, 2.236068896, 2.236067978

59. The values of c_n are approximately 2.236 (i.e., $\sqrt{5}$) for large values of n.

60. $\{u_n\}$ is the Fibonacci sequence, $\{v_n\}$ is the Fibonacci sequence preceded by 0.

61. $e^{0.2} = 1.2214000$; $e^{0.2} = 1.2214028$ (calculator—direct evaluation)

62. $e^{-0.5} \approx 0.6067708333$; $e^{-0.5} = 0.6065306597$, calculator

Exercise 11-2

1. 3 **2.** 12 **3.** 5 **4.** 1

5. P_1: $2 = 2\cdot 1^2$; P_2: $2 + 6 = 2\cdot 2^2$; P_3: $2 + 6 + 10 = 2\cdot 3^2$

6. $4 = 2(1)(1+1)$; $4 + 8 = 2(2)(2+1)$; $4 + 8 + 12 = 2(3)(3+1)$

7. P_1: $a^5 a^1 = a^{5+1}$; P_2: $a^5 a^2 = a^5(a^1 a) = (a^5 a)a = a^6 a = a^7 = a^{5+2}$;
P_3: $a^5 a^3 = a^5(a^2 a) = a^5(a^1 a)a = [(a^5 a)a]a = a^8 = a^{5+3}$

8. $(a^5)^1 = a^{5\cdot 1} = a^5$; $(a^5)^2 = a^{5\cdot 2} = a^{10}$; $(a^5)^3 = a^{5\cdot 3} = a^{15}$

9. P_1: $9^1 - 1 = 8$ is divisible by 4; P_2: $9^2 - 1 = 80$ is divisible by 4;
P_3: $9^3 - 1 = 728$ is divisible by 4

10. P_1: $4^1 - 1 = 3$ which is divisible by 3; P_2: $4^2 - 1 = 15$ which is divisible by 3;
P_3: $4^3 - 1 = 63$ which is divisible by 3

11. P_k: $2 + 6 + 10 + \cdots + (4k - 2) = 2k^2$
P_{k+1}: $2 + 6 + 10 + \cdots + (4k - 2) + (4k + 2) = 2(k + 1)^2$

12. P_k: $4 + 8 + 12 + \cdots + 4k = 2k(k + 1)$;
P_{k+1}: $4 + 8 + 12 + \cdots + 4k + 4(k + 1) = 2(k + 1)(k + 2)$

13. P_k: $a^5 a^k = a^{5+k}$; P_{k+1}: $a^5 a^{k+1} = a^{5+k+1}$

14. P_k: $(a^5)^k = a^{5k}$; P_{k+1}: $(a^5)^{k+1} = a^{5(k+1)}$

15. P_k: $9^k - 1 = 4r$ for some integer r; P_{k+1}: $9^{k+1} - 1 = 4s$ for some integer s

16. P_k: $4^k - 1 = 3r$, $r \in N$; P_{k+1}: $4^{(k+1)} - 1 = 3s$, $s \in N$

23. $n = 4$, $p(x) = x^4 + 1$ **24.** $n = 15$

25. $n = 23$ **26.** $a = 1$, $b = 7$, $c = 5$, $d = 5$

43. P_n: $2 + 4 + 6 + \cdots + 2n = n(n + 1)$

44. $\dfrac{1}{1\cdot 2} + \dfrac{1}{2\cdot 3} + \dfrac{1}{3\cdot 4} + \cdots + \dfrac{1}{n(n + 1)} = \dfrac{n}{n + 1}$

45. $1 + 2 + 3 + \cdots + (n - 1) = \dfrac{n(n - 1)}{2}$, $n \geq 2$

46. $2 + 3 + 4 + \cdots + (n - 2) = \dfrac{n(n - 3)}{2}$, $n > 3$

51. $3^4 + 4^4 + 5^4 + 6^4 \neq 7^4$ **52.** Prime up to $n = 17$; fails at $n = 18$

Exercise 11-3

1. (A) Arithmetic with $d = -5$; -26, -31 (B) Geometric with $r = -2$; -16, 32
  (C) Neither (D) Geometric with $r = \dfrac{1}{3}$; $\dfrac{1}{54}$, $\dfrac{1}{162}$

2. (A) Neither (B) Both with $d = 0$, $r = 1$; -5, -5
  (C) Arithmetic with $d = -0.5$; 5.5, 5 (D) Geometric with $r = \dfrac{1}{2}$; 64, 32

3. $a_2 = 11$, $a_3 = 16$, $a_4 = 21$ **4.** $a_2 = -7$, $a_3 = -3$, $a_4 = 1$

5. $a_{21} = -153$, $S_{21} = -1{,}743$ **6.** $a_{12} = -46$, $S_{12} = -156$

7. $S_{25} = 1{,}775$ **8.** $a_{30} = 205$ **9.** $S_{15} = 6{,}375$ **10.** $a_{29} = 272$

11. $a_2 = 3$; $a_3 = -\dfrac{3}{2}$; $a_4 = \dfrac{3}{4}$ **12.** $a_2 = 8$; $a_3 = \dfrac{16}{3}$; $a_4 = \dfrac{32}{9}$

13. $a_{10} = \dfrac{1}{243}$ **14.** $a_{13} = \dfrac{1}{64}$ **15.** $S_7 = 3{,}279$ **16.** $S_7 = 547$

17. $S_{50} = 3{,}925$ **18.** $S_{100} = 9{,}200$ **19.** $a_{64} = 56.5$ **20.** $a_{45} = -97$

21. $a_1 = 6$ **22.** $S_{10} = 230$ **23.** $a_{10} = 3$, $d = -\dfrac{1}{9}$

24. $a_{12} = 13$, $d = \dfrac{16}{11}$ **25.** $r = \pm\sqrt{10}$ **26.** $r = \pm\dfrac{1}{\sqrt{3}}$ **27.** $S_{10} = 42{,}625$

28. $S_{12} = 81{,}900$ **29.** $a_2 = 60$, $a_3 = 90$

30. $a_2 = -250$, $a_3 = 100$, $a_4 = -40$, $a_5 = 16$ **31.** $S_{51} = 4{,}131$ **32.** $S_{40} = 1520$

33. $S_7 = 547$ **34.** $S_7 = 3279$ **35.** $-1{,}071$ **36.** 320

37. $\dfrac{1{,}023}{1{,}024}$ **38.** 2046 **39.** $4{,}446$ **40.** $60{,}000$

43. $x = 2\sqrt{3}$ **44.** $x = 4\sqrt{3}$ **45.** Yes **46.** No

47. 66 **48.** 11 **49.** 133 **50.** 122

51. $S_\infty = \dfrac{9}{2}$ **52.** $\dfrac{64}{3}$ **53.** no sum **54.** no sum

55. $S_\infty = \dfrac{8}{5}$ **56.** $\dfrac{147}{8}$ **57.** $\dfrac{7}{9}$ **58.** $\dfrac{5}{9}$

59. $\dfrac{6}{11}$ **60.** $\dfrac{3}{11}$ **61.** $3\dfrac{8}{37}$ or $\dfrac{119}{37}$ **62.** $5 + \dfrac{7}{11} = \dfrac{62}{11}$

65. $a_n = (-2)(-3)^{n-1}$ **66.** $S_n = \dfrac{-2 - (-2)(-3)^n}{1 - (-3)} = \dfrac{(-3)^n - 1}{2}$

67. Hint: $y = x + d$, $z = x + 2d$

68. 25   **71.** $x = -1$, $y = 2$ **72.** 40; -24

73. Firm A: \$501,000; Firm B: \$504,000   **74.** Firm A: \$35,800; Firm B: \$35,200

75. \$4,000,000   **76.** \$1400

77. $P(1 + r)^n$; approximately 12 yr   **78.** $A_0(1 + r)^t$; 35 years

79. \$700 per year; \$115,500

80. (A) arithmetic sequence   (B) $T_n = 80 + (n)(-5)$

81. 900   **82.** 100 inches   **83.** 1,250,000

84. $2^{20} = 1,048,576$ **85.** (A) 336 ft   (B) 1,936 ft   (C) $16t^2$ ft

86. (A) 624 feet   (B) $a_t = 32t - 16$ **87.** $A = A_0 2^{2t}$ **88.** 15th day

89. $r = 10^{-0.4} = 0.398$ **90.** (A) 1.059   (B) 475 cps

91. 9.22×10^{16} dollars; 1.845×10^{17} dollars   **92.** 68 miles

93. 0.0015 pounds per square inch   **94.** 1 min

95. 2   **96.** $\frac{1}{2}$, 1.4   **97.** 3,420°

Exercise 11-4

1. 5,040   **2.** 120   **3.** 210   **4.** 6,840

5. 144   **6.** 362,880   **7.** 56   **8.** 45

9. 1   **10.** 1   **11.** 720   **12.** 604,800

13. $\dfrac{9!}{8!}$ **14.** $\dfrac{12!}{11!}$ **15.** $\dfrac{8!}{5!}$ **16.** $\dfrac{12!}{8!}$

17. 715   **18.** 792   **19.** 3,432   **20.** 12,870

21. 161,700   **22.** 161,700

25. $8x^3 - 36x^2y + 54xy^2 - 27y^3$ **26.** $27u^3 + 54u^2v + 36uv^2 + 8v^3$

27. $x^4 - 8x^3 + 24x^2 - 32x + 16$ **28.** $81p^4 - 108p^3q + 54p^2q^2 - 12pq^3 + q^4$

29. $32x^5 - 80x^4y + 80x^3y^2 - 40x^2y^3 + 10xy^4 - y^5$

30. $64x^6 - 192x^5y + 240x^4y^2 - 160x^3y^3 + 60x^2y^4 - 12xy^5 + y^6$

31. $5,005u^9v^6$ **32.** $495a^8b^4$ **33.** $180m^2n^8$ **34.** $702x^{11}y^2$

35. $392,445w^{16}$ **36.** $-1,400,000x^3y^5$ **37.** $-48,384x^3y^5$ **38.** $-15,120p^4q^3$

39. 5   **40.** 7   **41.** (A) $a_4 = 0.251$ (B) 1

42. (A) $a_7 = 0.267$ (B) 1   **43.** 1.1046   **44.** 0.9415

45. True   **46.** False   **47.** True   **48.** True

54. 1   5   10   10   5   1   and   1   6   15   20   15   6   1

Exercise 11-5

1. 2,730   **2.** 380   **3.** 1   **4.** 25

5. 84   **6.** 21   **7.** 1,820   **8.** 816

9. 6,720   **10.** 56   **11.** 132,600   **12.** 154,440

13. 1,287   **14.** 715   **15.** 2,598,960   **16.** 116,280

17. $5 \cdot 3 \cdot 4 \cdot 2 = 120$ **18.** $3 \cdot 5 \cdot 2 = 30$ **19.** $P_{10,3} = 10 \cdot 9 \cdot 8 = 720$

20. $P_{50,5} = 254,251,200$ **21.** $C_{7,3} = 35$ subcommittees; $P_{7,3} = 210$

22. (A) $P_{9,3} = 504$ (B) $C_{9,3} = 84$ **23.** $C_{10,2} = 45$ **24.** $C_{7,2} = 21$

25. No repeats: $6 \cdot 5 \cdot 4 \cdot 3 = 360$; with repeats: $6 \cdot 6 \cdot 6 \cdot 6 = 1,296$

26. No repeats: $P_{10,3} = 720$; with repeats: $10^3 = 1000$ **27.** $C_{13,5} = 1,287$

28. $C_{12,5} = 792$, $C_{8,5} = 56$

29. $26 \cdot 26 \cdot 26 \cdot 10 \cdot 10 \cdot 10 = 17,576,000$ possible license plates; no repeats: $26 \cdot 25 \cdot 24 \cdot 10 \cdot 9 \cdot 8 = 11,232,000$

30. $10^5 = 100,000$; $P_{10,5} = 30,240$ **31.** $C_{13,5} \cdot C_{13,2} = 100,386$

32. $C_{13,2} \cdot C_{13,3} = 22,308$ **33.** $C_{8,3} \cdot C_{10,4} \cdot C_{7,2} = 246,960$

34. $P_{12,2} \cdot P_{15,2} \cdot P_{18,2} = 8,482,320$

35. (B) $r = 0, 10$

(C) Each is the product of r consecutive integers, the largest of which is n for $P_{n,r}$ and r for $r!$.

36. (A) They are equal.   **37.** $12 \cdot 11 = 132$

38. $6 \cdot 5 = 30$ **39.** (A) $C_{8,2} = 28$ (B) $C_{8,3} = 56$ (C) $C_{8,4} = 70$

40. (A) $C_{5,2} = 10$ (B) $C_{5,3} = 10$

41. two people: $5 \cdot 4 = 20$; three people: $5 \cdot 4 \cdot 3 = 60$; four people: $5 \cdot 4 \cdot 3 \cdot 2 = 120$; five people: $5 \cdot 4 \cdot 3 \cdot 2 \cdot 1 = 120$

42. 28,800   **43.** (A) $P_{8,5} = 6,720$ (B) $C_{8,5} = 56$ (C) $C_{2,1} \cdot C_{6,4} = 30$

44. (A) $C_{9,4} = 126$ (B) $C_{7,2} = 21$ (C) $2C_{7,3} = 70$

45. There are $C_{4,1} \cdot C_{48,4} = 778,320$ hands which contain exactly one king, and $C_{39,5} = 575,757$ hands containing no hearts, so the former is more likely.

46. There are $C_{26,10} = 5,311,735$ hands whose cards are all red and $C_{48,6} = 12,271,512$ hands containing all four aces, so the latter is more likely.

47. 21   **48.** 165

CHAPTER 11 REVIEW

1. (A) geometric   (B) arithmetic   (C) arithmetic
     (D) neither   (E) geometric   (*11-1, 11-3*)

2. (A) 5, 7, 9, 11   (B) $a_{10} = 23$ (C) $S_{10} = 140$ (*11-1, 11-3*)

3. (A) 16, 8, 4, 2   (B) $a_{10} = \dfrac{1}{32}$ (C) $S_{10} = 31\frac{31}{32}$ (*11-1, 11-3*)

4. (A) −8, −5, −2, 1   (B) $a_{10} = 19$ (C) $S_{10} = 55$ (*11-1, 11-3*)

5. (A) −1, 2, −4, 8   (B) $a_{10} = 512$ (C) $S_{10} = 341$ (*11-1, 11-3*)

6. $S_\infty = 32$ (*11-3*)   **7.** 3,628,800   (*11-4*)   **8.** 17,100,720   (*11-4*)

9. 1,287   (*11-4*)   **10.** $P_{8,4} = 1,680$; $C_{8,4} = 70$ (*11-5*)

11. (A) 12 combined outcomes: (B) $6 \cdot 2 = 12$

$(11-5)$

12. $6 \cdot 5 \cdot 4 \cdot 3 \cdot 2 \cdot 1 = 720$ $(11-5)$ **13.** $P_{6,6} = 6! = 720$ $(11-5)$

14. P_1: $5 = 1^2 + 4 \cdot 1 = 5$; P_2: $5 + 7 = 2^2 + 4 \cdot 2$; P_3: $5 + 7 + 9 = 3^2 + 4 \cdot 3$ $(11-2)$

15. P_1: $2 = 2^{1+1} - 2$; P_2: $2 + 4 = 2^{2+1} - 2$; P_3: $2 + 4 + 8 = 2^{3+1} - 2$ $(11-2)$

16. P_1: $49^1 - 1 = 48$ is divisible by 6; P_2: $49^2 - 1 = 2,400$ is divisible by 6;
P_3: $49^3 - 1 = 117,648$ is divisible by 6 $(11-2)$

17. P_k: $5 + 7 + 9 + \cdots + (2k + 3) = k^2 + 4k$
P_{k+1}: $5 + 7 + 9 + \cdots + (2k + 3) + (2k + 5) = (k + 1)^2 + 4(k + 1)$ $(11-2)$

18. P_k: $2 + 4 + 8 + \cdots + 2^k = 2^{k+1} - 2$
P_{k+1}: $2 + 4 + 8 + \cdots + 2^k + 2^{k+1} = 2^{k+2} - 2$ $(11-2)$

19. P_k: $49^k - 1 = 6r$ for some integer r
P_{k+1}: $49^{k+1} - 1 = 6s$ for some integer s $(11-2)$

20. $n = 31$ is a counterexample $(11-2)$

21. $S_{10} = (-6) + (-4) + (-2) + 0 + 2 + 4 + 6 + 8 + 10 + 12 = 30$ $(11-3)$

22. $S_7 = 8 + 4 + 2 + 1 + \frac{1}{2} + \frac{1}{4} + \frac{1}{8} = 15\frac{7}{8}$ $(11-3)$

23. $S_\infty = \frac{81}{5}$ $(11-3)$ **24.** $S_n = \sum_{k=1}^{n} \frac{(-1)^{k+1}}{3^k}$; $S_\infty = \frac{1}{4}$ $(11-3)$

25. $C_{6,3} = 20$ $(11-5)$ **26.** $d = 3$, $a_5 = 25$ $(11-3)$

27. $a_1 = -9$, $d = \frac{19}{5}$ $(11-3)$ **28.** 336; 512; 392 $(11-5)$

29. $\frac{8}{11}$ $(11-3)$ **30.** (A) $P_{6,3} = 120$ (B) $C_{5,2} = 10$ $(11-5)$

31. 190 $(11-4)$ **32.** 1,820 $(11-4)$ **33.** 1 $(11-4)$ **34.** $\frac{987!}{493!}$ $(11-4)$

35. $\binom{1000}{501}$ $(11-5)$ **36.** $x^5 - 5x^4y + 10x^3y^2 - 10x^2y^3 + 5xy^4 - y^5$ $(11-4)$

37. $-1760x^3y^9$ *(11-4)*   **41.** 29   *(11-4)*

42. 26   *(11-1)*   **43.** $2 \cdot 2 \cdot 2 \cdot 2 \cdot 2 = 32$; 6   *(11-5)*

44. $\dfrac{49g}{2}$ feet; $\dfrac{625g}{2}$ feet   *(11-3)*   **45.** 12   *(11-5)*

46. $x^6 + 6ix^5 - 15x^4 - 20ix^3 + 15x^2 + 6ix - 1$ *(11-4)*

47. $P_{5,5} = 120$ *(11-5)*

53. $n = 5$ *(11-1)*

54. $\{a_n\}$ is neither arithmetic nor geometric; $\{b_n\}$ is geometric   *(11-3)*

CHAPTER 12

Exercise 12-1

1.

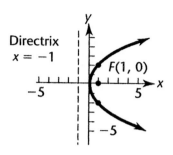

2.

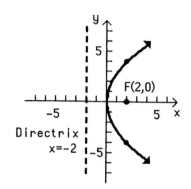

3.

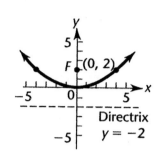

4.

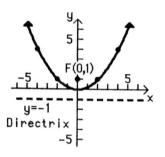

5.

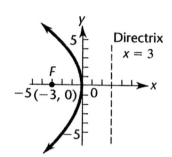

6.

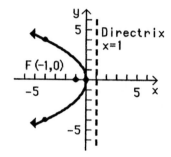

7.

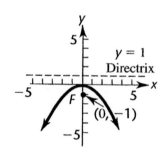

8.

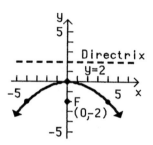

9.

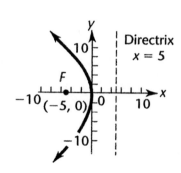

10.

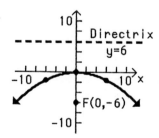

11.

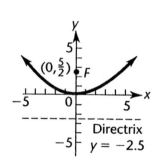

12.

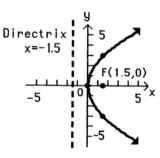

13. $(9.75, 0)$

14. $F(0, 14.5)$

15. $(0, -26.25)$

16. $F(-23.25, 0)$

17. $(-19.25, 0)$

18. $F(0, -51.25)$

19. $y^2 = -24x$

20. $x^2 = -32y$

21. $x^2 = 20y$

22. $y^2 = 12x$

23. $x^2 = -\frac{4}{3}y$

24. $x^2 = 2y$

25. $y^2 = -100x$

26. $x^2 = -60y$

27. $x^2 = -3y$

28. $y^2 = x$

29. $y^2 = -\frac{1}{2}x$

30. $x^2 = \frac{2}{3}y$

31.

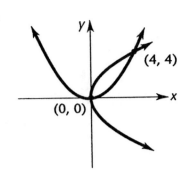

(4, 4)

(0, 0)

32.

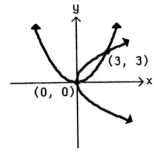

(3, 3)

(0, 0)

33.

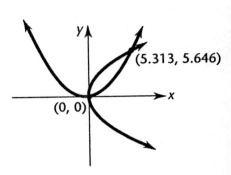

(5.313, 5.646)

(0, 0)

34.

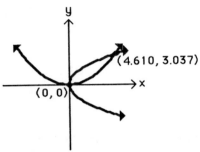

(4.610, 3.037)

(0, 0)

35. (A) 2; $x = 0$ and $y = 0$ (B) (0, 0), ($4am$, $4am^2$)

36. (0, 0), ($4\sqrt[3]{a^2 b}$, $4\sqrt[3]{ab^2}$) **37.** ($\pm 2a$, a) **38.** $|4a|$

39. False **40.** True **41.** True **42.** False

43. $x^2 - 4x - 12y - 8 = 0$ **44.** $x^2 + 6x - 8y + 41 = 0$

45. $y^2 + 8y - 8x + 48 = 0$ **46.** $y^2 - 8y - 8x + 8 = 0$

47. (−0.78, 0.08), (40.78, 207.92) **48.** (−6.52, 14.15), (1.27, 0.53)

49. (−6.84, −5.85), (0,0) **50.** (0.31, −1.37), (134.19, 28.37)

51. $x^2 = -200y$ **52.** (A) $x^2 = 60y$ (B) 15 inches

53. (A) $y = 0.0025x^2$, $-100 \leq x \leq 100$ (B) 25 ft

54. (A) $y^2 = 6x$, $0 \leq x \leq 6$ (B) depth = 6 inches

Exercise 12-2

1. Foci: $F'(-\sqrt{21}, 0)$, $F(\sqrt{21}, 0)$
Major axis length = 10
Minor axis length = 4

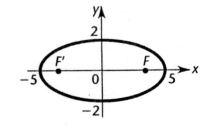

2. Foci: $F(\sqrt{5}, 0)$, $F'(-\sqrt{5}, 0)$
major axis length = 6
minor axis length = 4

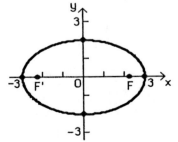

3. Foci: $F'(0, -\sqrt{21})$, $F(0, \sqrt{21})$
   Major axis length = 10
   Minor axis length = 4

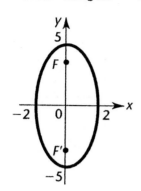

4. Foci: $F(0, \sqrt{5})$, $F'(0, -\sqrt{5})$
   major axis length = 6
   minor axis length = 4

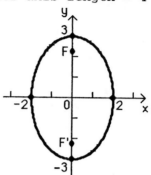

5. Foci: $F'(-\sqrt{8}, 0)$, $F(\sqrt{8}, 0)$
   Major axis length = 6
   Minor axis length = 2

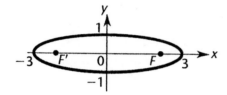

6. Foci: $F(0, \sqrt{3})$, $F'(0, -\sqrt{3})$
   major axis length = 4
   minor axis length = 2

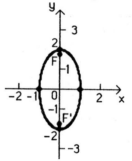

7. Foci: $F'(0, -4)$, $F(0, 4)$
   Major axis length = 10
   Minor axis length = 6

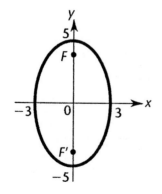

8. Foci: $F(3, 0)$, $F'(-3, 0)$
   major axis length = 10
   minor axis length = 8

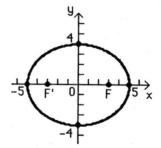

9. Foci: $F'(0, -\sqrt{6})$, $F(0, \sqrt{6})$
Major axis length $= 2\sqrt{12} \approx 6.93$
Minor axis length $= 2\sqrt{6} \approx 4.90$

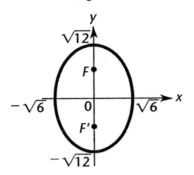

10. Foci: $F(0, \sqrt{2})$, $F'(0, -\sqrt{2})$
major axis length $= 2\sqrt{8}$
minor axis length $= 2\sqrt{6}$

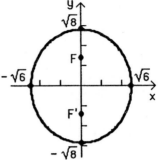

11. Foci: $F'(-\sqrt{3}, 0)$, $F(\sqrt{3}, 0)$
Major axis length $= 2\sqrt{7} \approx 5.29$
Minor axis length $= 4$

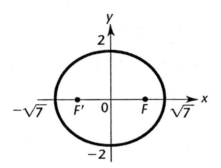

12. Foci: $F(0, 2)$, $F'(0, -2)$
major axis length $= 2\sqrt{12}$
minor axis length $= 2\sqrt{8}$

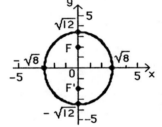

13. $x^2 + \dfrac{y^2}{9} = 1$ **14.** $\dfrac{x^2}{256} + \dfrac{y^2}{225} = 1$ **15.** $\dfrac{x^2}{41} + \dfrac{y^2}{25} = 1$ **16.** $\dfrac{x^2}{15} + \dfrac{y^2}{64} = 1$

17. $\dfrac{x^2}{143} + \dfrac{y^2}{144} = 1$ **18.** $\dfrac{x^2}{629} + \dfrac{y^2}{4} = 1$

19. It does not pass the vertical line test.

20. The ellipse is nearly circular when the focus is close to the origin, but becomes more elongated as the distance from focus to origin increases.

21.

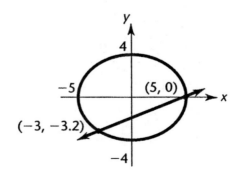

22.

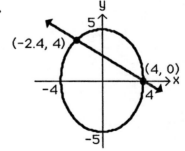

23.

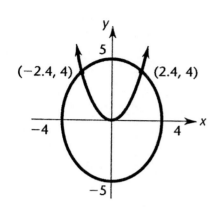

24.

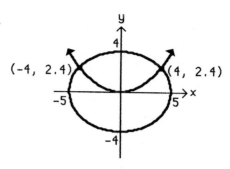

25. (2.201, 4.402)   **26.** (3.775, 1.887)   **27.** (3.565, 1.589)

28. (3.673, 1.124)   **29.** False   **30.** False   **31.** True

32. True   **33.** $\frac{x^2}{16} + \frac{y^2}{12} = 1$: ellipse

34. $\frac{x^2}{63} + \frac{y^2}{144} = 1$: ellipse   **35.** (-0.46, 2.57), (4.08, -1.06)

36. (-13.86, -7.68), (13.86, -7.68)   **37.** (±3.64, ±9.50)

38. No points of intersection   **39.** $\frac{x^2}{400} + \frac{y^2}{144} = 1$; 7.94 feet approx.

40. $4 - \sqrt{12} \approx 0.54$, distance from edge to focus
length of string = 8 ft

41. (A) $\frac{x^2}{576} + \frac{y^2}{15.9} = 1$ (B) 5.13 ft   **42.** (A) $\frac{x^2}{36} + \frac{y^2}{6.26} = 1$ (B) 2.38 ft

Exercise 12-3

1. Foci: $F'(-\sqrt{13}, 0)$, $F(\sqrt{13}, 0)$
Transverse axis length = 6
Conjugate axis length = 4

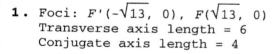

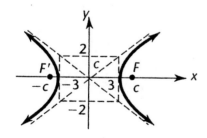

2. Foci: $F'(-\sqrt{34}, 0)$, $F(\sqrt{34}, 0)$
conjugate axis length = 10
transverse axis length = 6

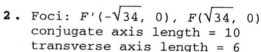

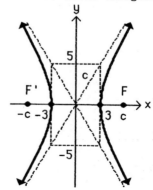

3. Foci: $F'(0, -\sqrt{13})$, $F(0, \sqrt{13})$
Transverse axis length = 4
Conjugate axis length = 6

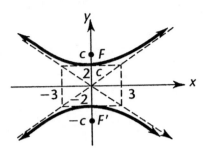

4. Foci: $F'(0, -\sqrt{34})$, $F(0, \sqrt{34})$
transverse axis length = 10
conjugate axis length = 6

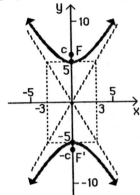

5. Foci: $F'(-\sqrt{20}, 0)$, $F(\sqrt{20}, 0)$
Transverse axis length = 4
Conjugate axis length = 8

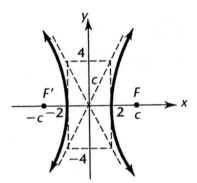

6. Foci: $F'(-\sqrt{10}, 0)$, $F(\sqrt{10}, 0)$
transverse axis length = 6
conjugate axis length = 2

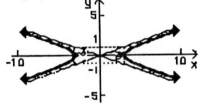

7. Foci: $F'(0, -5)$, $F(0, 5)$
Transverse axis length = 8
Conjugate axis length = 6

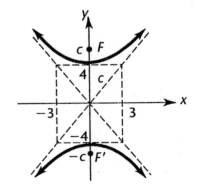

8. Foci: $F'(0, -\sqrt{29})$, $F(0, \sqrt{29})$
transverse axis length = 10
conjugate axis length = 4

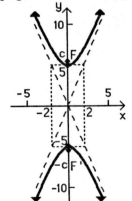

9. Foci: $F'(-\sqrt{10},\ 0)$, $F(\sqrt{10},\ 0)$
   Transverse axis length = 4
   Conjugate axis length = $2\sqrt{6} \approx 4.90$

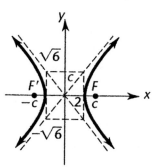

10. Foci: $F'(-\sqrt{14},\ 0)$, $F(\sqrt{14},\ 0)$
   transverse axis length = $2\sqrt{8} \approx 5.66$
   conjugate axis length = $2\sqrt{6} \approx 4.90$

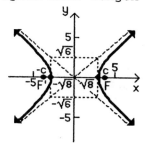

11. Foci: $F'(0,\ -\sqrt{11})$, $F(0,\ \sqrt{11})$
   Transverse axis length = 4
   Conjugate axis length = $2\sqrt{7} \approx 5.29$

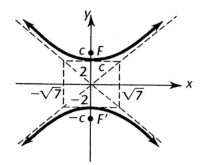

12. Foci: $F'(0,\ -\sqrt{20})$, $F(0,\ \sqrt{20})$
   transverse axis length = $2\sqrt{8} \approx 5.66$
   conjugate axis length = $2\sqrt{12} \approx 6.93$

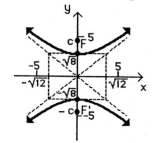

13. $\dfrac{y^2}{25} - \dfrac{x^2}{81} = 1$ **14.** $\dfrac{x^2}{121} - y^2 = 1$ **15.** $\dfrac{x^2}{49} - \dfrac{y^2}{32} = 1$ **16.** $\dfrac{y^2}{400} - \dfrac{x^2}{225} = 1$

17. $\dfrac{y^2}{36} - \dfrac{x^2}{36} = 1$ **18.** $x^2 - \dfrac{y^2}{575} = 1$

19. (A) Infinitely many; $\dfrac{x^2}{a^2} - \dfrac{y^2}{1 - a^2} = 1$ $(0 < a < 1)$

   (B) Infinitely many; $\dfrac{x^2}{a^2} + \dfrac{y^2}{a^2 - 1} = 1$ $(a > 1)$

   (C) One; $y^2 = 4x$

20. Infinitely many; $\dfrac{x^2}{a^2} - \dfrac{y^2}{4a^2} = 1$, $\dfrac{y^2}{a^2} - \dfrac{4x^2}{a^2} = 1$ $(a > 0)$

21.

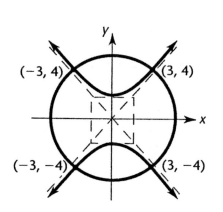

22.

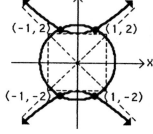

23.

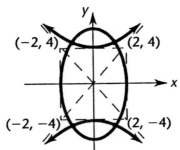

24.

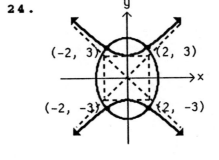

25. (-1.389, 3.306), (6.722, 7.361)

26. (-2.667, 3.333)

27. (±3.266, ±3.830)

28. (±2.160, ±2.380)

29. True   **30.** True

31. False   **32.** True

33. $\dfrac{x^2}{4} - \dfrac{y^2}{5} = 1$; hyperbola

34. $\dfrac{y^2}{9} - \dfrac{x^2}{7} = 1$; hyperbola

35. (-4.73, 2.88), (3.35, -0.90)

36. (-1.06, -3.37), (1.06, -3.37)

37. (±1.39, ±2.96)

38. No points of intersection

39. $\dfrac{y^2}{16} - \dfrac{x^2}{8} = 1$; 5.38 ft above vertex

40. 141 ft, top radius; 254 ft, base radius; 100 ft, radius of smallest circular cross section

41. $y = \dfrac{4}{3}\sqrt{x^2 + 30^2}$

Exercise 12-4

1. (A) $x' = x - 3$; $y' = y - 5$ (B) $x'^2 + y'^2 = 81$ (C) Circle

2. (A) $x' = x - 3$, $y' = y + 2$ (B) $x'^2 = 8y'$ (C) parabola

3. (A) $x' = x + 7$, $y' = y - 4$ (B) $\dfrac{x'^2}{9} + \dfrac{y'^2}{16} = 1$ (C) Ellipse

4. (A) $x' = x + 2$, $y' = y + 6$ (B) $x'^2 + y'^2 = 36$ (C) circle

5. (A) $x' = x - 4$, $y' = y + 9$ (B) $y'^2 = 16x'$ (C) Parabola

6. (A) $x' = x + 5$, $y' = y - 9$ (B) $\dfrac{y'^2}{10} - \dfrac{x'^2}{6} = 1$ (C) hyperbola

7. (A) $x' = x + 8$, $y' = y + 3$ (B) $\dfrac{x'^2}{12} + \dfrac{y'^2}{8} = 1$ (C) Ellipse

8. (A) $x' = x + 7$, $y' = y - 8$ (B) $\dfrac{x'^2}{25} - \dfrac{y'^2}{50} = 1$ (C) hyperbola

9. (A) $\dfrac{(x - 3)^2}{9} - \dfrac{(y + 2)^2}{16} = 1$ (B) hyperbola

10. (A) $(y + 2)^2 = 12(x - 3)$ (B) parabola

11. (A) $\dfrac{(x + 5)^2}{5} + \dfrac{(y + 7)^2}{6} = 1$ (B) ellipse

12. (A) $\dfrac{(y - 5)^2}{2} - \dfrac{(x - 3)^2}{3} = 1$ (B) hyperbola

13. (A) $(x + 6)^2 = -24(y - 4)$ (B) parabola

14. (A) $\dfrac{(x - 7)^2}{7} + \dfrac{(y - 3)^2}{4} = 1$ (B) ellipse

15. $\dfrac{(x - 2)^2}{9} + \dfrac{(y - 2)^2}{4} = 1$; ellipse

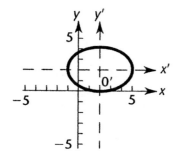

16. $\dfrac{(x + 2)^2}{9} + \dfrac{(y + 3)^2}{16} = 1$: ellipse

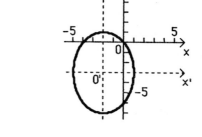

17. $(x + 4)^2 = -8(y - 2)$; parabola

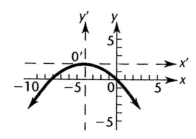

18. $(y + 2)^2 = -12(x - 3)$: parabola

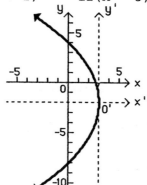

19. $(x + 6)^2 + (y + 5)^2 = 16$; circle

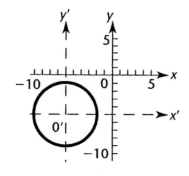

20. $(x - 4)^2 + (y - 3)^2 = 25$: circle

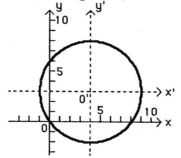

21. $\dfrac{(y-3)^2}{9} - \dfrac{(x+4)^2}{16} = 1$; hyperbola

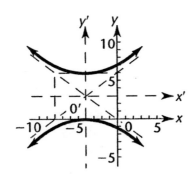

22. $\dfrac{(x-5)^2}{25} - \dfrac{y^2}{16} = 1$: hyperbola

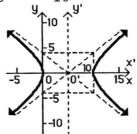

23. $h = \dfrac{-D}{2A}$, $k = \dfrac{D^2 - 4AF}{4AE}$

24. $h = \dfrac{E^2 - 4CF}{4CD}$, $k = \dfrac{-E}{2C}$

25. $x^2 - 10x - 32y + 121 = 0$

26. $y^2 - 4x - 6y + 13 = 0$

27. $36x^2 + 25y^2 + 216x - 200y - 176 = 0$

28. $16x^2 - y^2 - 32x - 16y - 192 = 0$

29. $3x^2 - y^2 - 24x + 2y + 44 = 0$

30. $25x^2 + 16y^2 + 150x - 96y - 31 = 0$

31. $4x^2 - 3y - 4 = 0$

32. $6y^2 - 25x - 24y - 126 = 0$

33. $x^2 + 5y^2 + 4x + 10y = 0$

34. $15x^2 - 4y^2 - 60x + 32y = 0$

35. $F'(-\sqrt{5} + 2, 2)$ and $F(\sqrt{5} + 2, 2)$

36. $F(-2, \sqrt{7} - 3)$, $F'(-2, -\sqrt{7} - 3)$

37. $F(-4, 0)$

38. $F(0, -2)$

39. $F'(-4, -2)$, $F(-4, 8)$

40. $F(\sqrt{41} + 5, 0)$, $F'(-\sqrt{41} + 5, 0)$

41. $(1.18, 1.98)$, $(6.85, -6.52)$

42. $(-2.06, -3.03)$, $(3.45, -0.52)$

43. $(-1.72, -1.87)$, $(-0.99, 2.06)$

44. $(1.30, 2.40)$, $(2.39, -2.23)$,
$(3.43, -1.86)$, $(4.19, 1.38)$

Exercise 12-5

1. $y = -2x - 2$;
straight line

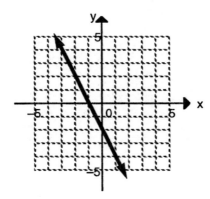

2. $y = x + 1$,
straight line

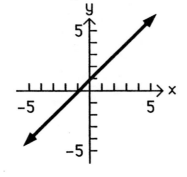

3. $y = -2x - 2$, $x \leq 0$
a ray (part of a
straight line)

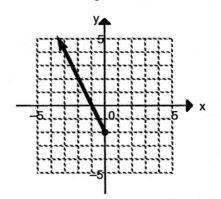

4. $y = x + 1$, $x \geq 0$
a ray (part of a
straight line)

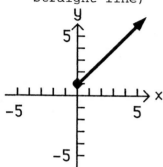

5. $y = -\frac{2}{3}x$;
straight line

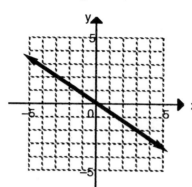

6. $y = \frac{1}{2}x$, straight line

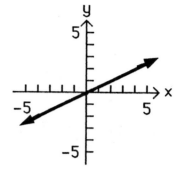

7. $y^2 = 4x$; parabola

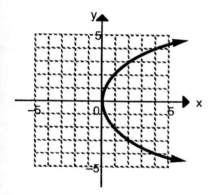

8. $x^2 = 4y$; parabola

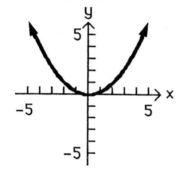

9. $y^2 = 4x$, $y \geq 0$;
parabola (upper half)

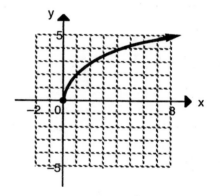

10. $x^2 = 4y$, $x \geq 0$;
parabola (right half)

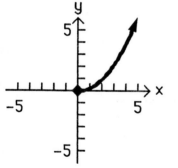

11. $\frac{x^2}{9} + \frac{y^2}{16} = 1$; ellipse

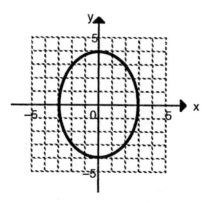

12. $x^2 + y^2 = 9$; circle

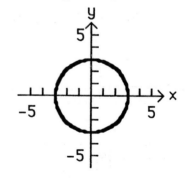

13. $(x - 2)^2 + (y - 3)^2 = 4$; circle **14.** $\dfrac{(x - 3)^2}{16} + \dfrac{(y - 2)^2}{4} = 1$; ellipse **15.** $y = -\dfrac{2}{x}$; hyperbola

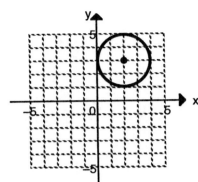

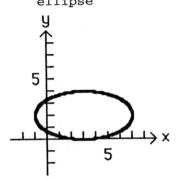

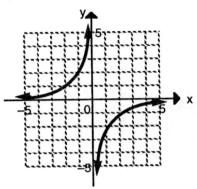

16. $y = \dfrac{2}{x}$, hyperbola **17.** $y^2 = x + 1,\ y \geq 0,\ x \geq -1$; parabola (upper half) **18.** $y = x^{2/3} + 1$

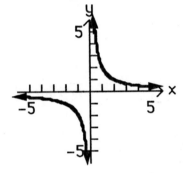

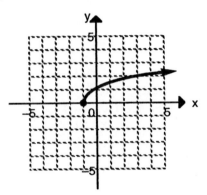

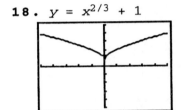

19. $x = t,\ y = \dfrac{At^2 + Dt + F}{-E},\ -\infty < t < \infty$; parabola

20. $x = \dfrac{Ct^2 + Et + F}{-D},\ y = t,\ -\infty < t < \infty$; parabola

21. $y = \dfrac{1}{x},\ x > 0$; hyperbola (one branch) **22.** $y = \dfrac{1}{x},\ x > 0$; hyperbola (one branch) **23.** $y^2 = -8(x - 1),\ -1 \leq x \leq 1$; part of a parabola

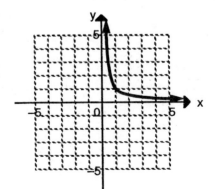

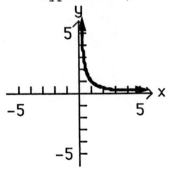

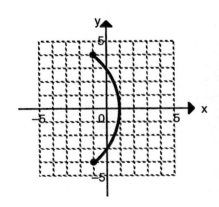

24. $y = \frac{2}{3}x - 2$, $x \geq 3$
a ray (part of a
straight line)

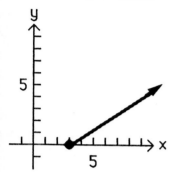

25. $x^2 + y^2 = 2x$, $x \neq 0$ or
$(x - 1)^2 + y^2 = 1$, $x \neq 0$;
circle (note hole at
origin)

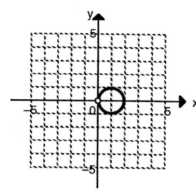

26. $x^2 + y^2 = 4y$, $y \neq 4$ or
$x^2 + (y - 2)^2 = 4$; circle
[note hole at $(0, 4)$]

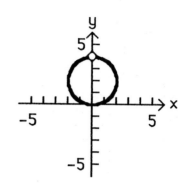

27.

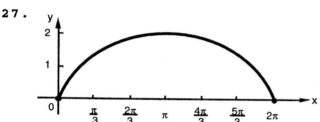

28.

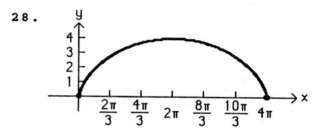

29. $\frac{(x - 3)^2}{36} + \frac{(y - 2)^2}{16} = 1$;
ellipse with center $(3, 2)$

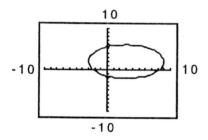

30. $\frac{(x - 1)^2}{9} - \frac{(y + 2)^2}{4} = 1$;
hyperbola with center $(1, -2)$

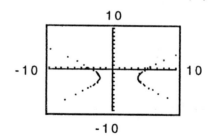

31. $\frac{(y + 1)^2}{25} - \frac{(x + 3)^2}{4} = 1$;
hyperbola with center $(-3, -1)$

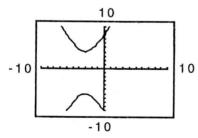

32. $\frac{(x + 4)^2}{25} + \frac{(y - 1)^2}{64} = 1$;
ellipse with center $(-4, 1)$

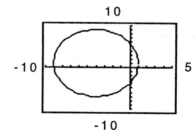

33. $5x - 2y = 0$

34. $9x^2 - y^2 = 0$

35. $\dfrac{(y + 1)^2}{25} - \dfrac{(x - 4)^2}{9} = 1;$
hyperbola with center $(4, -1);$
$x = 4 + 3 \tan t, \ y = -1 + 5 \sec t,$
$-\dfrac{\pi}{2} < t < \dfrac{3\pi}{2}, \ t \neq \dfrac{\pi}{2}$

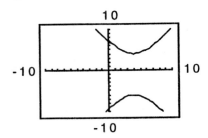

36. $\dfrac{(x + 5)^2}{4} + \dfrac{(y - 1)^2}{36} = 1;$
ellipse with center $(-5, 1);$
$x = -5 + 2 \cos t, \ y = 1 + 6 \sin t,$
$0 \leq t \leq 2\pi;$

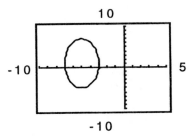

37. $\dfrac{(x - 3)^2}{49} + \dfrac{(y + 4)^2}{4} = 1;$ ellipse
with center $(3, -4); \ x = 3 + 7 \cos t,$
$y = -4 + 2 \sin t, \ 0 \leq t \leq 2\pi$

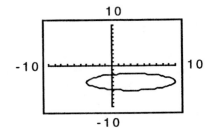

38. $\dfrac{(x + 1)^2}{9} - \dfrac{(y + 2)^2}{16} = 1;$ hyperbola
with center $(-1, -2);$
$x = -1 + 3 \sec t, \ y = -2 + 4 \tan t,$
$\dfrac{-\pi}{2} < t < \dfrac{3\pi}{2}, \ t \neq \dfrac{\pi}{2}$

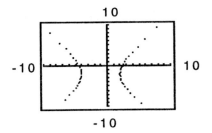

39. (A) $(4.8, -1.5)$
(B) $x^2 + y^2 = 25;$ circle

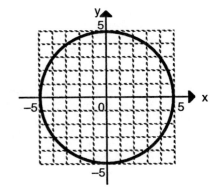

40. (A) $(1.2, 1.9)$
(B) $\dfrac{x^2}{16} + \dfrac{y^2}{4} = 1,$ ellipse

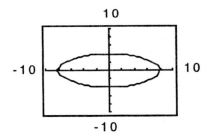

41. (A) 43.292 sec   (B) 9,183.619 m, 9.184 km   (C) 2,295.918 m

42. (A) 39.354 sec   (B) 9,044.153 m, 9.044 km   (C) 1,897.236 m

CHAPTER 12 REVIEW

1. Foci: $F'(-4, 0)$, $F(4, 0)$
Major axis length = 10
Minor axis length = 6

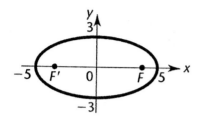

$(12-2)$

2.

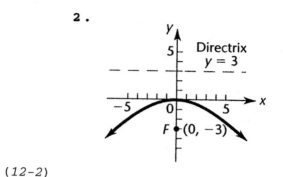

$(12-1)$

3. Foci: $F'(0, -\sqrt{34})$, $F(0, \sqrt{34})$
Transverse axis length = 6
Conjugate axis length = 10

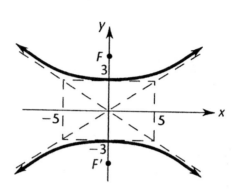

$(12-3)$

4. (A) $\dfrac{(y + 2)^2}{25} - \dfrac{(x - 4)^2}{4} = 1$ (B) hyperbola $(12-4)$

5. (A) $(x + 5)^2 = -12(y + 4)$ (B) parabola $(12-4)$

6. (A) $\dfrac{(x - 6)^2}{9} + \dfrac{(y - 4)^2}{16} = 1$ (B) ellipse $(12-4)$

7. $y^2 = -7x$ $(12-1)$ **8.** $\dfrac{x^2}{4} + \dfrac{y^2}{965} = 1$ $(12-2)$ **9.** $\dfrac{x^2}{25} - \dfrac{y^2}{11} = 1$ $(12-3)$

10. $y = \dfrac{1}{2}x + 1$, $x \leq 0$; a ray (part of a straight line)

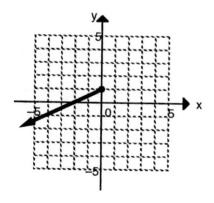

$(12-5)$

11.

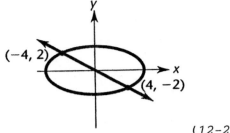

(−4, 2)

(4, −2)

$(12-2, \; 9-3)$

12.

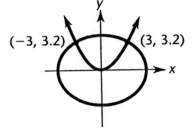

(−3, 3.2)   (3, 3.2)

$(12-1, \; 12-2, \; 9-3)$

13.

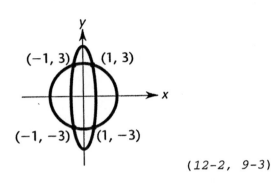

(−1, 3)   (1, 3)

(−1, −3)   (1, −3)

$(12-2, \; 9-3)$

14. $\dfrac{(x+3)^2}{4} + \dfrac{(y-2)^2}{16} = 1$; ellipse

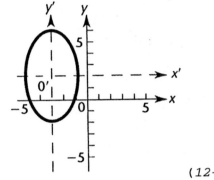

$(12-4)$

15. $(x-2)^2 = 4(2)(y+3)$; parabola

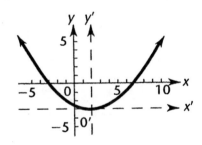

$(12-4)$

16. $\dfrac{(x+3)^2}{9} - \dfrac{(y+2)^2}{4} = 1$; hyperbola

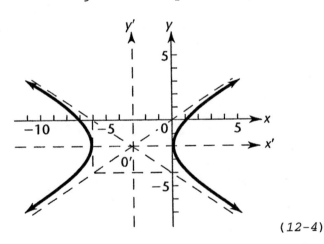

$(12-4)$

17. $\dfrac{(x+2)^2}{4} + \dfrac{(y-3)^2}{16} = 1$; ellipse

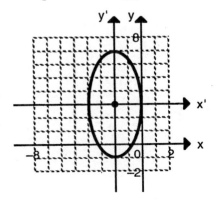

$(12-5)$

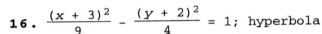

18. $m = 0.2;$ $x^2 = 50y$ is a magnification by a factor 50 of $x^2 = y$ (*12-1*)

19. $(y - 4)^2 = -8(x - 4)$ or $y^2 - 8y + 8x - 16 = 0$ (*12-1*)

20. $\dfrac{x^2}{4} - \dfrac{y^2}{12} = 1;$ hyperbola (*12-3*)   **21.** $\dfrac{x^2}{36} + \dfrac{y^2}{20} = 1;$ ellipse (*12-2*)

22. $F'(-3, -\sqrt{12} + 2)$ and $F(-3, \sqrt{12} + 2)$ (*12-4*)   **23.** $F(2, -1)$ (*12-4*)

24. $F'(-\sqrt{13} - 3, -2)$ and $F(\sqrt{13} - 3, -2)$ (*12-4*)

25. $y = \dfrac{1}{x},$ $x > 0;$ hyperbola (one branch)

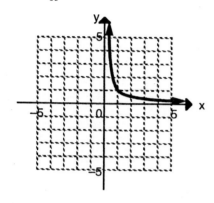

(*12-5*)

26. $(2.09, 2.50), (3.67, -1.92)$ (*12-4*)   **27.** 4 feet (*12-1*)

28. $\dfrac{x^2}{5^2} + \dfrac{y^2}{3^2} = 1$ (*12-2*)   **29.** 4.72 feet deep (*12-3*)

CUMULATIVE REVIEW EXERCISE (Chapters 11 and 12)

1. (A) Neither (B) Arithmetic (C) Both (D) Geometric (E) Geometric
   (F) Neither *(11-3)*

2. (A) -2, 4, -8, 16   (B) $a_8 = 256$ (C) $S_8 = 170$ *(11-3)*

3. (A) 1, 7, 13, 19   (B) $a_8 = 43$ (C) $S_8 = 176$ *(11-3)*

4. (A) -20, -16, -12, -8   (B) $a_8 = 8$ (C) $S_8 = -48$ *(11-3)*

5. (A) 5,040   (B) 13,800   (C) 210   *(11-4)*

6. (A) 924   (B) 126   (C) 6,720   *(11-4, 11-5)*

7. Foci: $F'(-\sqrt{61}, 0)$, $F(\sqrt{61}, 0)$
   Transverse axis length = 12
   Conjugate axis length = 10

8. Foci: $F'(-\sqrt{11}, 0)$, $F(\sqrt{11}, 0)$
   Major axis length = 12
   Minor axis length = 10

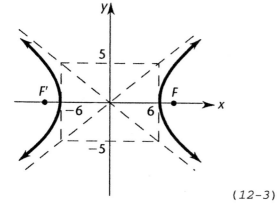

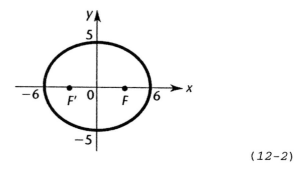

(12-2)

(12-3)

9.

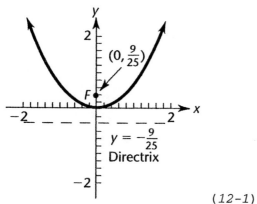

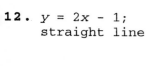

(12-1)

10. (A) 8 combined outcomes:

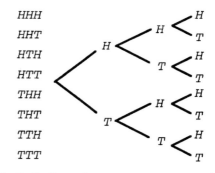

HHH
HHT
HTH
HTT
THH
THT
TTH
TTT

(B) $2 \cdot 2 \cdot 2 = 8$ *(11-5)*

11. (A) $4 \cdot 3 \cdot 2 \cdot 1 = 24$ (B) $P_{4,4} = 4! = 24$ *(11-5)*

12. $y = 2x - 1$;
    straight line

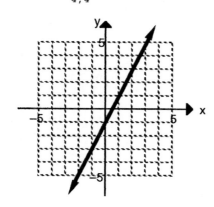

(12-5)

13. P_1: $1 = 1(2 \cdot 1 - 1)$; P_2: $1 + 5 = 2(2 \cdot 2 - 1)$; P_3: $1 + 5 + 9 = 3(2 \cdot 3 - 1)$ *(11-2)*

14. P_1: $1^2 + 1 + 2 = 4$ is divisible by 2; P_2: $2^2 + 2 + 2 = 8$ is divisible by 2;
P_3: $3^2 + 3 + 2 = 14$ is divisible by 2   *(11-2)*

15. P_k: $1 + 5 + 9 + \cdots + (4k - 3) = k(2k - 1)$
P_{k+1}: $1 + 5 + 9 + \cdots + (4k - 3) + (4k + 1) = (k + 1)(2k + 1)$ *(11-2)*

16. P_k: $k^2 + k + 2 = 2r$ for some integer r
P_{k+1}: $(k + 1)^2 + (k + 1) + 2 = 2s$ for some integer s *(11-2)*

17. $y = -2x^2$ *(12-1)*   **18.** $\dfrac{x^2}{25} + \dfrac{y^2}{16} = 1$ *(12-2)*   **19.** $\dfrac{x^2}{64} - \dfrac{y^2}{25} = 1$ *(12-3)*

20. $1 + 4 + 27 + 256 + 3{,}125 = 3{,}413$ *(11-1)*   **21.** $\displaystyle\sum_{k=1}^{6} (-1)^{k+1} \dfrac{2^k}{(k + 1)!}$ *(11-1)*

22. 81   *(11-3)*   **23.** 360; 1,296; 750   *(11-5)*   **24.** $n = 22$ *(11-3)*

25. $\dfrac{(x - 2)^2}{49} + \dfrac{(y + 3)^2}{25} = 1$; ellipse

26. (A) 6,375,600
(B) 53,130
(C) 53,130   *(11-4, 11-5)*

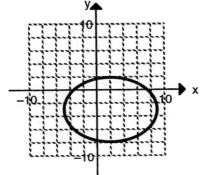

(12-5)

27. $a^6 + 3a^5b + \dfrac{15}{4}a^4b^2 + \dfrac{5}{2}a^3b^3 + \dfrac{15}{16}a^2b^4 + \dfrac{3}{16}ab^5 + \dfrac{1}{64}b^6$ *(11-4)*

28. $153{,}090x^6y^4$; $-3{,}240x^3y^7$ *(11-4)*   **31.** 61,875   *(11-3)*

32. $\dfrac{27}{11}$ *(11-3)*   **33.** $a_{22} = 0.236$; 8 terms   *(11-4)*

34. $4(x + 3) = (y - 2)^2$; parabola   **35.** $(y + 2)^2, 4) - \dfrac{(x + 1)^2}{16} = 1$; hyperbola

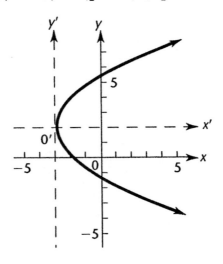

(12-1)

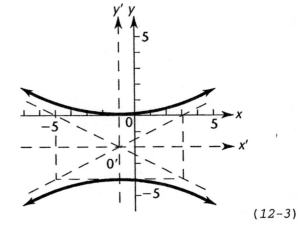

(12-3)

36. $\dfrac{(x - 2)^2}{9} + \dfrac{(y + 3)^2}{4} = 1$;
ellipse

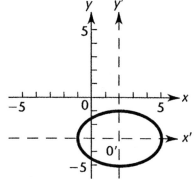

(12-2)

37. 10^9; 3,628,800 zip codes *(11-5)*

38. (-2.26, -4.72), (1.85, 3.09)   *(12-4)*

40. $x^6 - 12ix^5 - 60x^4 + 160ix^3 + 240x^2 - 192ix - 64$ *(11-4)*

41. $x^2 - 12x + 4y + 28 = 0$ *(12-1)*   **42.** $\pm 2\sqrt{3}$ *(12-2)*

43. 8   *(12-3)*   **44.** Geometric   *(11-3, 11-4)*

45. Neither   *(11-3)*   **46.** Both   *(11-3)*

47. Arithmetic   *(11-3)*   **48.** False   *(11-2, 11-4)*

49. True   *(11-2, 11-4)*   **50.** False   *(11-2, 11-4)*

51. True   *(11-2, 11-4)*   **52.** True   *(12-2)*

53. False   *(12-1)*   **54.** False   *(12-3)*

55. True   *(12-2)*   **56.** False   *(12-3)*

57. One parabola; $y^2 = 8x + 9$ *(12-4)*   **58.** $y + 4 = \pm\dfrac{1}{2}(x - 5)$ *(12-3, 12-4)*

59. $4\sqrt{10}$ *(12-2)*   **60.** $C_{7,3} = 35$ *(11-5)*

61. $x + 4 = (y - 1)^2$, $y < 1$; lower half of a parabola (excluding the vertex)

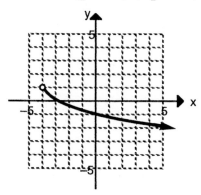

(12-5)

64. $x^2 - 8y^2 - 2x - 8y + 17 = 0$; hyperbola   *(12-3)*

65. $6,000,000   *(11-3)*

66. 4 in.   *(12-1)*   **67.** 32 ft, 14.4 ft   *(12-2)*